FINANCIAL DECISION MAKING— THEORY AND PRACTICE

text and problems

FINANCIAL DECISION MAKING— THEORY AND PRACTICE

text and problems

PRENTICE-
HALL, INC.
ENGLEWOOD
CLIFFS,
NEW JERSEY

AVERY B. COHAN

Professor of Finance
University of North Carolina at Chapel Hill

© 1972 by PRENTICE-HALL, INC., Englewood Cliffs, New Jersey

10 9 8 7 6 5 4 3 2

Library of Congress Catalog Number: 72–166041

ISBN: 0–13–314831–9

Printed in the United States of America

PRENTICE-HALL INTERNATIONAL, INC., London
PRENTICE-HALL OF AUSTRALIA, PTY. LTD., Sydney
PRENTICE-HALL OF CANADA, LTD., Toronto
PRENTICE-HALL OF INDIA PRIVATE LIMITED, New Delhi
PRENTICE-HALL OF JAPAN, INC., Tokyo

To my family

CONTENTS

PREFACE

My purpose in writing this book, has been to present the modern theory of corporation finance—but in a nonabstract way so that it would be readily comprehensible to the typical beginning student.

Three caveats:

First, I have put everything—current assets, machines, acquisitions—into a capital budgeting framework on the grounds that I could see no difference in principle between investing in a lathe and investing in liquidity, or in accounts receivable, or in another firm. You will therefore find no separate sections, outside the main theme of the book, on managing working capital, or on mergers and acquisitions.

This device, which leads us first down one side of the balance sheet and then down the other, works to make the student feel that he has been presented with a "well organized" body of material.

Second, the book is entirely "problem oriented" and inductive. I have chosen to present the modern theory of corporation finance—plus a bit of modern portfolio theory—by applying it to real financial problems. This manner of presentation works to make the student feel that the theory is "relevant"—to use a word which has not yet, perhaps, lost all its meaning.

Third, except for parts of Chapter 16, you will find no descriptive material as such. I have brought in "descriptive" material only when it was itself part of the problem under discussion. Nevertheless, the book contains more "descriptive" material than may, at first, meet the eye.

A large number of friends have read and reacted to various preliminary versions of this book and, thereby, helped make it a better book than it would otherwise have been. I thank each of them warmly. They are: Erma L. Adams, Ronnie N. Anderson, Leo Barnes, Robert S. Carlson, Dewitt C. Dearborn, Frank DeFelice, Arthur T. Dietz, Robert R. Dince, Herman A. Ellis, Sidney Finkel, C. Jackson Grayson, Jr., William Hale, W. F. Hardin, John A. Haslem, Frank C. Jen, Charles P. Jones, O. Maurice Joy, Robert A. Kavesh, James P. King, Burton G. Malkiel, Richard W. McEnally, Morris Mendelson, Robert Phillips, Charles F. Poston, C. U. Rao, Ed Renshaw, Donald S. Shannon, Gordon Shillinglaw, John A. Swiger, J. E. Thornton, Robert H. Trent, L. Frederick Van Eck, Jr., Harold E. Wyman.

In addition, I should like to thank the Graduate School of Business Administration, University of North Carolina at Chapel Hill, and its Dean Maurice W. Lee for many administrative kindnesses bestowed generously and without stint. I should like also to thank the Central Carolina Bank and Trust Company of Durham, North Carolina, The North Carolina National Bank of Charlotte, and The Wachovia Bank and Trust Company of Winston-Salem for permission to use various of their Loan Forms; Arnold Bernhard and *The Value Line Investment Survey* for permission to quote from various Value Line Reports; Dun and Bradstreet for permission to reproduce several sample credit reports; Sidney Homer and the Salomon Brothers for permission to reproduce parts of their various publications.

But perhaps I am indebted most of all to the participants in The Eighth Management Development Program at IMEDE (Lausanne, Switzerland) who encouraged me steadily, over a period of eight months, to try to write a basic text in finance which would show some pity for those beginning students who, although genuinely interested in principles and theory, have (like most of us) little flair for abstraction. Whether I have succeeded in this or not is, of course, for others to judge.

Avery B. Cohan
The University of North Carolina at Chapel Hill

FINANCIAL DECISION MAKING— THEORY AND PRACTICE

text and problems

INTRODUCTION

FINANCE AND THE FIRM

THE RELATIONSHIP OF FINANCE TO THE FIRM

What is *Finance*? And what is the relationship between Finance and the other parts of the firm?

the crossroads of finance

In order to answer these questions, let's watch, for a minute, what is happening in the office of Dale Martin, Vice President of Finance for the Butcher Company. The Butcher Company, with its head office in New York City, is a medium sized, diversified manufacturer of small hand tools, machine tools, plastics, chemicals, blended and synthetic fabrics, and a variety of other products.

1. The marketing vice president, Carter, has sent the president a six page memorandum proposing that he, Carter, be allowed to sell hand tools to a large group of slower paying customers. Carter estimates that these customers would buy $850,000 worth

of merchandise a year. These additional sales would contribute about $170,000 to Butcher's profit before taxes. The memo is full of facts and figures, the marketing people obviously have done a lot of research on the proposal and take it seriously. An addendum lists the names and addresses of the 132 proposed new customers.

The president has put five question marks across the top of the memo and has passed it on to Martin.

2. Carter, the marketing vice president, who has obviously been keeping busy, sends the president another memo, asking that his advertising budget for the next quarter be increased by $600,000. This memo is also six pages long and, again, is full of facts and figures. The president has sent this memo also to Martin with the comment: "Looks good to me."

3. The vice president for production, Hastings, estimates capital expenditures for the tool division for the first six months of the next year at $4,970,000. The tool division also wants to increase its parts inventory by $750,000. A memo, requesting approval of these expenditures, has been passed to Martin by the president with the comment: "He's always thinking up ways to spend money."

4. The controller tells Martin that the advertising manager has only $9,000 left from his budget for the fourth quarter—with six weeks still to go.

5. Martin finds a note from the president saying: "I think we should pay an extra fourth quarter dividend. "How much can you spare?"

6. Jim Barton, the manager of the basic research division, a Ph.D. in organic chemistry, sends Martin a memo requesting permission to order two more electron microscopes. He offers no explanation as to why they are needed and does not bother to indicate how much they cost.

7. The sales manager writes a memo to Martin, passing on a salesman's report containing the following remarks:

> Page (A. W. Page Company) told me the banks have turned down renewal of his note and that he will need 150 days on the enclosed order. I enclose his latest (unaudited) income statement and balance sheet.

The enclosed order is for $50,000 worth of small tools which, the financial vice president knows, will be obsolete in eighteen months. The order was at regular prices and would contribute $11,000 to Butcher's profits.

8. The purchasing manager calls Martin to say that the wool

buyer for the company's textile division has found some South African raw wool that he can pick up at bargain prices—at a total cost of $500,000. The wool buyer says: "This is just a temporary increase in inventory. We'll be back to normal in six weeks."

Martin thinks: "I've heard that before."

9. Kelley, Martin's assistant, tells Martin that Raimondi at Chase Manhattan is betting three to one that 90 day bill prices will continue to go down for at least thirty days. Kelley says: "I think we should sell half of what we've got."

10. Hastings, the vice president for production, wanders into Martin's office and says: "I'm getting very worried about the Tampico plant. The situation there is getting worse and worse. I think perhaps we should take our money and get out. Let's talk about it."

11. Martin receives a memo from the president containing two brief paragraphs:

> I have just read an article in the *Harvard Business Review* on the advantages of using preferred stock to raise money. We have never used preferred stock nor have you ever recommended doing so. Why? *We should look into this.* I suppose we'll have to raise long-term money again this year.
>
> I have also read an article in the *Bulletin of the Federal Reserve Bank of St. Louis* on commercial paper. We've never used that either. Why? *It's cheaper than short-term bank credit.* We should look into this, too.

After he read this memo, Martin had an impulse to steal the president's reading glasses.

12. Martin himself looks up the bond page in the *Wall Street Journal* and finds that good quality industrial bonds are yielding more than 8 percent. He says: "Ugh, everything's going up."

The last time Butcher borrowed money, in 1966, the cost was 5.5 percent.

analyzing the problem

Now, let's look over the financial vice president's shoulder and watch his initial reactions to the problems which have been put on his desk.

First, Martin made a list of all those proposals which would require new allocations of funds. The results of his handiwork are shown in columns (1) and (2) of Table 1.1. He then added another column, labelled "Rate of Return," indicating whether or not a rate of return had been calculated for each proposal. He noted that no rates had been calculated for the increase in parts inventory, for the two electron microscopes, for the increase in the wool inventory, or for either of the proposals from the marketing division.

He then called in Kelley, his assistant, and handed him a copy of the table. He said: "Tell me whether we'll have to go outside to get money if all the projects in column two are approved. You've got fifteen minutes."

He then called in his secretary and dictated the following memo to the president:

> Re the proposed extra dividend: I have now received proposals for capital expenditures totaling $7,583,000 for the first six months of next year. The final total will probably be at least 20 percent higher: I have not yet heard from textiles or plastics or chemicals. An eighty cent extra dividend would cost us $1,750,000.
>
> I suggest that we wait until the Finance Committee meets

TABLE 1.1

THE BUTCHER COMPANY*
PROPOSED NEW PROJECTS

PROPOSED CAPITAL EXPENDITURES	SHORT TERM	LONG TERM	EXPECTED RATE OF RETURN
	(thousands)		
	(1)	(2)	(3)
1. Increase in accounts receivable	$ 50.	$ 680.	N.C.
2. New plant and equipment (Tools division)	—	4,970.	14% (average)
3. Increase in parts inventory (Tools division)	—	750.	N.C.
4. Two electron microscopes at $16,500 each	—	33.	N.C.
5. Increase in raw wool inventory	$ 500.	—	N.C.
6. Increase in advertising expenditures	—	600.	N.C.
TOTAL	$ 550.	$7,033.	
7. Extra dividend at 80 cents a share	$1,750.		

Note: N.C. = not calculated.
* As of November 1968.

before drawing up any recommendations to the board. I'm getting sick of borrowing money to pay extra dividends.

Martin then sent for the controller and pointed out to him that, as usual, rates of return had not been calculated by the marketing people either on the increase in accounts receivable or on the increase in their advertising budget. Moreover, the production manager of the tools division had not calculated a rate on the proposed increase in parts inventory, "and that's not like him." Martin also asked the controller "to see what he could do" to get enough information from Barton, the chemist, about the electron microscopes so that he (the Controller) could calculate a rate himself. He wanted to know how much money the wool buyer thought he would save by buying that wool now, "and when, please, would the wool be used." Finally he gave the controller the memo from sales on A. W. Page Company (see page 4) and requested a recommendation.

Martin then scribbled a note to Kelley at the top of the president's memo:

> At the next meeting of the Finance Committee, be prepared to explain why we don't (and won't) use preferred stock. The old boy apparently still doesn't understand that it's twice as expensive as debt. You'd better look up the article that got him all excited.
>
> Also, find out what goes on in the commercial paper market.
>
> Also, call your pal at Fidelity Mutual and ask him what we'd have to pay for $3 million for ten years.

He then marked the memo "Kelley" and put it in his "out" box.

When Kelley got the memo he wiped the sweat off his brow and said to himself: "Now, tell me, what would Martin do without me." Then he buzzed his secretary and said: "Get me Morton at Fidelity Mutual. Please."

Martin then called Kelley in again and asked him to see whether enough cash could be spared in the next month or so to pay for $500,000 worth of raw wool.

"The answer is yes," said Kelley.

"OK," said Martin. "Thanks."

As he was leaving, Kelley asked: "What about the 90 day bills?"

"Let that go until next week. We don't need the cash now, do we?"

"No," said Kelley, "but we'd pick up a very nice capital gain."

"Next week. Right now, I'm going down to the bank."

the role of finance

What do the foregoing incidents tell us about Finance and the role of Finance in the firm?

They tell us, first, that the various parts of the firm periodically propose expenditures which, each believes, will improve his ability to do his respective job. The *marketing vice president* wants to sell to new customers or increase his advertising budget in order to increase sales. The *production manager* wants to spend money on new machinery and the plant in order to increase production or efficiency. The *wool buyer* wants a temporary increase in his inventory in order to take advantage of a bargain. The overeager *advertising manager* is about to exceed his budget for this quarter—which means that someone will have to decide whether he should be given additional funds. Or the *finance officer* himself may believe that the firm should hold more cash and liquidity so that he will be better able to meet unforeseen financial contingencies. And the *president,* in order to please the stockholders (of which he is one), wants to pay an extra fourth quarter dividend.

The foregoing incidents tell us, in short, that in the Butcher Company—which we may assume to be more or less typical—*everyone wants money,* for one purpose or another.

The incidents also tell us that Finance receives these various proposals and bears the primary responsibility for worrying about:

1. Whether they should be undertaken;
2. How they should be financed.

The incidents tell us (albeit indirectly) that these decisions will determine whether the firm will grow, and how fast it will grow.

And the incidents tell us, finally, that these decisions are *not* the private domain of the chief financial officer, even though he must do the basic worrying about them. These decisions are in fact made by the top management group: by the president or the Finance Committee or the Board of Directors or, as in the case of Butcher, by all three acting together on the basis of advice and counsel provided by the chief financial officer and his staff. Providing such advice and counsel constitutes the central preoccupation of *Finance.*

THE GOAL OF THE FIRM

But no organism—animal, vegetable, or mineral—can make sensible decisions *unless it has a goal.*

choosing a goal

When a freshman arrives at a university, a wide spectrum of opportunities is available to him and he is placed in a difficult and complex situation, although, in his innocence, he may not realize it.

Let's consider Freddy Ferguson who chooses to spend his four years playing his guitar and pursuing the opposite sex from one end of the campus to the other. His goal is "fun" in the conventional sense. Of course, if he chooses this goal, he'll have to study just enough to stay in school. His goal, then, is to have as much fun as possible, consistent with a passing average. With this goal in mind, he begins to see how, at the outset, to allocate his time and money.

In the middle of Freddy's sophomore year, complications arise. In order to have *more* fun, he decides to buy a car, a stereo, and some new clothes. He also needs a haircut. But all these things will cost money, which he doesn't have. His father offers to lend him $2,000, to be repaid after he graduates provided he maintains a "B" average. If he doesn't maintain a "B" average, his allowance will be cut by 35 percent until the loan is repaid, and Freddy knows his father is ruthless.

Now our young friend has a real problem. Should he borrow the money from his father or should he not? He still wants to have as much fun as possible. And he knows he could maintain a "B" average if he spent four hours a week studying—instead of thirty minutes, as he does at present. Will the additional fun he will obtain from the car, the stereo, and the clothes be worth their cost in terms of fun sacrificed?

But our young friend knows what he wants—he wants fun. He is therefore able to sit down and coolly weigh one consideration against the other and come to some (more or less) sensible conclusion.

But suppose he had no goal, or suppose he didn't know what his goal was. He wouldn't know how to deal with his problem. He wouldn't know what to compare with what. He would founder, feel frustrated and gloomy, and growl at people when they said hello. And, in the end, he would probably make a decision which was wrong in terms of what he himself really wanted. (Actually, of course, everyone has a goal—although most people do not know what their goals are.)

Families, also, have goals. A family may, for example, try to maximize the happiness of its members, or it may try to maximize the happiness of some single member, or it may try to maximize educational opportunities for its children, or it may try to maximize the number of new Cadillacs it can afford to buy each year, or it may try to maximize the income which will be available to the senior members of the family in their old age—and so on without end. The family's goal may, of course, change as the circumstances of the family change. But only if the goals are known and made explicit will the family be able to allocate its resources efficiently, that is, to achieve those goals.

goals in business

What should be the goal of the business firm? Clearly, a firm could have a variety of different goals. It could choose to maximize the happiness of its employees (a very complex and difficult goal to define and achieve!) or it could choose to maximize the number of months its managers were able to spend each year on the sands in the Bahamas. Or it could choose to maximize some *economic* magnitude, such as its profits, or its sales, or the wealth of its stockholders. The goal a firm in fact chooses to pursue will be determined by the tastes and values of its managers, the tastes, values, and vigilance of its stockholders, and by its market situation. A firm which is engaged in a bitter competitive struggle to survive is not likely to find itself in business very long if its managers spend all their time playing cribbage.

This book defines the goal of the firm as follows:

> **The Goal of the Firm is the maximization of the market value of its own common stock—the maximization, that is, of the value of the equity owned by its stockholders—subject to whatever constraints, legal or moral, exist in the firm's environment.**

We should bear continuously in mind that this goal is merely an expository device. It does not mean that all firms *do* try to maximize the market value of their common stock. They do not. Nor does it mean that all firms *should* try to maximize the market value of their common stock. They should do whatever they want to do. The goals which firms in the real world in fact choose to pursue are very complex and varied indeed.

The goal given above has been chosen because we must have a relatively simple economic goal in order to be able to describe the *allocative process*. And maximization of the market value of the firm's common stock is, for reasons which are explained in Chapter 2, a more satisfactory goal than maximization of sales or of profits.

In any event, our definition leaves out of account—as falling beyond the scope of a theory of the financial management of the privately-owned business enterprise—two broad classes of money-making units:

1. Professional people, such as doctors, lawyers, engineers, and architects, to the extent that they are inseparable from their respective enterprises;

2. Those government-owned enterprises, such as the Post Office, which are run so as to maximize their contribution to something vaguely called "the general welfare" and which, in any case, have no market value.

The definition given above implies that the firm has a more or less readily ascertainable current market value; which in turn implies that it is corporate in form and that its shares are traded publicly; or if its shares are not traded publicly, or if it is noncorporate in form, that the owners are primarily interested in maximizing the sum they could obtain for the enterprise if they chose to sell it as a going concern.

We are concerned here, then, with the private enterprise which produces and sells goods and services with the object of maximizing the market value of its own common stock.

The next chapter explains why this, rather than some other, economic goal has been chosen.

CONCLUSION

In this introductory chapter, we have made the following assertions:

1. Finance bears the primary responsibility for worrying about how money should be spent and how much money should be *raised*.

   Should Butcher invest more money in new plant or equipment or should it not? Or should it, perhaps, sell off some of the present plant and, if so, what should it do with the proceeds? Should it invest more money or less in cash, in marketable securities, in accounts receivable, in inventory? Should it spend more money or less on advertising, sales promotion and coffeebreaks?

   And how should Butcher raise the necessary funds, if any? In the same old way? Or should it explore new possibilities?

2. But *decisions* on these matters are *not* made by Finance alone. They are made by the top management group on the basis of advice and counsel provided by Finance.

3. But decisions of this kind cannot be made intelligently unless the decision maker has an explicitly formulated goal, or set of goals, which he is striving to achieve.

4. In this book we assume that the firm's primary purpose in life, its goal, is the maximization of the market value of its own common stock—that is, of the value of the pieces of engraved paper which identify the owners of the firm. The next chapter discusses this goal.

REVIEW
OF
FINANCIAL ACCOUNTING

The following problems will help you to review the financial accounting you will need to understand this book.

BALANCE SHEETS AND INCOME STATEMENTS

(1) You have the following assets and liabilities: An Alfa-Romeo 1750 GT which you bought new in Italy two years ago for $3,250. This figure includes the cost of transport to the United States. When you arrived in the United States, you paid $110 in customs duty on the car, bringing your total landed cost to $3,360. The car has a market value now in the United States of $2,850. In addition, you own clothing which cost $800 (but which would bring barely $100 now), books which cost $80 (which you will be able to sell for about $40 at the end of this semester), two guitars—one twelve string and one electric—which you bought second hand several years ago at a total cost of $180. Because of inflation, the two guitars, together, are now worth $40 more than you paid for them. You have a checking account with a balance of $52.18, a savings account with a balance of $418, and two savings bonds, which you received two years ago when you graduated from high school. Each of these bonds has a face value of $100, but if you cashed them now you would receive only about $79 for each bond. You have $9.83 in currency in your pocket and a meal ticket—still good for $47 worth of meals. You have, finally, about $500 (original cost) worth of assorted debris, including a sterling silver ball point pen, a moth-eaten raccoon coat which once belonged to your father, and a pair of ice skates which no longer fit. You have paid your tuition ($800) and your room rent ($330), in advance, for the first semester. You owe your father $500, which you will not have to repay until two years after you graduate—and only *if* you graduate. You haven't yet paid miscellaneous outstanding bills totaling $62, because, as usual, your father is late with your monthly allowance ($200).

A day or so ago (in mid-September) you went to the local bank to borrow $200 to buy a stereo outfit. The loan officer asked you to draw up your personal balance sheet. He gave you a form, *Exhibit 1*, to use.

Fill in the form. What figure will the loan officer be especially interested in? Why?

(2)   After the loan officer has seen your balance sheet, he asks you to draw up a statement of revenue and expense on an annual basis. Do so, given the following figures: allowance, $200 a month for nine months; summer earnings (construction job), $1,400, before deduction for social security and income tax; summer earnings *after* deduction for social security and income tax, $1,190; room rent, nine months, $660; food, nine months, $900 (You live at home, free, during the summer and your mother packs your lunch.); tuition, $1,600 (reimbursed to you by your father); books, $200; laundry, $110; beverages, $180; clothing, $250; miscellaneous entertainment, $500.

After the loan officer has seen your statement, what, do you suppose, his reaction will be?

(3)   You are given the following assortment of figures for Keller Metal Fabricating, Inc., a small company with which Butcher is considering a merger. Draw up an income statement and balance sheet using all the following figures. Income statement items are for the year 1970. Balance sheet items are as of the end of 1970. All figures in thousands.

Accounts payable, $73; sales, $2,500; notes payable, $51; accrued taxes, $38; interest expense, $87; net income after taxes, $416; cash on hand and in banks, $37; treasury bills and notes (90 days), $105; net income before taxes, $816; 7 percent preferred stock, $1,300; federal income tax, $400; accounts receivable, $420; raw materials, $106; retained earnings, $1,835; work-in-process, $702; preferred dividends, $91; earnings before interest and taxes, $903; finished goods, $2,016; plant and equipment (net), $2,111; common stock ($10 par), $1,000; long-term notes, $1,200; cost of goods sold, $1,415 (including depreciation expense of $308); dividend on common stock, $150; selling, general and administrative expense, $182 including amortization of organization expense, $25.

SOURCES AND USES OF FUNDS

(4)   The company's balance sheet as of the end of 1969 is given in Table 1.2. Using the information given in that table and in problem 3 above, draw up a Sources and Uses statement for the company. *List each item separately.* Do *not* net out working capital.

(5)   "Cash Flow" is sometimes defined as earnings after taxes plus noncash expenses. Using this definition calculate Keller's cash flow for 1970. Under what circumstances would this sum produce a corresponding increase in the cash account?

(6)   List five different kinds of noncash expenses. Why are they called "noncash"?

EXHIBIT 1

FINANCIAL STATEMENT

NAME _____   WIFE'S NAME _____

OCCUPATION OR BUSINESS _____   ADDRESS _____

TO THE **NORTH CAROLINA NATIONAL BANK:**

    For the purpose of obtaining credit, direct or indirect, and any other accommodations or benefits from the North Carolina National Bank, from time to time, I/we submit below and on the reverse side hereof the statement of my/our financial condition as of _____ 19 _____ .
In consideration of the premises, I/we agree to notify the North Carolina National Bank of any changes affecting my/our financial responsibility and will at any time upon request furnish the North Carolina National Bank a then current statement of my/our financial condition, said statement to be in such form as required by said bank.

(PLEASE FILL IN ALL BLANKS, SHOWING "NONE" WHERE APPROPRIATE.)

ASSETS		LIABILITIES	
CASH		NOTES PAYABLE (Schedule 3—A)	
ON HAND		TO NORTH CAROLINA NATIONAL BANK	
IN NORTH CAROLINA NATIONAL BANK		OTHER BANKS	
OTHER DEPOSITORIES		OTHERS	
NOTES RECEIVABLE			
UNSECURED		ACCOUNTS PAYABLE (Schedule 3—B)	
DUE WITHIN 12 MONTHS		INSTALLMENT ACCOUNTS	
DUE BEYOND 12 MONTHS		OTHERS	
SECURED			
DUE WITHIN 12 MONTHS			
DUE BEYOND 12 MONTHS			
ACCOUNTS RECEIVABLE		TAXES DUE	
		MORTGAGES (Schedule 2)	
		DUE WITHIN 12 MONTHS	
		DUE BEYOND 12 MONTHS	
INVESTMENTS (Schedule 1)			
U. S. GOVERNMENT SECURITIES			
MARKETABLE SECURITIES			
OTHER INVESTMENTS			
		OTHER LIABILITIES — (Specify)	
REAL ESTATE (Schedule 2)			
CASH VALUE LIFE INSURANCE			
OTHER ASSETS — (Specify)			
		TOTAL LIABILITIES	
		NET WORTH	
TOTAL ASSETS	$	TOTAL LIABILITIES AND NET WORTH	$

SCHEDULES

1. INVESTMENTS—STOCKS AND BONDS

DESCRIPTION	NO. OF SHARES	PAR VALUE	MARKET VALUE	ISSUED IN NAME OF
TOTAL			$	

2. REAL ESTATE

LOCATION	DESCRIPTION TYPE OF BUILDING	SIZE OF LAND	COST	CURRENT MKT. VALUE	MORTGAGE	HOW PAYABLE	TITLE HELD IN NAME OF
TOTAL			$	$	$		

FIRE INSURANCE CARRIED $

3. LIABILITIES

A. TO BANKS (itemize) NAME OF BANK	COLLATERAL OR ENDORSEMENT	HOW PAYABLE	UNPAID BALANCE
TOTAL NOTES PAYABLE TO BANKS		$	$
B. TO OTHERS (List Names of Creditors)			
		$	$

MY ANNUAL INCOME IS: $	FROM:
MY TAXES ARE PAID IN FULL THROUGH	MY LIABILITY AS ENDORSER OR GUARANTOR DOES NOT EXCEED $
I CARRY $	LIFE INSURANCE PAYABLE TO:
THE EXECUTOR OF MY WILL IS :	☐ I HAVE NOT MADE A WILL

I/we certify as a basis for credit that, to the best of my/our knowledge and belief, the information furnished and all representations made herein constitute the true and correct statement of my/our financial condition; that I/we have no assets or liabilities other than as shown on this statement; that all my/our assets are free of lien or assignment except as shown herein and that there are no judgments outstanding or suits pending against me/us.

WITNESS: _____   SIGNATURE: _____

WITNESS: _____   SIGNATURE: _____

RECEIVED BY: _____ ON _____ 19 __

☐ DELIVERED IN PERSON   ☐ RECEIVED BY MAIL

TABLE 1.2

KELLER METAL FABRICATING, INC.,
BALANCE SHEET AS OF DECEMBER 31, 1969

ASSETS

Cash	$ 79
Marketable securities	40
Accounts receivable	118
Inventories	2,407
Plant and equipment (net)	1,739
Other assets	25
TOTAL	$4,408

LIABILITIES AND EQUITY

Notes payable	$ 480
Accounts payable	42
Accrued taxes	26
Long-term notes	600
Preferred stock	850
Common stock ($10 par)	750
Retained earnings	1,660
TOTAL	$4,408

(7) You are given the following forecasted figures for Keller for the month of January, 1971, (all figures in thousands):

(a) expected gross profit before taxes, $55
(b) depreciation, $24
(c) expected increase in inventories, $63
(d) expected decrease in accounts receivable, $18
(e) expected decrease in accounts payable, $2
(f) expected decrease in accruals, $4
(g) selling and general expense, $39
(h) construction costs, $7

No other transactions are expected during the month. If all these forecasts prove to be correct, how much cash will Keller have at the end of the month?

(8) Actually, Keller's cash declined by $20,000 in January 1971. At 5:00 P.M., on January 31, you are given the following forecasts for February, (all figures again in thousands):

(a) gross profit, $140
(b) depreciation, $23

(c) decrease in inventories, $33
(d) decrease in accruals, $4
(e) increase in accounts receivable, $177
(f) increase in accounts payable, $15
(g) selling and general expense, $47
(h) construction costs, $45
(i) interest paid, $13

Calculate the expected change in the cash account for February.

(9) Review carefully each separate item in problems 4 and 5. Be sure you understand why its impact on the cash account is positive or negative, as the case may be.

RATIO ANALYSIS

(10) Calculate the following ratios for Keller, for 1969 and 1970:
(a) acid test
(b) current ratio
(c) profits after taxes to sales (1970 only)
(d) total debt to equity
(e) total debt to total assets
(f) long-term debt to equity
(g) long-term debt to total capital
(h) long-term debt plus preferred stock to common equity
(i) long-term debt plus preferred stock to total capital

After you have calculated each of these ratios, ask yourself whether (and, if so, how) you are wiser than you were before you calculated it. In what circumstances would you use each ratio and how would you use it?

(11) Calculate the following "turns" for Keller for 1970:
(a) accounts receivable
(b) inventory four ways: cost of goods sold and sales, *and* ending inventory and average inventory
(c) net worth turn
(d) total assets turn
(e) fixed assets turn

(12) Keller sells on net 30 day terms. Calculate the average collection period for 1970. What does the figure mean to you?

(13) Calculate Keller's earnings per common share for 1970.

Suppose Keller had no long-term debt and no preferred stock but, instead, 145,000 shares of common stock ($10 par). Calculate EPS in such circumstances.

(14) Calculate Keller's rate of return, after taxes:
(a) on total assets
(b) on net worth

How do you explain the difference?

RISK, RETURN, AND THE GOAL OF THE FIRM

As Chapter 1 has suggested, a decision maker without a clearly stated, explicit goal is not likely to make consistent and efficient decisions. This is true whether the decision maker is an individual, a family, a firm, a government or just a drinking club. A clearly stated, explicit goal is the litmus paper which enables a decision maker to decide consistently and efficiently among alternatives. A decision maker without such a goal is a lost soul—en route to oblivion.

In Chapter 1 we defined the firm as that organism, among all organisms, whose goal is to "maximize" the market value of its own common stock. In this chapter we discuss this goal in detail—but before doing so we discuss the meaning we will give, in this book, to the word *maximize*. Many people believe that the process of "maximizing" consists in squeezing the last drop of blood out of widows and orphans—especially poor widows and orphans. This is *not* the meaning we will give to the word in this book, as we shall now see.

THE MEANING OF "MAXIMIZE"

At any moment in time, the firm has available to it two kinds of investment opportunities. It can invest in projects whose shape and dimensions are clear and visible and which are expected to increase income *now or in the very near future*. Most of the proposals lying on Dale Martin's desk are of this sort: the production manager's proposed projects, and the marketing vice president's proposed increase in accounts receivable. Each of these proposals would be expected to generate additional income soon.

Alternatively, the firm can invest in attempts, sometimes called *research*, to develop projects which would increase income later on—money spent to find new products, or to develop new processes, or to explore new markets. The proposed purchase of new electron microscopes is of this sort. These microscopes would generate no income now or in the near future. They would presumably, however, be useful to the research division in its search for new products and new processes.

These two types of opportunities, together, constitute the sum total of Butcher's *currently available opportunities*.

Of course, after the president, the Finance Committee and the Board of Directors examine these opportunities, they may be disappointed in them. And, if so, they may criticize the research division, or the marketing vice president, or the manager of the mergers and acquisitions division. And they may insist hard on the importance of finding better opportunities for the future. But they must allocate funds *now* and they cannot allocate funds to opportunities they do not have.

Whatever its goal may be, the firm can hardly try to achieve it by choosing alternatives which do not exist.

> By the term *maximize* we mean choosing from among the total of *currently available opportunities* those which will contribute most to the achievement of the firm's goal.

available alternatives

As we all know, individuals try to maximize something called their "utility." Each tries, that is, to make himself as happy as possible. Some individuals (perhaps you among them) do so consciously. Some do so unconsciously. But one way or another, each tries to do so by choosing as well as he can from among the alternatives available to him. But some of the alternatives available now would, if chosen now, improve the alternatives available in the future. Suppose, for example, you have an income of $5,000 a year from property left to you by a rich uncle. What are your alternatives now? You could obviously squander the whole sum now on wine, women, and rock. Or you might decide to spend less now in order to have more to spend later. If you chose the latter alternative, you would be investing money now in order to improve the alternatives from which you would be able to choose later. You might, for example, decide to spend only $3,000 a year and invest $2,000 a year, for some period of time, in stocks and bonds. Or you might decide to invest $2,000 a year for three years to further your education in hopes of improving your subsequent earning power. In either case, you would be investing some money now in order to be able to spend more later on.

And you would choose from among these available alternatives, so as to maximize your total utility over your lifetime. If you thought that an increase in spending power later on would more than offset your present sacrifices you would sacrifice now. In short, you would choose among your *currently available opportunities* so as best to achieve your desired goal.

So, too, does the firm *maximize* by choosing from among its *currently available opportunities* those which will contribute most to the achievement of its goal.

We turn now to consideration of the goal itself.

maximization of what

In elementary economic theory, you doubtless learned that the firm should maximize profits—short-term or long-term. This is a workable goal—provided profits are known *with certainty in advance*. If you are sure that you can earn 10 percent by buying Bond A, and 8 percent by buying Bond B, you will surely buy Bond A. And your choice will be correct. But the world inhabited by elementary economic theory is not the real world. And in the real world, you can rarely be sure—Bond A will probably yield more profit than Bond B—but then, unhappily, it may yield less. How, then, do you decide which to buy?

Suppose, for example, that you are offered the following two alternatives:

1. You can invest $10,000 now in a one year bond with a guaranteed yield of 7 percent. If you invest in it, you will be certain to receive $10,700 at the end of a year—your original principal of $10,000 plus $700 in interest.

2. You can invest $10,000 in a risky venture which will yield either nothing or 14 percent—with a fifty–fifty chance of either. In other words, at the end of the year you would receive either $10,000 or $11,400. In the first case your money would have earned nothing (a yield of 0 percent). In the second case, your money would have earned $1,400, a yield of 14 percent—or twice as much as you would have earned had you invested in the guaranteed bond.

These two alternatives are real alternatives. You will find their counterparts all around you. The bond with a guaranteed yield of 7 percent might, for example, be a bond issued by the Federal Government. The risky venture might be a speculative common stock, such as Butcher to which we were introduced in Chapter 1. As you try to decide which of these two alternatives is best for you, you find yourself mumbling as follows:

> If I invest in the guaranteed bond I will have $700 extra at the end of the year. If I invest in Butcher, I will have either nothing extra or $1,400 extra. Well, nothing plus $1,400 equals $1,400. Fourteen hundred dollars divided by two is $700—which is just the average of the two possible outcomes. Hooray! The two investments are the same. They offer the same average profit. So I'll buy the guaranteed bond and be sure of getting at least $700.

But as you reach for the phone to call your broker, you stop short and shake your head slowly. You shake your head because you have suddenly realized that the two investments are *not* the same, and that if you decide between them on the assumption that they are the same, you will be deceiving yourself. The two investments are not the same because the guaranteed bond offers a certain profit of $700—no more, no less. On the other hand, the risky venture offers you the chance of making a profit of $1,400—if you are willing to run the risk of making no profit at all. In short, you have realized that you cannot use *profits* as a guide because you do not really know what the profit from the risky venture will be; you know only that it will be very high or very low. The choice has two dimensions, not just one: you are offered a chance of higher profits provided you are willing to run the risk of no profits at all.

Now that you see the full dimensions of the problem, how would you decide what to do? What would your decision be? And what would your decision be if the risky venture offered profits of either zero or $2,000?

considering the alternatives

Let's look at the Clay Company of Richmond, Virginia, which has a problem very much like the one above. The Clay Company specializes in building moderately priced, partially prefabricated homes. It is now trying to decide whether to invest about $3 million (a large sum of money in relation to its total assets) in one of the two following projects:

1. To build another batch of its medium-priced, partially pre-fabricated houses, which would require a substantial investment in land and some additional investment in plant and machinery. The company is experienced in this type of project and is almost certain that it would recover its capital investment in two years and would earn a rate of return of somewhere between 9 and 11 percent. If everything went smoothly, the company would earn 11 percent; if minor difficulties arose, the company would earn 9 percent. The management believes that the chances are fifty-fifty that everything will go smoothly. They see no chance whatever of major difficulty. Forty percent of the stock of Clay is held by the public-at-large and is actively traded on the New York Stock Exchange.

2. Alternatively, Clay, for about the same amount, can buy all the outstanding common stock of Mobile Residences, Inc., of Austin, Texas, a company which has been struggling for five years to establish itself in the mobile home market. The mobile home market looks very promising, but its long-run future is highly uncertain. Mobile Residence's product is moderately well known in the Southwest, but sales have been disappointing and the company's capital is disappearing rapidly. In exchange for $3 million, the stockholders of Mobile Residences would pay off all the company's debts and turn over all their stock in Mobile Residences to Clay. The Clay Company would thus acquire plant and machinery which cost $2.9 million five years before, a skilled labor force, a small ineffective sales organization, and miscellaneous other assets. With the exception of the production manager, who has agreed to stay for at least eighteen months, Clay would have to provide a whole new management team.

The Clay Company management, especially F. S. Paul, President, and S. C. Williams, Chairman of the Board, are impressed with the possibilities of the mobile home market. Moreover, they would be acquiring the plant and equipment of Mobile Residences at less than half their present cost. They thought that if things went well, within a couple of years Clay would begin to earn a return of between 40 and 50 percent on its original investment. And if things continued to go well, further growth would be substantial and rapid.

On the other hand, problems would be many: finding a new management team, finding the right product, developing an effective sales organization. And Austin, Texas is nearly 1,500 air miles from Richmond. Clay had a good deal of "know-how" about land development and about building and selling medium-priced houses. But how much of this "know-how" could be applied to building and selling mobile homes?

After a long series of meetings, during which they discussed this alternative (of buying Mobile Residences, Inc.) and its related problems in depth, Paul, Williams, and their associates had concluded that if things went badly, the Clay Company might lose 30 percent or more of its investment. And they felt that the chances were fifty-fifty that things would go very well or very badly.

Which alternative would you choose? On the one hand, the first alternative—increasing production of its own product—promises a maximum return of 11 percent and a minimum return of 9 percent, with about equal chances of either. We may say, therefore, that the project, on balance, promises an average return of about 10 percent. The main characteristic of this alternative is the narrow range within which the return is expected to fall: the return is almost certain to be somewhere between 9 and 11 percent. And there is no risk of loss of capital.

On the other hand, the second alternative—purchasing Mobile Residences, Inc.—provides a fifty-fifty chance of a very high return, and a fifty-fifty chance of a loss of $1 million. Where the return would actually fall is obviously highly uncertain and the possible range of returns is large. In short, the second alternative is very risky.

choosing an alternative

How should Clay, or any company faced with a similar choice, decide which alternative to choose—assuming that it will choose one or the other?

Let us restate the essential difference between the two alternatives. If Clay chooses the first alternative, it would be choosing a virtually riskless, moderate return of 10 percent—a rate about the same as the rates it has been earning year in and year out on most of its new projects. If it chooses this project, the company could be virtually certain that when the project ended two years hence the investment of $3 million would have grown at a compound annual rate of 10 percent or, in dollars, by $300,000 the first year and by $330,000 the second year—after taxes. In short, after the project had ended, and the original investment had been recovered, the company would have $3.63 million available to reinvest or to pay in dividends to its stockholders.

On the other hand, if the company chooses the second alternative, it might earn a very high return beginning in four or five years. And this return would continue, and perhaps grow, over a long period of time: if the mobile homes company were successful, the Clay Company would, of course, retain its investment. On the other hand, if it could not rehabilitate Mobile Residences, Clay might lose a third of its original investment.

Suppose you were F. S. Paul and S. C. Williams rolled into one. How would *you* make this decision? Obviously, you cannot use profits alone as a guide—simply because you do not know what profits from Mobile Residences would be. You know only that they will be very high, very low, or something in between. You must choose between a virtually certain return of about 10 percent and a risky return which will be much higher than 10 percent, or much lower.

How do you make this decision?

INCREASED RISK

Let's reconsider Butcher which, as we saw in Chapter 1, has a similar problem.

As we saw earlier, Dale Martin, Vice President of Finance for Butcher, has received requests for new long-term capital investments, totaling $6.433 million. If approved by the Board, these investments would be made during the next year. With Kelley's help, Martin has estimated that $4.56 million would be available from profits and other internal sources to pay for these investments. But he is very much aware that this estimate may be wrong. And he believes that he may have to raise as much as $3 million from outside sources during the coming year. But he knows that neither the President nor the Board would approve the sale of additional common stock now. He would, therefore, have to borrow the money at long term, to be repaid over the life of the new assets, which he estimates would be ten to twelve years. He must decide, therefore, how money should be spent and how much money should be raised. Tables 2.1 and 2.2 give an estimated balance sheet and income statement for the year which will end on December 31, 1968, only a month or so away.

Martin knew that borrowing more money, even a small amount, would make the company seem more of a gamble to some of the present stockholders, and to the investing public as a whole. Why was this so?

Martin had been over all the relevant considerations, two years before, in mid-1966 when Butcher had borrowed $36.8 million at 5½ percent from a large insurance company. (One payment of $2.3 million had already been made on this loan.) Butcher had needed a lot of money to improve its own efficiency and to diversify. At that time, the company had had two alternatives: it could have borrowed the necessary money, as in fact it finally decided to do, or it could have sold about 1.3 million

TABLE 2.1

THE BUTCHER COMPANY, ESTIMATED CONSOLIDATED BALANCE SHEET AS OF DECEMBER 31, 1968

ASSETS

Cash and marketable securities	$ 10,528,385
Accounts receivable (net)	48,007,580
Inventories	84,148,980
Prepaid expenses	443,955
Other current assets	14,209,035
Land, plant, and equipment (net)	34,035,310
TOTAL	$191,373,245

LIABILITIES AND EQUITY

Accounts payable	$ 28,189,530
Accrued expense	10,721,330
Accrued federal income tax	6,446,190
Long-term debt	34,500,000
Common stock ($10 par)	21,875,000
Retained earnings	89,641,195
TOTAL	$191,373,245

TABLE 2.2

THE BUTCHER COMPANY, ESTIMATED INCOME STATEMENT, AS OF DECEMBER 31, 1968

Net sales	$283,594,305
Cost of merchandise sold (including depreciation)	—218,259,790
Operating profit	$ 65,334,515
Selling, administrative and general expense before deduction of interest	—45,500,150
Earnings before interest and income taxes	19,834,365
Interest expense	—1,897,500
Earnings before taxes	$ 17,936,865
Federal and other income (including surtax)	—8,789,064
Earnings after taxes	$ 9,147,801
Earnings per share, based on 2,187,500 shares outstanding	$4.18

shares of common stock at $30 a share. At that time Martin, the Finance Committee, and the Board had been almost exclusively concerned about earnings per share—which had been very low in the early sixties (see Table 2.3).

TABLE 2.3

THE BUTCHER COMPANY,
SALES, EARNINGS, AND EARNINGS PER SHARE, 1959-1968

YEAR ENDED DECEMBER 31:	NET SALES	EARNINGS AFTER TAXES	PER SHARE†
		(thousands)	
(1)	(2)	(3)	(4)
1959	$196,590	$11,520	$5.27
1960	196,210	9,065	4.14
1961	123,415	1,021	.47
1962	136,275	1,710	.78
1963	134,000	815	.37
1964	123,085	1,685	.77
1965	155,780	4,125	1.89
1966	167,580	4,170	1.91
1967	213,785	7,990	3.65
1968 *	283,594	9,147	4.18

* Estimated.
† Based on 2,187,500 shares.

Martin had done the calculations given in Tables 2.4 and 2.5 at that time. Martin had thought these two tables were very striking. They had been done for the purpose of illustrating the effect of each of the two alternatives on earnings per share at a low level of earnings and at a high level. At that time, of course, Butcher had no long term debt on its books.

First, let's consider Table 2.4: In 1965, Butcher had earned $4.125 million after taxes or about $8.25 million *before* taxes. The new investments being contemplated in mid-1966 were expected to earn a bit more than 12 percent after taxes and were expected to add $9.12 million to earnings before taxes, beginning in 1967. Total earnings before taxes for 1967 were, thus, estimated at $17.37 million ($8,250,000 + $9,120,000 = $17,370,000).

Both the Finance Committee and the Board considered this figure to

TABLE 2.4

THE BUTCHER COMPANY, EFFECTS OF BORROWING ON EARNINGS PER SHARE AT MODERATELY HIGH LEVEL OF EARNINGS AS OF JULY 1966

	BORROW	SELL COMMON STOCK
	(thousands)	
Earnings before interest and taxes	$17,370	$17,370
Interest first year at 5½ percent on $36,800,000	—2,024	——
Earnings before taxes	15,346	17,370
Taxes at 50 percent	7,673	8,685
Earnings after taxes	$ 7,673	$ 8,685
Number of common shares:		
Old	2,187.5	2,187.5
New	——	1,300.0
TOTAL	$ 2,187.5	$ 3,487.5
Earnings per share for common stock	$ 3.51	$ 2.49

be moderately high but not necessarily a maximum. If earnings before taxes reached this figure, Butcher would earn $3.51 a share if it used debt, but only $2.49 if it used common stock—as column (1) of Table 2.4 shows.

But when earnings before interest and taxes were as low as anyone thought they could possibly go, earnings per share would be *lower,* not higher, if the company borrowed—as shown in Table 2.5. If earnings before interest and taxes fell about halfway between the low and high figures (at about $10.5 million) earnings per share would be $1.94 if the company borrowed, but only $1.51 if it sold additional common stock—as shown in Table 2.6. In other words, if Butcher borrowed $36.8 million to pay for the new assets instead of selling additional common stock, and if earnings were high, the present common stockholders would be much better off. But if earnings were low, they would be worse off, perhaps much worse off. Borrowing would, therefore, be a gamble.

It would give the common stockholders a chance to earn more money, and receive higher dividends, than would otherwise have been possible; but it would also make the company much riskier—the stockholders

TABLE 2.5

THE BUTCHER COMPANY, EFFECT OF BORROWING ON EARNINGS PER SHARE AT LOW LEVEL OF EARNINGS AS OF JULY 1966

	BORROW	SELL COMMON STOCK
	(thousands)	
Earnings before interest and taxes	$3,600	$3,600
Interest first year at 5½ percent on $36,800,000	2,024	——
Earnings before taxes	1,576	3,600
Taxes at 50 percent	788	1,800
Earnings after taxes	$ 788	$1,800
Number of common shares	2,187.5	3,487.5
Earnings per share for common stock	$ .36	$ .52

might earn less money, and receive lower dividends, than would otherwise have been the case. And if earnings remained low for several years in succession the company might be seriously embarrassed financially. If this happened, the price of Butcher stock would drop drastically. It was the same old problem Martin and the company had encountered many times before—the choice between risk and return: higher return, more risk; lower return, less risk.

Actually, in 1966, Butcher had decided to borrow. Both the Finance Committee and the Board gave a great deal of weight to the difference of $1.02 (see Table 2.4) in earnings per share at a moderately high level of earnings. They were also impressed by the fact that, if earnings were only "average," as shown in Table 2.6, earnings per common share would be nearly one-third higher if they borrowed. Also, they hoped that diversification would, at least in the long run, reduce risk, since they hoped to acquire companies with a sales cycle opposite to that of machine tools—so that when sales of machine tools were low, sales of other products would be high.

Martin felt that Butcher had been lucky. Sales had gone up since 1966 by 69 percent; and earnings after taxes and earnings per share had more than doubled (see Table 2.3). And the price of the stock, which had risen from $30 to $35 a share the day after the announcement had been made, in 1966, had traded yesterday (just three years later) at $51.

TABLE 2.6

THE BUTCHER COMPANY, EFFECT OF BORROWING ON EARNINGS PER SHARE AT AVERAGE LEVEL OF EARNINGS AS OF JULY 1966

	BORROW	SELL COMMON STOCK
	(thousands)	
Earnings before interest and taxes	$10,500	$10,500
Interest first year at 5½ percent on $36,800,000	—2,024	——
Earnings before taxes	8,476	10,500
Taxes at 50 percent	4,238	5,250
Earnings after taxes	4,238	5,250
Number of common shares		
Old	2,187.5	2,187.5
New	——	1,300.0
TOTAL	2,187.5	3,487.5
Earnings per share for common stock	$ 1.94	$ 1.51

But, for the longer run, Martin had good reason to feel very uncertain. Butcher's earnings *were* highly volatile, as Table 2.3 shows. In 1967, for example, Butcher had earned about $7.99 million after taxes. But in 1965, the company's earnings after taxes were only $4.125 million and in 1966, $4.17 million. In 1964 they were only $1.685 million and in 1963, just five short years ago, they had been a mere $815,000. And prior to 1967, the company had had no long-term debt and had paid only nominal amounts of interest (to its local banks on occasional short-term loans). If Butcher had had long-term debt on its books in 1963 and 1964, interest payments would have reduced earnings to zero or below.

In thinking about the problem he faced today, that is, whether to borrow an additional $3 million, Martin was very much aware that if a recession in business coincided with a recession in the demand for machine tools, consolidated earnings after taxes might conceivably fall as low as $800,000—unless Butcher were able to diversify further before a recession occurred. On the other hand, even without additional outside funds, Martin thought earnings as high as $12 million after taxes would not be impossible in boom years. In short, then, Martin thought that over the next five years or so, earnings after taxes could fall anywhere between $800,000 and $12 million, depending on general business conditions and the demand for machine tools.

If earnings were in the upper range, the company's present debt would be no problem. Nor would a small amount of additional debt. Interest on the present long-term debt at 5½ percent was $1,897,500. And annual required repayments on principal were $2.3 million in each of the next fifteen years. Interest on $3 million of additional debt would be about $220,000 and amortization, about $300,000. With earnings in the upper range, all these required payments could be made easily as Table 2.7 shows. With earnings after taxes at $10.8 million—his forecast for next year—earnings *before* taxes but after deduction of interest would be about $21.6 million. Earnings before deduction of taxes *and* interest, but after deduction of all other expenses, would, therefore, be $23,497,500, as shown in Table 2.7. In such circumstances, Butcher would

TABLE 2.7

THE BUTCHER COMPANY, FORECAST FOR 1969

Earnings before deduction of interest and taxes but after deduction of all other expenses	$23,497,500
Interest on present long-term debt	—$1,897,500
Earnings before taxes	21,600,000
Taxes at assumed rate of 50 percent	—10,800,000
Earnings after taxes	$10,800,000
Amortization of present long term debt	—2,300,000
	$ 8,500,000
Regular and extra dividend of $2.35 on 2,187,500 shares	—5,140,000
Balance	$ 3,360,000

obviously have no difficulty whatever paying interest and amortization, both old and new.

But if earnings fell to $800,000 after taxes, Butcher would be in moderate trouble. It would be unable to pay amortization out of earnings and would have to reduce cash or borrow short-term from the banks. And it would doubtless be forced to cut the dividend drastically. If earnings continued to be poor for a number of years, Butcher might be in serious trouble. It could not go on reducing cash or borrowing short-term indefinitely to pay amortization. And it might have to sell productive assets in order to meet its obligations.

Martin felt, therefore, that the problem he faced in 1968 was no different in principle from the problem he had faced in mid-1966, although of course, the amount involved was much smaller now. The additional borrowing would create the possibility of even higher returns for the stockholders. But it would also increase the risk of lower returns—and of bankruptcy.

What should he do? What would you do if you were Martin? Would you borrow another $3 million?

Here also, then, as in the case of the Clay Company, Martin cannot look merely at profits. He cannot look merely at profits because if he borrows more money he will, true, have created the possibility of higher maximum and average profits for Butcher's stockholders—but only by increasing the risk of lower profits and bankruptcy. He was thus faced again with the problem of risk versus return: higher return, more risk; lower return, less risk. *How should he make this decision?*

subjective decision making

To shed some light on this problem, let's go back now to the individual (perhaps it was someone just like you) who was trying to decide whether to invest $10,000 either in a bond with a guaranteed profit of $700 or, alternatively, in a risky venture on which profits would be either zero or $1,400. How should you make this decision? The answer is that no one, except yourself, can tell you what you should do. You should do whatever you are disposed to do. And what you are disposed to do will depend on your own subjective willingness to gamble—that is, on your temperament, and on your circumstances. If you are timid and "conservative" you will probably choose the first alternative and will criticize, as gamblers, those who choose the second alternative. And, of course, you will be envious if the gamblers win. If you are a gambler you will probably choose the second alternative, and you will be full of scorn for those dreary souls who choose the first alternative.

In short, the decision you make, given the above situation, will depend on your own subjective attitude toward risk. But at bottom, most of the common stock in most corporations in the United States is owned directly or indirectly by individuals who, like the individual described above, have their own subjective attitudes toward risk. Much of the stock, for example, in companies like U.S. Steel or RCA or AT&T, is owned directly by individuals. And some stock is owned by financial institutions such as mutual funds, which are themselves owned by individuals.[1]

To repeat, each of these individuals will have his own subjective attitude toward risk. Some individuals enjoy risk; those who do will buy risky common stocks or speculate in wildcat oil wells. On the other hand, some individuals dislike risk (widows and orphans) and they will buy high quality bonds or stable common stocks. This is just another way of saying that each individual will invest so as to make himself feel comfortable—given his own subjective attitude toward risk. This being so, we may say that those individuals who now own stock in Clay or in Butcher are reasonably happy with the combination of risk and return being offered by each company. *Otherwise, they would have sold their stock in those companies and would not now be stockholders.*

Now, obviously, a corporation should be responsible to its owners, which means, in plain language, that it should do what its owners want it to do. And this means, among other things, that it should run the degree of risk its owners want it to run. But how can a company which is considering doing something which will make the company riskier find out what its stockholders think?

STOCKHOLDER PARTICIPATION IN CHOOSING ALTERNATIVES

Now let's go back and watch S. C. Williams and F. S. Paul as they try to decide whether or not to buy Mobile Residences, Inc. What they are trying to do, actually, is to answer the question: Is the chance for a very high return worth to our stockholders the risk of losing one third of $3 million? Why "to our stockholders"? Simply because, as noted above, the $3 million which would be invested in Mobile Residences belongs to Clay's stockholders.

Let's suppose, first, that the Clay Company, instead of being owned in part by the public-at-large, were owned entirely by its managers and

---

[1] Some common stock is owned by pension funds and mutual insurance companies, which are not really owned by individuals. In any case, beneficiaries of pension funds and policy holders in mutual insurance companies have no way to make themselves heard if they happen to dislike the investment policies being followed by such companies. They cannot transfer their interest from one pension fund to another, or their life insurance policies from one insurance company to another. Investors in a mutual *fund*, on the other hand, can transfer their holdings out of that fund if, for any reason, they choose to do so, simply by selling their shares back to the fund.

their families—as is the case with many small and medium-sized companies. If this were the case, Paul and Williams of the Clay Company would simply discuss the matter between themselves and with those of their associates who owned stock in the company. The conversation might go as follows:

"Oh, it's risky all right," Williams would say. All heads would nod in agreement. "But I'm sick of being so conservative. Our earnings are stagnating. Mobile Residences would give us a chance for real, maybe phenomenal, growth. Frank agrees with me."

"I do," said Paul. "I'm willing to gamble."

"I'm not," said Knox, the vice president for production.

"I'm not willing to risk that much of my capital. Everything I've got is invested in Clay. That's not the case with you and Frank. And as you know, I need the dividends to help support my mother and sister. If Mobile Residences goes under, the Clay dividend would be cut, drastically, maybe to zero. And who knows whether we would ever recover."

After half an hour of talk, it became clear that Knox was the only stockholder who would be unhappy if Clay invested in Mobile Residences.

Williams said to him, "How much stock do you own?"

"Three thousand shares," said Knox.

"Worth about $33 a share at book value," said Williams.

"Yes," said Knox.

"I'll buy it from you," said Williams, "at $35 a share."

"I want some," said Paul.

"Me, too," said three or four others.

"Okay," said Knox, "but I don't want to sell all of it."

"Oh," said Williams, "You'd like to keep some? How much?" Williams was relieved. He wanted all key personnel to own stock in the company.

"Maybe a thousand shares," said Knox. "I'll tell you in the morning. I'd like to talk it over with my wife."

"Okay," said Williams, and the meeting ended.

What, in effect, had Williams done? He had polled the stockholders in order to ascertain their subjective feelings about the gamble represented by Mobile Residences. He had found one stockholder who, because of his temperament or his circumstances or perhaps both, was not willing to gamble. That stockholder had been given a chance to sell his stock at what both buyer and seller thought was a fair price and, as a result, everyone was happy. And Williams himself was not only gratified that Knox wanted to keep a thousand shares, he was amused, as well.

In reality, however, the Clay Company stock was not all held by the managers and their families. Unhappily, 40 percent of the stock of Clay was held by the public—by 750 stockholders scattered all over the East. Holdings among the public ranged from 25 to 10,000 shares, the average being about 300 shares. The stock was traded actively in the New York Stock Exchange. Williams knew a few of the larger stockholders personally and he thought they would be in favor of buying Mobile Residences. But what about the others?

Williams soon realized that after Clay announced the purchase of Mobile Residences, any Clay stockholder who wished to do so could sell all or part of his Clay stock if he thought the company had now become too risky, too much of a gamble. But he did not want those stockholders who chose to sell to have to take a loss, perhaps a big loss. But neither he nor the company had the resources to support the price of the stock—to buy whatever was offered in order to maintain the present price of about $33 a share. He felt he had to consider the welfare of the outside stockholders not only because they owned part of the company but also because they could be a nuisance if they got angry. In addition, Williams himself owned 100,000 Clay shares presently worth $3.3 million. He did not, most decidedly, want to see the price of the stock drop by a third, or even by 10 percent—even though he was sure that the price of the stock would treble, or more, if Mobile Residences worked out well. He knew that if the price of the stock dropped, it would not move much again until clear results began to come in from Mobile Residences, but that would not be for a year or more.

He was sure that some stockholders would be unhappy at the decision and would sell their stock. But the real question was what would happen to the demand for the stock. Perhaps some of the present stockholders would buy more and perhaps investors who now held no stock in the company would buy some. If demand for the stock exceeded supply at the present price, the price would go up. Those stockholders who wished to sell would be able to sell at a profit over the present price and everyone would be happy.

So the basic question was: would demand for the stock increase after the announcement was made? This question could be put differently. The Clay Company would be much more of a gamble after the acquisition of Mobile Residences than it was now. And some of the present stockholders, among them Williams' mother-in-law, would be displeased. They were the ones who would sell all or part of their stock or, at the very least, write him nasty, crackpot letters. (He wanted to be able to write back saying that if they did not like Clay's plans, they could sell their stock—and at a 10 percent profit.) But he was sure there were many investors who did not presently own Clay stock because they thought the company was too conservatively managed. They cared less about stable earnings and a stable dividend than they did about a chance for growth—and capital gains. And they were willing to gamble in order to obtain a chance for growth. Such investors would find the Clay Company more attractive, not less, after the purchase of Mobile Residences than they had before. Williams did not, of course, know whether enough new investors would be attracted to Clay stock to keep the price from going down. But he felt, intuitively, that the chances were about even that the stock would remain at its present level or go up a point or two. He decided to talk the matter over with two large stockbrokers who had always shown an interest in Clay stock. Both expressed the opinion that the company's stock would not go down. They said they did not know whether it would go up, but they did say that as soon as the public announcement was made, they would buy small amounts of Clay Company stock for their own portfolios. Williams was encouraged. A few days later Clay acquired Mobile Residences, and Williams made a public announcement to that effect.[2]

Williams had thus made his decision by guessing, as best he could, *what the effect would be on the price of Clay common stock*. He could not, rationally, have made this decision in any other way if he wished to take account of the economic interests of the company's stockholders.

Williams might, of course, have made the decision, perfectly rationally, on *noneconomic* grounds. He might have decided, for example, that the present stockholders were perfectly happy. And as evidence of this he could have pointed to the fact that sales of Clay stock were few and usually in small amounts. Why, therefore, should he "rock the boat"? If things went wrong with the purchase of Mobile Residences he would be confronted at the next meeting by a mob of angry stockholders. And for weeks or months thereafter much of his time would be taken up answering letters and talking personally to those stockholders who insisted on seeing him. But if Williams had made the decision in this way, he would have been looking at his own interests rather than those of the owners of the company—the stockholders. As things turned out, of course, everyone was better off. And even if Mobile Residences turned out to be a total loss, he would always be able to say to any angry present stockholder: "You could have sold your stock at $80. You knew what the risks were." And he would be able to say to any new stockholder: "You shouldn't have paid $80 for the stock. You knew what the risks were."

---

[2] A few days after the announcement was made to buy Mobile Residences, the Clay stock was selling at $40. After only four months, long before Mobile Residences had begun to earn money, the stock had risen to $80. Williams had grossly underestimated the number of gamblers in the East!

In short, Williams had gone through a four step mental process. He had said to himself:

1. If I were the only stockholder in this company, I'd be able to do exactly as I please. I'd be able to take any risk I chose to take.
2. But I'm not the only stockholder. There are more than 750 others —no two of whom, very likely, have the same attitude toward risk.
3. Obviously, I can't please them all. Even if I called a stock-holders' meeting and the proposal carried by a big majority, some stockholders would still be unhappy—those who had voted No.
4. But if we buy Mobile Residences, and the price of our stock does not go down, anyone who thinks we've become too risky would be able to sell out and be no worse off than he was before. The only way to deal with the problem, then, is by trying to assess the effect of the purchase on the price of our stock.

And Williams had done some talking and thinking and had come to the conclusion that the investing public as a whole—*not* just Clay's present stockholders—would, on balance, support the purchase of Mobile Residences. Some of Clay's present stockholders would sell. But enough outsiders would buy so that the price of Clay's stock would not go down, and it might go up. Thus any of Clay's present stockholders would be able to sell his stock, if he chose to do so, at no loss. It was as if Williams had polled Clay's stockholders and had said to those who opposed the purchase: "I'll get someone to buy you out at the current price."

What do the foregoing illustrations tell us?

They tell us, first, that the firm in the real world cannot simply try to "maximize profits." It cannot simply try to maximize profits because the alternatives available to it differ not only in expected profits but also in risk. By "risk," we mean simply the fact that actual profits may be very different from expected profits—and especially that they may be substantially lower. And in choosing from among the alternatives available to it the firm must, therefore, consider *both* expected profits and risk.

Second, the firm can take account of *both* expected profits *and* risk by looking at the effect of the choices it makes on the price of its com-mon stock, provided its stock is held by the public. (If its stock is not held by the public but, rather, by a small group, such as a family or management, the small group must itself decide what to do on the basis of its own composite, subjective attitude toward risk. We saw this happen in our initial discussion of Clay's problem, above.)

Third, the conclusion that a firm should try to maximize the price of its common stock follows from three basic propositions:

1. The firm is owned by—that is, is the property of—its current stockholders.
2. Managers should manage the firm in the interests of the firm's owners—that is, its current stockholders.
3. If the price of the firm's stock goes up, the value of the property owned by the current stockholders will have increased and they (the current stockholders) will be better off.

FINANCE AND THE PRICE OF THE FIRM'S STOCK

In short, then, the finance officer must try to assess the effect his allocative decisions will have on the price of the firm's common stock. He must try, in other words, in the language we have used above, to *maximize* the price of the firm's stock.

We said, above, that the firm maximizes by making the most of the opportunities available to it at the moment when the allocative decision must be made. The firm must, therefore, separate those opportunities which can be expected to increase the price of its stock from those which can be expected to reduce it or leave it unchanged.

How does the firm do so—that is, how does the firm separate those opportunities which can be expected to increase the price of its stock from those which can be expected to decrease it or leave it unchanged? It does so in one or the other of two ways: it does what Williams and Paul of the Clay Company did in the situation described above—that is, it conducts a piece of informal market research, among a few selected investors, aimed at answering the question: if we do something which simultaneously increases expected return and risk (for example, if we buy Mobile Residences), what will happen to the market for our common stock? Will the investing public run away from our stock or will they rush to buy it?

Or, as an alternative to this more or less unsystematic and highly subjective procedure, the firm can do what Dale Martin did when he resolved Butcher's $3 million problem. Let's reconsider what Martin did.

Martin had been accustomed for some time to calculating for Butcher a mysterious number called the *cost of capital*. Martin knew that the "cost of capital" was affected by the degree of risk a company took, as we shall see in Part IV of this book. And he knew, or thought he knew, that Butcher's present cost of capital was about 10.8 percent. He did a calculation or two and concluded that if Butcher borrowed another $3 million, its cost of capital would probably fall slightly, but surely would go no higher. He then looked at the expected rate of return on each proposed new project and rejected all those which promised returns less than 10.8 percent. If "the expected rate of return" on a project were higher than the "cost of capital", and the project were undertaken, the price of Butcher's stock would go up—other things remaining unchanged.

CONCLUSION

This chapter has made the following points:

1. By the term *maximize* we mean simply "making the most of existing opportunities," given the goal of the firm.

2. Expected profits are not a feasible economic goal for the firm when the firm, in the real world, must choose among alternatives which differ not only in expected profits but also in risk. The firm, that is, is always trying to decide whether or not to accept more risk in order to obtain a chance to earn a higher return.

3. The firm *can* choose among such alternatives, however, by assessing the effect of each on the price of its (the firm's) common stock. A choice which raises the price of the firm's stock is a good choice, and vice versa.

4. The firm can assess the effect of each alternative on the price of its common stock by (a) calculating an expected rate of return on each alternative and then (b) comparing each such rate of return with its cost of capital.

5. The firm should invest in every opportunity which promises a rate of return higher than its cost of capital. It should invest in none which promises a rate of return lower than its cost of capital.

THE STRUCTURE OF THIS BOOK

If this brief description of what Martin did confuses you, remember that *the purpose of this book, in a sentence, is to tell you what "rates of return" are and what the "cost of capital" is and to show you how to use them to maximize the price of the firm's common stock.*

We cannot understand what expected rates of return are or what the cost of capital is unless we have particular kinds of knowledge. What, for example, are the peculiarities (idiosyncrasies might be a better word) of each of the assets the firm uses to do its job? What, for example, is cash (it's not what you think it is)? What are 90 days bills? What are accounts receivable, inventory and fixed assets? And what, for example, is common stock, and what is a bond, and what are the differences between them? What are the other "external" sources of funds, short term and long? What is a bank and why, generally, are bankers so conservative? And how do you go about inducing a bank to lend you money? What is a factor (again, not what you think it is)?

But even if we had more facts in our possession than the authors of the *Encyclopaedia Britannica,* we would not be able to maximize the market value of our common stock unless we knew how to use various and sundry tools of analysis, which we shall now consider.

tools of analysis

As indicated above, two tools are at the center of the allocative process in the firm. They have been introduced above: expected *rates of return* and the *cost of capital.* There are four more.

PRESENT VALUE

By the term "present value" we mean the value *now* of money to be received at some time in the future. If someone were to promise to pay you $10,000 one year from now, what would you be willing to pay for that promise? Chapter 3 explores this question.

PROBABILITY DISTRIBUTIONS

In estimating expected rates of return on physical assets or expected profits, or expected cash receipts, we will always be looking into the future. We will be trying, that is, to see what lies ahead. We cannot know what really lies ahead—which is simply another way of saying that more than one actual outcome is possible. If more than one outcome is possible, we will get better results over the long run if we take account of the different possibilities of each outcome instead of trying to predict a single outcome. A probability distribution is merely a device which enables us to take account of these different possibilities.

If, for example, a car salesman tells you that the car he is trying to sell you "will last ten years," you know perfectly well that he does not really mean what he says. What he really means is that the car will probably last ten years or perhaps that it *may* last ten years—given reasonable care. But there are obviously other possibilities: the whole thing may fall to the ground the first time you open the door; or the transmission may drop out the first time your wife tries to put the car in reverse without throwing out the clutch; or after five great years, it may dig in and refuse to go any farther; or it may last fifteen years with nothing but an oil change every 50,000 miles. And in order to know what you can really expect from the car, you must know (or estimate) the probability that the car will last one year, two years, three years and so forth. Chapters 6 and 7 discuss probability distributions and some of the ways they are used in finance.

FORECASTING TECHNIQUES

The finance officer is always forecasting six months or a year or more ahead. This book uses three forecasting techniques: *cash budgets, pro forma balance sheets and income statements,* and *correlation analysis,* both simple and multiple. Cash budgets and pro forma balance sheets and income statements are discussed in Chapters 9 and 15 and correlation analysis in Chapter 11.

FINANCIAL RATIOS

The finance officer must also be able to draw conclusions, as an outsider, about the financial condition of other companies, especially customers, suppliers and merger prospects. Financial ratios are sometimes helpful for this purpose. (These have been introduced in the Appendix to Chapter 1.)

In sum then, the structure of the book is as follows: Part II discusses tools of analysis: present value rates of return, financial ratios probability and Part III discusses the various types of assets held by the firm and applies present value and rate of return analysis to each. Part IV discusses sources of funds, both short and long term, and the cost of capital, both short and long term.

PROBLEMS

1. Be sure you understand how Tables 2.5, 2.6, and 2.7 were constructed.

   Construct a similar table for EBIT of $16.5 million.

2. Under the rules and regulations of the Board of Governors of the Federal Reserve System, "Margin requirements are 70 percent." This means that if you want to buy a common stock, such as RCA or AT&T, traded on the New York Stock Exchange or the American

Stock Exchange, you must reach into your own pocket for 70 percent of the price. You may borrow the remainder (30 percent) from your stockbroker or your bank. Thus if you have $700 you would be able to buy stocks worth $1,000—if you were willing and able to borrow $300 from a broker or a bank.

While your roommate is having his morning beer and steak tartare, he rouses you from a sound sleep and says: "Hey, look at this! Roan Selection Trust is selling at $5 a share! That's what you should do with that $700." You open one eye and see him standing next to your bed flourishing the Wall Street Journal. A few weeks ago you inherited $700 from a rich uncle. Your roommate is jealous and he's been trying to persuade you, ever since, to do something foolish with it.

You say, "Go away and let me sleep." You close your eye.

He rants on: "You could buy 200 shares on margin by borrowing $300 from a broker. There's a good chance that Roan will go to $10 a share in less than three months!"

You know:

That Roan could also go to $3 a share in less than three months;

That your broker is now charging 9 percent a year (= 9/12 of 1 percent a month) on margin loans;

That Roan pays a dividend of twenty cents a share every three months. If you bought the stock now and held it for three months, you would receive one such dividend.

(a) Assume you buy the stock, it goes to $10 a share in the next three months, and you sell then. Calculate your profit in dollars if you borrow $300 and buy 200 shares. Don't forget to take account of both the dividend you will receive and the interest you will pay on the money you borrow. And don't forget either that after you sell the stock, you will have to repay the money you have borrowed.

(b) Now assume the price goes down to $3 a share instead of up to $10. Calculate your loss in dollars, again remembering that you will receive a dividend and will have to pay interest as above. And, of course, as soon as you sell the stock, you will have to repay the loan.

(c) Now, instead of borrowing $300 in order to buy 200 shares, you buy only 140 shares ($700/$5 = 140). Calculate your dollar profit if the price of the stock goes up to $10 a share and your dollar loss if it goes down to $3.

3. Why are both profit and loss larger if you borrow in order to buy the 60 extra shares? Explain in precise numerical terms.

4. Now try as hard as you can to imagine that you are in the situa-

tion described in problem 2. Which alternative would you chose? Why?

5. In order to make the above decision intelligently, you need one additional piece of information. What do you think that piece of information might be?

6. Now, suppose that you decide that you will buy only 140 shares of Roan. You have two alternatives: you can buy them outright, that is, not borrow; or you can borrow any amount up to $210 (.30 × $700 = $210). If you borrow, you will put whatever you yourself do not invest in a savings bank at 5 percent. That is, if you decide to borrow $210, you will pay for the 140 shares with $490 of your own money and $210 in borrowed money. You will put $210 of your own money into the savings bank.

   Calculate your profit and loss, as in problem 2 above, on the assumptions that you would borrow
   (a) $50
   (b) $100
   (c) $210
   How much would you borrow? Why?

7. You now realize that despite the pressure being put on you by your roommate, you can, if you wish, put all or part of your money in a savings bank at 5 percent interest. If you save all of it, you will have earned $8.75 in interest in three months and, at the end of three months, you will have $708.75 with no chance of loss. If you had to choose between buying 140 shares of Roan (no borrowing) and investing in a savings account at 5 percent, which would you do? Why?

8. Thinking about the foregoing choice makes you realize that you really have a large number of alternatives available to you, as follows: Invest $700 in a savings account; invest $1,000 in Roan, borrowing the additional $300 from your broker; anything between these two alternatives. (But remember: if you buy Roan, you must buy at least 20 shares, the minimum order your broker will accept.)

   Look up Roan Selection Trust in a recent issue of the Value Line Investment Survey or Standard and Poor's or some other investment advisory service. Then decide how you would invest your $700:
   (a) all in Roan, borrowing $300
   (b) all in a savings account
   (c) something in between (a) and (b).
   Support your decision with appropriate computations.

9. Suppose that:
   (a) Butcher accepts all the proposed new projects and its earn-

ings after taxes, but before deduction of additional interest,
increase by $900,000;

(b) Butcher could borrow $3 million to pay for the assets repre-
sented by these projects, with the additional interest amounting to about $220,000;

(c) Butcher's stock is now selling at $51 a share.

Calculate Butcher's additional EPS (earnings per share) after
taxes and interest if Butcher finances the new projects by:

(a) borrowing

(b) selling common stock.

II

TOOLS AND TECHNIQUES

3

PRESENT VALUE

"At $10,650 installed, this lathe is an absolute bargain." Ex-Cello's regional sales manager was talking enthusiastically. He held up the picture of the lathe again and looked at it fondly. "This thing," he said, "will save you $1,800 a year, after taxes, for at least seven years, even if labor costs don't go up. If labor costs do go up, it will save you that much more."

"It may be a bargain to you," said Hastings, Butcher's production manager, "but it's no bargain to me. On the basis of your figures and my calculations, that lathe isn't worth—to me—one cent more than $8,400. And even at that price, I have my doubts."

"Well," said Ex-Cello's man, "I've sold ten of these things in the last three months."

"Oh," said Hastings, "I didn't say it couldn't be worth $10,650 to someone else. Just not to me, that's all."

On what basis had Hastings decided that the lathe was *not* worth $10,650 to him, only $8,400?

Finance must continually determine the value *now* to the firm of proposed new investments. The value now to the firm of a proposed new investment is called, in the jargon of finance, the *present value* of that investment. Why does the firm have to worry about "present value"? The firm has to worry about present value for one simple reason: *because money earns interest.*

Look at the matter from your own individual point of view. If money did not earn interest, a dollar to be received in the future, say one year from now, would have the same value to you as the dollar you own now. And that would be that. And you might be perfectly willing to give up a dollar now in exchange for a dollar to be received one year from now or two years from now. But you aren't willing to give up a dollar now in exchange for a dollar to be received in the future. Suppose you walked into the local savings bank to open an account and the girl behind the counter said: "You do realize that we don't pay interest. In return for this $100 you will have exactly $100 a year from now." What would your reaction be?

Your roommate feels the same way you feel—as you learned to your sorrow yesterday. You walked into your cold, bare dormitory room, threw your beaver hat on the floor, peeled off your beard, and said to him:

"Hey, I need to borrow $100."

"OK," he said "for how long?"

You raised an eyebrow. "Whadyya mean, how long? What kind of a dirty question is that? I'll pay you back when I can."

"No," he said. "I must know how long you want it for."

"What's gotten into you?" you asked. "You'll know how long I wanted it for when I pay you back."

"No good," he said. "I must know it beforehand".

"Why?" you asked. "You don't trust me?" You advanced on him glaring.

He stood his ground. "No," he said piously, "if I didn't trust you, I wouldn't lend you the money at all. How long do you want it for?"

"Why do you want to know?"

"So I can figure out how much you'll have to repay."

"Whadyya mean how much I'll have to repay? If I borrow $100, I' repay $100!"

"No," he said. "Times have changed. I now charge interest."

"You charge what!"

"Interest," he said. "You know—interest."

You said, "Okay, loan shark, I'll pay you back in one year. How much?"

He did some rapid calculating on the back of a dirty sweatshirt and said "Okay, you pay me back $110 at noon one year from today."

You said, $110! That's 10 percent!"

"That's right," he said, "but my expenses are going up. Look at the time I've wasted on you already. My required rate of interest is 10 percent. Take it or leave it."

One hundred and ten dollars to be repaid a year from now didn't really seem to you to be much money and you needed that $100 badly right now. But you once heard your father say "Never accept their first offer." And you decided therefore to play it cool. You said: "Never mind, buddy. I'll try the local bank."

He said: "Whoa! Wait a minute! I'll tell you what I'll do. I'll charge you only 8 percent provided you're willing to pay me back at the rate of $9 a month for twelve months."

You remembered from your multiplication tables that $9 times 12 is $108, which is $2 less than the $110 he originally wanted. Also, you felt it would be easier to make twelve payments of $9 each month than one payment of $110. And so you said: "Okay, gimme the money."

He pulled out his wallet, extracted ten $10 bills. You reached for them. "Whoa!" he said. "Just a minute. Don't be in such a hurry. Sign here." He passed a piece of paper under your nose.

You said: "What's this?"

He said, "Just a note. Sign it." You mumbled something under your breath. But you signed. You grabbed the ten $10 bills and dashed out the door. As you reached your car you felt your stomach sinking. Something told you that you'd been tricked. In fact, you had—you should have accepted his first offer. The offer you did accept implies an annual rate of interest of about 14 percent, as we shall see later on.

Now then, what did you learn from this little experience?

First, you learned that your roommate had suddenly become a "maximizer." When you walked into the room and asked for $100, you became one of his "available opportunities" and he made the most of you.

Second, you learned that your roommate had "discovered" interest. He was not willing to give you $100 now in return for your promise to repay $100 one year from now. You had to promise to repay more than $100. Your roommate was saying, in effect, that he would not (repeat *not*) give you $100 now except in return for a promise with a *future value* greater than $100.

How much greater? When he made his first offer he was, as you were quick to see, using an interest rate of 10 percent. And to get the *future value* of the sum you wanted to borrow, your roommate had simply multiplied $100 by 10 percent and added, thus:

$100   Loan
  10   Required interest
─────
$110   Future value

This is equivalent to multiplying the amount of the loan by 1 plus the rate of interest: $100 × 1.10 = $110.

DETERMINING PRESENT AND FUTURE VALUE

But suppose now that you had walked into your room and said to your roommate: "I promise to pay you $110 at noon one year from today. What will you pay for that promise *now?*" What would your roommate have said? Obviously, he would have said, as quick as a flash: "$100." Whether he knew it or not (and he probably did), he would have been saying that the *present value* to him, the value to him *now*, of the $110 you had promised to pay him one year from now was $100. To obtain this figure, your roommate would simply have *divided* the amount you promised to pay him one year hence by 1 plus his required rate of interest: $110/1.10 = $100.

Thus when your roommate calculated the required *future* value of the loan you wanted, he was looking *forward* from the present to the future. When he calculated the *present* value of your promise to pay him $110 one year from now, he was looking *back* from the future to the present. To obtain the future value of the $100 loan, he *multiplied* by 1 plus his required rate of interest, that is, by 1.10. This seems sensible because we know that the sum you will have to repay a year from now will be larger than the amount he lends you now.

But when he calculated the *present* value of your promise to pay him $110 one year from now, he *divided* by 1.10. This seems sensible, too, for the same reason. The amount he would pay now for your promise would have to be smaller than the amount of the promise. *Present value is future value in reverse—and vice versa.*

We can sum up the situation as follows:

1. Calculating the *future* value of a present dollar—that is, of a dollar you have now—is easy. You do it all the time. If you deposit $100 in a savings bank that pays interest at the rate of 5 percent a year, you know that at the end of a year you'll have $105.

2. Calculating the *present* value of a dollar someone promises to pay you a year from now is easy too, provided you realize that

when you do so you are looking back from the future, instead of forward from the present.

3. In order to calculate the *future* value of a present amount of money, we need to know the *present* amount and we need to know, also, a required rate of interest.

4. In order to calculate the *present* value of an amount of money someone promises to pay you a year from now, you need to know the future amount and you need to know, also, a required rate of interest.

We have mentioned repeatedly, above, something called "a required rate of interest." What is a required rate of interest and where does it come from? Why, for example, did your roommate insist on 10 percent rather than 9, 11, 6, 4 or 2? We will take up this question after we have talked a bit about the present value of promises longer than one year.

COMPOUND INTEREST

When, in the situation discussed above, you borrowed $100 from your roommate, you borrowed it for just one year. But suppose, now, that the next time you need money, you walk into your room and say, "Hey, Joe!" You don't see him anywhere. "Hey, Joe, where are you?"

He says, "I'm under the bed." You don't ask him why he's under the bed because you know why: he's looking for a quarter he lost four weeks ago and on which he has already lost almost two-tenths of a cent in interest. You say: "Give up the search a minute and hear my question."

He says, "Okay, but make it snappy. Time is money."

You say, "I promise to pay you $57.62 at noon, one year from today and $57.62 at noon, two years from today. What'll you pay for my promise?"

Joe responds immediately (he has a computer in his head), "$100 subject of course to a note and a chattel mortgage on your car."

Then you say, "Okay, now suppose I promise to pay you $40.21 at noon one year from today, $40.21 at noon two years from today and $40.21 at noon three years from today. How much?"

He says, "$100 subject of course . . ."

You say, "Yes, yes. I know all that. I'll take the two-year deal."

He says: "Okay, take the money out of my wallet and sign a note and a mortgage before you leave. You know where they are." He's now running his loan office cafeteria-style.

We know that Joe's required rate of interest is 10 percent. If he can't get 10 percent, he'd rather keep his money in his wallet. But what calculations did he do before he said "$100" to your first proposal? He went through the following three step process:

1. This man, he said, is really making two promises, not just one. He promised to pay me $57.62 one year from now. And he promises to pay me $57.62 two years from now.
2. My required rate of interest is 10 percent a year. This means that the present value of the first promise is $57.62/1.10 = $52.38. He checked his arithmetic by multiplying $52.38 by 10 percent and adding, thus:

$$52.38 \times .10 = \$ \quad 5.24$$
$$\text{Loan} \quad \quad 52.38$$
$$\overline{\text{Total} \quad \$ \quad 57.62}$$

"Okay," he said, "I'll give him $52.38 for that first promise and when, a year from now, he pays me $57.62, I will have earned interest at 10 percent on the amount I gave him."

3. "But now, what about that second promise?" he thinks. "What's it worth to me now? This is tricky. Whatever I give him for that promise must earn 10 percent the first year. And it must earn compound interest at 10 percent the second year—which means that the interest I earn the first year must *itself* earn interest the second year. Tricky," he said, "but no trickier than putting $100 in a savings bank for two years at 10 percent a year. At the end of the first year, I'd have $110 (= $100 × 1.10). Now if I left the interest in the bank, I'd have $121 (= $110 × 1.10) at the end of the second year. I just have to work this thing in reverse."

He then drew up a little table, in his mind, as follows:

$$\$ \quad 100$$
$$\times 1.10$$
$$\overline{\$ \quad 110}$$
$$\times 1.10$$
$$\overline{\$ \quad 121}$$

Thus he saw that the interest earned the first year ($10) had itself earned interest, at 10 percent, during the second year ($10 × .10 = $1).

"Now then," he said to himself, "what's the *present* value of the $57.62 he promised to pay me two years from now? Let's see. The sum

I loaned him—let's call that x—has to earn interest at 21 percent over the two year period. That would be .21x. And, of course, I have to get the amount of the loan back. In other words, the $57.62 he promises to pay me two years from now must be equal to the sum of whatever I loaned him (x) plus 21 percent of that amount (.21x). So,

$$x + .21x = \$57.62$$
$$1.21x = \quad 57.62$$
$$x = \$47.62$$

"If I give him $47.62 now in return for his promise to pay me $57.62 *two* years hence, I will have earned 10 percent compounded when he pays me, thus:

Loan	$47.62
Interest, 1st year at 10 percent	4.76
	52.38
Interest, 2nd year at 10 percent	5.24
TOTAL	$57,62

You should note, especially, that the interest your roommate would earn during the second year includes interest at 10 percent on the interest earned during the first year. Thus the interest earned during the second year would be *compound interest*.

In short, then, the present value of *both* promises was $100, as follows:

Present value first promise	$52.38
Present value second promise	47.62
Present value both promises	$100.00

Now, just to test yourself, prove that the present value of your second set of promises—to pay $40.21 at the end of *each* of the next three years—is also $100. First figure out what the compound rate of interest would be at 10 percent for a *three* year period.

We can sum up as follows:

1. Calculating the *future* value of a present dollar over a period longer than one year is easy. You do it all the time. If you deposit $100 in a savings bank at 5 percent a year for two years and *do not withdraw your interest at* anytime during the period, how much money will you have at the end of the second year?
2. Calculating the *present* value of a dollar someone promises to pay you two years or more from now is easy too, provided you

realize that you are looking back from the future to the present and provided also that you realize that if you buy a promise from someone to pay you $1 two years or more from now, the amount you pay for the $1 must earn *compound* interest, at your required rate, over the whole period.

3. In order to calculate the *future* value of a present dollar we need to know your required rate of compound interest and we need to know how long the dollar will remain invested. Appendix A, *Growth Factors,* shows compound growth factors ($=1$ plus compound *rates*) for up to fifty periods (years, months, days, etc.) and for all rates of interest from 1.0 percent to 100.0 percent a period. It will tell you, for example, how much $1 will become in ten years if it earns compound interest at 12.0 percent a year—or for any other combination of rate and period up to 100 percent and fifty periods. To get the future value of a present sum of money, you simply *multiply* the sum of money by the correct growth factor: $1 invested now at 18 percent compounded per period for fifty periods will have become $3,927.40 by the end of the fiftieth period. Look this up in Appendix A.

4. In order to calculate the *present* value of an amount of money someone promises to pay you two or more years from now you need to know the future amount, you need to know when you will receive that amount, and you need to know also your *compound* required rate of interest for the period of the promise. To get the *present* value of a promise to pay you a sum of money at some time in the future, you simply *divide* the future sum by the correct growth factor. If someone promises to pay you $3,927.40 at the end of fifty periods, the present value of that sum is $1—if your required rate of interest is 18 percent compounded per period: $3,927.40/3,927.40 $=$ $1.

EXERCISES

1. $100 today will be worth how much at the end of three years:
   a. assuming an interest rate of 10%?
   b. assuming an interest rate of 100%?
   c. assuming an interest rate of 0%?
2. $100 at the end of three years is worth how much today:
   a. assuming an interest rate of 10%?

b.   assuming an interest rate of 100%?

c.   assuming an interest rate of 0%?

3.   What is the present value of $500 received at the end of each of the next three years:

a.   assuming an interest rate of 4%?

b.   assuming an interest rate of 25%?

4. $100 is to be received at the end of one year, $500 at the end of two years, and $1,000 at the end of three years. What is the present value of these receipts:

a.   assuming an interest rate of 4%?

b.   assuming an interest rate of 25%?

5. $1,000 is to be received at the end of one year, $500 at the end of two years, and $100 at the end of three years. What is the present value of these receipts:

a.   assuming an interest rate of 4%?

b.   assuming an interest rate of 25%?

6. $1,000 is to be received at the end of each of the next three years. What is the present value of these receipts:

a.   assuming interest rates of 4% in the first year, 10% in the second year, and 25% in the third year?

b.   assuming interest rates of 25% in the first year, 10% in the second year, and 4% in the third year?

THE REQUIRED RATE OF INTEREST

Let's talk now about your "required rate of interest." The required rate of interest for a company is its *cost of capital*, which will be discussed in Part IV; we will not, therefore, discuss it further here. We will simply assume, until we get to Part IV, that each of the companies we talk about knows its particular cost of capital.

But what about individuals such as you? Where do their "required rates of interest" come from, and what do they mean? Where, for example, did your roommate get his required rate (of 10 percent)?

As you have good reason to know, your roommate is the shrewd type who reads the *Wall Street Journal* everyday. And he knew, when you asked him to lend you $100, that he could lend money to the Federal Government at nearly 8 percent simply by calling his bank and buying treasury bills or bonds. And if he did so, he would be absolutely certain of being repaid—no worry, no sleepless nights asking himself whether or not you'd meet your next payment. Moreover, if he loaned money to the government—by buying a one year treasury bill, for example—and he needed money in the meantime, he would be able to sell the treasury bill on the open market and recover his principal plus interest at 8 percent a year up to the moment he sold it. But suppose he tried to sell the note you had signed before it came due? Who would buy it? No one, except perhaps your mother, and she, very likely, only at a substantial discount. In short, the treasury bill is readily *negotiable*; your note is not negotiable at all.

Thus your roommate can invest his money in riskless treasury bills, which are readily negotiable, at a yield of 8 percent. This is what we will call your roommate's *basic opportunity cost*. But he is surely entitled to charge you something more than 8 percent because your note is not negotiable and because you may not repay the loan. And if you did not, he would have the bother and the expense of foreclosing the chattel mortgage on your car. In general, an individual's required rate of interest (yours, for example) is the sacrifice he makes by not investing in his next best opportunity, adjusted for the difference in risk between the best opportunity and next best opportunity. Your roommate added two percentage points to the yield on one year treasury bills, thus arriving at the 10 percent he charged you. Some part of those two percentage points was an adjustment for the difference in risk between a treasury bill and your note.

ANALYZING "PROMISES"

Now, let's go back to Hastings of the Butcher Company and his lathe. Ex-Cello's salesman had told Hastings that the new lathe would save Butcher $1,800 a year in labor costs each year for seven years, which meant merely that the new lathe was more efficient than the lathes Butcher was now using; the new lathe would use less labor to turn out the same amount of product. We may say that, in effect, Ex-Cello's lathe was making a series of seven promises—to pay Butcher $1,800 at the end of the first year, $1,800 at the end of the second year, $1,800 at the end of the third year, and so forth for seven years, as shown in column (2) of Table 3.1. What was this set of promises worth to Butcher *now*? Or in the language we used above, what is the *present value* to Butcher of each of the seven promises, and what is their sum? In order to calculate the present value to Butcher of each of the seven "promises" being made by the lathe, we need to know Butcher's required rate of interest. As we saw in Chapter 2, Butcher's cost of capital was about 11 percent; this means simply that if Butcher cannot earn 11 percent on a new project, Butcher prefers to keep its money in the bank or,

TABLE 3.1

PRESENT VALUE OF EX-CELLO'S LATHE TO THE BUTCHER COMPANY

LENGTH OF PROMISE (IN YEARS)	AMOUNT OF PROMISE	1 PLUS REQUIRED COMPOUND RATE OF INTEREST *	PRESENT VALUE OF EACH PROMISE †
(1)	(2)	(3)	(4)
1	$1,800	$(1.11)^1 = 1.1100$	$1,621.62
2	1,800	$(1.11)^2 = 1.2321$	1,460.92
3	1,800	$(1.11)^3 = 1.3676$	1,316.17
4	1,800	$(1.11)^4 = 1.5181$	1,185.69
5	1,800	$(1.11)^5 = 1.6851$	1,068.19
6	1,800	$(1.11)^6 = 1.8704$	962.36
7	1,800	$(1.11)^7 = 2.0762$	866.97
		TOTAL	$8,481.92

* From Appendix A.
† Column (2) divided by column (3).

perhaps, to pay it out in dividends to its stockholders. Butcher's attitude is analagous to your roommate's, who would have kept his money in his wallet unless you were willing to pay him 10 percent on his money.

Now that we know Butcher's required rate of interest (its cost of capital), we can calculate the present value of each of the seven "promises" and their sum. This is done in Table 3.1 Column (1) lists the length in years of each of the seven "promises." Column (2) lists the amount of each of the seven promises (they are all the same). Column (3) lists the required compound rates of interest and multiplies them out, thus: $(1.11)^1 = 1.11$; $(1.11)^2 = 1.2321$ and so forth. These latter numbers were simply copied from the first seven rows under "11.0" in Appendix A. Column (4) is simply column (2) divided by column (3), thus: $1800/1.11 = 1621.62, $1800/1.2321 = 1460.92 and so forth. The numbers in column (4) simply answer the question: What should I pay *now* for each of the promises listed in column (2) so that I will have earned my required compound rate when each promise is kept? If you do a little arithmetic, you will see that if you pay $1,621.62 for the first promise, and that promise is kept, you will have earned 11 percent for one year on the amount you paid for the promise. Likewise, if you pay $1,460.92 for the second promise, and that promise is kept, you will have earned 11 percent, *compounded for two years,* on the amount you paid for the promise. And so forth for each of the other promises.

different kinds of promises

A great variety of promises is available in the real world—some of them are made by financial assets, such as stocks and bonds, and some of them are made by real assets, such as Ex-Cello's lathe. Moreover, they vary widely in what we will call their *time pattern*. Ex-Cello's lathe promised to pay Butcher $1,800 at the end of each of seven years. But conceivably it might have promised to pay $1,800 at the end of the first year, $2,000 at the end of the second year, $2,200 at the end of the third year, and so forth. You would calculate the present value of such a set of promises in the same way you calculated the present value of the set of promises the machine actually did make, as in Table 3.1. *The principle and the technique of calculation are the same regardless of the time pattern of the promises.*

We illustrate this point by using various types of financial assets You have $100 to invest. After shopping around in the financial markets for a while—which means that you've scanned the *Wall Street Journal*

TABLE 3.2

COMPARISON OF BONDS

LENGTH OF PROMISE (IN YEARS)	6% GOVERNMENT GUARANTEED BOND	E-BOND *	LEVEL PAYMENT BOND *
(1)	(2)	(3)	(4)
1	$ 6	——	$13.60
2	6	——	$13.60
3	6	——	$13.60
4	6	——	$13.60
5	6	——	$13.60
6	6	——	$13.60
7	6	——	$13.60
8	6	——	$13.60
9	6	——	$13.60
10	106	160	$13.60

* Amount to be received at end of each year.

every day and talked to your very knowledgable roommate—you find three government bonds as follows:

1. A bond which promises to pay you $6 a year at the end of each of the next nine years, and $106 at the end of the tenth year. See Table 3.2, column (2).
2. A single payment bond which promises to pay you $160 at the end of ten years—but nothing else. One payment, that's all. See Table 3.2, column (3).
3. A "level-payment" bond which promises to pay you $13.60 a year for ten years—as in column (4) of Table 3.2. The set of promises made by this bond resembles in time pattern the set of promises made by Ex-Cello's lathe—although, of course, the two sets of promises differ in amount.

The question is: What is each of these three bonds worth? Or in other words, what is the present value of each of these three sets of promises?

These bonds are government bonds and you, therefore, assume they are riskless: the promises will be kept as made. Your required rate of

TABLE 3.3

COMPARISON OF PRESENT VALUE OF BONDS

LENGTH OF PROMISE (IN YEARS)	1 PLUS REQUIRED COMPOUND RATE OF INTEREST (AT 8%) *	GOVERNMENT GUARANTEED BOND	E-BOND	LEVEL PAYMENT BOND
(1)	(2)	(3)	(4)	(5)
1	1.0800	$ 5.56	——	$12.59
2	1.1664	5.14	——	11.66
3	1.2597	4.76	——	10.80
4	1.3605	4.41	——	10.00
5	1.4693	4.08	——	9.27
6	1.5869	3.78	——	8.57
7	1.7138	3.50	——	7.94
8	1.8509	3.24	——	7.35
9	1.9990	3.00	——	6.80
10	2.1589	49.10	74.11	6.30
TOTAL		$86.57	$74.11	$91.28

* Determined from Appendix A.

interest is, therefore, your basic opportunity cost, which, your room-mate tells you, is 8 percent. At 8 percent, the present value of the government guaranteed bond would be $86.57; the present value of the bond like an E-Bond, $74.11, and the present value of the "level-payment" bond—which resembles Ex-Cello's lathe, $91.28. The calculations are shown in Table 3.3. And as you can see, the *method* of calculation is the same for all three bonds; it is the same as the method used to calculate the present value of the set of promises made by Ex-Cello's lathe. In other words, each of the various promises is divided by 1 plus that compound rate of interest appropriate to the length of time, in years, the promise will be outstanding. Thus in column (2) of Table 3.2, the first $6 promise, which will be outstanding one year, is divided by .08 plus 1 ($= 1.08$) because (given your 8 percent required rate), 8 percent is the rate appropriate to a promise which will be outstanding one year (column (3) of Table 3.3). The second $6 promise is divided by .1664 plus 1 ($= 1.1664$), because 16.64 percent is the compound rate appropriate to a promise which will be outstanding two years, and so forth. The single promise made by the single payment bond is divided by 1.1589 plus 1 ($= 2.1589$) because 115.89 percent is the compound rate appropriate to a promise which will be outstanding ten years—again given your required 8 percent rate. And if you bought the single payment bond *now* for $74.11, you would receive back in ten years $85.89 in compound interest on your investment plus the amount of the investment itself, thus:

Investment $= \$74.11$ $(= 74.11 \times 1.0000)$
Compound interest on your
investment at 8 percent
for 10 years $= 85.89$ $(= \$74.11 \times 1.1589)$
TOTAL $\$160.00$ $(= 74.11 \times 2.1589)$

Whether you would in fact buy any of the three bonds would depend on their prices. At the beginning of the 1970s, bonds like the government guaranteed bond, maturing in ten years were selling at about $82. This was *less* than the present value to you of such a bond ($86.57) and you might, therefore, have bought one.

THE PRESENT VALUE OF A SHARE OF STOCK

Suppose, now, that instead of buying a bond, as you did in the situation above, you decide you would prefer to invest $100 in common stock. You have heard of several: IBM, AT&T, Polaroid. Xerox, RCA, to mention just a few. You pick up the morning paper and look up yesterday's closing prices, as follows:

NAME	PRICE PER SHARE
IBM	$318.00
AT&T	56.375
Polaroid	109.50
Xerox	272.00
RCA	43.50

You rule out IBM, Polaroid and Xerox because $100 would buy only a fraction of a share. You decide to concentrate your attention on RCA and AT&T. What is the present value to you of each of these stocks? Is it higher than the quoted price or lower?

As we have seen above, you must have three figures in order to be able to calculate the present value of an investment:

1. A required rate of interest.
2. The *amount* of each of the "promises" being made by the investment.
3. The *length* of each of the "promises."

REQUIRED RATE OF INTEREST

We will assume that your required rate of interest is 10 percent. You do not know quite why you have chosen 10 percent, rather than 9 or 11 percent, but you feel, subjectively, that if you cannot earn 10 percent for either AT&T or RCA, you will invest in some kind of long term government bond.

AMOUNT OF PROMISES

In fact, of course, common stocks do not make promises in any formal way as bonds do. Except in rare cases, a bond will list explicitly the promises it makes—that is, how much interest it will pay and when, and when and how principal (your investment) is to be repaid. A share of common stock, on the other hand, makes no *explicit* promise to pay you anything. But if a share of stock did not carry with it the *implicit* promise to pay you something at sometime, it would be a worthless piece of paper, that is, its price would be zero. Part of the job of deciding whether to invest in a particular common stock—the most difficult part—lies in deciding how much you think the stock will in fact pay you, and when.

A share of stock is capable of putting money in your pocket in *two* different ways:

1. The company which has issued the stock may pay you something

every three months or every six months or every year. These payments are called *dividends*.

2. After you have bought the stock, you may decide to sell it. If you do, the stock has put into your pocket whatever you happen to get for it. If the stock has gone up in price, you will have made what is called a *capital gain*. Thus if you buy a share of stock on January 2, 1968, for $10, and sell it on December 31, 1968, at $12, you have made a capital gain of $2. If, meanwhile, you have received a dividend of fifty cents, we may say that during the year the share of stock has put $12.50 into your pocket—your original principal ($10), a dividend (50¢), and a capital gain ($2).

Of course, when you buy a share of stock you cannot predict when you will in fact sell it. But in order to estimate the present value to you of the share, you must make some assumption about when you will sell it and at what price, or whether you will sell it at all. If you assume that you will never sell it, the only payments you will expect to receive will be whatever dividends you expect the company to pay.

LENGTH OF "PROMISES"

As we have indicated above, bonds almost always have a fixed life which is stated explicitly in the bond contract. It may range from one to a hundred or more, years. By the end of the life of the bond, all the original principal will have been returned to the investor.

Common stock does not have a fixed life; it will exist until the company (whose ownership it represents) goes out of existence. But common stock can be sold by the investor whenever he wishes, provided, of course, a market exists in the stock. Large markets exist for both AT&T and RCA, and you can, of course, make any assumption you like about the life of the share, or you can make several assumptions and compare the results. But we will assume here that you would plan to hold for ten years whatever stock you buy, and then sell it.

determining present values of stocks

In Table 3.4, the present value of a share of AT&T and a share of RCA are calculated on the assumption of a ten-year life for each, at the end of which time we would sell the shares at the price we paid for them. We assume also that the present dividend paid by both companies will remain unchanged for the next ten years.

Columns (2) and (3) of Table 3.4 show the payments expected

TABLE 3.4

PRESENT VALUE,* ONE SHARE OF AT&T AND RCA
(WITH CONSTANT DIVIDEND)

YEAR	EXPECTED PAYMENTS ON AT&T	COMPOUND EXPECTED PAYMENTS ON RCA	1 PLUS REQUIRED RATE OF INTEREST † AT 10%	PRESENT VALUE AT&T	PRESENT VALUE RCA
(1)	(2)	(3)	(4)	(5)	(6)
1969	$ 2.40	$ 1.00	1.1000	$ 2.182	$ .909
1970	2.40	1.00	1.2100	1.983	.826
1971	2.40	1.00	1.3310	1.803	.751
1972	2.40	1.00	1.4641	1.639	.683
1973	2.40	1.00	1.6105	1.490	.621
1974	2.40	1.00	1.7716	1.335	.564
1975	2.40	1.00	1.9487	1.232	.513
1976	2.40	1.00	2.1436	1.120	.467
1977	2.40	1.00	2.3579	1.018	.424
1978	58.78 ‡	44.50 §	2.5937	22.663	17.157
				$36.465	$22.915

* Required rate of interest is 10 percent.
† See Appendix A under "10.0."
‡ The sum of $2.40 dividend plus sales proceeds of $56.38.
§ The sum of $1.00 dividend plus sales proceeds of $43.50.

to be generated by each share. For the first nine years, the payment is simply assumed to be equal to the present dividend—$2.40 for AT&T and $1.00 for RCA. For the tenth year, the payment is, in each case, the present dividend plus the *present* price of the stock. You have not made a capital gain nor have you suffered a capital loss. *On these assumptions* column (5) gives the present value of a share of AT&T ($36.47) and column 6, the present value of a share of RCA ($22.92). *If the assumptions we have made about expected payments are correct,* neither share is worth buying. You would have to pay for AT&T nearly $20.00 more than its present value to you; and for RCA, nearly $21 more. Obviously, if the assumptions are correct, you would be better off to buy a government bond.

But are the assumptions in fact correct? And if they are, how can the two stocks be selling at their present prices? We have made two critical assumptions: the first, about the discount rate, and the second about the payments the two stocks would make.

In mid-1969, interest rates were very high and 7 to 8 percent, ten-year, riskless opportunities were plentiful. On the whole, therefore, the 10 percent discount rate would seem reasonable. It would seem unlikely that any investor would use a lower rate as his basic opportunity cost. And the use of a higher rate would reduce the present value of both shares even farther. This is so because the higher the required rate, the lower the present value of a dollar to be received at some time in the future (see Appendix A). Moreover, the adjustment made for risk —two to three percentage points—does not seem too big. If you could be sure of earning 7 or 8 percent, without risk, in a government bond, would you invest in a risky common stock at less than 10 percent?

On the other hand, we have assumed that both the AT&T and the RCA dividends will remain constant over the next ten years. Most investors in both AT&T and RCA would probably argue that this assumption is very wrong. In 1968 it was a fact that AT&T's dividend

TABLE 3.5

PRESENT VALUE,* ONE SHARE OF AT&T AND RCA (GROWING DIVIDENDS AND PRICES)

YEAR	EXPECTED † PAYMENTS ON AT&T	EXPECTED ‡ PAYMENTS ON RCA	1 PLUS REQUIRED COMPOUND RATE OF INTEREST AT 10%	PRESENT VALUE AT&T	PRESENT VALUE RCA
(1)	(2)	(3)	(4)	(5)	(6)
1969	$ 2.40	$ 1.00	1.1000	$ 2.182	$ .909
1970	2.50	1.14	1.2100	2.066	.942
1971	2.60	1.30	1.3310	1.953	.977
1972	2.70	1.48	1.4641	1.844	1.011
1973	2.81	1.69	1.6105	1.745	1.049
1974	2.92	1.93	1.7716	1.648	1.089
1975	3.04	2.20	1.9487	1.560	1.129
1976	3.16	2.51	2.1436	1.474	1.171
1977	3.29	2.86	2.3579	1.395	1.213
1978	3.42)	3.25)	2.5937	1.319)	1.257)
	78.00)	105.00)		30.073)	40.483)
				$47.259	$51.230

* Required rate of interest is 10 percent discount rate.
† Growth rates of 4 percent a year in dividends and 3.5 percent a year in price of stock.
‡ Growth rates of 14 percent a year in dividends and 9 percent a year in price of stock.

had increased steadily for ten years, from $1.62 to $2.40, at the rate of 4 percent a year. RCA's dividend grew, during the same period, from $.27 to $1.00, at the rate of 14 percent a year. Investors in AT&T and RCA would argue that both dividends would grow over the next ten years. They will not remain stable.

Table 3.5 calculates the present value of both stocks on the assumption that both dividends will continue to grow at the prior rates—the AT&T dividend at the rate of 4 percent a year, and the RCA dividend at the rate of 14 percent a year.

But if the dividends grow at the above rates, the two stocks will probably not, ten years from now, be selling at their present prices. In 1959, for example, AT&T was selling at about $40 a share while in 1969, it sold at $56. This increase represents a growth rate over the ten year period of about 3.5 percent a year—a rate not very different from the growth rate of the dividend itself. In 1959, RCA was selling at about $18 a share; in 1969, it sold at $43.50 a share. This increase represents a growth rate of about 9 percent a year—a rate somewhat lower than the growth rate of the dividend. Table 3.5 assumes that during the ten years following 1968, the price of AT&T will go up steadily at the rate of 3.5 percent a year, and the price of RCA by 9 percent a year. On these assumptions, columns (5) and (6) of Table 3.5 indicate that the present value of a share of AT&T would be $47.26 and of a share of RCA $51.23. The former is $9 below the 1968 price, and the latter, $8 above. RCA (but not AT&T) looks like a "buy."

The foregoing results obviously depend heavily on the two forecasts. If the growth rate of dividends and the growth rates of the prices of the two stocks had been lower, present value would have been lower.[1]

In any event, every investor makes his own estimate of the present value of a share of stock—whether he knows it or not. He may not do it consciously and deliberately, as we have above. But every time he rushes into the market to buy a share of stock, he is saying, in effect, that the market price of the stock is below the present value to him of the stock. And every time he rushes in to sell, he is saying that the market price of the stock is higher to him than the present value of the stock. And the market prices of all stocks—and for that matter of all investments both real and financial—are determined by the interaction of a whole multitude of individual estimates of the present value of those investments. These individual estimates are, of course, continually being revised as new information becomes available.

---

[1] In mid-1969, The Value Line Investment Survey, forecast dividends for AT&T and RCA for 1972–74 of $3.20 and $1.40 respectively. These figures imply a rate of growth for AT&T of 7.5 percent and for RCA of 9.0 percent.

CALCULATING DISCOUNT FACTORS

When we calculated the present value, above, of the promises you made to your roommate and the various other promises discussed above, we used the *growth factors* given in Appendix A. Sometimes it's easier to use the reciprocals of the growth factors that is, the growth factors divided into one. When your roommate divided $57.62 by 1.10 to obtain the present value of your first promise, he could have equally as well multiplied $57.62 by 1/1.10 or by .9091. He would have gotten the same answer in either case:

$$\frac{\$57.62}{1.10} = \$57.62 \times .9091 = \$52.38.$$

When the number 1 is divided by the growth factor, the quotient we get is called a *discount factor*. Discount factors for selected rates of interest and periods are given in Table 3.6. The discount factors given in Table 3.6 were obtained by dividing into the number 1 the appropriate growth factors given in Appendix A. The discount factors are thus nothing more than the growth factors looked at upside down.

Throughout the rest of this book we will sometimes use growth rates and sometimes their reciprocals (discount factors) in calculating estimates of present value.

CONCLUSION

This chapter has covered the following ground:

(1) Present value is, so to speak, future value "in reverse." *Future value* responds to the question: If I have $1 now and I can earn interest at 10 percent compounded annually, how much will my dollar have become one year hence, or two years hence, or ten years hence? The answer, as we have seen, is $1.10, or $1.21, or $2.5937. When we calculate the future value of a present sum at some rate of interest, we are looking *forward* from the present.

Present Value responds to the question: If someone promises to give me $1.10 one year hence, or $1.21 two years hence, or $2.5937 ten years hence, and I can earn interest at 10 percent compounded annually, what is each of those promises worth to me

TABLE 3.6
PRESENT VALUE OF $1

PERIODS HENCE	1%	2%	4%	6%	8%	10%	12%	14%	15%	16%	18%	20%	22%	24%	25%	26%	28%	30%	35%	40%	45%	50%
1	0.990	0.980	0.962	0.943	0.926	0.909	0.893	0.877	0.870	0.862	0.847	0.833	0.820	0.806	0.800	0.794	0.781	0.769	0.741	0.714	0.690	0.667
2	0.980	0.961	0.925	0.890	0.857	0.826	0.797	0.769	0.756	0.743	0.718	0.694	0.672	0.650	0.640	0.630	0.610	0.592	0.549	0.510	0.476	0.444
3	0.971	0.942	0.889	0.840	0.794	0.751	0.712	0.675	0.658	0.641	0.609	0.579	0.551	0.524	0.512	0.500	0.477	0.455	0.406	0.364	0.328	0.296
4	0.961	0.924	0.855	0.792	0.735	0.683	0.636	0.592	0.572	0.552	0.516	0.482	0.451	0.423	0.410	0.397	0.373	0.350	0.301	0.260	0.226	0.198
5	0.951	0.906	0.822	0.747	0.681	0.621	0.567	0.519	0.497	0.476	0.437	0.402	0.370	0.341	0.328	0.315	0.291	0.269	0.223	0.186	0.156	0.132
6	0.942	0.888	0.790	0.705	0.630	0.564	0.507	0.456	0.432	0.410	0.370	0.335	0.303	0.275	0.262	0.250	0.227	0.207	0.165	0.133	0.108	0.088
7	0.933	0.871	0.760	0.665	0.583	0.513	0.452	0.400	0.376	0.354	0.314	0.279	0.249	0.222	0.210	0.198	0.178	0.159	0.122	0.095	0.074	0.059
8	0.923	0.853	0.731	0.627	0.540	0.467	0.404	0.351	0.327	0.305	0.266	0.233	0.204	0.179	0.168	0.157	0.139	0.123	0.091	0.068	0.051	0.039
9	0.914	0.837	0.703	0.592	0.500	0.424	0.361	0.308	0.284	0.263	0.225	0.194	0.167	0.144	0.134	0.125	0.108	0.094	0.067	0.048	0.035	0.026
10	0.905	0.820	0.676	0.558	0.463	0.386	0.322	0.270	0.247	0.227	0.191	0.162	0.137	0.116	0.107	0.099	0.085	0.073	0.050	0.035	0.024	0.017
11	0.896	0.804	0.650	0.527	0.429	0.350	0.287	0.237	0.215	0.195	0.162	0.135	0.112	0.094	0.086	0.079	0.066	0.056	0.037	0.025	0.017	0.012
12	0.887	0.788	0.625	0.497	0.397	0.319	0.257	0.208	0.187	0.168	0.137	0.112	0.092	0.076	0.069	0.062	0.052	0.043	0.027	0.018	0.012	0.008
13	0.879	0.773	0.601	0.469	0.368	0.290	0.229	0.182	0.163	0.145	0.116	0.093	0.075	0.061	0.055	0.050	0.040	0.033	0.020	0.013	0.008	0.005
14	0.870	0.758	0.577	0.442	0.340	0.263	0.205	0.160	0.141	0.125	0.099	0.078	0.062	0.049	0.044	0.039	0.032	0.025	0.015	0.009	0.006	0.003
15	0.861	0.743	0.555	0.417	0.315	0.239	0.183	0.140	0.123	0.108	0.084	0.065	0.051	0.040	0.035	0.031	0.025	0.020	0.011	0.006	0.004	0.002
16	0.853	0.728	0.534	0.394	0.292	0.218	0.163	0.123	0.107	0.093	0.071	0.054	0.042	0.032	0.028	0.025	0.019	0.015	0.008	0.005	0.003	0.002
17	0.844	0.714	0.513	0.371	0.270	0.198	0.146	0.108	0.093	0.080	0.060	0.045	0.034	0.026	0.023	0.020	0.015	0.012	0.006	0.003	0.002	0.001
18	0.836	0.700	0.494	0.350	0.250	0.180	0.130	0.095	0.081	0.069	0.051	0.038	0.028	0.021	0.018	0.016	0.012	0.009	0.005	0.002	0.001	0.001
19	0.828	0.686	0.475	0.331	0.232	0.164	0.116	0.083	0.070	0.060	0.043	0.031	0.023	0.017	0.014	0.012	0.009	0.007	0.003	0.002	0.001	0.001
20	0.820	0.673	0.456	0.312	0.215	0.149	0.104	0.073	0.061	0.051	0.037	0.026	0.019	0.014	0.012	0.010	0.007	0.005	0.002	0.001	0.001	
21	0.811	0.660	0.439	0.294	0.199	0.135	0.093	0.064	0.053	0.044	0.031	0.022	0.015	0.011	0.009	0.008	0.006	0.004	0.002	0.001		
22	0.803	0.647	0.422	0.278	0.184	0.123	0.083	0.056	0.046	0.038	0.026	0.018	0.013	0.009	0.007	0.006	0.004	0.003	0.001	0.001		
23	0.795	0.634	0.406	0.262	0.170	0.112	0.074	0.049	0.040	0.033	0.022	0.015	0.010	0.007	0.006	0.005	0.003	0.002	0.001			
24	0.788	0.622	0.390	0.247	0.158	0.102	0.066	0.043	0.035	0.028	0.019	0.013	0.008	0.006	0.005	0.004	0.003	0.002	0.001			
25	0.780	0.610	0.375	0.233	0.146	0.092	0.059	0.038	0.030	0.024	0.016	0.010	0.007	0.005	0.004	0.003	0.002	0.001	0.001			
26	0.772	0.598	0.361	0.220	0.135	0.084	0.053	0.033	0.026	0.021	0.014	0.009	0.006	0.004	0.003	0.002	0.002	0.001	0.001			
27	0.764	0.586	0.347	0.207	0.125	0.076	0.047	0.029	0.023	0.018	0.011	0.007	0.005	0.003	0.002	0.002	0.001	0.001				
28	0.757	0.574	0.333	0.196	0.116	0.069	0.042	0.026	0.020	0.016	0.010	0.006	0.004	0.002	0.002	0.002	0.001	0.001				
29	0.749	0.563	0.321	0.185	0.107	0.063	0.037	0.022	0.017	0.014	0.008	0.005	0.003	0.002	0.002	0.001	0.001					
30	0.742	0.552	0.308	0.174	0.099	0.057	0.033	0.020	0.015	0.012	0.007	0.004	0.003	0.002	0.002	0.001	0.001					
40	0.672	0.453	0.208	0.097	0.046	0.022	0.011	0.005	0.004	0.003	0.001	0.001										
50	0.608	0.372	0.141	0.054	0.021	0.009	0.003	0.001	0.001	0.001												

For easy reference, this table also appears at the back of the book.

now? The answer in each case is $1. When we calculate the present value of a sum to be received in the future, we are looking *backwards* from the future to the present.

But present value and future value are really just opposite sides of the same set of facts: at 10 percent, $1.10 is the future value of the dollar you have now, and $1 is the present value of the $1.10 you will receive a year from now.

(2)   In order to be able to calculate the present value of a set of promises, companies and individuals must know their *required rate of interest*. A company's required rate of interest is its *cost of capital*, which will be discussed in Part IV. An individual's required rate of interest is the sacrifice he would make by *not* investing in his best available riskless opportunity plus an adjustment for any difference in risk between the riskless opportunity and the investment he happens to be considering.

(3)   All kinds of sets of "promises" are for sale in the real world. They vary in riskiness, in length and in time pattern. Using present value techniques, we estimated the present value of your promises to your roommate, the promises made to Hastings of Butcher by Ex-Cello's lathe, the promises made by the government when it sells bonds, and the promises (albeit implicit) made by a share of AT&T and RCA. And we saw that in each case the method of calculating present value was the same.

(4)   When you have calculated at your required rate of interest the present value of a set of promises being made by some asset—a loan, a bond, a share of stock, or a real asset such as a lathe—you are able to decide whether the asset is, in your opinion, worth the price being asked for it—or, alternatively, to fix the maximum price you would pay for the asset. *This is the whole point of the chapter.* By using present value techniques, Hastings was able to decide that he would not pay $10,650 for Ex-Cello's lathe, your roommate was able to fix the amount he would pay for your various promises, and you were able to form an opinion as to whether various government bonds and two common stocks were overpriced or underpriced.

PROBLEMS

1.   Suppose you deposit $100 in a savings bank paying interest at the rate of 5 percent a year. At the end of each year you withdraw $5 to buy yourself a Christmas present. You do not make any further

deposits. How much money will you have in the account at the end of the tenth year?

2. Now suppose that you make no withdrawals (and no further deposits). How much money will you have at the end of the tenth year in the account described in problem 1? Why is this amount so much larger than the amount you would have had if you had withdrawn $5 at the end of each year? Be specific!

3. Divide into the number 1 each of the numbers given in column (4) of Table 3.5. Compare your results with the first seven rows under "10.0" in Table 3.6.

4. Using the results you obtained in problem 3 above, go back to Table 3.5 and calculate the present value of one share of RCA.

5. The discount factors described in this chapter above, can also be interpreted as the present value of $1.00 to be received any number of years hence. Thus if your required rate of interest is 10 percent, the present value to you of $1.00 to be received one year hence is $.9091; of $1 to be received two years hence is $.8264, and so forth. Why is this so?

6. You will notice that the heading over the first column in Table 3.6

TABLE 3.7

DETERMINING REQUIRED RATE OF INTEREST

LENGTH OF PROMISE IN MONTHS	PROMISED PAYMENT (END OF MONTH)	PERCENTAGE OF GROWTH RATE	PRESENT VALUE *
(1)	(2)	(3)	(4)
1	$9		
2	9		
3	9		
4	9		
5	9		
6	9		
7	9		
8	9		
9	9		
10	9		
11	9		
12	9		
		TOTAL	$100

* Column (3) divided by growth rates.

does not say "years." It says "periods." (It might just as well have said "length of promise in periods.") A period can be anything you like—a day, a week, a month, a year or a tenth of a second.

Under the terms of the final "deal" you worked out with your roommate, you agreed to pay him $9 each month for twelve months. Using the growth factors in Appendix A, find the required rate of interest per month which would make the present value of the twelve promises you made to your roommate equal to $100.

Proceed as follows:

(a) regard the periods as months.

(b) set up a table like Table 3.7.

Your problem is to find a set of growth factors which, when inserted in column (3), divided into column (2), and the results carried to column (4), will add up to $100.

After you have done this you will have discovered the rate of interest you were charged per month. If you multiply this by 12, you will discover the extent to which you were tricked by your roommate's apparent generosity.

7. Suppose your roommate invested your $9 payments as he received them at 10 percent a year (= 5/6 of 1%, or .833 percent a month). How much money would he have accumulated by the time you made your last $9 payment?

8. Your roommate offered you $100 for two annual payments of $57.62 each (a total of $115.24). He would also have offered you $100 for a payment of $10 at the end of the first year and $110 at the end of the second year (a total of $120). He would also have offered you $100 for one payment of $121 to be made at the end of the second year. The totals all differ, but the present values are all the same. What do you make of this?

9. Look up AT&T and RCA in the Value Line Investment Survey or in Standard and Poor's. What dividend did each actually pay in 1970 and 1971? What is the present price of each stock? Decide whether you would now buy or sell either. Support your conclusion with appropriate present value calculations.

4

RATES
OF
RETURN

When Hastings, Butcher's vice president for production, got home one Friday night, he found his son Johnny there for the weekend. Johnny was a sophomore at the University of Connecticut.

"Hi, Dad," said Johnny, "I got that clipping you sent me. What's the point?"

Hastings had sent Johnny a newspaper clipping which reported that college graduates with B.A. or B.S. degrees earned through their working lives, on the average, $7,000 a year more than high school graduates.

"I hadn't seen those figures before," said Hastings. "That's a fantastically high rate of return on the investment in a college education. If your working life is thirty-five or forty years, the rate of return would be more than 40 percent."

"So what," said Johnny, "I want a car and I want to get married. I need some money *now*."

"How much more money do you think you will need," asked Hastings, "in addition to what I give you and to what you can make during the summer?"

"I figure I'll need an extra $3,000 next year and $3,000 the year after—$6,000 altogether."

"I tell you what I'll do," said Hastings. "I'll take you down to the bank and we'll arrange to borrow up to $6,000, as you need it. You sign the note and I'll endorse it. You can start to repay the loan two years after you graduate at the rate of $1,200 a year.

"$1,200 a year! That's a lot!"

"Of course it's a lot but even so you'll be much better off than you would be if you quit school now. You'll have more money in your pocket then. Do you realize that on the basis of those figures, you could afford to pay $100,000 for a college education and still break even? At a cost of $16,000 a college education is the biggest bargain since Manhattan Island."

"Yeah," said Johnny, "it's even more of a bargain if you can get your old man to pay for all of it."

On what basis had Hastings decided that at $16,000 a college education was the biggest bargain since Manhattan Island? And what did he mean when he said that Johnny would have "more money in his pocket" if he borrowed to pay for his college education?

ESTABLISHING PRESENT VALUE

The main message of Chapter 3 can be summarized as follows:

If we know the present value of a promise, or a set of promises, we can fix the maximum price we would pay for the promise, or the set of promises.

This is what your roommate did when he offered you $100—"take it or leave it"—for each of the various sets of promises you made. If you had insisted on having $100.01, he would doubtless have said: "No, thanks."

And Hastings did the same thing when he rejected Ex-Cello's lathe. He had estimated that the present value to Butcher of the set of seven promises made by the lathe was about $8,400—which was $2,250 less than the price of the lathe. Butcher, being in its right mind, would not, of course, pay $10,650 for a set of promises estimated to be worth only $8,400.

And we did essentially the same thing when we estimated the present value of the three bonds, a share of AT&T and a share of RCA. We were, that is, trying to answer the question: What is the maximum price I would be willing to pay for each of these assets? Or alternatively, should I buy these assets at their present prices? In the case of AT&T, for example, the answer was no. In the case of RCA, the answer was perhaps. (It was perhaps rather than yes in the case of RCA, primarily because you had only $100 to invest, and you might have been able to find something else which would have been a better buy.)

But as we saw in Chapter 3, we can calculate the present value of a set of promises only if we know our required rate of interest or, if we happen to be a company, our cost of capital. Every individual can (and should) know his required rate of interest. But not every company knows its cost of capital at every moment of time. The cost of capital changes from time to time for various reasons, as we shall see in Part IV. It can be affected, for example, by the kind of projects a company undertakes, as we shall also see in Part IV. But even if a company does know its cost of capital, it will often wish to know for each and every proposed new project not only the present value but also the rate of return.

WHAT IS A RATE OF RETURN

A rate of return is a number, stated as a percent per period. The period is usually a year, but as we saw in Chapter 3, it can be anything you choose to make it: you can earn rates of return of 5 percent a year or 6 percent a month or 10 percent a day or, if you happen to strike oil in your back yard, 600 percent an hour. In its simplest terms, a rate of return tells you how much better off you will be, in terms of percent per period, if you invest in some proposed project. When your roommate offered to lend you $100 for a year in return for your promise to pay him $110 at the end of the year, he expected to be 10 percent —or $10—better off at the end of the year than he was at the beginning.

one-period rates of return

You can rapidly calculate rates of return on simple one-period projects. A simple one-period project is a project which:

1. Begins at the beginning of a period and ends at the end of that period;
2. Calls for one payment by you (at the beginning of the period) and one payment to you (at the end of the period).

Your roommate's original offer to you was such a project. The period was a year. He would have made one payment to you ($100) at the beginning of the period and would have received one payment from you ($110) at the end of the period. Your roommate's expected rate of return was, thus, 10 percent a year $(= \dfrac{\$110 - 100}{100})$.

Or suppose you had bought a share of RCA for $47 on January 2,

1967 and sold it one month later for $51.70. Your rate of return would have been 10 percent a *month* ($51.70 − 47.00/$47.00 = .10). Or suppose you bought the single payment bond described in Table 3.2 and held it for ten years. You would have received $160 at the end of the tenth year, and your return would have been 60 percent per *decade*.

complications

But now suppose that you invest in the bond like an E-Bond. And suppose, also, that you couldn't care less about the rate of return per decade. You want to know the rate of return *per year*. What do you do then? An intuition tells you that you cannot simply divide 60 percent by 10 and conclude that the rate of return is 6 percent a year.

Or suppose that your roommate wants to know the rate of return per year on the loan he actually made to you (the one you are repaying at the rate of $9 a month) so that he can compare the rate of return on the loan with his basic opportunity cost—which happens to be stated as a percent per year. What does he do then?

In order to dispel these complications, we will have to define a rate of return somewhat more carefully than we have. We said above that if your roommate had given you $100 in return for your promise to pay him $110 one year from now, his expected rate of return would have been 10 percent. We obtained the rate of return by subtracting $100 from $110 and dividing the remainder by the amount of the loan ($10/100 = .10). But curiously enough, *10 percent is also the rate which, when added to the number 1 and divided into the amount of your promise ($110), makes that promise equal to the amount of the original loan.* Thus, $110/1.10 = $100. This means that we could have found the expected rate of return on the loan—if we had not known it—by finding the *growth factor* (Appendix A) which would make the amount of the promise equal to the amount of the loan. As we have seen above, the growth factor which does the job is 1.10.

Thus we have the following definition:

> The rate of return on an asset is that rate which, when added to the number 1, *makes the present value of a set of promises equal to their cost.*[1]

This definition enables us to resolve the "complications" described above.

---

[1] Rates of return as defined above are often called *DCF* rates of return. DCF stands for discounted cash flow.

As you can see, then, calculating the rate of return on a set of promises is nothing more than a somewhat different kind of present value problem. When we calculated the present value of the three bonds listed in Table 3.2, we simply used a rate *which was given to us,* added the number 1 to it, converted it into appropriate compound form, and divided each corresponding rate into the corresponding promise (see Table 3.1). In order to calculate a rate of return, everything is given to us—except the rate. We know the amount of each promise, the length of time each promise will be outstanding, and the present price of the set of promises. We are asked to find the rate which will make the present value of the set of promises equal to their cost. You did exactly this, by the way, when you found the answer to problem 6 at the end of Chapter 3.

CALCULATING RATES OF RETURN

Now then, what is the rate of return on Ex-Cello's lathe? Unhappily, calculating a rate of return is a somewhat tedious trial-and-error process. We try one rate and if it does not work, we try another until we find the right rate.[2]

In order to get the rate of return on Ex-Cello's lathe, let's try 8 percent first. We are, in effect, asking the question: Is 8 percent the rate which will make the present value of the seven promises equal to $10,650—the price of the lathe. (The answer is no). Table 4.1 shows the calculations. As in Table 3.1, we specify first the length and the amount of each promise. Column (3) lists compound, 8 percent, growth factors taken from the first seven rows of Appendix A under "8.0." We then divide each promise by the appropriate growth factor to obtain the present values listed in column (4). Next, we add up the present values, at 8 percent, of the seven promises. The total, $9,371.49, is substantially less than $10,650—which means that we have reduced each promise by too much. This, in turn, means that we have used compound growth factors which are too high. In other words, we have divided each promise by a number which is too large.

Next let's try 4 percent, going through the same step-by-step procedure (see Table 4.2). The total of present values in Table 4.2 is now too large, which means that we have not reduced the promises *enough.* This, in turn, means that the growth factors in column (3) are too small. But the total at the bottom of column (4) is only slightly too large and

---

[2] Appendix 4.A describes a short cut method of finding the rate of return on a set of promises. The method can be used only if all, or some, of the promises made by an asset are identical in amount.

TABLE 4.1

FIRST CALCULATIONS OF RATE OF RETURN ON $10,650 LATHE

LENGTH OF PROMISE (IN YEARS)	AMOUNT OF PROMISE	COMPOUND GROWTH FACTORS AT 8%	PRESENT VALUE *
(1)	(2)	(3)	(4)
1	$1,800	1.0800	$1,666.67
2	1,800	1.1664	1,543.21
3	1,800	1.2597	1,428.91
4	1,800	1.3605	1,323.04
5	1,800	1.4693	1,225.07
6	1,800	1.5869	1,134.29
7	1,800	1.7138	1,050.30
		TOTAL	$9,371.49

* Column (2) divided by column (3).

TABLE 4.2

SECOND CALCULATION OF RATE OF RETURN ON $10,650 LATHE

LENGTH OF PROMISE (IN YEARS)	AMOUNT OF PROMISE	COMPOUND GROWTH FACTORS AT 4%	PRESENT VALUE *
(1)	(2)	(3)	(4)
1	$1,800	1.0400	$ 1,730.77
2	1,800	1.0816	1,664.20
3	1,800	1.1249	1,600.14
4	1,800	1.1699	1,538.59
5	1,800	1.2167	1,479.41
6	1,800	1.2653	1,422.59
7	1,800	1.3159	1,367.89
		TOTAL	$10,803.59

* Column (2) divided by column (3).

this fact suggests that the rate of return is not far from 4 percent. We therefore try 4.4 percent and lo and behold, the result is just $4.20 less than the cost of the lathe. This is close enough and we conclude, therefore, that the true rate of return on the lathe is just slightly *less* than 4.4 percent. (Do you see why we say "less" than and not "more" than? If not, you'd better reread the last three paragraphs and look closely again at Tables 4.1 and 4.2.)

TABLE 4.3

THIRD CALCULATION OF RATE OF RETURN ON $10,650 LATHE

LENGTH OF PROMISE (IN YEARS)	AMOUNT OF PROMISE	COMPOUND GROWTH FACTORS AT 4.4% *	PRESENT VALUE †
(1)	(2)	(3)	(4)
1	$1,800	$1.0440 = (1.044)$	$ 1,724.14
2	1,800	$1.0899 = (1.044)^2$	1,651.53
3	1,800	$1.1379 = (1.044)^3$	1,581.86
4	1,800	$1.1880 = (1.044)^4$	1,515.15
5	1,800	$1.2402 = (1.044)^5$	1,451.38
6	1,800	$1.2948 = (1.044)^6$	1,390.18
7	1,800	$1.3518 = (1.044)^7$	1,331.56
		TOTAL	$10,645.80

* Computed on a desk calculator in 20 seconds.
† Column (2) divided by column (3).

Thus, finding the rate of return offered by a set of promises is simple (!). It's just the rate (plus the number 1) which equates the present value of a set of promises to the cost of those promises.

But why do we define a rate of return in this involved and peculiar way? Why don't we just divide $1,800 by $10,650 (=16.9 percent) to get a rate of return on the lathe? This is a good question—to which we will return after we have calculated a few more rates of return. (But you should, by now, begin to have a hint of the answer. Ask yourself whether at the end of seven years, you would really be 16.9 percent a year "better off" if you bought the lathe. If you don't remember what we mean by "better off," go back and reread the initial definition of a rate of return.) In any case, we may note that the difference between 4.4 percent and 16.9 percent is certainly not small.

the single payment bond

When we calculated the present value of the bond like an E-Bond, we used three figures:

1. The amount of the promise being made by the bond ($160);
2. The length of time the promise would be outstanding (10 years);
3. Your required rate of interest (8 percent).

Knowing that your required rate of interest was 8 percent and knowing also that the promise to pay you $160 would be outstanding for ten years, we knew that whatever you paid for the bond would have to earn compound interest at 8 percent for ten years. We were thus able to say:

$$PV(1.08)^{10} = \$160 \quad \text{or} \quad PV = \frac{\$160}{(1.08)^{10}},$$

where PV simply stands for the present value we were trying to find. We simply looked up $(1.08)^{10}$ in Appendix A, ten rows down under "8.0," and found it was 2.1589 (see Table 3.3). We then simply divided $160 by 2.1589 to obtain the answer: $74.11.

We now suppose that the government has put a price of $100 on the bond. And the question we are asking is: If you pay $100 for the bond, what will your rate of return be? (We already know, of course, that if you were able to buy the bond for $74.11, your rate of return would be 8 percent.)

We are, in other words, asking the question:

$$\$100 (1 + r)^{10} = \$160$$

or

$$(1 + r)^{10} = \frac{\$160}{\$100}$$
$$= 1.60$$

In order to find the rate of return, then, we need only look up 1.60, opposite ten periods in Appendix A. We run our eye across the tenth row and under "5.0" we find 1.6289—which is as close as the tenth row comes to 1.60. And this tells us that the rate of return on the bond is slightly less than 5.0 percent, say 4.8 percent.

What have we done? *We have found the rate which, plus the number 1, makes the present value of the promise made by the bond equal to the cost of the bond*: For,

$$\$160/(1.048)^{10}$$
$$= 160/1.5981$$
$$= \$100 \text{ (approximately)}$$

And this means that if you buy the bond for $100, your investment will have grown at a compound rate of 4.8 percent in ten years. The compound growth process is illustrated in Table 4.4. But, of course, if your

TABLE 4.4

HOW $100 BECOMES $160 IN TEN YEARS
AT COMPOUND GROWTH RATE OF 4.8 PERCENT

Original investment	$100.00
Interest, first year, at 4.8%	4.80
Principal, end first year	104.80
Interest, second year, at 4.8%	5.0304
Principal, end second year	109.8304
Interest, third year, at 4.8%	5.2719
Principal, end third year	115.1023
Interest, fourth year, at 4.8%	5.5249
Principal, end fourth year	120.6272
Interest, fifth year, at 4.8%	5.7901
Principal, end fifth year	126.4173
Interest, sixth year, at 4.8%	6.0680
Principal, end sixth year	132,4853
Interest seventh year, at 4.8%	6.3593
Principal, end seventh year	138.8446
Interest, eighth year, at 4.8%	6.6656
Principal, end eighth year	145.5102
Interest, ninth year, at 4.8%	6.9844
Principal, end ninth year	152.4946
Interest, tenth year, at 4.8%	7.3197
Principal, end tenth year	$159.8143

required rate of interest is 8 percent, you won't buy a bond—or anything else—returning only 4.8 percent.

the government-guaranteed bond

The rate of return on the single payment bond was easy to calculate because we needed to look up only one figure in Appendix A. The rate

of return on one other type of investment is also easy to calculate—
on an investment, such as the government bond described in Table 3.2.
If you bought such a bond when it was first issued you would, usually,
pay a specified amount for it, say $100, and that amount would be
returned to you at the end of the last year of the life of the bond. And
you would receive the same amount of interest each year. The rate of
return on such an investment is simply the amount of interest you would
receive each year divided by the price of the investment. If annual
interest were $6, the rate of return on the bond would be $6/$100 or
6 percent.

But as Table 4.5 shows, 6 percent is also the rate which makes the
present value of the set of promises made by the bond equal to the cost
of the bond.

a level payment bond

Now suppose you are considering a bond, also at a price of $100, which
promises to pay you $14.90 a year for ten years—and that is all. You

TABLE 4.5

COMPARISON OF PRESENT VALUE OF PROMISES WITH THE COST OF A $100 BOND

LENGTH OF PROMISE (IN YEARS)	AMOUNT OF PROMISE	COMPOUND GROWTH FACTORS AT 6%	PRESENT VALUE *
(1)	(2)	(3)	(4)
1	$ 6	1.06	$ 5.66
2	6	1.1236	5.34
3	6	1.1910	5.04
4	6	1.2625	4.75
5	6	1.3382	4.48
6	6	1.4185	4.23
7	6	1.5036	3.99
8	6	1.5938	3.76
9	6	1.6895	3.55
10	106	1.7908	59.19
		TOTAL	$99.99

* Column (2) divided by column (3).

would receive no other payments. The annual payment obviously must include both principal and interest because you will receive no other payments. But how much of the annual payment is interest and how much is principal? In other words, what is the rate of return on such a bond and how do we calculate it? This type of investment is, of course, similar to Ex-Cello's lathe.

Again, the rate of return on such a bond is the rate which, when added to the number 1, makes the present value of the promises made by the bond equal to the cost of the bond. The process of finding the rate is again a trial and error process—and this time in Table 4.6 we use discount factors (see Table 3.6) instead of growth factors, just to give you a chance to see which you prefer. We try 6 percent first.

TABLE 4.6

CALCULATION OF RATE OF RETURN ON $100 WITH PROMISED PAYMENT OF $14.90 A YEAR FOR TEN YEARS

LENGTH OF PROMISE (IN YEARS)	AMOUNT OF PROMISE	At 6% Discount Factor		At 10% Discount Factor		At 8% Discount Factor	
		FACTOR	PRESENT VALUE *	FACTOR	PRESENT VALUE †	FACTOR	PRESENT VALUE ‡
(1)	(2)	(3)	(4)	(5)	(6)	(7)	(8)
1	$ 14.90	.943	$ 14.05	.909	$ 13.54	.926	$ 13.80
2	14.90	.890	13.26	.826	12.31	.857	12.77
3	14.90	.840	12.52	.751	11.19	.794	11.83
4	14.90	.792	11.80	.683	10.18	.735	10.95
5	14.90	.747	11.13	.621	9.25	.681	10.15
6	14.90	.705	10.50	.564	8.40	.630	9.39
7	14.90	.665	9.91	.513	7.64	.583	8.69
8	14.90	.627	9.34	.467	6.96	.540	8.05
9	14.90	.592	8.82	.424	6.32	.500	7.45
10	14.90	.558	8.31	.386	5.75	.463	6.90
TOTAL	$149.00	7.359	$109.64	6.144	$91.54	6.710	$99.98

* Column (2) *multiplied by* Column (3).
† Column (2) *multiplied by* Column (5).
‡ Column (2) *multiplied by* Column (7).

As shown in Table 4.6, at 6 percent, the sum of present values given in column (4), $109.64, is too high by $9.64, so we try 10 percent. At 10 percent, the sum of present values listed in column (6), $91.54, is too low by $8.46, so we try 8 percent. At 8 percent, the present value of promises is almost exactly $100. The rate of return on the bond is therefore almost exactly 8 percent.

DEFINING "RATE OF RETURN"

Now then, why do we define the rate of return on a proposed investment as *the rate which, when added to the number 1, will make the present value of the promises made by the investment equal to the cost of the investment?*

We define rate of return in this complicated way because such a rate is what we will call a *break-even rate.* What do we mean by a break-even rate? A break-even rate is the rate at which we could raise money to pay for the investment and be no better or no worse off after the investment had fulfilled all its promises.

Refer again to Table 4.6. We see in that table that the rate of return on the level-payment bond is almost exactly 8 percent. This means that if we went to a bank and borrowed $100 to buy the bond, and agreed to pay the bank interest at the rate of *8 percent* a year, we would find that at the end of the tenth year, we had broken exactly even. We would

TABLE 4.7

PAYMENT OF INTEREST AND PRINCIPAL ON 8 PERCENT BOND

YEAR	AMOUNT INVESTED AT BEGINNING (OF YEAR)	PROMISED PAYMENT	INTEREST AT 8% ON OUTSTANDING PRINCIPAL	TO REDUCTION * OF PRINCIPAL	AMOUNT INVESTED AT END OF YEAR †
(1)	(2)	(3)	(4)	(5)	(6)
1	$100.00	$ 14.90	$ 8.00	$ 6.90	$93.10
2	93.10	14.90	7.45	7.45	85.65
3	85.65	14.90	6.85	8.05	77.70
4	77.70	14.90	6.20	8.70	69.00
5	69.00	14.90	5.50	9.40	59.60
6	59.60	14.90	4.75	10.15	49.45
7	49.45	14.90	3.95	10.95	38.50
8	38.50	14.90	3.08	11.82	26.68
9	26.70	14.90	2.14	12.76	13.92
10	13.95	14.90	1.12	13.78	.14 ‡
TOTAL		$149.00	$49.04	$99.96	

* Promised payment (column (3)) minus interest on outstanding balance (column (4)).
† Amount invested at beginning of year (colum (2)) minus loan reduction (column(5)).
‡ Should equal zero. Does not because of rounding.

find, that is, that our receipts had been just sufficient to repay the loan, and to pay the bank interest at 8 percent a year on the outstanding balance of the loan.

This is illustrated in Table 4.7. At the end of the first year you would receive $14.90. Interest at 8 percent on $100 for one year would be $8 and this would leave $6.90 with which to reduce the principal amount of the loan. At the beginning of the second year, therefore, the principal remaining outstanding would be $93.10 ($100 – $6.90). At the *end* of the second year, you would receive a second payment of $14.90. Interest at 8 percent for one year on $93.10 would be $7.45 and this would leave $7.45 to reduce principal. At the beginning of the third year, therefore, the principal remaining outstanding would be $85.65 ($93.10 – $7.45). And so forth, through the remaining years of the life of the investment. We should note:

1. The total sum you have received from the investment, $149, has been just sufficient to pay interest and repay principal. Nothing is left over. You would have just "broke-even" if you had raised money at 8 percent to buy the bond. But, *if you had been able to raise money at less than eight percent to buy the bond, you would have made money.*

2. Principal is going steadily down because part of each annual payment is being used to reduce it. Interest is being paid only on the principal remaining outstanding. For this reason a rate of return, such as that calculated above, is also called a *rate of return on the outstanding balance.* It is *not* a rate of return on the original investment.

3. It makes no difference whether you actually do repay the bank each year the amount given in column (5) of Table 4.7. You might, for example, use the funds instead to invest in something else. The point is rather that your investment *in the bond* is being reduced each year by the amount listed in that column. But, of course, if you did *not* repay the bank each year, you would have to pay the bank interest at 8 percent a year on the whole $100. But this means merely that the amounts you did *not* repay would themselves have to earn interest at 8 percent. If they did not, you would not "break-even." (You should be able to show why this is so!)

4. We can, if we choose to do so, say that in buying the bond, you are making not one loan of $100 but rather *ten* loans *totaling* $100, as shown in Table 4.6 under Present Value at 8% Discount Factor. The first loan would be for $13.80 to be repaid with interest at 8 percent at the end of the first year, at which

time you would receive $14.90, representing principal of $13.80 plus interest of $1.10. $1.10 is simple interest for one year at 8 percent on $13.80.

The second loan would be for $12.77 for *two* years, as shown in Table 4.6. At the end of the second year, you would again receive $14.90, representing principal of $12.77 and interest of $2.13. $2.13 is compound interest for *two* years at 8 percent on $12.77. And so forth for each of the remaining eight loans. The tenth loan, for $6.90, as shown in Table 4.6, would be repaid with compound interest for ten years at 8 percent. Compound interest at 8 percent for ten years on $6.90 is $8, and $8 plus $6.90 is equal to $14.90, the amount you would receive at the end of the tenth year.

TABLE 4.8

PAYMENTS OF INTEREST AND
PRINCIPAL ON EX-CELLO'S LATHE

YEAR	AMOUNT INVESTED AT BEGINNING OF YEAR	PROMISED PAYMENT	INTEREST AT 4.4% OUTSTANDING PRINCIPAL	REDUCTION OF PRINCIPAL	AMOUNT INVESTED AT END OF YEAR
(1)	(2)	(3)	(4)	(5)	(6)
1	$10,650.00	$ 1,800	$ 468.60	$ 1,331.40	$9,318.60
2	9,318.60	1,800	410.02	1,389.98	7,928.62
3	7,928.62	1,800	348.86	1,451.14	6.477.48
4	6,477.48	1,800	285.01	1,514.99	4,962.49
5	4,962.49	1,800	218.35	1,581.65	3,380.84
6	3,380.84	1,800	148.76	1,651.24	1,729.60
7	1,729.60	1,800	76.10	1,723.90	5.70
TOTAL	$44,447.63	$12,600	$1,955.70	$10,644.30 *	

* Does not add to $10,650 due to rounding.

Table 4.8, referring to Ex-Cello's lathe, is analogous to Table 4.7 and shows that with interest calculated at 4.4 percent on the outstanding balance, everything "comes out even"—except for a rounding error. This means, to repeat, that if Butcher had been able to buy the lathe with funds obtained at 4.4 percent, it would have just "broken-even" on the lathe—it would have lost nothing and would have gained nothing. But, of course, Butcher's cost of capital is about 11 percent—which explains why Hastings rejected the lathe.

CONCLUSION

In this chapter:

1. We have defined a discounted cash flow (DCF) rate of return as that rate which, when added to the number 1, makes the total present value of the set of promises made by an investment equal to the cost of that investment;
2. We have illustrated the calculation of such rates of return for various types of investments—investments in *financial* assets, such as your roommate's loan to you, and bonds of various kinds; and in *real* assets, such as Ex-Cello's lathe;
3. And we have shown that DCF rates are break-even rates—which means that if your required rate is *less* than the DCF rate on a proposed project, that project will be profitable—and vice versa.

EXERCISES

1. An investment of $1,000 today will return $2,000 at the end of 10 years. What is the rate of return on this investment?
2. An investment of $1,000 today will return $500 at the end of each of the next three years. What is its rate of return?
3. An investment of $1,000 today will return $100 at the end of one year, $500 at the end of two years, $1,000 at the end of three years. What is its rate of return? What is its present value at an interest rate of 10 percent?
4. An investment of $1,000 today will return $1,000 at the end of one year, $500 at the end of two years, and $100 at the end of three years. What is its rate of return? What is its present value at an interest rate of 10 percent?
5. An investment of $1,000 today will return $50 per year forevermore. What is its rate of return?

PROBLEMS

1. *Find the rate of interest which would make the cash flows given in Table 3.5, for both AT&T and RCA, equal to their respective market*

prices, assuming these market prices are $56.375 for AT&T and $43.50 for RCA.

2. Suppose that Ex-Cello's lathe promised $1,800 a year for eight years instead of for seven. What would the rate of return be? For nine years? For ten years? Use the shortcut procedure described in Appendix 4.A.

3. In Table 4.4, how much interest is the interest itself earning? Why can't you divide the total increase $59.81 ($159.81 −$100) by 10 in order to find the rate of return?

4. Using the information Hastings gave his son, calculate the rate of return on a college education? Assume that you must choose between:
    a. borrowing $16,000 to pay for your college education;
    b. not going to college. Would you borrow the necessary money if you had to pay interest at 12 percent a year on the outstanding balance of the loan?

5. Assume that you do borrow the $16,000 on the following terms:
    a. rate on outstanding balance is 12 percent;
    b. you pay nothing—neither interest nor principal—until two years after you graduate (assume you do graduate).

    Draw up a repayment schedule, beginning exactly two years after you graduate, which would pay off the entire loan plus interest by the end of the seventh year after you graduate—neither sooner nor later. The five annual payments must all be equal in amount. Don't forget that the whole $16,000 will have accumulated compound interest for six years at 12 percent.

6. You want to buy a car. You borrow $1,000 from an auto finance company which advertises 6 percent loans. You sign a note for $1,066—$60 in interest plus a $6 fee plus the $1,000. You are to repay the loan at the rate of $88.83 a month for twelve months. What rate of return is the bank really earning on its investment?

7. In the situation described in problem 6, how much would your monthly payments be if the finance company's true rate of return were 6 percent a year?

8. After you have found the true rate of return the bank is earning on your car loan in problem 6, make up a break-even table for your payments like Table 4.8.

9. Using the figures given in Table 3.5, in Columns (2) and (3), calculate rates of return on investing in AT&T and RCA, assuming their current prices to be $56.375 for AT&T and $43.50 for RCA.

10. Early in this chapter, the following question was raised: To get the rate of return on Ex-Cello's lathe, why not divide $1,800 (the annual promise) by $10,650 (the cost of the lathe)? Why not?

SHORTCUT METHOD
FOR CALCULATING
RATES OF RETURN

If we have a set of level promises, such as those made by Ex-Cello's lathe, we can shorten the process of calculating a rate of return, as follows:

1. Divide the cost of the investment by one of the promises thus: $\dfrac{\$10,650}{\$\ 1,800} = 5.917$

2. Find the number closest to 5.917 along the seventh row of Table 4.9 (Present Value of $1 received annually). It is 6.002. Thus 5.917 lies between 4 and 5 percent.

3. Interpolate, in the following manner between 4 percent and 5 percent:

   a. $\begin{array}{r} 6.002 \\ -\ 5.786 \\ \hline .216 \end{array}$ (4 percent)
   (5 percent)

   b. $\begin{array}{r} 5.917 \\ -\ 5.786 \\ \hline .131 \end{array}$

   c. $\dfrac{.131}{.216} = .61$

   d. Subtract .61 from 5.00 percent:

   $\begin{array}{r} 5.00 \\ -\ .61 \\ \hline 4.39 \end{array}$ (rounded to 4.4)

Therefore: Rate of return equals 5 percent *minus* .61 × one percent, or 4.39 percent which, after rounding, is equal to 4.4 percent, the rate we found in Table 4.8.

What's the underlying meaning of this somewhat mechanical procedure? Refer back to Table 4.3.

In that table, we were really setting up an equation—although you may not have realized it at the time. We were saying that:

$$\$10,650 = \frac{\$1,800}{(1+x)} + \frac{\$1,800}{(1+x)^2} + \frac{\$1,800}{(1+x)^3} + \frac{\$1,800}{(1+x)^4} + \frac{\$1,800}{(1+x)^5} +$$

$$\frac{\$1,800}{(1+x)^6} + \frac{\$1,800}{(1+x)^7}$$

Where:

$10,650 = cost of lathe
$1,800 = annual promise
x   = unknown rate of return

All this equation means is that we will have found the rate of return on the lathe when the right hand side of the equation is equal to the left hand side or, in other words, *when the total present value of the seven promises is equal to the cost of the lathe.*

Because all the annual promises are equal to each other we can *factor out* $1,800 and rewrite the equation as follows:

$$\$10,650 = \$1,800\left[\frac{1}{(1+x)} + \frac{1}{(1+x)^2} + \frac{1}{(1+x)^3} + \frac{1}{(1+x)^4} + \frac{1}{(1+x)^5} + \frac{1}{(1+x)^6} + \frac{1}{(1+x)^7}\right]$$

Now, we can transfer the $1,800 to the left hand side, thus:

$$\frac{\$10,650}{\$1,800} = 5.917 = \frac{1}{(1+x)} + \frac{1}{(1+x)^2} + \frac{1}{(1+x)^3} + \frac{1}{(1+x)^4} + \frac{1}{(1+x)^5} + \frac{1}{(1+x)^6} + \frac{1}{(1+x)^7}$$

But we know that each of the terms on the right hand side is the reciprocal of a growth factor. And the reciprocal of a growth rate is a *discount* factor. Therefore the equation is simply telling us that the *sum* of the compound discount factors which will make both sides of the equation equal is 5.917. Table 4.9 gives us *sums* of discount factors for selected rates for fifty periods.

Using a computer we constructed Table 4.9 by simply adding up, for all periods up to fifty, the individual discount factors given in Table 3.6. Table 3.6 does not give discount factors for 4.4 percent

TABLE 4.9

PRESENT VALUE OF $1 RECEIVED PERIODICALLY FOR n PERIODS

PERIODS	1%	2%	4%	6%	8%	10%	12%	14%	15%	16%	18%	20%	22%	24%	25%	26%	28%	30%	35%	40%	46%	50%
1	0.990	0.980	0.962	0.943	0.926	0.909	0.893	0.877	0.870	0.862	0.847	0.833	0.820	0.806	0.800	0.794	0.781	0.769	0.741	0.714	0.690	0.667
2	1.970	1.942	1.886	1.833	1.783	1.736	1.690	1.647	1.626	1.605	1.566	1.528	1.492	1.457	1.440	1.424	1.392	1.361	1.289	1.224	1.165	1.111
3	2.941	2.884	2.775	2.673	2.577	2.487	2.402	2.322	2.283	2.246	2.174	2.106	2.042	1.981	1.952	1.923	1.868	1.816	1.696	1.589	1.493	1.407
4	3.902	3.808	3.630	3.465	3.312	3.170	3.037	2.914	2.855	2.798	2.690	2.589	2.494	2.404	2.362	2.320	2.241	2.166	1.997	1.849	1.720	1.605
5	4.853	4.713	4.452	4.212	3.993	3.791	3.605	3.433	3.352	3.274	3.127	2.991	2.864	2.745	2.689	2.635	2.532	2.436	2.220	2.035	1.876	1.737
6	5.795	5.601	5.242	4.917	4.623	4.355	4.111	3.889	3.784	3.685	3.498	3.326	3.167	3.020	2.951	2.885	2.759	2.643	2.385	2.168	1.983	1.824
7	6.728	6.472	6.002	5.582	5.206	4.868	4.564	4.288	4.160	4.039	3.812	3.605	3.416	3.242	3.161	3.083	2.937	2.802	2.508	2.263	2.057	1.883
8	7.652	7.325	6.733	6.210	5.747	5.335	4.968	4.639	4.487	4.344	4.078	3.837	3.619	3.421	3.329	3.241	3.076	2.925	2.598	2.331	2.108	1.922
9	8.566	8.162	7.435	6.802	6.247	5.759	5.328	4.946	4.772	4.607	4.303	4.031	3.786	3.566	3.463	3.366	3.184	3.019	2.665	2.379	2.144	1.948
10	9.471	8.983	8.111	7.360	6.710	6.145	5.650	5.216	5.019	4.833	4.494	4.192	3.923	3.682	3.571	3.465	3.269	3.092	2.715	2.414	2.168	1.965
11	10.368	9.787	8.760	7.887	7.139	6.495	5.988	5.453	5.234	5.029	4.656	4.327	4.035	3.776	3.656	3.544	3.335	3.147	2.752	2.438	2.185	1.977
12	11.255	10.575	9.385	8.384	7.536	6.814	6.194	5.660	5.421	5.197	4.793	4.439	4.127	3.851	3.725	3.606	3.387	3.190	2.779	2.456	2.196	1.985
13	12.134	11.343	9.986	8.853	7.904	7.103	6.424	5.842	5.583	5.342	4.910	4.533	4.203	3.912	3.780	3.656	3.427	3.223	2.799	2.468	2.204	1.990
14	13.004	12.106	10.563	9.295	8.244	7.367	6.628	6.002	5.724	5.468	5.008	4.611	4.265	3.962	3.824	3.695	3.459	3.249	2.814	2.477	2.210	1.993
15	13.865	12.849	11.118	9.712	8.559	7.606	6.811	6.142	5.847	5.575	5.092	4.675	4.315	4.001	3.859	3.726	3.483	3.268	2.825	2.484	2.214	1.995
16	14.718	13.578	11.652	10.106	8.851	7.824	6.974	6.265	5.954	5.669	5.162	4.730	4.357	4.033	3.887	3.751	3.503	3.283	2.834	2.489	2.216	1.997
17	15.562	14.292	12.166	10.477	9.122	8.022	7.120	6.373	6.047	5.749	5.222	4.775	4.391	4.059	3.910	3.771	3.518	3.295	2.840	2.492	2.218	1.998
18	16.398	14.992	12.659	10.828	9.372	8.201	7.250	6.467	6.128	5.818	5.273	4.812	4.419	4.080	3.928	3.786	3.529	3.304	2.844	2.494	2.219	1.999
19	17.226	15.678	13.134	11.158	9.604	8.365	7.366	6.550	6.198	5.877	5.316	4.844	4.442	4.097	3.942	3.799	3.539	3.311	2.848	2.496	2.220	1.999
20	18.046	16.351	13.590	11.470	9.818	8.514	7.469	6.623	6.259	5.929	5.353	4.870	4.460	4.110	3.954	3.808	3.546	3.316	2.850	2.497	2.221	1.999
21	18.857	17.011	14.029	11.764	10.017	8.649	7.562	6.687	6.312	5.973	5.384	4.891	4.476	4.121	3.963	3.816	3.551	3.320	2.852	2.498	2.221	2.100
22	19.660	17.658	14.451	12.042	10.201	8.772	7.645	6.743	6.359	6.011	5.410	4.909	4.488	4.130	3.970	3.822	3.556	3.323	2.853	2.498	2.222	2.000
23	20.456	18.292	14.857	12.303	10.371	8.883	7.718	6.792	6.399	6.044	5.432	4.925	4.499	4.137	3.976	3.827	3.559	3.325	2.854	2.499	2.222	2.000
24	21.243	18.914	15.247	12.550	10.529	8.985	7.784	6.835	6.434	6.073	5.451	4.937	4.507	4.143	3.981	3.831	3.562	3.327	2.855	2.499	2.222	2.000
25	22.023	19.523	15.622	12.783	10.675	9.077	7.843	6.873	6.464	6.097	5.467	4.948	4.514	4.147	3.985	3.834	3.564	3.329	2.856	2.499	2.222	2.000
26	22.795	20.121	15.983	13.003	10.810	9.161	7.896	6.906	6.491	6.118	5.480	4.956	4.520	4.151	3.988	3.837	3.566	3.330	2.856	2.500	2.222	2.000
27	23.560	20.707	16.330	13.211	10.935	9.237	7.943	6.935	6.514	6.136	5.492	4.964	4.524	4.154	3.990	3.839	3.567	3.331	2.856	2.500	2.222	2.000
28	24.316	21.281	16.663	13.406	11.051	9.307	7.984	6.961	6.534	6.152	5.502	4.970	4.528	4.157	3.992	3.840	3.568	3.331	2.857	2.500	2.222	2.000
29	25.066	21.844	16.984	13.591	11.158	9.370	8.022	6.983	6.551	6.166	5.510	4.975	4.531	4.159	3.994	3.841	3.569	3.332	2.857	2.500	2.222	2.000
30	25.808	22.396	17.292	13.765	11.258	9.427	8.055	7.003	6.566	6.177	5.517	4.979	4.534	4.160	3.995	3.842	3.569	3.332	2.857	2.500	2.222	2.000
40	32.835	27.355	19.793	15.046	11.925	9.779	8.244	7.105	6.642	6.234	5.548	4.997	4.544	4.166	3.999	3.846	3.571	3.333	2.857	2.500	2.222	2.000
50	39.196	31.424	21.482	15.762	12.234	9.915	8.304	7.133	6.661	6.246	5.554	4.999	4.545	4.167	4.000	3.846	3.571	3.333	2.857	2.500	2.222	2.000

For easy reference, this table also appears at the back of the book.

and therefore Table 4.10 does not give their sum. But we can calculate them ourselves, as follows:

PERIOD	DISCOUNT FACTORS AT 4.4%
1	$.95785 = 1/1.044$
2	$.91752 = 1/(1.044)^2$
3	$.87881 = 1/(1.044)^3$
4	$.84175 = 1/(1.044)^4$
5	$.80632 = 1/(1.044)^5$
6	$.77232 = 1/(1.044)^6$
7	$.73975 = 1/(1.044)^7$
TOTAL	5.91432 *

* Which is very close to 5.917.

Table 4.10 shows the relationship between the *individual* discount factors (Table 3.6) and the *sums* (Table 4.9) for a rate of 4 percent.

TABLE 4.10

DERIVATION OF 4 PERCENT SUMS FROM 4 PERCENT FACTORS

PERIOD	1	2	3	4	5	6
1	.962† / .962*	.962)†	.962)†	.962)†	.962)†	.962)†
2		.925) / 1.886*	.925)	.925)	.925)	.925)
3			.889) / 2.775*	.889)	.889)	.889)
4				.855) / 3.630*	.855)	.855)
5					.822) / 4.452*	.822)
6						.790) / 5.242*

NOTE: Sums indicated by arrows are listed under "4%" in Table 4.9. Factors do not add to sums due to rounding.

† From Table 3.6, under "4%."

* From Table 4.9, under "4%."

RATES OF RETURN OR PRESENT VALUE?

In Chapters 3 and 4 we described two tools—present value and rates of return—*both* of which can be used to assess the worthwhileness of proposed projects. Which is better and which should we use? The answer is: "That depends . . ."

NET PRESENT VALUE

Let's go back for a minute to Chapter 2, where we said that the firm maximizes the price of its common stock by calculating rates of return on proposed new projects and then comparing those rates with its cost of capital. And, of course, when we said "rates of return," we meant discounted cash flow (DCF) rates of return as defined in Chapter 4. But we saw in Chapter 3 that we can use a predetermined required rate of interest to calculate the value to you now (the present value) of a set of promises. In Table 3.5, for example, we found that the present value of a share of AT&T was $47.26, and the present value of a share of RCA, $51.23. For the purpose of making these calculations we assumed that your required rate of interest was 10 percent. Using that rate, we found the present value to you, as given above, of a share of AT&T and of a share of RCA. After we found these two figures, we could have subtracted from each the *cost* of each share, thus:

Present value of share of AT&T	$47.26
Cost of share of AT&T	— 56.38
Net Present Value	— $9.12

Or in the case of RCA:

Present value of share of RCA	$51.23
Cost of share of RCA	— 43.50
Net Present Value	$ 7.73

In other words, the *net* present value of each share is simply its present value, calculated at your required rate of interest, minus the price (cost) of each share.

A DCF rate of return and an estimate of net present value are thus two different ways of measuring something we might call "the worthwhileness of an investment." And, intuitively, both measures would seem to be equivalent. To calculate a *DCF rate of return*, we use three figures to obtain a fourth—we use the price of the asset, the promises made by the asset, and the expected life of the asset. By a trial and error process, we find the rate which makes the sum of the present values of each of the promises, equal to the price of the asset.

To obtain the *net present value* (net PV) of an asset, we use the promises made by the asset, the length of time each promise will be outstanding, and a rate. Using the rate, appropriately compounded, we calculate the present value of each promise and add them. From this sum we then subtract the cost of the asset. The remainder is the *net* PV which would be generated by the asset. Net PV can, of course, be either positive or negative. In the illustration above, the net PV of a share of AT&T was negative—which meant simply that, for you, the price of AT&T was too high.

In other words, when we calculate a DCF rate of return on an asset, we equate price and present value. We have, in effect, answered the question: What rate of return would make the net present value of this asset equal to zero? When we calculate the net present value of an asset, we answer the question: At our required rate, is this asset worth anything to us beyond its cost and, if so, how much?

Is there any real difference between the two measures, given the fact that they merely look at the same numbers—promises, life and price— from a different vantage point? Before we discuss the differences, let us emphasize an important similarity. *Both measures enable us to compare rates of return with the cost of capital.* One measure requires us to make the comparison consciously and explicitly; the other measure makes the comparison implicitly. After we have calculated DCF rates of return on all the proposals in a capital budget, we can rank the proposals as we have in Table 5.1, which is simply an expanded version of Table 1.1.

TABLE 5.1

PROPOSED NEW PROJECTS, DECEMBER, 1968 *

PROJECT	COST (thousands)	DCF RATE †	NET PRESENT VALUE AT 11% (thousands)
1. Increase in accounts receivable	$ 680	42%	$ 83
2. Increase in parts inventory	750	28%	52
3. Chemical storage tanks	1,525	24%	600
4. Tank and other trucks	190	19%	60
5. New plant and equipment (Lima, Ohio)	925	18%	22
6. Machinery-Plastics division	1,225	16%	68
7. New heat pump, etc. (Old Forge, N.Y.)	730	12%	12
8. Materials handling equipment	504	12%	10
9. Electron microscopes	33	8%	(—20)

* This table includes some proposals made after Martin had drawn up Table 1.1.
† After taxes.

Hence using its cost of capital as a cutoff rate, Butcher simply could glance at the budget and accept all projects which show expected rates of return higher than 11 percent. Butcher would thus accept all the proposed projects except the electron microscopes.

But Butcher could just as well, and with identical results, simply accept all projects which show positive present value—that is, with present value greater than zero—as indicated under Net Present Value in Table 5.1.

Why would the results have been identical: *If the promises made by a project show positive net present value at the cost of capital, then the rate of return on the project must be higher than the cost of capital.* Why is this so? It is so because the rate which would make net PV on that project zero—that is, the DCF rate on the promises—must be higher than the cost of capital. You will see in Table 5.1 that every project which promises a rate of return higher than the cost of capital (11 percent) also shows net PV at 11 percent.

TABLE 5.2

RATE OF RETURN WITH PROMISED ANNUAL OPERATING SAVINGS OF $2,333

LENGTH OF PROMISE (IN YEARS)	AMOUNT OF PROMISE	DISCOUNT FACTORS AT 12%	PRESENT VALUE
(1)	(2)	(3)	(4)
1	$2,333	.893	$ 2,083.37
2	2,333	.797	1,859.40
3	2,333	.712	1,661.10
4	2,333	.636	1,483.79
5	2,333	.567	1.322.81
6	2,333	.507	1,182.83
7	2,333	.452	1,054.52
		TOTAL	$10.647.82

TABLE 5.3

RATE OF RETURN WITH PROMISED ANNUAL OPERATING SAVINGS OF $2,260

LENGTH OF PROMISE (IN YEARS)	AMOUNT OF PROMISE	DISCOUNT FACTORS AT 11%	PRESENT VALUE
(1)	(2)	(3)	(4)
1	$2,260	.901	$ 2,036.26
2	2,260	.812	1,835.12
3	2,260	.731	1,652.06
4	2,260	.659	1,489.34
5	2,260	.593	1,340.18
6	2,260	.535	1,209.10
7	2,260	.482	1,089.32
		TOTAL	$10,651.38

Suppose, for example, that Hastings, in the course of shopping around for lathes, found two, each made by a different manufacturer, but each priced at $10,650. The first promised $2,333 savings a year, after taxes, for seven years; the second, $2,260, after taxes, also for seven years. As Table 5.2 shows, the rate of return on the first lathe is almost exactly 12 percent. And, as Table 5.3 shows, the rate of return on the second lathe is almost exactly 11 percent. Thus the rate of return on the first lathe is higher than the rate of return on the second lathe. But if this is so, the set of promises made by the first lathe should have higher net PV than the set of promises made by the second lathe—*when each set is discounted at the cost of capital.* This is exactly what Tables 5.4 and

TABLE 5.4

PRESENT VAULE OF LATHE PROMISING $2,333 SAVINGS

LENGTH OF PROMISE (IN YEARS)	AMOUNT OF PROMISE	FACTORS DISCOUNT AT 11%	PRESENT VALUE
(1)	(2)	(3)	(4)
1	$2,333	.901	$ 2,102.03
2	2,333	.817	1,906.06
3	2,333	.731	1,705.42
4	2,333	.659	1,537.45
5	2,333	.593	1,383.47
6	2,333	.535	1,248.16
7	2,333	.482	1,124.51
		TOTAL	$11,007.10

TABLE 5.5

COMPARISON OF NET PRESENT VALUES

	FIRST LATHE	SECOND LATHE
Present Value	$11,007	$10,651
Cost	10,650	10,650
Net Present Value	$ 357	$ 1

5.5 show. The set of promises made by the first lathe shows net PV of $357, and the set of promises made by the second lathe, shows net PV of about zero.

Thus, if a project shows net PV at the cost of capital, the DCF rate of return on that project will be higher than the cost of capital.

What's the fuss? If this is so, what difference does it make which we use? The answer is none—most of the time. The explanation of this anomaly follows.

CHOOSING DCF RATES OR NET PV

First, the two measures are stated in different terms. The DCF rate of return is, of course, stated as a rate. Net PV, on the other hand, is stated in dollars—as the difference between the present value of a project and its price. This means that the two measures will not always *rank* proposed new projects in the same way—if those projects differ in *size*. Table 5.1 makes this clear. The highest rate of return is expected to be earned by proposal Number 1—which ranks only third in terms of net present value.

Second, this means that in certain circumstances, a project with a lower rate of return will be preferable to a project with a higher rate of return. In what circumstances will this be so? Suppose that in mid-1966, the following incident occurred *after* the Butcher Company had sold all the debt it thought it would need and did not wish to sell any more: Hastings stopped by to see Dale Martin, Butcher's financial vice president, and said, "Dale, I have another project I'd like to get into the budget."

Martin said, "The budget's already been approved. You know that."

"I know," said Hastings, "but this one is only $50,000. I thought you might squeeze it in somehow."

"I don't see how," said Martin, "we had only $35,000 left over. And there's no chance whatever of borrowing any more money—not right now."

"Well," said Hastings, "suppose I give up those two new fork lifts at $7,500 each, that's $15,000. With the $35,000 you have left over, I'd just be able to pay for this new compression moulding machine."

"What's the return?" asked Martin, reaching for his capital budgeting "book," a loose leaf affair in which he kept all the relevant data on all projects approved for the coming year by the Finance Committee and the Board.

"Twelve percent," said Hastings.

"But the fork lifts show 14 percent," said Martin. "Here, look." He pushed the book to Hastings.

"Yes, I know," said Hastings. "But the net present value of the moulding machine is larger." He showed Martin Tables 5.6 and 5.7.

TABLE 5.6

FORK LIFT

YEAR	ANNUAL PROMISE	DISCOUNT FACTORS AT 14%	PRESENT VALUE	DISCOUNT FACTORS AT 11%	PRESENT VALUE
(1)	(2)	(3)	(4)	(5)	(6)
1	$3,235	.877	$ 2,837.10	.901	$ 2,914.73
2	3,235	.769	2,487.71	.817	2,643.00
3	3,235	.675	2,183.62	.731	2,364.78
4	3,235	.592	1,915.12	.659	2,131.87
5	3,235	.519	1,678.97	.593	1,918.35
6	3,235	.456	1,475.16	.535	1,730.73
7	3,235	.400	1,294.00	.482	1,559.27
8	3,235	.351	1,135.48	.434	1,403.99
TOTAL			$15,007.16		$16,666.72

TABLE 5.7

COMPRESSION MOULDING MACHINE

YEAR	ANNUAL PROMISE	DISCOUNT FACTORS AT 12%	PRESENT VALUE	DISCOUNT FACTORS AT 11%	PRESENT VALUE
(1)	(2)	(3)	(4)	(5)	(6)
1	$10,065	.893	$ 8,988.05	.901	$ 9,068.57
2	10,065	.797	8,021.81	.817	8,223.11
3	10,065	.712	7,166.28	.731	7,357.52
4	10,065	.636	6,401.34	.659	6,632.84
5	10,065	.567	5,706.86	.593	5,968.55
6	10,065	.507	5,102.96	.535	5,384.78
7	10,065	.452	4,549.38	.482	4,851.33
8	10,065	.404	4,066.26	.434	4,368.21
TOTAL			$50,002.94		$51,854.91

Both projects had eight year lives. Table 5.6 gives the figures on the fork lifts; Table 5.7 the figures on the compression moulding machine. Hastings had listed the discount factors corresponding to the rate of return on each project—14 percent for the fork lifts and 12 percent for the compression moulding machine. He had then calculated present values, at those rates, of the promises expected to be generated by each project. When calculated at the rate of return on each project, the present value of each project was, of course, equal to its cost—and *net* present value was, of course, zero—except for small rounding errors.

Thus, the tables showed merely that the rate of return on the fork lifts was 14 percent and on the moulding machine, 12 percent. Hastings then calculated the present value of each project, using as his discount rate Butcher's cost of capital, which was approximately 11 percent. He thereby obtained the figures shown in the final column of Tables 5.6 and 5.7. These columns show that the present value of the promises made by the fork lifts is about $16,667; the present value of cash flows expected to be generated by the moulding machine is about $51,855. Hastings then calculated *net* present values, as follows:

FORK LIFT

Present value at 11%	$16,667
Cost	—15,000
Net Present Value	$ 1,667

MOULDING MACHINE

Present value at 11%	$51,855
Cost	—50,000
Net Present Value	$ 1,855

"And so the net present value of the moulding machine is larger—even though the rate of return is less," said Martin.

"Yes," said Hastings.

"Well, then, take your pick," said Martin.

"No chance of having both?" asked Hastings.

"Sorry. Not enough M-O-N-E-Y."

"Okay, I'll settle for the moulding machine," said Hastings, as he left.

advantages of using net PV

The moulding machine had a higher net present value and therefore meant more dollars of profit to the company—merely because it was a larger project. (If you have difficulty seeing this point, ask yourself which is larger, 5 percent of $2,000 or 7 percent of $1,000. And if you had $2,000, and no more, to invest, which project would you choose—

the 5 percent project or the 7 percent project—provided you had to choose one or the other?)

Moreover, if the cost of capital is known, the net present value of an asset is easier to calculate than its DCF rate of return—especially if promises vary in amount from year to year. When Hastings in Chapter 3 calculated the present value of Ex-Cello's lathe (see Table 3.1) all he had to do was write down the 11 percent growth factors, divide and add the present values. To obtain *net* present value, he would merely have had to subtract the price of the lathe. But when we calculated the DCF rate of return on the lathe (see Table 4.3), we had to go through the multiplication and adding procedure with several different rates. This was tedious. And the process of calculating the rate of return took about three times as long as the process of calculating net present value. This consideration is not very important if a firm uses a computer to calculate rates of return, as many firms do. But it is important if you do not have access to a computer and are forced to use a desk calculator or a slide rule.

In sum then, we may say that the net PV method is preferable to the DCF rate of return method as a way of deciding whether or not to accept proposed investments—provided the cost of capital is known—primarily for two reasons:[1] *first*, if money is scarce, using the net PV method will not mislead a firm into choosing a smaller project with a higher rate of return but less net present value. *Second*, net PV is easier to calculate if the cost of capital is known. And, if the cost of capital is known, all proposed investments which show positive net present value should be accepted. But, unhappily, the cost of capital will not always be known, because it often depends on the method used to finance the proposed new investments, and also on the riskiness of those new investments relative to the riskiness of the firm's present assets. This matter will be discussed further in Part IV.

OTHER MEASURES

Sometimes other measures are used as alternatives to DCF rates of return and net PV to assess the worthwhileness of a proposed investment. Most of them are misleading. But you will encounter them from time to time and therefore you should know *why* they are misleading. These other measures are:

---

[1] There are technical reasons, as well, which need not detain us here because they are not very important. In rare situations, for example, a rate of return calculation may lead to more than one rate. See J. T. S. Porterfield, *Investment Decisions and Capital Costs*, (Englewood Cliffs, N.J.: Prentice-Hall, Inc., 1965), pp. 24-29.

1. The payback period
2. The rate of return on *original* investment
3. The rate of return on *average* investment.

payback period

The payback period is exactly what its name suggests—the period of time, measured *in years*, an investment will take to return (that is, to "payback") its cost.

The price of Ex-Cello's lathe, you will remember, was $10,650 installed. Ex-Cello's salesman said it would save Butcher $1,800 a year after taxes (for seven years) in labor cost—which meant simply that in Ex-Cello's opinion, Butcher's labor cost would be reduced by $1,800, net, each year for seven years for each one of the new lathes it bought.

How long would it take the new lathe to return its cost, or in other words, to pay for itself? We divide cost by labor savings to obtain the answer, thus:

$$\frac{\$10,650}{\$\ 1,800} = 5.92 \text{ years}$$

or five years and eleven months. Five years, eleven months is, thus, the *payback period* for the lathe, calculated on the basis of Ex-Cello's figures. In other words, five years and eleven months after the lathe had been installed, the sum of the labor savings generated by the lathe would have paid for the lathe.

The foregoing calculation assumes that the labor savings expected to be generated by the lathe would be level at $1,800 for at least the payback period or would *average* that amount over the payback period. If the labor savings are not expected to be level, the payback period can be most simply calculated by subtracting the annual savings successively from the cost of the investment until the balance becomes negative. Suppose that Hastings believed that the savings on the lathe would not be level although they would average $1,800 over a seven year period, as shown in the upper half of Table 5.8. In the lower half of the table, the annual savings given in the upper half are subtracted successively from the cost of the lathe. The subtraction is continued until the balance becomes negative. The payback period is found by this process to be 6.30 years, or about six years and four months.

At one time, business used the payback period extensively to assess the worthwhileness of investments. But the payback period has many defects:

TABLE 5.8

PAYBACK PERIOD WITH UNEVEN LABOR SAVINGS

YEAR	LABOR SAVINGS
1	$ 800
2	1,200
3	1,400
4	1,800
5	2,200
6	2,400
7	2,800
TOTAL	$12,600

CALCULATION OF PAYBACK

Cost of lathe	$10,650
Saving, Year 1	800
Balance	9,850
Saving, Year 2	1,200
Balance	8,650
Saving, Year 3	1,400
Balance	7,250
Saving, Year 4	1,800
Balance	5,450
Saving, Year 5	2,200
Balance	3,250
Saving, Year 6	2,400
Balance	850
Saving, Year 7	2,800
	—$1,950

$$\frac{\text{Balance End of Year 6}}{\text{Saving, Year 7}} = \frac{850}{2,800} = .30$$

Payback Period = 6.30 Years

First, it is stated in years and therefore cannot be compared with the cost of capital, which is stated as a percent.

Second, the payback period does not distinguish between two investments which make the same annual promise but *which have different lives.* This is illustrated in Table 5.9. The two investments have the same cost and each promises $1,800 a year. But the second will last a

TABLE 5.9

TWO INVESTMENTS WITH SAME PAYBACK PERIOD, BUT DIFFERENT LIVES

INVESTMENT NUMBER 1		INVESTMENT NUMBER 2	
Cost	$5,400	Cost	$5,400
Annual promise	$1,800	Annual promise	$1,800
Payback	3 Years	Payback	3 Years
Life	3 Years	Life	4 Years

Rate of Return = Less than 0.   Rate of Return = More than 12%.

year longer and will therefore bring in $1,800 more. The payback period makes both investments seem equally worthwhile, despite the fact that they obviously are not.

Third, the payback period cannot distinguish between two investments with the same lives that offer promises with different time patterns, as in Table 5.10. Investment Number 1 in Table 5.10 promises its largest payment in the first year and its smallest in the third. Invest-

TABLE 5.10

TWO INVESTMENTS WITH THE SAME PAYBACK PERIOD, THE SAME LIVES, AND THE SAME AVERAGE ANNUAL PROMISE, BUT WITH DIFFERENT TIME PATTERNS OF PROMISES

YEAR	INVESTMENT NUMBER 1 ANNUAL PROMISE	INVESTMENT NUMBER 2 ANNUAL PROMISE
(1)	(2)	(3)
1	$2,200	$1,200
2	2,000	2,000
3	1,200	2,200
4	1,800	1,800
5	1,800	1,800
6	1,800	1,800
Payback	3 Years	3 Years
Life	6 Years	6 Years
Present Value at 6%	$8,903	$8,800

ment Number 2 promises its largest payment in the third year and its smallest in the first. And as we would expect, investment Number 1 has the larger present value and is, therefore, worth more now than the second.

rate of return on original investment

This measure is simply the *net income* on the investment, after taxes, divided by the total amount originally invested. Net income is *not* the same as the promise made by the investment. The promise is net income *plus depreciation.*

When Ex-Cello's salesman discussed the new lathe with Hastings, he said it would save Butcher $1,800 a year in labor cost, after taxes, for at least seven years. This statement meant, in effect, that Butcher's saving *before taxes* would be $2,080, as shown in Table 5.11. This latter sum can be regarded as the gross difference in Butcher's labor cost attributable to the lathe—on the assumption that sales of the products produced by the lathe *remain the same.* In other words, Butcher would be producing with the new lathe the same physical volume of products it is now producing, but the new lathe would be more efficient, that is, it would use less labor and, therefore, Butcher's labor cost would be less. This is where the $2,080 comes from. This sum would be saved annually for seven years.

TABLE 5.11

GROSS LABOR SAVINGS BEFORE TAXES FROM EX-CELLO'S LATHE

1.	Gross labor saving before taxes	$2,080
2.	Less depreciation $(= \dfrac{10,650}{7})$	— 1,520
3.	Increase in taxable income	560
4.	Less taxes on increase at 50%	— 280
5.	Increase in net income, after taxes, attributable to lathe	280
6.	Plus depreciation (as above)	1,520
7.	Savings, after taxes, attributable to lathe	$1,800

Using this gross figure as the starting point, Table 5.11 shows the additional net income which would be generated by the new lathe (line 5). We start with $2,080, the *gross* labor saving. Next, the annual depreciation charge is obtained by dividing the installed cost of the machine by its expected life ($10,650/7 = $1,520). This procedure assumes that depreciation will be taken in equal annual amounts, with no allowance for salvage value at the end of the useful life of the machine. Depreciation is thus $1,520 a year for seven years. This amount is deducted from the gross saving to obtain the increase in taxable income, $560. This sum is taxable at a rate of 50 percent, meaning that half of it goes to the federal and state governments, and half of it is kept by Butcher.

Out of the original gross savings of $2,080, Butcher retains the amount represented by depreciation, plus the additional net income,

$$\$1,520 + \$280 = \$1,800.$$

Thus, $1,800 represents the after-tax savings estimated by Ex-Cello's salesman.

Now in order to calculate the rate of return on original investment, we simply divide the increase in net income ($280) by the original investment ($10,650), thus:

$$\frac{\$ \quad 280}{\$10,650} = .0263$$

or 2.63 percent which seems rather low.

rate of return on average investment

Why is the rate of return on the *original* investment so low? As we know, the original investment is progressively reduced each year. This means that a return based on the original investment is *understated*: to repeat, net income is the same each year, but the amount invested is progressively reduced.

One way of dealing with this problem is to divide the original investment by two. This assumes that at the beginning of the *first* day of the life of the investment, the whole amount ($10,650) is invested. This amount would be steadily and evenly reduced during the life of the investment, and at the end of the *last* day of the life of the investment, would be zero. Thus, the average investment would be:

$$\frac{\$10,650 + 0}{2} = \$5,325.$$

If, in fact, $5,325 does really represent the average amount invested over the life of the machine (it doesn't), then the rate of return on that amount would be:

$$\frac{\$\ 280}{\$5,325} = .0526$$

or 5.26 percent, which is, of course, exactly twice the rate calculated on the original investment. It is twice the rate because the original investment has been divided by two.

This method of calculation—that is, dividing the original investment by two—assumes, as we have indicated above, that the original investment is recovered steadily and evenly over the life of the asset. This happens very rarely and in all cases when promises are level, return of capital will *not* be level. It will be smaller in the earlier years and larger in the later years of the life of the asset as shown in Tables 4.8 and 5.12.

Thus, the two rates of return described above either overstate or understate, as the case may be, the outstanding investment in the asset, and therefore either understate or overstate the rate of return on the asset.

misleading calculations

What do we mean, concretely, by the terms "understate" and "overstate?" In Chapter 4 we defined a DCF rate of return as the *rate of return on the true outstanding balance*. We defined it, in other words, as the rate of return which would *just* enable you, over the life of the asset, to pay interest at a rate equal to that rate of return, on funds raised to buy the asset, and to repay in full the amount of the loan. In order to refresh your memory on this point look again at Tables 4.7 and 4.8. In other words, a DCF rate is a "break-even" rate. It specifies the rate of interest we could pay on money raised to buy the asset, and still "break-even."

But what about the two rates calculated above? Both would lead us astray. The rate of return on *original* investment would lead us *not* to invest in the lathe if our cost of capital were higher than 2.63 percent. And the rate of return on *average* investment would lead us not to invest in the lathe if our cost of capital were just less than 5.26 percent. Both decisions would be wrong.

This is illustrated in Tables 5.12 and 5.13. Table 5.12 assumes that the true rate of return on the lathe is 2.63 percent; Table 5.13 assumes the true rate is 5.26 percent. These tables are analogous to Tables 4.7 and 4.8.

TABLE 5.12

ALLOCATION OF ANNUAL LABOR SAVINGS TO INTEREST AND PRINCIPAL ON ASSUMPTION THAT TRUE RATE ON LATHE IS 2.63 PERCENT

YEAR	AMOUNT INVESTED BEGINNING OF YEAR	ANNUAL LABOR SAVING	INTEREST AT 2.63% ON OUTSTANDING BALANCE	TO REDUCTION OF PRINCIPAL	AMOUNT INVESTED AT END OF YEAR
(1)	(2)	(3)	(4)	(5)	(6)
1	$10,650.00	$1,800	$280.10	$1,519.90	$9,130.10
2	9,130.10	1,800	240.12	1,559.88	7,570.22
3	7,570.22	1,800	199.10	1,600.90	5,969.32
4	5,969.32	1,800	156.99	1,643.01	4,326.31
5	4,326.31	1,800	113.78	1,686.22	2,640.09
6	2,640.09	1,800	69.43	1,730.57	909.52
7	909.52	1,800	23.92	1,776.08	— 866.56

TABLE 5.13

ALLOCATION OF ANNUAL LABOR SAVINGS TO INTEREST AND PRINCIPAL ON ASSUMPTION THAT TRUE RATE ON LATHE IS 5.26 PERCENT

YEAR	AMOUNT INVESTED BEGINNING OF YEAR	ANNUAL LABOR SAVINGS	INTEREST AT 5.26% ON OUTSTANDING BALANCE	REDUCTION OF PRINCIPAL	AMOUNT INVESTED AT END OF YEAR
(1)	(2)	(3)	(4)	(5)	(6)
1	$10,650.00	$1,800	$560.19	$1,239.81	$9,410.19
2	9,410.19	1,800	494.98	1,305.02	8,105.17
3	8,105.17	1,800	426.33	1,373.67	6,731.50
4	6,731.50	1,800	354.08	1,445.92	5,285.58
5	5,285.58	1,800	278.02	1,521.98	3,763.60
6	3,763.60	1,800	197.97	1,602.03	2,161.57
7	2,161.57	1,800	113.70	1,686.30	475.27

What do we see when we look at Table 5.12? We see that principal has been reduced to zero by the middle of the seventh year, but that about $900 is still to be received during the seventh year. What does *this* mean? It means that a rate of 2.63 percent has induced us to allocate too much of the annual labor saving to principal and not enough to interest. And this, in turn, means that Butcher could have paid interest at a rate *higher* than 2.63 percent (on money borrowed to buy the lathe) and still broken even.

Now look at Table 5.13. In this table, at 5.26 percent, too much, rather than too little, is being allocated to interest. And the amount to be received during the seventh year is *not* sufficient to pay interest at 5.26 percent on the remaining balance of the loan, and to repay that balance. Thus, if Butcher had borrowed money at 5.26 percent to buy the lathe, it would *not* have broken even. It would have been "out-of-pocket" at the end of the seventh year by $475.27.

What *is* the true rate on the lathe? The true rate—the rate which just equates the present value of the promises to the original cost of the lathe—was calculated in Table 4.3 and was found to be about 4.4 percent. Table 4.8 showed that when 4.4 percent is used to allocate labor savings to interest and principal, everything "comes out even," except for a small rounding error.

In short, rates of return on original and average investment, although easy to calculate, are often highly misleading. They should *not* be used for the purpose of estimating the return on a proposed investment.

CONCLUSION

In this chapter we have compared various types of rates of return with each other. And we have compared DCF rates of return with net present value.

We have come to two conclusions: first, rates of return based on original investment or on rough and ready estimates of "average" investment are unsatisfactory. They are unsatisfactory because they either understate or overstate the rate of return on a proposed invest-ment. They understate or overstate, as the case may be, because they erroneously assume that the time pattern in which the project will return its original cost can be determined before the rate on the project has been calculated. As we have seen above, this is not so. The time pattern in which the project will return its original cost can be determined only after the DCF rate on the project has been calculated.

We have concluded, second, that net PV is preferable to a DCF rate of return as a test of the worthwhileness of a proposed project —provided the firm knows its cost of capital. If the cost of capital is *not* known we must calculate DCF rates for each new proposal.

PROBLEMS

1. Using the promises and cost figures given in Table 5.14, calculate DCF rates of return on both lathes to two decimal places. Then calculate the net PV of each at 11 percent. What do you see?

TABLE 5.14

COMPARISON OF ANNUAL PROMISES ON TWO $10,650 LATHES

YEAR	LATHE NUMBER 1	LATHE NUMBER 2
1	$ 800	$ 2,800
2	1,200	2,400
3	1,400	2,200
4	1,800	1,800
5	2,200	1,400
6	2,400	1,200
7	2,800	800
TOTAL	$12,600	$12,600

2. After you have calculated the rates of return in problem 1, use those rates to allocate the annual payments, as in Table 4.8, to interest and reduction of principal.
3. Calculate the net present value of the two projects given in Table 5.15 at a cost of capital of 2 percent, 1 percent and 0 percent.
4. At what rate of return on the materials handling equipment would the net PV on the two projects be approximately the same?
5. Go back to Tables 5.2 and 5.3. Calculate, for each lathe, the gross savings that is, before taxes. Make the same assumptions made in Table 5.11.
6. Two sets of promises have the same cost and the same lives. Using simple algebra, prove that if one has a higher rate of return that the other, it will also have more net PV.

TABLE 5.15

COMPARISON OF ANNUAL PROMISES

YEAR	MATERIALS HANDLING EQUIPMENT * (thousands)	PLASTICS MACHINERY †
(1)	(2)	(3)
1	$128.5	$219.7
2	128.5	219.7
3	128.5	219.7
4	128.5	219.7
5	128.5	219.7
6	128.5	219.7
7	128.5	219.7
8	128.5	219.7
9	128.5	219.7
10	128.5	219.7

* Based on proposal number 8, Table 5.1.
† Based on proposal number 6, Table 5.1.

6

PROBABILITY DISTRIBUTIONS

Early in 1965, the following story appeared in many European newspapers:

FOUR AMERICAN AND BRITISH STATISTICIANS BARRED FROM MUNICH CASINO

Munich (Western Germany), February 3, 1965: Four American statisticians were barred from the Munich Casino today after winning one million Deutsche Marks ($250,000) at roulette in one evening's play. The owners of the casino refused to comment. But rumors circulating in local gambling circles indicated that the four had been barred because they had developed an "unbeatable system."

Over a period of several months, they had noted down the results of 6,000 spins of each of the casino's four wheels, and had had the results analyzed on a computer in London. They were gone a week. When they returned, they each played one wheel for four hours—with the results described above.

DETERMINING PROBABILITY

What had the four statisticians done? *First,* they had realized that no roulette wheel is absolutely true, that each one has its own peculiar defects.

Second, they decided to see whether they could find the defects in each of the Munich casino's four wheels, by analyzing the results of a large number of spins.

Table 6.1 tabulates results for one of the four wheels. It shows that of the thirty-seven numbers, four—16, 17, 18 and 19—each won nearly 10 percent of the time. And it shows also that eight adjacent numbers—12, 13, 14, 15; and 20, 21, 22, 23—each won hardly at all. Many other numbers won less often than they should have. The wheel was badly balanced.

The statisticians knew, of course, that if the wheel were absolutely

TABLE 6.1

FREQUENCY OF OCCURRENCE OF ROULETTE WHEEL NUMBERS (AFTER 6,000 SPINS)

	Frequency of Occurrence			Frequency of Occurrence	
NUMBER	NUMBER OF TIMES	PERCENTAGE OF TIMES	NUMBER	NUMBER OF TIMES	PERCENTAGE OF TIMES
(1)	(2)	(3)	(1)	(2)	(3)
0	160	2.47	19	591	9.11
1	162	2.50	20	17	0.26
2	163	2.51	21	59	0.91
3	161	2.48	22	23	0.35
4	164	2.53	23	31	0.48
5	165	2.54	24	128	1.97
6	162	2.50	25	135	2.08
7	159	2.45	26	142	2.19
8	158	2.44	27	150	2.31
9	157	2.42	28	161	2.48
10	145	2.24	29	163	2.51
11	130	2.00	30	162	2.50
12	30	0.46	31	164	2.53
13	16	0.25	32	158	2.44
14	25	0.39	33	160	2.47
15	60	0.92	34	164	2.53
16	585	9.01	35	162	2.50
17	576	8.88	36	159	2.45
18	580	8.94	TOTAL	6,487	100.00

free of defects (and were run fairly), each number would win about 2.7 percent of the time. Thus in 1,000 spins of the wheel, each of the thirty-seven numbers (0 through 36) would have won about twenty-seven times $(27 \times 37 = 999)$.

And in 6,000 spins, each number should have won 162 times $(6 \times 27 = 162)$.

Now, if a roulette wheel is perfectly balanced and the game itself is fair, the best you can do at roulette in the long run is "break even." You will win 2.7 percent of the time and lose 97.3 percent of the time. If you start with $100 and place 1,000 bets of ten cents each, you will lose 973 of them or $97.30. But you will win twenty-seven of them, each of which will return $3.70 to you (odds of 36 to 1 plus the ten cents you bet). Twenty-seven wins at $3.70 each is equal to $99.90—you lost ten cents due to rounding—and you have almost exactly "broken even."

But now suppose you find, as a result of careful analysis, that the *true odds* on some number are 9 to 1—which means that, in ten spins, the number will lose nine times, or 90 percent of the time, and win once, or 10 percent of the time. But when it *does* win, you will receive odds of 36 to 1. And suppose, that instead of $100, you have $10,000, and place 100 bets of $100 each. You will lose ninety of them, or $9,000. But you will win ten—each of which will return $3,700 to you, or $37,000 in total. Your net profit would be $27,000 (= $37,000 — $10,000), that is, the $37,000 you received when you won minus the $10,000 you started with.

This, in effect, is what the four statisticians did. They found the *true odds* on each number on each wheel—or we might, equally, say the *probability* that each number on each wheel would win. And when they discovered these *probabilities,* they knew something that the operators of the casino did not know—namely, that each wheel had serious defects which caused certain numbers to win nearly 10 percent of the time. And they took advantage of the fact that whenever one of their numbers won, the casino, in its ignorance, would give them $37 instead of $10 for each dollar they had bet. The four statisticians had, in effect, taken the gamble out of playing roulette. There are many situations in business in which the simple principles used by the four statisticians can be applied—with equally happy results.

APPLYING PROBABILITY DISTRIBUTIONS

Perhaps the best-known users of probability distributions in the United States are the life insurance companies. They use them, of course, to remove the risk involved in selling life insurance. The probability distributions they use are called *mortality tables*. Mortality tables are

TABLE 6.2

DEATHS PER 1,000 LIVING

AGE	DEATHS PER 1,000
0	25.93
1	1.70
2	1.04
3	.80
4	.67
5	.59
6	.52
7	.47
8	.43
9	.39
10	.37
11	.37
12	.40
13	.48
14	.59
15	.71
16	.82
17	.93
18	1.02
19	1.08
20	1.15
21	1.22
22	1.27
23	1.28
24	1.27
25	1.26

Source: *Life Insurance Fact Book, 1970.*

simply summaries of mortality experience over some prior period. They give data on deaths per 1,000 by age. Table 6.2 gives an extract from those tables for ages zero (born but not yet one year old) through twenty-five years old. The table tells us, for example, that of all males aged eighteen, 1.02 out of 1,000 will die before they reach the age of nineteen, and so forth.

Suppose that on your eighteenth birthday, you decide to insure your life for exactly one year for $1,000—just so that a fund would be available to pay your accumulated bills should you die suddenly from an overdose of intellectual activity—or beer. How would the insurance agent decide what premium you should pay? He would look at the mortality tables, find that one-tenth of 1 percent of all eighteen year olds will die before they are nineteen. He would then reason about as follows:

1. For any group of insured, the premiums paid should be just sufficient, if mortality experience is normal, to pay death claims and pay the costs of administering the fund. In other words, if 1,000 men, aged eighteen, each bought a $1,000 one term policy, the basic premium should be about one-tenth of 1 percent of the face amount of the policy—simply because the mortality rate (in the United States) among men aged eighteen is (approximately) one-tenth of 1 percent. Thus with normal mortality experience, one of the 1,000 men will die, and his beneficiaries will be entitled to receive $1,000. If each of the 1,000 men insured had paid a premium of $1, the fund would be just sufficient to pay this claim.

2. But collecting the premiums at the beginning of the year, holding them, running the risk that mortality experience would *not* be normal, and paying the death claims would cost something and for this reason the premium would have to be something more than $1.

3. And, of course, we have to make a reasonable profit. Past experience suggests that we should add about 25 percent for expenses and 10 percent for profit after taxes. The premium therefore should be about $1.35 for each $1,000 of insurance sold ($1 plus 35 percent of $1 equals $1.35).

By fixing the premium at this price, the insurance company must make money—regardless of what happens to *you*—provided only that mortality experience is normal.

After you have passed the medical examination, paid your premium and received your policy, you will notice ads in national magazines, paid for by various life insurance companies, urging you to stop smoking, to be careful crossing streets, to take your vitamins everyday—all part of a conscious campaign to prolong your life. Why do the life insurance companies spend money in this way? The reason is simple: If you do as they say, and as a result live longer, mortality experience will improve and the odds in their favor will have increased. And until the mortality tables they use are officially revised—as they are periodically—the life insurance companies' profits will increase.

WHAT IS A PROBABILITY DISTRIBUTION

Probabilities are nothing more than weights which describe in quantitative terms the likelihood of some future, unknown occurrence. We saw above that the probability was one-tenth of 1 percent ($= 1/10\%$) that a man of eighteen would die before reaching the age of nineteen. Probabilities are usually expressed as fractions or decimals but they can, equally, be expressed as percentages: one-tenth of 1 percent, for example, equals $\frac{1}{1,000}$ or .001.

A probability *distribution* is simply the system of individual weights assigned to the events in some group of events—one or another of which will occur in the future. If the probability that you will die before you reach age nineteen is 1/10 of 1 percent, or 1/1,000, or .001, then the probability that you will *not* die is 99.9 percent, or $\frac{999}{1,000,}$ or .999. The two events in the group are:

EVENT	PROBABILITY
Die before age 19	.001
Not die before age 19	.999
TOTAL	1.000

forecasting the weather

Suppose, now, that you ask your roommate whether he thinks it will rain this afternoon.

He says, "I don't know."

You say, "You don't know whether you think it will rain this afternoon? That doesn't make any sense. I didn't ask you whether it *would* rain this afternoon. I asked whether *you thought* it would rain. Either you think it will rain or you think it won't rain."

He says, "I don't think."

You say, "Come on. This is important to me and I value your opinion. You're a good weather forecaster."

He says, "Go away and leave me alone." And then, "Why do you want to know?"

You say, "Just look out the window and tell me what you think."

He staggers over to the window, looks out, staggers back to the couch and collapses. "There's a 1 percent chance of a short light rain between now and 6:15."

You say, "Thanks. Here's your umbrella back." With only a 1 percent chance of rain, you don't want to be bothered carrying it around.

Your roommate has (you believe) suggested the following probability distribution:

Rain this afternoon

FUTURE EVENT	PROBABILITY
Rain	.01,
No rain	.99,
Rain or no rain	1.00,

We should note a few of the characteristics of this probability distribution:

> The term *probability distribution* means a distribution of probabilities over the events being contemplated.

1. When your roommate said the probability of rain was 1 percent ($= .01 = 1/100$) he implied, presumably, that the probability of no rain was 99 percent ($= .99 = 99/100$). The distribution of the two probabilities over the two events is a *probability distribution*. A probability distribution can assign probabilities to many events or to as few as one. The roulette wheel distribution given in Table 6.1, for example, assigned probabilities to thirty-seven events.

2. All the events covered by a probability distribution are *mutually exclusive*. This means merely that if one event occurs, the others cannot occur. It can either rain or not rain before 6:15 P.M., but it cannot do both. And the events must be defined so that they are, in fact, mutually exclusive.

3. All possible events must be clearly specified in the distribution either explicitly or implicitly. If they are not, the meaning of the probabilities will be unclear and the distribution misleading. In the above distribution, for example, your roommate meant, presumably, a 1 percent probability of a light, short rain *or more*. And, presumably, he also meant to imply zero probabilities of a heavy short rain, or a heavy long rain, or snow. (You cannot be sure about this, of course, because you didn't ask him.) But, conceivably, he may have deliberately misled you—just to get his umbrella back. He may actually have had in mind a probability distribution which looked like this:

Rain this afternoon

EVENT	PROBABILITY
Short light rain or less	.01
Short heavy rain	.24
Long light rain	.25
Long heavy rain	.25
Snow	.24
No rain or snow	.01
TOTAL	1.00

4. The total probabilities must add to 1.00 or, if they are being expressed as percentages, to 100. If they do not, they will not be probabilities.

Why is this so? It is so because a probability distribution must cover all the possibilities—or, in other words, 100 percent of the possibilities. And 1.00 is simply 100 percent in decimal form $(100 \times 1.00 = 100)$. If the probabilities add to less than 1.00, some event which could occur is being ignored or, if not, the events which could occur are not being given their correct weights. And conversely, if the probabilities add to more than 1.00, then some event which could not occur has been included or, if not, the events which could occur have been assigned incorrect weights.

odds in horseracing

Suppose, for example, that you find the following odds on the horses in the eighth race at Arlington Park for tomorrow:

HORSE NUMBER	ODDS	EQUIVALENT PROBABILITY OF WINNING
1	1-1	.500
2	2-1	.333
3	5-1	.167
4	7-1	.125
5	9-1	.100
6	19-1	.050

Horse number 3, at 5 to 1, is one of your favorite animals and you have won on him several times in the recent past. You grab your sock (which contains your last ten dollars) and rush out to the track. You glance up at the pari-mutuel machine and see that horse number 3 is being ignored by the crowd and will pay 8 to 1. You have two inflexible rules about betting: you *never* bet more than $10.00 on a race, and you *never* bet on a horse unless the odds at which you will be paid are 60 percent higher than the odds on the horse quoted in the morning paper. Your horse was 5 to 1 in the morning paper but you will be paid at 8 to 1 if he wins. You rush to the window and bet your $10. The window slams down and "They're off!"

Suddenly, you notice that the equivalent probabilities in the table, above, do not add to 1.00 but rather 1.275 as follows:

HORSE NUMBER	PROBABILITIES
1	.500
2	.333
3	.167
4	.125
5	.100
6	.050
TOTAL	1.275

You do some quick arithmetic and divide each of the individual probabilities by the total and obtain new probabilities which do add to 1.00, as follows:

HORSE NUMBER	PROBABILITIES	APPROXIMATE EQUIVALENT ODDS
1	.393	1.54-1
2	.262	2.82-1
3	.130	6.69-1
4	.098	9.20-1
5	.078	11.82-1
6	.039	24.64-1
TOTAL	1.000	

You breathe a slight sigh of relief as you note that the adjusted odds on horse number 3 are 6.69 to 1—which is not as good as 5 to 1, but still less than the 8 to 1 at which you will be paid—if number 3 wins. You look up from your arithmetic just in time to see your horse come in last. "Oh, well," you say, as you quietly pull the stopper and slide down the drain.

A *probability* is then a weight assigned to a particular future event. The weight indicates the likelihood of the occurrence of that event. And a probability distribution is simply the system of weights assigned to the events in a given, exhaustive, mutually exclusive set of possibilities.

You may, by the way, be puzzled by the fact that a horse which is really 5 to 1 can "payoff" at 8 to 1. If you are puzzled then you don't understand how so-called professional gamblers earn their living. They earn their living, in brief, by *not* gambling. They are not gamblers at all. Their method of operation is much like the method of operation of insurance companies, as we shall see.

About $10,000 *in total* was bet by individuals on the six horses in the race described above. Of this sum, $1,100 was bet on horse number 3. As their profit the track owners simply deduct 1 percent of the total amount bet. They then divided the remainder by $1,100 in order to determine the payoff per dollar on horse number 3, if it won, thus:

$$\begin{array}{r} \$10,000 \\ -\quad 100 \quad (1 \text{ percent}) \\ \hline \$\ 9,900 \end{array}$$

$$\$9,900 \div \$1,100 = \$9$$

Thus each dollar bet on horse number 3 would receive $9.00 if horse number 3 won. This includes, of course, the $1.00 bet. Subtract that from the $9 and you find that you would have won $8 for each dollar bet on horse number 3. This is just another way of saying that you would have been paid off at odds of 8 to 1. You would, that is, *win $8* for each dollar you bet. You can see, thus, that pari-mutuel machines take no risk at all. They are not betting on anything—they simply take a fixed percentage of the total amount bet—and sometimes it's much more than 1 percent. They then divide whatever is left among those individuals who happen to have bet on the winning horse. Obviously, they couldn't care less which horse wins.

You can see, also, that the payoff on any given horse can be at a rate higher or lower than your estimate of the true odds—for it depends on the amount bet on any single horse *relative to the total amount bet*. On any given day, for example, the people at the track may be fun-loving, wide-eyed, optimistic and devoted to bright colors. And they may bet too much on horse number 6 merely because his name happens to be Scarlett. But this would mean that too little had been bet on horse number 3 whose name happens to be Somber Lad. The pay off on number 6 would then be *below* the true odds, as the pay off on number 3 would have been above—if number 3 had won. Or on some other day, the crowd at the track may be made up largely of pessimistic, unhappy people who don't like to take too much risk. And they may bet too much on horse number 1, the favorite, merely because his chance of winning seems to be best. On such a day, the payoff on horse number 1, if he won, would be at a rate well below the true odds. And the payoffs on the other horses, if they won, above.

expected payoffs

When you placed your $10 bet, above, on horse number 3 at Arlington Park you had in mind what we will call an *expected payoff*. Look first at Table 6.3. There are two mutually exclusive events in the distribution:

TABLE 6.3

EXPECTED PAYOFF FROM $10 BET,
TRUE ODDS AT 5-1; PAYOFF AT 8-1.

EVENT (1)	DOLLAR GAIN OR LOSS (2)	PROBABILITY EVENT WILL OCCUR (3)	AVERAGE GAIN (4)
Horse number 3 wins	+ $80	.1667	+ $13.33
Horse number 3 loses	− $10	.8333	− $ 8.33
TOTAL		1.000	+ $ 5.00

either the horse wins or it loses. There are no other possibilities. We see the payoff in dollar terms if the horse wins and if he loses. If the horse wins, you will receive $90—your $10 bet plus $80. Your gain, therefore, is $80. You will, that is, be "+ $80." But if the horse loses you will lose the $10 bet. You will be "− $10."

Column (3) gives the two probabilities which constitute the probability distribution over the particular set of events given in Column (1). But these probabilities also constitute a probability distribution over the set of events given in column (2)—because the events in column (2) are simply the events in column (1) translated into dollar terms. The sum of the two probabilities is, of course, 1.00.

Column (4), which is harder to understand than the other three columns, is simply the product of columns (2) and (3): .166 × $80 = $13.33 and .833 × − $10 = − $8.33. And the total at the bottom of column (4) is the algebraic sum of the two products:

$$\$13.33 - \$8.33 = \$5.00.$$

What does this last figure mean? The answer is that if we are talking about just one horse race, it does not mean much. It does not mean much because if you bet on just one race, you will either win $80 or lose $10. There will be no "average" payoff.

But suppose instead you have set aside $1,000 as an amusement fund and you are using it to find out whether you can "beat the races." You prepared long and hard for this experiment by comparing the odds given in the morning newspaper with the results, and you found that the newspaper seemed highly reliable for odds of 5 to 1 and below. You found, that is, the results given in Table 6.4.

TABLE 6.4

TRUE ODDS AND TRUE PROBABILITIES OF WINNING A HORSE RACE

QUOTED ODDS	WINNERS	LOSERS	APPROXIMATE TRUE ODDS	APPROXIMATE PROBABILITY OF WINNING
(1)	(2)	(3)	(4)	(5)
1-1	50	48	1-1	.50
2-1	40	81	2-1	.33
3-1	40	118	3-1	.25
4-1	40	163	4-1	.20
5-1	31	149	5-1	.167

You found also:

1. that at odds above 5 to 1 the morning paper is not reliable at all;
2. that the average payoff on horses quoted at 3 to 1 and below is at a rate *below* the true odds;
3. that the average payoff on horses quoted at 4 to 1 and 5 to 1 is at a rate above the true odds.

With all this information in hand, you decided to place one hundred $10 bets on horses quoted at 4 to 1 and 5 to 1 but only when the promised payoff is at 7 to 1 (for 4 to 1 horses) and 8 to 1 (for 5 to 1 horses). You feel you can't lose and in fact you can't—provided the odds quoted in the paper are really the *true* odds or close to the true odds. But, of course, you feel they are. Table 6.5 shows the results of your little experiment. The table assumes that you have bet only on 5 to 1 horses which have paid off at 8 to 1, on the average, when they have won.

Now, what does Table 6.5 mean? It means simply that of the 100 horses, eighty-three have lost—at a cost to you of $833. But about seventeen have won, and on these seventeen you have gained $1,334. You have in hand, therefore, $1,334—your net *gain* on the seventeen winning horses, plus the $10 you bet on each—to a total of about $1,500. You are, therefore, almost exactly $500 better off than you were at the start.

What are the probabilities telling us in this case? They are telling us that if we make 100 bets, we will lose about eighty-three and will win

TABLE 6.5

GAIN FROM $10 BET,
TRUE ODDS AT 5-1;
PAYOFF AT 8-1.

EVENT	DOLLAR GAIN OR LOSS	PROBABILITY EVENT WILL OCCUR	AVERAGE GAIN
(1)	(2)	(3)	(4)
100 horses at 5-1 win	+ $8,000 *	.1667	+ $1,334
100 horses at 5-1 lose	— $1,000	.8333	— $ 833
		1.000	+ $ 501

* Payoff at 8-1 if win. If you win, you also receive back the $10 you have bet.

about seventeen.[1] And the final column is telling us that the gain on the seventeen winning horses was (or will be) $1,334 and the loss on the eighty-three losing horses was (or will be) $833.

When the four statisticians returned from London with their findings they, too, had a probability distribution in mind—which looked very much like the distributions given in Tables 6.6 and 6.7. The distribution in Table 6.6 is for one bet of $100 on number 16. The distribution in Table 6.7 is for one hundred such bets. This latter distribution is telling us that, provided the probabilities are accurate, the gain from one hundred $100 bets will be about $27,000.

In the above two cases, we may say, in summary, that both the horse-player and the statisticians have used probability distributions to calculate average payoffs on playing roulette at Munich and on betting on the horses at Arlington Park. By doing so they have eliminated the risks involved in each enterprise. *They have, that is, taken the risk out of gambling.* And for the benefit of those of you who may have prejudices about "gambling," we may say that neither the statisticians nor the horse-player were gambling. They were betting on "sure things." The

---

[1] We say "about," because even when you place a large number of bets, as in this case, the results will deviate somewhat from the true odds.

TABLE 6.6

RESULTS OF PLACING ONE $100 BET

EVENT	DOLLAR GAIN OR LOSS	APPROXIMATE PROBABILITY EVENT WILL OCCUR	AVERAGE GAIN
(1)	(2)	(3)	(4)
Number 16 wins	+ $3,600	.10	+ $360
Some other number wins	— $ 100	.90	— 90
		1.00	+ $270

TABLE 6.7

RESULTS OF PLACING ONE HUNDRED $100 BETS

EVENT	DOLLAR GAIN OR LOSS	APPROXIMATE PROBABILITY EVENT WILL OCCUR	AVERAGE GAIN
(1)	(2)	(3)	(4)
Number 16 wins	+ $360,000	.10	+ $36,000
Some other number wins	— $ 10,000	.90	— 9,000
		1.00	+ $27,000

probability distributions enabled them to predict, with virtual certainty, what the outcome of their respective "experiments" would be. Both were relying on one basic scientific proposition: if a large number of draws is made from an accurate probability distribution, the distribution of outcomes will be approximately the same as the distribution of the probabilities.

Suppose now that instead of placing a large number of small bets, the horse-player and the statisticians had decided to bet their entire respective resources—$1,000 for the horse-player and $10,000 for the statisticians —on just one race or on just one spin of the wheel. Would the probability distributions given in Tables 6.2 and 6.5 be of any use to them? The answer is nearly none. The essence of each distribution is, of course, the calculation of average expected gain. But if they were to place just one bet, this figure would be meaningless, as we saw above. It would be meaningless because they would either win at high odds or lose their entire respective stakes. There could be no "average gain." To repeat: *the average gain has meaning only if they place a large number of bets.*

Conversely, it would be pointless to play a "fair" game a large number of times. As Table 6.8 indicates the average gain to be expected

TABLE 6.8

**AVERAGE EXPECTED GAIN FROM 1,000 BETS OF $1
TRUE ODDS AT 5-1; PAYOFF AT 5-1**

EVENT	DOLLAR GAIN OR LOSS	PROBABILITY EVENT WILL OCCUR	EXPECTED AVERAGE GAIN
(1)	(2)	(3)	(4)
1,000 horses, at 5-1, win	+ $5,000	.1667	+ $833
1,000 horses, at 5-1, lose	— $1,000	.8333	— $833
		1.00	0

from playing a fair game a large number of times is zero. This is so because a fair game is one which pays off at the rate indicated by the true odds. Thus if you bet, at fair odds, on 1,000 horses at 5 to 1, you would win 167 races, each worth $5, and you would lose 833 races at $1 a piece. Your winnings thus would be exactly equal to your losses, as Table 6.8 shows. After the last race was over you would have in hand the $833 you had won on 167 races plus the $167 you bet on those races. You would, in short, be exactly where you were when you started. People play fair games only in the hope of having a "streak of luck." But the odds against "streaks of luck" are very high.

CONCLUSION

In this chapter we have defined a probability as a decimal or a percent which measures the likelihood that some specific future event will occur. And we have defined a probability distribution as a *set* of decimals or percents which measure the likelihood that *each* of the events in an exhaustive, mutually-exclusive set will occur. We explained why each set had to be exhaustive and why the events in the set had to be defined so as to be mutually exclusive. And we explained why the probabilities had to add to 1.00 (if they are expressed as decimals) or 100 (if they are expressed as percents).

And, finally, we showed how probabilities, provided they are reasonably accurate, can be used to take the risk out of gambling. In Chapter 7 we shall discuss some of the ways probability distributions are used in finance.

PROBLEMS

1. Toss a coin 100 times and note down the number of times it comes up heads and the number of times it comes up tails. Toss the same coin 100 times again and note the results again. Go through the same procedure with a different coin. Look at the results of tossing both coins. What do you see?

2. Your roommate likes to toss coins, betting a quarter a toss he can call it right. You pick the coin, he tosses it, and you call, or vice versa. Given the results in problem 1, which coin would you pick and how would you call?

3. After the first 100 tosses of his coin, your roommate insists on changing the procedure. You are now to toss the coin and he will call. What odds do you now insist on in order to be reasonably sure that you will break even?

4. In the table on page 116, where do the "equivalent odds" come from, and what do they mean?

5. Suppose that instead of betting $100 on number 16, one hundred times, the statisticians had bet $400 twenty-five times—$100 on 16, $100 on 17, $100 on 18 and $100 on 19. Draw up a payoff table

and calculate the average expected gain. Which plan is safer? Why? Given the results, which course of action would you choose?

6.   *It would be pointless for the statisticians to bet their entire stake on one spin of the wheel. Why?*

7.   *In Table 6.4 we assumed you bet only on horses quoted at 5 to 1. Assume instead, that you bet half your money $10 at a time on 4 to 1 horses paying off at 7 to 1, and half on 5 to 1 horses paying off at 8 to 1. Construct a payoff table and calculate your average expected gain.*

8.   *You know that Jim O'Brien of the Baltimore Colts has successfully kicked 42 percent of all the field goals he has tried. You are watching a game in Los Angeles between the Rams and the Colts and, with eight seconds left to play and the Rams leading 14-12, O'Brien is about to try a field goal from the Ram's thirty-nine yard line. An enthusiastic Los Angeles fan sitting next to you slaps you on the back and says: "$15 to $5 he doesn't make it."*

   Do you bet or not—and why?

9.   *Suppose in problem 8 you do bet and you lose. And you decide you should now draw up a more sophisticated probability distribution on O'Brien's efforts. How would you do so?*

10. *You have just bought a car. Your insurance agent tells you that for $120 you can buy a "full-coverage policy"—which means that the insurance company will pay for all damage to the car for which you are responsible or for which an unknown person is responsible. Or, he tells you, for $100 you may have a "$100 deductible" policy— which means that you would pay for damage up to $100, done by yourself or by an unknown person. The insurance company would pay the balance. Thus if some unknown person backed hard into your car in a parking lot, did $110 worth of damage, and drove off without leaving his name, you would contribute $100 to the repair bill, and the insurance company would contribute $10.*

   What questions do you ask yourself before deciding whether or not to pay $20 extra for full coverage?

7

PROBABILITY
DISTRIBUTIONS
IN
FINANCE

Probability distributions are used in many different ways in finance: to obtain better estimates of the present value of an investment (or of the rate of return on that investment), to obtain better estimates of expected cash balances, to obtain better estimates of the additional risk to the firm of borrowing money or of investing in speculative projects, and for many other purposes. The probability distributions used in finance are no different in structure from the probability distributions discussed above—although they are different in other ways, as we shall see below.

This chapter illustrates the use of probability distributions in finance by describing the way they might be used:

1. To obtain a better estimate of the present value to Butcher of Ex-Cello's lathe.
2. To obtain an estimate of the additional risk and average gain, to Butcher in 1966, of adding $36.8 million in debt to its capital structure.
3. To obtain better estimates of the present value, to you, of a share of AT&T and RCA.

CALCULATING PRESENT VALUE

Ex-Cello's salesman had said that the lathe would save Butcher $1,800 a year for at least seven years. Hastings knew, of course, that both figures were subject to error. He kept careful records on machine tools, listing each by its manufacturer. When he went through Ex-Cello's file after Ex-Cello's salesman had left, he found the two frequency distributions given in Tables 7.1 and 7.2. A frequency distribution relates to the *past* and is simply a tabulation of events in some class, which have occurred in the past. When the four statisticians sat in the Munich casino for a month, beer steins and pencils in hand, watching the roulette wheel spin, they were constructing what is called a frequency distribution (see Table 6.1). They were constructing it in order to be able to derive a probability distribution from it. Nearly all the probability distributions used in finance are derived from tabulations of past experience, that is, from frequency distributions summarizing past experience.

TABLE 7.1

*FREQUENCY DISTRIBUTION ON MACHINE TOOL SAVINGS OVER TEN YEARS ***

SALESMAN'S FORECAST OF SAVINGS	MID-POINT OF ERROR IN FORECAST	NUMBER OF TOOLS	PERCENTAGE OF TOTAL NUMBER	ERROR IN SALESMAN'S FORECAST †
(1)	(2)	(3)	(4)	(5)
0% to 5% too low	− 2.5%	1	2.38%	− 5.95%
As stated	0.0%	4	9.52%	0.00%
0% to 5% too high	+ 2.5%	16	38.10%	+ 95.25%
5.1% to 10% too high	+ 7.5%	14	33.33%	+ 249.98%
10.1% to 15% too high	+ 12.5%	7	16.67%	+ 208.38%
		42	100. %	+ 547.66%

$$\frac{547.66}{100.00} = 5.48\% \text{ Average Error.}$$

* Includes only machine tools which had been replaced.
† Average discrepancy multiplied by percentage of total.

Hastings wasn't sure, as he looked at Table 7.1, why Ex-Cello's previous forecast of savings had been, for the most part, too high in comparison to actual savings. But he suspected that in making its calculations, Ex-Cello had used average industry wage rates. The rates Butcher paid were somewhat below the industry average. Therefore, a machine which was attractive because it saved labor would be less attractive to Butcher than to those companies in the industry which paid higher wage rates. In other words, Butcher, by buying the machine, would save the same amount of labor, but fewer dollars than those companies whose labor costs were higher. But there were doubtless other factors also—not the least of which was, perhaps, the rosy optimism of salesmen.

Hastings believed that the frequency distribution enabled him to adjust, with reasonable accuracy, for both of the foregoing influences. He knew, of course, that ideally he would have liked to have had data on *actual man-hours saved by a large sample of the new lathes*. But he knew, of course, that was not possible. He had to do the best he could with the data he had. He realized, of course, that he was making the assumption that if he did have such data, it would not differ much from the data he already had.

Table 7.1 gives what are called *class intervals*. The class intervals ask: In how many cases was the Ex-Cello salesman's estimate of savings between 0 percent and 5 percent too low? In how many cases was it just about right? In how many cases was the Ex-Cello salesman's estimate between 0 percent and 5 percent too high; between 5.1 percent and 10 percent too high? And so forth. Column (2) gives the average error of these estimates. In the next column we have the number of Ex-Cello tools which fell in each class interval: the Ex-Cello salesman's estimate was too low in just one case. It was about correct in four cases. It was between 0 percent and 5 percent too high in sixteen cases, and so forth. Next we see the percentage of each class interval in comparison to the total number of tools bought from Ex-Cello.

Table 7.2 is similar to Table 7.1. It is simply Hasting's attempt to measure the extent to which the Ex-Cello salesman's estimates of the lives of its lathes had been too high or too low. Butcher's experience indicated that Ex-Cello's estimates of the expected lives of its lathes fell in a range from 5.0 percent too low to 5.0 percent too high. If the life of a lathe turned out to be less than expected, the rate of return on that lathe would be less than expected. And if the life of a machine tool turned out to be higher than expected, the rate of return on that tool would be higher than expected. Of the forty-two tools, thirty fell in the "too low" category—that is, the Ex-Cello salesman had *underestimated* their lives by about 2.5 percent. And twelve fell in the "too high" category.

TABLE 7.2

*FREQUENCY DISTRIBUTION FOR LIFE OF MACHINE TOOLS OVER TEN YEARS ***

SALESMAN'S FORECAST OF LIFE	MID-POINT OF ERROR IN FORECAST	NUMBER OF TOOLS	PERCENTAGE OF TOTAL NUMBER	ERROR IN SALESMAN'S FORECAST †
(1)	(2)	(3)	(4)	(5)
0% to 5% too low	− 2.5%	30	71.43%	− 178.58%
0% to 5% too high	+ 2.5%	12	28.57%	+ 71.43%
		42	100.00%	− 107.15%

$$\frac{-107.15}{100.00} = -1.07\% \text{ Average.}$$

* Includes only machine tools which had been replaced.
† Average error multiplied by percentage of total.

Hastings had calculated the averages given at the bottom of each table by multiplying the mid-point of each class interval by the corresponding percentage, totaling the final column, and dividing that total by the sum of the weights (=100). [The mid-points of each class interval are given in Column (2).] In reading these two tables be careful to realize that the percents in Column (2) are being multiplied *not* by the numbers given in Column (3) but by the mid-points given in Column (2): Hastings wanted, of course, an estimate, in percent, of the extent to which the Ex-Cello salesman's past forecasts had been wrong. Hastings' arithmetic showed (bottom of Table 7.1) that *on the average* the Ex-Cello salesman had *over*estimated labor savings by 5.48 percent and (bottom of Table 7.2) had *under*estimated lives by 1.07 percent.

Hastings ignored the latter figure because it was negligible: 1.07 percent of seven years is less than a month. But he adjusted Ex-Cello's estimated savings on the proposed lathe ($1,800) downward by 5.48 percent, to $1,700 (5.48% × $1,800 = $100 approximately). Hastings then calculated the present value of $1,700 received annually, using 11 percent—the company's approximate current after-tax cost of capital[1]— as his discount rate. He allowed $1000 in the final year for the trade-in

---

[1] See Chapter 2.

value at that time of the lathe. His calculations are shown in Table 7.3.

TABLE 7.3

PRESENT VALUE OF EX-CELLO LATHE, PROBABILITY BASIS

YEAR	ESTIMATED SAVINGS	DISCOUNT FACTORS AT 11%	PRESENT VALUE
(1)	(2)	(3)	(4)
1	$1,700	.901	$1,532.70
2	1,700	.812	1,380.40
3	1,700	.731	1,242.70
4	1,700	.659	1,120.30
5	1,700	.593	1,008.10
6	1,700	.535	909.50
7	2,700 *	.482	1,301.40
		TOTAL	$8,495.10

* Savings plus estimated trade-in value of lathe at end of seventh year.

After he had added the figures in the last column of Table 7.3, Hastings called Gordon Roberts, Ex-Cello's salesman.

"Look Roberts," Hastings said, "I've done a few more calculations on that lathe."

"You've decided to buy it" said Roberts.

"Not exactly," said Hastings. "I've just called to say that if the price of that lathe should drop to $8,400, let me know. I might buy one or two."

"Are you dickering with me?" asked Roberts.

"Certainly not," said Hastings. "I'm just giving you a few facts to mull over."

"Thanks," said Roberts.

"That price is $8,400, *installed*", said Hastings, and hung up.

DETERMINING *EBIT*

After the meetings of the Finance Committee and the Board in mid-1966 —at which the decision was reached to borrow $36.8 million—Martin and Kelley walked back to their offices together. Kelley was a recent graduate of a business school in the Midwest and was somewhat overloaded,

Martin thought, with new-fangled ideas. At that time, Kelley had been with Butcher just a few months.

"What did you think of that?" asked Martin.

"Very interesting," said Kelley. "I do think, though, that we could have done a better job on the risk-return problem."

"What do you mean?" asked Martin. He thought he *had* done a good job on the risk-return problem.

"I think we could have brought out more clearly the implications of putting so much debt in the capital structure."

"That sounds pretty vague," said Martin. "What do you mean?"

"I'd like to try to apply probability analysis to the problem," said Kelley.

"Probability analysis?" said Martin.

"Yes," said Kelley.

"Everything happens to me" thought Martin. But he said, "How would you do it?"

As they entered Martin's office Kelley said, "The best way to explain is to show you an example. Will you let me waste a day working up some figures?"

"Okay," said Martin. He didn't want Kelley to think he had a closed mind.

"Great," said Kelley. "Do you have a minute now to answer a couple of questions?"

"Sure," said Martin.

"First," asked Kelley, "how high do you think EBIT [earnings before interest and taxes] could go—after the rebuilding program is completed, and assuming current prices and a two-shift operation? It seems to me that $25 million is an absolutely outside figure."

"I'd say that's about right," said Martin. "Our average figure is $10.5 million, assuming one shift at 88 percent of capacity." He picked up his slide rule. "*Two* shifts at *full* capacity," he said, "would be just about $25 million."

"Do you think there's any chance EBIT could go to zero or below?" asked Kelley.

"To zero, maybe," said Martin. "A very small chance. But not below. Of course, I'm assuming we won't have another great depression in this country. We may have some minor ups and downs and, for the time being, until we can diversify, we'll be affected by the machine tool cycle. But nothing more serious than that."

"Do you really think the chance of a severe depression is absolutely zero?" asked Kelley.

"Not really," said Martin. "I think the chance of a severe long depression is zero. I'd say the chance of a severe short depression is about one in a hundred."

"Thanks," said Kelley. "I'll have something for you tomorrow afternoon."

After he got back to his office, Kelley went methodically about the business of constructing a probability distribution over EBIT, as shown in Table 7.4.

TABLE 7.4

PROBABILITIES FOR EBIT

EBIT	MID-POINT OF EBIT	PROBABILITY THAT EBIT WILL FALL WITHIN CLASS INTERVAL
(millions)		
(1)	(2)	(3)
$20.1 - 25.0	$22.5	.10
15.1 - 20.0	17.5	.20
10.1 - 15.0	12.5	.40
5.1 - 10.0	7.5	.15
0.1 - 5.0	2.5	.10
— 5.1 - 0.0	— 2.5	.05
		1.00

First, he established class intervals, using the maximum Martin had given him as the upper limit of the highest class, as in Column 1 of Table 7.4. After he had done this he set up a second column in which he simply put down the mid-point of each class interval (Column (2) of Table 7.4).

He then put down in Column (3) an initial estimate (taken, more or less, out of his hat) of the probability that EBIT would fall within each of the original class intervals given in Column (1): .10 that EBIT would fall within the interval $20.1 to 25.0 million; .20 that it would fall within the interval $15.1 to 20.0 million; and so forth. He was fairly confident that the interval $10.1 to 15.0 million would be the most popular interval. He therefore gave it 40 percent of the total weight. Thus he gave the three upper intervals, together, 70 percent of the total weight. He wondered whether this were, in fact, enough.

Kelley felt that the only years which would fall below $10.1 million would be those in which sales of machine tools were adversely affected either by the machine tool cycle or by a recession in general business activity. In such years, EBIT might fall between zero and $10.0 million, depending on the severity of the cycle. But recessions in business activity were getting scarcer and scarcer and were now occurring at the rate of one every ten years or so. Machine tool recessions tended to occur once every four or five years, or between 20 and 25 percent of the time. This meant that in three or four years out of every fifteen (or between ¼ and ⅓ of the time), EBIT might fall between zero and $10.0 million. It would fall in the lower range only if a general recession and a machine tool recession coincided, or if either were severe or long. He assigned a probability of .15 to EBIT between $5.1 million and $10.0 million, and a probability of .10 to EBIT between $0.1 million and $5.0 million.

This left 5 percent of the weight to outcomes below zero—which would occur, he felt, only as a result of a severe depression. He realized, of course, that Martin had said the chances of a severe depression were "one in a hundred," not five in a hundred. But for the moment he left the figure unchanged.

As he sat back and looked at the results of this initial effort, Kelley suddenly realized that the basic *events* over which he was trying to establish a probability distribution were really *expected economic conditions*. If boom conditions prevailed, EBIT would be very high; if business conditions were very favorable (but not booming) EBIT would be high, but less than the absolute maximum, and so forth. He was really, he decided, trying to answer *two* questions, not just one. First, what were the chances that next year would be a boom year, a very good year, a good year, and so forth? In answering this question, he realized that he would have to rely very heavily on past experience. Out of the past twenty years, how many, for example, had been boom years, how many very good years, and so forth.

Second, he was asking: If a boom year occurred, how high would EBIT be—assuming that Butcher remained efficient and competitive? He was sure he would be able to answer this question by establishing relationships between business conditions in the past and Butcher's performance in the past. For example, at what percent of capacity had Butcher operated during 1968, which had been a very good year for the economy as a whole?

MULTIPLICATIVE LAW OF COMPOUND PROBABILITY

Kelley decided to recast his original probabilities as shown in Table 7.5. He listed five different phases of the general business cycle, describing each by an adjective *and* by a rate of unemployment. He decided to use the rate of unemployment for a variety of reasons: so that the events would be objectively defined ("boom" was really a vague word) and so that he could be sure his class intervals were mutually exclusive and exhaustive, that is, so he could be sure that all possible events were included and that the events did not overlap. He then assigned each phase a probability, again, taken right off the top of his head.

TABLE 7.5

PROBABILITY DISTRIBUTION OVER GENERAL BUSINESS CONDITIONS

PHASE	RATE OF UNEMPLOYMENT	PROBABILITY
Boom	1% to 2%	.15
Very Good	2.1% to 3%	.25
Good	3.1% to 5%	.45
Recession	5.1% to 7%	.10
Depression	over 7%	.05
	TOTAL	1.00

After he finished Table 7.5, Kelley tried to take account of the machine tool cycle. He knew that on the average a machine tool recession occurred in one year out of five, or in other words, with a probability of .20. The probability that a machine tool recession would *not* occur in any given year was therefore .80 (1.00 − .20 = .80). He knew also that a machine tool recession could occur at any time—in a boom year, in a very good year, in a good year, and so forth. And Kelley knew that no matter when it occurred, Butcher's results would not be as good as they would otherwise have been. Now, what was the probability that a boom and a machine tool recession (MTR) would occur *simultaneously*? Or that a very good year and an MTR would occur simultaneously? Or a recession and an MTR? He felt a little fuzzy on this problem until he realized he was dealing with what is called a *compound event*. If he tossed a fair coin once, he knew the chances of getting one head were ½, on the assumption that the coin did not decide to land on its edge. And if he tossed it twice he knew the odds of getting two heads were 1/2 times 1/2, or 1/4. Why? He enumerated the possibilities as follows:

TWO TOSSES

Head, head
Head, tail

Tail, head
Tail, tail

In other words, if he tossed a coin twice, there would be four possible outcomes: a head first and then a second head; a head first and then a tail, and so forth. Of these four possible outcomes, only one is "head, head." Therefore, the chance of getting two heads in two tosses is $\frac{1}{4}$. If he repeated the two-toss experiment a thousand times (a thousand *pairs* of tosses) about 25 percent of the pairs would be "head, head." This result can be calculated by multiplying $\frac{1}{2} \times \frac{1}{2} \ (= \frac{1}{4})$. And with three tosses of a coin, the probability of getting three heads in succession can be calculated by multiplying $\frac{1}{2} \times \frac{1}{2} \times \frac{1}{2} \ (= \frac{1}{8})$ as follows:

ONE TOSS	TWO TOSSES	THREE TOSSES
H	H, H	H, H, H
	H, T	H, T, H
		H, H, T
		H, T, T
T	T, H	T, H, H
	T, T	T, T, H
		T, H, T
		T, T, T

Well, Kelley thought, if an MTR can occur at any time (and it can), then I'm dealing with two *independent* events—like tossing two separate coins or tossing the same coin twice. Therefore the probability that a boom and an MTR will occur *simultaneously* is simply the probability that a boom will occur, (calculated as .15 in Table 7.5), multiplied by the probability that an MTR will occur, which probability Kelley had guessed to be .20. Thus, .15 $\times$ .20 = .03. Kelley therefore found that the probability of a boom and an MTR occurring simultaneously was .03. Hurray, he said to himself quietly.

Kelley had thus found that the probability that two *independent* events will occur *simultaneously* can be calculated by multiplying together the separate probabilities of each. This is called the *multiplicative law of compound probability*.

Kelley next proceeded to compute the probabilities as shown in Table 7.6. The probability that a boom and an MTR would occur together was, as stated above, .03. The probability of a boom without an MTR was simply the probability of a boom (.15) multiplied by the probability that an MTR would *not* occur, or .80. Since .80 $\times$ .15 = .12, the probability of a boom without an MTR was .12. And so forth for each of the other intervals.

TABLE 7.6

PROBABILITY OF BUSINESS PHASE OCCURRING

PHASE	WITH MTR	WITHOUT MTR
Boom	.03	.12
Very Good	.05	.20
Good	.09	.36
Recession	.02	.08
Depression	.01	.04
TOTAL	.20	.80

.20 + .80 = 1.00

After Kelley finished Table 7.6, he regarded his handiwork with pleasure. Everything balanced perfectly: the "with MTR's" totaled .20; the "without MTR's" totaled .80; and the whole thing totaled 1.00.

TABLE 7.7

PROBABILITIES OVER EBIT *WITH* CONSIDERATION OF MTR

PHASE	EBIT	MID-POINT	PROBABILITY
	(millions)		
Boom			
With MTR	$15.1 to 20.0	$17.5	.03
Without MTR	20.1 to 25.0	22.5	.12
Very Good			
With MTR	10.1 to 15.0	12.5	.05
Without MTR	15.1 to 20.0	17.5	.20
Good			
With MTR	5.1 to 10.0	7.5	.09
Without MTR	10.1 to 15.0	12.5	.36
Recession			
With MTR	0.0 to 5.0	2.5	.02
Without MTR	5.1 to 10.0	7.5	.08
Depression			
With MTR	—5.0 to —0.1	—2.5	.01
Without MTR	0.0 to +5.0	2.5	.04
		TOTAL	1.00

Next, Kelley set up Table 7.7. The first column listed all the ten events given in Table 7.6. The fourth column simply listed the probabilities given in Table 7.6. He then filled in Column 2. With a boom and no MTR, EBIT would fall in the interval $20.1 to 25.0 million. He filled in that line first and, in Column 3, the corresponding mid-point, $22.5 million. He then filled in the other Without MTR rows—*very good,* $15.1 to 20.0 million; *good,* $10.1 to 15.0 million, and so forth. He filled in the With MTR rows on the assumption that if an MTR occurred, EBIT would be one class interval less than it otherwise would have been. Thus if an MTR occurred simultaneously with a boom in economic conditions, EBIT would fall in the range $15.1 to 20.0 million. If an MTR occurred simultaneously with a very good year, EBIT would be $10.1 to 15.0 million, and so forth.

Next, Kelley transferred the mid-points of each class interval to Table 7.8. He then calculated earnings per share of common stock (EPS) for each level of EBIT on two assumptions:

1.   Butcher borrows $36.8 million at 5½ percent to finance the rebuilding program.
2.   Butcher, instead, sells to its present stockholders about 1.3

TABLE 7.8

AVERAGE EARNINGS PER SHARE AT VARIOUS LEVELS OF EBIT

PHASE	EBIT MID-POINT (millions)	Earnings per Share DEBT	STOCK
(1)	(2)	(3)	(4)
Boom			
With MTR	$17.5	$3.54	$2.51
Without MTR	22.5	4.68	3.23
Very Good			
With MTR	12.5	2.40	1.79
Without MTR	17.5	3.54	2.51
Good			
With MTR	7.5	1.26	1.08
Without MTR	12.5	2.40	1.79
Recession			
With MTR	2.5	0.11	0.36
Without MTR	7.5	1.26	1.08
Depression			
With MTR	—2.5	—2.06	—0.72
Without MTR	2.5	0.11	0.36

million shares of new stock at $30. The sale, after costs, would net about $37 million. This would raise the total number of common shares outstanding from 2,187,500 at present to about 3,487,500.

Kelley knew that EBIT depended only on operating earnings: it was simply sales minus cost of sales and general expenses (*not* including interest). It depended therefore only on general business conditions, the machine tool cycle, and the company's own efficiency and competitiveness. *It would not depend on the method of financing the new assets.*

DETERMINING EARNINGS PER SHARE

Earnings per share, however, *did* depend on the method of financing for two reasons: first, if Butcher sold 1.3 million additional shares of common stock, earnings would have to be divided among 3,487,500 shares instead of among 2,187,500. But on the other hand, if Butcher sold $36.8 million of debt, instead of the additional shares of common, it would have annual interest charges of about $2 million, and this would reduce earnings after taxes. In short, if debt were used, EBIT would be reduced by interest and taxes. The remainder would then be divided by the *present* number of shares. If new stock were sold, EBIT would be reduced only by taxes (no interest). But the remainder, after taxes, would be divided by a much larger number of shares. Tables 7.9 and 7.10 illustrate the calculations for two levels of EBIT: $22.5 million,

TABLE 7.9

EARNINGS PER SHARE
DURING BOOM PHASE

	WITH DEBT	WITH COMMON STOCK
EBIT	$22,500,000	$22,500,000
Interest	2,000,000	0
Earnings after interest	20,500,000	22,500,000
Taxes at 50%	10,250,000	11,250,000
Earnings after taxes	$10,250,000	$11,250,000
Number of shares (000)	2.188	3.488
Earnings per share	$ 4.68	$ 3.23

TABLE 7.10

*EARNINGS PER SHARE
DURING DEPRESSION PHASE*

	WITH DEBT	WITH COMMON STOCK
EBIT	—2,500,000	—2,500,000
Interest	2,000,000	0
Earnings after interest	—4,500,000	—2,500,000
Taxes *	0	0
Earnings after taxes	—4,500,000	—2,500,000
Number of shares	2.188	3.488
Earnings per share	—2.06	—0.72

* No taxes on losses (negative income).

and a loss of $2.5 million. In order to simplify the arithmetic, Kelley assumed interest charges of $2 million (instead of $2.024 million) and a tax rate of 50 percent (instead of 48 percent). He disregarded the small amount of interest Butcher paid from time to time on short term bank debt.

The actual computations were very simple: EBIT minus interest minus taxes divided by the number of shares. Interest would, of course, be zero for common stock financing, but the number of common shares would be larger. Table 7.8 gives EPS, calculated in the above manner, for each of the business cycle phases. (Kelley was interested to see that as EBIT went down the difference between EPS with debt and EPS with stock decreased.) Kelley next set up Table 7.11 using the two sets of EPS figures from Table 7.8, and the probabilities from Table 7.6.

Finally, Kelley was ready to calculate average expected EPS (a) with debt financing, and (b) with stock financing. The results are given in Table 7.11: with debt financing, average expected EPS would be $2.55; with common stock financing, $1.90. These figures were much lower than the figures given in Table 2.6 because the figures in that table had attached no weight at all to levels of EBIT below $17.5 million.

Kelley then wrote the following memorandum to Martin:

> I attach my first attempt at a probability analysis of earnings. I also attach my worksheets so you can see how I obtained the final results.

TABLE 7.11

AVERAGE EXPECTED EARNINGS PER SHARE

	EARNINGS PER SHARE		PROBA-	AVERAGE EXPECTED EPS	
PHASE	DEBT	STOCK	BILITIES	DEBT	STOCK
(1)	(2)	(3)	(4)	(5)	(6)
Boom					
With MTR	$3.54	$2.51	.03	$ .11	$ .08
Without MTR	4.68	3.23	.12	.56	.39
Very Good					
With MTR	2.40	1.79	.05	.12	.09
Without MTR	3.54	2.51	.20	.71	.50
Good					
With MTR	1.26	1.08	.09	.11	.10
Without MTR	2.40	1.79	.36	.86	.64
Recession					
With MTR	0.11	0.36	.02	—*	.01
Without MTR	1.26	1.08	.08	.10	.09
Depression					
With MTR	—2.06	—0.72	.01	—.02	—.01
Without MTR	0.11	0.36	.04	—*	.01
			1.00	$2.55	$1.90

* Less than one half of a cent.

I'd just like to make three points:

1. Table 7.11 contains all the information we presented to the Board plus some we did not present—for example, the full range of possibilities, with a weight attached to each. In the Board meeting, everyone had weights on his mind, but they were not discussed explicitly and no concensus on them was reached—although everyone did agree that the likelihood of really low earnings was small.

Also, with the attached figures we are better able to assess the advantages and disadvantages of using debt. Average expected EPS is 66 cents higher with debt, but the variability of earnings is very much increased. The maximum possible negative figure is a $2.06 loss as compared with a 72 cent loss for common stock. And the swings with debt are much greater—from $4.68 to a loss of $2.06, a difference of $6.74. The swing with common is only $3.95—from $3.23 to a 72 cent loss.

2. The main virtue of this approach, I believe, is that it brings

all the elements of the problem to the surface and forces us to think about them critically. In different words, some probability distribution or other over EBIT and EPS underlay the decisions taken by the Board. Our thinking would have been clarified if that probability distribution had been made explicit and discussed critically.

3. The figures are really just illustrative and I'd like your permission to put in a few days doing a little more research.

I hope I'll have your permission later to pass the study around for comment to a few people and to keep it up to date.

A day or so later, Kelley received his memo back. Martin had scrawled across the top the words: "Okay. But don't spend more than two or three days on it."

THE PRESENT VALUE OF RCA

In Chapter 3 we calculated the present value of a share of RCA on the assumption that the dividend would grow at the rate of 14 percent a year, and the price of the stock at the rate of 9 percent a year. But now we wish to calculate the present value of a share of RCA on the more realistic assumption that the rate of growth in the dividend may take any one of a number of values—that it is, in fact, *subject to a probability distribution.*

Unfortunately, as outsiders, we have virtually no information about what is really happening inside RCA. We know that RCA manufactures television sets, industrial electronic equipment and computers. And we know that they operate successful radio and TV networks and publish books. But we do not know which of these products are presently being emphasized—as television sets were in the ten years 1959–1968. We know also that RCA is doing a good deal of product research, but we do not know and, without "inside information" (which we are not likely to be able to obtain!) we cannot know what specific products are being developed—and much less, what their prospects for success are.

Occasionally, a stockbroker will prepare and distribute to the public a careful study of the prospects of individual companies. Such studies are based on information which is publicly available plus information obtained from company officers and are often useful for assessing the prospects of individual companies. But nothing of this sort, up-to-date, is available on RCA. We have only two kinds of information available. We have first, the eighteen year record of earnings and dividends—available from any stock service—given in Table 7.12. And we have the

TABLE 7.12

RCA, VARIOUS DATA ON EARNINGS AND DIVIDENDS, 1952-1969

YEAR	EPS	RATE OF GROWTH (EPS)	DIVIDEND	RATE OF GROWTH (DIVIDEND)	PAYOUT RATIO
(1)	(2)	(3)	(4)	(5)	(6)
1952	$ .58	—	$ .27	—	46.6%
1953	.63	8.6%	.40	48.1%	63.5%
1954	.73	11.6%	.37	— 7.5%	50.7%
1955	.87	11.9%	.41	11.1%	47.1%
1956	.73	—16.1%	.44	7.3%	60.3%
1957	.70	— 4.1%	.41	— 6.8%	58.6%
1958	.55	—21.4%	.41	0%	74.5%
1959	.72	13.1%	.27	—34.1%	37.5%
1960	.55	—23.6%	.27	0.1%	49.1%
1961	.56	1.8%	.28	3.7%	50.0%
1962	.82	46.4%	.29	3.6%	35.4%
1963	1.07	30.5%	.44	51.7%	41.1%
1964	1.34	25.2%	.62	40.9%	46.3%
1965	1.69	26.1%	.64	3.2%	37.9%
1966	2.18	29.0%	.78	21.9%	35.8%
1967	2.26	3.7%	.85	9.0%	37.6%
1968	2.35	4.0%	1.00	11.8%	42.6%
1969	2.50 *	6.4%	1.00	0%	40.0%

* Estimated.

following brief estimate of prospects taken from the *Value Line Investment Survey* for February 28, 1969:

> RCA is in a buying range, especially for conservative accounts. The equities of most color TV makers have been weak in recent months probably reflecting the belief in some quarters that 1969 volume gains will be modest. It is noteworthy that RCA shares have declined less than those of its major competitors. This fact may be due to the company's wide diversification in electronics and other fields which could enable it to post a 1969 earnings gain even if color TV sales are not brisk. We believe that RCA stock will outperform the market this year. Moreover, this good quality issue could command a considerably higher quotation in the 1971-73 period based on the earnings progress we envision over the coming 3 to 5 years.
>
> The trusts [mutual funds] do not share our optimism. All trans-

actions [by mutual funds] late last year, according to latest reports, were on the sell side. Thirteen large trusts, though, continue to own over two million Radio Corp. shares. Officer Mills exercised an option for 8993 shares bringing his holdings to 26,700.

Results in 1969 set a record by a small margin. The gain would have been considerably better [by about 17 cents a share] had it not been for the income tax surcharge. Advances in color television, the NBC network and the Hertz subsidiary all contributed to the rise in pre-tax profits.

Further progress is estimated for the current year. Profits from color television, a significant portion of the total, may be little changed this year reflecting a more moderate advance in industry sales, higher costs, and the probability of lower selling prices. On the other hand, greater earnings are expected from the network as advertisers become increasingly aware of the advantages of color. In addition, Hertz is expected to continue its strong growth pattern this year as is the RCA Communications subsidiary.

Computers could boost 1971-73 results. This activity was unprofitable last year, largely reflecting the fact that most machines were leased rather than sold outright. Inasmuch as leasing revenues rose substantially in 1969 [about 45%] there is reason to hope that this division may start to become profitable by the early 1970's.

The *Value Line* report also tells us that RCA's capital structure consists of:

Debt	$422.9 million
Preferred stock	$140.4 million
Common stock	62,728,980 shares

This then is all the information we have and we must form our probability beliefs on the basis of it. We know also that dividends depend on two things: earnings and the payout ratio. The payout ratio is simply the percentage of earnings paid out in dividends. In 1968, for example, earnings (per share) were $2.35, the dividend was $1.00 and the payout ratio 42.6 percent (= $1.00/$2.35). We can obtain a figure for expected dividends by constructing a probability distribution over earnings. We will then assume a payout ratio in order to obtain an average expected dividend.

We notice in Table 7.12 that EPS fluctuated a good deal from year-to-year and in some years actually declined. And, in percentage terms, some of the declines were not negligible—for example, from 1957 to 1958, earnings declined by 21.4 percent, and from 1959 to 1960, by 23.6 percent. The overall growth rate between 1957 and 1967, (12.4 percent, see Table 7.13), was, therefore, the resultant of two large declines in

TABLE 7.13

RCA AVERAGE GROWTH BY TEN YEAR PERIODS
1952-69

PERIOD	AVERAGE RATE OF GROWTH (EPS)	AVERAGE RATE OF GROWTH (DIVIDEND)	AVERAGE PAYOUT RATIO
(1)	(2)	(3)	(4)
1952-62	3.5%	0.7%	52.1%
1953-63	5.4%	1.0%	51.6%
1954-64	6.3%	5.3%	50.1%
1955-65	6.9%	4.6%	48.9%
1956-66	11.6%	5.9%	47.9%
1957-67	12.4%	7.6%	45.8%
1958-68	15.6%	9.3%	44.3%
1959-69	13.3%	14.0%	41.2%

earnings plus five successive large increases. The five large increases occurred between 1962 and 1966. After the last large increase in 1966, the rate of growth in earnings declined sharply: from 29.0 percent in 1966 to 3.7 percent in 1967. We guess that the large increases were due to rapidly increasing sales of color television sets. But clearly, by 1967, RCA and the other TV manufacturers had begun to saturate this market.

This, in turn, suggests that RCA's earnings are likely to grow at a high rate in the *next* ten years *only if RCA can develop a new product and market it successfully*. What might that product be? On the basis of the limited information we have, the product might be electronic computers. The *Value Line* comment (above) tells us that "leasing revenues (from computers) rose by 45 percent in 1968" and that "there is reason to hope that this division [computers] may start to become profitable by the early 1970's." We know, simply because we read the newspapers, that IBM—the dominant company in the computer industry —has been hit with a large number of antitrust suits. If IBM's operations are curtailed, RCA will be in an especially strong position to benefit: it has "know-how" in the field and a very good name. And we know that the surface of the computer market has barely been scratched. We decide to assume, as a point of departure, that *at the very most*, by 1978, RCA's revenues from computers will have reached one fourth of IBM's *present* (1968) revenues. IBM's total revenues in 1968 were about $8.7 billion (RCA's were $3.1 billion), on which IBM earned $7.70 a share, or about $870 million in total. But RCA's costs would probably be higher than IBM's, and we assume therefore that computer revenues would add, *at the very most*, only $200 million to RCA's earnings after taxes. This would be approximately $3.20 a share.

Our initial reaction to this figure is that it is too high. But we then note from Table 7.12 that between 1958 and 1968, color television sales, plus normal growth in other products, added nearly $2.00 to RCA's earnings per share. We note also that between 1966 and 1968, that is, *in just two years*, IBM's revenues increased by more than $2.6 billion and its earnings after taxes by about $340 million. We are assuming, *as a maximum*, that RCA's revenues from computers over a *ten* year period will increase by $1.75 billion and its earnings after taxes by $200 million. Against this background the figures do not seem to be unreasonably high—and indeed may prove to be conservative—*if* RCA really penetrates the computer market.

But, of course, RCA may not succeed in doing so. By 1979, additional revenue from computers may be zero, or any other figure—up to 25 percent of IBM's present revenues. If additional revenues from the computer division add nothing to revenues, then EPS will grow only as population and living standards rise or at the rate of perhaps 5 percent a year.[2]

We are now in position to begin to construct a probability distribution over RCA's EPS for 1978, as shown in Table 7.14. First, we list all possible events. From the discussion above, we have concluded that *at the very worst* RCA's earnings during the next ten years will grow at the rate of 5 percent a year even if they fail altogether to penetrate the computer market. We have concluded, also, that *at the very most*, by 1970 RCA's revenues from its computer division will have grown by 20 to 25 percent of IBM's present revenues. In between these two extremes are a multitude of other possibilities which in Table 7.14 have been compressed into five class intervals: an increase in computer revenues by 1979 of between zero and 5.0 percent of IBM's present revenues; of between 5.1 and 10 percent of IBM's present revenues,

---

[2] Assuming, of course, that no other new products are introduced, about which we now know nothing.

and so forth. Each of the "events" is thus "mutually exclusive" and the distribution as a whole exhausts all the possibilities.

The next column of Table 7.14 simply lists the mid-points of the class intervals. (The first event is not a class interval and therefore has no mid-point.)

TABLE 7.14

ESTIMATED EARNINGS PER SHARE FOR RCA FOR 1978

INCREASE FROM COMPUTER REVENUE *	MIDPOINT	INCREASE IN PROFITS AFTER TAXES (millions)	INCREASE IN EPS †	EPS †
Without computers (Normal growth only)		$ 92.8	$1.48	$3.83
0 - 5%	2.5%	20.0	0.32	4.15
5.1 - 10%	7.5%	60.0	0.96	4.79
10.1 - 15%	12.5%	100.0	1.59	5.42
15.1 - 20%	17.5%	140.0	2.23	6.06
20.1 - 25%	22.5%	180.0	2.87	6.70

* Percentages based on IBM's present (1968) revenues.
† Based on 62.7 million shares, and EPS of $2.35 in 1968.

As we see in Table 7.14, normal growth at the rate of 5 percent a year would add $92.8 million to RCA's total profits by 1978. If by 1978, RCA's computer revenues have increased by 2.5 percent of IBM's present revenues, $20.0 million will have been added to earnings after taxes. (This amount is, of course, *in addition to* the amount added by normal growth.) If by 1978, RCA's computer revenues have increased by 7.5 percent of IBM's present revenues, $60.0 million will have been added to earnings after taxes, and so forth.

The table translates the total dollar increases in profits into increases *per share*. The addition of $92.8 million through normal growth would add $1.48 to earnings per share since $92.8 million ÷ 62.7 million shares = $1.48. An increase of $20 million would add $.32 to earnings per share, and so forth.

The final column in Table 7.14 translates the *increases* in EPS into *total* earnings per share for 1978. With only normal growth, EPS in 1978 would be $3.83, that is,

$2.35   EPS in 1968
1.48   Normal growth
$3.83   EPS in 1978

If, in addition, the computer division added $.32 a share, EPS in 1978 would be $4.15 ($3.83 + $.32). If the computer division added $.96 a share, EPS in 1978 would be $4.79 (= $3.83 + $.96), and so forth. Maximum EPS in 1978 would be $6.70 ($3.83 + $2.87).

We now transfer the 1978 EPS figures from Table 7.14 to Column (1) of Table 7.15 and attach probabilities to them. The probabilities are

TABLE 7.15

AVERAGE EXPECTED EARNINGS FOR RCA
FOR 1978

EPS	PROBABILITY	AVERAGE EXPECTED EPS
(1)	(2)	(3)
$3.83	.20	$0.77
4.15	.30	1.25
4.79	.20	0.96
5.42	.15	0.81
6.06	.10	0.61
6.70	.05	0.34
	1.00	$4.74

really, of course, the probabilities associated with the basic events listed in Column (1) of Table 7.14.

Where do the probabilities come from? They are, we must admit, purely subjective. They are, that is, what *we* think they are—subject to two conditions: first, they must add to 1.00; and second, they must seem to us to be reasonable.

The idea of "subjective probabilities" is not new to you, although you may think it is. Suppose, your roommate suggests you toss a coin for 25 cents a toss. If heads come up he will pay you 25 cents. If tails come up, you will pay him 25 cents. He pulls a coin out of his pocket. You look at it, toss it once or twice and say "Okay." What have you done? You have made the subjective judgment that heads will come up at least as often as tails. In other words, you have made the subjective judgment that the probability of heads is at least one half. And when the four statisticians, discussed above, returned to Munich after having analyzed their data, they made the subjective judgment that the four wheels in Munich would continue to behave as they had behaved in the past. In short, *no* probability distribution is entirely objective. It is equally true, of course, that some distributions are more subjective than others and that the probability distribution given in Table 7.15 is very subjective indeed!

We now calculate average expected EPS by multiplying each event by its associated probability. This process yields an average expected EPS, for 1978, of $4.74. We now multiply this by .40, our assumed average payout ratio, in order to obtain an average expected dividend for 1978, $4.74 $\times$ .40 = $1.90. But our growth tables tell us that a dividend of $1.90 in 1978 implies a compound growth rate of 6.6 percent between now and then. We assume that the dividend will grow steadily at this rate between 1968 and 1978—as indicated under Expected Dividend in Table 7.16 (We are aware that this assumption is un-

TABLE 7.16

PRESENT VALUE OF ONE SHARE OF RCA

YEAR	EXPECTED DIVIDEND	DISCOUNT FACTOR AT 8%	PRESENT VALUE
(1)	(2)	(3)	(4)
1969	1.07	.926	$ .99
1970	1.14	.857	.98
1971	1.22	.794	.97
1972	1.30	.735	.96
1973	1.39	.681	.95
1974	1.48	.630	.93
1975	1.58	.583	.92
1976	1.68	.540	.91
1977	1.79	.500	.90
1978	1.90 *	.463	.88
			38.43*
		TOTAL	$47.82

* Price of stock assumed to grow at same rate as dividend. $38.43 is obtained by applying the .463 factor to the anticipated stock price of $83.00, $83 $\times$ .463 = $38.429.

realistic but it greatly simplifies the arithmetic and does not materially change the result—provided only that the dividend is raised as earnings increase.) We assume also that the price of the stock will have risen at the same compound rate and, in 1978, will be $83.[3]

---

[3] The price of the stock in 1978 will be determined by expectations *then* as to future earnings and dividends.

Now, using 8 percent discount factors, we proceed to calculate the present value to us of a share of RCA. We find that at 8 percent, a share of RCA is worth to us now, in 1968, $47.82—or $4.32 more than its present price. We, of course, rush out and buy a share.

But no matter what we do, the results we obtained in Table 7.16 are better than the results obtained in Table 3.7 for one simple reason: in order to try to construct a probability distribution, we have been forced to examine some of the real factors likely to affect RCA's earnings. We are better informed than we were before we began. We have not simply projected the past into the future. And, of course, had we been able to do more research, we would have had more information about the real forces underlying RCA's earnings—and our results would have been that much better.

CONCLUSION

In finance, as in almost everything else, every decision we make implies a prediction about the future—and every prediction about the future runs the risk of being wrong. If Hastings, of the Butcher Company, buys that lathe, he is predicting that the savings it generates will be high enough to make the rate of return on the lathe at least 11 percent.

If Dale Martin sells Government bonds now, even though he does not need the cash now, he is predicting that he will be no worse off than he would have been had he not done so. If he sells, and interest rates continue to go up, bond prices will go down and Martin will have avoided a capital loss. If they remain stable, bond prices will remain stable but Martin will have lost interest on his money. If interest rates go down, bond prices will rise, and Martin will have lost a capital gain. Therefore if he sells now, he is, in effect, predicting that interest rates will continue to go up at least enough to offset loss of interest.

Predictions can be made in three ways:

(1) By guessing on the basis of hunch and intuition. Good predictions can often be made in this way by people who have had experience and who have developed a flair for interpreting—almost unconsciously—the inner meaning of a complex assortment of facts. Such people almost *smell* the future. They sniff here and sniff there and announce confidently that horse number 5 will win or that the stock

market will go down by ten points in two weeks. And horse number 5 does win and the stock market does go down by ten points in exactly fourteen days. Such people do not need probability distributions because they can divine the future. There is no risk or uncertainty for them. But fortunately, such people are rare.

(2) By mechanically projecting the past into the future. In deciding whether or not to sell Government bonds now, Martin might simply argue that interest rates have gone up for six months and will doubtless continue to go up for a few months more. Therefore, we sell. (In the spring of 1969, this would have turned out to be a good prediction.)

(3) By assigning to each of the possibilities in a given set an appropriate weight determined by analyzing those real, underlying forces which will determine the future outcome. Sometimes this is easy to do, especially when the "analysis" consists merely in keeping good records of past experience and that past experience can be expected to apply to the future—as with the four statisticians and Hasting's lathe. But sometimes the necessary analysis is complex and difficult, as Kelley found when he tried to construct a probability distribution over Butcher's earnings, and as we found when we tried to construct a probability distribution over RCA's dividends for the next ten years.

And in some cases, the probabilities have a highly subjective character. But such probabilities can always be revised in the light of subsequent experience. And in any event, the analytic quest for probabilities means that we will be better informed about real underlying forces.

And this means that our performance will be better than it otherwise would have been.

The illustrations used in this chapter may have raised a question or two in your mind: suppose as Hastings has assumed, that the frequency distribution given in Table 7.1, which (as we have indicated above) relates to the *past*, can be taken to represent an accurate probability distribution over events to occur in the *future*. Hastings will not use this individual distribution often and, therefore, his estimate of average savings is not likely to be a meaningful figure. Only if he bought 100 or 500 or 1,000 machine tools from the same company in a short period of time could he feel reasonably certain that savings would, on the average, be reasonably close to 5.48 percent below the manufacturer's estimate.

We may say two things about this point of view. First, Butcher expects to be in business a long time, perhaps forever. And over a long period of time it will in fact buy a large number of machine tools from Ex-Cello, perhaps as many as 200. Over the long run, therefore, if the probability distribution is accurate and stable, actual savings will average about 5.48 percent below Ex-Cello's estimates.

Second, during any short period of time, say a year, Butcher will make a large number of decisions each of which, individually will involve an amount of money which is small relative to the company's total assets. Butcher will, for example, in any given year make several thousand purchases of raw materials—which may or may not be up to standard. It will conduct several dozen independent market surveys. It will place advertising in a thousand different publications. Every year it will invest $5,000 in training each of five or ten new junior executives. It will make fifty independent decisions to buy or sell $25,000 worth of treasury bills and notes. It will postpone decisions to pay bills in twenty different foreign currencies at twenty different times in the belief that each such country is about to devalue its currency, in which case fewer dollars would be required to pay each bill. It will decide to increase investment in finished goods inventory of ten different products in the belief that their prices are going up. And so on, *ad infinitum*.

In short, Butcher will make thousands of decisions every year *each of which will imply a prediction about some future event.* The aggregate payoff on all these decisions, taken together, will be determined by the probability distribution underlying each. And the aggregate payoff can be estimated in advance—provided all the decisions involve about the same amount of money—and provided all the probability distributions are known and independent of each other.

Suppose that our four friends, the statisticians, had analyzed 100 roulette wheels scattered all over the world from Nome, Alaska to Lagos, Nigeria, instead of just four located in Munich, Germany. And suppose they placed a $100 bet (by telegram, of course) on one number on one spin of each wheel. Each number they bet on carried favorable but *different* odds. What is their expected average gain? Their average expected gain is the average of the one hundred separate average expected gains.

"All right," you say. "But the probability distributions we are using are not really probability distributions. They are history, they describe the past. They may or may not be good predictors of the future."

But after you've made that remark, you realize two things:

(1) That you can examine prior probability distributions in the light of current experience and revise them if necessary;

(2) That, more importantly, *whether he does so consciously and explicitly or not, the businessman is always acting on the basis of some probability distribution or other.*

Every decision the businessman makes implies an underlying probability distribution. And this being so, his decisions will be better if he brings such distributions to the surface and analyzes them critically in order to make them as accurate as possible. And the more accurate they are, the more reliable and useful they will be.

A final word of warning: we said in Chapter 6 that if we plan to place just one bet, an average expected payoff is not a meaningful figure. Sometimes a company (like Clay Company in Chapter 2) must decide whether to make a large bet on just one spin of the wheel. Is a probability distribution of any help in making such a decision? The answer is yes—but not because the average expected payoff has much meaning. The average expected payoff has meaning, as we have seen above, only when the bettor expects to make a relatively large number of small independent bets. In such case, the average expected payoff will be a useful guide to action, provided the underlying probability distribution is reasonably accurate.

But betting $3.5 million on a single toss of a coin? Well, that's a different matter—to which we will return in Part IV.

EXERCISES

1. You have a fair coin and two fair cubes, A and B. The six sides of cube A contain the numbers 1, 2, 3, 3, 4, 4 while the six sides of cube B contain the numbers 1, 1, 2, 2, 3, 4. Consider the following experiment. First, throw cube A; second, toss the coin; and third, throw cube B.
    a. Calculate the following probabilities:
        1. a 4 on the throw of cube A;
        2. a 3 on the throw of cube A followed by a tail on the toss of the coin;
        3. a 2 on the throw of cube A followed by a head on the toss of the coin followed by a 2 on the throw of cube B.
    b. Which event has the greater probability:
        1. (1, H, 4) or (3, T, 1);
        2. (2, T, 2) or (3, T, 3);
        3. (1, H, 1) or (3, H, 3)?

PROBLEMS

1. Outline, step-by-step, the process Kelley went through in calculating average expected EPS with debt and with stock.

2. Pay a visit to your local haberdasher or department store. Ask a buyer what rules he uses to decide how many sport jackets to order in each size. Ask him where he learned the rule.

3. Toss a coin once, then toss it a second time. Note the results. Repeat this procedure four times. How many head, head combinations should you get? How many did you get? Make a list of all possible outcomes.

4. Hastings calls Roberts at Ex-Cello and says: "That lathe is worth exactly $9850 to me, installed, and not a penny more!" Hastings has reached this conclusion intuitively, without explicit reference to any past experience with Ex-Cello's lathes.

   Assuming an 11 percent cost of capital and trade-in value of $1000 at the end of the seventh year, draw up a probability distribution over savings which would justify Hastings' figure. Assume savings are the same each year for seven years.

5. You are Kelley, Martin's assistant. Assume Butcher is considering, as a third alternative, raising $36.8 million by borrowing $20 million at 5½ percent and selling about 590,000 shares to present stockholders at $30 a share—which would net about $17 million to the company.

   Calculate:

   (a) EPS at each level of EBIT

   (b) average expected EPS, using the mid-points and probabilities given in Table 7.7.

   What assumption is involved in using the mid-points?

6. Actually, to obtain the EPS figures given in Table 7.8, Kelley had shortcut the computations by using the following formula when EBIT was greater than interest.

$$2 \text{ EPS} = \frac{EBIT}{\text{Number of shares}} - \frac{\text{Interest in dollars}}{\text{Number of shares}}$$

Using Table 7.9 see if you can derive this formula. Note that for any proposed amount of debt, the first term is a constant—that is, it does not change as EBIT changes.

What would the formula be when interest was greater than EBIT?

7. *Table 7.18 gives AT&T's earnings and dividends per share for the years 1954-1968. Using this information and the most recent Value Line assessment, draw up, as best you can, a list of all possible rates of growth for AT&T for the next ten years and assign a probability weight to each.*

    Next calculate an average expected rate of growth in the dividend and the present value of a share of AT&T at 8 percent.

8. *Subjective probability distributions can always be revised in the light of subsequent experience. One year after having bought a share of RCA at $43.50, you learn that in 1969 RCA earned $2.59 and will pay a dividend of 40 cents for the fourth quarter. This brings the total dividend for the whole year to $1.15. In announcing these figures, Robert Sarnoff makes the statement that "our computer divi-*

TABLE 7.18

AT&T EARNINGS PER SHARE AND DIVIDENDS, 1954-1969

YEAR	EPS	DIVIDEND PER SHARE
(1)	(2)	(3)
1954	$1.90	$1.50
1955	2.05	1.50
1956	2.00	1.50
1957	2.14	1.50
1958	2.25	1.50
1959	2.59	1.61
1960	2.71	1.65
1961	2.76	1.76
1962	2.86	1.80
1963	3.02	1.80
1964	3.18	2.00
1965	3.39	2.00
1966	3.67	2.20
1967	3.79	2.25
1968	2.74	2.40
1969 *	4.00	2.40

* Estimated.

sion contributed a small amount to profits for the first time, this year."

In the light of this new information, revise the probability distribution given in Table 7.15.

You then turn to the New York Stock Exchange quotations in the Wall Street Journal and find that RCA, which has moved up steadily during the year, is selling at $62—up two points since yesterday. Would you buy another share? Why or why not?

9. After you have done the calculations in Table 7.16, you do not rush out to buy a share. Instead you say to yourself: "I've given too much weight to earnings from the computer division."

Find a probability distribution over the intervals in Table 7.14 which would lead to a figure for the present value, at 8 percent, of a share of RCA about equal to its present price.

8

CONCLUSION TO PART II
where are we now?

In Chapter 1 you will surely remember we said that finance wrestles continuously with two questions:

1. How much money should the firm invest in new projects?
2. How should any necessary new money be raised?

We said also that the answers to these two questions would together determine *whether the firm would grow and how fast it would grow.* Obviously, if Butcher invests in all the new assets listed in the upper half of Table 1.1, Butcher will grow—which is just another way of saying that its total assets will have increased. And the more new assets Butcher buys, the faster it will grow.

But the number of new assets Butcher will buy, will depend on two things:

1. The number of new projects proposed by Butcher's various divisions—and the expected rates of return on each of those projects.
2. Butcher's cost of capital.

Thus if Butcher's cost of capital had been 4 percent instead of

11 percent, Hastings would have found Ex-Cello's lathe much more attractive. In fact, he would have bought it.

But the cost of capital itself depends on how money is raised. And this being so, we can restate the two questions above in a somewhat more enlightening way:

1. How much money should Butcher invest in new projects—*given its cost of capital?*
2. How should new money be raised—*so as to minimize Butcher's cost of capital,* that is, so as to make the cost of capital as low as possible.

Putting these two questions in this way, gives us—or should give us— a bit more insight into what Dale Martin, Butcher's financial vice president, was doing in Chapter 2. In Chapter 2, you will recall, we said that Martin resolved his problem by first reestimating Butcher's cost of capital and then comparing that cost with the expected rates of return on the proposed new projects.

We still know very little about the cost of capital—only that it is a number which bears some vague resemblance to an individual's opportunity cost.

But we *do* know something now about *expected rates of return.* We know first what a proper rate of return is—it's a discounted cash flow (DCF) rate of return. And we now can define the word "expected" as the mean of a probability distribution. And we know, therefore, that an *expected rate of return* is a DCF rate which is the mean of a probability distribution.

Where do we go now?

In the next six chapters, we will apply what we have learned about expected rates of return to the various assets in the firm's portfolio. As we know, the typical firm holds a variety of assets. It holds cash and marketable securities, which together we will refer to as *liquidity.* It holds accounts receivable. It holds various kinds of inventory—raw materials, work-in-process and finished goods. Liquidity, receivables and inventory together are called *current* assets, for reasons which will become clear in the next chapter. The firm also holds a variety of *long-term* assets, primarily buildings and machinery which are used in combination with labor and raw materials to produce the goods and services the firm sells.

And we will now, in effect, proceed down the asset side of the firm's balance sheet, calculating rates of return as we go. We must bear in mind, of course, that at this stage we will be calculating rates of return on *proposed additions* to the firm's portfolio of assets—*not on the assets the firm already holds:* the marketing vice president wants to invest *more money* in accounts receivable; the production manager of the tools division wants to invest *more money* in parts inventory; the plastics division wants *more* plant and equipment, and so forth.

After we have completed this excursion down the asset side of the balance sheet, we will, in Part IV, examine *the cost of capital*.

RATES
OF
RETURN
AND
THE NEED
FOR
FUNDS

INVESTING
IN
LIQUIDITY
/
the normal cash cycle

9

"Sit down," said Barclay to Vaughn. "Stop pacing. You're making me nervous."

"What do we do if Philbrook says no?" said Vaughn, half to himself. *"What do we do?"*

"He won't say 'no' ", said Whitman.

"But suppose he does," said Vaughn "suppose he does."

"All of you keep quiet," said Roberts. "Here he comes."

Barclay, Vaughn, Whitman, and Roberts were four young electronics engineers in search of money to finance the production and sale of a new micro-relay—which had been developed a few months before by Barclay. Philbrook had lots of money. He was the head of a group of wealthy investors who were interested in new ventures, especially in electronics. This was the ninth meeting Barclay, Vaughn, Whitman, and Roberts had had with Philbrook. The first few meetings had been simply exploratory. They had talked about themselves, about Barclay's invention, about their plans, and about electronic circuitry in general. Then they had met with Philbrook's engineers—with whom they had gone over their patents in detail. Then Philbrook had asked his lawyers to search the patents. Then Philbrook had gone over with them their production and marketing plans. And then, finally, at their last meeting, which had taken place two weeks ago, Philbrook had suggested they organize the company, incorporate it in Delaware, and draw up a detailed financial plan. They had the plan with them today and hoped that at the end of the meeting, Philbrook would agree to provide the money they needed.

They all stood up. Philbrook shook hands all around.

"Well," he said, "to come to the point quickly, how much money do you think you need?"

"About $300,000," said Barclay, adjusting his steel-rimmed spectacles.

"Let's see the figures," said Philbrook. "That's just about the amount my group would be prepared to put up. Very good. I must tell you frankly that our technical people think the odds are 50 to 50 that this innocent looking thing,"—he held a tiny chip in the center of his hand— "may well revolutionize electronic circuitry. And our legal people say your patents are good patents."

"Thanks," said Barclay. "Here are the figures." He passed a sheet of paper across the conference table. "The actual amount is $302,000."

Philbrook briefly studied the estimates (see Table 9.1). "So you are

TABLE 9.1

ESTIMATE OF AMOUNT NEEDED TO ESTABLISH COMPANY

Renovation of leased plant	$130,000
Machinery	220,000
Four months supply of raw materials	70,000
Rent on plant (one year, payable in advance)	18,000
Office furniture and supplies (second hand)	4,000
Total required	$442,000
To be invested by us	140,000
Needed from Philbrook group	$302,000

planning to put up $140,000."

"Yes," said Barclay, "$35,000 a piece. That's all the money we have. It includes all our money plus some we've borrowed from our parents."

Philbrook looked at Table 9.1 briefly and tossed it on the table. "You haven't asked for enough money," he said. "You show no cash, no liquidity. *And you can't operate a business without liquidity.* And that piece of paper," he gestured at Table 9.1, "is *not* a financial plan."

He got up from the table and went to a large blackboard at the end of the room.

"Let me show you something," he said, picking up a piece of red chalk. "I'm going to put three balance sheets on the board: The first as of right now—assuming that my group puts up $302,000; the second, as of the moment you open the doors of the fully equipped plant; and the third, one month later. For the benefit of those of you who don't know what a balance sheet is, it's simply a statement of what the firm *owns*—its assets, and what is *owes*—its liabilities."

"We know that," said Barclay.

Philbrook said to Barclay, "You have a trial order from IBM?"

"Yes, for 250,000 pieces."

"How long will it take you to manufacture that many pieces?"

"About a month," said Barclay.

Philbrook then put on the blackboard the three balance sheets, given in Tables 9.2, 9.3 and 9.4.

TABLE 9.2

BALANCE SHEET MICRO ELECTRONICS, INC.
AS OF JUNE 30, 1969

ASSETS	
Cash	$442,000
TOTAL	$442,000

LIABILITIES	
Long term notes payable (parents)	20,000
Philbrook group	302,000
Common stock bought by Barclay group	120,000
TOTAL	$442,000

"Now," said Philbrook, "the first thing I want you to notice that is common to all three balance sheets—they balance. They balance because everything the company possesses is *owed* to its creditors or *owned* by its stockholders. So the right side is always equal to the left side. If the company makes money, the amount owned by the stockholders increases and, I might add, vice versa.

"The second thing I want you to notice is that as of the day you start up, you have a bank balance of exactly zero. But you have to start hiring and paying labor and you yourselves can't live on nothing. And you have to run your plant—lights, heat, power, and so forth.

TABLE 9.3

BALANCE SHEET MICRO ELECTRONICS, INC.
AS OF START-UP DATE

ASSETS

Cash	$ 0
Raw materials	70.000
Factory (leasehold improvements)	130,000
Machinery and tools	220,000
Office furniture	4,000
Prepaid rent	18,000
TOTAL	**$442.000**

LIABILITIES

Long-term notes payable	20,000
Philbrook group	302.000
Common stock (Barclay group)	120,000
TOTAL	**$442,000**

"That's why the third balance sheet shows accrued salaries, accrued wages and other accruals. But your families can't live on money the company owes you. And your labor will really insist on being paid every week."

"But the company's making money," interjected Vaughn.

"Right," said Philbrook, "but it won't be in business next week —because you can't pay your bills with money IBM owes you."

"All right," said Barclay, "let's add $25,000. Or maybe IBM would pay us in advance."

"Not likely," said Philbrook, "and if you asked them to, you might very well lose the order."

"Well," Barclay repeated, "let's add the $25,000. That should do it."

"Not enough," said Philbrook. "And where would you get it?"

"I thought your group might . . ." Barclay said.

"No," said Philbrook, "My group will put up exactly $302,000—on the following basis: The company will issue to us $302,000 worth of bonds, secured by a chattel mortgage on the machinery and leasehold improvements. The bonds will run for five years and will carry an interest rate of $7\frac{1}{4}$ percent. They will be convertible into 2,500 shares of common stock at our option—any time before June 30, 1974."

TABLE 9.4

BALANCE SHEET MICRO ELECTRONICS, INC.
AS OF ONE MONTH AFTER START-UP

ASSETS

Cash	$ 0
Accounts Receivable (IBM)	17,500
Raw materials	65,000
Factory (leasehold improvements)	130,000
Machinery and tools	220,000
Office furniture	4,000
Prepaid rent	16,500
TOTAL	**$453,000**

LIABILITIES

Accrued salaries	$ 2,000
Accrued wages	6,650
Accrued Social Security taxes	700
Other accruals	500
Long term notes payable	20,000
Philbrook group	302,000
Barclay group	120,000
Retained Earnings	1,150
TOTAL	**$453,000**

"That would give your group more than twice as many shares as we have," said Barclay.

"Yes," said Philbrook, "but we're putting up more than twice as much money as you are. But we would give your group the right to buy back from us—at book value—at that time enough stock to give your group 51 percent of the stock."

"Well, I guess it sounds all right," said Barclay. "I suggest we go ahead on that basis." He looked around. Vaughn, Whitman and Roberts all nodded their heads.

"No," said Philbrook, "not until you have drawn up a satisfactory financial plan for the first year of operation, which *each* of you fully understands and can defend. And also not until you've thought hard about my proposal and decided that it's in your own best interests. Do you realize," Philbrook continued, "that of all the new firms that fail each year more than 80 percent fail because they don't know how to manage money? They're started by people, such as you, who've invented an interesting new product or a new process, or by a person who has a knack for selling. New firms are rarely started by finance men."

"But Mr. Philbrook," said Barclay unhappily, "we've got production, sales and research well covered—as our resumes show—and we're eager to get started. And what about the IBM order? Why couldn't we hire a finance man, or why couldn't you help us?"

"No," said Philbrook, "I'd be glad to help from time to time. In fact I'd insist on doing so. But I can't participate in day-to-day operations. And you can't afford a finance man—at least not right now. You'll have to learn something about finance yourselves. I suggest you begin by trying to understand why you can't operate a business without liquidity."

> We define *liquidity* as petty cash plus demand deposits plus savings deposits plus marketable (usually short-term government) securities.

Chapters 9 and 10 discuss two questions:

1. *Why* does a company need to hold (invest in) liquidity.
2. *How much* liquidity should it hold?
3. *In what form* should the liquidity be held?

The need for liquidity is created by two facts of life in business. It is created, first, by the fact that most businesses grant credit to their customers. This means that there is almost always a lag between the time disbursements are made to pay for goods produced and the time payment for those goods is received. And every firm will have a normal "cash cycle"—a normal period from disbursements to receipts—the length of which will depend on its production period and the credit terms it grants its customers. But, second, the normal cash cycle is often upset by "unforeseen contingencies" beyond the control of the firm—a big customer doesn't pay his bill on time, sales decline suddenly, a strategic machine breaks, labor goes on strike. If a firm wishes to be able to weather "unforeseen contingencies," it must be able to pay its bills, until its affairs return to "normal."

We discuss the "cash cycle" first.

THE "CASH CYCLE"

In order to make this lag clear, let's go back to the four young men who had underestimated the amount of money they needed in order to start manufacturing microminiature circuitry. And let us suppose that they start in business with the balance sheet given in Table 9.3, which shows lots of real assets but nothing in the bank.

Now (and perhaps obviously) if the company could produce a few relays each day, sell them the same day and receive payment for them the same day, they would need no initial cash balance. Suppose they produced $2,000 worth of relays a day (at direct cost) and sold them for $2,500. By the end of the first week they would have accumulated enough money to pay the labor they had employed, and by the end of the first month, enough to pay the other bills which would then come due—including their own salaries. This is shown in Tables 9.5, 9.6, and

TABLE 9.5

MICRO ELECTRONICS, INC. BALANCE SHEET
ONE WEEK AFTER START-UP
"CASH AND CARRY" BASIS

	AMOUNT	CHANGE SINCE START-UP
ASSETS		
Cash on hand (or in bank)	$12,500	+ $12,500
Accounts receivable	0	0
Raw materials	66,000	— 4,000
Work in progress	0	0
Finished goods	0	0
Machinery, equipment and supplies (net)	219,577	— 423
Leasehold improvements (net)	129,750	— 250
Prepaid rent	17,654	— 346
Office furniture	3,980	— 20
TOTAL	$449,461	+ $7,461
LIABILITIES AND EQUITY		
Accrued wages	$ 6,000	+ $6,000
Accrued salaries	1,000	+ 1,000
Accrued social security	200	+ 200
Accrued income taxes	0	0
Miscellaneous accruals *	545	+ 545
Convertible debentures	$302,000	0
Notes payable (parents)	20,000	0
Common stock	120,000	0
Retained earnings	(284)	— 284
TOTAL	$449,461	+ $7,461

* Interest $447.00; heat, light and power $90, and supplies, $8.

TABLE 9.6

INCOME ACCOUNT FOR FIRST WEEK OF OPERATION
"CASH AND CARRY" BASIS

Net Sales		$12,500.00
Cost of Sales:		
Labor	$6,000.00	
Raw materials	4,000.00	
Production manager's salary	250.00	
Company share of social security	162.50	
Depreciation	673.00	
Heat, light, power, etc.	90.00	11,175.50
Operating profit		$ 1,324.50
Administrative and selling expense:		
Salaries	750.00	
Rent	346.00	
Company share of social security on salaries	37.50	
Supplies	8.00	
Depreciation on office furniture	20.00	1,161.50
Profit before interest and taxes		163.00
Interest		447.00
Profit (loss) after taxes LOSS		$ 284.00

9.7. The balance sheet given in Table 9.5 is dated as of the end of the first week—just a few minutes *before* the wages are due to be paid for labor for five days. It shows the amount then available for each balance sheet item and indicates the change in each item from the preceding balance sheet, which had been based on the actual start-up date. What does each change mean? Let's consider them in order.

1. *Increase in Cash from Zero to $12,500.* This represents five day sales at $2,500 a day, for which payment is received daily. No cash outlays are necessary during the week for raw materials used because they have already been paid for (see Table 9.2). Labor and other operating expenses have not yet been paid and the total amount of sales revenue has therefore gone into the company's bank account. The total sum, $12,500 is carried to the income (profit and loss) account for the purpose of calculating profit for the period (Table 9.6).

2. The company has no *accounts receivable* simply because it is

being paid *in cash* for everything it sells. Only if the company were granting credit would accounts receivable appear on its balance sheet.

3. *Decrease in raw materials by $4,000 from $70,000 to $66,000.* Raw materials which cost $4,000 have been used to manufacture the relays which have been sold. No new purchases of raw materials have been made and therefore the stock of raw materials has declined by $4,000.

4. The company will not have any *work in process* until the following Monday morning when production is started again. The company sells everything on the day it is finished and therefore carries no *finished goods* in stock.

5. *The decrease in the value, by $673 on the books of the company, of machinery, equipment and leasehold improvements.* This represents an arbitrary assessment of the value of physical capital "used up" during the week in the process of producing $12,500 worth of relays. A ten-year depreciation period is assumed both for the machinery and equipment and for the leasehold improvements. Equal amounts are assumed to be "used up" each year.

   Of course, none of this physical capital has really been "used up" in any meaningful sense. All the decrease in these items really means is that $673 of the original cost of these investments had been returned to the company in the form of cash. This sum also appears on the income account (Table 9.6) as a deduction from sales.

6. *Decrease of $20 in the value of office furniture.* This furniture is being depreciated at the rate of $1,000 a year, or about $20 a week. This item also appears on the income statement as a deduction from sales revenue.

7. *Decrease of $346 in prepaid rent.* The company has paid $18,000 in advance for one year's rent. This is no different in principle from buying a year's supply of raw materials (or anything else) in advance. The deduction simply means that the company has used one week's rent ($18,000 ÷ 52). We may say also that the company has converted one week's worth of prepaid rent into cash. This item also appears on the income statement as a deduction from sales revenue.

8. *Increase in accrued wages by $6,000 and in accrued salaries by $1,000.* The word *accrued* simply means "owed but not yet paid." The $6,000 represents five days work (40 hours) at an average rate of $3.00 an hour by fifty skilled and semiskilled workers (including one combination secretary and bookkeeper). They are paid weekly and wages have accrued to them at the

end of each day. After they are paid, this item will be reduced to zero and cash will be reduced by $6,000. (They cannot be paid with anything but cash.) Each of the four officers of the company is to receive a salary of $250 a week, payable every four weeks. Each has worked one week and the company therefore owes them a total of $1,000 (4 × $250). Both *accrued wages* and *accrued salaries* appear on the income statement as deductions from sales revenue.

9. *Increase in accrued Social Security taxes.* This represents the portion of Social Security taxes which the firm itself must pay. After labor has been paid at the end of the week a new item will appear on the balance sheet called "social security and withholding taxes payable (on behalf of employees)." In other words, when wages and salaries are actually *paid,* income taxes and Social Security taxes are withheld by the company to be paid later to the government. Hence, until these withholdings are in fact paid to the government, they are owed to the government.

10. *Increase in miscellaneous accruals of $545.* This simply represents the sum of other expenses which have been incurred but are not yet payable—such as heat, light, power ($90); interest due for one week at 7¼ percent a year on the convertible bonds held by the Philbrook group; 6½ percent on the notes payable to parents ($447); plus $8 due for supplies.

11. *Decrease in retained earnings of $284.* This represents the loss on the week's operations after deduction of all expenses. During the week the firm has sold relays for $12,500. In order to produce these relays it has "mixed together" $4,000 worth of raw materials, $6,000 worth of labor, $1,000 worth of management, $346 (rent) worth of plant, $693 worth of capital equipment and furniture, and small amounts of heat, light, power and so forth.

After subtracting the total cost of all these ingredients from its total revenues, the company finds itself $284 worse off than it was at the beginning of the week (see Table 9.6). This $284, its loss for the week, is shown as a decrease in "retained earnings." Because the company had no prior earnings, this loss is really a reduction in the company's original capital.

Now let us look briefly at the cash account which contains what seems to be an impressive sum—$12,500, where nothing had been before. Table 9.7 shows that of this total sum, $7,745 is due to outsiders—$6,000 to labor, $1,000 to the managers (they are not the company, they are its managers), $98 to utility companies, $447 to lenders, $200 to the

TABLE 9.7

CASH ACCOUNT AS OF ONE WEEK AFTER START-UP
"CASH AND CARRY" BASIS

Cash	$12,500
Belongs to labor	6,000 *
Subbalance	6,500
Belongs to management	1,000 *
Subbalance	5,500
Belongs to utility and supply companies	98 *
Subbalance	5,402
Belongs to lenders	447 *
Subbalance	4,955
Belongs to government (Social Security)	200 *
Subbalance	4,755 †
Recovery of raw materials cost	4,000
Subbalance	755
Recovery of part of capital investment in machinery, equipment and furniture	693
Subbalance	62
Recovery of part of prepaid rent	346
Balance (negative figure)	$284 ‡

* These sums are due to outsiders and when paid will reduce bank balance.
† This sum belongs to company and was obtained in manner indicated.
‡ This sum represents reduction in capital.

federal government. Only $4,755 really belongs to the company. But at the end of its first four weeks of operation, assuming the same level of sales, the company would have four times this amount, or about $19,000   (4 × $4,755 = $19,020) in cash *net of its obligations to its employees, its lenders, and so forth.* About one fourth of its raw materials would be gone by that time, but it would have money enough to replace them—and to expand operations somewhat if it wished to do so.

The foregoing illustration makes clear, then, that if Micro Electronics could produce, sell and be paid on a single day (or within a single week) —in other words if there were *no lag* (or only a very short lag) between production, sale, and receipt of proceeds—the company, at start-up, would need only enough cash in the bank to buy the new telephone operator a double chocolate sundae.

THE NORMAL CYCLE

But virtually every manufacturing company in the United States (and most wholesalers and retailers as well) must grant credit to their customers. Merchandise is manufactured and shipped but, in the normal course of events, is paid for only ten, twenty, thirty or sixty (calendar, not working) days thereafter. In the electronics industry the terms vary a good deal depending on the product. But let us assume that Micro Electronics would sell on a net thirty days basis, i.e., payment in full, without any discount, within thirty days of the date of the invoice. Would the company, in such case, be able to start business with no cash in the bank? No, it would not.

It would not for two primary reasons. First, the production period for the type of relays the company plans to make is estimated to be three weeks—after all the "bugs" have been removed from the production process. No one really knows precisely how long the production period will be because this particular type of relay has never been manufactured before. But let us assume that all production runs, including the first, take four weeks. Each run is about 30,000 relays, worth about $2,000 at direct cost (materials and labor). A new run is started each day, which means that on the first day of the fifth week following start-up, 30,000 finished relays will come off the lines, will be inspected, and will be shipped on thirty day terms. And 30,000 will come off the lines each day thereafter and will be shipped on the same terms.

What does this mean? It means that for the first four weeks it is in business, Micro Electronics will be spending money at the rate of $6,000 a week for wages, $1,000 a week for salaries, plus small amounts a week for other expenses. In short, during the first eight weeks of its existence the company will have disbursed nearly $50,000 in *cash*. And during that period it will have received no payments of any kind from its customers or from anyone else. Table 9.8 gives expected receipts and expenditures, by four-week periods, for the company for its first year of operations assuming:

1. The first sale (shipment), of $2,500, takes place on the first day of the fifth week following start up.
2. Shipments are made steadily at the rate of $2,500 a day ($12,500 a week) from week 5 through week 28. Thereafter, until the

end of the year, shipments are made at the rate of $5,000 a day, or $25,000 a week.

3. All merchandise is found satisfactory by customers.
4. All customers pay their bills on the thirtieth day following date of invoice, which is the same as the date of shipment.

What does the table show? Let's consider it line by line:

1. *Sales.* This simply represents the dollar value of merchandise expected to be shipped during each four week period. Sales (shipments) are $2,500 a day, $12,500 a week, and $50,000 for each four week period from the second through the seventh. Thereafter, they are $100,000 for each four week period until the end of the year. This is *not* a cash item. Cash is not received on account of sales until payment is actually made. This item is included in Table 9.8 simply to illustrate the lag between the time merchandise is shipped to a customer and the receipt of cash for it.

2. *Receipts.* Receipts include both cash payments received for merchandise shipped, and other cash receipts—such as the proceeds of a bank loan deposited to the firm's account. The first cash payment for merchandise shipped is received on the thirtieth day following the day the first shipment is made. This is so because the company is selling on terms of thirty days net. Thus the buyer is to make payment to the seller on the thirtieth (calendar) day following the date of the invoice. Collections during weeks 9-12 total $47,250 instead of $50,000 because during this period there are only nineteen business days beginning with the thirtieth day after the first shipment. Thereafter collections match sales with a lag of thirty calendar days and are therefore $50,000 in each four week period from the fourth period through the end of the eighth period. Thereafter receipts are at the rate of $100,000 for each four week period.

3. *Total Receipts.* This is the same as collections on accounts receivable, no other cash receipts being, for the moment, anticipated.

4. *Wages.* The company's wage bill is $6,000 a week, payable every Friday, or $24,000 for each of the first seven periods. But Social Security and income tax, averaging about 15 percent of total wages, are withheld (to be paid to the government later) and the *actual cash* received by the workers is, therefore, only $20,400. Beginning in the eighth period, wages double.

5. *Salaries.* Each of the four members of the management team receives $250 a week, payable every fourth Friday, for a total

TABLE 9.8

CASH RECEIPTS AND CASH EXPENDITURES FOR FIRST YEAR OF OPERATION

	Weeks					
	1-4	5-8	9-12	13-16	17-20	21-24
EXPECTED SALES:		$50,000	$50,000	$50,000	$50,000	$50,000
RECEIPTS:						
Collections on A/R			$47,250	$50,000	$50,000	$50,000
Other						
Total receipts			$47,250	$50,000	$50,000	$50,000
DISBURSEMENTS						
Wages	$20,400	$20,400	$20,400	$20,400	$20,400	$20,400
Salaries	3,400	3,400	3,400	3,400	3,400	3,400
Social security and with-holding taxes				16,800		
Heat, light, power, telephone		360	360	360	360	360
Interest						
Convertibles				5,475		
Parents				325		
Raw materials					16,000	16,000
Supplies			100			100
Estimated federal income tax				500		
Total disbursements	$23,800	$24,160	$24,260	$47,260	$40,160	$40,260
RECEIPTS LESS DISBURSEMENTS	$23,800 *	$24,160 *	$22,990	$ 2,740	$ 9,840	$ 9,740

of $4,000 (4 × 250 × 4). But again Social Security and income taxes are withheld and total cash actually paid out is therefore only $3,400.

6. *Social Security and Withholding taxes.* Every three months the company must pay to the government Social Security and income taxes withheld plus its own share (another 5 percent of wages and salaries) of the total Social Security tax. For each of the

TABLE 9.8 (Con't)

			Weeks				
25-28	**29-32**	**33-36**	**37-40**	**41-44**	**45-48**	**49-52**	**TOTALS**
$50,000	$100,000	$100,000	$100,000	$100,000	$100,000	$100,000	$900,000
$50,000	$ 50,000	$100,000	$100,000	$100,000	$100,000	$100,000	$797,250
$50,000	$ 50,000	$100,000	$100,000	$100,000	$100,000	$100,000	$797,250
$20,400	$ 40,800	$ 40,800	$ 40,800	$ 40,800	$ 40,800	$ 40,800	$387,600
3,400	3,400	3,400	3,400	3,400	3,400	3,400	44,200
16,800				36,800		31,200	101,600
360	360	450	450	450	450	450	4,770
5,475			5,475			5,470	21,895
325			325			325	1,300
32,000	32,000	32,000	32,000	32,000	32,000	32,000	256,000
		100			100		400
	500					500	1,500
$78,760	$ 77,060	$ 76,750	$ 82,450	$113,450	$ 76,750	$114,145	$819,265
$28,760 *	$ 27,060 *	$ 23,250	$ 17,550	$ 13,450 *	$ 23,250	$ 14,145 *	$ 22,015

*** Excess of disbursements over receipts.**

first seven periods, income taxes withheld on wages and salaries
were $2,800 (10 percent of $28,000). The employees' share of
the Social Security tax was $1,400 and the company's share of
the Social Security tax is $1,400. The total to be paid over
to the government, during the fourth four week period, is
thus $5,600 ($2,800 + $1,400 + $1,400) multiplied by three, or

$16,800. A similar payment will have to be made every three months. It increases substantially after wages double.

7. *Heat, light and power.* The company receives a bill once a month from the local power, telephone and oil companies. These bills are payable when rendered and the company pays them on the tenth day of each month. Heat, light, power and telephone are expected to run about $90 weekly, or about $360 every four weeks until production is doubled at which time utilities costs will increase to $450 every period thereafter.

8. *Interest.* Micro Electronics is obliged to pay interest every three months to the parents of its four managers and to Philbrook and Company. Interest to Philbrook and Company at 7¼ percent on $302,000 is $21,900 a year, or about $5,475 every three months. Interest to parents at 6½ percent on $20,000 is $1,300 a year, or $325 every three months. These payments are made every three *calendar months* and the first payment is therefore due at the beginning of the thirteenth week.

9. *Raw Materials.* The company started business with a stock of $70,000 of raw materials—about four months supply. It is using this stock up at the rate of $4,000 a week (see Table 9.3). By the end of the sixteenth week, the company is down to less than two weeks supply but decides it cannot afford to order more than four weeks supply, that is $16,000 worth. The company has, as yet, no credit standing, and the raw materials will have to be paid for in cash (a certified check) on delivery. The raw materials are ordered during the sixteenth week and will be delivered one week later, that is, during the seventeenth week. Micro Electronics places another order for $16,000 at the end of each period for delivery during the first week of the following period. Payments for raw materials double (to $32,000) in the seventh period.

10. *Supplies.* These are factory and office supplies. Disbursements are expected to be $100 in the third period and $100 every three months thereafter.

11. *Income tax.* The company expects to earn money during its first year of existence. Under the revised tax law, it will have to estimate its tax and make quarterly payments on it. In order to estimate its tax, the company draws up the "pro forma" income statement given in Table 9.9. The company finds that its expected profit after taxes is $12,238 and its estimated tax for the year, $3,452. It decides to make quarterly payments of $500, paying the balance due, if any, in the next year. The first such payment will be made at the beginning of the thirteenth week.

TABLE 9.9

PRO FORMA INCOME STATEMENT FOR FIRST YEAR OF OPERATION

Sales		
Six periods at $ 50,000 = $300,000		
Six periods at $100,000 = 600,000		$900,000
Cost of sales		795,470
Operating profit		104,530
Administrative and selling expense		60,350
Profit before interest and taxes		44,180
Interest		28,490
Profit before taxes		15,690
Federal taxes at 22 percent		3,452
Profit after taxes		$ 12,238

12. *Total disbursements.* This line represents the sum of all disbursements for each four week period. Total disbursements for the first period are expected to be $23,800; for the second period (weeks 5-8), $24,160, and so forth.
13. *Total receipts minus total disbursements.* This line shows negative figures for the first two periods, namely $23,800 loss for weeks 1-4; $24,160 loss for weeks 5-8; and losses for weeks 25-28, 29-32, 41-44, and 49-52.

Table 9.10 summarizes for each four week period, the total receipts, the total disbursements and the difference between the two. Table 9.10 also shows the firm's expected cash balance at the end of each four week period, based on the assumption that *the company had no cash balance at the beginning of the first week.*

what the figures show

The figures in Table 9.8 (which in effect represent a "cash budget") and the figures in Table 9.10 show that the company in the first eight weeks of its existence can expect to pay out nearly $50,000 more than it will take in. This means that *if it does not have this sum in the bank when it starts operations, it will not be able to pay wages and its other bills* and will not be in existence very long. This, of course, is what

Philbrook had in mind when he said that another $25,000 would not be enough. The largest figure shown in the last column of Table 9.10 ($58,470) is thus an estimate of the *minimum* amount of *cash* the company must have in the bank, or otherwise available, when it starts operations.

TABLE 9.10

SUMMARY OF EXPECTED CASH RECEIPTS AND DISBURSEMENTS, FIRST YEAR

WEEKS	TOTAL RECEIPTS	TOTAL DISBURSEMENTS	DIFFERENCE	CASH BALANCE
(1)	(2)	(3)	(4)	(5)
1- 4		$ 23,800	$23,800 *	$23,800 *
5- 8		$ 24,160	$24,160 *	$47,960 *
9-12	$ 47,250	$ 24,260	$22,990	$24,970 *
13-16	$ 50,000	$ 47,260	$ 2,740	$22,230 *
17-20	$ 50,000	$ 40,160	$ 9,840	$12,390 *
21-24	$ 50,000	$ 40,260	$ 9,740	$ 2,650 *
25-28	$ 50,000	$ 78,760	$28,760 *	$31,410 *
29-32	$ 50,000	$ 77,060	$27,060 *	$58,470 *
33-36	$100,000	$ 76,750	$23,250	$35,220 *
37-40	$100,000	$ 82,450	$17,550	$17,670 *
41-44	$100,000	$113,450	$13,450 *	$31,120 *
45-48	$100,000	$ 76,750	$23,250	$ 7,870 *
49-52	$100,000	$114,145	$14,145 *	$22,015 *

* Negative.

THE CIRCULAR FLOW

The figures given in Tables 9.8 and 9.10 also illustrate what we may call "the circular flow of working capital" in the typical manufacturing firm.

During the first two to three weeks of operation, Micro Electronics is using machinery to transform labor and raw materials into semi-finished goods (work in process). During weeks 3-4 the company transforms these semifinished goods into finished goods ready for shipment to customers. In other words, the company first turns money into raw materials. It then uses more money (the money it pays in wages and salaries and for heat, light and power, etc.) to turn the raw materials first into work-in-process and then into finished goods.

The finished goods are then shipped to customers and become accounts receivable. When the accounts receivable are eventually paid, they are in effect turned into cash and the first cycle is complete: cash to raw materials to work-in-process to finished goods to accounts receivable and, finally, back to cash. In other words, cash moves successively down through each current asset and then finally back to cash. If everything goes according to plan, cash will increase as each cycle is completed because the company is operating at a profit—i.e., included in accounts receivable is, of course, a markup over cost—and also, of course, because it is turning prepaid rent and the investment in plant and equipment into cash (see Table 9.7).

UNFORESEEN CONTINGENCIES

This cycle will keep repeating itself, will keep going around and around, like a ferris wheel, almost automatically, *if everything remains stable:*

1. If sales remain level at $50,000 every four weeks;
2. If there is no defective production—companies using microminiature relays and other electronic components, have very rigid systems of quality control;
3. If accounts receivable are paid when due;
4. If labor or other difficulties do not interfere with the production processes.

If anything goes wrong, the cycle will *not* repeat itself automatically. And if Micro Electronics did not have enough liquidity to tide itself over, production would be brought to a halt. This is equivalent to saying that the wheel will keep turning only if unforeseen, adverse events, beyond the control of the company, do not occur.

returns

Suppose after fifteen to twenty weeks of operations, during which Vaughn, the sales manager, has been setting the countryside on fire, Barclay receives the following call:

"John?"

"Yes."

"You remember the relays we sold to Arbuckle, the little guy up in Northampton."

"Yes."

"They're coming back."

"Who's coming back?"

"The *relays* are coming back. He says they're no good. Sloppy was the word he used."

"How much?"

"$26,000."

"$26,000! That was payable tomorrow—I need that money and I need it tomorrow. Hang up. I'm going to call him."

"I wouldn't if I were you. He's really angry. He had counted on those relays. His whole production schedule is upset—and so is he. Try the bank instead." Vaughn hangs up.

Arbuckle's failure to pay on time (whatever the reason) had slowed the cash cycle down. And, obviously, without sufficient money in the bank, or liquidity of other kinds, Micro Electronics might be unable to pay its bills.

production slow down

Or suppose Whitman, the production manager, comes in on a sunny Wednesday morning after the company has been in operation for a year or so, has grown some, and sales are running at the rate of $25,000 a week. He says:

"John, they're slowing down out there."

"Whaddya mean?"

"I mean they're slowing down. We won't ship our $25,000 this week. We'll be lucky if we hit fifteen next week, too. And maybe the week after that, and the week after that, *ad infinitum*."

"What's the trouble?"

"I don't know. And they won't tell me. We need a labor relations man."

"How long will it last?"

"I told you I don't know." And he walks out.

You see a strike or a walkout impending and you realize that if you can't produce relays, you can't sell them. And if you can't sell them, no money will be coming in. True, if the factory goes on strike, you won't have to pay *them*. But you have a two-inch stack of bills to pay plus interest on outstanding debt plus overhead—including your own salary. Where will the money come from? You see bankruptcy and ruin sitting there, a few weeks away, grinning at you maliciously. Do you have enough liquidity to tide you over until the strike is settled?

The same kind of problem would arise, if business, because of a recession, fell off. The amount of money coming in might not in such case be sufficient to pay bills, labor, interest and other overhead. And again, without sufficient liquidity you might have to sell real assets—machinery or inventory—in order to stave off bankruptcy.

Clearly, then, in order to cover the lag between disbursements and receipts and in order to meet adverse unforeseeable contingencies, a company must allocate a portion of its funds to liquidity—to cash, to demand deposits, to marketable securities—and so forth. And, of course, any company whose real assets are working profitably will almost always be able to borrow money—provided, of course, it hasn't borrowed too much already.

And so, we see, the question is: How much liquidity should a company hold and how much borrowing power should it keep in reserve? This question can be restated as follows: How do we measure the costs of holding liquidity and how do we measure the benefits? And after having answered these questions, we must decide how the liquidity should be held. How much, for example, should be held in cash-in-the-bank and how much in marketable securities?

In Chapter 10 we will discuss these rather complex questions.

CONCLUSION

This chapter has explained why firms must hold liquidity. Firms must hold liquidity for two reasons—

(1) To cover the lag between receipts and expenditures;
(2) To meet unforeseeable adverse contingencies.

One aspect of the discussion in this chapter deserves special notice. When Micro Electronics set up a cash budget for its first year of operations, it used *unique* figures for each receipt and disbursement. This is simply another way of saying that Micro Electronics did not construct probability distributions. It did not construct probability distributions because it was a new company and had no past experience. And having had no past experience, it had no basis on which to construct probability distributions.

But as we shall see in Chapter 10, receipts and disbursements cannot be predicted with absolute accuracy, even if unforeseen contingencies do not occur. And we must take account of this fact in deciding how much liquidity to hold.

PROBLEMS

1. As the text indicates, Micro Electronics, Inc., has not had enough experience to be able to put its cash budget on a "probability basis." Examine carefully each of the items listed in Table 9.8 and decide which, when experience permits, would be more accurate if put on a probability basis.

2. Using Table 9.8, construct a cash budget weekly for weeks 13-16 on the following assumptions:

> Receipts = $12,500 each week
> Wages and salaries = $5,950 each week
> Social Security taxes, etc. = $16,800, paid at end of week 13
> Heat, light and power = $360, paid at end of week 13
> Interest = $5,800, paid at beginning of week 13.
> Federal income tax = $500, paid at end of week 13.

Be sure and obtain total receipts and total disbursements for each week.

3. Draw up weekly budgets, as described in problem 2 for weeks 25-28 and 41-44. Assume that receipts are $12,500 weekly for weeks 25-28; and $25,000 for weeks 41-44. Wages and salaries are $5,950 weekly for weeks 25-28; and $11,050 weekly for weeks 41-44. All other disbursements are made in week 25 for weeks 25-28; and in week 41 for weeks 41-44.

4. In week 15, Vaughn calls and tells Barclay that Arbuckle is returning $26,000 (at selling price) worth of circuitry. What are the effects of this on the budget for weeks 13-16 and on the cash position at the end of the year? Assume that when the circuitry is returned, it is found to be worthless and is thrown away.

5. At the end of week 32 (see Table 9.8), the whole factory force goes on strike and production stops. The strike lasts for 20 weeks—that is, until the end of the year. Estimate the cash position as of the end of week 52. Specify your assumptions carefully.

6. After the strike described in problem 5 is settled (a 4 percent increase in wage rates), only half the original work force returns. The other half found satisfactory jobs elsewhere during the strike. Micro Electronics hires thirty new, inexperienced workers and trains them for two weeks at a cost of approximately $3,000 a week. The thirty experienced workers resume production immediately—that is, on January 2. Backorders total $400,000.

    Estimate the effect on cash as of the end of the fourth week of the new year. Specify your assumptions clearly.

10

INVESTING
IN
LIQUIDITY
II
cash or securities?

Shortly after Kelley had drawn up the probability distribution described in Chapter 7, he received the following note from Dale Martin attached to a folder marked "Marketable Securities":

> Here is my folder on marketables. Look it over. I'm not able to give our portfolio as much time as it needs and I suspect our yield is lower than it should be. Maybe you can improve it.

"Maybe," said Kelley to himself. He opened the folder and found Table 10.1 lying on top. Kelley noted the total at the bottom—nearly $13 million. He knew that Butcher had cash of nearly $2 million. Butcher thus held *total* liquidity—not including reserve borrowing power—of nearly $15 million. This was about 8 percent of total assets. He had no idea whether that amount of total liquidity was too much for a company like Butcher—or too little or about right.

Kelley noted the date on the table—June 17, 1966—the preceding day. He looked down the maturity column and saw that about $2.4 million worth of "repurchase agreements" would mature on June 19 (Kelley didn't know what a repurchase agreement was.) That meant, he assumed,

TABLE 10.1

MARKETABLE SECURITIES PORTFOLIO
AS OF JUNE 17, 1966

TYPE OF SECURITY	AMOUNT	MATURITY
90 day Treasury bills	$ 3,630,000	$1,300,600 July 15. Balance, August 1
Repurchase agreements	$ 3,752,902	Two-thirds, June 19. Balance, June 30
Bankers acceptances	$ 1,342,897	July 4
U.S. Treasury certificates	4,200,000	August 11
TOTAL	$12,925,799	

that tomorrow (or the next day), Butcher would have to reinvest $2.4 million in something or other—if it weren't needed to pay bills. (He found himself wondering whether Martin expected *him* to assume responsibility for reinvesting that sum!)

He put the table down, turned pages in Martin's folder, and came across a little blue booklet entitled *Short-term Investments* published by a Wall Street investment banking firm. (See Appendix 10.A at the end of this chapter.) Kelley looked in the Table of Contents of the booklet, found "Repurchase Agreements" listed, and breathed a long sigh of relief. He turned pages quickly until he came to that section and read avidly.

The description wasn't exactly vivid but Kelley derived the impression that a repurchase agreement was just about what its name suggested: the investing company (Butcher, in this case) paid cash to someone and received in return a batch of securities plus an agreement from the other party, to *repurchase* those securities at a specified time for a specified price. "I suppose the transaction's arranged through the bank," said Kelley to himself.

Next, Kelley reached into the bottom drawer of his desk, pulled out a thin folder labeled "Money Management" which he had started to put together during his last semester at business school. (Kelley had foresight.) It contained one article—"Managing the Corporate Money Position"—which had been published five years before by the Federal Reserve Bank of Philadelphia. It made the following points:

1. Interest rates are high. ("They're higher now than they were five years ago," thought Kelley.) Every dollar held in cash, as demand deposits, represents lost interest. ("The lost interest is the cost of holding cash," said Kelley to himself.)

2. On the other hand, if a company doesn't hold enough cash, it may run short. If it ran short, it would have to sell some securities. If it did sell, it might take a capital loss. ("The capital loss would be the cost of being caught short of cash," said Kelley to himself.)

3. The first step in deciding *how much* to invest and *how* to invest—in *what* and for *how long*—is the preparation of a cash budget. The cash budget will tell us when cash outflow is expected to exceed cash inflow (see Chapter 9). We would then be able to invest cash *which is excess now* so that it will be available when needed. ("Okay," said Kelley to himself, "the first step is a cash budget. Based on a probability distribution, of course," he added. Kelley knew that Butcher's controller prepared a cash budget for each division. But Kelley did not know whether those budgets were prepared on a probabilistic basis.)

4. Corporate portfolios of marketable securities are heavily concentrated in short-term government securities. ("Which means," said Kelley, "that most corporations care more about safety and liquidity than they do about yield.")

5. But corporations vary a good deal in the degree of aggressiveness with which they manage their portfolios.

"Okay," said Kelley putting the problem in a nutshell, "earn interest, cash budgets, mostly government securities and how aggressive should we be?"

The next day Kelley had lunch with Sam Morton, his friend at the Fidelity Mutual Life Insurance Company. Fidelity held all of Butcher's long-term debt.

"You've got a three part problem," said Morton:

"First, how much *total liquidity*—cash plus securities plus reserve borrowing power—should Butcher hold? In my opinion, Butcher's always held too much liquidity. And it's holding too much now.

"Second, of the total, *how much should be in cash*—in demand deposits? You now hold about $2 million in cash in twelve or thirteen banks around the country. That's rock bottom it seems to me. Those banks collect checks for you, handle your securities portfolio, give you advice and so forth. The compensation they receive in return for those services is what they are able to earn on the balances you keep with them.

"Third, *how should you invest the rest*—that is, the difference between total liquidity and cash?"

"Why do you say we're holding too much liquidity?" Kelley asked.

"You just are—$15 million is just too much. And that doesn't include reserve borrowing power. It's a matter of judgment. Butcher's finance committee has too many old fogies on it who lived through the Great Depression. Despite the fact that Butcher has diversified some, and will diversify further, and despite the fact that all kinds of stabilizers have been built into the economy—despite all that, some of the members of Butcher's finance committee would still attach a probability of .20 to a cash short-fall of $20 million—which Butcher would be unable to cover by borrowing! Absolutely unbelievable!

"I don't know what Butcher is earning on its portfolio of marketable securities. But it's certainly less than the interest rate on the money they've borrowed from us. And it's much less than they could earn by investing in more working assets."

"All right," Kelley said. "But how do we decide how much total liquidity to hold?"

"The first thing I'd do," said Morton, "is draw up a probability distribution over EBDIT—earnings before interest, taxes and depreciation. Do it in consultation with Martin. You want to know, especially, how low he thinks EBDIT could go—and with what probability."

EBDIT is better than EBIT for this purpose because it represents *total pre-tax cash flow*. And total pre-tax cash flow is what you would have available to pay fixed obligations such as interest and amortization.

Kelley said, "I've already done it for EBIT. All I'd have to do would be to add back depreciation."

"Good," said Morton. "That should give you a rough impression of the situation on an annual basis. But you'll have to draw up, also, monthly or biweekly probability distributions over net cash flow—receipts minus disbursements—at a high level of sales, a moderate level and the lowest level imaginable. Perhaps, Butcher already has such distributions."

"They have monthly cash budgets," said Kelley. "But I'm sure they're not based on probability distributions."

"Anyway," said Morton. "You'll surely find some months—especially when sales are low—when expected net cash flow will be negative. Most companies cover short-term swings by short-term borrowing. But not Butcher."

"How much reserve borrowing power do you think Butcher has?" Kelley asked.

"I should think they'd certainly be able to borrow $5 to $10 million short-term on short notice," answered Morton.

"Now?"

"Now," said Morton.

"During a severe depression?"

"How do I know," said Morton. "How could anybody answer *that* question?"

HOW MUCH TOTAL LIQUIDITY?

"Thanks," said Kelley. He paid the lunch check (out of his own pocket) and returned to the office. He made an appointment to see Martin later on that afternoon. Meanwhile he did two things:

First, he took Table 7.7 and added back $3 million in depreciation to obtain EBDIT. (He noted that *all* of the figures were now positive.) Then, using the probabilities in column (4) from Table 7.7, he calculated an expected value. The results of his handiwork are shown in Table 10.2.

Second, he took the lowest level of EBDIT ($500,000)—the level, that is, that would be expected to occur during a depression combined with a machine tool recession—and wrote it down on a separate sheet of

TABLE 10.2

EXPECTED VALUE OF EBDIT 1966

BUSINESS PHASE	MIDPOINT OF EBDIT (millions)	PROBABILITY	EXPECTED VALUE (thousands)
(1)	(2)	(3)	(4)
Boom			
With MTR	$20.5	.03	$ 615.0
Without MTR	25.5	.12	3,060.0
Very Good			
With MTR	15.5	.05	775.0
Without MTR	20.5	.20	4,100.0
Good			
With MTR	10.5	.09	945.0
Without MTR	15.5	.36	5,580.0
Recession			
With MTR	5.5	.02	110.0
Without MTR	10.5	.08	840.0
Depression			
With MTR	0.5	.01	5.0
Without MTR	5.5	.04	220.0
		1.00	$16,250.0

paper. He subtracted from it a $1 dividend (= $2,187,500) annual amortization of the loan held by Fidelity (= $2,300,000 × 2), and interest payable to Fidelity the first year. These calculations are given in Table 10.3.

TABLE 10.3

CASH DRAIN AT
LOWEST ANTICIPATED LEVEL OF EBDIT

Lowest expected level of EBDIT	$ 500,000
Pre-tax value of $1 dividend on 2,187,500 shares	—2,187,500
Balance	—$1,687,500
Pre-tax value of annual amortization of Fidelity loan	—2,300,000
Balance	—$3,987,500
Interest on Fidelity loan *	2,000,000
TOTAL	—$5,987,500

* First year. This would decline as loan amortized.

Kelley noted that the final figure—a negative $5,987,500 was nearly $5 million less than the total amount of liquidity Butcher now held. What did this mean? It meant that Butcher was holding enough liquidity to carry it through more than two years of severe depression. And the final figure included a dividend of $1 on the common stock. Kelley doubted that Butcher would pay a common dividend if EBDIT fell to $500,000. The dividend would surely be passed. And if the total dividend were added back, the expected cash drain would be reduced to $3.8 million (= $5,987,500 − 2,187,500). This meant that present total liquidity of about $15 million would carry Butcher through nearly four years of severe depression ($15 million ÷ $3.8 million is approximately 3.9)!

"Does seem conservative," thought Kelley. "Yes, it does. Especially when we bear in mind that Martin thinks that the chances of a prolonged severe depression are zero [see Chapter 7] and of a short severe depression (combined with an MTR) are about one in a hundred.

"What is all this liquidity costing us," Kelley asked himself. "Let's assume that we're earning about 4 percent—before taxes—on our portfolio of marketables. That's about 2 percent after taxes—or roughly

$250,000 [= .02 × $12.50 million]. If we invested the whole thing in working assets at our present *aftertax* expected rate of return on new projects—about 10 percent—we'd pick up about $1,250,000 [= .10 × $12.5 million]. That's a difference of nearly $1 million—or about 20 percent of expected after-tax earnings. And it's equal to about 45 cents a share [= $1 million/2,187,500]."

"In other words," said Kelley, "we're paying 45 cents a share in order to protect ourselves against a possibility Martin doesn't believe exists. And if our expected earnings went up by 45 cents a share, our stock would go up by perhaps $6—assuming it continued to sell at 15 times earnings.

"Suppose," Kelley went on, "that we cut liquidity to $8 million—$2 million in cash and $6 million in marketables. We'd then be paying about $450 thousand a year to protect ourselves against one chance out of a hundred of not having enough money and not being able to borrow enough money to pay interest and principle on our debt to Fidelity. But I can't believe we'd be unable to borrow short-term, or find the money somewhere."

Kelley wondered what Martin would say if the matter were put to him in the above way—that is, in terms of the cost of holding so much liquidity. How could the cost, he wondered, possibly be justified?

The telephone rang. Martin's secretary reminded Kelley, in a sharp voice, that he was already ten minutes late for his appointment with Martin.

"Sit down," said Martin. Kelley sat down.

"I need some guidance," said Kelley. "On the marketables problem."

"Oh yes, of course," said Martin. "The Finance Committee drew up a policy statement a year or so ago. It should be in that folder."

"No," said Kelley, "it's not."

"I'll get you a copy," said Martin. "But meanwhile the rules are as follows:

"First, nothing but U.S. governments—bills, notes, certificates, bonds—plus repurchase agreements secured by U.S. governments.

"Second, nothing but short maturities—a year or less. That means, of course, that you can buy U.S. Government bonds *only* when they're within a year of maturity. No commercial paper. No bankers acceptances. No finance company paper. And no corporate securities of any kind—not even AAA's. In short, nothing which carries any risk whatever of default.

"Third, the maturity pattern should match the cash flow pattern. In other words, if the cash budget indicates a net cash outflow of $600 thousand in March, you should have $600 thousand worth of securities maturing on March 1. You'll have to get the cash budget from Jamerson. It's done every month twelve months ahead. That means that on the first of every month, Jamerson will send you a computer printout containing monthly net cash flow figures forecast twelve months ahead— plus actual receipts and expenditures for the preceding month.

"Fourth, within these limits, you're supposed to earn as much as you possibly can. That's about it," said Martin. "Clear?"

"Sounds like a full-time job," said Kelley.

"Maybe," said Martin. "Do you have any questions?"

"A few," said Kelley. "First, why no long term securities?"

Martin said, "Too much risk of capital loss if interest rates go up— and we're forced to sell something unexpectedly. Long-term governments are now selling at a 30 to 40 percent discount—because of the recent rise in interest rates."

"Second," asked Kelley, "why no corporates? Some corporate yields are really very high."

"Corporates—even AAA's—default," answered Martin. "We just don't want to be bothered. We don't think that the slight additional yield is worth the worry and trouble. If we had a big diversified portfolio of long-term corporates, we'd probably do better *in terms of yield*—but the market risk would be too great. We'd take a terrible bath if interest rates started moving up—as they have in the last year or so. If we had held long-term corporates at the end of last year [1965], we would by this time have had a capital loss of perhaps 20 percent."

"Third," Kelley asked, "Why don't we borrow short term to cover short-term negative swings in net cash flow?"

"We do," said Martin, surprised. "If something unexpected happens and we don't want to sell anything. The Finance Committee has authorized me to borrow up to $10 million, at short term, if necessary. Right now, we have a $5 million line of credit at 7 percent, good for a year. The line is renegotiated every year. Costs us one-half of 1 percent. What made you think we didn't borrow short-term?"

"I had lunch with Sam Morton. He said so."

"Morton knows less about this company than he thinks he does," said Martin. "Anything else?"

"One last question. Why do we need $15 million in total liquidity?"

"Why do you ask?"

"Morton raised a question about it—and after I got back here I did a few quick calculations—based on the probability distribution I drew up after the last Finance Committee meeting (Chapter 7). It seems to me we're carrying enough total liquidity to carry us through four years of severe depression. But we think the probability of a prolonged severe depression is zero. We're paying $1 million, in effect, to be able to weather a storm which, we believe, will never occur. Why?"

"I'll tell you why," said Martin. "But first tell me how *you* think we should decide how much liquidity to hold."

Kelley said he thought Butcher should not pay more to avoid "the storm" than the damage the storm could be expected to do. "By 'expected to do,' I mean simply the damage which would be done by the storm multiplied by the probability that the storm will, in fact, occur. You live in a big house in the country?"

"Not so big," said Martin.

"You carry fire insurance on it?"

"Of course," said Martin, "also wind, water, hail and falling aircraft."

"Let's suppose it's insured for $100,000."

"Much less," said Martin.

"If the house were totally destroyed by fire," said Kelley, "you'd lose $100,000. But now suppose that the probability that the house would catch fire were zero."

"What kind of a house is it?" asked Martin. "Asbestos?"

"Yes," said Kelley. "Well, now—how much would you pay for a fire insurance policy on the house?"

Martin said, "That's just the point. I'd be prepared to believe that the house was fireproof. And so I'd buy no fire insurance. But we have a lot of old fogies on our Finance Committee who lived through the Great Depression. They'd never believe the house was fireproof. They'd think that the probability was .20 it would be totally destroyed by fire in any given year. And so they would be willing to pay an annual premium of $20,000 for fire insurance.

"But I see what you're getting at," Martin continued. "You're saying that we ought not to pay more to *avoid* the cost of being short of liquidity *than the cost of being short would be.* (Right! said Kelley.) And the cost of being short is not a unique figure. It's an expected value."

"Right," said Kelley. "And Table 10.2 tells us that there are about seven chances out of a hundred that EBDIT would be less than $6.6 million—in which case we'd be unable to pay interest and amortization in full on our long-term debt—out of earnings. ($6.6 million equals twice our amortization plus interest—$2.3 million ($\times$ 2 plus $2.0 million.)

"And," said Martin, "if we could just estimate the cost of being $1 short, $2 short, $3 short—on up to $6.6 million short, we'd be able to solve the problem in a rational way. The cost of being short up to $5 million—which is the amount of our line of credit—isn't worth discussing.

It would simply be the rate of interest we were then being charged on the line of credit—or, this year, 7 percent.

"But if we were short much more than $5 million, I have no idea what the cost would be. And it would depend entirely on the circumstances. If it weren't our fault, we probably would be able to borrow enough additional money to tide us over. But if it *were* our fault—that is if it were due to mismanagement—we probably would not be able to borrow enough. And conceivably, we might be forced into bankruptcy.

"The cost of that," Martin continued, "would be roughly the market value of our common stock—say, $65 million—on the assumption that if we did go bankrupt, our stockholders would lose everything." Martin glanced back at the figures shown in Tables 10.2 and 7.7.

"Your probabilities suggest", Martin said, "that there's a 1 percent chance that EBDIT might fall somewhere between minus $2 million and plus $3 million (midpoint = $500,000) —if we hit a severe depression combined with a machine tool recession. If EBDIT went as low as minus $2 million, we'd be perhaps $6 to $8 million short. We'd have to pay interest and amortization—about $4.3 million—and we might have to rebuild cash.

Martin continued, "But if the cost of being $6 to $8 million short were the market value of our common stock, then the *expected* cost would be $65 million $\times$ .01, or $650,000—because there's a 1 percent chance that we might find ourselves $6 to $8 million short. In other words, we'd be willing to pay an annual $650,000 'premium' for an 'insurance policy' which would cover the 'damage' if we found ourselves short by $6 to $8 million—and were, as a result, forced into bankruptcy. That's the way you want me to think about this problem, isn't it?"

"Yes," said Kelley.

"Well," Martin continued, "if we held $8 million in liquidity—instead of $15 million—the cost would be about $600,000. We'd hold $2 million in cash and invest $6 million—on which we'd pick up about 2 percent after taxes or about $120,000. But if we invested the $6 million in new working assets we'd pick up, say, 12 percent after taxes or about $720,000. The net cost therefore of holding $6 million in marketables would be $600,000 [= $720,000 − $120,000]. That's the way you'd argue, isn't it?"

"Right!" said Kelley.

"Well," Martin went on, "there are just a few things wrong with that:

"First, where would we find the additional 12 percent projects? And if we found them, would we be able to digest them? If we couldn't find them, our opportunity cost of holding $8 million of liquidity would be much less than $600,000. In fact, it might be zero."

"We could always buy back our own common stock," said Kelley, "or proportionate amounts of our stock, and the debt held by Fidelity. The return would be our cost of capital."

"All right," said Martin. "But, second, I don't really believe that if we found ourselves short by $8 million, we'd be unable to find the necessary funds somewhere—especially if we had maintained our efficiency and were simply the victims of circumstances—a depression or whatever. But, of course, I'm not sure. And so the fact of the matter is that I don't have the least idea what the cost of being short would be. And if I can't estimate the cost of being short, then I can't estimate the *expected* cost of being short.

"But there's one other point," said Martin. "And perhaps it's the main point. Suppose we could persuade the Finance Committee that the probability really was 1 percent that EBDIT would fall between minus $2 million and plus $3 million. What would they see? Would they see a simple actuarial problem? Hardly. They'd see, rather, a 1 percent probability that Butcher would be short $7 to $8 million which, to them, would be the same thing as 1 percent probability that Butcher would go bankrupt. And they'd want to protect themselves against that possibility at almost any cost. That means they would insist on holding $7 to $8 million in liquidity even if the opportunity cost were several million dollars a year.

"And why? For one simple reason—if we went bankrupt, our stockholders might lose everything they had invested in the company. And they would not be able to 'spin the wheel' again."

"Suppose the four statisticians," said Kelley to himself, "had bet their whole stake—$10,000—on one spin of the wheel—and had lost? The law of large numbers would have been unable to operate in their favor—because they would have been unable to go on playing."

Martin continued, "You own a house too, don't you?"

"Yes," said Kelley.

"What's it worth?"

"Oh, about $20,000."

"How much does your insurance on it cost a year?"

"About $100."

"All right. Suppose now that the fire insurance business in the United States suddenly became an unregulated monopoly. And suppose your agent called one day and raised your premium for the next year to $500. You know, of course, that $100 is more than the *actuarial* value of the premium—simply because the company had been making money [see Chapter 6]. What would you do?"

"I'd scream," said Kelley.

"But you'd pay."

"I'd pay."

"You'd pay because the house represents almost all your wealth. And, in fact, if you hadn't been able to buy insurance on the house, you wouldn't have bought it in the first place."

"That's right," said Kelley.

"All right," continued Martin. "Suppose now that the agent comes back the next year and raises the premium to $1,000—which would be more than ten times the actuarial value of the premium. You'd pay."

"I would," said Kelley. "But beyond some point, I'd sell the house—and move into a tent."

"What point?"

"I don't know," said Kelley. "But obviously, it would be well above the actuarial value of the premium."

"Well," said Martin, "you're sort of an old fogie too. In any case, the Finance Committee's attitude toward this business isn't very different from your attitude toward your house. They just don't choose to take any risk at all of total loss."

"You don't mean to suggest, do you," Kelley asked, "that every Finance Committee in every company would behave the same way?"

"Oh no," said Martin. "Some would view the risks differently. And some would be willing to take more risk than ours is willing to take. I'm sure there are lots of people who have most of their wealth invested in a house but carry no insurance. And there must be lots of others whose houses are not insured in full.

"And so, in my opinion," said Martin, "*how much total liquidity,* is partly a matter of judgment, partly a matter of how one views the risks and partly a matter of cost. We have to bear in mind that some of the people on our Finance Committee have lived through some very hard times. They're very sensitive to the possibility of going bankrupt.

"But, on the other hand, cost is obviously relevant. If they were made to see that, in fact, we are paying nearly $1 million for more than absolute safety—well, maybe we'd be able to persuade them that the probability of a severe depression is *not* 20 percent! I myself am now absolutely convinced—thanks to those probabilities of yours,"—Kelley made a mental note to pat himself on the back before he left for home—"I'm absolutely convinced that we *are* carrying much too much liquidity. Sam Morton's right. But there's one thing Sam Morton doesn't know."

"What's that?" asked Kelley.

"In order to get the old fogies on the Finance Committee to agree to let me borrow $36 million from Fidelity, I *had* to agree to maintain liquidity at $15 million. I felt then that $15 million was too much. But even if I'd been absolutely sure, I couldn't have done anything about it.

Getting permission to borrow $36 million at long-term was much more important than reducing liquidity by a few million dollars.

"But I do think now," said Martin, "that we ought to try to bring liquidity down to $10 million during the next two years. When you get time, write me a memo that I can pass on to the members of the Finance Committee."

"It'll be a pleasure," said Kelley. "When you say liquidity, do you include the line of credit?"

"Just cash and securities—for the time being," said Martin.

HOW MUCH CASH?

Kelley now turned to the problem of how much cash—that is, how should total liquidity be divided between demand deposits on the one hand, and securities on the other? He knew that Butcher held, and would continue to hold, about $2 million in cash—as demand deposits—in order to compensate its banks for services rendered. (The banks, in effect, compensated themselves by using Butcher's deposits to make loans to individuals and business.) But did this mean, Kelley wondered, that the whole balance, about $13 million, should be invested automatically in securities?

What was the problem? Kelley knew that *in principle* the problem was the same as the total liquidity problem. If he invested Butcher's portfolio in such a way that not enough cash was available on Tuesday to pay Tuesday's bills, he'd have to sell securities—on which he might take a capital loss. If the capital loss were larger than the interest he had earned on the securities, he would have lost money for Butcher.

Suppose that he had invested $500,000 in Treasury notes due to mature in sixty days—on the assumption that that sum would be needed then but not before then. The notes would yield about $4,000 in interest if held for sixty days. At the end of the tenth day, however, the cash forecast proves to be wrong and therefore Butcher has to sell the notes before maturity. But meanwhile, interest rates have shot up, and as a result, the notes—which cost $500,000—are now worth only $499,200. Butcher has earned about $700 in interest on the notes—but is, in total, $100 worse off (= $800 − $700). *The net loss would be Butcher's cost of being short of cash*—that is, if Butcher had not been caught short of cash, it would not have been forced to sell and would have had no capital loss. (Kelley couldn't avoid the capital loss by reducing his bank balance. If he reduced his bank balance, he'd have to build it back up immediately—and he could do so only by selling something.)

Now this cost (that is, the capital loss) could have been avoided by holding everything in cash. But if we held everything in cash we'd give up interest plus the possibility of a capital gain—if interest rates should, by some chance, go down. "And so, here again, Kelley said, "I'm weighing one cost against another—*the cost of being short against the cost of avoiding being short.* What do I do?"

Suppose we were *certain* that exactly sixty days from now, our net cash flow for the day would be minus $100,000. Cash from securities would have to be available to cover the deficit.

And suppose also that two investment alternatives are available: We could invest either in:

1. Treasury notes maturing in exactly sixty days and yielding 4 percent (per annum), or
2. Notes, selling at par, maturing in a year and yielding about 5 percent.

And suppose, finally, that we were certain that, between now and 60 days from now, interest rates:

1. Would be absolutely stable, or
2. Would go down, or
3. Would go up—but not enough to offset the additional interest we would earn on the long-term bonds.

In all three cases we would, of course, invest in the long-term bonds because, at worst, we'd be better off by doing so—obviously. But if we knew that interest rates would go up by *more* than enough to offset the additional interest we would earn on the long-term bonds, *we would buy the notes maturing in sixty days.*

"In short, if I could just predict *both* cash flows *and* the behavior of interest rates with certainty," Kelley said to himself, "I'd be able to handle this problem with one hand tied behind my back."

"But perhaps," he said, "I can use *expected values.* If I had probability distributions over net cash flow [NCF] by periods, and probability distributions over changes in interest rates between now and each future period—perhaps I could, somehow, rely on the law of large numbers. Perhaps, that is, I could behave *as if* I could predict with certainty both net cash flows and interest rates."

In order to be sure he knew what he was talking about, Kelley drew up the two hypothetical distributions shown in Tables 10.4 and 10.5. The first was over net cash flow (NCF) for September 1966. It showed a range from minus $40.0 thousand to minus $100.0 thousand.·The expected value of the distribution was minus $77 thousand. The second distribution was over the level of yields, two months hence—that is, as of September 15—on one-year Treasury notes. The expected value of this

TABLE 10.4

PROBABILITY DISTRIBUTION OVER NET CASH FLOW
SEPTEMBER 1966

EXPECTED NET CASH FLOW (thousands)	PROBABILITY	EXPECTED VALUE * (thousands)
(1)	(2)	(3)
$90.0 † — 100.0 †	.20	$19.0 †
80.0 † — 89.9 †	.30	25.5 †
70.0 † — 79.9 †	.20	15.0 †
60.0 † — 69.9 †	.15	9.75 †
50.0 † — 59.9 †	.10	5.5 †
40.0 † — 49.9 †	.05	2.25 †
	1.00	$77.00 †

* Midpoint of Expected Net Cash Flow. (NCF), multiplied by probability.
† All figures are negative.

TABLE 10.5

PROBABILITY DISTRIBUTION OVER YIELDS ON ONE-YEAR NOTES
AS OF SEPTEMBER 15, 1966

YIELD	PROBABILITY	EXPECTED VALUE *
(1)	(2)	(3)
4.65% — 4.75%	.10	.46%
4.76% — 4.85%	.20	.94%
4.86% — 4.95%	.50	2.45%
4.96% — 5.05% †	.125	.625%
5.06% — 5.15%	.05	.255%
5.16% — 5.25%	.025	.130%
	1.00	4.860%

* Midpoint of class interval over yield.
† Present level of yields on 90 day bills.

distribution was 4.86 percent. The distribution indicated a probability of .075 that yields would rise between the present date and September 15.

This meant, of course, that if Butcher held one-year notes on September 15 and was forced on that date to sell some in order to pay its bills, the chances were 7.5 out of 100 it would suffer a capital loss.

"All right," said Kelley, "now what do I do with these two distributions? How do I use them?

"First, I look at the NCF distribution and I see that the chances are 100 out of 100 [= 1.00] that I'll be short in September—if I hold no excess cash. Then I look at the second distribution and I see that if I *am* short, the chances are 7.5 out of 100 that I'll suffer a capital loss. The two events—being short and suffering a capital loss—are independent and compound. Therefore, the probability of suffering a capital loss *is the product of the two separate probabilities or .075 [= 1.00 × .075].*

"But," said Kelley, "I can't decide what to do unless I know the expected value of the loss. I'll have to convert the table [Table 10.5] into a profit and loss table." He thereupon jotted down the figures—all hypothetical—shown in Table 10.6. Kelley was primarily concerned, at this

TABLE 10.6

PROBABILITY DISTRIBUTION ON PAYOFF IF FORCED TO SELL NOTES ON SEPTEMBER 15

YIELD	PAYOFF *	PROBABILITY	EXPECTED VALUE ‡
(1)	(2)	(3)	(4)
4.65% — 4.75%	+ 1.5%	.10	+.15%
4.76% — 4.85%	+ 1.0%	.20	+.20%
4.86% — 4.95%	+ 0.5%	.50	+.25%
4.96% — 5.05% †	—	.125	—
5.06% — 5.15%	− 0.3%	.05	−.015%
5.16% — 5.25%	− 0.8%	.025	−.02%
		1.000	+.565%

* Capital loss or gain adjusted for interest earned.
† Present level of yields on 90 day bills.
‡ Payoff multiplied by probability.

moment, about *how to use* the distributions—if he had them. He'd worry about their accuracy later on.

The Yield and Probability columns were simply taken from Columns (1) and (2) of Table 10.5. Payoff was simply a very rough estimate of the loss Butcher would suffer ("−") or the gain it would earn ("+") if yields on notes on September 15 were as indicated. If the yield on notes on September 15 was approximately 4.70 percent—as compared with 4.96 at present—the price of bills would have *risen* and Butcher would have earned a capital *gain* of, say, 1.2 percent which, plus interest earned for (about) sixty days, would give Butcher a total profit of 1.5 percent. On the other hand, if yields went *up,* Butcher would suffer a capital *loss*—from which interest earned would be subtracted. Because of interest earned, the gain, if a gain occurred, would be *larger* than the *capital* gain. And the loss, if a loss occurred, would be *less* than the capital loss.

Kelley then multiplied Payoff by Probability, and found that the expected gain was .565 percentage points—a bit more than one half of 1 percent.

"Now," said Kelley, "what does this mean? It means that there is a positive probability [= .075] of incurring a *short cost.* I can protect myself against the possibility of incurring that cost by holding $100,000 in cash—for this other table [Table 10.4] tells me that the chances are zero that I will need more than that. But if I hold that much cash, I sacrifice interest and the substantial probability [= .925] of a capital gain. And on balance, Table 10.6 is telling me that if I draw repeatedly from the distribution given in that table, I'll be more than one half a percentage point better off in the long run."

Let's be perfectly clear now on what Kelley had done (and on *why* he had done it):

First, (Table 10.4) he had drawn up a probability distribution over NCF for the month of September. All the possibilities were negative (column 1) and the expected value, $77,000, was negative. Thus, if Butcher made a large number of draws from this distribution, the mean of all those draws would be approximately—$77,000.

All right, you say. If that's the case, what Kelley should do is make sure that securities worth $77,000 mature on or about September 15. Sometimes he'd have too much maturing and sometimes too little but on the average $77,000 would be about right.

Would Kelley agree to this? Certainly not! He'd say: "No, no, no! Suppose I'm certain that interest rates will not go *up.* If I am, then I know that if I do have to sell, I will earn at least the yield I expected to earn. In other words, if I'm certain that interest rates will *not* go up, then I can't go wrong by investing *all* my excess cash in the highest yielding securities I can find, regardless of whether I expect NCF to be positive or negative."

That's why Kelley drew up Tables 10.5 and 10.6—to see what the expected value of his gain or loss would be if he bought notes now (that is, in mid-July) and sold them on or about September 15. The tables told him two things: First (Table 10.5) that the range of possibilities (column 1) and the subjective probabilities (column 2) he had used indicated that the expected value of the yield, 60 days hence, on notes was 4.86 percent, or 10 basis points *less* than the present yield, which was 4.96 percent.

Kelley then, in effect, translated the decline in expected *yield* into an expected *gain*. (Table 10.6) If the expected yield, as of September 15, had been *higher* than the present yield, the figure at the bottom of the last column of Table 10.6 would have been negative instead of positive.

"Okay," said Kelley to himself, "where am I?"

First, in a situation such as that represented by Table 10.6, I have no problem. I have no problem because the expected short cost is not a cost at all. It's a *profit*. And therefore everything goes into securities. Over a reasonably large number of such decisions, I can't go wrong.

But, now what do I do if, for example:

1. The expected value of NCF is positive—but not all possibilities are positive *and* the expected value of the payoff, if I'm forced to sell securities, is negative or
2. The expected value of NCF is *negative*—but not all possibilities are negative and the expected value of the payoff, if I'm forced to sell is negative.

Kelley thought about these two problems for a day or so (off and on!) and then finally saw the light. *In every case, he would have to compare the expected cost of holding cash with the expected cost of holding securities—given probability distributions over NCF and interest rates. And he would choose that course of action which involved the least cost.* Kelley suddenly realized that he had done exactly that in the first illustration (Tables 10.4 through 10.6). And if he had wished to do so he could have compared the two alternatives—holding cash and holding securities by drawing up payoff tables as in Table 10.7. The comparison in that table indicates that given the information in Tables 10.5 and 10.6, the expected pay-off of holding cash—in order to avoid the cost of being short—is zero. This simply reflects the fact that demand deposits do not earn interest. On the other hand, the expected pay-off of holding securities is positive, +.565 percent. Holding securities is obviously the superior strategy—given the facts set forth in Tables 10. 5 and 10.6.

Kelley now drew up Table 10.8 on the following assumptions:

1. Probability of running short of cash = .25
2. Expected pay-off on investing in notes = −.05 percent
3. Interest to be earned by investing for 30 days in notes = .004 percent.

After examining Table 10.8 carefully, Kelley realized that the outcome depended entirely on the size of the numbers he had chosen—that is, on the size of the payoffs and on the probability of being short. In order to make this point clear to himself, he drew up Table 10.9 on the following assumptions:

TABLE 10.7

COMPARISON OF ALTERNATIVE STRATEGIES

EVENT: EXPECTED NET CASH FLOW (1)	PROBABILITY (2)	EXPECTED PAYOFF IF EVENT OCCURS (3)	EXPECTED VALUE OF PAYOFF (4)
		Hold Cash	
—	1.00	0%	0%
+	0.00	0%	0%
	1.00		0%
		Hold Securities	
—	1.00	+.565%	+.565%
+	0.00	+.004% *	0%
	1.00		+.565%

* Assumes interest earned for one month and no subsequent capital loss.

TABLE 10.8

SECOND COMPARISON OF ALTERNATIVE STRATEGIES

EVENT: EXPECTED NET CASH FLOW (1)	PROBABILITY (2)	EXPECTED PAYOFF IF EVENT OCCURS (3)	EXPECTED VALUE OF PAYOFF (4)
		Hold Cash	
—	.25	0 *	0%
+	.75	0%	0%
	1.00		0%
		Hold Securities	
—	.25	—.05% †	—.0125%
+	.75	+.004	+.0030%
	1.00		—.0095%

* By holding cash, avoids expected short cost, but earns nothing.
† By holding securities and being forced to sell, incurs short cost.

TABLE 10.9

THIRD COMPARISON OF ALTERNATIVE STRATEGIES

Hold Cash

EVENT: EXPECTED NET CASH FLOW	PROBABILITY	EXPECTED PAYOFF IF EVENT OCCURS	EXPECTED VALUE OF PAYOFF
(1)	(2)	(3)	(4)
—	.025	0%	0%
+	.975	0%	0%
	1.000		0%

Hold Securities

—	.025	—.06	—.0015
+	.975	+.0045	+.0044
	1.000		+.0029

1. Probability of running short of cash = .025
2. Expected payoff on investing in notes = —.06 percent
3. Interest to be earned by investing for 30 days in notes = .0045 percent.

On these assumptions, clearly, the correct strategy would be to buy securities, as Table 10.9 indicates, instead of holding cash, as in Table 10.8.

"Okay" said Kelley, "sounds fine in principle, but how do I make it operational?"

First, I forecast the expected yield on one-year notes, monthly, twelve months ahead. I revise every month. I convert each expected yield into an expected gain or loss. (I'll have to learn something about the behavior of interest rates, he found himself thinking. I really should have taken a good money markets course, he added a bit regretfully. But maybe Sidney Homer would be willing to give me some advice. He brightened up at that idea and made a note on his desk calendar: "Call Sidney Homer".)

Second, I get probability distributions over NCF.

Third, I calculate for each month, twelve months ahead, the expected value of each strategy—holding cash or holding securities.

Fourth, I invest my $13 million.

Fifth, as I go along, I iron out the bugs—of which there will surely be plenty. But nothing ventured, nothing gained. And I don't see how this system can produce a worse result than the system Martin is now using.

What I need now, he said, are some probability distributions.

Kelley spent the next two hours with Jamerson, Butcher's controller. They went over several reams of cash forecasts—Jamerson had them daily for the next sixty days, weekly for the next twenty-six weeks and monthly for the next twelve months. A new forecast was done every day sixty days ahead, every week twenty-six weeks ahead, and every month, twelve months ahead. Jamerson had them for each division and, consolidated, for the company as a whole. None were on a probability basis.

"Which do you want?" asked Jamerson.

"I'll take a small one to start with," said Kelley. "Let me have the monthly forecasts—and the results if possible—for the last six years—as of January 1, for the Plastics Division. I just want to try out some ideas."

"Right," said Jamerson. He gave Kelley tables—two each for each of the years 1960-1965—twelve forecasts and actual results. The forecast as of January 1965 is shown in Table 10.10.

Kelley took the tables back to his office and studied them. He realized immediately (or almost immediately) that only a few of the inflows and outflows were subject to probability distributions. He drew up the following list:

Cash Flows Subject to Probability Distributions:

  Collections from customers
  Payments to suppliers
  Manufacturing payroll
  Freight payments
  Miscellaneous cash expenses

Cash Flows *Not* Subject to Probability Distributions:

  Salary payroll
  Rent payments
  Dividend payments
  Capital equipment expenditures
  Payments to profit sharing fund
  Income tax payments
  Dividends and bond interest revenue

Those flows listed as *not* subject to probability distributions were known with virtual certainty—at least several months in advance. This meant that he could concentrate his attention on the five flows which *were* subject to random variation—that is, to probability distributions.

A hundred questions crowded into his head: should he try to draw

TABLE 10.10

PLASTICS DIVISION
CASH FORECASTS FOR 1965
AS OF JANUARY 1, 1965
(IN THOUSANDS)

	JANUARY	FEBRUARY	MARCH	APRIL	MAY	JUNE	JULY	AUGUST	SEPTEMBER	OCTOBER	NOVEMBER	DECEMBER
CASH RECEIPTS:												
Collection from customers	168.7	151.4	155.3	160.5	185.3	171.5	187.5	216.4	199.7	199.8	235.8	203.9
Dividends and interest											0.1	0.8
TOTAL	168.7	151.4	155.3	160.5	185.3	171.5	187.5	216.4	199.7	199.8	235.9	204.7
CASH DISBURSEMENTS:												
Payments to suppliers	50.9	98.5	95.3	162.4	149.0	133.8	74.9	69.9	129.7	148.5	200.9	135.8
Manufacturing labor	19.9	25.1	19.7	21.9	28.2	25.8	26.1	31.4	25.6	33.4	23.1	25.7
Freight payments	4.6	4.7	5.7	6.2	5.4	6.3	7.8	8.1	5.7	6.7	6.1	6.3
Miscellaneous cash expenses	13.1	8.9	21.7	12.4	18.3	13.4	20.1	11.7	16.6	20.8	22.3	18.5
Rent	0.5	0.5	0.5	0.5	0.5	0.5	0.5	0.5	0.5	0.5	0.5	0.5
Administration salaries	5.6	5.6	5.6	5.6	6.1	6.1	5.9	5.7	5.7	5.7	5.7	7.4
Purchase of equipment		0.4	6.2	1.4	1.2	1.2	2.0	0.7	1.2	1.3	2.6	10.9
Payments to profit sharing fund	31.3	28.2										
Income tax payments				6.0	27.0						30.0	
TOTAL	125.9	171.9	154.7	216.4	235.7	187.1	137.3	128.0	185.0	216.9	291.2	205.1
Net cash flow in (out)	42.8	(20.5)	0.6	(55.9)	(50.4)	(15.6)	50.2	88.4	14.7	(17.1)	(55.3)	(0.4)

* Disbursements in excess of receipts.

up distributions separately for *each* cash flow or should he work with totals? What period should he use—days, weeks, or months? Should the data be adjusted for seasonal variation? And so forth. He decided he'd better talk the problem over with Butcher's computer chief, a Ph.D. in statistics and operations research.

Kelley explained what he had in mind to the computer chief. He showed him Tables 10.4, 10.5, 10.6 and 10.7. He said that he would worry about the probability distributions over interest rates if he, the computer chief, would worry about the probability distributions over NCF.

The computer chief, after asking a few questions, said, "Kelley, you really must be out of your mind. What you've described is a huge, unmanagable job. It's probably a full time job for one person and a clerk. You can't possibly do it yourself."

Kelley said, "Do you realize that we have a securities portfolio of $13 million—on which we're now earning about 3 percent before taxes? We should be earning close to 6 percent. Our yield is so low because we've taken too many large, unexpected capital losses. Anyway, if we can improve our yield by one percentage point—just one percentage point— our additional gross would be $130,000. That would more than pay for one portfolio manager and one clerk."

"Hadn't thought about it that way," said the computer chief. "But what's Martin likely to say about all these subjective probability distributions?"

"Oh, I think by this time he realizes that nothing's perfect, but that some information's better than none. In fact, I think that's what he'd say: 'Nothing's perfect, but some information is better than none!' "

The computer chief then said, "We could certainly write a program which would turn the actual figures into probability distributions. In principle, we would remove all the variation in the figures due to assignable causes—to growth, to cyclical fluctuation and to seasonal fluctuation. We would try to remove irregular fluctuations in process of removing the seasonal fluctuations. Irregular fluctuations are fluctuations, up or down, due to such things as strikes, which, for example may affect shipments, sales and, subsequently, collections of accounts receivable.

"I won't bore you with the technical details. Worrying about the technical details is our problem—not yours. But if we were lucky, we'd be left with nothing but random fluctuations—that is, with a probability distribution over net cash flow for each week or month—or whatever period we had used. It would look *very much* like your table [Table 10.4].

"But the process of obtaining a set of distributions for every division this way would take time and it would be expensive. And, frankly, I doubt that I'd have a programmer available to work on it for perhaps two months. And I couldn't spend that much money on such a project without approval from Martin.

"But I'll tell you what I'll do. I'll do the Plastics Division for you now—on one condition."

"What condition?" asked Kelley.

"That you conduct an experiment. After I give you the distribution you would invest, *on paper*, two ways—the way they do now and your way. Do it for six months. At the end of that time you'll be able to compare the results. Then we'll see. If your system does better, we'll persuade Martin to let us do NCF distributions for each division—and for the company as a whole."

"Done!" said Kelley. "How long will it take to get the distributions for the Plastics Division?"

"A week," said the computer chief.

"I can't wait," said Kelley. And he left.

CONCLUSION

This chapter made the following points:

(1) The amount of *total liquidity* a company will hold will be determined, at bottom by the relative weights assigned by management to risk and return. If a management is unduly sensitive to risk and unwilling therefore to run any risk whatever of bankruptcy, it will probably hold more liquidity than it really needs—and its return, of course, will suffer. And vice versa—if a management is too ready to sacrifice safety to return it may run too much risk of being unable to meet its obligations.

(2) The decision as to how total liquidity should be divided between cash and marketable securities depends on two variables—the probability of being short of cash and the expected cost of being short. As we have seen, the expected cost of being short of cash will depend almost solely on the expected behavior of interest rates.

PROBLEMS

1. *How much total liquidity do you have? Is this amount more or less then you had, on the average, last year? If the total has gone up or down significantly, could you—if asked to do so—explain why?*

2. *Presumably, you get an allowance from someone, or a stipend, to*

enable you to pay your bills while you are in college. Or perhaps you are working part time.

What do you do with your money when you receive it—put it into a checking account? In a savings account? Hold it in cash? If you hold it in cash or put in into a checking account, what annual sacrifice are you making by doing so?

3. *Go back to Chapter 9. You are Barclay. You are trying to decide, in a rational way, how to divide your $442,000 (Table 9.1) between real assets and liquidity. You must assume that, for the time being, you would have no short-term borrowing power and, also, that $442,000 is the total amount of money you would be able to raise. Obviously, you have very little information on which to base a decision—but you must make a decision nevertheless. You would, of course, be free to seek information if you wished. What kind of information would you seek and from whom?*

4. *As Barclay, how would you estimate the cost of being short of liquidity?*

5. *How would you estimate the cost of holding whatever amount of liquidity you choose to hold?*

6. *You read the following summary (in Solomon Brothers weekly letter) of the week's developments in the money markets:*

    > *Week Ending September 25, 1970*
    > *Most departments of the bond market rallied early this week following the prime rate reduction from 8 to 7½ percent. As the week progressed, however, prices eased off, but in most sectors not enough to offset the earlier gains. On balance, Government bond prices, both intermediate and long, rose about three-eighth of a point, on the week. The three month Treasury bill rate declined dramatically by as much as 40 basis points to below 5.70 percent, the lowest level in two years. Most other money market rates also showed marked declines. Federal fund rates declined further, averaging about 5.90 percent, the lowest level since late 1968. Euro-dollar rates however, were about unchanged.*
    > *Corporate bond prices advanced and then eased. It became apparent that aggressive bidding on the week's new issues was meeting investor resistance. The largest price improvement was in the seasoned issue; deep and medium discount issues rose over a point. The large corporate calendar next week will continue to offer a wide variety of issues. The October calendar now totals $1.7 billion.*
    > *Municipal bond prices also advanced at first and then declined. Prices generally closed unchanged on the week. Next week's calendar will be moderate and the calendar for all*

of October is presently estimated at a little over $1 billion. Answer the following questions:

(a) What is meant by the phrase "the bond market rallied"?

(b) When yields on bonds go down, what happens to bond prices?

(c) What do you suppose is meant by the term (2nd paragraph) "basis points"?

(d) You are asked what you think the chances are that yields on 90 day bills will go down next week. What's your answer? Why?

7. You are Kelley's assistant. He has hired you to manage Butcher's portfolio of securities. On September 15 he hands you Table 10.11

TABLE 10.11

PROBABILITY DISTRIBUTION OVER GAINS AND LOSSES ON ONE-YEAR NOTES AS OF OCTOBER 15, 1966

YIELD	PAYOFF *	PROBABILITY	EXPECTED VALUE ‡
(1)	(2)	(3)	(4)
4.95% — 5.05%	+ 0.004%	.50	.0020%
5.06% — 5.15%	— 0.3%	.20	—.0600%
5.16% — 5.25%	— 0.8%	.15	—.1200%
5.26% — 5.35%	— 1.3%	.125	—.1625%
5.36% — 5.45%	— 1.8%	.02	—.0360%
5.46% — 5.55%	— 2.3%	.005	—.0115%
		1.000	—.3920%

* Capital loss or gain adjusted for interest earned.
† Approximate present level of yields on 90 day bills.
‡ Payoff multiplied by probability.

which represents his latest prediction of the yields, on October 15, on notes due to mature one year thereafter. What do you do if the probability of being short of cash in October is .25? .18? .01? 0? Assume that the interest to be earned for 30 days by investing in notes is 0.0042 percent.

8. Suppose you were asked to estimate a rate of return on investing x number of dollars in total liquidity. Assume, for the purposes of this problem, that you would hold the entire amount in cash. How would you go about trying to put the benefits into dollar terms?

**APPENDIX
10.A**

SHORT-TERM INVESTMENTS [1]

**Direct Obligations
of the United States Treasury**

UNITED STATES TREASURY BILLS

Treasury bills are issued on a discount basis in bearer form only and are paid at the face amount at maturity.

At the present time two new issues of bills are sold each week at competitive bidding; one is due in 91 days, the other in 182 days. In addition to those weekly series of bills, the Treasury issues nine month and one-year bills at monthly intervals. The holders of maturing series of bills have not been given any privilege of exchange.

Treasury bills are traded in the open market on a discount basis from par. The bid and offer quotations and all transactions are at a yield to maturity on a bank discount basis. The smallest par value denomination available is $1,000.

UNITED STATES TREASURY
CERTIFICATES OF INDEBTEDNESS

Certificates of indebtedness are issued only in bearer form with an original maturity at date of issue not exceeding one year. In recent years, however, the Treasury has relied mainly on the issuance of bills to raise short-term funds, and has only infrequently offered certificates.

UNITED STATES TREASURY NOTES AND BONDS

Treasury notes are offered with original maturities of from one to seven years—United States Treasury bonds generally with maturities of over seven years. Through the passage of time, these issues come into the category of short-term investments and as such are of interest to the short-term investor.

---

[1] Excerpted by permission from *Short-Term Investments*, seventh ed. New York: Solomon Brothers, 1969.

Treasury notes and bonds are available in coupon or registered form. The smallest denomination available in Treasury notes is $1,000, in bonds $500.

UNITED STATES TREASURY TAX ANTICIPATION SECURITIES

In recent years the United States Treasury has raised cash during the period when its tax receipts are not sufficient to cover current expenditures through the issuance of tax anticipation securities— both bills and very inferquently certificates.

FEDERAL INTERMEDIATE CREDIT BANKS

The twelve Federal Intermediate Credit Banks were organized by act of Congress in 1923 and operate under supervision of the Farm Credit Administration. They were established to provide a permanent and dependable source of funds for certain types of institutions that make loans to farmers and stockmen.

These Banks finance their lending operations principally through the public sale of consolidated collateral trust debentures usually issued in bearer form only for a term of nine months or less, although they are permitted under present law to issue obligations with maturities up to five years. The smallest denomination available is $5,000.

FEDERAL HOME LOAN BANKS

The eleven Federal Home Loan Banks were created in 1932 by act of Congress and operate under the supervision of the Federal Home Loan Bank Board. They were established to provide a central credit agency for approved thrift and home financing institutions such as savings and loan associations, savings banks, insurance companies, and other like organizations that qualify for membership.

The Federal Home Loan Banks generally finance their lending operations through the sale of consolidated notes with maturities of a year or less, although longer issues have from time to time been issued. The notes are not subject to redemption prior to maturity. They are issued in bearer form in minimum denominations of $5,000.

FEDERAL LAND BANKS

The twelve Federal Land Banks were organized pursuant to the Federal Farm Loan Act of 1916 and operate under the supervision of the Farm Credit Administration. They were established primarily to provide long-term farm mortgage loans at reasonable rates of interest. All loans made by the Banks are made through and with the endorsement of Federal Land Bank Associations which were created by the same legislation.

The Banks finance their lending operations largely through the sale to the public of consolidated Federal Farm Loan bonds supplemented by some borrowings from commercial banks. Maturities of these bonds vary from a few months to about 10 years. They are issued in coupon or registered form in minimum denomination of $1,000 (a few issues are available in $100 sizes). They can be called, in whole or in part upon prescribed notice, on any interest date beginning with optional retirement date (if specified).

FEDERAL NATIONAL MORTGAGE ASSOCIATION

The Federal National Mortgage Association, familiarly known as "Fannie Mae," was organized by act of Congress in 1938, rechartered in 1954, and restructured in 1968. The function of the new FNMA is to provide a greater degree of liquidity to the mortgage market by purchasing and selling mortgages. To accomplish this task, it may issue its own obligations and also issue securities backed by pools of FHA and VA mortgages which are to be guaranteed by the Government National Mortgage Association.

FNMA is authorized to issue, upon approval of the Secretary of the Treasury, and have outstanding at any time, obligations having a wide range of maturities from short-term notes to long-dated bond issues.

The obligations of FNMA are not guaranteed by the United States and do not constitute a debt or obligation of the United States or any of its agencies.

Minimum denominations on FNMA debentures range from $1,000 to $5,000 to $10,000 depending on the issue. They are issued in bearer form only and cannot be called for redemption prior to maturity.

FNMA discount notes are issued with maturities of from 30 to 270 days, in amounts ranging from $5,000 to $1,000,000 with a minimum $50,000 purchase.

BANKS FOR COOPERATIVES

The twelve district Banks for Cooperatives and the Central Bank for Cooperatives were organized pursuant to the Farm Credit Act of 1933 to provide credit on a sound business basis to eligible farmers' cooperatives to assist them in the effective merchandising of agricultural products, in meeting their needs for operating capital, and in constructing or acquiring physical facilities essential to their operations.

The Banks for Cooperatives finance their lending operations principally through the public sale of consolidated collateral trust debentures which generally have a six month maturity. The debentures are issued in bearer form only in minimum denominations of $5,000.

EXPORT—IMPORT BANK

The Export-Import Bank of the United States (popularly known as Eximbank), was founded in 1934 and is a wholly-owned corporate agency of the United States Government. Its function is to assist in the financing of foreign trade of the United States. The Bank makes loans directly to overseas buyers of American goods and services, by guaranteeing and issuing short and medium-term export transactions, and by discounting export debt obligations held by commercial banks.

To enable the Bank to conduct these operations, the Bank is authorized to borrow and to issue and sell promissory notes and other debt obligations. It issues short-term discount notes ranging from 30 to 360 days in maturity depending on period selected by investor and agreed to by the Bank, in the form of promissory notes payable to bearer. The notes are available to investors in multiples of $5,000 each with a minimum purchase of $100,000 required.

TENNESSEE VALLEY AUTHORITY

The Tennessee Valley Authority (TVA), a wholly—owned corporate agency and instrumentality of the United States, has from time to time since 1963, issued short term notes (frequently referred to as "Power Notes") to provide capital for its power programs. The notes are offered through auctions to certain banks and dealers.

The notes are issued in bearer form, on a discount basis in denominations of $5,000, $10,000, $100,000 and $1,000,000 usually with, but not necessarily restricted to, a maturity of about four months.

Other Short-Term Investments

COMMERCIAL PAPER

"Commercial paper" is the trade name for the unsecured promissory notes usually issued at a discount from par by businesses to finance short-term cash requirements. At one time industrial firms were the primary issuers of this paper, but in recent years its use has spread to utility, transportation and one bank holding companies. It is usually sold through dealers. A similar form of note is sold by sales finance companies. This is referred to as "finance paper" and is usually sold directly to the investor by the issuer.

Paper is issued, with maturities of from 5 to no longer than 270 days with the exact maturity date usually tailored to fit the needs of the purchaser. The rate of discount is determined by the length of time for which the note has been written, as well as the general level of short-term interest rates and the credit standing of the issuer.

DEPARTMENT OF HOUSING AND URBAN DEVELOPMENT PROJECT NOTES

Project Notes issued by the Department of Housing and Urban Development are advantageous for the investment of short-term funds held by taxable investors. The Department of Housing and Urban Development, an executive agency of the United States Government, administers a broad range of programs to provide financial assistance to cities and local public agencies. Among these programs are the urban renewal program—including a variation known as the neighborhood development program—and the public housing program. These three programs involve Federal grant payments but also employ borrowed capital which is for the most part raised in the private money market.

Project Notes are issued in bearer form and interest is paid at maturity. Initial maturities range from sixty days to one year. Denominations for individual notes are specified at the time of bid opening by the initial holder of the note. Once notes are issued, denominations cannot be changed. The following denominations are normally specified: $1,000; $5,000; $10,000; $25,000; $50,000 and $100,000.

BANKERS' ACCEPTANCES

A banker's acceptance is a bill of exchange (frequently called a time draft) drawn on and accepted by a banking institution. In this manner the bank guarantees the payment of the accepted bill at maturity and enables its customer, who pays a commission to the accepting bank for this accommodation, to secure financing readily and at a reasonable interest cost. Bankers' acceptances are used to finance the movement or storage of merchandise, principally commodities, and to finance dollar exchange transactions. Acceptances usually have maturities of 30, 60 or 90 days although longer maturities—120 and 180 days—are frequently available.

CERTIFICATES OF DEPOSIT

In early 1961 several of the major money center banks initiated issuance of negotiable certificates of time deposit. These certificates, generally issued in sizeable amounts and with maturities chosen by the investor of from 30 days to one year, evidence deposits of specified sums with the bank. Such deposits may not be withdrawn prior to the stated maturity date, at which time interest at the rate originally agreed upon is paid. The rate of interest paid on such deposits is limited by regulations of the Federal Reserve Board. Since the deposit is not subject to withdrawal prior to maturity, the investor must dispose of the certificae if funds are required at an earlier date. A sizeable secondary market does exist.

These certificates of deposit represent short term private paper with a maximum degree of safety. They are quoted on a bond yield equivalent basis. Negotiable CDs do not come in denominations of less than $100,000.

REPURCHASE AGREEMENTS

The term "repurchase agreement" is used to identify an investment transaction that permits the employment of temporary funds for a period of time exactly suited to an investor's money requirements, and which assures him of a specific rate of return while eliminating any risk of loss to him resulting from a fluctuation in the market price of the securities involved. Such repurchase agreements can be arranged to mature on a definite date or to terminate on one day's or longer notice given by either the investor or the dealer.

The mechanics of this type of transaction are: (1) the purchase by an investor of specified securities which are delivered to him or his designated depository against payment, and (2) the simultaneous sale of the securities back to the dealer, with delivery and payment to be made on the future date on which the investor will require the funds. After arranging the transaction, the investor will receive two of the customary confirmation tickets, one covering the purchase, the other covering the repurchase of the securities by the dealer. The confirmation ticket on the repurchase will show the sale price, the delivery date (if a definite one has been agreed upon) and the rate of return which the investor will receive on his funds. In addition to holding the securities as collateral, the investor, as further protection, holds the repurchase contract (confirmation ticket) of the security dealer.

Repurchase agreements are secured by United States Treasury issues, Federal agency issues, certificates of deposit or commercial paper.

INVESTING IN ACCOUNTS RECEIVABLE

In Chapter 1, you will surely recall, Butcher's marketing vice president had sent Martin a memo requesting permission to sell hand tools to 132 new customers known to be slow payers. Martin had passed this memo on to the controller—who in turn had passed it on to Kelley. When Kelley got the memo, a note was attached which read as follows: "Didn't I hear you say, a week or so ago, that you had some ideas on how this sort of thing should be handled???" The memo and the note were now lying in the middle of Kelley's desk and he was glaring at them hostilely. "Ideas?" he said to himself. "What ideas?"

Two other memos were also lying on Kelley's desk. One was from the controller to Martin recommending that the order from A. W. Page be turned down—with just the brief comment: "I think this is too risky." The order, you will recall, was for $50,000 worth of hand tools which would soon be obsolete. Martin had scribbled a note to Kelley across the top of the controller's memo: "I hate to turn this down. What do you think?" Kelley said to himself: "Ugh. He wants to take the order—but he wants to be able to blame me if Page goes bankrupt."

The last memo was from the manager of the machine tool division to Martin. It recommended that in a limited number of cases the division be allowed to sell machine tools on an installment basis. The memo simply pointed out that because money was so tight and interest rates so high, some of the division's smaller customers could not finance the purchase of Butcher's more expensive machine tools, which sold for as much as $40,000. The manager of the machine tools division thought— but he wasn't sure—that forty or fifty customers would buy something more than $1.2 million worth of tools (in total) if an installment plan were available. Martin wanted Kelley's reaction to this idea.

Suppose, now, that you were Kelley. How would you resolve these three problems? Would you recommend that marketing be allowed to sell hand tools to 132 small store keepers—any of whom might go bankrupt tomorrow? Would you sell $50,000 worth of obsolete tools to A. W. Page Company—who might be bankrupt now? And would you invest $1.2 million in installment loans in order to sell forty expensive machine tools—each of which would be custom built to the specifications of each individual buyer?

If Kelley says "yes" to any or all of these proposals, *he will, in effect, have recommended that Butcher invest a large amount of additional money in accounts receivable.*

DECIDING HOW MUCH TO INVEST

What are accounts receivable? And why does the amount carried on Butcher's balance sheet as "accounts receivable" represent an investment?

As we saw in Chapter 9, most business firms, both those who sell at retail and those who sell to other business firms, sell "on credit." Very few individuals and very few companies these days are unable to say "charge it" to their respective suppliers. And everytime a supplier agrees to allow you to charge it, he has made an investment in you, a risky investment perhaps, but an investment nevertheless.

Why is this so? When Butcher's hand tools division uses cash to pay for raw materials and labor, it is, in effect, turning cash into finished tools. It is, in other words, changing the form of its investment—and the appearance of its balance sheet. Its cash balance is now somewhat less and its inventory of finished goods somewhat larger. And correspondingly, when it sells finished tools on credit to 132 small hardware stores scattered through the Midwest, Butcher's investment in finished tools is being converted into something else—into promises on the part of those hardware stores to pay for the tools they have bought. These promises are carried on Butcher's balance sheet as *accounts receivable*.

If Butcher does, in fact, sell $850,000 worth of tools to these proposed new customers, its accounts receivable will have increased by that amount—that is, by $850,000. But this is *not* (repeat *not*) the amount which Butcher would, in fact, have invested in those receivables. It is *not* the amount Butcher would have invested in those receivables *because $850,000 is the sum of both the amount invested in those receivables and the dollar return on those receivables.* If all 132 customers pay their accounts in full, Butcher will receive $850,000 at most. This sum must, therefore, include *both* the amount invested *and* a dollar return.

Investing in receivables is very much like investing in a single-payment bond (see Table 3.2). When you invest in such a bond you invest a lump sum now in return for a larger lump sum to be received later on. The larger lump sum to be received later on includes the amount you invested *plus* a dollar return. Table 3.2 shows that for the $100 you invest now you will receive $160 in ten years.

Correspondingly, when a company invests in receivables, it invests a lump sum now in the expectation of receiving back a larger lump sum later on. We know that if Butcher sold to all 132 proposed new accounts, it would expect to receive back $850,000. But how much would Butcher have invested in those accounts?

It would have invested one or the other of the following two amounts —or something in between:

1. $680,000—which is the amount by which the inventory of finished tools would have decreased.
2. $582,000—which happens to be the *direct* cost of the materials and labor which would be used to manufacture the tools.

Which amount is correct?

This is the kind of question that makes strong men quake and turn green. But unhappily it cannot be avoided. It cannot be avoided because without the answer we would be unable to calculate a rate of return on the proposed investment in accounts receivable. In other words, if we do not know the *amount* of the investment, we can hardly calculate a rate of return on that investment.

incrementals

What does the answer depend on? Let's go back to the investment your roommate made in you when he loaned you $100. He had reached into his cavernous wallet (which tended to make him list to the west—like the Tower of Pisa) and had extracted a sheaf of ten-dollar bills. He had counted out ten of them and given them to you in return for a note and a chattel mortgage on your car. The note you signed and the chattel mortgage were, of course, *printed*—on good bond paper—and each had cost your roommate about ten cents. In addition, both the note and the mortgage had been prepared by a lawyer—who had charged your roommate a fee of $50. Now then, how much did your roommate invest in you when he gave you the ten ten-dollar bills? Did he invest just the ten ten-dollar bills? Or did he invest also the cost (twenty cents) of the two notes you had signed? Or did he invest also an allocated portion of the lawyer's fifty dollar fee? Which?

This question brings us face-to-face with a word we will meet often in the subsequent pages of this book. That word is *incremental*. We will often find ourselves using the expressions "incremental investment" and "incremental operating savings." What does the word *incremental* mean? It means plainly and simply "additional." And when we say "incremental investment," we mean merely "additional investment." Now your roommate's incremental investment in you was $100—*not* $100.20 and *not* $100.20 plus an allocated portion of the lawyer's fee. This is clear enough—simply because he had paid for the note and the mortgage forms and the lawyer's advice long before you walked into his loan office. To repeat—his *incremental* investment in you was $100—not a penny more or less. And he calculated his expected return by comparing the additional dollars he would receive—as a direct result of investing in the loan to you—with the amount of that investment. His expected rate of return was therefore an *incremental* rate calculated on his *incremental* investment.

So far so good. But *why* did your roommate calculate his expected rate of return in this way—that is, *incrementally*? He did so for one simple reason—because he would have been worse off if he hadn't. Suppose he had assumed that he was investing in you the ten ten-dollar bills plus the cost of the forms plus some allocated portion of the lawyer's fee—say one dollar—to a total of $101.20. If he had calculated his rate of return on *this* sum, it would have been less than his opportunity cost, thus:

$$\frac{\$10}{\$101.20} = .0988$$

or 9.88 percent. He would, of course, have rejected the loan—because it would have appeared to offer a return of less than 10 percent. You, on the other hand, would have gone down to the local bank—where you would have been able to borrow at 10 percent. And he would have been worse off by 10 percent of the dollars he had *not* loaned you—minus his *incremental* cost of funds.

In short, because your roommate's *incremental* cost of funds was less than 10 percent (say 9.9 percent), he would always be better off to lend those funds at 10 percent than *not* to lend them. By lending them, he would have recovered some part—albeit small—of the money he had spent on forms and legal advice. We will revert to the word "incremental" again later on.

Let's go back now to the marketing VP's proposal. What would be Butcher's *incremental* investment in the additional accounts receivable ($850,000 at selling price)? Would it be total factory cost ($680,000) or would it be just additional direct labor and materials ($582,000)?

We really cannot answer this question without knowing a few more facts, as follows:

1. Butcher's Hand Tools Division had enough excess capacity to be able to produce $850,000 worth of tools (at selling price) in the present plant.
2. Additional direct cost would be the sum of additional materials and labor (= $582,000) plus additional power, and additional maintenance.

The additional power and maintenance would be necessary because existing machinery would be used more intensively. Additional power would be about $220 a month for twelve months. Additional maintenance (at overtime rates for present factory maintenance employees) and parts would be about $300 a month, also for twelve months.

Total direct cost would therefore be:

Additional labor and materials	$582,000
Additional power ($220 monthly)	2,640
Additional maintenance and parts ($300 monthly)	3,600
TOTAL	$588,240

This sum, then, represents the *additional* (incremental) amount Butcher would have to spend in order to be able to sell $850,000 worth of hand tools. It is, then, the additional amount Butcher would have invested in the additional accounts receivable.

rate of return

How should an expected rate of return on this investment be calculated? In order to illustrate the process, we assume:

1. That equal dollar amounts of tools would be produced and sold monthly (about $70,000). This assumption is incorrect—sales of hand tools at retail are "seasonal," that is, they tend to be

much larger in spring and at Christmastime than at other seasons of the year. Kelley will adjust for this fact later on.

2. That all the proposed new customers will pay on Butcher's usual terms—2 percent, ten days, net thirty. This jargon simply means that if the customer pays within ten days of receipt of the invoice, he pays 2 percent less than the amount of the invoice. If he pays after the tenth day, he pays the full amount of the invoice. If he does not pay within thirty days, his account is considered overdue. Of course, few if any of the proposed new customers would pay within ten days, because all of them are known to be operating on a shoe-string and slow-paying. Kelley will adjust later on for this fact also. But meanwhile, we assume that none of the new customers will pay within ten days—but that all of them will pay within thirty days.

TABLE 11.1

RECEIPTS AND DISBURSEMENTS ON SALES TO NEW CUSTOMERS

AT END OF MONTH	AMOUNT INVESTED	AMOUNT RECEIVED	NET RECEIPTS
(1)	(2)	(3)	(4)
0	$ 49,020	$ ——	−$49,020 *
1	49,020	70,000	20,980
2	49,020	70,000	20,980
3	49,020	70,000	20,980
4	49,020	70,000	20,980
5	49,020	70,000	20,980
6	49,020	70,000	20,980
7	49,020	70,000	20,980
8	49,020	70,000	20,980
9	49,020	70,000	20,980
10	49,020	70,000	20,980
11	49,020	70,000	20,980
12	——	70,000	70,000
TOTAL	$588,240	$840,000	

* Net outflow.

These two assumptions together mean that Butcher will invest $49,020 ($588,240)/12 at the beginning of each month and, at the end of each month, will receive $70,000—as shown in Table 11.1. We assume also that no sales will be made after the beginning of the twelfth month. This is equivalent to saying that Butcher will invest $49,020 at the beginning of the first month and will receive, *net*, $20,980 at the end of each month, except the twelfth, as shown in Table 11.1. At the end of the twelfth month, Butcher will receive $70,000, net. In Table 11.2 we see

TABLE 11.2

RATE OF RETURN ON SALES TO NEW CUSTOMERS

AT END OF MONTH	NET RECEIPTS *	DISCOUNT FACTORS AT 43%	PRESENT VALUE
(1)	(2)	(3)	(4)
1	$20,980	.699	$14,665.02
2	20,980	.489	10,259.22
3	20,980	.342	7,175.16
4	20,980	.239	5,014.22
5	20,980	.167	3,503.66
6	20,980	.117	2,454.66
7	20,980	.082	1,720.36
8	20,980	.057	1,195.86
9	20,980	.040	839.20
10	20,980	.028	587.44
11	20,980	.020	419.60
12	70,000	.014	980.00
			$48,814.40

* From Table 11.1.

that 43 percent is the approximate rate of discount which makes Butcher's net receipts equal to $49,020.

The rate of return on the investment in the new accounts is thus 43 percent per month—or 516 percent a year! The size of the rate is the resultant of two forces—Butcher's markup over direct cost, and the number of times during the year that markup is earned.

Alternatively, we could reach the same result by simply subtracting $49,020 from $70,000 (= $20,980) and dividing by $49,020, thus:

$$\frac{\$70,000 - \$49,020}{\$49,020} = 43 \text{ percent}$$

In short, then, *if all the new customers pay on time,* the investment in additional accounts receivable will have been highly (!) worthwhile.

But, unfortunately, all the proposed new customers are marginal—and everyone knows they *won't* pay on time. And so the question really is: When will they pay, *on the average?* (Some of them, of course, may go bankrupt tomorrow.) This is the question, then, with which our friend Kelley—to whom we now return—must wrestle.

MARGINAL ACCOUNTS

subjective probability distributions

Kelley had decided to dispose of the A. W. Page Company problem first because it seemed to be the simplest of the three. He sent for the credit department's file on Page and found a batch of miscellaneous information—some of it badly out-of-date. The unaudited statements which Page had given to the Butcher salesman were included. Page was *not* a "small shopkeeper." The company owned and operated ten discount hardware and appliance stores in ten shopping centers in and around Indianapolis, Indiana. Total sales last year had been nearly $2 million, and until eighteen months ago, Page had grown consistently and had made modest amounts of profit. The file contained a Dun and Bradstreet's report, dated six weeks before, which indicated that Page was at that time sixty to ninety days late in paying its bills.

In addition, Butcher's controller had received just a few days ago a confidential letter from the Third National Bank of Indianapolis summarizing its view of Page's present situation. The letter was addressed to Butcher's New York bank, which at Butcher's request had written to its correspondent bank in Indianapolis.

> We have provided Page with seasonal and other short term financing for nearly fifteen years—primarily for the purpose of enabling it to build up inventory in early spring and in the fall. Until two years ago, Page was always able to take care of its indebtedness to us within a month or so after the end of the spring and Christmas selling seasons—that is, as soon as its charge customers began to pay for their spring and Christmas purchases.
>
> In February of last year, A. W. Page, Sr., asked for a 90 day extension. He gave two reasons for the request. He said first that Christmas sales had been off and his inventory was therefore higher than it should have been at that time of year. He said, second, that in October he had opened two more stores—bringing the total to ten. This, of course, had increased his need for

working capital—mostly inventory—by almost 20 percent. This was really a violation of the understanding between us. Given his heavy indebtedness to us, Page should not have opened two new stores without obtaining our prior consent. In effect, we have since then been providing Page with long-term financing.

Nevertheless, we would not have called his loan if we had not begun to have serious doubts about the future of so-called discount stores. All of them are presently running into very heavy competition—not only from each other, but also from the traditional type of retail store. And we believe that, at least in the Indianapolis area, the situation will get worse before it gets better. There will surely be some bankruptcies. We do not believe that Page will be among them—but of course, we can't be sure. A. W. Page, Sr., is one of the shrewdest merchants in town and his son, a recent graduate of the Indiana Business School, is bright and energetic.

We will continue to supply them with seasonal financing—but only after the $200,000 which has been outstanding since February of 1967 has been paid off—sometime in the next 90 days. This will force Page to sell off excess inventory and probably at unfavorable prices. We feel we had no alternative—Page's Christmas sales were off again this year, and our loan committee felt very strongly that we should stop providing long-term financing—unless Page, Sr., were willing to endorse a $200,000 note personally and provide satisfactory collateral. Page was not willing to do so.

"Well," said Kelley. "There's only one way to decide this." He called the sales manager of the tools division and asked him what he would do with the obsolete tools if they were not sold to Page.

"Oh," said the sales manager, "we could always get rid of them at cost."

"Which would be how much?" asked Kelley.

"About $39,000," said the sales manager.

"Thanks," said Kelley and hung up.

Kelley then went to the controller's office where the following conversation took place:

Kelley said, "Mr. Jamerson, on this order from Page, I'd like to try a little experiment with you and Johnson." Johnson was Butcher's general credit manager.

"Another exercise in subjective probabilities?" asked Jamerson.

"Yes," said Kelley.

Jamerson sent for Johnson. When he arrived, Kelley explained that Butcher could probably sell the tools elsewhere for $39,000. The question was therefore whether Butcher would do better than that if the tools were sold to Page.

"I've told Martin what I think," said Jamerson.

"And I've told Jamerson what *I* think," said Johnson.

"Not *everything* you think," said Kelley. "Look, you two men have seen hundreds of cases like this. Not all of them go sour."

"No two cases are really alike," said Jamerson. "But, true enough, not all of them go sour."

"Well, what that means," said Kelley, "is that somewhere off there in space are probability distributions over *how much* an account like this will pay and *when* it will pay. And each of you ought to be able to put down on paper your subjective feelings about what those probabilities are. As a personal favor to me."

"All right," said Jamerson. "As a personal favor to you. When? Right now?"

"As soon as possible," said Kelley. "But take enough time so that you're satisfied with what you've done. And I wish you'd do it independently."

"I can't just fill in numbers right here and now," said Jamerson. "I'd like to think about it. Might take me a couple of hours."

"Okay," said Kelley, "so much the better."

When he came in the next morning, Kelley found the two reports waiting for him on his desk. He used the figures in them to set up Tables 11.3 and 11.4. The controllers' figures had a note attached which said:

> I was a bit puzzled by the whole process. It seems to me—and to Johnson, too—that what we have done assumes that the two sets of probabilities are independent of each other—that is, that we can decide first *how much* Page would pay us and then, second, *when* he would pay us. In our experience, this is not the way life is. On an account like Page, if we get our money sooner, we're likely to get all or most of it. If we get it later, we're likely to get less—maybe much less. But we're not statisticians and so we'll let *you* worry about what to do about *that problem.*

"Ugh," said Kelley. "Complications. Not as simple as I'd thought. Means that for each class interval over days, there's a separate probability distribution over amount."

Kelley then set up Table 11.5, leaving Average Amount (Column 2) blank for the moment. "All I want you to do," he said to Jamerson and Johnson, "is to put down your best guess as to the amount we'd receive if Page paid us in 150 days or less, in 151 to 180 days and so forth."

After Jamerson and Johnson had spent four or five hours providing this information for column (2), Kelley took their figures and calculated annual yields, based on the average amounts in column (2) and the mid-points for the class intervals (Periods) given in column (1). Thus if Page paid the full amount due in seventy-five days (the mid point

TABLE 11.3

PROBABILITIES THAT A. W. PAGE COMPANY PAYS WITHIN SPECIFIED TIME

PERIOD (days)	CONTROLLER	CREDIT MANAGER	AVERAGE
(1)	(2)	(3)	(4)
0-150	.01	—	.005
151-180	.01	—	.005
181-210	.02	—	.010
211-240	.02	.03	.025
241-270	.02	.05	.035
271-300	.02	.07	.045
301-330	.05	.10	.075
331-360	.10	.10	.100
361-390	.50	.40	.450
391-420	.20	.20	.200
over 420	.05	.05	.050
	1.00	1.00	1.000

TABLE 11.4

PROBABILITIES THAT A. W. PAGE COMPANY PAYS SPECIFIED AMOUNT

AMOUNT	CONTROLLER	CREDIT MANAGER	AVERAGE
(1)	(2)	(3)	(4)
$ 0- 5,000	.02	—	.01
5,001-10,000	.02	—	.01
10,001-15,020	.02	—	.01
15,001-20,000	.02	.02	.02
20,001-25,000	.03	.03	.03
25,001-30,000	.04	.05	.045
30,001-35,001	.05	.10	.075
35,001-40,001	.20	.25	.225
40,001-45,001	.40	.37	.385
45,001-49,000	.18	.16	.170
50,000	.02	.02	.020
	1.00	1.00	1.000

TABLE 11.5

EXPECTED YIELD ON SALES TO A. W. PAGE COMPANY

PERIOD (days)	AVERAGE AMOUNT	APPROXIMATE ANNUAL YIELD	PROBABILITY	EXPECTED YIELD *
(1)	(2)	(3)	(4)	(5)
0-150	$50,000	137.3%	.005	0.7%
151-180	50,000	62.3%	.005	0.3%
181-210	49,000	47.9%	.010	0.5%
211-240	48,000	37.4%	.025	0.9%
241-270	47,000	29.3%	.035	1.0%
271-300	46,000	22.9%	.045	1.0%
301-330	45,000	17.9%	.075	1.3%
331-360	44,000	13.5%	.100	1.4%
361-390	43,000	10.0%	.450	4.5%
391-420	35,000	—9.2%	.200	—1.8%
over 420	25,000	—28.7%	.050	—1.4%
			1.000	+8.4%

* Before taxes.

of the first class interval) the yield on the sale would be 137.3 percent as follows:

$$\frac{\$50,000 - 39,000}{39,000} \times \frac{365}{75} = 1.373$$

or 137.3 percent. In other words, the "raw yield" on the sale would be

$$\frac{11,000}{39,000} \text{ or } \frac{\$11,000}{\$39,000} = .282$$

or 28.2 percent. But this raw yield would be earned in just seventy-five days. On an annual basis, therefore, the yield would be $28.2 \times \dfrac{365}{75}$ or, as above, 137.3 percent.

After he had calculated all the yields, column (3), Kelley multiplied by the probabilities, given in column (4). (These were taken from column (4) of Table 11.3.) He added up column (5) and found that the expected yield on the sale to Page was 8.4 percent.

He then wrote the following memo to Martin—copies to Jamerson and Johnson.

> To: Dale Martin
> From: R. Kelley
>
> Subject: Proposed sale of hand tools to A.W. Page Company
> Using subjective probabilities supplied by Messrs. Jamerson and Johnson, I have calculated an expected yield on the order from A. W. Page for $50,000 worth of hand tools. It is 8.4 percent before taxes—or noticeably *less* than our cost of capital.
>
> Messrs. Jamerson and Johnson have seen hundreds of situations of this kind. The probabilities are merely their attempt to put numbers on their experience.
>
> Before deciding for or against the sale, you may wish to reflect on the fact that A. W. Page has been a very good customer —especially in the last three years. The chances are that they will *not* work their way out of their present difficulty. But suppose they do? Will their attitude toward us be affected in future years? We are not, as you well know, the only manufacturer of hand tools. In fact, we are not the only manufacturer of *good* hand tools. If we turn Page down now—when he needs us—and he survives and grows, we may lose $2 million worth of business over the next ten years.

A few days later Kelley got this memo back from Martin. Scrawled across the top—in Martin's illegible handwriting—were the words: "Thanks. I've approved the sale to Page. I suppose that's what you wanted." The following note, also in Martin's handwriting, was scrawled in the margin:

> But, by the way, why did you ignore the reinvestment part of the problem? If Page paid us within 150 days, we'd be able to reinvest the proceeds—at no less than our cost of capital—sooner than if he paid us in 180 days. And if he paid us in 180 days, we'd be able to reinvest the proceeds sooner than if he paid us in 210 days. An so forth. I don't think that taking this into account would raise the average rate much, but the rates you have averaged are just not comparable. I'm surprised at you, Kelley.

"Well, well," said Kelley to himself, "sometimes *he* surprises *me!*"

objective probability distributions

Kelley turned next to the marketing VP's memo. He saw at once that with each of the 132 accounts, he could go through a process similar to the process he had gone through on the Page account. He could, that is, sit down with Jamerson and Johnson and try to persuade them to construct a subjective probability distribution for each account. Maybe they would be willing to do so—and maybe they wouldn't. But "objective" probability distributions would be better if, somehow, they could be obtained. (Kelley had to admit, from time to time, that he was no longer sure what an "objective" probability was. Even when he tossed coins with his wife—for a quarter a throw—he knew that he was making the subjective judgment that the coin was a "fair" coin.)

A few months before, Kelley had read an article in a financial magazine which had described certain statistical techniques the author had used successfully in predicting bankruptcies from financial ratios. Kelly had saved the article, and he now took it out of his files to reread. He had thought at the time that similar techniques could be used to assess credit risks—and perhaps, he now said to himself, the opportunity to apply the idea had presented itself. Kelley knew a little about statistics—but not as much as he would have liked. And he decided, therefore, to take his problem to Butcher's computer chief.

Kelley gave the computer chief (CC) a copy of the article and the memo from the marketing VP. He then went over carefully what he, Jamerson and Johnson had done in the Page case. "But," he said, "the conclusion we came to was pretty heavily subjective." It had struck him, he went on, as he had listened to Jamerson and Johnson discussing the Page case, that each of them had had a great deal of experience in credit analysis and had, as a result, developed a kind of "sense of smell" about marginal accounts. They could usually separate those which would work out satisfactorily from those which would not. Oh, yes—they made mistakes. But they were right much more often than not.

"Well," said Kelley to the CC, "I don't believe in crystal balls and witchcraft. If Jamerson and Johnson are right more often than not, then they've learned by experience to detect subsurface differences among marginal accounts. And if they've learned to detect subsurface differences among marginal accounts, those differences must exist. And if they exist, we should be able to detect them by statistical means. And if we could detect them by statistical means, we would probably be able to improve on the credit department's more or less intuitive procedures. And we'd be able to speed up the whole process of reviewing new applications for credit. And we'd be able to keep old marginal accounts under constant review."

The computer chief, who had glanced through the article while Kelley was talking, agreed to help and suggested that Kelley proceed as follows:

"First, write a memorandum to Martin explaining, in general terms, what you want to do. If he approves, he'll send the memo on to me.

"Second, decide what you want to predict. In the Page case, you predicted expected yield. Is that what you want to do here? You could, for example, predict payoff in dollars instead of percent."

"Yield is what I want to predict," said Kelley. "The trouble with expected payoff in dollars is that it doesn't take account of differences in time. If one customer paid off in full in thirty days and another paid off in full in six months, the dollar payoffs would be the same, but the second customer is really less attractive than the first. If we could predict the yield on a proposed sale to a new marginal customer, we'd be able to compare that yield with our current cost of capital—and decide whether to make the sale or not."

"Third," the CC went on, "sit down with Jamerson and Johnson and see if you can drag out of them the things they look at when they decide whether or not to sell to marginal accounts—current ratio, acid test, size of order, ratio of debt to equity, trend in profits, or what not. They don't try to estimate the yield on a sale. They simply try to decide, I suppose, whether a customer will default or not. But the things you would take into account would be much the same as the things they take into account.

"Fourth, go to the credit department and get a complete list of all the marginal hand tool accounts who have applied for credit in the last year or so—*including those who were turned down.* Calculate yields on those sales which were actually made. And you'll have to be sure to take account of all collection costs—including legal fees, if any. Then —and this won't be easy—you'll have to try to estimate what the yield would have been on those sales that were, in fact, turned down."

"What!" said Kelley. "And just how would I do that?"

"I don't know," said the CC. "That's *your* problem—but it has to be done."

"Why can't we simply analyze the accounts we've actually done business with?" asked Kelley.

"You can," said the CC, "if you want to get biased results. The accounts we have actually done business with would just not be typical of the accounts who would want to do business with us in the future. Why? Simply because the accounts we have actually done business with have been sifted by the credit department from among all those who wanted to do business with us. The poorer accounts have been sorted out.

"Here," continued the CC, "let me see that memo from marketing." Kelley handed it over. "Here, look," said the CC, indicating the list of 132 accounts attached to the memo. "The credit department has already eliminated some of these accounts—twenty-six of them in fact." He pushed the list under Kelley's nose.

"You're trying to develop an objective technique which would, in effect, better enable the credit department to do its job—enable it, that is, to put 'yes' or 'no' beside each name on a list such as this—with greater confidence in the final outcome. If you analyze only the accounts we've done business with, your sample will contain a much smaller percentage of rotten apples than exists out there in the world. In fact, if you drew a sample from just those accounts which had been approved for credit a year or so ago, you might find *no* rotten apples. You'd be totally unable to make comparisons of the characteristics of good apples and rotten apples."

"Okay," said Kelley, "don't rub it in. I understand. But I'm getting discouraged—it sounds like an impossible job."

"Not impossible," said the CC, "just very difficult."

"Well," said Kelley, "I just don't see any way in the world of estimating—with any degree of accuracy—the hypothetical yield on an account we didn't sell to."

"You'll have to do it," said the CC, "otherwise the experiment will be worth exactly nothing."

"No," said Kelley suddenly, "I just got a brilliant idea. These 132 accounts are probably what you would call a representative sample of marginal hardware accounts. But some of them will turn out to be good and some of them will turn out to be sour. Let's sell to all of them and see what happens. Then, six months from now, we'll analyze them —using this computer of yours—to see whether we can find the distinguishing characteristics of those that went sour."

"That would do the trick," said the CC. "You'd be deliberately selling to twenty-six shaky accounts. Might be expensive. Put it to Martin and let's see what he says."

Kelley rushed back to his office and wrote Martin a long memo explaining what he wanted to do. He devoted special care to explaining why he wanted to sell to all 132 accounts—including those which had been disapproved by the credit department. He sent the memo marked "urgent," off to Martin, with copies to Jamerson, Johnson, the marketing VP and the CC. He then did fifty pushups and sat back and waited for Martin to explode. It was then 4:30 in the afternoon. By 5:15 nothing had happened and at 5:45 Kelley left for home.

The next morning, a note from Martin was sitting in the middle of Kelley's desk. It read as follows:

> Kelly: You've really gone absolutely crazy. There will be a short meeting in my office at ten o'clock to discuss the dimensions of your successor. You may attend if you wish.

"Very funny," said Kelley to himself. He sent his secretary out for two large containers of black coffee. At ten o'clock he straightened his tie, put on his jacket and marched himself down to Martin's office. Jamerson, Johnson and the CC were already there.

"All right," said Martin. "We can begin."

Kelley asked whether the marketing VP was coming. "No," said Martin, "he's not. But we all know what he'd think. You have the floor," he said to Kelley.

Kelley took a deep breath and made the following points in rapid succession:

"One. We should invest in an account receivable in the same way we invest in anything else—that is, only if the expected return on it is greater than our cost of capital.

"Two. We could estimate expected rates of return subjectively, as we did in the Page case. The credit department would sit down with the facts and figures on each proposed new marginal account and then set up a subjective probability distribution over rate of return for each. They would then calculate an expected rate of return which could be compared with our current cost of capital. And so forth.

"Three. I am suggesting merely that we may be able to estimate expected rates of return on marginal accounts in a somewhat more objective way. We feel fairly certain, for example, that if one marginal account is bigger or has more net worth than another, it's likely to be a better risk, if everything else is the same. And if we examined two marginal accounts of the same size and the same net worth, the account with more working capital would probably be the better risk. And so forth.

"Four. Statistical techniques are available which would enable us to analyze past experience. We would take a representative sample of marginal accounts and we would analyze our past experience with them. First, we would calculate the yield we had actually earned on each marginal account—some would be well above our costs of capital, some would be less and of these some, perhaps, would be negative. We would then try to explain each yield in terms of the financial condition—and perhaps also the competitive situation—of the account on which we had earned that yield.

"Five. This process would give us an equation which we could use *to predict* yields on new accounts. That is, we would 'plug into the equation' the relevant data on a proposed *new* account, turn a crank, and out would come a predicted yield—on a sale of a certain size to that account. The prediction would be subject, of course, to a certain margin of error.

"Six. The trouble is that we do not have records on a representative sample of marginal accounts. We have records only on those accounts we have chosen to sell to—that is, on the better marginal accounts.

"Seven. The proposal from the marketing department provides us with an opportunity to obtain the necessary data from what is probably a representative sample of marginal hardware accounts."

"Questions please," ended Kelley.

"How expensive is this likely to be?" Martin asked.

"I don't know," said Kelley. "Expected sales would be $850,000. And incremental cost, about $588,000 or, on the average, about $4,500 a customer [= $588,000/132]. The credit department has indicated that of the 132 accounts, twenty-six are likely to go sour."

"But," Jamerson interjected, "that average sales figure is an annual figure. Orders would probably not exceed $1,000 in any individual case. That would be about $690 at cost. We would not ship a second order until the first had been paid for. Also, some of the twenty-six accounts —maybe six or seven—will turn out to be good accounts. That leaves twenty or so. The whole experiment might cost us $14,000.

"Is it worth it?" Martin asked. "Do you think a system of this kind would be better than the present rule-of-thumb system?"

"I don't know," said Jamerson, "It might be. If it worked, it might narrow considerably the area in which we had to rely on judgment. We now employ twenty-two credit analysts throughout the whole company at an annual cost of about $180,000. Is that right, Johnson?"

"Just about," said Johnson.

"We might cut that figure in half," said Jamerson. "Also it might help us enormously with the credit limit problem on marginal accounts —if I've understood what you've said." Jamerson said that as he understood what Kelley had said, size of order would be taken into account in the analysis. And presumably the analysis would show that beyond a certain point, the larger the order, the lower the yield on the account would be.

"We can't be sure," said the CC, "but probably."

"All right," said Martin. "I'd like to think about this overnight."

CONCLUSION

Any company would, of course, sell to any other company or to any individual for cash-on-delivery (C.O.D.). But in the United States, virtually every company which hopes to prosper must grant credit to its customers. And this being so, every company must know how to decide whether or not to do so.

In this chapter we have said that every company must in one way or another calculate an expected return on each and every proposed sale—which is just another way of saying that it must estimate the degree of risk (of default) in every proposed sale. But obviously no company will waste much time calculating the degree of risk of default on a sale to AT&T, or RCA, or General Motors—or to any other customer who is as rich as Croesus.

And obviously any company which is able to sell everything it produces to such customers will not need a credit department. But, in fact, most companies depend heavily on so-called marginal customers—on customers, that is, whose financial strength is *not* beyond question—who are, in fact, always just one step ahead of the sheriff. Without such customers many companies could not exist. Marginal accounts are, therefore, the central preoccupation of every credit department.

How should expected returns on marginal accounts be calculated? In this chapter, we have suggested that such returns can be calculated by extracting subjective probabilities from experienced credit men. We should bear in mind in this connection that no matter how a credit man decides what should be done in any given instance, a subjective probability distribution over the yield on the account underlies whatever decision he makes—whether he knows it or not. Even if he does nothing but bite hard on a prospective customers latest balance sheet, he is making implicit assumptions about the probabilities—again, whether he knows it or not. He is saying, in effect, that the probabilities are such that "the expected return on this sale is (or is not) higher than our cost of capial."

But objective techniques are available which will often reduce the subjectivity of subjective probabilities. And they should be used by any company which must sell to large numbers of marginal accounts.

PROBLEMS

1. *The credit department, under the general supervision of the chief financial officer, must decide not merely how much should be sold to which marginal customers but also what the company's credit terms should be, and how much money should be spent trying to collect overdue accounts.*

   Credit terms stipulate the length of the credit period—that is, the number of days within which the bill is to be paid, and the amount of the cash discount, if any. Thus the term "net 10 days" means that the full amount of the bill (no discount) is to be paid in ten days or less. The terms "2/10 net 30" mean that if the bill is paid in ten days or less, the customer may deduct 2 percent from the face amount of the bill. But if he doesn't "discount the bill," he must pay it within thirty days of the date of shipment—or his account will be considered to be overdue.

Credit terms vary widely from industry to industry but within any given industry, they tend to be much the same.

Your name is Kelley. You know that the hand tools division has for eight years been selling to small hardware stores on credit terms of "net 30 days," which means "this invoice cannot be discounted and must be paid in full in thirty days." Martin has passed on to you a memo from the marketing department urging that these terms be changed to "2/10 net 30." Put this problem in a rate of return context. How much would Butcher's investment in this "project" be, and what would have to happen as a result of changing terms if that investment were to turn out worthwhile? Assume that other hand tool manufacturers are all selling "net 30 days."

What do you think would really happen in the above case if Butcher did change its terms from "net 30" to "2/10 net 30"?

2. If a hardware store which buys $1,000 worth of hand tools from Butcher on terms of "2/10 net 30," does not take the discount, but does pay in thirty days, it is in effect borrowing $1,000 from Butcher for twenty days at a cost of $20 (= $1,000 × .02).

What annual rate of interest is the hardware store paying?

Prove that the hardware store would be better off to borrow $980 for twenty days at an annual rate of 24 percent and use the funds so borrowed to take the discount on Butcher's bill.

3. As Kelley suggested in his memo to Martin on the A. W. Page situation, if Butcher turned Page down and Page survived its present difficulty, Butcher might lose $2 million worth of business over the next ten years.

Assign probabilities to the following events:

(a) Page survives and buys $200,000 worth of hardware from Butcher during each of the next ten years if Butcher sells to Page now

(b) Page survives and buys $200,000 worth of hardware from Butcher during each of the next ten years if Butcher does not sell to Page now

Using the above probabilities and the information given in Table 11.5, recalculate the expected yield on the sale to Page.

4. The manager of Butcher's machine tools division has suggested, as you know, that he be allowed to sell machine tools to certain smaller customers on a twelve months installment basis. Butcher would add 6 percent to the selling price of each tool to obtain the total time

price. Butcher would then divide the total time price by 12 to obtain each monthly payment. For example, on a $40,000 machine tool, the time price would be $42,400 (= $40,000 × 1.06) and each monthly payment would be $3,533. The direct cost of manufacturing a $40,000 machine tool would be about $30,000. Butcher's current cost of capital is about 11 percent.

If you were Kelley, what recommendation would you make to Martin on the suggestion made by the manager of the machine tools division?

5. When a new customer applies to the Butcher Company for credit, Butcher requires up-to-date income statements and balance sheets, as in the Exhibits. It also requests a credit report from a national credit agency such as NCO or Dun and Bradstreet. Look these exhibits over carefully and decide which data you would be most likely to consider (and why) if you were trying to predict the yield on a proposed sale to a new account. But before you do so consider the following remarks, made some time ago by Butcher's credit manager in a talk to a group of credit analysts:

> What makes an account a marginal account? In general, marginal accounts tend to be small although they need not be small. But all of them are undercapitalized relative to their sales. By the term undercapitalized, I mean that they do not have enough money to be able to pay on time for all the things they buy. They buy tools from us on credit and sell them (perhaps on credit) before they have paid for them. When their customers pay them, they are able to pay us.
>
> Many such companies are reasonably well-managed— but some are not. The credit analyst's problem is to separate those that are reasonably well-managed from those that are not. The mere fact that they pay their bills slowly does not mean they are poorly managed. It often means just the opposite.

6. You will recall that Martin criticized the way Kelley had prepared Table 11.5. He said the yields in (3) were not comparable because Kelley had forgotten to take account of the fact that if A. W. Page paid sooner rather than later, Butcher would be able to reinvest the founds received for a longer rather than a shorter period of time.

Assume that Butcher would reinvest the funds, whenever they were received, to yield 1 percent a month, compounded.

Recalculate

(a) each of the yields in Table 11.5

(b) the expected yield

EXHIBIT 11.1

nco. specialized credit report

C & K KNITTING MILLS INC.
8 Tudor St.
York, Pa.

MFR. UNDERWEAR
Dept. 651
Analyst: Edwin P. Kellerman

SEPTEMBER 17, 197

CREDIT SUGGESTION - (C) - OPERATING PERFORMANCE BETTER THAN AVERAGE. CONDITION HEAVY BUT FINANCES UNDER CONTROL. GENERAL LINE OF $25,000 SUGGESTED.

ANTECEDENT COMMENT - Records clear. Incorporated 1957. Pennsylvania laws. Acquired assets and assumed liabilities of predecessor partnership formed 1931. Under experienced, capable and well regarded management. Manufactures infants', misses', and boys' underwear as well as athletic shirts and shorts.

FINANCIAL -	12/31/6-	12/31/6-	6/30/7-
Cash	$ 95,000	$ 32,000	$ 82,000
Receivables	495,000	427,000	581,000
Merchandise	412,000	453,000	418,000
Current Assets	1,002,000	912,000	1,081,000
Current Liabilities	921,000	816,000	897,000
Working Capital	81,000	96,000	184,000
Fixed Assets	214,000	182,000	185,000
Net Worth	271,000	308,000	383,000
Sales	2,987,000	2,824,000	1,854,000 (6 Mos.)
Profit	56,000	37,000	76,000

Auditor: Carl A. Casper, CPA., Philadelphia, Pa.

TRADE - SATISFACTORY

HIGH CREDIT	OWING	PAST DUE	TERMS	PAYMENTS
Ex. $100,000	Ex. 50,000	0	70+60X	ppt
Ex. 50,000	5,000	0	EOM	ppt
Ex. 50,000	15,000	0	3%/10 EOM	dis
Ex. 50,000	22,000	0	60+dtg.	ppt

Miller & Co., Phila., Pa.
A.B. Factors Corp., NYC

Monroe Cotton Mills, Monroe, N.C.
Pennsylvania Dye Works, Inc., Phila., Pa.

ANALYSIS - Over-all trend has been one of progress. Particularly good performance noted for the first half of this year with better than average operating profit recorded. This coupled with profit on sale of equipment (treated as capital gains), has added further relief to working position. On the surface, condition heavy, with indebtedness in excess of working capital and net worth; however, December and June statements are seasonally unbalanced.

Operating in an industry which is highly competitive, the company has more than held its own in recent years. Financing is accomplished through good sized seasonal bank support with depository currently reporting active but proper use made of its lending facilities. Accordingly, felt to merit supplier confidence.

EXHIBIT 11.2

nco.® specialized credit report

MANAGEMENT & PRODUCTS

C & K KNITTING MILLS INC.
8 Tudor St.
York, Pa.

MFR. UNDERWEAR
Dept. 651
Analyst: Edwin P. Kellerman

SEPTEMBER 17, 197

Horace B. Clark, Pres.
Robert M. Rogers, Sec.-Treas.

E. Paul Kollar, Vice Pres.

DIRECTORS - The officers and Thomas Long.

HISTORY - Incorporated under Pa. laws 1957. Acquired assets and assumed liabilities of predecessor partnership formed 1931. The original firm was a partnership of Horace B. and James H. Clark - the latter died 1951 leaving his interest to Horace B. who at that time became sole owner. A former contracting subsidiary, Puritan Underwear Inc. was merged into subject early 1964.

PERSONNEL - <u>Clark</u>, born 1906. Graduate of the Southern Textile Institute. One of the original founders. Active in all phases of the business. At one time sole owner; however, now retains 50% of the stock. His life is insured for $100,000 (corporation beneficiary).

<u>Kollar</u>, born 1924, Employed in this line throughout his business career. 1949 discharged from the U.S. Army as a Captain. Employed by Best Underwear Co. elected Sales Manager 1955 and Vice President 1958. Joined subject 1961 as Vice President in charge of sales. Became a 25% stockholder 1963.

<u>Rogers,</u> born 1914. Graduate of Harvard Business School - majored in accounting. Employed by Jack & Jill Underwear 1932 to 1951. Rose to the office of Vice President. Joined subject in 1952 and became a 25% stockholder in 1963. <u>Long,</u> born 1905. Attorney by profession and a partner in Long, Gottlieb & Schwartz, Philadelphia, Pa.

METHOD OF OPERATION - LINE - Manufactures principally women's and children's underwear in the moderate priced range utilizing cottons and synthetics.
DISTRIBUTION - Sells to jobbers and mail order firms through affiliate, Pride Underwear Co. Inc. on 2/10/N/30 day terms.
EQUIPMENT - Owns a five-story brick building at caption address affording 100,000 sq. ft. of floor space. Equipment includes 150 knitting and 325 sewing machines plus auxiliary equipment. Employs 125.

AFFILIATE - <u>Pride Underwear Co. Inc.</u>, caption address - incorporated under Pa. laws 1952. Selling agent for subject corporation. No other inter-company relations such as loans, guarantees or endorsements exist. Similar officers.

BANK - First National Bank of Pennsylvania, York, Pa.

EXHIBIT 11.3

FINANCIAL STATEMENT SUBMITTED TO **NATIONAL CREDIT OFFICE**

Name ... C & K Knitting Mills, Inc.　　Business ... **Mfr. Underwear**

Street and No. ... 8 Tudor Street　　City ... York,　　State ... Pa.　　ZIP ...

STATEMENT OF (DATE)　　　June 30,　19 7

ASSETS			LIABILITIES	
CASH IN BANK........$			ACCOUNTS PAYABLE............	$ 681,212
ON HAND......$	$ 82,324		DUE CONTRACTORS (without offset)	
U. S. GOVERNMENT SECURITIES...........			UNSECURED LOANS PAYABLE	
RECEIVABLES for Mdse. Sold to Customers (Age at Foot of Page)			To Banks................	80,000
ACCOUNTS $591,125			To Partners or Officers..........	
Less Res. for Discounts $ 10,043			To Others...........	
Less Res. for Doubtful ......$	581,082		SECURED LOANS PAYABLE	
			Owing to..........	
NOTES & TRADE ACCEPTANCES			ACCRUED WAGES & EXPENSES...........	53,911
(Less $........—discounted)			TAXES—Accrued and Payable: a. Withholding & Payroll....	9,597
DUE from FACTOR or FINANCE CO.			b. Federal & State Income.........	
			c. All Other...........	
PHYSICAL INVENTORY OF MDSE. (Valued at lower of Cost or Market)			RESERVE for Income Taxes since last closing	72,384
Raw Materials......$ 82,432			MORTGAGE—DEFERRED DEBT— Due within 12 mos........	
In Process..$161,195				
Finished Mdse......$174,358	417,985		**CURRENT LIABILITIES**	897,104
			MORTGAGE—DEFERRED DEBT— Due after 12 mos.........	
CURRENT ASSETS	1,081,391			
Due from Partners, Officers, or Employees			LOANS Subordinated until...........(date)	
Due from Affiliated or Assoc. Companies				
LAND & BUILDINGS $			**TOTAL LIABILITIES**	
Less Depreciation..$			IF CORPORATION	
MCHY., EQUIP., FURN., & FIXT. $ 600,832			Capital Stock Pfd. $ Com. $ 25,000	
Less Depreciation..$415,621	185,211		Capital Surplus......$ Earned Surplus......$ 358,101	
INVESTMENTS (Describe on opp. page)			Undist. Earnings (Sub-Chapter S) $	
PREPAID & DEFERRED............	13,603		Deficit (red)......$	
			CORPORATE, PARTNERSHIP or INDIVIDUAL............**NET WORTH**	383,101
TOTAL ASSETS	$1,280,205		**TOTAL LIABILITIES & CAPITAL**	$1,280,205

ACCOUNTANT—Was above statement prepared by an outside accountant? Yes ☒ No ☐ Is he C.P.A.? ☒ Registered? ☐ Licensed? ☐
Accountant's Name ... Carl A. Casper
Address ... 124 Broad St., Phila., Pa.
On what date are your books closed? ... 12/31
How often are books audited? ... Annually

MERCHANDISE—If not valued at Lower of Cost or Market, state
basis used ...
Is original inventory record retained by you ☐ or outside auditor ☐
Is any merchandise pledged as security for any debt? ... No
If so, state amount so pledged. $ ...

INSURANCE—Fire: Mdse. $500M ; Bldg. & Fixt. $150M
Use & Occup. $ 50M ; Burglary $; Life, Benefit
Business $100M on ... Horace B. Clark

RECEIVABLES
For goods shipped during months of:
a. June $ 512,115
b. May $ 65,082
c. April $ 13,928
d. Prior Months........... $ -

Do these include any consigned goods, uncredited returns, or unshipped merchandise? Yes ☐ No ☒
Have all bad accounts been charged off or reserved? Yes ☒ No ☐
During the past year have you sold, pledged, or assigned any receivables? Yes ☐ No ☒. If so, name financing concern and describe transaction: ...

69

EXHIBIT 11.4

Dun & Bradstreet® ANALYTICAL REPORT

PLEASE NOTE WHETHER NAME, BUSINESS AND STREET ADDRESS CORRESPOND WITH YOUR INQUIRY.

RATING UNCHANGED

SIC	D-U-N-S	© DUN & BRADSTREET, INC.	STARTED	RATING
20 51	01-112-3189	A-AD 37 APR 11 197-	1958	--
20 52	NEVILLE BAKING CO INC			

44 E 18TH ST; 21 Littleton Ave.

H NEWARK N J 07102
TEL 201 676-3333

SUMMARY

NEVILLE LANDLESS, PRES & TREAS &
CHIEF EXECUTIVE

PAYMENTS	DISC SLOW 60
EMPLOYS	175 (142 here)
RECORD	CLEAR

PAYMENTS

HC	OWE	P DUE	TERMS	MARCH 15 197-	SOLD
8000	6000		2-10	Disc	Over 3 yrs
3000	cur		2 10	Disc	Over 3 yrs
1000	cur		2 10	Disc	Over 3 yrs
2000			draft	Ppt	2 yrs
1800	770		30	Ppt	2 yrs
12000	7000	2736	1 10 30	Slow 7	2 yrs
9106	9106		Notes	Slow	
5200	3080	1600	1 10 30	Slow 15	
3400	3000	2000	1 10 30	Slow 45	Last sale Oct 197-
1100			2 10 30	Slow 5	
700	252		1 10 30	Slow 30	1 yr
324	134	134	10	Slow 20	
200	120	80	1 10 30	Slow 10	Over 3 yrs
178	178	178	2 10 30	Slow 60	

On April 11, 197- N. Landless, Pres.-Treas., declined to comment on slowness.

HIGHLIGHTS

Financial statements and specific operating information have been declined in recent years. However, investigation discloses that the company has a sizable net worth, represented to a considerable extent by fixed assets valued by the management in the past in high six figures. Latest statement submitted is dated Dec. 31, 196- and showed a net worth of $1,287,691. While specific comment relative to the nature and extent of liabilities has been declined at this time, management has acknowledged that debt includes notes payable for machinery as well as accounts payable and accruals.

The current survey with sources of supply (see Payments) showed 9 of the 14 suppliers responding reporting slowness with 6 of them showing past due amounts owing. Increased slowness has been evident during the past year. One year earlier only 4 of 14 suppliers reported slowness ranging from 7 to 14 days. Two outside sources consulted reported that increased slowness resulted from expansion of facilities and expenses incurred in introducing a new product line.

CURRENT

On April 11 197- N. Landless, Pres.-Treas. declined a financial statement. He stated that sales for the past year increased 11% over the prior year. The increase was attributed largely to the new biscuit and cookie line which was introduced last May. Advertising and other expenses rose sharply as a result. It was reported that new automated equipment was purchased last year to permit increased productivity of traditional and new lines.

CURRENT
(CONT'D)

Records of Sept. 15, 197- showed that a suit for $4,360 was brought against, Neville Baking Co., Inc. by Acme Flour Co., Inc. This arose from a dispute over the quality of a shipment of flour and is being contested. A check of records on April 7, 197- showed the above suit still open.

Banking
At a local bank low to moderate five figure balances are maintained. Loans have been granted to moderate 6 figures, secured by machinery and equipment. Presently a moderate six figures amount is owing with payments being made as per agreement.

At another local bank moderate to medium four figure balances are maintained. In the past loans had been granted on a secured basis to medium 5 figures, nothing presently owing.
4-11-7- (803-49)

EXHIBIT 11.5

NEVILLE BAKING CO INC
NEWARK N J

A CD PAGE I
4-11-197-

SUPPLEMENTAL
DATA

This corporation has not provided a financial statement during the past 4 years. The latest figures were dated Dec. 31, 196-, and are summarized as follows:

Current Assets	1,056,783
Current Liabilities	765,875
Other Assets	1,960,554
Long Term Debt	963,771
Worth	1,287,691

The following financing statements are on file:

File No.	Date Filed	Secured Party	Collateral
39,070	Jan. 15, 196-	Vendor Motor Co.	14 Trucks
41,003	Feb. 11, 196-	Baking Equipment Co.	Machinery
107,395	April 20, 197-	Bakery Equipment Co. Assigned to First Mercantile	Machinery
108,903	May 1, 197-	First Mercantile	Specified Equipment and Machinery

HISTORY

Incorporated: Under New Jersey laws April 30, 1958 as Landless Baking Co., Inc. The corporate name was changed to present style by corporate amendment on August 30, 1962.

Authorized Capital Stock: 5,000 shares of $100 par value Common Stock.
Outstanding Capital Stock: Not disclosed.

This business was established in 1934 and was originally conducted by Helena Bakeries Corp., a subsidiary of Landless Bakeries, Inc. In 1958 the assets of Helena Bakeries Corp. were purchased for a consideration reported in excess of $750,000 by subject. Landless Bakeries, Inc. had been controlled by an uncle of Neville Landless, President who has been chief executive and majority stock owner of this corporation since its inception.

Related Companies: Neville Landless is also the majority stockholder and President of the following:

North Newark Baking Corp. This address, chartered New Jersey laws May 1, 1958. That corporation owns certain equipment and machinery valued about $125,000 which is leased to the subject. There are no guarantees or endorsements reported.

Neville Holding Corp. Chartered New Jersey laws Dec. 1, 1964. Corporation owns real estate 21 Littleton Ave. Newark and the property at this location. Both properties are leased to the subject. Properties reportedly have a market value exceeding $400,000. and are subject to mortgages totalling $190,000. Inter-company relations confined to that of landlord and tenant.

OPERATION

Products: Bakes raisin, pound, layer, sponge, and other varities of cakes and cookies, which are sold under name "Neville". A line of biscuits and cookies sold under "Helena" name account for 10% of volume.

Distribution: To supermarkets, delicatessens, and restaurants.
Accounts: 3,000.
Territory: Metropolitan Newark and Northern New Jersey.
Terms: Cash and weekly.
Seasons: Fairly steady.
Employs: 175 including 25 salesman on a commission basis.
Delivery Equipment: 25 trucks.

EXHIBIT 11.6

NEVILLE BAKING CO INC
NEWARK N.J.

A CD PAGE 2
4-11-197-

Facilities: Rents from an affiliated concern a two and three-story brick building with about 60,000 square feet of floor space. The building extends from North 13th Avenue to North 14th Avenue. It is equipped with mixing machines, ovens, conveyors, racks, slicing and wrapping machines. Property is old, but well maintained and is located in a light industrial area next to a railroad siding. A distributing station is maintained at 21 Littleton Ave., Newark, where a one story building containing 20,00 square feet is leased from an affiliate.
4-11-7- (803-49)

- - - - - - - o - - - - - - - -

Neville Landless, President-Treasurer
Ann (Mrs. N.) Landless, Vice President
James R. Fox, Vice President
Franklin A. Landless, Secretary
Directors: The officers and Arthur M. Boynton.

(Management Background section of report omitted).

12

INVESTING
IN
INVENTORY

You had left the office early, hoping to surprise your bride of two months in the shiny new house you had just bought. But when you reached home, full of expectation, the house was dark. Of course you feared the worst. She had been injured in an accident (she wasn't a very good driver). You phoned the emergency room at the hospital. No, they said, no one by that name had been brought in lately. In fact, they said, we haven't had a real auto accident since the day before yesterday.

She's had a flat tire, you thought, on some dark and lonely country road. She tried to change the tire herself and the car fell on top of her. Or worst thought of all, she suddenly found herself dissatisfied with the way you did the dishes and had gone home to her mother.

As you reached for the phone—to call you didn't know whom—two pairs of headlights pulled into the driveway. You rushed to the door. It opened and there she was.

"Hold this dear," she said briskly, pushing a case of what-you-thought-was-canned-goods into your arms. She rushed out the door and reappeared with a second case—and with two men, each of whom was also carrying a case. "Put that down, dear," she said, "and come help."

The whole "operation"—which reminded you somehow of an infantry brigade fording a small river—took fourteen minutes. When it was over, the kitchen and the living room were piled high with cases of crunchy peanut butter—thirty cases, each containing twenty-four jars, twenty-four ounces each—or exactly 1,080 pounds of peanut butter.

You did a rapid calculation which told you that at your present rate of consumption of peanut butter, you would be eighty-six years old before the last jar had been eaten. You are now twenty-seven.

"What happend, dear?" you asked. "No, don't tell me," you said. "Let me guess. You went to a bridge party and won the door prize."

"I don't play bridge," she said, "and you know it. They were on sale at the A&P and I just thought I'd stock up. I saved ten cents a jar —can you imagine—seventy-two whole dollars! I bought myself a dress."

"What did the whole lost cost?" you asked.

"That's my secret," she said. "But I *would* like to borrow some money against next month's allowance."

"We'd better have some children in a hurry," you said. "Quintuplets, if possible."

"Let's have a drink," she said.

"Okay," you said. "What's for dinner?" As soon as the words were out, you realized that you should *not* have asked *that* question. "Don't tell me," you said quickly. "Let me guess."

KINDS OF INVENTORY

Manufacturing companies, in general, hold four different kinds of inventory: *raw materials, work-in-process, finished goods,* and *supplies.* Supplies are things such as pencils, paper, forms, electric light bulbs, and so forth, without which the company could hardly carry on its business, but which do not constitute part of its "stock-in-trade." The amount of each type of inventory any company holds depends almost uniquely on the kind of business (or businesses) the company is in. If a company manufactures a product which must be "aged in the wood" for seven years, it will, in the nature of its business, carry much more "work-in-process" inventory for the same volume of sales than a company which produces pasteurized milk or fresh eggs. If a company operates a large number of (expensive) cracking plants which use large quantities of a scarce mineral, it is likely, in the nature of its business, to hold a larger inventory of "raw materials"—either on the surface or under-ground—than a company which manufactures synthetic fibers out of thin air.

In sum, the amount of inventory any company holds will depend (to repeat) almost uniquely on the nature of its business. This does not mean, of course, that some companies do not hold too much inventory and others too little.

additional inventory

A company invests in *additional* inventory for one or the other of two reasons—in order to reduce costs or in order to increase sales. When the wool buyer asked for $500,000 to pick up a lot of raw wool at a bargain price, he expected that the temporary increase in investment in wool inventory would reduce the cost of producing fabric. When Norton, the production manager of the tools division asked that his inventory of parts be increased by $750,000, he hoped, first, to be able to reduce machine "down time" because part of the additional parts would be spare parts. But the bulk of the increase in parts inventory ($698,000) would be necessary to support a big increase in sales which had been forecast by the marketing people.

How do we decide whether to say "yes" or "no" to such requests? How do we decide, that is, whether to allow the wool buyer to increase his inventory of raw wool and the tools division, its inventory of parts? And what would *you* have said to your bride if she had approached you *beforehand* with the suggestion that she be allowed to buy a lifetime inventory of crunchy peanut butter—in order to be able to save ten cents a jar? Would you have known what to say—or would you not?

When the wool buyer of the Butcher Company got Martin's note via the controller and the purchasing manager (see Chapter 1), he sat down, sharpened his pencil and wrote the following memo to the purchasing manager:

> The lot of wool in question consists of 514,000 pounds of raw South African wool of the kind we would use to manufacture heavy tweeds. The lot is now sitting in the Cobham Street warehouse in Boston, duty paid. South African wool of this same grade is now being offered at $1.06 a pound, duty paid, for delivery three months from now. I could perhaps do a bit better than that—say $1.04—for an order of this size.
>
> This lot has been offered to me at 98 cents, duty paid. I have an option on it until 5 P.M. tomorrow. There is nothing the matter with the wool. I have inspected it myself, and it is a good average lot. It is for sale because the dealer to whom it was consigned has been in shaky condition and must liquidate the lot in order to stay alive. He cannot afford to hold it until early spring.
>
> We would have no additional storage charges. There's plenty of room for the lot at the mill. And, therefore, according to my

calculations, we are being offered a chance to earn an annual return of 24.4 percent as follows:

$$\frac{1.04 - .98}{.98} = .061$$

or 6.1 percent for about three months, or 24.4 percent on an annual basis.

The wool buyer gave the memo to his secretary, stood over her shoulder as she typed it and then sent it off to the purchasing manager marked "urgent."

RATE OF RETURN

When, Norton, the production manager of the tools division got Martin's note via the controller and the production vice president (see Chapter 1), he separated his calculations into two parts. First, he calculated a rate of return on that part of the increase represented by the spare parts, which would cost $52,000. The tools division ran forty-eight machines—lathes, and stamping and milling machines primarily—one and one half shifts, six days a week, fifty weeks a year. The division was responsible for about $22 million a year in sales, or slightly less than 10 percent of Butcher's total sales. Principal products were hand and power-driven small tools (saws, drills, sanders, grinders, and so forth) aimed at the commercial and "do-it-yourself" markets.

Norton kept detailed records. He knew therefore that each machine was down, waiting for spare parts, on the average sixteen one hundredths of 1 percent of the time. Norton translated this figure into lost production of $36,000 at selling price—or about $25,200 at direct cost. But the machine operator was paid anyway when a machine was down, and therefore the only additional cost of obtaining the additional $36,000 in sales would be materials plus a small amount of additional power. Materials averaged about 40 percent of selling price and on $36,000 worth of sales, would amount to about $14,400. This meant that $36,000 in additional sales would contribute $21,600 (= $36,000 − $14,400) to overhead. The $52,000 in additional inventory of spare parts would be a "permanent" addition to the supplies inventory. The rate of return on the additional inventory was slightly more than 40 percent a year, thus:

$$\frac{\$21,600}{\$52,000} = .415$$

or 41.5 percent a year. Norton was saying, then, that the investment in spare parts would make possible increased sales of $36,000—*with no additional labor cost*. The contribution on the additional sales would, therefore, be $21,600.

Norton, of course, realized that if there were no additional sales, the rate of return on the additional inventory would be zero. Norton knew, however, that an increase of about 8 percent in sales (= $1.8 million) had been forecast for the coming year for the tools division—this included $850,000 in sales to slow paying customers (see Chapter 11.)

Norton turned next to the remainder of the parts inventory—$698,000. As indicated above, these additional parts were necessary to support the increase in sales forecast by the marketing people. If sales of tools were to increase by $1.8 million next year, the division's inventories would have to increase correspondingly. The division would need not only additional inventories of raw materials and supplies but also of work-in-process and finished goods. The tools division's inventory-turn based on sales, was about 2.58 times. And the $698,000 figure for the proposed increase had been obtained simply by dividing the forecast increase in sales by 2.58, thus:

$$\frac{\$1,800,000}{2.58} = \$698,000$$

To obtain an expected rate of return on the proposed additional investment, Norton simply divided $698,000 into the contribution which would be made by the additional sales, thus:

$$\frac{\$1,800,000 \ (.30)}{\$698,000} = .774$$

or 77.4 percent.

Norton put these calculations and his calculations on the spare parts inventory into a memo which he sent to Hastings and which Hastings, in turn, passed along to Martin.

When Martin got Norton's memo, he read it through quickly, wrote across the top: "Something's wrong here," and passed it on to Kelley. When Kelley got it, he read it and said to himself: "Well, first, both rates are calculated before taxes—and so both rates should be cut in half. But what else?" He gazed meditatively out the window.

"Ah, ha," he said at last. "*Double counting*—or maybe it's triple counting this time."

What did Kelley mean by this? He meant simply that when an expected rate of return had been calculated on the additional sales to slow accounts (see Chapter 11) , the numerator in the fraction had been the contribution, before taxes, expected from the additional sales, thus:

$$\frac{\$70,000 - 49,020}{49,020} = .43$$

or 43 percent.

But now, Kelley realized, Norton had calculated an expected return on the additional inventory necessary to achieve the additional sales by using *the same contribution*. Actually, as Kelley knew, neither the additional sales nor the additional contribution would take place without additional investment in *both* receivables *and* inventory. Moreover, Norton had calculated an expected return on the spare parts inventory by using for the numerator the contribution which would be generated by the first $36,000 of the expected increase in sales. Therefore, this part of the contribution had been counted three times!

Kelley recalculated the two rates of return in the following way:

The saving from spare parts would not be the after-tax contribution on the additional sales. It would be, rather, the after-tax labor cost of sixteen one hundredths of 1 percent of present sales, thus:

$$\frac{(\$36,000 \times .30) \, .50}{\$52,000} = \frac{\$5,400}{\$52,000} = .1041$$

or 10.4 percent. In other words, with the additional inventory of spare parts, idle time would be reduced because machine operators would be doing nothing while their machines were down, awaiting repair. The idle time cost Butcher $10,800 (= $36,000 × .30). This idle time would now be eliminated and Butcher's after-tax profits would be increased by about half of $19,800, or by $5,400 (= .50 × $10,800). (This assumed, of course, that if sales did *not* increase, any unnecessary labor would be released.)

Kelley turned next to the increases, in inventory and receivables, necessary to support the forecast increase in sales of $1.8 million.

The tools division's inventory turn was, as stated above, 2.58 times, based on sales. This meant simply that if sales were to increase by $1.8 million, additional inventory of $698,000 would be required. This figure included raw materials and supplies, work-in-process and finished tools. The tools division's *receivables* turn was about 6 times. Kelley obtained this figure by dividing the division's sales by average receivables outstanding monthly. The figure meant simply that the division's accounts were outstanding about sixty days on the average since (360 days/6 = 60) . Under normal circumstances, this would have meant that

Butcher's receivables would increase by $300,000 (= $1.8 million/6).
But of the expected increase in sales, $850,000 would be to accounts
which were known to be very slow in paying their bills. Kelley decided
to assume therefore that these accounts would turnover only three times
a year. These accounts would thus be responsible for an increase in
receivables of about $283,000 (= $850,000/3). The rest of the increase
in sales, $950,000 (= $1,800,000 — $850,000), would turn over normally
and would be responsible for an increase in receivables of about $158,000
(= $950,000/6). The total increase in average receivables would thus
be $441,000 (= $283,000 + $158,000). Butcher's investment in these
receivables would be about $309,000 (= $441,000 × .70) which was
approximately equal to the direct cost of producing tools worth $441,000
at selling price.

Therefore, the *total* increase in investment, necessary to support the
expected increase in sales was thus:

Increase in average annual investment in inventories:	$698,000
Increase in average annual investment in receivables (direct cost):	309,000
TOTAL	$1,007,000

The additional sales would contribute $540,000 (= $1.8 million × .30)
before taxes or $270,000 after taxes. The expected return on the addi-
tional investment was then about 27 percent, thus:

$$\frac{\$270,000}{1,007,000} = .268$$

or 26.8 percent. This rate assumed, of course, that *no additional costs*
(for example, selling costs) *would be incurred in obtaining the additional sales.* It assumed also that no unusual expenses (for example,
legal fees) would be necessary to collect on sales to the 132 slower
paying customers.

REDUCING "SET-UP" COSTS

The "investment in inventory" problem can raise its head in a variety
of other ways. For example, Norton, the production manager of the
tools division, begins to wonder one day whether, somehow, machine
"set-up" costs can be reduced. Machine "set-up" costs, he has found,

have been increasing much more rapidly than sales. Machine "set-up" costs are incurred whenever a lathe or grinding or milling machine is "changed over" to manufacture a different component. Butcher produces hundreds of different tools—saws, drills, sanders, planes, polishers, wood-lathes, grinders, buffers and many others—each in a large number of sizes and shapes. Butcher itself manufactures all metal parts and components. It buys sheet metal and cuts, presses, stamps and grinds it until the necessary components of each tool have been produced. These components are stored briefly and then assembled into finished tools on a moving line along with certain components Butcher does *not* itself manufacture.

Thousands of components are thus manufactured each year. Several weeks prior to the beginning of each year, Norton and his assistant Jim Marks sit down with the sales forecast (prepared by the marketing department for each type of tool) and make long lists of each necessary component—including those bought from other manufacturers—for example, drive belts, electric cords and motors. Norton then draws up production schedules for each manufactured component, and purchasing schedules for each purchased component.

The size of each production run is determined in approximately the following way: The total number of pieces of each component presently in inventory is subtracted from the total number needed; the remainder is divided by twelve and multiplied by an appropriate seasonal factor. For example, in late November of 1968, Norton received the sales forecast for 1969 from the marketing department. The forecast indicated that expected sales of 7-inch, $1\frac{1}{4}$ HP power-driven circular saws (suggested retail: $22.50) would be 10,200 units. This meant that 10,200 7-inch circular saw blades would be needed. Nine hundred such blades were in inventory; therefore 9,300 would have to be manufactured. This figure was divided by 12 ($= 775$). This number was then multiplied by an appropriate seasonal factor as given in column (2) of Table 12.1. This process yielded the "adjusted production" figures given in column (3) of Table 12.1. The seasonal adjustment was made, of course, because sales of tools are seasonal. Sales (at retail) were highest in March-April and November-December. This meant that Butcher's shipments to retailers would be highest in February and October. This, in turn, meant that Butcher's production would be highest in January and September. (All seasonal adjustments were done by Butcher's computer using programs obtained from the National Bureau of Economic Research.)

The production schedule given in Table 12.1 meant that the tools division "set up" lathes and cutting machines to produce 7-inch blades twelve times a year. Each run took just a few minutes. Everytime the necessary machines were set up to produce 7-inch blades, Butcher

TABLE 12.1

MONTHLY PRODUCTION SCHEDULE
FOR 7-INCH CIRCULAR SAW BLADES

MONTH	AVERAGE PRODUCTION *	SEASONAL FACTOR	ADJUSTED PRODUCTION
January	775	1.28	992
February	775	1.12	868
March	775	1.11	860
April	775	1.10	853
May	775	1.00	775
June	775	.56	434
July	775	.60	465
August	775	.75	581
September	775	1.34	1,039
October	775	1.15	891
November	775	1.02	791
December	775	.97	752
TOTAL	9,300	12.00	9,301

* Total sales minus current inventory, divided by 12.

incurred extra labor cost of $18. This process was repeated each month and therefore Butcher's total annual set-up costs for 7-inch blades was $216 (= 12 × $18). When this figure—which was a good average—was multiplied by more than 4,000 components, the total bill for set-up cost for the tools division as a whole came to more than $800,000.

"That's a lot of money," thought Norton. "Obviously, we could produce all the 7-inch blades we need in a couple of hours in January. If we did so, our set-up costs for blades would be reduced by eleven twelfths. And *in total*, we could save about eleven twelfths of $800,000, or perhaps as much as $730,000. Or if we ran twice a year, instead of twelve times a year, on each component we might save as much as $665,000.

Norton, thereupon took his idea to Hastings. Hastings asked a few hundred questions, of which the following were typical:

"One. Do we have room enough to store all that additional inventory?"

Norton: "Most of it."

"Two. What would our additional storage and insurance costs be?"

Norton: "Very low—perhaps an additional $10,000, if that much. The inventory itself, all stainless steel and chrome, is not perishable and the only real risks are fire and theft."

"Three. By how much would our inventory go up?"

Norton: "We manufacture about $10 million worth of components a year. We now carry a components inventory of about $3 million. The increase would therefore be about $7 million—at the present level of sales."

"Four. How would you go about shifting over to the new system?"

Norton: "We'd have to do it gradually. Instead of producing 990 7-inch blades in January, we'd produce, say 20 percent more. Those extra 198 blades would go into the new components inventory. And so forth for the other components. The entire build-up might take a year or so."

"Five. What happens if fashions in tools change or if sales are below the forecast?"

Norton: "As you know, fashions in tools don't change rapidly. And the inventory of components would turn over once a year—at the present sales level. I'd like to hear what the marketing people have to say on that point. But in my opinion, there's very little risk that changes in fashion would make the inventory obsolete in a year. But one year's inventory would be enough. I wouldn't want to hold more than that. And if sales fell off permanently, the inventory would have to be worked down. But sales are not very likely to go down."

"All right," said Hastings after Norton had finished. "Why don't you calculate a rate of return on an increase of $7 million in components inventory. And then we'll draft a memo to Martin. But you'd better do it very carefully because it looks very doubtful to me: $800,000 looks like a lot of money—but it's barely 11 percent of $7 million, before taxes, and our latest cost of capital—so I hear—is about 11 percent, *after* taxes."

After a couple of weeks of hard work, tabulating components (he found 4,126) and calculating set-up costs, Jim Marks, Norton's assistant, presented him with Table 12.2. Norton raised a few questions about the table.

"One. The saving of $198 per component is based on twelve set-ups a year for each component at $18 each. Is that right?"

Marks: "Yes. And it assumes that if we adopt the plan, we will set-up only once for each component."

"Two. Why have you left out additional storage charges?"

Marks: "You told me to. You said that present storage space would be adequate. I checked and found you were right."

"Three. But shouldn't we take the opportunity cost of that storage space into account?"

Marks: "The finance people would say it's not incremental. And they're right—it's *not* incremental."

TABLE 12.2

RATE OF RETURN ON ADDITIONAL
$7 MILLION INVENTORY

Savings in Set-up Time		
4,126 components at $198		$816,948
Less:		
Additional insurance costs	$7,200	
Additional property taxes	7,000	
Additional storage costs	0	
		14,200
Net savings, before taxes		$802,748

Annual rate of return after build-up complete

$$\frac{\$802,748}{7,000,000} = 11.5$$

"Four. The machine tool division keeps saying it may want that space back. If they take it back, we'd have to find space somewhere, build bins and so forth. Might cost $200,000, maybe much more, for enough space to store all this additional inventory. What about that?"

Marks: "It's irrelevant. The components inventory would turn over once a year. In other words, *the proposal has a one year life.* We would always be free to let the inventory run down and return to the old system. If we had to build storage bins at some time in the future, we'd have to recalculate the expected rate of return on holding the additional inventory—taking the cost of the bins into account."

"Five. Why do you calculate the rate of return in this way—the net savings divided by the additional investment?"

Marks: "I'm assuming the investment itself would never be recovered —that is, that $7 million would remain permanently invested in components inventory. But it doesn't really make much difference. If we assume that the project terminates at the end of the fifth year—because the machine tool division wants its space back—the project would show a return of about 11.5 percent, as shown in Table 12.3."

After reviewing his assistant's calculations, Norton drafted a brief memo to Hastings, Hastings passed the memo on to Martin who, in turn, passed it on to the Finance Committee. That august body rejected the proposal for one simple reason—the expected rate of return, after taxes, was much too low.

TABLE 12.3

RATE OF RETURN ON ADDITIONAL $7 MILLION INVENTORY
(ASSUMING A FIVE YEAR LIFE)

YEAR	NET SAVINGS (thousands)	11.5 PERCENT DISCOUNT FACTORS	PRESENT VALUE
1	$ 802.7	.897	
2	802.7	.804	
3	802.7	.721	$2,929.
4	802.7	.647	
5	802.7	.580	
5	7,000.0 *	.580	4,060.
		TOTAL	$6,989.

* Return of capital Invested.

One day, shortly after he had heard that his proposal had been rejected, Norton found himself pondering the following problem:

1. We've been producing components here on a hand-to-mouth basis. When we need them—which is about once a month—we produce them—all 4,126 of them.
2. But, obviously, we have all kinds of alternatives. We could "set-up" for each component once a year or twice a year or three times or four times or, as we do now, twelve times a year. But there's probably one set-up system which is cheaper than the others. If we produce more often, we increase total set-up costs, but carry less inventory. If we produce less often, we reduce total set-up costs but carry more inventory. How should we decide what to do?

He mentioned the problem to Hastings, who said, "Go see Kelley in Martin's office. Maybe he can help you."

Norton went over the problem with Kelley, who said, "You've got a plain old rate of return problem. You're putting money into additional components inventory. In the jargon we use around here, you're *investing* in inventory. And anything we invest in must show an expected rate of return at least equal to our cost of capital. You ought to calculate rates of return on producing each component twice a year, three times a year—an so forth. Do you have a copy of your original project proposal with you? The one the Finance Committee turned down?"

Norton did and handed it to Kelley (see Table 12.2).

"Something wrong here," said Kelley. "Your investment in inventory is overstated. It's twice as high as it should be. If you set-up once a year—say in January—you'd produce a year's requirements in a month."

"Less than a month," said Norton.

"By the end of the year, your inventory of components would be all used up. You'd have nothing on hand."

"We'd have some odds and ends left over," said Norton.

"Oh, of course," said Kelley, "but we can ignore them for this purpose.

"So if you set-up once a year, your average inventory would be $7 million, divided by two—assuming you used up your stock of components more or less evenly through the year. And your rate of return, before taxes, on the project would really be twice as high as Table 12.2 shows it to be—or 23.4 percent. I'm surprised that nobody caught that. I didn't catch it, Martin didn't catch it, and the Finance Committee didn't catch it. Maybe I was on vacation."

"You were here," said Norton, "but I should have caught it. I'll resubmit it immediately."

"It should go through," said Kelley. "But before I resubmitted it, if I were you, I'd calculate rates of return on setting up twice a year, three times a year, four times a year, and so forth. They won't all be the same."

"Good idea," said Norton. And he left.

A few days later, the project was resubmitted with the expected rate of return recalculated.

CONCLUSION

In this chapter we have described ways and means of calculating rates of return on increases in various kinds of inventory—raw materials, spare parts and components.

One point should be stressed. We have been talking, in part, in this chapter and in the preceeding chapter about rates of return on spontaneous, independent increases in accounts receivable and inventory. But increases in sales will often require not merely increases in accounts receivable but also, increase in inventories—and in other assets. If so, we must be careful, in calculating expected rates of return to take the *total* required additional investment into account.

PROBLEMS

1. Suppose Norton's proposal, to set up once a year, is approved. Calculate his average monthly *inventory* on the following assumptions:

   (a) $7 million worth of components are produced in January. Production of components begins the first workday of the month and ends on the last.

   (b) The tools division uses components at the following rates:

MONTH	PERCENTAGE OF TOTAL DOLLAR INVENTORY VALUE
January	7.0
February	12.0
March	8.7
April	9.7
May	9.8
June	8.0
July	4.5
August	4.0
September	7.0
October	12.1
November	9.2
December	8.0
	100.0

2. Suppose instead that the Finance Committee authorizes Norton to set-up twice instead of once.

   Calculate, as in problem 1, his average monthly inventory.

3. While Norton was working on the set-up cost problem, he suddenly realized that he could apply the same kind of analysis to his inventory of purchased components. The tools division, for example, bought each year approximately 300,000 small motors, ranging in size from one-sixth to two horsepower. The total cost of these motors last year had been about $3.25 million net.

   Norton normally bought 25,000 to 30,000 motors each month, depending on expected production. But obviously he could place one order a year for all 300,000 motors, or two orders for 150,000 each, or three orders for 100,000 motors, and so forth.

   You are Norton and you now realize that this problem is a rate of return problem. What figures would you need in order to be able to decide how often to order motors?

4. Inventories can be reduced as well as increased. But a reduction in inventory—raw material, work-in-process, finished goods—is not likely to occur except as a result of investing in something else, usually in a fixed asset of some kind—for example, a better materials handling system or a more efficient control system.

   Investment in such (fixed) assets is discussed in Chapter 13. But suppose you are offered an accounting machine for $5,200, which (its manufacturer asserts) will "give you better control over your inventories and show a DCF return of about 15 percent a year, after taxes."

   What specific kinds of operating savings do you suppose the manufacturer has in mind?

5. At the breakfast table one bright and shining Thursday morning, your bride of two months jumps up and shouts:

   "Look! Crunchy peanut butter! On sale at the A&P! Ten cents off!"

   She rushes for the hall closet and reappears seconds later in her maxi coat. She starts out the door, stops, comes back in. She says: "Tell me quickly! How many cases shall I buy?"

   The facts are as follows: You have no peanut butter in stock. Each jar contains twenty-four ounces and, after the saving, would cost sixty-nine cents. You consume peanut butter at the rate of one such jar a month. All your excess funds are now invested in a savings account at 5 percent. You know that crunchy peanut butter will never again be available at this low, low price and will soon be selling again at seventy-nine cents, or perhaps more. There's room enough in the living room to store up to thirty cases.

   What advice do you give your wife?

6. After a few minutes of intensive figuring and a quick reference to the discount tables (Table 3.6) which you now carry around in your pocket, you tell her how much to buy. She asks, "Did you take account of the fact that if I make a special trip to the A&P now, I will spend fifteen cents worth of gas plus forty-two cents worth of wear and tear on the car and tires that I would not otherwise spend?"

   You say, "No dear, I didn't."

   She says, in an exasperated way: "Well, don't you think you'd better?"

   Do so.

13

INVESTING IN LONG-TERM ASSETS / internal growth

In the immediately preceding chapters we have described the process of calculating rates of return on, and the present value of, investments in *current* (short-term) assets. We turn now to *long-term* assets. By "long-term assets," in this context, we mean, of course, *physical* assets —such as buildings and machines—rather than *financial* assets such as stocks and bonds.

WHAT IS A LONG TERM ASSET?

A short-term asset, as we have seen previously, is an asset which is expected to turn over—that is, to convert itself into cash—within the firm's "normal operating cycle," which for most firms is a year. When Butcher decided to invest $628,000, at cost, in additional accounts receivable, it expected that a predetermined portion of that sum plus profits—that is, the face amount of the receivables minus an allowance for bad debts—would flow back into the company's bank account within a few months. Not every new customer would pay on time and some of them might not pay at all. But the bulk of them would pay within thirty to sixty days. And this would mean that Butcher's investment in those accounts had been converted into cash—that is, had *turned over* in that period of time. Similarly, with investment in short-term marketable securities—when Butcher invested $100,000 in 90 day bills, it expected (with virtual certainty) that in ninety days or less, it would get its money back—plus interest. Not all current assets will convert themselves into cash when they are supposed to—or in the amount at which they are carried on the company's balance sheet. Some of them, such as finished goods which no longer suit the public's taste, may be sold only after having been carried for a long period of time—and then sold at a loss. But all current assets, nevertheless, are *expected* to convert themselves into cash in a year or less.

A long-term asset, on the other hand, is an asset which is expected to convert itself into cash only over a period of time longer than a year—usually much longer. For this reason, the process of calculating expected rates of return on long-term assets is full of pitfalls and difficulties—as we shall see below—and the expected rates of return themselves, are surrounded by uncertainty: The pitfalls, difficulties and uncertainties become greater, as every fortune-teller knows, the farther ahead one tries to peer—that is, as the life of the asset is longer.

Moreover, long-term assets are, in general, expensive. They are, in general, expensive because, in general, they are "indivisible." A company can invest "just a few" more dollars in marketable securities, in accounts receivable or in inventory. But it cannot invest "just a few" more dollars in a complex of machines or in a new factory. These two peculiarities of long-term assets—their cost and the inevitable uncertainty surrounding the ultimate outcome—mean that proposals to invest in long-term assets provide managers with multiple opportunities to make big mistakes.

This latter fact means that expected rates of return on long-term assets must be calculated with special care. And it explains why, in most companies, proposals to spend money on long-term assets are reviewed not only by the originating division, but also by the finance division, by the Finance Committee and by the Board of Directors.

SPECIAL PROBLEMS

Moreover, when we calculate rates of return on long-term assets, we find ourselves beset with a variety of irritating special problems which are not present when we calculate rates of return on current assets.

First, the net (incremental) cost of an asset is often either more or less than it appears to be. It will be less than it appears to be if the new asset is replacing an old asset, and the old asset has trade-in or salvage value. The incremental cost of the new asset will be *more* than it appears to be if the old asset has no trade-in or salvage value but will have to be removed, at a cost, from its present site. Actually, when we estimated the cost of Ex-Cello's lathe in Chapter 4, we neglected to take into account the trade-in value of the old lathe the new lathe would have replaced. If we had subtracted trade-in value on the old lathe from the cost of the new lathe, to obtain *the incremental cost* of the new lathe, the rate of return on the new lathe would have been higher than the 4.4 percent we calculated.

In addition, the incremental cost of a new asset can be affected by the extent to which the old asset—the one being replaced—has been depreciated. If the trade-in value of the old asset is less than its present book value, buying the new asset will create a *capital loss* which will *save* taxes (*not* the other way around). And the incremental cost of the new asset will be its list price minus trade-in value minus the tax saving. On the other hand, if trade-in value exceeds book value, buying the new asset will create a capital *gain* on which additional taxes will have to be paid. And the *incremental* cost of the new asset would be its list price minus trade-in value plus (*not* minus) the additional taxes due to the capital gain.

We will call this problem the "incremental" problem. It applies not only to estimating the cost of an asset but also to estimating the contribution that asset will make to overhead.

Second, when we calculate a rate of return on a long-term asset, we must estimate its life. And this means that we must first decide what we mean by "life." Do we mean physical life or technological life or product market life—or what? We will call this problem the "life" problem.

Third, the lives of long-term assets vary widely. Suppose, for example, you have to choose between two lathes—one shows a rate of return of 14 percent and has an expected life of nine years. The second shows a rate of return of 16 percent and has an expected life of seven years. Which do you choose? Not necessarily, we may say, the one which shows the higher apparent rate. Or suppose a new project consists of a number of parts—each of which has a different life. How should the rate of return be calculated on the project as a whole? We will call this problem the "uneven lives" problem.

Fourth, of all the irritating problems which beset us in calculating rates of return on long-term assets, perhaps the most irritating is "depreciation and what to do about it." This problem presents itself in two forms:

First, what should be done, in general, about depreciation? Suppose that we are buying a machine which will perform an operation which had previously been done by hand—as for example, a dishwashing machine in a restaurant. In order to obtain a figure for operating savings, we compare the cost of doing the operation by hand with the cost of doing it by machine. Is depreciation on the machine part of the cost of doing the operation by machine? We will call this problem the "depreciation" problem.

Second, suppose we are buying a machine to replace a machine which is itself being depreciated—as Hastings, was considering doing with Ex-Cello's lathe? We will refer to this problem as the *"differential* depreciation" problem.

In short, then, we have five special problems to worry about:
1. the *incremental* problem
2. the *life* problem,
3. the *uneven lives* problem
4. the *depreciation* problem
5. the *differential depreciation* problem.

We illustrate these special problems by tracing through the early stages of the proposed expenditure by Butcher of $504,000 for materials handling equipment and additional inventory bins (see Table 5.1). This proposal originated in Butcher's recently acquired textile division, located in Nashua, New Hampshire.

The textile division manufactured two products: pure and blended woolen and worsted cloth, which was sold to clothing manufacturers; and upholstery fabric, which was sold primarily to automobile manufacturers. The company was vertically integrated—that is, it bought raw wool and synthetic fibers and turned out fully finished fabric. The manufacturing process itself was as efficient as it could be in a mill made up of three separate three-story buildings, all of which were forty years (or more) old. The receiving and warehousing operations, however, were grossly inefficient.

Raw wool was bought by Butcher's own buyers throughout the United States and the rest of the world, Texas, South Africa, Argentina, Uruguay, and Australia. The wool reached the Nashua plant's receiving room in the same condition it came off the sheep's back—"in the fleece"—packed in large burlap bales, each of which weighed about 500 pounds. Each year the Nashua plant received between 20,000 and 30,000 such bales. When a shipment arrived, each bale was identified by a receiving clerk and deposited, one bale at a time, by a fork-lift operator on the open floor of the warehouse in whatever space happened to be available. Every effort was made to deposit any given bale near bales from the same source and of the same quality. But this was not always possible. The result was that particular bales of wool often could not be found when they were needed and many had been "permanently" lost. A bale of raw wool was worth $500 or more, depending on its origin and grade.

After the wool had been received and stored in the above manner, it was sent—sooner or later—to the sorting room where each fleece was inspected for color and grade. It was then sent to the scouring rooms where it was washed to remove dirt, and chemically cleaned to remove grass, burrs, twigs and so forth. The sorting room and the scouring plant were in a second building, about fifty feet away from the receiving room warehouse.

After it had been cleaned, the wool was rebaled, and restored on the second floor of the warehouse to await the manufacturing process. Each bale of wool was thus handled manually (that is, with small fork lifts) four times: once when it was received and stored on the first floor of the warehouse; once when it was taken across the way to sorting and cleaning; once again when it was brought back to the warehouse to await manufacture; and finally when it was taken to the carding room— the first stage in the manufacturing process—located next to the cleaning room.

This situation had arisen, in part, because the Nashua division, prior to its acquisition by Butcher, had not bought raw wool. It had bought sorted and cleaned wool through dealers and brokers in Boston. Previously, therefore, wool had to be handled manually only twice—once when it was received from the supplier, and again when it was sent to the carding room.

At present five men were occupied full time, one shift, just moving bales around with the help of ten battery-driven "low-reach" fork lifts. Each lift could carry one bale of wool at a time. At peak periods (four months a year) all ten fork lifts were fully employed, two shifts a day.

Shortly after Butcher had acquired the Nashua division and Nashua had begun to buy its own raw wool, Hastings visited the plant. He cast his eye over the operations in the receiving room and warehouse and especially at the several precariously stacked mountains of wool. And he watched several fork-lift operators as they searched, often in vain, for particular bales of wool. After half an hour or so, he said to the plant manager: "This has really gotten pretty bad. I've never seen such a mess." The plant manager agreed and asked Hastings whether he could have "a couple of industrial engineers for a month or so to see what could be done." Hastings readily agreed.

Two industrial engineers arrived within ten days. They observed operations closely and discussed the problems at length with the plant manager. After a few weeks, they made the following three-part proposal (based on the assumption that the sorting and cleaning rooms could not be moved) :

1. A system of large shelved inventory bins would be installed on both floors of the warehouse. Those on the first floor would be used to store specified grades of raw wool. Those on the second floor would be used to store cleaned and sorted wool. The bins themselves would keep bales from being "lost" and the shelves would make each bale readily accessible to "high-reach" fork lifts. Much time would be saved both in storing raw and cleaned wool and in finding it again when it was needed.

2. Two covered conveyor belts would be installed—one to carry raw wool from the first floor of the warehouse to the sorting and cleaning rooms and the other, to carry sorted and cleaned wool from the sorting and cleaning rooms to the second floor of the warehouse—where it would be stored to await the manufacturing process. (Sufficient storage space was not available in or near the carding room to store sorted and cleaned wool there.) Running a conveyor belt from the sorting and cleaning operation to the second floor of the warehouse would make it unnecessary to use the warehouse elevator. This elevator had always been a bottleneck because it could hold only one small fork lift and moved exasperatingly slowly. A third conveyor might be added later on, moving directly from the second floor of the warehouse to the carding room—but not until an attempt had been made to use the second conveyor both ways.

3. Four new "high-reach," high-capacity, battery-driven fork lifts would replace the ten now in use. One would be stationed on the first floor of the warehouse, one on the second floor, one in the sorting-cleaning area, and one would be a spare. The fork lifts would no longer shuttle back and forth from the first and second floors of the warehouse to the sorting, cleaning, and carding areas across the way. They would merely load and unload conveyor belts and store both raw and cleaned wool. The ten small fork lifts, which were only a year or two old, would be traded in against the new fork lifts.

net cost

In order to get started the engineers called in a local contractor and a local dealer in fork lifts, described to them the proposed new system, and obtained, verbally, the figures given in Table 13.1. In addition, the fork-lift dealer said the ten old fork lifts would have trade-in value of $30,000.

The two engineers knew, as a result of bitter experience, that pre-

TABLE 13.1

PRELIMINARY ESTIMATE OF COST OF INSTALLING NEW EQUIPMENT AT NASHUA DIVISION

Two heavy duty enclosed conveyors (Installed)	$270,000
Shelved steel bins (Installed)	100,000
Reinforcing of second floor of warehouse to carry bins	25,000
Four fork lifts (list price)	60,000
Chargers, extra batteries, etc	10,000
TOTAL	$465,000

liminary estimates, obtained in this casual way, were likely to be too low. After the proposal had been tentatively approved, drawings would be made of the bins and conveyors, materials would be specified, and so forth, and firm bids obtained. The two engineers believed, on the basis of past experience, that the probability was about .80 that the lowest firm bid would be about 20 percent higher than the preliminary estimate. Or in other words, the probability was .80 that the lowest firm bid would be about $558,000 (= $465,000 × 1.20). This meant that, given the preliminary estimate (Table 13.1), the best estimate of actual cost would be $539,400, thus:

COST	PROBABILITY	EXPECTED VALUE
$465,000	.20	$ 93,000
$558,000	.80	$446,400
TOTAL	1.00	$539,400

This figure, $539,400, was carried to Table 13.2. The cost of the drawings ($1,500) and of certain extra labor costs (which would have to be borne by Nashua) were added, bringing the expected total to $541,750. Two deductions were then made. The first deduction represented the trade-in value of the ten old fork lifts, $30,000. The fact that the old fork lifts had trade-in value of $30,000 meant that the net out-of-pocket cost of the project would be $30,000 less than gross cost.

But, in addition, the ten fork lifts had cost $75,000 and were being depreciated on a straight-line basis at the rate of $15,000 a year. They were about two years old and therefore only $30,000 of their original cost had been written off. This meant that the present book value of the

TABLE 13.2

REVISED ESTIMATE OF COST OF INSTALLING
NEW EQUIPMENT AT NASHUA DIVISION

Expected cost of bins and equipment		$539,400
Extra labor		850 *
Drawings, etc.		1,500
	Subtotal	$541,750
Subtract trade-in value		
Ten fork lifts	$30,000	
Tax saving on same	7,500	$ 37,500
	Net Cost	$504,250

* Cost of preparing warehouse for bins and of storing bales in bins.

fork lifts was $45,000. But the trade-in value of the fork lifts was only $30,000. This meant a capital loss on the fork lifts of $15,000, thus:

Cost of ten fork lifts	$75,000
Depreciation taken	
(= amount of original cost recovered)	30.000
Unrecovered cost	45,000
Trade-in value	30,000
Capital loss	$15,000

This capital loss could be deducted from ordinary income and would save Butcher $7,500 in taxes ($7,500 = .50 × $15,000) —that is, because of the capital loss, Butcher's out-of-pocket outlay for taxes this year would be $7,500 less.

These two deductions together reduced the expected cost of the proposed project from $541,750 to $504,250 (see Table 13.2).

savings

The engineers turned next to the problem of estimating savings—which, they saw, would have two parts:

1. Operating savings—that is, savings in labor, power, maintenance and so forth: the new system would be cheaper to run than the old system.

2. The savings which would accrue because the new system would keep bales from getting lost.

The engineers attacked first, the problem of estimating operating savings.

OPERATING SAVINGS

First they tabulated from company records the cost of the labor required under the present system in a good year. These figures are given in Table 13.3. They are rounded averages of figures for the last two

TABLE 13.3

ESTIMATE OF OPERATING COSTS, IN A GOOD YEAR, UNDER PRESENT SYSTEM AT NASHUA

PRESENT LABOR COST	
5 full-time fork lift operators at $4,200 a year, 1st shift	$21,000
5 extra operators, four months a year, 1st shift	7,000
10 extra operators, four months a year, 2nd shift	16,000
Total labor	$44,000
MAINTENANCE	
10 fork lifts	5,000
Total labor and maintenance	$49,000

years. The figures include the company's share of payments for social security and all fringe benefits. Total labor cost came to about $44,000. Next they tabulated maintenance costs for the ten fork lifts for the last two years and averaged them. Maintenance came to about $500 a lift a year, or $5,000 in total.

The engineers turned next to the calculation of labor and other costs *under the proposed new arrangements* also in a good year. They estimated labor cost by riding around themselves in a borrowed high-reach fork lift, moving bales to and from imaginary bins and conveyors. They concluded after a week of experimentation on the first and second floors and in the sorting-cleaning area that three full-time fork-lift operators would be able to do the job with parttime assistance from a fourth operator. A very large amount of time would be saved because the fork lifts would no longer travel between the two buildings and up and down in the elevator. They would simply run back and forth for the most part, from bins to conveyor and vice versa—on a single floor. Estimates of labor and other direct costs in a good year under the proposed new arrangements, are given in Table 13.4. The labor cost is simply the cost

TABLE 13.4

ESTIMATE OF OPERATING COSTS
UNDER NEW SYSTEM AT NASHUA

ESTIMATED LABOR COST

3 full-time fork-lift operators at $4,200 a year	$12,600
1 extra operator, half-time	2,100
Total labor	$14,700

ESTIMATED MAINTENANCE

4 fork lifts	$ 2,000
2 conveyors	3,000
Total labor and maintenance	$19,700

of three full time fork-lift operators plus the cost of a fourth parttime operator. Maintenance on each of the new fork lifts would be about $500 a year, and about $1,500 on each of the two conveyors.

But the two engineers knew that in the textile industry, as in machine tools, one out of every three of four years would be an "off-year." In an off-year, labor cost would be less. They therefore calculated the

TABLE 13.5

COMPARISON OF LABOR COST AT NASHUA

Event	Cost		Probability		Expected Value	
	OLD SYSTEM	NEW SYSTEM	OLD SYSTEM	NEW SYSTEM	OLD SYSTEM	NEW SYSTEM
Good year	$44,000	$14,700	.66	.66	$29,040	$ 9,702
Off year	32,765	12,700	.34	.34	11,140	4,318
TOTAL			1.00	1.00	$40,180	$14,020

expected value of labor cost under the old system and the new.

In a good year, labor cost under the *present* system would be $44,000 as in Table 13.3. In an off-year, however, less overtime would be necessary and total labor cost would therefore be reduced to $32,765. The engineers used probabilities of .66 and .34 for, respectively, good years and off-years. The *expected* labor cost under the present system was thus found to be $40,180 (Table 13.5). Using the basic data contained in Table 13.4, they then calculated *expected* labor cost under the *new* system and found it to be $14,020 (Table 13.5).

MAINTENANCE AND POWER

The engineers then went through a similar process for maintenance costs—but did not construct a probability distribution. They assumed that maintenance costs would not vary much from good years to bad.

They then noticed they had forgotten to add electric power to run the three conveyors. They corrected this omission by adding $2,000 to the cost of operating the new system (Table 13.6). The fork-lift batteries

TABLE 13.6

ESTIMATED COSTS AND SAVINGS, BEFORE TAXES, AT NASHUA

	OLD SYSTEM	NEW SYSTEM
Labor cost	$40,180 *	$14,020 *
Maintenance	5,000	5,000
Electric power		2,000
TOTAL	$45,180	$21,020

* See Table 13.5.

had to be recharged daily, but the cost of recharging ten small batteries under the old system would not differ much from the cost of recharging four large ones under the new system.

after tax savings

Expected annual operating savings *before* taxes would thus be $24,160—which was equal to expected operating costs, before taxes, under the old system ($45,180) minus expected operating costs, before taxes, under the new system ($21,020), as shown in Table 13.7.

TABLE 13.7

ESTIMATED OPERATING SAVINGS, AFTER TAXES, AT NASHUA

Annual Operating Costs			
Old System		$45,180	
New System		21,020	
Savings before taxes			$24,160
Annual Depreciation on New System			
Bins ($100,000, 20-year life)	$ 5,000		
Conveyors ($270,000, 10-year life)	27,000		
Fork lifts ($60,000, 6-year life)	10,000		
Reinforcing ($25,000, 5-year life)	5,000		
		$47,000	
Annual Depreciation on Old System			
10 fork lifts		— 15,000	
Differential Depreciation			32,000
Change in taxable income			— 7,840
Tax savings (at 50% of $7,840)			3,920
Plus operating savings			24,160
TOTAL SAVINGS			$28,080

Thus under the new system *before depreciation* taxable income would be increased by $24,160—simply because operating costs would be reduced by that amount, sales and everything else remaining, on the average, the same.

But under the new system, because of the cost of the bins and the conveyors, depreciation charges would be large and would more than offset the additional taxable income. Depreciation under the old system was $15,000 (the ten old fork lifts). Under the new system, depreciation would be about $47,000 (see Table 13.7). Additional ("differential") depreciation under the new system would thus be $32,000.

The engineers were delighted to see that this was more than enough to offset the operating savings. There would therefore be no additional taxes. In fact, taxes for the Nashua plant as a whole would be less under the new system instead of more—by 50 percent of the amount by which depreciation exceeded operating savings. And this tax saving would be directly attributable to installation of the new system. The excess depreciation was $32,000 minus $24,160, or $7,840. At a tax rate of 50 percent, the overall tax saving would be $3,920 (= $7,840 × .50). In order to obtain net operating savings after tax, therefore, the engineers *added* $3,920 to the pretax operating savings. The total after-tax saving would therefore be $28,080 ($24,160 + $3,920). (See Table 13.7.)

The easiest way to understand this peculiar result is to compare Nashua's total operating funds-flow under the present system with total operating funds-flow under the proposed new system. Total funds-flow √ is equal to earnings after taxes plus depreciation (see Table 5.9). Table 13.8 shows this comparison. Under the old system the Nashua plant was

TABLE 13.8

COMPARISON OF OPERATING FUNDS-FLOW, AFTER TAXES

	OLD SYSTEM	NEW SYSTEM
EBTD *	$1,500,000	$1,524,160
Depreciation	150,000	182,000
EBT (= taxable income)	1,350,000	1,342,160
Taxes at 50%	675,000	671,080
EAT †	675,000	671,080
Add Back Depreciation	150,000	182,000
Total Funds-Flow	$ 825,000	$ 853,080
Total Operating Funds-Flow, New System		$ 853,080
Total Operating Funds-Flow, Old System		− 825,000
Additional Operating Funds-Flow Under New System		$ 28,080

* Earnings before taxes and depreciation.
† Earnings after taxes.

expected to contribute $1.5 million to earnings before taxes and depreciation. Under the new system this contribution would be $24,160 higher because operating costs would be that much less. Under the new system, annual depreciation would be $32,000 more than depreciation under the old system—because of the new equipment. Therefore, both **EBT** (earnings before taxes) and **EAT** (earnings after taxes) under the new system would be *less* under the new system than under the old system because the additional depreciation under the new system would more than offset operating savings. EBT would be $7,840 less and EAT $3,920 less. But when depreciation was added back, the engineers found that the total funds-flow under the new system would be $28,080 larger than the total funds-flow under the old system. This is exactly the same figure as that given at the bottom of Table 13.7—$28,080.

In sum then, annual expected operating savings, after taxes, under the new system would be $28,080.

We should pause here for a moment to note carefully what Brody and S:ms, the engineers, did, and did *not*, do about depreciation:

1. They did *not* add depreciation to the cost of operating the new system (see Table 13.6).
2. They did use depreciation, however, to calculate taxes on the additional contribution to overhead (see Table 13.7).
3. In order to obtain additional taxable income and additional taxes, they did *not* subtract all the depreciation on the new system. They subtracted, rather, *differential depreciation*—that is, depreciation on the new system ($47,000) minus depreciation on the old system ($15,000). They were, in effect, subtracting *additional* depreciation from *additional* contribution to overhead (the operating savings) to obtain *additional* taxable income—and *additional* taxes.

lost bales

Next the engineers tried to decide how many of the lost bales of wool, raw and cleaned, would be found after the bins had been installed. This would give them, at the same time, an estimate of the number of bales which would be likely to be lost in the future if the present system remained in effect.

The wool would be found as follows: the bins would be built by a local steel fabricator at his own plant in sections twenty feet high and four feet wide. They would be trucked to the mill during the two-week shutdown in July and bolted into place by the steel fabricator's employees. During the preceding week the five fork-lift operators would have provided space for the bins by moving all bales away from the walls, toward the center of each floor of the warehouse. About 2,500 bales of raw wool and 2,000 bales of cleaned wool would then be in inventory—including an unknown number of bales which had previously been "lost." After the bins had been installed and marked, the bales would be stored in them according to grade and quality, beginning with the intact lots of raw wool which had been most recently received.

Thus the head of the receiving room would take his inventory sheets and, reading down from the top, would tell the fork-lift operators to find, for example, twenty bales of Australian 80s. Suppose that eighteen such bales were found readily. They would be stored in the bins marked "Australian 80s." This process would continue until all whole lots had been stored. Left in the middle of the floor would be, for example, the two odd bales of Australian 80s—plus those bales which had previously been lost. The fork-lift operators would look first for all odd bales of new lots. These would then be stored. After this second stage of the process had been completed, all bales remaining on the floor would be bales which had previously been lost. The process would be repeated on the second floor with wool which had been sorted and cleaned. This process of storing the wool in bins was expected to take five men about one week and would cost Nashua about $500.

How many lost bales would be found? In order to answer this question, the engineers equipped themselves with inventory sheets and with copies of all requests for raw wool from the sorting-cleaning area and for cleaned wool from the carding room. They studied each fork lift operator for a week and found, to their great surprise, that on the average each request for inventoried raw wool was sent to the sorting-cleaning area .8 percent short. In other words, over a period of one week, .8 percent of all bales of raw wool could not be found. If every order from the sorting and cleaning area was filled .8 percent short, and Nashua received 25,000 bales of raw wool a year—then it followed that 200 bales of raw wool, at $500 each ($100,000) were being lost in each good year. The engineers were astonished. And needless to say, they attacked their job with new zest.

The engineers had also observed that when a fork lift operator could not find a particular bale of wool, he spent an unusual amount of time frantically looking for it. In the process, of course, he not only lost time but he also multiplied future confusion by turning over bales and mixing them into lots of wool to which they did not belong. The situation on the second floor—where the cleaned wool was kept—was somewhat better. There, "only" .4 percent of all bales were lost or mislaid. The engineers knew that wool shrank about 20 percent, on the average, during cleaning. Therefore, 25,000 bales of raw wool were equal to about 20,000 bales of cleaned wool. And if a bale of raw wool weighing about 500 pounds was worth about $500, a bale of cleaned wool weighing 500 pounds would be worth more than $625. And .4 percent of 20,000 cleaned bales, worth $625 each, was worth a total of $50,000 (20,000 × $625 × .004). The engineers began to feel, of course, that the savings in lost bales alone would pay for the project in a very short period of time.

The engineers then turned to the problem of finding out how many "lost" or mislaid bales were eventually found again. They discussed the matter with the plant manager.

"It all depends on the fork lift operator," he said. "I'm sure that there are some bales over there," he gestured at the several mountains of raw wool, "which were supposed to have been used two years ago. They're probably all moths by this time. But once in a while a good fork lift operator will come across a bale which he remembers was ordered out two weeks or two months or a year ago—but which couldn't then be found. If he comes across such a bale, he pushes it into that room near the elevator—the one with the 'Lost and Found' sign over the door. He gets $5 for finding the bale—and we have to decide what to do with it. Sometimes we can use it immediately. Sometimes we know we'll be able to use it in the near future—in which case we push it back where it's supposed to be and flag it. But sometimes it will get lost again. Sometimes we know we won't be able to use it and so we sell it— usually at a loss.

"'But," continued the plant manager, "most of the fork-lift operators don't care or can't remember. So if a bale is once lost, it's likely to stay lost. And we don't take physical inventory. We don't have the time or the help to be able to struggle through that mountain, bale by bale." Again he gestured toward the mountains of wool, in some parts of the room piled 25 feet high. "I'd say that 80 percent of the bales that are lost are never found again."

"How confident are you of that figure?" asked the senior engineer.

"Not very," said the plant manager.

"Where did it come from?" asked the senior engineer.

"Off the top of my head, of course," said the plant manager. "Where else? You wanted a figure and so I gave you one."

"Well," said the senior engineer, "we have a pretty good estimate of bales initially lost. Is there any way of getting an estimate, for each of the last two years, of those found? What about the $5 bonus you pay for found bales? Would there be separate records of the number paid?"

"No," said the plant manager. "Why should we have kept separate records of *that*? Record keeping costs money. It's all mixed in with the regular payroll. Would have to check the weekly payroll every week for two years."

"But only five men are involved," said one of the engineers.

"Closer to fifteen," said the plant manager. "We've had turnover in here. But try it if you like. You'll have to look at about 1,500 payroll slips. The bonus would be shown separately on the slip. Take you about a week."

"Wouldn't the inventory records show it?" asked the other engineer.

"The inventory records would show occasional odd bales in stock. But in order to be sure that those odd bales were lost bales, you'd have to check the inventory against sorting and cleaning orders for raw wool and against manufacturing orders for cleaned wool. There must be a thousand such orders. Take about a week, too. Here," he said, reaching for his book and a blank carding-room order form, "you look for odd lots on the inventory sheets. Here's one. Number 8242: 1,050 pounds cleaned wool, Texas 70s, two bales received back from sorting and cleaning on September 6, 1966. Whole lot was 16 bales, 8,010 pounds. The inventory sheet doesn't tell us whether fourteen or sixteen bales were ordered to the carding room. It just tells us that we have two bales in inventory. If sixteen bales were ordered to the carding room, those two bales are lost. If only fourteen were ordered, then they're not lost. Do you follow?

"Now," he continued, "let's look through the carding room orders for lot Number 8242. Every lot of raw wool keeps the same number through the whole manufacturing process. I can go through the finished goods inventory, piece by piece, and tell you where the raw wool came from, what it cost, how much it shrank in cleaning, what the carding waste was, how much the carding waste was sold for, what the combing waste was, and so forth. We now look for a carding room order for lot Number 8242 cleaned wool, issued some time after September 6, 1966. Should be easy. Here we are. Sixteen bales, 8,010 pounds, ordered out to carding on September 16, 1966. Sixteen bales ordered to carding, fourteen bales sent. Two bales presumed missing. We know that they were not found again because they're still carried in inventory. Q.E.D., two lost bales of cleaned Texas 70s, lost since September 16, 1966—nearly two years.

"You can get the answer this way," he concluded, "but it will be pretty tedious. The payroll records would probably be easier."

"But this would give us almost an exact count of lost bales," said one of the engineers. "And we'd be able to make a better estimate of annual savings—and of the windfall we expect to get when the bins are installed. Especially if you think it will only take a week to do the job. You don't happen to have someone who could do the job for us?"

"Not a chance," said the plant manager. "But I'll get the records together for you. Don't take them out of this office. You can work at that table over there." He indicated a table in the corner of his office which was piled high with samples of raw wool, cleaned wool and finished fabric. "I'll have it cleaned off for you."

"A few other questions before we break up," said the senior engineer. "First, how should we value the lost bales? We've got to put a dollar figure on the windfall." In reply to this question, the plant manager suggested they tabulate lost bales by lot number, weight, quality, and cost—lot Number 8242, two bales, 1,050 pounds Texas 70s, $1.43. After they'd finished, he would value each lot at the current market price.

Next, they asked what would happen to the lost wool if the bins were not installed. "It would stay lost, I suppose," said the plant manager.

The engineers said they weren't so sure. They pointed out that if bales continued to be lost at the rate of, say, 300 a year, the situation would soon become intolerable. If nothing were done now, it would have to be done later. "We've been assuming," Sims said, "that lost bales are simply gone—money down the drain. But if, in fact, they would be found in two or three years, they would be sold or used then, and there would be a windfall *then* instead of now. The windfall would be made up *then* of all the bales which are lost as of now, plus all the bales which would be lost until something were done—two or three or four years from now."

"I see," said the plant manager. "I think we'd be able to live with the present situation until we build the new plant."

"What new plant?" asked Brody, the senior engineer.

"In five years we either build a new one-story plant somewhere in this area or we move south. This is one of the least efficient textile mills in the whole state of New Hampshire."

"I'm glad someone finally told us," said the senior engineer, sarcastically. "Means we assume a five-year life on the project."

"The fact that we may move south is a secret," said the plant manager. "If the word got out, we'd start having all kinds of labor turnover."

"Okay," said Brody. "What will the conveyors be worth in five years?"

"About a third of their cost," said the plant manager. "If we stay here we'd be able to use them—I think. If we moved south, we'd probably sell them."

"At one third of their cost?" asked the junior engineer.

"About one third," said the plant manager. "Probably."

Brody and Sims spent the next week tabulating lost bales. They found exactly 502 bales, as follows:

JULY 1, 1966—JUNE 30, 1967

Raw wool	121 bales	
Cleaned wool	77 bales	
TOTAL	198 bales	

JULY 1, 1967—JUNE 30, 1968

Raw wool	162 bales	
Cleaned wool	142 bales	
		304 bales
TOTAL		502 bales

They showed their tabulations to the plant manager. He put an average value of $520 on each bale of raw wool and a value of $635 on each bale of cleaned wool. The total windfall would thus be $286,225 at current market prices. "But," said the plant manager, "you'd better reduce that figure by 25 percent. A lot of those bales will be pretty badly moth-eaten."

They then proceeded to calculate the *expected* value of lost bales under the old system (see Table 13.9). They had discovered 283 bales

TABLE 13.9

ESTIMATED ANNUAL VALUE OF LOST BALES

	Number of Bales Lost		Cost		Probability		Expected Value	
	RAW WOOL	CLEANED WOOL	RAW WOOL	CLEANED WOOL	RAW WOOL	CLEANED WOOL	RAW WOOL	CLEANED WOOL
	(1)	(2)	(3)	(4)	(5)	(6)	(7)	(8)
Good Year	142	110	$73,840	$69,850	.66	.66	$48,734	$46,101
Off Year *	107	83	55,380	52,388	.34	.34	18,829	17,813
					1.00	1.00	$67,563	$63,913

* 75 percent of figure for good year.

of lost raw wool with an average value per bale of $520, and 219 bales of lost cleaned wool with an average value per bale of $635. These 502 bales had, of course, been lost over a *two-year period*. More bales were lost during the second year than during the first but they decided to take a simple average of both years. Thus they assumed that in good years, 142 bales of raw wool, to a total cost of $73,840 (= 142 × $520) would be lost—as would 110 bales of cleaned wool. The cost of the lost cleaned wool, in a good year thus would be $69,850 (= 110 × $635). In an off-year, receipts of wool would be reduced by about 25 percent and losses would, therefore, also be reduced by about the same percentage. In an off-year, then, losses of raw wool would be $55,380 (= $73,840 × .75), and of cleaned wool, $52,388 (= $69,850 × .75). These figures are given separately for raw wool and cleaned wool in Table 13.9. The combined expected value of losses of *both* kinds of wool was thus found to be $131,476 (= $67,563 + $63,913).

But the engineers did not expect to reduce lost and mislaid bales to zero. Bin space would be provided for 7,000 bales of raw wool and 5,000 bales of cleaned wool and, with average turnover, this should be about 15 percent more space than would be necessary. Bales would rarely, if ever, therefore be lying around loose. But an occasional bale might be stored in the wrong bin and, if so, it would be difficult to find when a sorting or carding order for it came through. But it would be more "visible"—each bin would be four bales deep and two bales wide—and lost bales would turn up more quickly afterwards. Now mislaid bales were simply pushed out of the way and new bales, as they arrived, were piled on top of them. Brody and Sims estimated, without any really good basis for doing so, that the new system would reduce losses by 95 percent—or in other words that under the new system, losses would be 5 percent of losses under the old system. Five percent of $131,476 was $6,574.

The engineers then paused briefly to catch their breath and take stock. They had already determined that annual operating savings would be $28,080 (see Table 13.7) and annual savings due to keeping wool from getting lost would be $124,902. The engineers set these figures down, as in Table 13.10, year-by-year for the next five years. They felt

TABLE 13.10

ESTIMATED TOTAL SAVINGS ANNUALLY AT NASHUA

YEAR	OPERATING SAVINGS (AFTER TAX)	NET SAVINGS FROM NOT-LOST BALES *	TOTAL SAVINGS (AFTER TAX)
(1)	(2)	(3)	(4)
1968	$28,080	$124,902	$152,982
1969	28,080	124,902	152,982
1970	28,080	124,902	152,982
1971	28,080	124,902	152,982
1972	28,080	124,902	152,982

* Cost of bales expected to be lost under old system ($131,476) minus expected cost of bales expected to be lost under new system ($6,574).

a strong sense of accomplishment.

You have doubtless noticed that the engineers, in calculating the savings due to lost wool, did *not in any way* take account of any additional taxes. The engineers assumed, that is, that savings due to lost wool would *not* increase taxable income and would *not* therefore be subject to tax. The savings due to lost wool would not be subject to tax because, in effect, they would be due merely to reduction in inventory.

If you have difficulty understanding this, suppose that Nashua, just to amuse itself and its stockholders, bought 200 extra bales of wool a year and locked them in the attic over the warehouse, and threw away the key. The 200 bales would represent additional investment in useless inventory—and they would not affect taxable income unless they were used or damaged. Taxable income is, of course, sales minus (among other things) the cost of raw materials *used* to manufacture goods actually sold. But they could not possibly have been used to manufacture anything—they were locked in the attic—and the key thrown away.

But suppose now that after five years, the Nashua plant is torn down. The wreckers, accompanied by the plant manager, reach the attic door, break it down and gaze inside.

"Wool!" exclaims the plant manager rushing in.

"Moths!" exclaim the wreckers, rushing out.

"Moths is right," says the plant manager sadly, "$100,000 worth."

He removes the tickets from the bags (so that he can take them out of inventory and claim a tax loss) and instructs the warehouse manager to "Get those bales out of there. Fast." He notifies the accounting office of the loss—and on Nashua's tax return for the year, the following item appears: "Loss on raw wool damaged by moths ($100,000)."

As a result Nashua's taxable income for the year was reduced by $100,000 and its taxes (at a rate of 50 percent), by $50,000.

In short, under the old system the lost bales would have no tax effects until they were found. And when they were found, they would create a tax loss if they were damaged (or, of course, if they were sold at a loss).

Under the new system, bales would not be "locked in the attic" and therefore they would not be there to be found when the mill was torn down. This meant that under the new system there would be no tax loss at the end of the fifth year. And this meant, in turn, that both taxable income and taxes would be *higher* (not lower) in the final year—under the new system.

other considerations

The engineers felt they were now in position to close in rapidly on a rate of return on the project—and on an estimate of its net present value. But first they needed a few more figures as follows:

1. The salvage value of the bins and conveyors five years hence—when the present plant would be torn down.
2. The market value of the "lost" bales—which would be found as soon as the bins were installed.
3. The market value of the bales which would be found five years hence if the new system were *not* installed.

4. The tax saving on the bales which would be found five years hence if the new system were *not* installed.

For *salvage value* they took the plant manager's estimates—bins, $40,-000; conveyors, $90,000, and fork lifts, nothing. For the value of the windfall, they again used the plant manager's estimate—he had suggested they use 75 percent of the current market value of the 502 bales. This came to $214,669 (= .75 × $286,225). This windfall would not occur simultaneously with the installation of the bins. The lost bales would be found then—but it would take time to inspect each bale and dispose of it. The engineers therefore assumed that Nashua would receive the windfall at the end of the first year under the new system.

Next the engineers assumed that if the present system were continued, and the present plant closed down in five years, 1,250 bales of wool would be found *then,* of which 750 would be more than two years old and probably worthless. The value of the remaining 500 bales would be about $200,000. This sum would be received five years hence, to repeat, *if the present system were continued.* This assumed, of course, that wool prices five years hence would be at about their present level.[1]

The 750 worthless bales at $500 each (= $375,000), would constitute a tax loss which would be taken in the fifth year if the present system

TABLE 13.11

ESTIMATED GAINS AND LOSSES FROM INSTALLATION OF NEW EQUIPMENT AT NASHUA

YEAR (BEGINNING JULY 1)	TOTAL ANNUAL SAVINGS (AFTER TAX)	OTHER GAINS OR LOSSES	TOTAL ANNUAL GAIN OR LOSS
(1)	(2)	(3)	(4)
1968	$152,982	$214,669	$367,651
1969	152,982	——	152,982
1970	152,982	——	152,982
1971	152,982	——	152,982
1972	152,982	387,500 *	104,518 *
		130,000	

* Negative figure.

[1] The engineers decided for the time being not to construct a probability distribution over wool prices five years hence. Considerable research would have been required which, at this moment, did not seem to be worthwhile.

were continued. The amount of the tax loss would be about $187,500
(= $375,000 × .50).

The engineers then set up Table 13.11 which simply brought together total annual savings from Table 13.10 and the other gains and
losses described above. Thus in the first year the value of the windfall
($214,660) was added—making the total gain during the first year,
$367,651.[2]

In the last year, there would be one other gain and two other losses.
The salvage value of the equipment, $130,000, would be a gain. The
two losses would be (a) the estimated value of the 500 good bales
which would be found ($200,000) at the end of the fifth year if the
present system continued and (b) the tax-saving ($187,500) on account
of the 750 worthless bales which would be found at the end of the fifth
year—if the present system continued.

Why are these two latter amounts considered to be losses? They are
losses, if the new system is installed, because they would be gains if the
present system were continued. In other words, these two amounts
would be sacrificed if the new system were installed. Therefore they
must be deducted from gains in the final year *in order to put the gains
and losses in that year on a net basis.*

We can look at this matter in the following way—disregarding, for
the moment, the time pattern of the cash flows:

1. Under the new system, annual savings, after taxes, would be
   $152,982 or, in total for five years, $764,910.
2. Of this total amount, $624,510 (= 5 × $124,902) would be due
   to wool which would not be lost.
3. But this amount overstates savings due to lost wool because
   under the old system the wool lost during each of the five years
   would be found at the end of the fifth year, when the Nashua
   plant was torn down.
4. Some of the wool found at the end of the fifth year (400 to 500
   bales) would be good wool capable of being used or sold. The
   value of such good wool would be $200,000. When this amount
   is deducted from the total value of lost wool, the *net* value of
   the wool which would be lost under the old system is found to
   be $424,510 (= $624,510 − $200,000).

---

[2] A further tax saving of about $35,000 was ignored. It would be created by the
difference between the cost of the bales which would be found (when the bins
were installed) and their market value. Twenty-five percent of the bales would be
worthless; they had cost about $70,000. If the remaining bales were not sold above
cost, Nashua would have a tax loss of $70,000 and a tax saving of $35,000
(= $70,000 × .50) during the first year.

5. Even though the remaining 750 bales of wool would be worthless as wool, they would constitute a tax loss which would reduce Butcher's taxes in the fifth year by $187,500. When this sum is subtracted from $424,510, the *net* dollar value of the saving under the new system from lost wool is found to be only $237,010.

This, then, is what the two "losses" in the fifth year mean. They simply adjust for the fact that part of the value of wool lost during the first five years, if the old system were continued, would be recovered at the end of the fifth year—when the mill was torn down. Part of the recovery would be in the form of good wool and part of it in the form of a tax saving. These adjustments would have been unnecessary if all the wool expected to be found at the end of the fifth year were expected to be totally worthless as wool—*and* Nashua and Butcher lived in a world in which there were no taxes.

downtime

Just as they were about to sit down at a desk calculator and calculate an expected rate of return on the proposed new system, the two engineers realized that they had forgotten to consider the "downtime" problem. Downtime occurred when carding was held up because particular bales of cleaned wool could not be found. After thinking about it a bit they found this problem very complicated indeed and, for the time being, they decided to postpone it. They found it complicated because they soon realized that downtime in the carding room could well lead to downtime in subsequent operations—in combing, twisting, spinning, weaving, and finishing. In order to estimate downtime, therefore, a full survey of the whole plant would be required. They felt that such a survey could not be justified for the present purpose. Moreover, inspection of the savings they had been able to tabulate suggested that the expected rate of return on the bins and conveyors would be much higher than Butcher's cost of capital. In their report they would simply point out that the actual return would probably be higher than the calculated expected return because of reduced downtime throughout the plant.

rate of return and present value

Brody and Sims next transferred the gains and losses from Table 13.11 to Table 13.12. They then calculated the present value of the gains and

TABLE 13.12

ESTIMATED NET PRESENT VALUE
OF PROPOSED NEW EQUIPMENT AT NASHUA

YEAR (BEGINNING JULY 1)	NET ANNUAL GAINS AND LOSSES	DISCOUNT FACTORS AT 11%	PRESENT VALUE
(1)	(2)	(3)	(4)
1968	$367,651	.901	$331,253
1969	152,982	.812	124,221
1970	152,982	.731	111,829
1971	152,982	.659	100,815
1972	104,518 *	.593	61,979 *
Totals			$606,139

Calculation of Net Present Value

Present value = $606,139
Expected cost = 504,250

Net present value $101,889

* Negative figure.

losses using 11 percent discount factors. Present value was $606,139 and *net* present value, $101,889.

They then calculated a rate of return and found (Table 13.13) that at 24 percent the sum of the present values of the annual gains and losses was almost exactly equal to the expected cost of the equipment. Therefore, the expected rate of return on the project was almost exactly 24 percent.

The engineers then wrote up their findings. They recommended: "In order to expedite matters that work be begun at once on the specifications and drawings for the bins and conveyors." They sent the original of the report to Hastings and a copy to Dale Martin. They gave a copy to the plant manager and kept a copy for themselves. They then congratulated themselves on a job well done, packed their bags and set off for a vacation at Tuckerman's Ravine, where they hoped to find some spring snow.

When they returned to Butcher's home office ten days later, Brody found the following memorandum, from Martin to Hastings, waiting for him in his "in" box. Hastings had put a big question mark at the top and passed it on to him. It read:

TABLE 13.13

ESTIMATED RATE OF RETURN ON
PROPOSED NEW EQUIPMENT AT NASHUA

YEAR (BEGINNING JULY 1)	NET ANNUAL GAINS AND LOSSES	DISCOUNT FACTORS AT 24%	PRESENT VALUE
(1)	(2)	(3)	(4)
1968	$367,651	.806	$296,327
1969	152,982	.650	99,438
1970	152,982	.524	80,163
1971	152,982	.423	64,558
1972	104,518 *	.341	35,536 *
TOTAL			$504,950

Cost = $504,250

Rate of return slightly more than 24 percent.

* Negative figure.

June 2, 1968
TO: Mr. Hastings
FR: Dale Martin, Finance
The financial analysis group has examined carefully the proposed materials handling project at the Nashua plant and has come to the following conclusions:

1. The rate of return and net present value are grossly overstated. The bulk of the savings would be in lost wool. But this wool could be found simply by taking physical inventory once a year during the two-week July shutdown. Ten men hired at overtime rates for two weeks could surely do the job. The extra labor cost would be about $2,500. (We simply do not understand, by the way, how Nashua has gotten away without taking physical inventory at least once a year.)

2. If there are savings to be obtained by installing bins and conveyors they would be of three sorts in addition to savings in warehouse labor cost:

(a) Downtime throughout the plant because particular bales cannot be found when they are needed.

(b) Damage to lost wool. This would not be entirely avoided by taking physical inventory once a year.

(c) Lost contribution to overhead due to short shipment of orders when particular bales cannot be found.

3. We suggest that this return be recalculated on *an incremental basis*. The choice is between the proposed new system (bins and conveyors, etc.) and the present system—with physical inventory taken once a year.

I suggest that Brody and Sims return to Nashua for another couple of weeks—in order to get reasonable estimates of downtime, damage to bales lost for a year, and lost contribution to overhead.

There is, by the way, an error in Table 13.7. Operating savings in the fourth and fifth years would be $35,080 instead of $28,080. Depreciation on the old fork lifts would run out at the end of the third year.

We found the report very interesting.

"In place of 'financial analysis groups', said Sims, "we can read 'Kelley.' "

"Yeah, said Brody. "But at least we haven't been fired—what a boner!"

"Oh, well," said Sims. "We were misled by the fact that we're industrial engineers. Instinctively, we just wanted to install an efficient materials handling system!"

"Off we go to Nashua," said Brody. And off they went.

ANALYZING THE PROBLEMS

Let's go back for a moment to the "special problems" we discussed at the beginning of this chapter. What has "the Nashua case" taught us about them?

1. The incremental cost of finding the bales which had been "lost" and of avoiding the loss of bales in the future was merely the cost of taking physical inventory now and once or twice a year in the future. It was *not* the cost of the bins and conveyors. Brody and Sims did not look closely enough at what they were doing. They allowed themselves to be carried away, as they themselves said, by the prospect of installing a "really efficient" inventory handling system. The expenditure they proposed would have made the warehouse neater and more appealing to the eye, but it could not be justified on the basis of the savings they had tabulated—that is, on the basis of savings after taxes of $28,080 as shown in Table 13.10.

The expected rate of return on their proposal should therefore have been calculated *incrementally*. A rate should have been calculated first on the investment in the labor necessary to take physical inventory annually. Such a rate would have been very high—it would have been equal to the value of lost bales found each year minus the value of damaged wool plus the tax saving due to the damaged wool, all divided by the annual labor cost of taking physical inventory.[3]

Conceivably, also, a second rate of return might have been calculated on the additional (incremental) investment in labor cost necessary to reduce damaged wool to zero. Suppose that damaged wool could be reduced from 10 percent of bales found to 5 percent by taking physical inventory twice a year instead of once. The *incremental* rate of return on taking physical inventory a second time would then be 5 percent of the value of lost bales divided by the cost of the *additional* labor required to reduce damaged bales from 5 percent to zero percent. This rate would also have been high. (Strictly speaking, only after these two rates had been calculated, could a rate have been calculated on the proposed investment in bins and conveyors.) [4] As Kelley suggested, the gains *directly* attributable to the investment in bins and conveyors would have been of three sorts: the saving in warehouse labor cost; the saving in downtime; and the lost contribution to overhead when, due to lost bales, orders were short-shipped.

2. We saw that Brody and Sims deducted two amounts from the gross cost of the new equipment: first, the trade-in value of the old fork lifts ($30,000); second, the tax saving ($7,500) created by the fact that the trade-in value of the fork lifts was less than their book value. Both were incremental because neither would have occurred if the old fork lifts were not traded in against new ones. Because they would be traded in, the net price of the new fork lifts and Nashua's total tax bill would both be less.

On the other hand, if the trade-in value of the old fork lifts had been *higher* than their book value, Nashua would have made a capital gain. In such case, its total tax bill would have been higher. And the incremental cost of the project would have been higher—by the amount of the additional taxes.

3. The various parts of the materials handling project had different lives—for example, the bins had an expected life of twenty years; the conveyors, an expected life of ten years; and the new fork lifts, an expected life of six years (see Table 13.7). But a rate of return could be calculated only on the project *as a whole*. What life should Brody and

---

[3] Such a rate would have to be calculated for each year separately. This is so simply because no rate, short of infinity, would make the sums of the discounted cash inflows equal to the sum of the discounted cash outflows. Why?

The NPV of the additional expenditure on labor could, of course, have been calculated at Butcher's cost of capital—11 percent.

[4] Actually, a whole series of incremental rates should be calculated—the rate on reducing damaged wool from ten percent to nine percent, from nine to eight, from eight to seven and so forth.

Sims have assumed—if they hadn't been lucky enough to have had the question decided for them—by the prior decision to build a new plant in five years? This problem, which is the *uneven lives* problem, can be resolved in either of two ways:

Brody and Sims could have assumed that at the end of the sixth year the four fork lifts would be replaced; at the end of the tenth year, the conveyors; and at the end of the twentieth year, the bins. They would have gone on into the future, replacing equipment in this way until at the end of the sixtieth year everything "came out even." The last set of fork lifts would have been bought at the end of the fifty-fourth year and would have expired at the end of the sixtieth year. The last set of conveyors would have been installed at the end of the fiftieth year and would also have expired at the end of the sixtieth year, and the last set of bins would have been installed at the end of the fortieth year and would also have breathed *their* last breath at the end of the sixtieth year.

They would have taken account of all these expenditures over a sixty-year period and of all savings over a sixty-year period. And they would have calculated a rate of return, based on a sixty-year life for the project as a whole—as shown in Table 13.14. This procedure doubtless seems absurd to you—and it would also have seemed absurd to Brody and Sims, not to mention Kelley and Hastings. In fact, it is absurd—for reasons which should be obvious to you.

Brody and Sims would therefore have assumed a six-year life for the project. They would have assumed, that is, that the project was over when the life of the shortest-lived component of the project had ended. They would have taken account of the remaining value of the bins and conveyors by estimating their *salvage value* as of the end of the sixth year. And they would have regarded this salvage value as *a gain to be received at the end of the sixth year*. They would very likely have assumed that the salvage value of the bins and conveyors, as of the end of the sixth year, was about equal to their remaining book value at that time—that is, their cost minus the depreciation which had, by then, been taken on them.

This procedure is very similar, of course, to the procedure Brody and Sims actually did use—except that they assumed a five-year life rather than a six-year life. And because the building was to be torn down at the end of five years, they preferred to use an estimate of the *market* value of the bins and conveyors five years hence—rather than their *book* value at that time.

The problem of uneven lives will also arise when you are trying to choose between two machines, both of which will do the same job but which have different lives. When the problem does arise, you will usually find it best to use the life of the shorter-lived machine and estimate the salvage value of the longer-lived machine as of the end of

TABLE 13.14

OUTLAYS AND SAVINGS ON ASSUMED
SIXTY-YEAR LIFE FOR NASHUA EQUIPMENT *

END OF YEAR	OUTLAY (thousands)	SAVING (thousands)
0	$504.3	
1-5	—	$153.0 ‖
6 †	60.0	
7-9	—	
10	270.0	
11	—	
12 †	60.0	
13-17	—	
18 †	60.0	
19	—	
20 ‡ §	370.0	
21-23	—	
24 †	60.0	
25-29	—	
30 † ‡	330.0	
31-35	—	
36 †	60.0	
37-39	—	
40 ‡ §	370.0	
42 †	60.0	
43-47	—	
48 †	60.0	
49	—	
50 ‡	270.0	
51-53	—	
54 †	60.0	
55-60	—	

* Outlay figures taken from Table 13.2, minus, for year 0, tax saving (—$7500) and trade-in value of old fork lifts $30,000. All salvage values disregarded.
† Replace fork lifts.
‡ Replace conveyors.
§ Replace bins.
‖ From Table 13.10, received each year for 60 years.

the life of the shorter-lived machine. There are, of course, exceptions to this rule—one of which we shall see below, when we discuss Butcher's Tampico plant.

4. We saw also that when Brody and Sims estimated the operating cost of the proposed new system (Table 13.6), they did *not* include depreciation. Were they right or wrong? They were right. Why?

In order to understand why they were right we must get one fact absolutely clear in our minds: when we calculate the rate of return on an asset, we are—in effect—comparing (a) the net *cost* of the asset with (b) the net gain, or *contribution,* we expect the asset to make. You do this sort of thing all the time—if you go down to the corner saloon and buy a can of beer, you have—in effect—consciously or otherwise, compared (a) the pleasure (?) you expect to get from the beer with (b) the cost of the beer. Or if you buy a car, you have compared (a) the pleasure you expect to get from the car with (b) the cost of the car. And so it was with Brody and Sims. They were comparing (a) the "pleasure" Nashua would get from the new system with (b) the net cost of the system. The expected net cost of the system was $504,250 (see Table 13.2) and the "pleasure" Nashua would get from the new system was represented by labor savings, tax savings, and (Brody and Sims thought!) savings on lost wool.

In sum, the two magnitudes being compared must be kept quite separate. But depreciation is just a part of the cost of an asset—and if you deduct it from contribution, you are not keeping the two magnitudes quite separate. You are mixing cost in with contribution.

Why do you feel impelled to deduct depreciation (which, as noted above, is just a proportionate part of cost) from contribution? Because your misguided instinct tells you that if you deduct annual depreciation from annual benefits, you will be left with a number representing annual *net* benefit. You will then, you feel, be able to divide this annual net benefit by the cost of the asset to obtain a rate of return. But as we saw in Chapter 5, a rate of return calculated in *this* way will be either too high or too low. (In order to refresh your memory on this point, refer to Tables 5.10 and 5.11.)

In short, if you wish to make an accurate comparison between (a) contribution and (b) cost, you must above all keep the two quite separate. That's obvious—how can you compare one with the other if you don't keep them separate?

And you must then, *and only then*, decide *how* to make the comparison. If, for some perverse reason, you prefer to make the comparison in the *wrong* way, simply deduct annual depreciation from contribution after taxes and divide by the original cost of the asset or by its average cost. You will be left with a rate of return—a misleading rate of return.

But if you prefer to make the comparison correctly, you will either (a) find the present value of the annual contributions at your cost of capital or (b) find the rate of return which equates the present value of the annual contributions to the cost of the asset.

5. But, you say, Brody and Sims *did* deduct depreciation (Tables 13.7 and 13.8). Weren't they mixing up cost and contribution? No, they weren't. They were simply trying to find out how much of the increased

contribution would have to be paid out in taxes—so they would know what the net contribution, after taxes, would be.

Brody and Sims knew that Butcher could recover its investment and earn a return only out of that portion of gross contribution it was allowed to retain. In a world of no taxes, depreciation would *not* be deducted because in a world of no taxes, taxes would not be calculated! Rates of return or NPV would be calculated on the basis of the original gross contribution. To repeat: depreciation is deducted from gross contribution solely for the purpose of ascertaining how much of the original gross contribution the investor will be allowed to keep.

In short, Brody and Sims were trying to answer a very simple question: How much better off will Butcher really be—that is, *after* the government has taken its share—if we replace the old system with the new system? (Brody and Sims would be the first to agree, of course, that in order to find the answer to this simple question, they had had to travel along a difficult, winding, uphill path.)

CLASSIFYING PROPOSALS FOR LONG-TERM INVESTMENTS

Proposals for the investment of funds in long-term assets can be classified, as follows, in terms of the purposes they are expected to serve:

1. Proposals which are expected to reduce costs, the level of sales remaining the same. Proposals of this type are called *cost reduction* proposals. The Nashua materials handling proposal falls in this category.
2. Proposals which would enable the company to increase output of a product presently in its product line. Proposals of this type are called *expansion proposals.*

    Proposals which would provide service facilities—such as salesmen's cars, executive aircraft, and computers which would keep the company's books and send out bills to customers, are sometimes cost reduction proposals and sometimes *both* cost reduction *and* expansion. Better, more efficient transportation, for example, would enable the company to service present customers with a smaller number of salesmen, or a larger number of customers with the present number of salesmen. An electronic computer would enable the company to handle the present volume of bookkeeping and accounts receivable with a smaller office force—or a larger volume with the same office force.
3. Proposals which would enable the company to produce a product

not now in *its* product line—but which is being produced by other companies. Butcher's Tampico plant, to be discussed below, falls in this category.

4. Proposals which would enable the company to produce a wholly new product—not now in *any* company's product line—and for which a market of measureable dimensions does not yet exist —for example, electronic computers just after World War II, or commercial aircraft just after World War I, or telephones in the late 1800s.

5. Intangible assets created by the expenditure of funds on advertising (or other forms of sales promotion), training programs, and research and development. Such expenditures are almost always "expensed" in the year in which they are made and are not, therefore, carried on the company's balance sheet as long-term assets. They are long-term assets, nevertheless, to the extent that they generate benefits for a period longer than one year. In other words, they do not really "turnover" in a year or less.

You may have noticed that the five types of proposals, above, are listed in decreasing order of the reliability of rates of return calculated on them. As we go from simple cost reduction proposals, to expansion proposals, to proposals for products new to the company's product line, to proposals for products for which no market presently exists, to proposals for product development, progressively less information is available on the basis of which to estimate expected contribution over the life of the asset. When Hastings estimated the net present value to Butcher of Ex-Cello's lathe, he knew his own present labor costs and he was able to estimate from the specifications of Ex-Cello's lathe how much money he would save annually. And when a company is thinking about expanding output of an existing product, it has available all its prior experience with that product, including an intimate knowledge of the market for that product.

But when a company decides to produce a product it has never before produced, it has no experience of its own to fall back on. And relevant information is often difficult and expensive to obtain indirectly. In order to bring out these difficulties somewhat more concretely, we describe briefly the process by which Butcher calculated an expected rate of return on its Tampico plant.

investing in a new product

In the early 1960s Butcher began to think about the possibility of diversifying. Since 1961, it had been successfully manufacturing—in addition to machine tools—industrial chemicals for use primarily in tanning, and in textile finishing, and had accumulated a substantial amount of technological and marketing "know-how." In 1962 Butcher's Board had authorized an expenditure of "up to $150,000" to explore the feasibility of manufacturing agricultural chemicals, somewhere in the Southeast, to serve the farmers of that area. The Southeast was growing rapidly and agricultural chemicals showed little, if any, cyclical behavior. Thus a successful venture in the Southeast in agricultural chemicals would add a steadily increasing amount to Butcher's profits each year.

Agricultural chemicals were, of course, primarily fertilizers—natural and synthetic, solid and liquid, organic and inorganic. The proposed plant would manufacture phosphorous anhydride and synthetic nitrogen. These two chemicals would be mixed with each other, in various proportions, and with potassium and other chemicals. The resulting mixtures would be sold, both in solid and liquid form, directly to farmers and farmers' cooperatives throughout the Southeast. Attached to the plant's sales force would be a small soil engineering staff who would develop mixtures, "custom tailored" to meet the needs of individual areas and crops.

The feasibility study was undertaken in four steps as follows:

1. First, a firm of marketing research consultants was hired to estimate the size of the market in the Southeast and Butcher's probable share of that market. Each of these estimates was broken down according to type of fertilizer. This study was done in close collaboration with Butcher's own marketing personnel.

    With the assistance of the Department of Agriculture, the problem of estimating total fertilizer sales in the Southeast was relatively simple. But how big was the market for the "custom-tailoring" service Butcher proposed to provide? In order to respond to this question, a field survey was done, using a random sample of 150 farmers and farmers' cooperatives scattered throughout the Southeast. This study produced a series of probability distributions over sales: one for each of the first five years of operation. This study took eight months.

2. After this study had been completed and reviewed by the Board, a firm of consulting chemical engineers was retained to design the proposed plant and equipment. They worked closely with a team of Butcher's own chemical and industrial engineers. This study took four months. The consulting engineers estimated that the necessary equipment would cost about $525,000.

3. After this study had been completed and reviewed, Butcher's industrial engineers looked for centrally located sites. Several

were found. The final selection, Tampico (South Carolina), was made primarily on the basis of the suitability of the local labor supply. After Tampico was chosen, Butcher's industrial engineers set about estimating production costs (on a probability basis) and a firm of local architects was retained to design the plant and estimate its cost ($618,000).

4. Butcher's finance group then spent a month or two estimating the amount of working capital the Tampico plant would need —primarily accounts receivable, and inventory—raw materials, work-in-process and finished goods (also on a probability basis). The need for working capital was expected to reach a seasonal peak in March of the first year at $985,000. The expected value of total investment in the Tampico plant would thus be something more than $2 million as follows:

Plant	$ 618,000
Equipment	525,000
Working capital	985,000
	$2,128,000

After these four studies had been completed, Butcher's finance and industrial engineering groups set about putting them together into a single report for presentation to the Board. The final document ran to about 200 pages—and weighed three pounds. It brought together all the data on expected sales, on expected costs, and on the choice of the Tampico plant site.

It concluded by estimating a rate of return on the project based on a ten-year life. Net investment in the venture was, as explained above, the sum of plant, equipment, and working capital or $2,128,000. Expected gains were profits after taxes plus depreciation for each of the first ten years—plus the estimated value of plant, equipment and working capital at the end of the tenth year. As a matter of policy, Butcher used ten-year lives on new plants primarily because looking more than ten years ahead seemed too unrealistic. (Looking ten years ahead, Butcher felt, was unrealistic enough.)

In any event, the expected return on the proposed new plant worked out to about 18 percent—or about seven percentage points above Butcher's estimated cost of capital. After a long series of meetings, during which the report was turned inside out and upside down and scrutinized from every conceivable point of view, Butcher's Finance Committee and Board approved the Tampico proposal.

When we compare the Nashua project with the Tampico project, what differences do we see? We see primarily a difference in the reliability of the basic figures used to calculate expected rates of return.

Virtually all the figures Brody and Sims had needed to calculate an expected rate of return on the Nashua project were available from Nashua's experience and records—especially labor costs and the value of lost bales. At Tampico, however, the only probability distribution which was not subject to a large degree of error was that for the cost of plant and equipment. The sales estimates, for example, were constructed as carefully as the most modern interviewing methods and statistical techniques allowed. But they were, at bottom, based on 150 subjective replies to questions such as:

1. Q: *How much fertilizer do you use a year?*
   A: "Don't know exactly. Maybe fifteen tons—give or take a ton or two."
2. Q: *Are you satisfied with it?*
   A: "I'm never satisfied with anything."
3. Q: *How would you react to a custom-tailoring service designed to give you exactly what you need for your crops and soil?*
   A: "Sounds great."
4. Q: *How much "custom tailored" fertilizer would you buy?*
   A: "Don't know. But I'd be willing to try it."

Estimates of labor supply and labor cost were equally precarious. Butcher's industrial engineers had spent several weeks in Tampico estimating the available labor supply (and its skills) on the basis of information provided by the United States Employment Service and the local Chamber of Commerce. These estimates were reasonably satisfactory as of the time they were made. But no one could foresee with accuracy what the situation would be eighteen to twenty-four months hence—after the plant had been built and equipped. This would depend on the extent to which, meanwhile, existing plants had expanded, and new plants had been established in Tampico and the surrounding area.

CONCLUSION

In order to calculate rates of return on long-term assets we need four figures, as follows:

(1) The incremental cost of the asset
(2) The life of the asset
(3) The expected value of the incremental benefits the asset will generate during its life

(4) The residual value—the salvage value of the asset—at the end of its life

The cost of the asset is, generally, the easiest figure to obtain. This is so because the cost of the asset is to be incurred now—or in the very near future. If Ex-Cello wants to sell us a lathe, it will have to quote us a firm installed price on that lathe. If we want to build a plant in Tampico, we will usually be able to obtain reasonably reliable estimates of the cost of land, plant and equipment. This does not mean that estimates of cost are always known with certainty when the decision to invest is made. But it does mean that estimates of cost are usually subject to only a small degree of error.

Sometimes, of course, investment in an asset will take place over an extended period of time—as, for example, in a large complex plant which takes several years to build. And sometimes firm contracts for the construction of such plants cannot be obtained. If not, estimates of the ultimate cost may be subject to a large degree of error.

Sometimes the life of an asset is easy to estimate but more often it is not. The life of the materials handling project at Nashua was easy to estimate—because a decision had already been made by Butcher's management to build a new plant in five years.

But what about the lathe that Ex-Cello said had a life of seven years? What did Ex-Cello mean, anyway, by this assertion? That the lathe had a physical life of seven years? That is, that at the end of seven years, it would fall apart and be nothing more than a pile of junk? Hardly. The lathe was well built, of first-grade materials, and was easy to maintain. It was capable of running at close to its present level of efficiency for fifty years. What then did Ex-Cello mean? Ex-Cello meant that in about seven years, the lathe would probably be obsolete—that is, that by the end of seven years new and better lathes would have been developed which would have reduced costs further by a significant amount. And at that time if Butcher Company itself wished to remain competitive, it would probably be forced to buy the new, more efficient lathe.

Thus when Ex-Cello's salesman said that the lathe had a life of seven years, he meant that the lathe had a *technological* life of seven years. Inasmuch as Ex-Cello was itself, even at this moment, developing new lathes, its estimate of the technological life of the present lathe was probably highly reliable. And Hastings knew that Ex-Cello had been highly reliable in the past.

But what about the Tampico plant? When Butcher used a life of ten years, it was not saying that at the end of the tenth year the plant and equipment would have taken their last breath and expired. With proper maintenance, the plant could go on producing agricultural chemicals for ten times ten years. Butcher knew, however, that during the next ten years more efficient manufacturing equipment would be developed. And it knew also that new agricultural chemicals would be found. Perhaps these new products would be revolutionary and perhaps they would be patented by competitors. If so, Butcher's Tampico plant might be rendered absolutely worthless. But even if such new products were not patented, Butcher might have to reequip the whole Tampico plant in order to produce them. In other words, Butcher had to ask itself how long Tampico's products would have an active, vigorous market—a market, that is, which would generate net benefit to Butcher.

In fixing the life of the Tampico plant at ten years, Butcher was simply saying that revolutionary new products would probably be found within ten years—that is, that it would be foolhardy to assume that the *product-market* life of the Tampico plant would be more than ten years.

In short, the life of a long term physical asset is rarely, if ever, its physical life. It is more often than not its technological life or its product-market life. One or the other of two eventualities can occur —new, more efficient methods will be found to produce existing products or new products will be developed which will render existing products obsolete. You can, with little difficulty, think of examples of developments of both types.

In general, the benefit an asset will generate is easier to estimate for cost-saving projects than for expansion projects. Sims and Brody had their problems at Nashua—but, for the most part, the figures they needed were readily available (labor saving) or could be obtained by energetic digging. Similarly, reasonably satisfactory records will be available on most cost-saving projects.

Expansion projects, on the other hand, are of two kinds—those which would increase production of existing products; and those which would involve producing products not previously produced by the company (for example, the Tampico plant). If a company plans to invest money in plant and machinery in order to increase output of a product presently in its line, it will have reliable information on costs. And usually, it will have, or will be able to develop, information on additional sales. (Normally, of course, a company does not consider expanding capacity unless it has reason to believe that sales will increase!)

But a company will usually have difficulty estimating the benefit which will be generated by new products—and especially, of course, if the product has never been produced or sold before by anyone. In such cases, the estimate of the benefit will often be highly subjective—and the rate of return calculations will be "acts of faith" which will depend more on the optimism or pessimism of the person doing the calculating than on anything else.

As we saw in the Nashua case, some types of benefit can be "tricky"—especially if they involve tax savings due to losses, or if a benefit is being obtained now but only at the cost of giving up what would be a benefit later—as in the case of the "windfall" at Nashua. We must remember that we are interested in the *differences* over time between two ways of doing something or other —the present way and some other way (or ways). The best way of isolating the differences is by tabulating *separately for each way*— and then subtracting—as in Tables 13.7 and, especially, 13.8.

PROBLEMS

1. Outline step-by-step, from beginning to end, the process Brody and Sims went through to obtain the figures given in Table 13.10.

2. Suppose that the ten old fork lifts (Table 13.1) had been depreciated for four years instead of two at $15,000 a year. Trade-in value remained at $30,000. What then would be the (preliminary) net cost of the proposed investment in materials handling equipment? What would (preliminary) net cost have been if the fork lifts had been depreciated for three years?

3. In Table 13.7, annual operating savings after taxes (OSAT) were estimated at $28,080, based on depreciation on the new equipment of $47,000. Calculate OSAT on the assumption that depreciation on the new equipment will be
   (a) $43,000 a year instead of $47,000
   (b) $54,000 a year instead of $47,000.

4. Calculate the grain (or loss) for the fifth year, (Table 13.10) on the assumptions that at the end of the fifth year
   (a) 1,250 bales will be found all of which will be worthless
   (b) 1,250 bales will be found, all of which will be intact and usable.

5. Calculate the NPV of the investment using the gains for the first four years as given in Table 13.12 and the gain (or loss) for the fifth year you obtained in response to problem 5(a) above.

6. When Brody and Sims estimated the gains and losses for the final year (Table 13.10), they forgot to take account of a capital loss on the bins, conveyors and fork lifts. Correct their figures.

7. After spending two more weeks at Nashua, Brody and Sims obtained the following figures for the cost of downtime, damage due to lost bales, and lost contribution to overhead due to lost bales (see Memo from the finance analysis group to Hastings):

Downtime	$ 28,000
Lost contribution to overhead	170,000
Damage to lost bales	10,000

    The downtime figure was obtained by applying a percentage obtained from the plant manager to an average, over good years and bad, of total annual labor cost. The figure was very rough. The lost contribution figure was obtained by assuming that 200 bales of wool (112 raw and 88 cleaned) would be lost each year. Each bale contained about 500 pounds of wool. Each bale of raw wool was equal to about 400 pounds of cleaned wool and each pound of cleaned wool was equal to about two yards of finished cloth. Each yard of finished cloth contributed on the average 63.7 cents to overhead.

    Cost of damage to lost bales was taken at 10 percent of the value of those bales found when physical inventory was taken once a year.

    Calculate a revised rate of return on the proposed materials handling equipment. Don't forget to include the labor saving, etc., as given in Table 13.6.

8. Go back to Table 13.14. Calculate the present value, at 11 percent, of all the outlays and all the savings. Then calculate the NPV of the project. Compare your results with the results Brody and Sims obtained in Table 13.12. Then calculate a rate of return on a 60-year life.

9. Dale Martin, in his memo to Hastings, said that operating savings after taxes would be $35,080 instead of $28,080 in the fourth and the fifth years. Do you agree? And, if so, where does the extra $7,500 come from?

14

INVESTING IN LONG-TERM ASSETS II
mergers and acquisitions

In the preceding chapter, we saw how a company evaluates long-term projects arising from inside the firm. But sometimes, a company can increase output of a product presently in its product line, or broaden the product line itself, by buying a going business or part of a going business. Why does a company choose to buy a going business (or part of one) instead of expanding internally? And how does it make this choice?

Mergers and acquisitions take place for a wide variety of *stated* reasons. One company may have a research division or a sales force or a production capability or an industrial engineering staff which it would take the other firm years to build up. Or one firm may produce just a single product and wish, for that reason, to diversify. Or a firm producing a number of products may wish to diversify further. Or two firms may think that if they joined forces they would be able to operate more efficiently together than either could alone—for example, by combining accounting or finance or purchasing or manufacturing, and so forth.

But whatever the *stated* reasons may be, one firm acquires another firm *because it believes that doing so is worthwhile in money terms.*

And the firm which is acquired must also consider itself to be better off in money terms. *Both conditions must be satisfied.* No merger (or acquisition) can take place unless both parties—buyer and seller—believe they will be better off than they are now. Thus the buyer must believe that the present value to him of the assets he proposes to buy is *higher* than the price he proposes to pay for those assets. And at the same time, the seller must believe that the present value to him of the assets he proposes to sell is *lower* than the price being offered by the prospective buyer. This is just a roundabout way of saying that the merger will not (or should not!) take place unless it seems worthwhile to both sides. But how can the same sum of money (namely, the price being offered for the seller's assets) be *less than* the present value of those assets to the buyer and *more than* the present value of those same assets to the seller?

This chapter describes the way in which buyer and seller look at mergers and how they decide whether or not merger with the other company would be worthwhile. The term "mergers and acquisitions" is used here to include all forms of "external growth"—buying all the outstanding stock of a company, or a majority of it, from that company's stockholders, or buying the *assets* of the company, or some of them, from the company itself.

REASONS FOR MERGER

Butcher acquired its Nashua division in mid-1966 for $980,000 in cash as part of its (Butcher's) program of diversification.

Nashua had opened its doors in 1902 to manufacture high quality woolens, especially tweeds and flannels, for men's suitings and women's coats and skirts. In 1902, cotton, wool and silk were the principal textile fibers and most woolen mills were located in New England.

All the stock in Nashua was owned by a Scots-English family named McEwen which had come to New Hampshire, in the 1840s, from Lancashire, the heart of the English woolen and worsted industry. They had worked in textile mills in New Hampshire for fifty years, and had saved their pennies. By the late 1890s, they had accumulated enough money ($40,000) to allow three grandsons of the original McEwen, all in their early thirties, to start the mill. They had needed only a small amount of supplementary assistance from local bankers. The family knew how to manufacture high quality woolens, and they were determined that their product would be the best available.

They were highly successful. Sales were $108,000 the first year and grew rapidly thereafter. The McEwens lived frugally, reinvested nearly all Nashua's earnings in the latest technology, and never lost sight of their basic policy—to produce woolens of the best possible quality.

By 1929, sales had grown to $12 million. Net profits fluctuated between $600,000 and $1 million a year. The McEwens had added a second building to the mill in 1915 and a third in 1928.

Nashua survived the Great Depression with small losses. During World War II, they produced heavy woolens for the military. Sales during the war rose to $35 million a year. Total net profits after taxes plus depreciation during the years 1941-1945 had totaled more than $11 million. And at the end of World War II, Nashua held nearly $13 million in cash and marketable securities. Of this sum, the McEwens spent $3 million to replace old and wornout machinery and to repair the three buildings—which, after four years of neglect, were showing their age.

The McEwens then wrestled hard with the problem of what to do with the remaining $10 million. They considered, briefly, the possibility of expanding by building an additional one-story plant in Georgia which would double Nashua's capacity. (Many of Nashua's competitors had moved south to take advantage of lower labor costs.) The McEwens decided against doing so because they felt that the skilled labor available in New Hampshire was, at bottom, the secret of their success. Many jobs in the mill had been handed down from father to son and every employee and, for that matter, everyone in Nashua took great pride in the quality of the mill's product, which by this time was very well known from coast-to-coast.

In order to get rid of excess funds, the family authorized the company to use $8.5 million to buy back 25 percent of the company's outstanding stock. Four of the descendants of the founders—all of whom were officers of the company and active in its management, received $1 million each in cash.

This was the beginning of the end. Within eighteen months two officers, both grandsons of the original founders, had resigned to enjoy their wealth. One was Vice President in Charge of Sales and the other was Vice President in Charge of Production. At the same time, developments in the textile industry and in the economy began to affect Nashua adversely. Cars and homes were better heated and, as a result, the demand for lighter weight clothing increased. The demand for Nashua's specialty, heavy woolens, began correspondingly to decline. Synthetics, such as dacron (with which Nashua had no experience), began to take hold—primarily because they could be blended with wool to produce the lighter weight fabrics then coming into style. As the heavy suiting market began to disappear, Nashua fell back on fabrics for sport coats and high-style skirtings. But the volume in these fabrics was small and Nashua's output began to fall drastically. In 1957, for the first time in its history. Nashua was forced to lay off labor. As a result, the town of Nashua, which had a very possessive attitude toward the mill, began to feel it had been "let down" by the McEwens. The town felt that if the McEwens' money had remained invested in the mill, the family would have had the incentive—and would probably have found the energy necessary—to adjust the mill to the new trends.

Losses continued, and in 1960, after two especially bad years, the two McEwens who had remained in the company, resigned. The family, which still held most of the outstanding stock, turned the management of the mill over to the plant manager, Dennis Evans. Evans, who was then about sixty years old and had been with Nashua for forty years, was elected President. He had no experience whatever in styling, sales, finance, or general management.

Table 14.1 gives selected figures for sales, earnings, costs and profits

TABLE 14.1

NASHUA MILLS SELECTED OPERATING FIGURES 1945-1965 (IN MILLIONS OF DOLLARS)

YEAR	SALES	COST OF GOODS	GROSS PROFIT	GENERAL EXPENSE	PROFIT OR LOSS BEFORE TAXES
(1)	(2)	(3)	(4)	(5)	(6)
1945	$34.9	$24.8	$10.1	$7.1	$3.0
1950	26.2	17.1	9.1	6.8	2.3
1955	22.7	15.9	6.8	5.6	1.2
1960	20.4	16.3	4.1	5.6	1.5 *
1961	21.4	17.3	3.9	5.8	1.7 *
1962	22.6	15.0	7.4	5.9	1.7
1963	21.6	15.6	6.0	5.8	0.2
1964	21.4	17.9	3.5	6.0	2.5 *
1965	20.2	17.9	2.3	5.8	3.5 *
1966 †	4.2	3.4	0.8	1.3	0.5 *

* Loss.
† Three months, unaudited.

for Nashua for selected years during the period 1945-1966. As this table shows, Nashua had lost money heavily between 1961-1965. In 1959, Evans had put in a line of dacron and worsted blends and in 1960, a line of automobile upholstery fabrics.

These two lines had required $3 million worth of additional machinery

—which sum was obtained on a fifteen-year loan at 5 percent from the Mutual Life Insurance Company of Boston. Nashua was required to reduce the principal amount of the loan by $200,000 each year. Interest was calculated on the outstanding balance. The loan had been personally guaranteed by members of the McEwen family—after heavy pressure had been put on them by two local bankers and the Nashua Chamber of Commerce. The family would have preferred to liquidate the mill.

In order to be better able to sell to auto manufacturers, Evans had opened a small sales office in Detroit. Both the worsted-dacron blends and the upholstery fabrics had lost money heavily, but heavy woolens had recovered somewhat with the rising demand for sport coats, and Nashua had, so far, been able to meet payments on the Mutual loan.

In late 1965, Evans, who was then about to retire, asked Butcher's regional sales manager for industrial chemicals whether Butcher might be interested in buying the mill. Butcher's industrial chemicals division had been selling chemicals to Nashua for four or five years. Butcher's regional sales manager passed the word along to headquarters and, within a week, Martin and Hastings were in Nashua looking the mill over. They spent several days with Evans, and several with the sales vice president who had come in from New York for their visit.

What did they see?

1. Nashua's machinery was up-to-date and in good condition. But plant layout was inefficient—primarily because operations were scattered through three buildings.

2. Nashua's labor was unionized and wage rates were 20 percent higher than they were in the South for comparable work. In general, Nashua's competitive position was poor and getting worse.

3. Nashua was losing cash rapidly and might not be able to pay interest and principal on the next installment of the loan held by Mutual Life. A payment of $300,000 would be due in six weeks. Of this sum, $100,000 was interest at 5 percent on the $2 million balance of the loan outstanding during the preceding year.

4. But, on the other hand, Nashua owned four well-known, highly regarded trademarks, and although it had lost a lot of skilled labor to electronics and other light industry, it still had a great deal of "know-how in the manufacture of high-quality fabric. It also had a good sales force—although the number of resignations had risen sharply during the last year or so, primarily because Nashua's recent heavy losses had created the fear that the ship was sinking rapidly.

After this brief survey of Nashua's situation, Martin and Hastings found themselves feeling that a merger with Nashua would have three primary advantages for Butcher. First, the textile cycle tended to be opposite to the machine tool cycle—so that if Nashua could be made profitable once again, Butcher's total earnings would tend to be more stable. In addition, Nashua had a $6 million tax loss (Table 14.1) worth about $3 million to Butcher almost immediately.

But even if Nashua could not be made profitable once again, its losses would represent tax savings to Butcher. And provided those losses did not exceed depreciation charges—which were now about $750,000 a year—Nashua would lose no cash and would be able to finance operations without help from Butcher. If Nashua earned some (but not all) of its depreciation charges, Butcher would be better off by the sum of depreciation earned plus one half of Nashua's loss. This assumed, of course, that Butcher would not have to spend money at Nashua on new machinery and equipment. If Nashua earned all its depreciation, Butcher would be better off by that amount.

In short, provided no capital expenditures had to be made at Nashua for the next four or five years, and if Nashua's losses in the next year or so did not exceed depreciation charges:

1. Butcher would receive an annual net cash inflow equal to whatever depreciation Nashua did earn plus one half of Nashua's losses.
2. As soon as Nashua reached a breakeven basis, Butcher would receive an annual net cash inflow equal to Nashua's annual depreciation charges, namely, $750,000 a year.
3. But, of course, if Nashua's losses did exceed depreciation charges, Butcher might have to invest more money in Nashua.

Two questions thus were uppermost in Martin's mind:

1. Would Butcher have to replace any machinery or equipment at Nashua during the next four or five years? Hastings had formed the impression that Nashua's machinery was reasonably up-to-date and in good condition. But this impression would have to be checked in detail.
2. Could Nashua's costs be cut so that losses would not exceed depreciation? Martin and Hastings felt that Nashua's manufacturing costs and its administrative costs were very high. Nashua's operating ratio had declined from 30.0 percent in 1955 to 11.4 percent in 1965. During this period gross profit had declined from nearly $6.1 million to $2.3 million on about the same volume of sales (see Table 14.1). In 1955, Nashua had

earned $1.2 million before taxes. In 1965, it had lost $3.5 million. If Nashua's operating ratio could be raised to 20 percent (and administrative costs cut by $1 million) Nashua would just about break even before depreciation.

CAPITAL EXPENDITURES AND OPERATING COSTS

After their return to New York and a brief talk with the president of Butcher Company, Martin and Hastings sent a team of industrial engineers off to Nashua with instructions to get complete machinery lists with name of manufacturer, model number and date of acquisition, and also to see what, if anything, could be done to improve the flow of work through the plant and to reduce manufacturing costs in other ways. The engineers spent a couple of weeks at the mill and on their return made recommendations for changes in work-flow which they estimated would save about $325,000 a year in labor cost. They also suggested that Nashua might be able to save as much as $800,000 a year in raw materials costs if it bought its own raw wool instead of buying cleaned wool from Boston dealers as it now did. They said that Evans, the President of Nashua, agreed with this suggestion. An investment in additional machinery of $360,000 would be required.

The industrial engineers had obtained machinery lists and had checked them with various textile machinery manufacturers. The engineers had concluded that major replacement expenditures would probably not be required during the next four to five years. They also expressed the opinion that the decline in Nashua's operating ratio during the past five years was due to bad management almost as much as to high labor costs and inefficient plant layout. Coordination between the mill and Nashua's New York sales office was poor. Designs, for example, often reached the mill too late to be included in the line for the coming season. Usually the mill went ahead and made the samples anyway, knowing full well that when the New York sales office received them, it would take orders for delivery dates which the mill would not be able to meet. In addition, general production scheduling was very poor and orders were rarely, if ever, shipped on time. This often resulted in cancellations. When their orders were not shipped on time, customers often cancelled—especially when business was poor. When orders were cancelled Nashua was left holding finished inventory, which it could not sell except at a large loss. In each of the years 1964 and 1965 it had been forced to sell $2 million worth of fabric at 50 percent of cost.

Production scheduling was done by the plant manager with a pencil and a piece of paper. Hastings knew, from Butcher's experience, that if production scheduling were computerized, late shipments could be virtually eliminated. The computer would always know where everything was and would run up a red flag if some salesman tried to take an order which the computer knew could not be delivered when the customer said he wanted it.

In short, Hastings and Martin saw a number of ways in which Butcher, by applying *its* "know-how" to Nashua's problems, could reduce Nashua's manufacturing costs substantially—by a total of something more than $2 million, as follows:

Improved work-flow	$ 325,000
Savings on raw wool	800,000
Savings due to improved production scheduling	1,000,000
TOTAL	$2,125,000

In addition, Butcher would provide tighter management all around, including better coordination between the mill and Nashua's New York and Detroit sales offices. And the merger itself would restore the confidence of Nashua's sales personnel in Nashua's future and, very likely, reduce turnover among them.

administrative costs

Nashua's administrative costs were full of "water" which, Martin knew, would be squeezed out by the merger. He had obtained from Evans a detailed breakdown of Nashua's administrative costs and had found to his astonishment that the four McEwens, who were no longer active in the company, (and now came to the office only rarely) were receiving $50,000 a year each in salary plus $25,000 in tax free expenses. In addition, each had a company car and the use of the company plane—a Piper Aztec which had cost about $90,000. The McEwens had insisted on being given these amenities when they guaranteed repayment of Nashua's loan from Mutual Life of Boston. The plane was almost never used by anyone else—except the wool buyer who occasionally flew it to wool markets in Texas or Ohio. These markets could be reached by commercial airline. Nashua had also given make-work jobs to six other members of the McEwen family at salaries of $7,500 a year each.

In addition, the accounting, finance and payroll sections which now employed a total of forty-one people, would no longer be necessary and would be closed down. Butcher would take over all three functions —with a negligible increase in its present staff.

When these savings—which were certain—were added to a large number of other small miscellaneous savings (including the annual cost of running and maintaining the Piper Aztec), the total came to $872,500.

Martin had thus obtained tentative answers to the two questions which had been uppermost in his mind: in all likelihood, no substantial replacement expenditures would be necessary at Nashua during the next four or five years; and costs could probably be cut so that during the same period losses would not exceed depreciation.

Martin then listed the operating advantages Butcher would get and those Nashua would get as a result of the merger, as shown in Table 14.2.

TABLE 14.2

OPERATING BENEFITS TO BUTCHER AND TO NASHUA FROM MERGER

BUTCHER GETS FROM NASHUA:	NASHUA GETS FROM BUTCHER:
1. Ready-made diversification	1. Tighter management
2. Four well-known trademarks plus considerable "know-how" in manufacture of high quality textiles	2. Reduced overhead
3. Some "know-how" in manufacture of blended worsted suitings and automobile upholstery	3. Reduced factory costs due to better work-flow and production scheduling
4. $6 million tax loss worth about $3 million immediately	4. Improved morale in New York and Detroit sales offices
5. Annual depreciation of $750,000 (if earned)	5. Strong financial support
6. A manufacturing plant in reasonably good condition	

Both companies, he found himself thinking, would be stronger as a result of the merger—provided no replacement expenditures were necessary at Nashua for four or five years, and provided also that Nashua's losses did not exceed depreciation. "Four plus two equals eight," he said to himself. "Very interesting."

Martin then called in Kelley, gave him his notes, as above, and asked him to estimate expected values for the foregoing cash flows, and the present value to Butcher, at 11 percent, of those expected values.

Martin and Hastings then drew up the following tentative plan to be submitted to the Board of the Butcher Company along with any proposal to acquire Nashua:

1. Nashua's indebtedness to the Mutual Life of Boston would be paid off out of the tax refund Butcher would receive on account of Nashua's $6 million tax loss.
2. Steps would be taken immediately to enable Nashua to buy and process raw wool. This would cost $360,000.
3. A new plant manager would be appointed to replace Evans who, in any case, was about to retire. Evans' assistant had been with Nashua for twenty years, was only forty-five years old and was eager to take over.
4. Hastings and Martin would take whatever measures were necessary to put Nashua on a break-even basis within eighteen months.
5. The mill would continue to operate at Nashua for five or six years. During that period Butcher would exert itself to learn as much as possible about the textile business.
6. At the end of the third or fourth year, depending on progress, Butcher would make two decisions: first, whether to remain in the textile business and, if so, second, whether to build a new one-story plant. A decision would be subsequently made as to where such a plant should be built—at the present location or in the South.

Let's go back now to Kelley who has been sitting at his desk, chewing his nails, mumbling to himself: "Mergers, mergers. I know perfectly well that there's no difference, in principal, between buying a machine and buying a company. It's just more complicated, that's all. Isn't that right," he said to himself. Then he heard himself answering back: "Maybe yes, maybe no."

He decided, first, that in order to get a hold on the problem somewhere, he would separate the two types of figures Martin had given him. Martin had given him rough and ready estimates of the various amounts of money that Martin believed Butcher would be able to save Nashua if the two companies merged. These would reduce Nashua's losses. Kelley listed these estimates in Table 14.3. They really were, he felt, rough and ready. On what basis could the industrial engineers have concluded that improved work-flow would save $325,000? And the other three figures (in Table 14.3) looked suspiciously like very rough "approximations." He thereupon went in to see Martin:

"I'd like to go up to Nashua for a couple of days," Kelley said.

"What for?" asked Martin, bristling slightly. He found himself thinking: "Why can't Kelley ever do as he's told?"

"To get a better fix on those figures you gave me."

"What's the matter with the figures I gave you?"

TABLE 14.3

NASHUA'S COST REDUCTIONS FROM MERGER

Improved work-flow	$ 325,000
Savings on wool	800,000
Reduction in administrative costs	1,000,000
Savings due to improved production scheduling	1,000,000
TOTAL	**$3,125,000**

"They're too rough."

"Look," said Martin, "I just want you to take those figures and get me a present value estimate."

"I can't do it," said Kelley, "I'd turn over in my grave. I only want two days. It will cost nearly nothing to get figures that are four or five times as good as these."

"Okay," said Martin, "Go. But if you're not back in this office exactly forty-eight hours from now," he looked at his watch, "you're fired."

Kelley spent two days in Nashua talking to the plant manager, the wool buyer and the office manager. He found some interesting facts.

First, the industrial engineers had not made the estimate of savings due to improved work-flow. It had been made by Evans himself in his spare time. He laid his charts and diagrams out in front of Kelley. They showed the present flow of work through the plant and the proposed flow. Evans had calculated labor cost, both ways, at the present level of sales and present wage rates. The proposed flow, simply by putting next to each other operations that belonged next to each other, would save thirty-three man-years in labor cost, or almost exactly $165,000. This saving, Evans repeated, was at present wage rates. If wage rates went up, the saving would be larger. Evans, of course, expected wage rates to go up. The present flow of work had just happened over time and no one had noticed how inefficient it was—until Nashua had begun to lose money.

In addition to saving labor, the proposed work-flow would make production scheduling easier and speed up production itself. This would mean fewer cancellations and fewer losses and write-downs on finished goods inventory. Evans had estimated this saving at $160,000. Kelley noted that if Butcher "computerized" Nashua's production scheduling, this saving would occur anyway. Evans agreed.

Kelley asked why Evans hadn't rearranged the work-flow before now. "No time and no money," Evans replied. "It would cost $25,000."

Second, Kelley discovered that the estimate of savings on wool had been based on the difference between the current price of raw wool and the current price of cleaned wool, and the cost of turning raw wool into clean wool. Raw wool was twenty-four cents a pound cheaper than cleaned wool. The cost of sorting and scouring raw wool plus the cost of shrinkage would be about eight cents a pound. The cost saving would therefore be sixteen cents = .24 — .08) a pound. Nashua used 5 million pounds of wool in the manufacture of woolens.[1] Thus at sixteen cents a pound, the total saving would be $800,000. The necessary washing and scouring equipment would cost $360,000. The wool buyer was careful to point out that the difference between the price of cleaned and raw wool varied as the prices themselves went up or down because of shrinkage.[2] But he believed that twenty-four cents was a good average figure. After questioning him closely, Kelley concluded that the wool buyer was (unconsciously) attaching a probability of about .25 to a difference of twenty cents, a probability of about .50 to a difference of twenty-four cents and a probability of about .25 to a difference of twenty-eight cents, thus:

DIFFERENCE IN PRICE (In Cents)	PROBABILITY	EXPECTED DIFFERENCE (In Cents)
.20	.25	.05
.24	.50	.12
.28	.25	.07
	1.00	.24

When Kelley left, he had the feeling that the wool buyer knew what he was talking about and that the $800,000 estimated saving was reliable.

Third, Kelley turned to the problem of production scheduling.

In 1965, Nashua had sold at distress (written-down) prices 1,048,000 yards of cancelled finished goods worth $2.18 a yard at direct cost (labor and materials only), or a total of $2,284,640. This yardage had been cancelled because Nashua had been unable to meet promised delivery dates. About half had been sold at 48 percent of direct cost and half was still carried in inventory. The half which was still in inventory had been written down by 50 percent but had not yet been sold. Evans believed this yardage could now be sold at ninety cents a yard. Nashua's total out-of-pocket loss for 1965 on cancelled finished

---

[1] It also used 5 to 6 million pounds in the manufacture of *worsteds*. But, for the time being no change would be made in this part of the operation.

[2] If raw wool shrank by, say, 10 percent during washing and scouring, ten cents worth of raw wool would be lost if raw wool were selling at $1 a pound, but twelve cents worth would be lost if it were selling at $1.20 a pound.

goods would thus be about $1,246,440. Losses because of cancellations in the previous five years had been as follows:

NASHUA'S CANCELLATION LOSSES, 1960-1964

1960	$ 896,240
1961	1,420,630
1962	250,266
1963	728,902
1964	1,114,329

Evans explained that Nashua always delivered about the same amount of yardage late. But cancellations tended to be far fewer when business was good. Hence when business was good, losses were always less. But when business was poor, Nashua's customers took advantage of any pretext whatever to cancel prior commitments.

"Last year and the year before were very poor years," said Evans. "So was 1961. 1962 was a very good year. 1960 and 1963 were just fair."

"Tell me something about the textile cycle," said Kelley, thinking back to the work he had done on the machine-tool cycle.

"Well," said Evans, "it's changing. Right now I'd say that one year in every five is a boom year, two in every five are good, and two are poor."

When he got back to his motel room that night, Kelley constructed the probability distribution over inventory losses given in Table 14.4, using the figures Evans had given him to determine the probabilities and the gross loss.

The next morning, bright and early, Kelley drew up a pro forma income statement which took account of all the expected reductions

TABLE 14.4

PROBABILITY DISTRIBUTION
OVER INVENTORY LOSSES AT NASHUA

EVENT	PROBABILITY	LOSS IF EVENT OCCURS	AVERAGE EXPECTED LOSS
(1)	(2)	(3)	(4)
Boom year	.20	$ 250,000	$ 50,000
Good year	.40	812,000	325,000
Poor year	.40	1,250,000	500,000
TOTAL	1.00		$875,000

TABLE 14.5

PRO FORMA INCOME STATEMENT FOR NASHUA

	AMOUNT	PERCENTAGE OF SALES
Sales	$21,300,000	100.0%
Cost of goods sold	17,060,000	80.1%
Gross profit	4,240,000	19.9%
Administrative and general	4,928,000	23.2%
Profit or (loss)	—$ 688,000	—3.3%

in cost. This statement is given in Table 14.5. The figures were derived as follows:

1. *Sales.* Nashua's sales had held steady during the past five years between $19 million and $22 million. For this reason, Kelley saw little point in constructing a probability distribution over sales. He simply averaged the sales figures, given in Table 14.1, over the past five years. This procedure gave him an estimated sales figure of $21.3 million.

2. *Cost of goods sold.* In order to obtain a figure for cost of goods sold, Kelley took the ratio of cost of goods sold to sales for 1965 —the worst year Nashua had experienced. This ratio was .886 ($17.9 million / $20.2 million = .886). He then multiplied his sales figure by this ratio and obtained a cost of goods sold figure of $18.9 million ($21.3 million × .886 = $18.9 million). This figure was thus an estimate of what cost of goods sold would be if sales were $21.3 million—*without* any of the new savings Butcher hoped to effect. Kelley then estimated cost of goods sold after expected new savings as follows:

Cost of goods sold in present operation with sales of $21.3 million		$18,900,000
Savings		
Work-flow	$ 165,000	
Wool	800,000	
Loss due to cancellations	875,000	
TOTAL	$1,840,000	
		1,840,000
Estimate of cost of goods sold after savings		$17,060,000

3. *Gross operating profit.* In order to obtain his figure for gross operating profit, ($4,240,000), Kelley simply subtracted his revised figure for cost of goods sold from sales.

4. *Administrative expense.* Kelley then estimated administrative and general expense by deducting expected savings from $5.8 million—which was his estimate of administrative and general expense without any savings. He thus arrived at a revised figure of $4,928,000 for administrative expense.

Seeing the final result of these calculations—a loss of $688,000 after all savings—made Kelley a bit glum, although he realized that the loss would represent a tax saving for Butcher.

DETERMINING THE PRICE OF PURCHASE

Kelley next drew up a list of cash inflows and outflows. Nashua had not put a price on its common stock and therefore the principal outlay could not be estimated. But Kelley realized that after he had estimated the benefits and calculated their present value at Butcher's cost of capital, he would have found the maximum price Butcher could afford to pay for Nashua.

The benefits were essentially very simple (see Table 14.6). They consisted almost solely of tax savings. Nashua had accumulated a tax loss of $6.12 million from prior years, which would be used immediately to reduce Butcher's income in 1965 and 1964. Butcher's taxes would be retroactively reduced for those years by about 50 percent of the reduction in its income. This came to about $3.06 million. Butcher would receive a refund of that amount during the first year after the merger took place. Butcher would also receive a sum equal to the present market value of the Piper Aztec which, Kelley knew, Butcher would sell. The plane was now worth about $45,000.

Nashua would also lose money the first year after the merger and probably also for sometime thereafter. The effects of tighter management and better coordination would not be felt immediately. Kelley therefore decided to assume that Nashua would lose $688,000 the first year after the merger and for four years thereafter. This meant that Butcher would get a tax saving for four or five years of half Nashua's loss, or about $344,000. And because Butcher would decide in four or five years whether to remain in textiles, Kelley decided to assume a four- or, at most, a five-year life for the project.

Kelley then set up the foregoing cash flows, as in Table 14.6, and calculated their present value at 11 percent. The final figure of $3.7 million represented the maximum amount Butcher could pay for Nashua

TABLE 14.6

ESTIMATED VALUES OF CASH OUTLAYS * AND BENEFITS
FROM NASHUA MERGER (IN THOUSANDS OF DOLLARS)

YEAR	OUTLAYS *	BENEFITS	NET BENEFITS	11 PERCENT DISCOUNT FACTORS	PRESENT VALUE
(1)	(2)	(3)	(4)	(5)	(6)
1	$385 †	$3,449 ‡	$3,064	.901	$2,761
2		344	344	.812	279
3		344	344	.731	251
4		344	344	.659	227
5		344	344	.593	204
				TOTAL	$3,722

* Excepting price.

†	360,000	New wool processing machinery
	25,000	Cost of obtaining improved work-flow
	$385.000	Total

‡	$3,060,000	Tax saving due to accumulated losses
	344,000	Tax saving due to annual loss
	45,000	Resale value of Piper Aztec
	$3,449,000	

and still "break even." Martin would use this figure, Kelley surmised, as a starting point in making up his mind how much to bid for Nashua. Kelley then wrote the following memorandum to Dale Martin:

To: Dale Martin
From: R. Relley
Subject: *Merger with Nashua*

1. I have tried to look at the proposed merger with Nashua as if it were a lathe. We must decide what we would be willing to pay for Nashua's stock but we cannot do so except by calculating the present value of the net benefits we expect to get out of Nashua. This, of course, is precisely what Hastings does when he tries to decide what one of Ex-Cello's lathes is really worth to Butcher. There is thus no difference in principle between the two cases.

2. But the benefits we would get out of the merger are much more difficult to isolate and estimate than the benefits we would get out of a lathe.

3. I have proceeded as follows:

First, I checked out the savings you and Mr. Hastings had estimated. My figures are somewhat lower than yours, primarily because yours were maximum savings whereas mine are the expected values of probability distributions.

Second, using my figures for savings, I drew up the pro forma income statement given in Table 14.5. This statement shows that Nashua's present loss of $3.5 million will be reduced to $688,000 as soon as all savings have been made.

Third, I assumed losses of this amount would continue during the first five years of operations. I did so because I did not know what other assumption to make. How Nashua would do after a merger is highly uncertain. I do not believe they would lose more than $688,000 a year. But on the other hand I do not believe that my opinion is worth very much. The difficulty is that I do not know anything about the market for woven textiles and Nashua's competitive position. And, frankly, I do not believe that you do either. We need an outside opinion —from someone who has a real feeling for textiles. If you asked me to tell you why I have chosen a loss of $688,000 instead of a loss of $1,376,000 or a profit of $688,000, I would be forced to say, "I don't know." What would you say if I asked you the same question?

The point is that our cost estimates are probably fairly good but our estimate of sales (yards sold times average price per yard) is very weak. Will Nashua go on selling present yardage at about present prices? Or will prices improve or weaken? *I don't know.* Only someone who knows the market can tell us.

In any case, my method indicates present value to us of $3,722,000 at 11 percent. All the benefits to Butcher are tax savings. I should think we would be able to get Nashua for a lot less than $3,722,000.

4. I have left two things out of account—salvage value at the end of the period and reduced interest if we in fact do pay off the long-term note to the Mutual of Boston. I left out salvage value because, in my opinion, Nashua's assets would be worth no more than their weight as junk if we decided to get out in five years. (The three buildings are for all practical purposes worthless now.) I left out the saving in interest because Nashua's business is seasonal and we will need to use our funds to help them carry inventory and receivables. This will cost us $60,000-$70,000 a year on our portfolio of marketables. (But why should we pay off the loan? Nothing in the agreement between Nashua and Mutual would require us to do so. And as of right now we can't borrow money at anything like 5 percent. If we simply invested the $2 million in short-term governments at 7 percent, we'd pick up $40,000 net before taxes.)

5. My calculations assume that if Nashua loses $688,000 or less, we would not have to put in any more money. But if Nashua's losses were larger than that amount, we might have

to put in more money in order to protect our investment. This is one of the reasons why I believe we should get an outside opinion from someone who knows something about woven textiles—and especially about Nashua's position in that market.

6. Finally, I wouldn't be doing my job if I didn't say that I'm suspicious of the whole thing. Why hasn't someone picked up Nashua as a tax loss? The saving of $3.06 million, less the loan, means that someone could pick up a neat clear profit of $1.06 million. How come? Are you sure we'd get the tax loss? And the machinery and inventory are, of course, worth something.

Martin held the memo for a day or so and then called Kelley in.

"Kelley," he said, "you're passing the buck."

"Of course I am," said Kelley.

"This thing has to be decided quickly. We can't wait for some expensive consultant to prepare a 250 page report."

"Why don't you discuss it with Goldberg at Smith, Horgan?" asked Kelley. "They do a lot of financing for some of the very big textile companies."

"Good idea," said Martin. "We can talk about some financing for ourselves at the same time. Call him and ask whether he can have lunch with us this week."

"Me, too?" said Kelley.

"You, too," said Martin. "Tell him what we want to talk about. Invite Hastings, too. And, by the way, you can't just buy tax losses. Go read Section 269 of the Internal Revenue Code."

At lunch, two days later, Martin, Hastings and Kelley described the situation at Nashua to Goldberg and his textile specialist and explained in detail the savings Butcher hoped to be able to make. Goldberg's assistant was fully familiar with woven textiles and with Nashua's position in the market. He discussed the industry in detail—reciting facts and figures by the yard. He had been following Nashua's situation closely through friends at Mutual of Boston, and he knew the company would either have to merge or face bankruptcy. He had, in fact, tried unsuccessfully to locate a merger prospect for Nashua. He looked at Kelley's figures and said he thought they were very conservative, given the savings Butcher expected to make at Nashua.

"With tight management," he said, "Nashua should be on a break-even basis in eighteen months. They've got first-class trademarks and first-class know-how. And woven fabrics will be around for a long, long time. And high quality textiles will get an increasing share of the market simply because living standards are going up and everyone's sick of junk. The trouble with Nashua has been that no one has been interested in putting it back on a money-making basis. Worse than that, really—the family's been milking it dry."

"How much do you think we should pay for it?" asked Martin.

"It would be a steal at $1 million," said Goldberg's assistant.

Goldberg nodded his head, and added, "Your bargaining position is very good—the family's not eager to make good on that Mutual of Boston note. And, of course, other things equal, they'd like to keep the mill running."

"All right," said Kelley. "Sounds great. But why haven't you been able to find a merger prospect?"

"Because I've approached only textile companies," said Goldberg's assistant. "They're all too busy diversifying."

Two days later Martin and Hastings had obtained the approval of the Board to pay up to $1 million for Nashua's common stock—either in cash or in Butcher stock. The next day they met with Nashua's Board—made up of members of the McEwen family and Evans—and after a week of negotiation agreed to a price of $980,000 to be paid to Nashua's stockholders in cash. The family, of course, felt they had been "robbed" —$980,000 was about 25 percent of Nashua's book value. But as Goldberg predicted, they were worried about their liability under the note to Mutual of Boston—and their worry increased as the April 15th deadline approached. On that day Nashua would be obliged to pay Mutual of Boston $100,000 in interest and $200,000 in principal on the note. As a condition of purchase, Butcher agreed to assume full responsibility for the note.

The merger was approved by Butcher's stockholders at a special meeting held early in April 1966.

THE NATURE OF MERGER

What does the Nashua story tell us? *No merger can take place unless both sides find it worthwhile.* Butcher found the merger with Nashua worthwhile primarily because Butcher would be able to obtain diversification *rapidly at low cost.* Diversification would make Butcher's earnings more stable and for that reason would probably raise the price of Butcher's common stock. Butcher, obviously, could have started in textiles on its own. But the learning process would have been long—and risky. And Butcher could hardly have established a textile division as large as Nashua for $980,000. The book value alone of Nashua's plant and machinery was nearly $5 million—although salvage value was, as noted above, much less. And it would have taken Butcher years (and a lot of money) to build up four trademarks as valuable as Nashua's.

Butcher would not, of course, get the benefits of diversification unless Nashua could be made profitable once again. But Butcher would earn a satisfactory return on investment even if Nashua lost $750,000 a year for the next five years.

What did the McEwen family see in Butcher? They were totally disinterested in the business (indeed, they were sick of it) and they were concerned about their liability to Mutual of Boston. They were afraid that if Nashua were liquidated and its plant, machinery and inventory sold at auction, not enough money would be realized to pay off Mutual of Boston. By merging, the McEwens got rid of the business and their liability. In addition, they received $980,000 in cash.

The whole is sometimes equal to more than the sum of its parts. Nashua would contribute diversification to Butcher—which Butcher had had only to a lesser degree before. Butcher hence became stronger as a result of the merger. Nashua also contributed a tax loss to Butcher with the result that the taxes which would be paid in the future by the combined companies would be less than the sum of the taxes they would have paid if they had not merged. On the other hand, Butcher would contribute to Nashua many things which Nashua, by itself, could not have afforded—tighter management, industrial engineering, computerized production scheduling and bookkeeping, stability and, last but not least, access to money if needed. In short, Butcher's strength was not diluted as the result of merger with a weak company. The merger made *both* companies stronger.

Assessing the worthwhileness of buying a going concern is, in principle, no different from assessing the worthwhileness of buying any other kind of asset. As the buyer you must estimate the net benefits you would expect the acquisition to generate and, using an appropriate rate of discount, you must estimate the present value to you of those expected net benefits.

Estimating the benefits a proposed acquisition or merger can be expected to generate will not be nearly as easy as falling off a log. A company, such as Nashua, is, most emphatically, not a machine such as Ex-Cello's lathe.

First, a company represents a complex, integrated system of assets —some of them are tangible (buildings and machines) and some of them, intangible (trademarks and goodwill). And you, as the buyer, will not be able to ascertain accurately, except in the simplest cases (and perhaps not even then), the condition of each separate asset and when it will have to be replaced. This means that you will not be able to estimate accurately the outlays which will be required to maintain the integrity of the system.

Second, you will have difficulty judging how the system of assets will respond to the exhortations of a new management. Will the system behave more efficiently or less? Except in rare cases, people will accompany the assets you have bought. How will they behave?

And, third, how will your new customers behave? Their "goodwill" has cost you a pretty penny, but many of them will wonder whether "things will change" and whether they will be able to rely on you as they had relied on your predecessor. And many of them will cast an eye at other suppliers.

Fourth, you will have difficulty translating into money terms your expected contribution to the efficiency and productiveness of the system. What do you expect to contribute to the system? Product research? Industrial engineering? Better sales promotion? General management? Money? When will your contribution begin to take effect? And by how much will it increase the efficiency of the system and the benefits you will derive from that system?

Now, having explored the Butcher-Nashua affair in detail, we are in position to make a few cynical remarks about mergers:

First, a merger is an alternative to internal growth. Butcher could obviously have gone into textiles on its own—just as it went into agricultural chemicals at Tampico on its own. And because a merger is an allocation of funds alternative to internal growth, it must pass the same test as any proposal for internal growth: the merger must show net PV at the buyer's cost of capital. Growth for the sake of growth may mean that the chairman (and perhaps the president, too) of the surviving company will be able to put his feet on a bigger desk. But from the stockholder's point of view, growth for the sake of growth is dull, boring and pointless. And sometimes it may be painful—it may reduce the value of their common stock.

Second, not many proposed acquisitions are likely to pass the foregoing test. Of those that do, most will be companies which for one reason or another seem to the potential buyer to be *undervalued*—that is, they will be available at prices which seem to potential buyers to be bargain prices.

Third, a company can be undervalued for a variety of reasons, for example: It is being mismanaged or, as in the case of Nashua, not being managed at all. And the potential buyer (as, for example, Butcher) believes it can provide better management which in turn will increase profits substantially.

Or even if the potential acquisition *is* well-managed, the potential buyer and the potential seller may view the future differently. They may, that is, have different probability distributions over the expected benefits the acquisition will generate in the future. If the potential buyer is optimistic and the potential seller is pessimistic, or if the buyer sees opportunities the seller does not see, the acquisition will appear undervalued to the potential buyer. When the Manhattan Indians sold their island to Peter Minuit in 1626 for beads and cloth worth twenty-four dollars, the two parties to the transaction had rather different views about the benefits the island would generate!

Or if the potential acquisition has a tax loss carry forward, as Nashua did, it will appear to be a bargain for that reason alone—and especially if the buyer believes, as in the case of Nashua, that prior losses were due to mismanagement—which the buyer will be able to correct.

Or small firms may seem riskier to the public than large firms merely because they are small. To the extent that this is so, a small firm will appear undervalued to a large firm. In other words, the buyer may believe that the value of the common stock of the small firm will rise as soon as the small firm becomes part of the large firm.

But, most bargains tend to disappear almost as soon as they are discovered by buyers. This means that no company is likely to be able actually to buy another company at a bargain price—unless the negotiations are isolated from the effects of competition—as were, for example, the Butcher-Nashua negotiations. Nashua's stockholders were worried about the possibility of foreclosure by Mutual of Boston, they had very little time in which to shop around further for a "better deal" and, as a result, were in a poor bargaining position: Butcher was the only buyer. And a seller who is being virtually forced, by circumstances, to sell and finds himself at the mercy of a single buyer, is likely to feel that he is being "robbed."

In short, Nashua appeared to Butcher to be a mismanagement bargain. But Butcher actually got Nashua at a bargain price because no other potential buyer saw Nashua in the same way.

Fifth, why is it that of those potential acquisitions which pass the rate of return—cost of capital test, most are likely to be undervalued? This is equivalent to saying that unless a company has been mismanaged or, if well-managed, is small or pessimistic about the future, it is not likely to promise a rate of return higher than the buyer's cost of capital. Why should this be so? It should be so because the only other type of acquisition likely to pass the test is one which brings with it the prospect of a reduction in unit costs. Butcher thought, for example, that it would be able to supply Nashua with tighter management and various administrative and computer services at little or no additional cost. This meant that the total overhead costs of the two companies after the merger would be much less than they had been before. This would mean, in turn, a reduction in overhead per unit of output—provided only that the combined output of the two companies did not decline.

But if this in fact turned out to be so, Nashua's overhead before the merger must have been too high—due to mismanagement (we know this was in fact the case), or Butcher's was too high—*for the same reason.* If, after the merger, Butcher was able to provide Nashua with tighter management or with various other services at little or no additional cost, then Butcher itself must have had more management or more computer capacity than it really needed before the merger took place. This may sound "too theoretical," but most companies try very hard not to hire unnecessary expensive resources, such as management and computers. And most successful, well-managed companies will tend to have about as much of such resources as they need. And they will tend to operate at a level which makes total unit cost as low as possible. This means that opportunities to reduce total unit cost by merging with some other successful, well-managed company are likely to be few and far between. This does not mean that mergers between successful, well-managed companies never take place. They do. But, in general, such mergers are not likely to improve the lot of the stockholders of either company—although they may make the managers of both companies feel bigger and more powerful.

PROBLEMS

1. Trace through, step-by-step, the process Butcher went through in deciding how much to offer for Nashua.

2. Using the net benefits given in Table 14.6, calculate Butcher's rate of return on the merger at a purchase price of $980,000.

3. In deciding whether or not to accept Butcher's offer of $980,000 for their stock, Nashua's stockholders must have estimated, explicitly or implicitly, the present value to them of Nashua's assets. This means that they must have estimated, explicitly or implicitly, the benefits Nashua's assets would generate—if no merger took place. Assume that you are one of Nashua's stockholders. Assuming no merger, draw up a pattern of expected benefits consistent with the facts of the case which, when discounted at some appropriate rate, would make you willing to accept Butcher's offer.

4. Butcher was able to buy Nashua at a bargain price because Nashua's stockholders were in a very poor bargaining position. They were not really free not to merge with Butcher.

    But suppose that instead of having lost money for the last three years (see Table 14.1), Nashua had in fact shown profits before taxes since 1961 as follows:

1962	$420,000
1963	619,000
1964	398,000
1965	521,000

Depreciation charges would be $750,000 a year for the next five years—and everything else would be the same, including the reductions Butcher thought it could make in Nashua's costs. In such circumstances, Nashua's stockholders would have had no sword hanging over their heads and would therefore have been perfectly free not to merge. And they would have been under no time pressure and would have been able, if they had wished, to shop around energetically for another buyer.

Given the revised figures, above, find the maximum price which, in your opinion, Butcher should have been willing to pay for Nashua. Also, using an appropriate rate of discount, find the minimum price which you, as a Nashua stockholder, would have been willing to accept. Would the merger have taken place? Assume no salvage value.

5. Actually, Kelley made a slight mistake (which Martin somehow failed to notice) in calculating the annual benefits in Table 14.6. Find the mistake. (Hint: Nashua's annual depreciation charges would be $750,000 a year in each of the next five years.)

6. A "spinoff" is, we might say, a unmerger or, if you prefer, a dismerger. It occurs when a company disposes of part of its assets, either to its own stockholders or to the public-at-large. The term "spinoff" was "invented" by a Wall Street financial writer whose name, by coincidence, was Spunoff. In late 1964, "dismergers" were going off all around poor Spunoff and they reminded him somehow of centrifugal force. He decided therefore to rename them spunoffs in honor of himself. The public insisted, however, on pronouncing "spunoff" as if it were spelled "spinoff"—to Spunoff's sorrow and dismay.

Meat-Ball, Goof-Ball, Golf Ball. A classic example of a spinoff occurred in 1967 when Ling-Temco-Vought (LTV), split Wilson and Company, which it had previously acquired, into three parts, each of which became a wholly-owned subsidiary of LTV. The three parts were: a meat company to be called Wilson and Company, Inc.; a drug company to be called Wilson Pharmaceutical and Chemical Corporation; and a sporting goods company to be called Wilson Sporting Goods Company. Wilson had, of course, been in all three businesses—meat, drugs, and sporting goods—for a long time prior to merging with LTV.

LTV then sold to the public at large through an investment banking syndicate, one million shares in the meat company, 600,000 shares in the sporting goods company, and 350,000 shares in the drug company. LTV retained 81.8 percent of the voting securities of the meat company, 77.4 percent of the voting securities of the drug company, and 75 percent of the voting securities of the sporting goods company. LTV listed all three subsidiary companies on the American Stock Exchange—where you will find them trading today.

The result of this interesting maneuver was an increase in the market value of Wilson and Company of about $60 million. Before the merger with LTV, the total market value of Wilson and Company's common stock had been about $120 million. After the merger and the three spinoffs, the value of the meat company was $100 million, the value of the drug company, about $23 million, and the value of the sporting goods company, about $60 million—to a total of $183 million.

Imagine that you are Ling, President of LTV. Using such data as you are able to find in Moody's and the Wall Street Journal, and bearing in mind the merger with Wilson had to precede the spinoffs, list the various benefits and outlays which you would take into account in deciding whether to make an offer to the holders of Wilson's common stock. (LTV actually made such an offer on December 21, 1966 of $62.50 for each share of Wilson stock.) You are not being asked to try to quantify the cash flows. You are being asked merely to list them.

7. As indicated in Chapter 1, Butcher's Tampico plant is in trouble. Martin and Hastings now have come to feel that they should not have gone into agricultural chemicals. The Board of Butcher and the Finance Committee agree and have asked Martin to suggest the best way of getting out. As usual Martin has asked Kelley to prepare a memorandum. Kelley sees three alternatives:

   (a) To accept an offer of $762,000 made by Allied Potash for the plant. This would be payable in cash immediately.

   (b) To set the Tampico plant up as a separate corporation and spin it off on a pro rata basis to Butcher's present stockholders. Each Butcher shareholder would receive one share in Tampico for each share of Butcher he held. Thus a stockholder who now owned 100 shares of Butcher would, after the spinoff, own in addition 100 shares of Tampico. Butcher itself (that is, as a company), would no longer own any part of Tampico. Those of Butcher's officers and employees who owned Butcher stock (among them Martin, Hastings and Kelley himself) would, of course, receive shares in Tampico. After such a spinoff about 15 percent of the stock of Tampico would be owned by Butcher employees.

(c)   To set the Tampico plant up as a separate company but sell
the stock in it to the public-at-large.

Kelley had read "the LTV story" and was bemused by the possibility of a spinoff. As Kelley, what information would you want in
order to try to make an intelligent decision among the foregoing
three alternatives?

15

CONCLUSION TO PART III
where do we go from here?

WHERE ARE WE NOW?

In the six preceding chapters we have, in effect, described how the need for funds arises: Butcher's sales manager wants to increase accounts receivable; the production manager wants a larger inventory of parts; Hastings wants to clean up the mess at Nashua; the tools and plastics divisions need more machinery; Martin and Hastings have found a new promising acquisition; Martin himself wants to build up liquidity, and so forth. In short, every one of Butcher's divisions wants to spend money on what appear to be worthwhile projects. And Butcher must decide which projects to accept. And as we shall see below, Micro Electronics, Inc., (see Chapter 9) is also beginning to have this same kind of problem.

This then is where we are:

We have surveyed *all* of Butcher's *currently available* (new) opportunities—both short and long term. And we have calculated proper rates of return on (and the NPV of) each of those opportunities (Table 15.1).

Now, if we knew how to calculate Butcher's cost of long-term capital, our problem would be simple. We would proceed as follows:

First, we would separate short-term projects from long-term projects. A short-term project is, of course, a project which will be over and done with within one year—as the temporary increase in wool inventory at Nashua. We would estimate our net need for external short term funds.

Second, we would look around for short-term sources of funds and, after weighing each one carefully, we would decide which to use.

We would then turn to our proposed new long-term projects. We would estimate how much money, if any, we would have to raise externally—that is, *outside* the firm—in order to pay for those projects. We would, next, decide *how* those funds should be raised—that is, what percent should be debt and what percent should be equity. (Long term funds should be raised, obviously, so as *to minimize our cost of long term capital*).

After we had decided how long term funds should be raised, we would know (as we shall see) our cost of capital. We would then be able to decide *which long-term projects we should in fact accept.* Suppose Butcher found that its current cost of capital were 9 percent, instead of 11. Nine percent would then be Butcher's cut-off rate—subject to certain assumptions which we will discuss in Chapter 23.

We would then look down our list of currently available opportunities —and accept all projects showing DCF rates of return higher than 9 percent. Thus, only the last four projects in Table 15.1 would be rejected.

WHERE DO WE GO NOW?

The foregoing discussion suggests that the following tasks remain before us:

First, we must estimate the net need for external funds, both short and long term. We will illustrate this process briefly in this chapter.

Second, we must explore the various sources of short-term funds, and decide how to choose among them. This is the subject matter of Chapter 16.

Third, we must explore the sources of long term funds and decide how to choose among *them*. Sources of long term funds are discussed in Chapter 16. The *cost* of long-term funds is discussed in Chapters 17-22.

Finally, we must remove a critical assumption on which much of the discussion in Chapters 9-22 is based—that is, that all projects which constitute the set of our *currently available opportunities* do not differ much, *in degree of risk*, from our present assets. But suppose this as-

TABLE 15.1

NEW PROJECTS FOR CONSIDERATION BY
FINANCE COMMITTEE AND BOARD (DECEMBER 1968)

PROPOSAL	COST (thousands)	DCF RATE *	NET PRESENT VALUE AT 11 % (thousands)
1. Increase in accounts receivable	$ 680	42%	$ 83
2. Increase in parts inventory (tools)	750	28%	52
3. Additional temporary increase in raw wool inventory (Nashua)	1500	24%	90
4. Chemical storage tanks (Tampico)	1525	24%	600
5. Plant to produce die castings and injection moulding machinery	1960	22%	205
6. Government contract (Tampico)	830	21%	56
7. Tank and other trucks (chemicals)	190	19%	60
8. New plant and equipment, Lima, Ohio (tools)	925	18%	22
9. Machinery-Plastics division	1225	16%	68
10. Materials handling equipment (Nashua)	504	12%	15
11. New heat pump, etc. (chemicals)	730	12%	12
12. Construction of facilities for loading and transfer of chemicals to barges—New Jersey	300	10%	10
13. Purchase of company to handle export sales and relations (all products)	200	8%	
14. Electron microscopes	33	8%	20 †
15. Modernization of Nashua office	150	4%	
16. Apartment in New York City to accommodate personnel traveling to New York from out-of-town plants	140	4%	40 †
TOTAL	$11,642		

* After tax.
† Negative figure.

sumption is not valid? Suppose some of the proposed new projects are much less risky—or much more risky—than Butcher's present assets? What then? We discuss this matter briefly in Chapter 23.

In the rest of this chapter, as indicated above, we will illustrate the process of estimating the net need for external funds.

ESTIMATING THE NEED FOR FUNDS

In mid-December of 1968 Dale Martin called Kelley in and said: "What does it all add up to? The Finance Committee meets next week."

"I know," said Kelley. "It's much more than we thought it would be."

"How much?" asked Martin.

Kelley put Table 15.1 on Martin's desk.

"Wow," said Martin. "Nearly $12 million for just six months. How did it get so big in such a hurry?"

"Last minute rush," said Kelley.

"And why have you included all these low rates of return? Our cost of capital is 11 percent."

"That was our cost of capital last year," said Kelley. "We don't know what it is this year. And besides, I don't think that 11 percent figure was calculated properly."

"Oh," said Martin. "You calculated it—using, I thought, the very best ingredients. Don't tell me *you* made a mistake."

"I may have," said Kelley.

"Well, how much will it be this year?"

"Don't know," said Kelley. "I just don't know. I've got some new ideas on the subject—but I haven't thought them through."

"Well, you'd better hurry up," said Martin. "You've got to have a figure for the Finance Committee meeting. You've got just five working days."

"I know," said Kelley. "Don't worry about it. I'll have a figure for you."

"The right figure?" asked Martin.

"Maybe," said Kelley.

"Suppose we take all these projects," said Martin, indicating Table 15.1. "How much outside money will we need?"

Kelley gave Martin the uses and sources statement shown in Table 15.2. "We'll have to go outside for $6,297,000."

"How much!" said Martin.

"$6,297,000," said Kelley.

"That's just out of the question," said Martin, grimly.

"It's not out of the question," said Kelley. "It all depends on the cost of capital."

"Why can't you be just a little bit realistic," said Martin. "The Finance Committee will never agree to it."

"They will if we persuade them to," said Kelley.

"And you've reduced cash and securities by $2 million. They won't

TABLE 15.2

*EXTERNAL FINANCING NEEDS
IF ALL PROPOSALS ACCEPTED*

PROPOSED USES

Short Term

Temporary increase in wool inventory (Nashua)	$ 1,500,000
Inventory build-up for government order for agricultural chemicals (Tampico)	830,000
Total short-term	$ 2,330,000

Long Term

Miscellaneous long term assets *	$ 9,312,000
Total short-term and long-term *	$11,642,000

EXPECTED SOURCES

Net profit after taxes, six months †	$ 5,400,000
Less two quarterly dividends of $.60 a share	2,625,000
Expected retentions	2,775,000
Plus depreciation for six months	1,720,000
	$ 4,495,000
Amortization of long term loan	$ 1,150,000
Balance	$ 3,345,000
Reduction in cash and securities	$ 2,000,000
Total available internally	$ 5,345,000
Needed from outside sources	$ 6,297,000
Total internal and external	$11,642,000

* See Table 15.1.
† See Table 2.7.

buy that either—and neither will I. We've been all over that before. Why do you bring it up again?"

"Because I'm persistent," said Kelley.

"Everybody just sleeps better when we have a lot of cash and governments," said Martin. "And that's that. No reduction in cash and securities."

"I don't," said Kelley.

"You don't what?" asked Martin.

"I don't sleep better," said Kelley. "I sleep worse. All that liquidity is costing us maybe $500,000 a year. And, besides, $2.3 million worth of those projects are short-term, self-liquidating, and virtually certain. The $2 million would be back in the bank in four months."

"Skip it," said Martin. "With no reduction in cash, we'll have to go outside for $8,297,000, instead of $6,297,000. You're out of your mind, Kelley."

"As I said," said Kelley, "it all depends on . . ."

"Yes, I know," said Martin. "It all depends on the cost of capital."

Kelley went back to his office and put his feet on his desk and fell asleep. He dreamed about absolutely nothing—not even the cost of capital.

A TEMPORARY INCREASE IN INVENTORY

Let's go back now to Barclay, Vaughn, Whitman and Roberts at Micro Electronics, Inc., who are also beginning to find they need funds.

After their last meeting with Philbrook (see Chapter 9), they had worked intensively for about 4 months, under the tutelage of James Moses, a loan officer at the Second National Bank of Rahway, (New Jersey). Moses was a friend of Barclay's and had made the original contact for him with Philbrook. After looking at the cash budget drawn up by Barclay (Table 9.8), Philbrook, on November 1, 1969, had agreed to go ahead with the venture and invest in Micro Electronics. His group had put up $302,000 on the terms described in Chapter 9. In addition, to provide Micro Electronics with the necessary liquidity, Philbrook had arranged a one-year loan to the company of $75,000 with Second National. Philbrook endorsed the note personally and thus assumed responsibility for its repayment. Micro Electronics started operation 8 weeks later—on January 2, 1970.

The first thirty-five weeks of operations have gone peacefully enough —and then one day during the thirty-sixth week of operations, Vaughn calls Barclay from Binghamton and, all excited, says "I have another order from IBM."

"How much?"

"$250,000."

"$250,000!"

"Yeah, $250,000."

"For delivery when?"

"Whole thing in four weeks."

"We can't do it."

"Whaddya mean we can't do it! Of course we can do it! I'm gonna take it. Go out and hire some more people. Good bye."

"Why'd you bother to call?"

"I didn't think you'd say no. Goodbye."

"If you take that order, you're fired."

"You can't fire me—I own as much stock in this thing as you do."
And he hung up.

When Vaughn came in the next day, Barclay simply told him that his suggestion was impossible—the order couldn't possibly be produced or financed on such short notice. They would have to buy more raw materials, hire more labor and set up another production line. All these things would take money—which they didn't have and couldn't possibly raise in a month.

Barclay said: "I'm just as interested in making this company grow as you are. And I'll listen to any reasonable suggestion. But your suggestion just isn't reasonable."

"Okay," said Vaughn, slightly (but only slightly) chastened.

TABLE 15.3

MICRO ELECTRONICS, INC., PRO FORMA BALANCE SHEET AS OF DECEMBER 31, 1970

ASSETS

Cash		$ 52,985
Accounts receivable		102,750
Raw materials		22,000
Work-in-process		41,200
Finished goods		0
Machinery and equipment (gross)	$220,000	
Accumulated depreciation	22,000	
Machinery and equipment (net)		198,000
Leasehold improvements (net)		117,000
Office furniture		3,000
Prepaid rent		0
Total assets		$536,935

LIABILITIES AND EQUITY

Notes payable bank	$ 75,000
Accounts payable	0
Accrued salaries and wages	0
Accrued federal income and other taxes	1,952
Other accruals	5,745
Convertible debentures	302,000
Long-term notes (parents)	20,000
Common stock ($120 par value)	120,000
Retained earnings	12,238
Total liabilities and equity	$536,935

CONCLUSION TO PART III: WHERE DO WE GO FROM HERE?

Then, a few weeks later, Vaughn—who is irrepressible—comes in and suggests that he'd like to build up finished inventory by $250,000 before the first of June (1971)—which is then about seven months away. "I hope that's sufficient notice," he says.

"What's up?" said Barclay.

"Beginning in June, I expect a real breakthrough—with some big ones. People like RCA and Control Data. I want to be able to deliver the goods. We'd be back to normal by October."

Barclay says: "We'll have to see." Vaughn grunts and leaves.

Barclay couldn't dismiss this suggestion as being wholly unreasonable. And he therefore set out to analyze its financial implications by drawing

TABLE 15.4

MICRO ELECTRONICS, INC., PRO FORMA BALANCE SHEET AS OF TWENTY WEEKS AFTER THE END OF THE FIRST YEAR

ASSETS

Cash	$ 25,000	
Accounts receivable	102,750	
Raw materials	22,000	
Work-in-process (at cost)	41,200	
Finished goods (at cost)	250,000	
Machinery and equipment (net)	189,540	
Leasehold improvements (net)	112,000	
Office furniture (net)	2,600	
Prepaid rent	10,500	
Total assets		$755,590

LIABILITIES AND EQUITY

Notes payable (bank)		$227,612 *
Accounts payable	—	
Accrued salaries and wages	—	
Accrued federal income and other taxes	46,140	
Other accruals	5,440	
Convertible debentures	302,000	
Long-term notes (parents)	20,000	
Common stock ($120 par value)	120,000	
Retained earnings	34,398	$527,978
Total liabilities and equity		$755,590

* $755,590
 — 527,978

 $227,612 required bank loan at end of period. A figure calculated in such a way is called a "plugged" figure.

up a proforma balance sheet as of June 1, 1971. But first he drew up a balance sheet as of the end of the year—which was then just a few weeks away. This pro forma balance sheet is given in Table 15.3. The pro-forma balance sheet as of June 1, 1971 is given in Table 15.4. The latter table showed that in order to build up finished goods inventory by $250,000 (at cost) a total bank loan of $227,612 would be necessary.

Several things struck Barclay immediately about this result:

First, a bank loan of this amount was absolutely out of the question. The company could not hope to borrow that much on its own signature. And he knew that Philbrook would not endorse a note of that size.

TABLE 15.5

MICRO ELECTRONICS, INC. NET INCREASES IN ASSETS AND LIABILITIES AS OF TWENTY WEEKS AFTER END OF FIRST YEAR

INCREASES IN ASSETS		
Finished goods inventory	$250,000	
Prepaid rent	10,500	
Total increases in assets		$260,500
DECREASES IN ASSETS		
Cash	27,985	
Machinery and equipment	8,460	
Leasehold improvements	5,000	
Office furniture	400	
Total decreases in assets		$ 41,845
Net increase in assets		$218,655
INCREASES IN LIABILITIES AND EQUITY		
Bank loan	$152,612	
Accrued taxes	44,188	
Retained earnings	22,160	
Total increase in liabilities and equity		$218,960
DECREASES IN LIABILITIES AND EQUITY		
Other accruals	$ 305	305
Net increase in liabilities and equity		$218,655

Second, he saw that the bank loan required at the end of the period was less (by about $23,000) (= $250,000 — 227,612), than the increase in finished goods inventory. This suggests to him that the company could build up finished goods inventory to some extent *without any bank loan* —and the more so (although not by the full amount) if Philbrook could just be persuaded to endorse another $75,000 short-term note.

In order to be sure about this, he first rearranged the figures in Table 15.4 and compared them with the pro forma end of year balance sheet, given in Table 15.3. The figures resulting from this comparison are given in Table 15.5. In drawing up this table Barclay, first, separated the increases in assets from the decreases. He saw immediately that the increase in assets between the two balance sheets, $218,655, was a *net* figure. Some assets had gone up (finished goods inventory and prepaid rent). But some had gone down (cash and fixed assets). He then drew, in sources and uses form, the figures given in Table 15.6 on the assumption

TABLE 15.6

MICRO-ELECTRONICS, INC., PRO FORMA USES AND SOURCES OF FUNDS, DECEMBER 31, 1970 TO MAY 31, 1971— ASSUMING NO INCREASE IN BANK LOAN

USES		
Increase in prepaid rent	$10,500	
Decrease in other accruals	305	
Increase in finished goods inventory	97,388	
		$108,193
SOURCES		
Decrease in cash	$27,985	
Depreciation on machinery, etc.	8,460	
Amortization of leasehold improvements	5,000	
Depreciation on office furniture	400	
Retained earnings	22,160	
Accrued taxes	44,188	
		$108,193

of no increase in the bank loan over the amount outstanding at the end of the first year. These calculations yielded a figure of $97,388 as the amount by which finished goods inventory could be built up with no *increase* in the bank loan. In order to find out how much finished goods inventory could be built up with *no* bank loan at all, he subtracted

$75,000 from the above figure and obtained $22,388—which checked with the figure he had obtained above.

Moreover, while he was sure his figures were right, (because everything balanced!) he was a bit puzzled about *why* they were right. The items on the uses side (Table 15.6) were easy enough to understand. On the preceding January 1, $18,000 would have had to be paid out for a year's rent in advance. Twenty weeks later, $7,500 of this would have been recovered out of sales. Thus, the *net* increase in pre-paid rent would be $10,500, between December 31, 1970 and May 31, 1971. He saw also, on the sources side, so far as depreciation and amortization were concerned, that the company's machinery and leasehold improvements had been paid for once (see Table 9.3) and would not have to be paid for again. As accounts receivable were collected, therefore, these amounts (the amounts called depreciation and amortization) would be recovered and would also find their way into the cash account. And they also, therefore, would be available to help pay for additional raw materials and labor. The same thing was true of the increase in retained earnings—which represented money above and beyond all expenses. It was also contained in collections of accounts receivable. But what about accrued taxes? How would this sum become available, if only temporarily, *as cash,* to help pay for additional raw materials and labor? By this time, Barclay realized that labor, employees and suppliers could be paid only with *cash.* They couldn't be paid with retained earnings, or with accrued taxes or with anything, to repeat, *except cash.* And Barclay did not see clearly how the $44,188 would find its way into cash so as to be available to be used to pay for raw materials and labor.

After puzzling over this problem for an hour or so, he finally realized that this sum was not unlike an increase in a short-term bank loan. At the end of the twenty-week period the company would owe the government $46,140 or $44,188 more than it had owed it at the end of the first year ($1,952, Table 15.3). This sum would be payable during the twenty-fifth week of the year—or five weeks *after* the end of the inventory buildup. If this sum had been payable *before* the end of the twenty-week period, cash would have been reduced by that amount and the required bank loan would have been that much larger—or $273,752 instead of $227,612 ($227,612 + 46,140 = $273,752).

In short, Table 15.6 told Barclay that he would be able to finance an increase of $97,388 in inventory *from internal sources alone,* provided Philbrook would allow them to maintain the present bank loan.

After he had completed Table 15.6, Barclay felt he was ready to meet with his associates on the proposed inventory buildup, and he called them in. He found himself thinking about how to handle Vaughn—who, he knew would be very unhappy (to put it mildly) about what the figures showed.

"Well," said Barclay adjusting his steel-rimmed spectacles, "you all know that Joe (Vaughn) wants to build up finished inventory by $250,000 during the first five months after the end of the year."

"Yeah," said Joe, "I've told everybody."

"I've been putting some figures together," said Barclay. "Here they are." He passed around copies of Tables 15.3 and 15.4.

"More balance sheets," said Vaughn.

"Let me just explain what I've done," said Barclay.

"We can all read balance sheets," said Vaughn. "Just give us the news in one word—yes or no."

"Let him explain," said Whitman, the production manager. "It will save time."

"Go on, Ed," said Roberts, who was in charge of quality control. "Don't pay any attention to him."

"Well," said Barclay, again fussing with his spectacles. "This is the first week in November. We've been in business for more than forty weeks and we're doing fairly well. The question really is how fast can we push sales up and still keep afloat. In my opinion, Joe wants to push too fast. These two tables explain why I think so.

"The first table," he continued, "is a pro forma balance sheet as of the end of the year. It's an attempt to estimate *each item* in the balance sheet as of the end of the year—how much cash will we have, how much will our customers owe us, and so forth." Barclay showed them Table 15.3.

"I see you estimate our profit for the year at more than $12,000," said Whitman. "Not bad. Ten percent on our investment and we haven't begun to scratch the surface."

"Yes," said Barclay.

"We're not going to be able to pay off the bank loan on January 2," said Roberts, looking up.

"That's right," said Barclay. "But I estimate that cash will build up by nearly $25,000 in January. So that we'd be able to pay off the loan by February 1 or a bit earlier."

"Philbrook won't like that," said Roberts.

"No," said Barclay, "he won't."

"This is all irrelevant," said Vaughn. "What about the $250,000?"

"Well," said Barclay, "I then projected the figures twenty weeks beyond the end of the year. I know that's a long way off and all kinds of things can happen. But these figures," he picked up Table 15.4, "represent the best estimates I can make, as of right now. What do the figures show? They show that in order to build up inventory by $250,000, we would need a total bank loan of nearly $225,000. In my opinion, that's just out of the question. No bank would lend us that amount of money on our own, and Philbrook won't endorse a note of that size."

"How do you know?" asked Vaughn.

"I just know," said Barclay.

"Have you asked him?" asked Vaughn.

"No," said Barclay. "He'd think I was out of my mind."

"I think you should ask him," said Vaughn, sulkily.

"Let me point out a couple of things," said Barclay, ignoring Vaughn and passing around copies of Table 15.6. "Even with no bank loan, we could increase finished goods by $22,000."

"$22,000!" said Vaughn, contemptuously. "I'm going to blow my top. $22,000! I say forget the whole thing." He got up from the table and started to walk out.

"Sit down," said Barclay. "Perhaps Philbrook would be willing to sign another $75,000 note. If he is, we could increase finished goods by nearly $100,000."

"Why can't we squeeze the raw materials inventory and work-in-process a little?" asked Roberts.

"We might squeeze raw materials a little. But no more than $5,000. That would leave us with barely two weeks supply. And that's cutting it pretty thin. We can't cut work-in-process at all. That would mean speeding up the line and that line is just not ready to be speeded up."

"But you do think you might get $5,000 out of raw materials?" asked Barclay.

"It would make me uncomfortable," said Whitman, "but I'd be willing to try."

"That's the old school spirit," said Vaughn. "There's one thing all of you seem to forget. The buildup will be over by June 1. The whole thing will be sold by the first day of July, and we would have received payment by the first of August. At which time the whole loan would be paid off. This is a real, short-term, self-liquidating loan. It's just the kind of loan that banks are made for."

"Yes," said Barclay. "If you can persuade them to make it. I think we ought to talk the whole thing over with Philbrook."

"Good," said Whitman.

"The sooner, the better," said Vaughn. "And don't any of you forget that the additional sales would contribute nearly $50,000 to profits. Over a period of six months, that's a DCF rate of return of more than 40 percent."

CONCLUSION

In this chapter we have illustrated the process of estimating the *net* need for external funds, both short and long term. Butcher may need as much as $12 million of which $2.3 million would be short term. Barclay "needs" about $225,000, all of which appears to be short term. In the next chapter we examine alternative sources of short-term funds and describe the process of choosing among them.

PROBLEMS

1. Using the information given in Table 9.3 and in this chapter, draw up a balance sheet for Micro-Electronics at start-up—that is, just after they received the proceeds of the $75,000 loan from Second National.

2. Using the information given in Table 9.8, and in chapter 9, show in detail how Barclay derived each item in the "pro forma" income statement for the first year of operations—that is, for the year ended December 31, 1970 (Table 15.3).

   (Hint: you'll have to go over chapters 9 and 15 very carefully and use every ounce of your ingenuity).

   Assume:

   (a) Depreciation on machinery and equipment, and on lease-hold improvements, is ten year, straight line with no salvage value.

   (b) The company's first year will end on a Friday afternoon at the end of the final (13th) four week period of the year. There would therefore be no accrued wages and salaries.

3. Now, using the same ingenuity as above, derive each of the items in Table 15.4. Assume Barclay has decided he wants to try to maintain a minimum cash balance of $25,000.

IV

SOURCES OF FUNDS AND THE COST OF CAPITAL

16

SOURCES OF FUNDS AND THE SHORT-TERM FINANCING DECISION

"Good morning," said Philbrook, shaking hands all around. "What's the problem today?" Philbrook, Barclay, Vaughn, Roberts and Whitman sat down around the long table in the big walnut-paneled conference room of Philbrook and Company.

"We'll try to take as little time as possible," said Barclay. He passed copies of Tables 15.3, 15.4 and 15.5 across the table. "The point is essentially this: Sales of trial orders have been going very well and Joe thinks that right after the first of June we'll get some fairly big orders for immediate delivery. And in order to deliver, he wants to build up finished goods inventory by $250,000, at cost, between January 1 and May 31. That's a lot of money for us. And in Tables 15.3 and 15.4, we've tried to bring out some of the financial implications."

"One of the financial implications that isn't brought out in those tables," said Vaughn, "is that the additional sales will mean a contribution of $50,000 to profits before taxes. That's a DCF rate of return of over 40 percent."

"Table 15.3 is as of the end of the year and Table 15.4, as of May 31," said Philbrook.

"Right," said Barclay.

"How are you going to pay off the bank loan on January 2?" asked Philbrook.

"I don't see how we can pay it off then," said Barclay. "I believe we'd be able to pay it off by the end of the month."

"I don't like that," said Philbrook, "and the bank won't like it either. That loan must be paid off, as promised, on January 2. Your future good relations with the bank depend on it."

"But how can we?" asked Barclay.

"Let's look at this end of year balance sheet again," said Philbrook. "What can we squeeze? I see you show no accounts payable. Does that mean you're still paying cash for raw materials?"

"It does," said Barclay.

"Well," said Philbrook, "you've now been in business for eleven months and you've done fairly well. Why don't you write your suppliers —who are they anyway?"

"Reed and Company, Worcester, Massachusetts," said Whitman.

"Write to Reed and Company and ask whether they'd give you their usual terms from now on. What are their terms, anyway?"

Barclay looked at Whitman. "Net thirty days," said Whitman.

"Good," said Philbrook. "And how much are you buying a month?"

"$32,000," said Whitman.

"Mmm . . . ," Philbrook murmured. "That would raise end of year cash by $32,000 to $84,985—more than enough to pay off the loan plus interest. When you write to Reed, send them copies of the November 1 income statement and balance sheet. Use the bank as reference."

"But," Barclay interjected, "when we include interest on the bank loan, we'd be left with a bank balance of less than $5,000 on January 3."

"And that makes you nervous," said Philbrook.

"Very."

"Well, let's see if we can squeeze something else. Why do you need $22,000 in raw materials inventory?"

"That's just a little less than three weeks supply," said Whitman.

"But how long does it take you to get delivery?" asked Philbrook.

"About four days."

"And how much are you using a week?"

"Now, about $8,000 worth. But as soon as we start the buildup—if we do—we'd use about $15,000 a week."

"Then," said Philbrook, "you really could work raw materials down to, say, $8,000 until the middle of January—that is until January collections begin to come in. That would push cash up by $14,000 to nearly $20,000."

"Yes, if we could be sure of getting delivery in four or five days," said Whitman. "But *that* would make *me* nervous. You're just pushing Ed Barclay's cash problem off on me!"

"Well," said Philbrook, "you'd better decide which of you is going to have the sleepless nights. Anyway, let's see what the balance sheet would look like early on January 2 just after you pay off the bank loan and assuming, first, that Reed and Company give you thirty day terms beginning now and, second, that you let raw materials run down to $8,000."

Philbrook went to the black board. "First," he said, "in mid-December you order no raw materials instead of $32,000 for which you would have had to pay cash. That means that cash disbursements in December will be $32,000 less and end of year cash $32,000 more, or $84,985. You then pay off the bank loan plus interest. How much is interest?"

TABLE 16.1

MICRO ELECTRONICS, INC. REVISED END OF YEAR BALANCE SHEET (BEFORE REPAYMENT OF BANK LOAN)

ASSETS

Cash	$ 84,985
Accounts receivable	102,750
Raw materials	8,000
Work in process	41,200
Finished goods	0
Machinery and equipment (net)	198,000
Leasehold improvements (net)	117,000
Office furniture (net)	3,000
Prepaid rent	0
Total assets	$554,935

LIABILITIES AND EQUITY

Notes payable (bank)	$ 75,000
Accounts payable	18,000
Accrued salaries and wages	0
Accrued federal income and other taxes	1,952
Other accruals	5,745
Convertible debentures	302,000
Long-term notes (parents)	20,000
Company stock	120,000
Retained earnings	12,238
Total liabilities and equity	$554,935

"$5,295," said Barclay.

"All right," said Philbrook, "cash then comes down by $75,000 plus $5,295 or $80,295. That leaves cash at $4,690. The two balancing items on the liability side are the bank loan and accrued interest. Where's accrued interest?"

"In other accruals," said Barclay.

"Yes," said Philbrook, "other accruals come down by $5,295." He put on the blackboard the figures given in Tables 16.1 and 16.2.

TABLE 16.2

MICRO ELECTRONICS, INC. REVISED END OF YEAR BALANCE SHEET (AFTER REPAYMENT OF BANK LOAN)

ASSETS

Cash	$ 4,690
Accounts receivable	102,750
Raw materials	8,000
Work in process	41,200
Finished goods	0
Machinery and equipment (net)	198,000
Leasehold improvements (net)	117,000
Office furniture (net)	3,000
Prepaid rent	0
Total assets	$474,640

LIABILITIES AND EQUITY

Notes payable (bank)	$ 0
Accounts payable	18,000
Accrued salaries and wages	0
Accrued federal income and other taxes	1,952
Other accruals	450
Convertible debentures	302,000
Long-term notes (parents)	20,000
Company stock	120,000
Retained earnings	12,238
Total liabilities and equity	$474,640

"What about the raw materials item," asked Whitman. "If we receive no deliveries in December, our end of year raw materials inventory will be *minus* $10,000!"

"Mmm," said Philbrook.

"You see," said Whitman, "we would normally order in the forty-eighth week for delivery in the forty-ninth week. We are using raw materials at the rate of $8,000 a week, so that by the end of the fifty-second week, our inventory would again be down to $22,000. Now, if we order *nothing* in the forty-eighth week for delivery in the forty-ninth week, we won't have any raw materials *at all* after the middle of the fifty-first week."

"Yes, of course," said Philbrook, "I was wrong. You have to order just enough in the forty-eighth week, in late November, so that your ending inventory will be $8,000. How much would that be?"

Whitman did some quick calculations. "$18,000," he said.

"Yes, of course," said Philbrook, "that's where the extra $14,000 comes from."

"What do you mean?" asked Roberts. "I don't understand a word you're saying."

Philbrook laughed. "Two things are happening here. First, you are not disbursing in December the $32,000 you had planned to disburse for raw materials. You are not disbursing it because Reed, we assume, is now giving you terms. I assume that that disbursement was in the cash budget and affected the cash figure shown in Table 15.3."

"Right," said Barclay.

"That means then," said Philbrook, "that at the end of the year cash will be higher by that amount."

"Right," said Barclay.

"Second," said Philbrook, "instead of ordering $32,000 worth of raw materials in the forty-eighth week, you order only $18,000 worth. These are delivered in the forty-ninth week, but you do not have to pay for them until thirty days later—meaning the first week of next year. Your end of year balance sheet would then show raw materials at $8,000 and accounts payable of $18,000."

Philbrook by that time had put on the blackboard all the figures shown in Tables 16.1 and 16.2. Table 16.1 gives the end of year balance sheet just before the bank loan is paid off; Table 16.2, just after—both tables are based on the assumptions that the company receives credit from its supplier and cuts raw materials inventory by $14,000.

"All right," said Whitman, "but now where's that extra $14,000 in cash. It's not there."

"Well," said Philbrook, "where is it?"

"Easy," said Vaughn. "Normally, the first week of the period we'd disburse $32,000 for raw materials. But this time we'll have to disburse only $18,000. And so after that disbursement is made, cash will be $14,000 higher than it otherwise would have been."

"Yes," said Barclay. "Cash during January will build back up faster, and by the end of the month it will be higher than expected by $14,000."

"There's a lesson here," said Philbrook. "You can often find some short-term financing in unexpected places—by squeezing some asset or by extending a liability. The $32,000 worth of credit from Reed and Company is no different from a bank loan—except that they charge no interest. And you can almost always defer payment of taxes for a brief period, if necessary. Now let's look at the inventory buildup. You need money—although I'm happy to say, less than you thought you needed."

SOURCES OF FUNDS

Sources of funds can be distinguished one from another in a variety of ways. Some are short-term, some medium-term, and some long-term. Some represent ownership (common stock) and some do not (all kinds of debt). Some are secured and others unsecured. Sources of funds can also be distinguished, one from another, in terms of cost and in terms of the type of institution from which they are available—banks, finance companies, insurance companies, small business development corporations, and so forth. But perhaps the most important distinction among sources, *for any individual company,* is the distinction between those sources which, as a practical matter, are in fact available to it and those which are not. We should also bear continually in mind that in a rapidly changing economy such as the one we have in the United States, nothing ever remains the same for very long. Business changes, its needs change, and new responses to those changing needs are continually being made.

The rest of this chapter is devoted to describing sources of funds —both long and short term—and to illustrating the process of deciding among alternative sources of short-term funds. Discussion of the differences in detail among the various types of long-term funds, and the sources from which they come, is put off to later chapters.

All funds come from either inside the firm or from outside the firm. When funds come from inside the firm they are called *internally generated,* or *from internal sources,* or just *internal.* And sometimes they are called *funds from operations.* When funds come from outside the firm they are said to be *from external sources* or sometimes just *external.* Internal funds consist, as we have seen above, of the sum of depreciation, amortization and profits after tax. When internally generated funds are reinvested in the firm, they usually remain invested as long as the firm remains alive.

long-term external sources

There are three principal types of long-term financing: common stock, debt, and preferred stock, of which two—common stock and debt—are "pure" types. Preferred is a hybrid which, although called *equity*, has more of the characteristics of debt than of common.

common stock

Those persons who hold a company's common stock "own" the company. The ownership of a company is similar to the ownership of anything else; the owners can do as they wish with it—pay all its earnings out in dividends, expand it, merge it, sell it, liquidate it—if more than 50 percent of them can agree on what should be done. But the owners of large publicly-held companies are not likely to be an organized, cohesive group and they are not likely, therefore, to do more than cast an occasional vote on matters presented to them for decision by the corporate officers.

Common stock is often sold to the original investors at a price above what is called *par value*. This was not the case with the Micro Electronics which sold 1,000 shares to its four original stockholders at a price exactly equal to its par value—$120. The stock might, however, have been issued with par value of $10, $20 or $100, or any other arbitrary sum. If the stock had carried a par value less than the price actually charged, the difference would have been carried on the balance sheet as Paid in Capital or, more accurately, as Capital Paid in, in Excess of Par Value of Common Stock. Suppose, for example, that the par value of each of the 1,000 shares issued had been $100. The capital entries on the balance sheet would then have been:

Common stock,	
1,000 shares par value $100	$100,000
Capital paid in, in excess	
of par value	20,000
TOTAL	$120,000

In the typical case, every share of common stock in any given firm is on an equal footing.

Common stockholders do not receive a fixed return. Instead they receive what is left over, if anything, after all contractual obligations have been paid, including interest on debt and dividends on preferred stock.

preferred stock

Preferred stock differs from common stock in two respects. First, it is fixed cost and hence does not participate in residual earnings. Cost to the company is stated in dollars, as a $5 preferred or a $6 preferred, and so forth, or in percent, as a 5% preferred or a 6% preferred and so forth.

Second, preferred stock generally has no voting rights, although if dividends are not paid when due the preferred stockholders may have the right to elect one or more members of the board of directors. In the typical case, if a company passes seven successive quarterly dividends, the preferred stockholders will have the right to elect one member of the board of directors.

In brief, then, unlike common stock, preferred stock (a) is limited in cost (to the company) to a specified percentage of par value and therefore does not participate in residual earnings, and (b) has no voting rights and no voice in management.

long-term debt

The essential characteristic of debt is not its fixed cost, which characteristic, as we saw above, it shares with preferred stock. The essential characteristic of debt is that the person or persons who hold the debt, that is, the lender, is always a creditor of the company. And if the borrower defaults, the lender can, in the extreme case, sell the borrower's assets, the proceeds being used first to pay off the creditors. Only if anything remains, after all the creditors have been paid off, will the preferred stockholders and common stockholders, in that order, receive payment for their stock.

This fact explains, in part, why debt carries a lower out-of-pocket cost than preferred: interest and principal on debt must be paid when due if the borrower wishes to avoid the risk of being forced into liquidation. Preferred dividends, on the other hand, can be passed with no such risk and, in general, with only relatively minor inconvenience. One type of long-term debt differs from another in maturity and in the kind of collateral (security) lenders require. Long-term debt instruments vary in maturity from as little as a year to a hundred years and more. And they can be secured merely by the general credit of the borrowing company, as in the case of debenture bonds, or at the other extreme, by a lien on all the borrowing company's fixed assets, as in the case of general mortgage bonds.

In addition, many small and medium-size firms obtain substantial amounts of long-term fianancing by renting assets instead of buying them. This form of fianancing is discussed in the appendix to Chapter 17.

short term external sources

Short term loans are of two sorts: unsecured, and secured by some specific, carefully defined asset. A company can also obtain short-term funds by *selling* some self-liquidating asset, such as accounts receivable.

UNSECURED DEBT

Unsecured loans of any maturity whatever up to a year are available from commercial banks—but only to established firms with high credit standing. In addition, large, established, well-known firms with high credit standing can often sell short-term unsecured notes to dealers or directly to nonbank investors, for example, individuals and to other companies which have excess short-term funds available. Notes of this type drafted by the firm itself and sold in the above way, are called *commercial paper*. This type of short-term borrowing is generally cheaper than bank borrowing but, as indicated above, is available only to a small, highly select group of large, well-known firms.[1]

installment loans

Some of the larger banks now lend money to business on an installment basis, interest and principal payable in equal amounts monthly. Interest

---

[1] An article by Frederick M. Struble published in November of 1968, indicates that, in 1952, 418 firms financed part of their short-term needs by selling commercial paper either to dealers in such paper or to ultimate investors. In 1965, about 425 firms did so. But in 1965, the total volume of commercial paper sold was $17.1 billion as compared with $1.8 billion in 1952. The bulk of this very large increase was due to the growth of finance companies of all types, and to the increase, relative to bank loans, in their use of the commercial paper market. In 1952 finance companies had total liabilities of $7.6 billion. In 1965, their liabilities had grown to $40.8 billion, or almost six-fold. But in 1965, commercial paper represented 34.6 percent of the total liabilities of finance companies as compared with 18.4 percent in 1952. See F. M. Struble, "The Commercial Paper Boom in Perspective," *Monthly Review* (Federal Reserve Bank of Kansas City, November 1968).

is calculated for the period of the loan on the amount of the original loan, at some specified rate. The amount of interest, so calculated, is added to the amount of the loan and the total is divided by the number of months the loan is expected to be outstanding. The amount so obtained is payable monthly. The effective rate on such loans is about twice the rate at which the total amount of interest is calculated. This kind of loan is analogous to the first loan your roommate made to you (see Chapter 3) and to the typical car purchase loan.

Suppose, for example, that a bank lends $10,000 to a company at a nominal rate of 5 percent for twelve months. Interest, which would thus be $10,000 $\times$ .05, or $500, would be added to the amount of the loan, yielding a total of $10,500. This sum would then be divided by twelve to obtain the amount of each monthly payment. The effective rate on such a loan would be about 10 percent (rather than 5 percent) because the principal amount of the loan is repaid monthly, along with interest, and therefore only about *half* the original amount of the loan is outstanding, on the average, over the year as a whole. The borrower, in other words, has the use on the average during the year of only about half the original amount of the loan, or $5,000. But the company is paying $500 for the right to use this sum for a year. The effective rate of interest is, therefore, about twice as high as the nominal rate. Installment loans of this sort are usually made on an unsecured basis but only in moderate amounts.

SECURED DEBT

A short-term loan can be secured by anything, however flimsy, a lender can be persuaded to accept as collateral. Most lenders, however, insist on collateral which could be liquidated readily if the borrower defaulted. Three types of collateral tend to provide the basis for most secured short-term loans to business—marketable securities, accounts receivable and inventory.

marketable securities

Most firms hold no marketable securities, except government bills, notes and bonds. They hold government bills, notes and bonds which are readily marketable, so as to provide for future cash needs, presently foreseen, or to provide for unforeseen contingencies. They would not be likely, therefore, to be willing to put up such securities as collateral for a loan. But sometimes members of a management group, or an interested outsider, such as Philbrook in the case of Micro Electronics, are willing to put up their own personal securities as collateral for a loan to a company.

accounts receivable

Accounts receivable are considered good security for short-term loans depending on their number, size and quality. The smaller the number of accounts, the larger their size and the better their quality, the greater the likelihood that a lender would be willing to accept them as security for a loan. Small and medium-sized companies rely heavily on loans of this type for short-term funds. In general such loans tend to be loosely administered or the reverse, depending on whether they are made by banks or commercial finance companies. Finance companies will almost always insist on regular inspection of records in order to be sure that the volume and quality of receivables continues to be sufficient to support the loan. Banks usually do not insist on regular inspection, especially if they know the borrower well, primarily because inspection takes time and therefore costs money.

inventory

Inventory is also often used as collateral for a short-term loan. Inventory loans are of two types: those under which the borrower retains physical possession of the inventory, merely pledging it as security for a loan, and those under which the lender retains physical possession until the loan is repaid. Under the latter type of arrangement (sometimes called a *field warehousing loan*), the lender in effect buys inventory for the borrower and stores it in or near the borrower's place of business. When the borrower wishes to use some portion of the inventory, he "buys" the inventory from the lender by paying off the loan. Both types of inventory loans are available from commercial finance companies and the larger commercial banks. In general, both types are cumbersome to administer and for this reason tend to be more expensive than more conventional arrangements.

Lenders, for obvious reasons, prefer inventory which is not perishable and in which a ready, stable market exists, preferably with published prices, as, for example, in the case of raw wool, cocoa, coffee and other basic commodities traded on the commodity exchanges.

SALE OF ACCOUNTS RECEIVABLE

Under this type of arrangement, receivables are sold outright to a special type of commercial finance company called a *factor*. The factor will usually buy only those receivables which satisfy his credit standards. On those he does buy, however, the factor assumes all risk of credit loss.

The charges made by factors are high and normally companies will not "factor" their receivables unless they are unable to obtain short-term financing in any other way. When receivables are sold, they are, of course, removed from the balance sheet inasmuch as they have been converted into cash.[2]

OTHER TYPES OF SECURITY

Every other tangible asset on a company's balance sheet can be pledged as security for a loan—provided, of course, the lender agrees. In addition to receivables and inventory, those tangible assets most often pledged as security are machinery and equipment and real estate. Although such assets could be pledged to secure short-term loans, they are almost always, rather, used to secure long-term loans.

In summary, short-term funds are, in general, supplied by four types of sources: the commercial paper market, commercial banks, commercial finance companies and factors. The commercial paper market, which is generally the cheapest source, is available only to established, well-known companies with high credit standing. Commercial banks also tend to be selective and are likely to lend to small firms whose prospects are uncertain only against good security—such as marketable securities, high quality receivables, or readily marketable raw materials inventory. For small firms which are unable to provide adequate security and which therefore are unable to obtain short-term financing from banks, commercial finance companies and factors are available. Their charges are high but not higher than required by the degree of risk they take. We may say, in general, that the biggest, best known firms will have the largest number of alternatives available to them. Small, new firms

---

[2] Whether the factoring of receivables constitutes "short" or "long" term financing is a question which need not detain us long. The typical factoring arrangement is continuous, but new funds are obtained regularly and the arrangement can be terminated at any time by either party.

will have the smallest, and, more often than not, will have to make substantial concessions in order to obtain short-term financing. The small firm should always begin its quest for short-term funds at its own bank. This is so simply because the bank knows the firm and, in general, will be more sympathetic to the firm's needs than a lender which has not had prior contact with the firm. And if the bank itself is unable to lend the necessary funds, it will often be able to guide the firm to the cheapest other sources.

"USURIOUS" RATES OF INTEREST

Finally, every borrower should realize that the rate charged by any lender must be high enough to cover defaults and return a reasonable margin of profit. Suppose a lender lends $10,000 for a year to each of 100 small, fairly risky companies at an effective rate of 15 percent a year. The lender will have lent a total of $1,000,000. If all borrowers repay interest and principal in full when due, the lender will have received $1,150,000 at the end of the year and he will have earned 15 percent on his investment.

But suppose that ten of the loans default during the year, and the lender is able to salvage only $5,000 from each—or $50,000 in total. His total receipts at the end of the year would then be:

10 defaulted loans at $5,000 each	$ 50,000
90 good loans at $10,000	900,000
Plus interest at 15% on good loans	135,000
	$1,085,000

The lender would thus have received a total of $1,085,000 in return for making loans totalling $1,000,000 for a year. His *actual* yield on his investment would thus be 8.5 percent rather than 15 percent, out of which he would have to pay expenses and earn a return on capital.

In a highly competitive capital market—such as the one we have in the United States—there is really no such thing as usury—that is, there is no such thing as an "excessive" rate of interest. No borrower need pay more for money than the riskiness of his business justifies—and, in fact, very few sensible borrowers do pay more.

THE SHORT-TERM FINANCING DECISION

Before the meeting had ended, Philbrook questioned Vaughn very closely in order to satisfy himself that the additional finished goods inventory would, in all likelihood, be sold within four to six weeks after

June 1. He asked very specific questions such as: "What makes you think you will be able to sell $250,000 worth (at cost) of finished circuitry between June 1 and July 31—and to whom?" Vaughn replied that ten large customers had each taken trial orders of $50,000 or more over the last six months. Each of these customers, Vaughn said, used at least a million dollars worth of circuitry a year. He had called on each of the ten once a week since the original orders had been placed. All of them, without exception, reported very good results. All of them said they were still testing but that additional orders would probably be forthcoming in the next six or seven months. They had asked whether the circuitry would be available in quantity by the first of June.

"And," said Vaughn, "we are selling to new customers every week. We have sold trial quantities to sixty different customers—not all large, but all very solid and all capable of using good quantities." Vaughn concluded by saying that he thought that $250,000 was a minimum estimate of reorders from these companies.

Philbrook then asked Whitman how he expected to produce the relays—where would the labor come from, for example, and would he really be able to produce an additional $250,000 without interfering with regular production. Whitman had replied that he would have to set up another line and train another twenty-five people. A few of the regular employees would be used to train the new people, but he didn't expect much interference with regular production. The company was using women on the line, most of them married, and they were perfectly willing to come in and be trained, with the full understanding that they would work for only fifteen or twenty weeks. They all understood also, Whitman had said, that if production increased permanently, they would be rehired.

Philbrook asked next whether training costs had been included in the budget. Barclay replied they had not and Whitman said they would be small, perhaps $5,000 in wages and spoiled materials.

Finally, Philbrook asked Vaughn what he thought would happen to sales after the $250,000 in additional inventory had been sold. Vaughn said they would continue to increase and might well reach $75,000 a week by the end of the year. He added that he thought the company should build up a permanent finished goods inventory of a least $250,000 —so as to have relays always available for immediate delivery. Philbrook had said that he did not see how that would be possible without bringing in additional outside capital. "You're trying to grow too fast," he said. He explained what he meant by putting on the blackboard the figures given in Table 15.5. He pointed out that:

1. An increase in inventory of $250,000 during the first twenty weeks of next year would mean a net increase in assets of $218,655.

2. This increase could only be financed by an increase in the bank loan of $152,612 less whatever credit they could get from Reed and Company.

This would mean a *total* bank loan of perhaps $175,000—which seemed out of the question. The bank would not lend the company that much on its own signature, and he would not endorse a note of that size.

He then pointed out that if the company tried to increase inventory permanently by $250,000 by the end of the year, they would still need a large amount of outside help, perhaps as much as $150,000. That was less than they needed now, because profits and depreciation would have contributed about $80,000.

But $150,000 would still be much more than they could hope to obtain from the bank. The bank, he said, would want to know when and how a loan of that size would be paid off. He thought it might take the company two and a half years to pay off a loan of that size —if everything went smoothly.

He said that for the time being the company should not try to grow by more than the amount of internally generated funds. This did not mean that they should not borrow moderate amounts of short-term funds from time to time. But, he added, he would absolutely insist that they pay off bank loans when they were due.

"The temptation is very great," Philbrook said, "if you find that you could go on using the money, to ask the bank to extend the loan. When you came in here this morning," he said, looking directly at Barclay, "you intended to do exactly that—you said you wouldn't be able to pay off the $75,000 loan on January 2."

"All right," said Barclay, "I learn something every day."

Philbrook continued: "What would have happened? I would have gotten annoyed and so would the loan officer at the bank. He would have been annoyed because you would have gotten him into trouble with his boss.

"I would have been annoyed," Philbrook continued, "because I don't want my collateral tied up any longer than necessary. Technically, the bank could throw you into liquidation. They wouldn't do so because they don't like liquidations and you're doing well. And it would be obvious to them that, sooner or later, the loan would be repaid. But your standing with them, and perhaps mine also, would have been hurt. And the next time you went in to ask for help, you might not have gotten it."

Philbrook concluded by pointing out that some clever manipulators can turn a thirty day loan into a five-year loan by continually forcing a bank to choose between liquidating the company and extending the loan. Invariably, the bank will extend the loan—if the company is making money. And the company has, in effect, obtained long-term financing which the bank would never have been willing to supply before the first loan was made.

Moreover, he pointed out, a short term loan runs for less than a year. "You should not try to renew a short term loan," he said. "You should pay it off when due and allow a month or so to elapse before you ask for a new loan. Why a month? Because that's the test the loan officer and the bank will apply in order to decide whether or not they are supplying long-term funds to the company. If the company can get along for a month without borrowing, the bank will feel it is supplying genuine short-term financing."

"How about borrowing from a second bank for a month in order to be out of the first one for a month?" asked Barclay. "It would show on your balance sheet," said Philbrook. "Banks talk to each other, and they would quickly see that, together, they were supplying long-term capital to the company. You might, then, get nothing from either one."

"I hear you," said Barclay, and the meeting ended.

The next morning, Barclay drew up a new pro forma balance sheet on the following assumptions:

1. Barclay would pay off the present bank loan, plus interest, on January 2.
2. Cash would be allowed to build up gradually to $25,000.
3. Raw materials inventory would be allowed to build back up to two weeks normal supply ($16,000).
4. The bank would not make a new loan until February 2.
5. The inventory buildup would not begin until the proceeds of the new bank loan had been received. The buildup would nevertheless be completed by May 31.
6. During January, but not until the bank had agreed to make the new loan, Barclay would set up a third production line and start hiring and training more labor. Training costs would be about $6,000.
7. Micro Electronics would receive Reed and Company's regular credit terms for purchases up to $60,000.
8. The first sale ($50,000) out of the built-up inventory would not be made until after the inventory buildup had been completed.

Table 16.3 gives the revised pro forma balance sheet, drawn up on the foregoing assumptions, as of twenty weeks after the end of the first year of operations. The only difference between the first pro forma (Table 15.4) and the revised version was due to the assumption that Reed and Company would now give Barclay credit up to $60,000. Barclay saw quite clearly now that trade credit was equivalent to an interest-free bank loan.

Barclay then made a list of outstanding accounts receivable customer

TABLE 16.3

MICRO ELECTRONICS, INC., REVISED PRO FORMA BALANCE SHEET (AS OF TWENTY WEEKS AFTER END OF FIRST YEAR) *

ASSETS

Cash	$ 25,000	
Accounts receivable	102,750	
Raw materials	16,000	
Work-in-process (cost)	41,200	
Finished goods (cost)	250,000	
Machinery and equipment (net)	189,540	
Leasehold improvements (net)	112,000	
Office furniture	2,600	
Prepaid rent	10,500	
Total assets		$749,590

LIABILITIES

Notes payable (bank)		$169,612 †
Accounts payable	52,000	
Accrued salaries and wages	0	
Accrued federal income and other taxes	45,590	
Other accruals	5,440	
Convertible debentures	302,000	
Long-term notes (parents)	20,000	
Common stock ($120 par value)	120,000	
Retained earnings	34,948	
		$579,978
Total liabilities and equity		$749,590

* After completion of inventory buildup.
† Plugged figure.

by customer. He then asked Vaughn to make a list of potential sales after June 1, customer by customer, indicating how much in total had been sold to each so far. He then called the bank and made an appointment for the next day to see James Moses, the loan officer who had authorized the original loan. He took Vaughn with him.

After Barclay had explained what he wanted, Moses asked all the questions Philbrook had asked and a few more. The first one, of course, was whether the original loan would be paid off when due. Barclay replied it would. Moses then spent half an hour raising questions about the various statements Barclay had put on his desk. He wanted to know whether the company's labor was unionized ("No"), what the average wage rate was ("$3.00 an hour"), whether they had had much labor turnover ("No"), where they would get raw materials on short notice if Reed and Company was unable to deliver ("Six other suppliers"), were they thinking about products other than relays ("Not yet"), and so forth.

Moses finally seemed satisfied and said he would call Barclay in a day or so. But he suggested that Barclay might also wish to call National Factors, a commercial credit and factoring company in order to have another alternative source available in case the bank said no. Moses gave Barclay the name of a loan officer at National whom Moses knew well. Barclay and Vaughn visited National the next day and went through the same kind of cross-examination they had gone through the previous day at the bank. They were pleasantly surprised to learn that Dermott, the National Loan Officer, had heard favorably of the company from Moses.

By the end of the week, Barclay had heard from both Moses and Dermott and had the following alternatives available to him:

Moses' bank offered the three following alternatives:

ALTERNATIVE 1.

$80,000 to be made available on February 1, one month after the present loan had been repaid. The company would put up its receivables to the bank as collateral for the loan but the company's customers would not be notified. They would pay the company directly as in the past. The rate of interest would be 7½ percent a year. Moses had explained that the rate was low—½ percent above the prime rate—because the company's receivables were of very high quality. The total amount of the loan would be payable by July 31—by which time the company would have begun to receive payment from the sale of the additional finished goods. Moses pointed out that as the company received payment between February 1 and July 31 on accounts receivable outstanding on February 1, it would be required to notify the bank of new shipments so as to maintain the required amount of security at approximately 80 percent of the loan. Otherwise, the difference would become due and payable to the bank at once. Thus if the company's receivables on February 1 included $20,000 due from IBM, and this amount were received from IBM on February 10, the security for the loan would have been reduced by $20,000. But the company, meanwhile, would have made new shipments either to IBM itself or to other customers, and would thus have created new receivables.

The company would be required to notify the bank every week of collections and shipments so that the bank would be able to assure itself that the security for the loan was being maintained at the required amount. In addition, a bank officer would probably drop in once in a while to look over the company's accounts. Close supervision was necessary, he explained, in order to protect the bank's legal position —just in case something went wrong. If something did go wrong the bank would have to prove, perhaps in court, that the receivables had really been security for the loan. This meant that the bank had to behave in a way that would convince a court that the receivables really had been security for the loan. He added quickly that the bank didn't expect anything to go wrong—or it wouldn't be making the loan. He said also that if the quality of the company's receivables declined, the amount of the loan might be reduced. He said finally that he regarded the loan as a short-term loan and would expect it to be paid off in full when due.

ALTERNATIVE 2.

In addition to the loan on receivables, Moses offered to make $50,000 available to Micro Electronics on February 1, unsecured, on a semi-installment basis. From February 1 to July 31 interest would be calculated at 8 percent. Interest for this six month period, $2,000, would be added on August 1 to the original amount of the loan; interest on the total sum, $52,000, would be calculated at a rate of $4\frac{1}{2}$ percent and again added on. The resulting sum, $54,340, would be payable in six installments of $9,056.67 each, beginning September 1. Moses said that if the company wished to pay the interest due at the end of the first six months, it would be free to do so. In that case, the six monthly payments would be $8,708.34 each. Moses was very careful to point out that under such an arrangement, the company would have the use of the full $50,000 for the first six months but on the average of only about half that amount for the second six months. The company would thus be paying $2,250 in interest for the privilege of using $25,000 (approximately) for the second six months. This was at the rate of about 9.0 percent for six months or 18 percent a year. Moses said he realized the rate was high, but they must understand that the loan would be unsecured and, although the company had done very well, it was still very young and to a large extent, untried. Moses added that under this arrangement they would be free to obtain receivables financing, either from the bank or elsewhere, up to $80,000. If they went elsewhere, the bank would expect them to obtain its prior consent.

ALTERNATIVE 3.

Alternatively, the bank offered to lend the company up to $160,000 on Philbrook's endorsement and security. The interest rate would depend on the quality of the securities Philbrook was willing to pledge as collateral but would probably be around 7½ percent. The loan would be due and payable on July 31.

ALTERNATIVE 4.

National Factors had added two alternatives to Barclay's choice by stating, first, that they would *buy* all the company's receivables, as of now, at 98 percent of their face value. They would guarantee the company against credit losses. Thus National would buy all the receivables now in Micro Electronic's books and credit the company immediately with 98 percent of $102,500, or $100,450. They would buy new receivables each succeeding month at the same rate.

ALTERNATIVE 5.

If the Barclay Company did factor its receivables with National, National would lend them an additional $50,000 unsecured. This amount would be made available to Micro Electronics as it was needed. Principal, plus interest of $2,750, would be repayable in twelve installments of $4,395.83 a month, beginning August 1.

After rereading the letters from Moses and Dermott several times, Barclay found himself a bit confused. He was also puzzled as to how to make a decision in a rational way, among the five alternatives. He started, for no very good reason, by putting together the data given in Table 16.4 on amount of loan, dollar interest cost and the effective rate

TABLE 16.4

MICRO ELECTRONICS, INC., ALTERNATIVE SHORT-TERM FINANCING ARRANGEMENTS

ALTERNATIVE	AMOUNT	INTEREST OR CHARGE (In Dollars)	EFFECTIVE RATE
Bank 1	$ 80,000	$ 3,000	7½%
Bank 2	50,000	4,340	8% and 18%
Bank 3	160,000	6,000	7½% *
Factor 1	100,450	12,300 †	24% †
Factor 2	50,000	2,750	11%

* With Philbrook's endorsement, for six months.
† For six months, beginning February 1, at $2,050 a month.

of interest. The factoring arrangement with National was by far the most expensive. Barclay estimated that he would have to factor his receivables each month for six months at a cost of $2,050 monthly ($= \$102,500 - \$100,450$). This was a total of $12,300 for six months ($\$12,300 = 6 \times \$2,050$).

After having done this, Barclay noted various other differences among the alternatives, as follows:

First, the maximum amounts available from the bank and the factor were different. The bank would lend the company $130,000 without Philbrook's signature and $160,000 with it. National, on the other hand, would make $150,450 available. Barclay had about half decided that the company should not ask Philbrook to endorse another loan. In any case, he (Barclay) was sure that Philbrook would not endorse a loan for more than $75,000 and then only if the receivables were neither pledged to someone else nor factored.

Second, that part of the bank loan secured by receivables would have to be paid off on July 31. If everything went well, more than enough money would be available. But something might go wrong. They would be hiring new people and setting up a new production line. It might be difficult to get quality up to standard. And it was conceivable that they might have no additional merchandise to sell until early July. If so, their collections during July might not be sufficient to pay off the loan on July 31. One clear advantage of the National proposal was that only (about) $4,400 would be due and payable on August 1.

Third, National would be willing to go on buying receivables from the company as long as the company needed financing. And as sales increased, increased financing would be available. Thus the arrangement with National could be used to provide short-term funds or long-term funds, as Barclay wished. National's proposal was more expensive than the bank's but, on the other hand, it was somewhat more flexible.

Fourth, National would assume all credit losses and be responsible for all credit investigations. This would not save the company any money now because it was selling only to AAA customers. But they would surely be selling to lower quality customers in the future.

Fifth, National would notify Barclay's customers that they should make payment directly to National. This would be embarrassing and some customers might think that Barclay was having financial difficulty and, perhaps, might not be in the business long. This conceivably might affect sales.

Sixth, making weekly lists of collections and shipments for the bank would be a nuisance.

After thinking about the problem for an hour or so, Barclay called in his associates to discuss it. He put Table 16.4 and his notes in front of them and said: "These things aren't comparable. National's offer would be more flexible. Moreover, under the arrangement with the bank, the full amount of the loan on receivables, $80,000, would be due on July 31. Suppose something should go wrong. On July 31 we would have to pay National only about $4,400. There is a big difference," he said, "between $80,000 and $4,400. Also, the National arrangement could be continued indefinitely."

Roberts, looking puzzled, said, "I don't understand the factoring arrangement and I wish someone would explain it to me."

"It's as if we were to go on a cash basis," said Barclay. "But instead of being paid by our customers, we'd be paid by National. At the beginning of February, next year, we'd have $102,500 in accounts receivable on the books. We would collect those during February in the regular way. But as we made new shipments during February, we'd send the invoices to National and they would buy them immediately at face value minus 2 percent. That means that during February we'd collect, in the regular way, the receivables on the books at the start of the month—about $100,000—*plus,* from National, the amount we shipped during February less 2 percent. That means that during February we'd collect slightly less than $200,000—or almost twice as much as we would collect otherwise. We'd use about half to finance our regular production and about half to finance the inventory buildup. Is that clear?"

"Yes," said Roberts, "but on the first of March we'd have no receivables on the books. Right?"

"Right," said Barclay, "because we'd sold them to National during February."

"Well then," said Roberts, "we'd collect nothing from our customers during March. And how would we finance regular production during March?"

"We'd have to go on selling receivables to National during March," Barclay said. "We'd probably remain in National's clutches for six months or so. That's why Table 16.4 shows that we'd pay National $12,300—which is $2,050 a month for six months."

"Lot of money," said Roberts. "Are you sure we'd be out of their clutches in six months?"

"I'm far from sure," Barclay said.

Whitman said they could always sell their receivables to National on July 31 in order to pay off the bank loan. Even if they had sold none of the additional finished goods and therefore had nothing but their regular accounts on the books, this would realize $100,450—which would be more than enough to pay off the loan on receivables and make the first two payments (of $9,056.67 each) on September 1 and October 1 on the $50,000 installment portion of the loan. He said he thought the main issue was whether the additional amount of money available from National was worth the additional cost. He scribbled on a piece of paper the figures given in Table 16.5. He passed the figures around

TABLE 16.5

MICRO ELECTRONICS, INC.,
ADDITIONAL CONTRIBUTION TO OVERHEAD

	BANK LOAN	NATIONAL
Additional sales	$287,500	$312,500
Additional cost of sales	230,000	250,000
Contribution to overhead and interest	$ 57,500	$ 62,500
Additional interest	7,340	15,050 *
Contribution to overhead after interest	$ 50,160	$ 47,450

* $15,050 = $12,300 + $2,750. See text describing National's offer.

pointing out that under the bank arrangement, the increase in finished inventory would be $20,000 less at cost and $25,000 less at selling price. Everyone was surprised to see that the contribution to overhead, after additional interest, was more with the bank loan. Vaughn said that with a larger inventory they would be able to service more customers —and that was important in order to build the right kind of "image."

Barclay then pointed out that they could *not* assume that National would buy their receivables on July 31.

"Call them," Whitman said.

"No," said Barclay, "Dermott would simply say that they would buy them if they had the money *then*." Barclay concluded by saying that in his opinion the question they had to decide was: is it more important not to be tied down to a big lump sum payment on July 31 than it is to pay more interest and, in fact, generate a smaller contribution to overhead? Whitman said he would put the question differently: if they borrowed from the bank, interest charges would be less. That was certain. But their ability to repay the loan was uncertain. They were weighing a certain advantage against an uncertain disadvantage. The question, he thought, was: How much risk do we want to take, if any at all, that we will be unable to pay the bank $80,000 on July 31?

What would you do if you were running Micro Electronics?

Now let's glance back briefly at Butcher—which, we saw, also needed short-term funds. After Kelley returned to his office—to wrestle quietly with Butcher's cost of capital—Martin picked up the phone and called Raimondi. The conversation went as follows:

"Rai," said Martin, "I'll probably need $2,500,000 for four months."

"When?" asked Raimondi.

"In about two weeks."

"Okay," said Raimondi. "Send us a note."

"How much?" asked Martin.

"Seven," said Raimondi. "That's still just ¼ over the prime rate."

"Okay," said Martin.

"Have we got copies of your last audited statements?" asked Raimondi.

"Don't know," said Martin. "Kelley was supposed to have sent them to you . . . One question before you hang up."

"Yes?" said Raimondi.

"Would I do better in the commercial paper market?"

"Maybe an eighth of a point," said Raimondi. "That's about $1,000 on $2,500,000 for four months. Just think of all the useful advice and information you get from me."

"Right," said Martin, "I'll send along the note. And thanks."

After he hung up, he called Kelley and said: "Kelley, find out what goes on in the commercial paper market."

CONCLUSION

In this chapter, we have reviewed alternative sources of short-term funds and have illustrated the process of choosing among them. Short-term funds, to labor the obvious, can be obtained only by selling an asset (for example, accounts receivable or marketable securities) or by borrowing money from someone: an individual (your rich uncle), a bank, a commercial credit company, a supplier (accounts payable), a government (accrued income or other taxes).

The various sources of short-term funds differ from each other in a variety of ways: in cost, in the type of collateral the lender will require, in terms—including repayment provisions. Of all short-term sources, trade credit (accounts payable) is the cheapest (unless discounts are not taken) and the easiest to obtain. Any company which pays its bills reasonably promptly and is not tottering on the edge of bankruptcy, will usually be able to obtain trade credit. This is *not* because business firms are inherently fun loving and generous. As we saw in Chapter 11 most business firms sell their merchandise at a substantial markup over cost. If a company sells $1,000 worth of merchandise every three months to a small concern, at a markup of 25 percent of selling price, and the firm pays its bills every three months, the seller will have earned a return of 33 1/3 percent every three months (= 133 1/3 percent a year) on an investment of $750. The seller, obviously can afford to take a risk or two.

Banks, on the other hand, tend to be niggardly relative to business firms—primarily because they are able to earn only relatively modest rates of return. Even if a bank lends money on an installment basis at an effective rate of 14 percent a year (a high rate for a bank), it can obviously take fewer (and less risky) risks than a business firm earning 133 percent a year. And, for this same reason, banks tend to be fussy about things like collateral, with any but the strongest firms.

In between trade credit at one extreme and commercial banks on the other, are a variety of other sources of short-term funds. They are usually willing to help any viable firm—provided the "price is right"—provided, that is, that the return to the lender is sufficient to cover the risks involved and the cost of doing business.

In the course of illustrating the process of choosing among alternative sources of short-term funds, or in connection with deciding whether to borrow at short-term (as in the case of Butcher), we looked merely at the cost of the funds and the terms and conditions of each proposed loan. *We did not look directly at additional risk to the borrower.* Nor did we, in the case of Butcher, look at the probable effect on the price of Butcher's stock. Does this mean that we violated the law laid down in Chapter 2?

Not really. In the case of Micro Electronics, all the common stock was owned by the four officers of the company. The probable return on the inventory buildup was high, and the four stockholders, by agreeing to go ahead, agreed implicitly that the probable return was worth the additional risk. The risk, of course, was that Vaughn would not make the additional sales he had promised to make and that if he did not, Barclay would not be able to repay the loans when they were due.

But why didn't Martin, before calling Raimondi, make an attempt to assess the effect of the additional borrowing on the price of Butcher's stock? Butcher would borrow an additional $2.3 million, its contractual obligations would be higher by that much (plus interest) and risk would apparently therefore be increased.

But in fact Martin *had* looked at the effect on the price of Butcher's common stock. He had done so without even knowing that he'd done so. What had happened?

First, he had looked at the two short-term projects (the wool purchase and the Government contract at Tampico) and had noted that they were small in size relative to Butcher's total assets and that they promised very high rates of return.

And he knew also that both rates of return were subject to a relatively small margin of error. Martin was virtually certain that four months from now, Tampico would have completed the Government contract and been paid. Nothing much could go wrong. Tampico would be producing things it knew how to produce. And the contract (with the Department of Agriculture) was firm and contained built-in protection against strikes and other unforeseen contingencies. And Martin was virtually certain, also, that during the next four months Nashua would have spent much more than $1.5 million on raw wool. Thus the wool buyer, by buying wool now, was merely anticipating purchases which would, anyway, be made later on. In short, the returns on the two short-term projects were very high and virtually certain. And both would have "turned over" in four months and, by doing so, would have provided at least enough money to pay back the borrowed funds with interest. Martin knew that additional borrowing created additional risk *only when large amounts were involved relative to total assets and only when returns were uncertain.*

Both short-term projects were, to repeat, small—in total they represented about 1 percent of Butcher's total assets. And the expected rates of return on both projects were high and virtually certain.

Martin concluded, therefore, (albeit, half-unconsciously) that the two projects would have a favorable effect on the price of Butcher's stock: both would increase earnings substantially with virtually no increase in risk.

But, on the other hand, suppose the two short-term projects had been large, relative to the firm's total assets (suppose they had required $25 million instead of $2.5 million) and the returns had been subject to a high degree of uncertainty. What would Martin have done then? He would have been much more careful—as we shall see in the succeeding chapters.

PROBLEMS

1. Exhibits 16.1, 16.2, 16.3, 16.4, and 16.5 show the forms used by various banks for, respectively,

   (a) An unsecured loan;

   (b) A secured loan;

   (c) An assignment of accounts receivable;

(d) A security agreement covering an assignment of accounts receivable;

(e) A general loan and collateral security agreement covering a loan on inventory.

Read the fine print and indicate the purpose of each agreement.

2. Assume that Barclay decides to accept National's offer. On January 2, Micro Electronics receives a check for $100,450 from National—which it deposits in its checking account at Second National. Make the necessary adjustments in Micro Electronics' revised year end balance sheet (see Table 16.2).

   During January, of course, Micro Electronics sells $100,000 worth of circuitry. Will these receivables also have to be sold to National? Why or why not? What about the receivables generated by February's sales—will they also have to be sold? Assuming no further inventory buildup after June 1, when will Barclay be able to stop factoring? Exhibit 16.6 may help you analyze the foregoing questions.

3. In considering the alternative offers from Second National and National Factors, Barclay noted that factoring could be used to provide long-term funds as well as short-term funds.

   After Vaughn has sold the additional $250,000 worth (at cost) of circuitry, and everything is back to normal (that is, no finished goods inventory), he tells Barclay that finished goods inventory "will just have to be built back up to $250,000 and kept there. With a permanent finished goods inventory of $250,000," he says, "I'd be able to increase sales by $50,000 (at selling price) a month. We can just start selling receivables again to National Factors."

   Assume Barclay agrees. How long would Micro Electronics have to go on selling receivables to National and in what amounts? Assume the buildup takes three months, beginning August 1. Sales rise by $50,000 a month—just as Vaughn had predicted—beginning in November.

4. Suppose you obtain the campus concession for the New York Times. You are required to pay the Times each Saturday in advance for the papers you will receive the following week. The bill amounts to about $90 a week. Until now you have been paying this amount out of your own pocket. One day it occurs to you that you could use the $90—which until now you have kept invested in inventory. You go to your roommate and ask him whether he would lend you $90 with your newspaper inventory as collateral. What do you suppose he would say? Why would he say it?

5. Suppose you were selling gold? Coffee? High style textile fabric? If you were asked to list those characteristics of inventory which

would make it ideal as collateral for a loan, what would those characteristics be?

6. A chattel mortgage is a mortgage on anything tangible (except real estate)—inventory, machinery, cars, trucks and so forth. Make a list of ten tangible things (in order of their acceptability) which would be acceptable—to a tough minded lender—as security for a chattel mortgage.

EXHIBIT 16.1

_____ 19 ____ $ _____

_____ DAYS AFTER DATE, FOR VALUE RECEIVED, _____ PROMISE TO PAY TO

▼▼ WACHOVIA BANK AND TRUST COMPANY, N.A.

OR ORDER, AT ITS OFFICE WHERE BORROWED

_____ **DOLLARS**

INTEREST RATE BEFORE MATURITY, _____ % PER ANNUM; AFTER MATURITY, AT HIGHEST RATE PERMITTED BY APPLICABLE LAW NOT EXCEEDING 12% PER ANNUM. ALL PARTIES TO THIS NOTE, INCLUDING THE MAKERS, ENDORSERS, SURETIES AND GUARANTORS, AND WHETHER BOUND BY THIS OR BY SEPARATE INSTRUMENT OR AGREEMENT, HEREBY WAIVE PRESENTMENT FOR PAYMENT, DEMAND, PROTEST, NOTICE OF NON-PAYMENT OR DISHONOR AND OF PROTEST, AND ANY AND ALL OTHER NOTICES AND DEMANDS WHATSOEVER, AND HEREBY CONSENT THAT AT ANY TIME, OR FROM TIME TO TIME, PAYMENT OF ANY SUM PAYABLE UNDER THIS NOTE MAY BE EXTENDED WITHOUT NOTICE, WHETHER FOR A DEFINITE OR INDEFINITE TIME. IN THE EVENT ANY SUCH PARTY TO THIS NOTE DEFAULTS IN THE PAYMENT OF ANY OBLIGATION DUE ANY CREDITOR, THEN, AT THE OPTION OF THE HOLDER HEREOF, THIS NOTE TOGETHER WITH ACCRUED INTEREST AND ALL OTHER LOAN CHARGES THEREON SHALL BECOME IMMEDIATELY DUE AND PAYABLE. ANY CREDIT LIFE INSURANCE SECURING THE PAYMENT OF THIS NOTE WAS EFFECTED SOLELY AT THE OPTION OF THE UNDERSIGNED INSURED. IN THE EVENT THE INDEBTEDNESS EVIDENCED HEREBY IS COLLECTED BY OR THROUGH AN ATTORNEY, THE HOLDER SHALL BE ENTITLED TO RECOVER REASONABLE ATTORNEY'S FEES TO THE EXTENT PERMITTED BY APPLICABLE LAW.

GIVEN UNDER THE HAND AND SEAL OF EACH PARTY HERETO.

DUE _____   _____ (SEAL)

ADDRESS _____   _____ (SEAL)

BUSINESS ADDRESS _____   _____ (SEAL)

629 New (Replaces 950) 8-69   ACCOUNTING INFORMATION ONLY — NOT TERMS OF THE NOTE

ACCOUNT NO.		LOAN NO.		BLOT CODE	BRANCH	OFFICER	AGREE-MENT	INTEREST PAID TO	INSURANCE PAID TO
RATE	D-T	TRAN	FRB CL	INSUR	SECURITY	TERM	FEES	INSURANCE PREM.	INTEREST

$ ___

___ after date, for value received and with interest ___

at ___% per annum, the undersigned promise(s) to pay

to   **NORTH CAROLINA NATIONAL BANK**   or Order

___ Dollars

PAYABLE AT ANY OFFICE OF THE NORTH CAROLINA NATIONAL BANK IN NORTH CAROLINA. INTEREST HEREON SHALL ACCRUE AFTER MATURITY OR DEMAND, UNTIL PAID, AT THE RATE STATED ABOVE.

To secure the payment of this note and liabilities as herein defined, the parties hereto hereby pledge and grant to said Bank (the word "Bank" wherever used herein shall include any holder or assignee of this note) a security interest in the collateral described as follows:

and any collateral added thereto or substituted therefor, including shares issued as stock dividends and stock splits and dividends representing distribution of capital assets. The Bank is hereby authorized at any time to charge against any deposit accounts of any party hereto any and all liabilities whether due or not. The Bank may declare all liabilities due at once in the event any party hereto becomes subject to any proceedings for the relief of creditors including but not limited to proceedings under the Bankruptcy Act or otherwise, or if in the judgment of Bank the collateral decreases in value so as to render Bank insecure and Bank demands additional collateral which is not furnished, or if Bank at any time otherwise deems itself insecure. In the event the indebtedness evidenced hereby or liabilities as defined herein be collected by or through an attorney at law, the holder shall be entitled to collect reasonable attorneys' fees.

Upon failure to pay any liability when due, Bank may sell the collateral at public or private sale, for cash or on credit, as a whole or in parcels, without notice, and Bank may at any such sale purchase the collateral or any part thereof for its own account, and the proceeds of any such sale shall be applied first to the costs of such sale and the expenses of collection, including reasonable attorneys' fees, and then to the outstanding balance due on said liabilities, the application to be made in the manner and proportions as Bank elects. The Bank may forbear from realizing on the collateral or any part thereof, by sale or otherwise, all as the Bank may decide, and the liabilities of the parties hereto shall not be released, discharged or in any way affected by any such forbearance, nor shall any of the parties hereto have any rights or recourse against the collateral unless such deterioration, waste, or loss be caused by the willful act or willful failure to act of the Bank. Upon payment of this note the Bank may release the collateral but shall have the right to retain the same to secure any unpaid liabilities. Upon any transfer of this note and the collateral, the Bank shall be fully relieved of responsibility with reference thereto. "Liabilities" or "Liability," as herein used, shall include this note and all obligations of every kind of any party hereto in whatever capacity to Bank, now or hereafter existing, whether arising directly or acquired from others as collateral or otherwise, whether absolute or contingent, joint or several, joint and several, secured or unsecured, due or not due, direct or indirect, including, but not limited to, liabilities arising by operation of law, contractual or tortious, liquidated or otherwise.

All persons bound on this obligation, whether primarily or secondarily liable as principals, sureties, guarantors, endorsers or otherwise, hereby waive presentment, protest, notice of dishonor and of acceleration of maturity and any right to require the Bank to retain any collateral pledged as security for this note or any other liabilities and agree that any extension of time for payment with or without notice shall not affect their joint and several liabilities.

Witness our/my hand(s) and seal(s).

Address ___

Due ___   No. ___

___(Seal)

___(Seal)

NCNB 2155 REV. 10-69

EXHIBIT 16.2

EXHIBIT 16.3

ASSIGNMENT OF ACCOUNTS RECEIVABLE
(For use with Security Agreement NCNB 2178)

FOR VALUE RECEIVED and as collateral security for the payment of indebtedness of the undersigned (hereafter called the "Borrower") to the NORTH CAROLINA NATIONAL BANK,

_____ (hereinafter called the "Bank"), under that certain Security

Agreement entered into by and between the Borrower and the Bank on the _____day

of _____, 19____, the Borrower hereby assigns, transfers and sets over unto the Bank, all the right, title and interest of the Borrower in and to the accounts receivable and all proceeds

thereof, aggregating in unpaid balance $_____, evidenced by invoices of the Borrower, copies of which are delivered to the Bank herewith, numbered as follows:

The Borrower represents and warrants to the Bank that the office where the Borrower keeps its records concerning all of its accounts is at the address stated in the above mentioned Agreement; that each assigned account receivable represents a bona fide sale from or a completed rendering of services by the Borrower to its customer; that the assigned accounts receivable have unpaid balances legally owing by such customers which are not past due in the amounts set forth in the respective invoices; that the goods or merchandise sold have been delivered to such customer or to the carrier or the services have been performed for such customers in accordance with the contracts or purchase orders; that said sales or rendering of services were not in violation of any law or governmental regulation or order; that no account receivable assigned hereby has been otherwise assigned or pledged, has not been subjected to any legal process and is not subject to any set-off, counter-claim or defense; and that the inventory, goods or merchandise, the sale of which gave rise to any said account receivable, were and are not subject to any security interest held or by any levy, lien or encumbrance in favor of anyone other than the Bank and no Financing Statement is on file with respect thereto.

IN WITNESS WHEREOF, the Borrower has duly executed this assignment of accounts receivable pursuant to the aforesaid Security Agreement, this the _____ day of_____, 19____.

_____

By :_____

NCNB 2163 Rev. 7/67

372

EXHIBIT 16.4

SECURITY AGREEMENT
(Accounts Receivable Revolving Credit)

STATE OF NORTH CAROLINA

COUNTY OF _____

THIS AGREEMENT entered into this_____day of_____, 19_____, by and between

_____ of
      Name   **Street Address**

_____, hereinafter
     City   **County**   **State**

called the "Borrower", party of the first part, and NORTH CAROLINA NATIONAL BANK, a national banking association of

_____, hereinafter called the "Bank", party of the second part.

WITNESSETH:

WHEREAS, the Borrower desires to establish with the Bank a basis upon which loans may be obtained by it from the Bank from time to time secured by the assignment of accounts receivable, the proceeds of which loans will be used in the normal course of the business of the Borrower and for its proper corporate purposes; and

WHEREAS, the parties hereto desire to state the terms, conditions, provisions and their respective rights and remedies with respect to any loan or loans which may be made hereunder:

NOW, THEREFORE, in consideration of the premises and the mutual promises of the parties hereto hereinafter contained, it is hereby agreed as follows:

1. The Borrower will execute a note or notes (such note or notes, including any extensions, modifications or renewals thereof, being hereinafter referred to in the singular as the "note" and in the plural as the "notes") in form satisfactory to the Bank to evidence loans made hereunder. As collateral security for the payment of the indebtedness evidenced by the note or notes, the Borrower hereby assigns to and the Bank shall have a security interest in all of its accounts receivable now existing or hereafter arising and all proceeds thereof, including but not limited to accounts receivable evidenced by invoices acceptable and delivered to the Bank having balances aggregating not less than_____percent of the principal amount of the note or notes at any time outstanding. All such assignments of accounts receivable shall be in manner, form and substance prescribed by or satisfactory to the Bank. As additional security for any and all loans made hereunder, the Borrower hereby assigns to and the Bank shall have a security interest in all of the Borrower's inventory now owned or hereafter acquired, including but not limited to goods held for sale or being processed for sale, including all materials, goods in process, finished goods and supplies customarily classified as inventory, and the proceeds in any form of all of the Borrower's inventory and accounts receivable, whether specifically assigned to the Bank or not. The security interest of the Bank in all of Borrower's inventory and accounts receivable and the proceeds therefrom, in any form, whether specifically assigned to the Bank or not, shall secure the Borrower's indebtedness to the Bank for all loans made by the Bank to the Borrower under this Agreement and also all other indebtedness of the Borrower to the Bank now existing or hereafter arising.

2. Prior to disbursement by Bank of any loan proceeds under this Agreement, Borrower shall have furnished the Bank a properly executed Financing Statement prescribed by the Uniform Commercial Code and approved by the Bank, and Borrower hereby agrees to execute if required by the Bank any necessary continuation statements so long as this Agreement remains in effect.

3. The Borrower will deliver, with each assignment of accounts receivable, copies of the invoices, which shall be in form and substance satisfactory to the Bank, evidencing the sale of goods, merchandise or services which created any assigned account receivable, and such copies of invoices shall bear a legend, printed or stamped thereon, as follows:

"The account receivable evidenced hereby is assigned to

North Carolina National Bank

of _____ to secure
loans of money."

With each assignment of accounts hereunder, the Borrower will deliver to Bank any and all other instruments and documents deemed by Bank necessary or desirable in support of such assigned accounts, including, but not limited to, the usual evidences of delivery of goods or performance of services such as bills of lading, waybills, freight bills or delivery receipts.

NCNB 2178 Rev. 7/67

4. By each assignment of accounts receivable, the Borrower shall be deemed to have represented and warranted to the Bank that the office where Borrower keeps its records concerning all of its accounts is at the address stated above; that each assigned account receivable represents a bona fide sale from or a completed rendering of services by the Borrower to its customer; that the assigned account receivable has an unpaid balance, legally owing by such customer but which is not past due, in the amount set forth in the invoice applicable thereto; that the goods or merchandise sold shall have been delivered to such customer or to the carrier or the services shall have been performed for such customer in accordance with the contract or purchase order; that said sale shall not have been in violation of any law or govermental regulation or order; that the assigned account receivable has not been otherwise assigned or pledged, has not been subjected to any legal process and is not subject to any setoff, counter-claim or defense; and that the inventory, goods or merchandise, the sale of which gave rise to said accounts receivable, were and are not subject to any security interest held by or any levy, lien or encumbrance in favor of anyone other than the Bank and no Financing Statement is on file with respect thereto.

5. The Bank shall have and succeed to all rights, remedies, interests, powers, securities and liens of the Borrower with respect to the assigned accounts receivable, and to the goods, merchandise or services the sale of which created the assigned accounts receivable (including but not limited to the right of stoppage in transitu), and shall have the right to enforce the same in its name or to direct the enforcement thereof by the Borrower for the benefit of the Bank.

6. The Borrower shall not, without the consent and approval of the Bank, grant or permit any extensions of time of pay-ment of the assigned accounts receivable or any part thereof; shall not compromise, compound or settle, or permit the compro-mise or settlement of, the assigned accounts receivable or any part thereof for less than the unpaid net balance thereof; shall not release in whole or in part any person or persons liable for the payment of the assigned accounts receivable or any part thereof; nor allow any credit whatsoever on the unpaid net balance of the assigned accounts receivable, except for the amount of cash paid thereon.

7. The Borrower does hereby acknowledge that the assignment of accounts receivable, is as well the assignment of the proceeds from these assigned accounts receivable and the Bank is therefore fully empowered by the Borrower to collect upon said assigned accounts receivable when due, and to hold the proceeds from such collections as security for the notes in lieu of the assigned accounts receivable collected upon.

8. The Borrower is hereby appointed the Agent of the Bank to make collection of the assigned accounts receivable subject to the direction and control of the Bank, which may without cause or notice curtail or terminate said authority and agency at any time. The Borrower will collect upon the assigned accounts receivable but only as Agent of the Bank and will hold all of the proceeds thereof so collected in trust for the Bank, will not commingle them with the Borrower's own funds in any manner whatever, and will deliver them to the Bank not later than the next business day after collection, or within that time deposit them in the Collateral Account hereinafter provided for. Such proceeds whether consisting of cash, checks, drafts, notes, trade acceptances, or other instruments for the payment of money shall be delivered to the Bank in the identical form received, except for the endorsement of the Borrower which shall be supplied when required.

9. All funds received by the Bank or by the Borrower as Agent of the Bank in the collection of the assigned accounts receiv-able shall be deposited in a separate bank account to be maintained with the Bank, or with such other depository as the Bank may designate, which shall be called "_____ Collateral Account, North Carolina National Bank, Assignee" (elsewhere referred to as "Collateral Account"), subject to withdrawal only in accord-ance with the terms of this agreement and with the approval of the Bank, and the sums on deposit in said account shall continue to be collateral security for the notes until applied thereon or released as hereinafter provided.

10. The Bank will periodically at such intervals as may be agreed upon, release to the Borrower, any funds on deposit in the Collateral Account over and above that amount required to maintain the total remaining collateral consisting of assigned accounts receivable and collected proceeds on deposit in the Collateral Account at an amount equal to _____ percent of the aggregate amount of the unpaid balances of the notes then outstanding hereunder; provided, however, that the Borrower shall not be in default in any of the terms and conditions of this Agreement or of any of the notes, and provided moreover, that the Bank shall have in its absolute discretion the right to refuse to release such funds or any part thereof and may instead apply such funds or any part thereof to the payment of the principal and interest on any of the notes outstanding hereunder, the order and method of such application to be in the sole discretion of the Bank.

The above release provisions contemplate that as collections are made on assigned accounts receivable and placed on deposit in the Collateral Account the Bank may release to Borrower all or any part of such funds if prior to or simultaneously with such re-lease the Borrower assigns to the Bank other accounts receivable which are acceptable to the Bank and have an aggregate unpaid balance in an amount sufficient to make the total amount of collateral security equal to not less than _____ percent of the unpaid balance due on the note or notes. The assigned accounts receivable thus substituted for funds released from the Collateral Account shall be assigned with all the formalities required for the assignment of accounts receivable in the first instance and shall be subject to all of the terms and condition of this Agreement.

11. If the unpaid net balance of any assigned account receivable is not paid within_____ days after it becomes due, the Borrower will pay into the Collateral Account the full amount of such past due invoices or with approval of Bank sub-stitute therefor other accounts receivable acceptable to the Bank and having unpaid balances not less than the aggregate amount of the unpaid balance upon the past due assigned account receivable. The past due accounts receivable and the invoices evidencing the same shall remain in possession of and under assignment to the Bank as surplus above the required _____ percent of the unpaid balances due on the note or notes outstanding and any excess cash on deposit in the Collateral Account resulting there-from shall be subject to the provisions of Paragraph 10 above.

12. The Borrower will receive and report to the Bank daily all goods or merchandise, the sale of which created an assigned account receivable, returned to or recovered (including by stoppage in transitu) by the Borrower and the Borrower will hold such goods or merchandise segregated and in trust for the Bank until an account receivable which is acceptable to the Bank is substituted for the assigned account receivable covering such returned or recovered goods or merchandise or at the option of the Bank until the Borrower pays into the Collateral Account the full amount of the invoice covering the returned or recovered goods or merchandise.

13. The Bank shall have the right at all times this Agreement is in effect to cause verification to be made of the assigned accounts receivable with the account debtor and with or without notice being given to the account debtor of the assignments here-

under and Bank may, during any business day, by such agent as the Bank shall designate, examine the ledgers, books of account, records and papers of the Borrower and all evidence in support thereof of any entry thereon; and the Borrower agrees to produce such ledgers, books, records and papers upon demand by the Bank.

14. All notes made by the Borrower held by the Bank may, at the option of the Bank, be declared and become immediately due and payable without demand or notice, which are hereby waived, if any representation or warranty of the Borrower made herein or pursuant hereto should prove untrue or misleading in any material respect, or in the event of any breach on the part of the Borrower of any of the terms, conditions and provisions contained in this Agreement or in any of the notes or other agreements given by the Borrower to the Bank, or upon the failure of the Borrower to pay any of the notes or interest thereon, or any installments thereof, or other obligations to the Bank when due by the terms thereof or declared to be due hereunder. In any such event the Bank may proceed to give notice of any such assignments hereunder to the account debtors on the invoices, collect the accounts directly from the account debtors, and sell all or any part of the collateral security in accordance with the terms and provisions contained in the notes made by the Borrower to the Bank and may apply the proceeds of such sales upon the balance owing upon such notes. Each and every term and provision contained in any such note is hereby incorporated herein by reference and is hereby made a part of this Agreement as if the same were set forth in full herein. In addition to but not in limitation of any of the foregoing, in the event of such a default by the Borrower under the terms of the Agreement or under the terms of any notes or other indebtedness secured hereby, the Bank may without notice to the Borrower proceed to enforce payment of the same and to exercise any or all of the rights and remedies afforded to the Bank by the provisions of the Uniform Commercial Code or available to the Bank under the note or notes then outstanding, or otherwise, with all such rights and remedies being cumulative and not alternative, and the Borrower agrees to pay the cost of collection including, in addition to the costs and disbursements provided by statute, reasonable attorney's fees and legal expenses which may be incurred by the Bank.

In the event the Borrower suspends the transaction of its business, requests a general extension of time within which to pay its debts, or makes an assignment for the benefit of creditors, or in the event a petition in bankruptcy, or in equity for receivership, or for reorganization under the Bankruptcy Act or any amendment thereof is filed by or against the Borrower, or a creditor's committee is named for the Borrower, or in the event of the occurrence of any act whatsoever amounting to a business failure by the Borrower, then upon the occurrence of any such events, all notes then outstanding shall become immediately due and payable without demand or notice, which are hereby waived.

15. Neither the failure nor any delay on the part of the Bank to exercise any right, power or privilege hereunder shall operate as a waiver thereof; nor shall any single or partial exercise of any such right, power or privilege preclude any other or further exercise thereof or the exercise of any other right, power or privilege of the Bank.

This Agreement shall be construed and its performance governed in accordance with the laws of the State of North Carolina.

IN WITNESS WHEREOF, the parties hereto have caused this Agreement to be duly executed in duplicate as of the day and year first above written.

ATTEST:

_____
Borrower

By:_____   By:_____
(Title)   (Title)

ATTEST:

NORTH CAROLINA NATIONAL BANK

By:_____   By:_____
(Title)   (Title)

EXHIBIT 16.5

Accounts Receivable and Contract Rights Security Agreement

This Assignment made this _____ day of _____, 19____, to CENTRAL CAROLINA BANK & TRUST CO.

(herein called "Bank") by _____
(herein called "Borrower"), provides:

1. **Location of Records.** Borrower warrants that the office where Borrower keeps its records concerning all of its accounts and contract rights is at the address appearing after Borrower's signature hereto, unless a different address is specified in the following space:

_____

Borrower will immediately advise Bank in writing of any change in the location of the place where said records are kept.

2. **Assignment Of Accounts Receivable, Contract Rights And Proceeds.** As security for the payment of all indebtedness of Borrower and all other parties thereto, and each of them, to Bank, now existing or hereafter incurred, matured or unmatured, direct or indirect, absolute or contingent, including any extensions and renewals thereof (herein called the "Indebtedness"), Borrower hereby assigns to Bank and grants to Bank a security interest in all of Borrower's existing accounts receivable and contract rights, all of Borrower's accounts receivable and contract rights which come into existence during the term of this agreement, and in all the proceeds of said existing and future accounts receivable and contract rights.

At the time of each borrowing hereunder, and at such intervals as may be prescribed by Bank, Borrower will give Bank a schedule (in the form required by Bank) of Borrower's accounts receivable and contract rights which describes each such account and contract right or such thereof as Bank may prescribe, together with copies of the contracts or invoices with evidence of shipment. Borrower warrants that each such account shown on such schedule meets and will continue to meet the following specifications until it is collected in full:

(a) The account arose from the performance of services or an outright sale of goods by Borrower, such goods have been shipped to the account debtor, and Borrower has possession of, or has delivered to Bank, evidence of such shipment.

(b) The account is not subject to any prior assignment, claim, lien or security interest, and Borrower will not make any further assignment thereof or create any further security interest therein, nor permit Borrower's rights therein to be reached by attachment, levy, garnishment or other judicial process.

(c) The account is not subject to set-off, credit, allowance or adjustment by the account debtor, except discount allowed for prompt payment, and the debtor has not complained as to his liability thereon and has not returned any of the goods from the sale of which the account arose.

(d) The account arose in the ordinary course of Borrower's business and no notice of the bankruptcy, insolvency or financial embarrassment of the account debtor has been received.

(e) Bank has not notified Borrower that the account or the account debtor is unsatisfactory.

Borrower will notify Bank in writing promptly of any account shown on such schedule as to which any of the above warranties are no longer correct.

3. **Collections.** Bank is authorized and empowered at any time in its sole discretion: (a) To require Borrower to notify or itself to notify, either in its own name or in the name of Borrower, any debtor named in the accounts receivable or any party obligated under contracts involved in the contract rights assigned to Bank, of the fact of this assignment or to request in its name, in the name of Borrower or in the name of a third party, confirmation from any such debtor or party of the amount shown by the accounts receivable or contracts to be payable or any other matter stated therein; (b) to demand, collect or compromise for any and all sums which are now or may hereafter become due or owing upon any of the accounts receivable or contract rights; (c) to enforce payment thereof either in its own name or in the name of Borrower; and (d) to endorse in the name of Borrower and to collect any negotiable instruments tendered or received in payment of the accounts receivable or contract rights. But Bank under no circumstances shall be under any duty to act in regard to any of the foregoing matters. The costs of such collection and enforcement, including attorneys' fees and out-of-pocket expenses, shall be borne solely by Borrower whether the same are incurred by Bank or Borrower.

Unless otherwise directed by Bank, Borrower will forthwith upon receipt of all checks, drafts, cash and other remittances in payment or on account of Borrower's accounts receivable or contract rights, deposit the same in a special bank account maintained with Bank, over which Bank alone has power of withdrawal and will designate with each such deposit the particular account receivable or contract right upon which the remittance was made. The funds in said account shall be held by Bank as security for the Indebtedness. Said proceeds shall be deposited in precisely the form received except for the endorsement of Borrower where necessary to permit collection of items, which endorsement Borrower agrees to make, and which Bank is also hereby authorized to make on Borrower's behalf. Pending such deposit, Borrower agrees that it will not commingle any such checks, drafts, cash and other remittances with any of Borrower's funds or property, but will hold them separate and apart therefrom and upon an express trust for Bank until deposit thereof is made in the special account. Bank may at any time and from time to time, in its sole discretion, apply any part of the credit balance in the special account to the payment of the Indebtedness, whether or not the same be due. Upon the full and final liquidation of the Indebtedness, Bank will pay over to Borrower any excess received by it from Borrower, whether received by it as a deposit in the special account or received by it as a direct payment on any of the Indebtedness.

4. **Other Agreements Of Borrower.**

(a) Borrower will at all times keep accurate and complete records of Borrower's accounts receivable, contract rights and performance under contracts involved in the contract rights. Bank, or any of its agents, shall have the right to call at Borrower's place or places of business at intervals to be determined by Bank, and without hindrance or delay, to inspect, audit, check and make extracts from the books, records, journals, orders, receipts, correspondence and other data relating to Borrower's accounts receivable, contract rights or to any other transactions between the parties hereto.

(b) If any of Borrower's accounts receivable or contract rights arise out of contracts with the United States or any department, agency, or instrumentality thereof, Borrower will immediately notify Bank in writing and execute any instruments and take any steps required by Bank in order that all monies due and to become due under such contracts shall be assigned to Bank and notice thereof given to the Government under the Federal Assignment of Claims Act.

(c) If any of Borrower's accounts receivable should be evidenced by promissory notes, trade acceptances, or other instruments for the payment of money, Borrower will, unless otherwise directed by Bank, deliver same to Bank appropriately endorsed to Bank's order and, regardless of the form of such endorsement, Borrower hereby waives presentment, demand, notice of dishonor, protest and notice of protest and all other notices with respect thereto. Bank shall not be bound to take any steps necessary to preserve any right of Borrower against any prior parties to such instruments which Borrower hereby assumes to do.

(d) If Borrower shall fail to pay when due any Indebtedness, or shall otherwise be in default under any obligation of Borrower to Bank, or shall fail to observe or perform any of the provisions of this agreement, Borrower shall be in default hereunder. When Borrower is so in default, all of the Indebtedness shall become immediately due and payable at Bank's option without notice to Borrower, and Bank may proceed to enforce payment of the same and to exercise any or all of the rights and remedies afforded to Bank by the Uniform Commercial Code or otherwise possessed by Bank. Borrower shall pay to Bank on demand all expenses, including legal expenses and attorneys' fees, incurred or paid by Bank in protecting and enforcing the rights of Bank hereunder.

(e) Borrower will not without the prior written consent of Bank pledge, or grant any security interest in, any of its accounts receivable or contract rights or any inventory to anyone except Bank, or permit any lien or encumbrance to attach to any of the foregoing, or any levy to be made thereon, or any financing statement (except Bank's statement) to be on file with respect thereto.

(f) Borrower agrees that it will not permit any return of merchandise, the sale of which gave rise to any of the accounts, except in the usual and regular course of business, and any merchandise thus returned will be segregated and held by Borrower in trust for Bank, which is hereby given a security interest in such merchandise and any proceeds thereof as security for the Indebtedness.

5. The term of this assignment shall commence with the date hereof and end on the termination date as herein defined. The termination date means the date when, after written notice from either party to the other that no further loans are to be made hereunder, all Indebtedness is paid in full.

6. The North Carolina laws shall govern the construction of this agreement and the rights and duties of the parties hereto. Bank's failure to exercise any right or take any action hereunder shall not constitute a waiver of that or any other right or action.

7. Borrower will deliver such instruments of further assignment or assurance as Bank may from time to time request to carry out the intent hereof, and will join with Bank in executing financing statements in form satisfactory to Bank and pay the cost of filing the same and continuation and termination statements and any other documents in any public office deemed advisable by Bank.

8. This assignment shall be binding upon Borrower, its successors and assigns, and the benefits hereof shall inure to Bank, its successors and assigns.

_____ (Seal)
(Borrower)

By _____ (Seal)
(name and title)

_____
(number and street)

_____
(city or county, state)

EXHIBIT 16.6

MICRO ELECTRONICS CASH RECEIPTS AND EXPENDITURES
BY FOUR-WEEK PERIODS
(FOR TWENTY-FOUR WEEKS AFTER END OF FIRST YEAR)

				Weeks			Total
	1-4	5-8	9-12	13-16	17-20	21-24	
Expected Sales							
Old	$100,000	$100,000	$100,000	$100,000	$100,000	$100,000	$600,000
New	0	0	0	0	0	50,000	50,000
Receipts							
Collections on A/R	100,000	100,000	100,000	100,000	100,000	100,000	600,000
Other	0	0	0	0	0	0	0
Total Receipts	$100,000	$100,000	$100,000	$100,000	$100,000	$100,000	$600,000
Disbursements							
Wages							
Old	$ 40,800	$ 40,800	$ 40,800	$ 40,800	$ 40,800	$ 40,800	$244,800
New	4,000	24,000	24,000	24,000	24,000	24,000	124,000
Salaries	3,400	3,400	3,400	3,400	3,400	3,400	20,400
Social Security and Withholding taxes	0	0	0	44,200	0	0	44,200
Heat, light, power, telephone	500	600	600	600	600	600	3,500
Interest							
Convertibles	0	0	0	5,475	0	0	5,475
Parents	0	0	0	325	0	0	325
Raw Materials	18,000	52,000	52,000	52,000	52,000	52,000	278,000
Supplies	0	100	0	0	100	0	200
Estimated Federal income tax	1,952	0	4,000	0	0	4,000	9,952
Total Disbursements	$ 68,652	$120,900	$124,800	$170,800	$120,900	$124,800	$730,852
Receipts less disbursements	$ 31,348	—$ 20,900	—$ 24,800	—$ 70,800	—$ 20,900	—$ 24,800	—$130,852

17

THE COST OF LONG-TERM CAPITAL / introduction

You returned to your room one day in mid-spring—after your roommate's small loan business had prospered to the point at which he had hired two assistants and a part time bookkeeper. It was late afternoon. He was sitting on his bed, sobbing wildly and pulling his hair out, slowly and deliberately, in big bunches.

You said, "Quiet, will you. You'll wake the dog. And stop pulling your hair out. You'll catch a head cold. Besides, the top of your head is beginning to look like a checkerboard."

He pulled out another bunch of hair.

You said, "What's the matter anyway?"

He said, "I have no friends and I'm losing all my money."

You said, "Losing all your money! Bah! I don't believe it."

He said, "I've just had a meeting with my accountant. I made 1,082 loans last year and I did make a little money. *But I would have done much better if I'd invested everything in treasury bills.*"

You said contemptuously, "Ha! You underestimated your cost of capital. You didn't realize that *the cost of capital is an opportunity cost.* How could you have been so stupid?"

He started sobbing again. Then suddenly he stopped and looked up. He said, "What's the cost of capital? And what's an opportunity cost?"

You said, "Listen, and I'll tell you . . ."

We discuss, first, the "cost of capital" problem in a small closely-held company such as Micro Electronics.

IN SMALL COMPANIES

Late in August of 1970, after Barclay had completed the initial inventory buildup—with financial assistance from National Factors—and had sold most of it, Vaughn appeared in Barclay's office.

"I've just sold the last $30,000 worth to IBM for immediate delivery," he said. "That runs our stock down to zero. We've got to build it back up again. We've got to be able to fill orders for immediate delivery. It will make a difference of $75,000 a month in sales—maybe as much as $100,000."

"You want a permanent finished goods inventory," said Barclay.

"Yes," said Vaughn.

"How much?" asked Barclay.

"$500,000," said Vaughn blandly.

"Why so much?" asked Barclay. "You yourself just said that additional sales wouldn't be higher than $100,000 a month. We can produce $100,000 worth in a month. If we had a permanent finished goods inventory of $200,000 and you sold $100,000 a month for immediate delivery, we'd always have $100,000 available."

"You confuse me," said Vaughn.

"Look," said Barclay. "We build finished goods back up to $200,000 by November 1. During November you sell $100,000 worth—at cost— of relays. As soon as you make the sale, we start building up finished goods again. Would take a month. But we've got the second $100,000 worth to cover the sale you'd make in December. Follow?"

"More or less," said Vaughn. "Okay, $200,000—for the time being."

After Vaughn left, Barclay quickly calculated a rate of return on a permanent finished goods inventory of $200,000 at cost. He assumed that additional sales would be $75,000 a month—on which the contribution to overhead would be about $12,000—or $144,000 a year. Thus he saw that if Vaughn were right, the rate of return would be very high—more than 70 percent on an annual basis ($144,000/$200,000 = .72).

But Barclay, who was trying to improve his mind, had gone to a talk the previous week on "The Application of Probability to Business Problems." And he suddenly realized that the rate of return he had calculated was a *maximum* rate of return—not an *expected* rate of return.

He began also to worry, slightly, about two things: first, Vaughn might not have taken account of the possibility that sales out of inventory might cut into regular sales; second, even if Vaughn had taken account of that possibility, Vaughn—who had more than his share of optimism—might simply have overestimated additional sales. Barclay decided therefore that he would try to draw up a probability distribution over the expected rate of return on the inventory buildup. He went to Vaughn's office and after an hour or so returned with the first three columns of Table 17.1 filled in. Vaughn (who thought subjective probabilities

TABLE 17.1

MICRO ELECTRONICS, INC. EXPECTED RETURN ON PERMANENT FINISHED INVENTORY OF $200,000

ADDITIONAL SALES PER MONTH	PAYOFF *	PROBABILITY	AVERAGE EXPECTED RATE OF RETURN
(1)	(2)	(3)	(4)
0-10,000	4.8%	.01	.048%
10,001-20,000	14.4%	.02	.288%
20,001-30,000	24.0%	.02	.480%
30,001-40,000	33.6%	.02	.672%
40,001-50,000	43.2%	.03	1.296%
50,001-60,000	52.8%	.10	5.280%
60,001-70,000	62.4%	.15	9.360%
70,001-80,000	72.0%	.40	28.800%
80,001-90,000	81.6%	.15	12.240%
90,001-100,000	91.2%	.10	9.120%
		1.00	67.584%

* Approximate rate of return before taxes if event occurs (assuming midpoint).

were nonsense) had said in effect that the nature of Micro Electronics business was changing.

"For the first ten to fourteen months," he said, "we were selling trial orders. People were trying to see how our product would perform and whether they'd be able to use it regularly. We are still selling trial orders—but most of our business now is from people who have become or are about to become regular customers. And we won't be able to give them the kind of service they must have, unless we can ship, at once, out of inventory—if they happen to need more than they've ordered in advance. In other words, if we want to grow, we'll have to sell increasing quantities to regular customers, but in order to do so, we'll have to carry a stock of finished goods. And as we grow our stock of finished goods will have to grow also."

When Barclay calculated the expected return on the buildup, he found it was about 68 percent.

He then drew up pro forma balance sheets as of August 31—now just a few days off—and as of October 30—by which time Vaughn's proposed buildup would have been completed. These balance sheets are given in Tables 17.2 and 17.3.

TABLE 17.2

MICRO ELECTRONICS, INC. BALANCE SHEET
AS OF AUGUST 31, 1969

Cash	$ 28,605
Accounts receivable	252,750
Raw materials	22,000
Work-in-process (at cost)	41,200
Finished goods (at cost)	0
Machinery and equipment (net)	184,040
Lease hold improvements (net)	108,750
Office furniture (net)	2,340
Prepaid rent	5,625
Total assets	$645,310
Notes payable (factor)	$ 46,021
Accounts payable	32,000
Accrued salaries and wages	0
Accrued Taxes	44,372
Other accruals	5,000
Convertible debentures	302,000
Long-term notes (parents)	20,000
Common stock ($120 par value)	120,000
Retained earnings	75,917
Total liabilities and equity	$645,310

The only unusual item was the large receivables balance as of August 31. This was due to sales by Vaughn out of the prior "buildup" in finished goods inventory—which, to repeat, had been financed by National Factors. The receivables balance would be back down to normal by the end of October. Barclay saw (Table 17.3) that in order to build finished goods back up to $200,000 a total loan of about $102,000 would

TABLE 17.3

MICRO ELECTRONICS, INC. PRO FORMA
BALANCE SHEET AS OF OCTOBER 30, 1969

Cash	$ 50,000	
Accounts receivable	100,000	
Raw materials	22,000	
Work-in-process (at cost)	41,200	
Finished goods (at cost)	200,000	
Machinery and equipment (net)	180,133	
Lease hold improvements (net)	106,500	
Office furniture (net)	2,160	
Prepaid rent	2,250	
Total assets		$704,243
Notes payable	$101,885 *	
Accounts payable	32,000	
Accrued salaries and wages	0	
Accrued taxes	45,000	
Other accruals	0	
Convertible debentures	302,000	
Long-term notes (parents)	20,000	
Common stock ($120 par value)	120,000	
Retained earnings	83,358	
		$602,358
Total liabilities and equity		$704,243

* $704,243
602,358
———————
$101,885   Required bank loan, end of period. Plugged figure.

be necessary. This included about $38,000 which, at the end of October, would still be due to National Factors on the supplementary $50,000 loan (see Table 16.4).

Barclay then went to see Moses at Second National. He took Vaughn along with him. Moses again asked a lot of questions—aimed primarily at finding out how Barclay was now doing business. Vaughn explained, as he had to Barclay, that their relays were being used by a large number of customers in their regular production. They anticipated their requirements in advance, as well as they could, but they expected to be able to obtain additional quantities for immediate delivery. "And if we want their business," Vaughn said, "we'll have to be able to deliver the goods."

Moses then spent half an hour trying to see what might go wrong. Vaughn didn't think anything could. "We've got the best circuitry in the business. And the way we've picked up regular business from all the top people in electronics proves it."

"Suppose someone invents a better relay. You've got all your eggs in one basket."

"Could be," said Vaughn. "But if they did, it wouldn't affect us for a year. There'd be plenty of time to get rid of the extra inventory."

Moses seemed satisfied and said he'd call them in a day or so—after he'd been able to discuss the matter with his loan committee.

Moses called the next afternoon and told Barclay that the loan committee "hadn't said yes and hadn't said no." They were concerned that Micro Electronics was a single-product company in a dynamic, rapidly changing industry and that it appeared to be doing nothing in product development. Barclay replied that he himself was primarily responsible for product development. But he had been too busy with finance and general administration to be able to give product development the amount of time it required. Moses suggested that perhaps the time had come for Barclay to hire a finance man who could help with general administration.

"You can afford it," said Moses.

"Perhaps," said Barclay. "I'd like to talk it over with Philbrook."

"Right," said Moses. "Call me back. I'm sure I could help you find some one."

"Okay," said Barclay. Then he added, "You're saying, aren't you, that the loan won't be made unless we show some signs of life in product development."

"Just about," said Moses.

"Okay, thanks," said Barclay and hung up.

Barclay and his brethren went to see Philbrook the next morning. Philbrook wasn't surprised that Moses had asked about product development. He had, he said, begun to wonder about it himself.

Philbrook then asked what other alternative sources of money they had.

Barclay said, "National Factors at 24 percent a year—but no restrictions. The bank would probably be a lot cheaper."

Philbrook then asked, "What would happen if sales went to $150,000 every four weeks—how much capacity would be left?"

"Nearly none without a second shift," said Barclay. "And getting married women to work a night shift would be very difficult."

Philbrook said that maybe they'd have to build an addition to the present plant (if the landlord would let them). If they did so, they might have to sell an issue of common stock (to the public) to raise the necessary money. Anyway, financial problems would be getting bigger rather than smaller. And he agreed that Barclay should spend more time on product development. Maybe, as Moses had suggested, Micro Electronics should hire a young finance man who could help also with general administration. They might be able to get someone with a couple of years of experience for $14,000 to $15,000. "Would be all right with me," Philbrook said.

When they got back to the office, Barclay called Moses and said Philbrook had agreed they should hire a young financial man. He said also that he himself would begin to put in more time immediately on product development. Moses said he would pass the word along. He asked how much they'd be willing to pay for a man with two or three years of experience.

"Philbrook suggested $14,000 to $15,000," said Barclay.

"You ought to get something respectable at that price," said Moses. "But its more than you're making."

"I know," said Barclay, "but we own the business."

Moses called back the next afternoon and offered a three-year term loan of $105,000. About $38,000 of this amount would be used to pay off the remaining balance of the loan from National Factors. This payment would be made directly to National by the bank. Micro Electronics would actually receive about $67,000. The loan would be payable in six semi-annual installments of $17,500 with interest at 10½ percent, also payable semi-annually, on the outstanding balance. The loan would be secured by Barclay's accounts receivable and inventory—both raw materials and finished goods. During the three-year period, Micro Electronics would be required to maintain net working capital of $225,000 and would not be free to pay dividends, raise officers' salaries by more than 10 percent a year, buy additional fixed assets, or borrow additional funds elsewhere, except on a note subordinated to the term loan. Moses explained that these restrictions were typical of term loan agreements and were designed to protect cash—so that the loan could be paid off, and to protect the bank's lien position—in case "problems" occurred. If any of these restrictions were violated, the loan would become due at once. He said Barclay could have a couple of days to think the matter over.

The next morning the four men who ran Micro Electronics sat down to talk the matter over.

Barclay said, "Seems to me the return is worth the risk."

Vaughn said, "Risk? What risk?"

Barclay said, "Until now, we've been producing only against firm orders. We get an order, we produce it, we inspect it, we ship it. No risk. Now, we'd produce $200,000 worth of relays—at cost—without having firm orders in advance. Suppose demand dried up suddenly. Or suppose someone *did* come along with something better. We'd be left holding $200,000 of worthless inventory."

Vaughn said, "The chance of that is zero."

"Small," said Barclay, "but not zero. Somebody could take the business away from us, just as we've taken it away from them. If they did, we wouldn't be able to pay off the bank loan and we might lose our whole equity."

"We'd have warning," said Vaughn.

"Maybe yes, maybe no," said Barclay. He added, "I just want to be sure that everyone understands what the risks are. As for me, I'm in favor of going ahead."

Everyone else was, too. Barclay called Moses and told him they'd take the three-year term loan.

What was Barclay's cost of capital? The answer is: We don't really know—although it was certainly not less than 10.5 percent—the rate the bank would charge for the term loan. But, as we shall see below, we really couldn't care less.

small closely-held companies

This little incident tells us two things:

It tells us, first, that companies which are controlled by a small group of stockholders, all known to each other, do not have to estimate their cost of capital. They need only decide whether they wish to take the risk, if any, of investing in new projects—either with additional funds of their own or with money borrowed from a bank or some other lender—such as an insurance company. If they borrow money, their cost of capital will be no less than the rate they pay for the borrowed funds. If they use additional funds of their own, their cost of capital will be their separate opportunity costs. If any stockholder has an opportunity cost *higher* than the expected return on the proposed project, he will probably refuse to invest additional funds of his own in that project. Or he may refuse, even if the expected rate of return is higher than his opportunity cost—simply because he wishes to diversify. In that case he might say: "I've got enough money in this business already."

This means, of course, that the stockholders of closely-held companies may disagree—either because they view the risks differently or because their separate opportunity costs are not the same. If disagreement occurs, the stockholders will have to discuss matters among themselves and compromise, if necessary—if they can. (We saw this happen, in Chapter 2, inside the Clay Company.)

In short, small closely held companies do not have a "cost of capital problem." (They have fights instead.) Only *publicly-held* companies need worry about estimating their cost of capital.

Second, the incident brings out—albeit, indirectly—one of the reasons why large publicly held companies—with hundreds or thousands of individual stockholders—must estimate their cost of capital. They must do so because in general they cannot, by themselves, undertake to arrange compromises and transactions among a widely scattered multitude of individual stockholders—some happy with its decisions and some, unhappy. Publicly held companies cannot, as Clay Company did in Chapter 2, buy stock from one stockholder and sell it to another. They cannot do so for reasons which should be obvious. They must allow this job to be done by the public market (e.g., the New York Stock Exchange). But the company must do its best to assure that if an unhappy stockholder wants to sell his stock—or some part of it—*he will not do so at a loss*. This means that no company should invest in new projects—*if doing so would, in its best judgment, lower the price of its stock*. A company can feel that it has done its best toward achieving this objective *if it invests in no project with an expected return less than the company's cost of capital*.

WHAT IS THE COST OF CAPITAL?

Now then, exactly what do we mean by the term "cost of capital"— which term we have bantered around somewhat cavalierly above and in the preceding sixteen chapters?

We mean something very simple—conceptually. We mean simply *the cost of the new funds which will soon be invested in new projects*. In Chapters 10 through 15 we heard Martin, Kelley, and Hastings, of the Butcher Company, suggest—or actually say—that Butcher's cost of capital was about 11 percent. What they meant, of course, was that 11 percent represented an estimate of the cost of the *new* money which would be invested in *new* projects—in Ex-Cello's lathe (perhaps), in a new plant at Tampico or in a materials handling system at Nashua. And they meant also that if the expected return on a proposed project *exceeded* Butcher's cost of capital, Butcher's stockholders would be better off— other things equal—with the proposed project than without it. And vice versa.

We can also put the problem in the following way:

1. If we buy something for five cents and sell it for six cents, we're *better* off. If we buy it for six cents and sell it for five cents, we're *worse* off.

2. All the new projects Butcher's Finance Committee has before it (see Table 15.1) have to be paid for with money. That money will be new money. And every dollar of new money Butcher raises—or we might say *buys*—will have a "price tag" attached to it.

3. Butcher wants to be sure that when it "sells" that money (that is, *invests* it), it does so at a profit. Therefore, Butcher must know what the cost of the new money is.

Our task in the rest of this chapter—and in the five succeeding chapters—will be to try to understand, in detail, the cost of capital. This task is not easy. But it will be easier than it would otherwise be *if we bear continually in mind what we are trying to do.*

We are trying to find out what money costs us—so that when we sell it—that is, invest it—we will do so at a profit. We do not want to wake up one day, as did your roommate, to find that we've been paying six cents for money and selling it—that is, investing it—for five. That way lies madness—and debtors' prison.

DETERMINING EXPLICIT COSTS

Let's look in now on Kelley, who had just come to life with a start—and a headache. It was almost five o'clock in the afternoon. He sent his secretary out to get two large containers of black coffee and then took four aspirin. He phoned his wife and said he wouldn't be home for dinner. While he waited for his secretary to come back, he found himself mumbling:

"The cost of capital! Bah! If Martin and I owned this company, we'd sit down at a table and decide, just between us, how much additional return was worth how much additional risk. We might not take all these projects and we might not borrow $6 million, or $8 million. But if we talked for an hour, man to man, we'd be able to decide what to do. He'd have his attitude toward risk and I'd have mine. And if we disagreed we'd compromise. Simple!

"But here we've got all these ridiculous stockholders—20,192 of them—so we have to decide what will happen to the market for our stock when we do this or that, which means we have to estimate our cost of capital—or maybe it's the other way around." Kelley felt himself getting annoyed. Then he mumbled, "Maybe if I looked hard, I could find a job as finance officer in a small privately-held growth company. In electronics."

Kelley knew that the worst was yet to come from Martin. He knew he never should have suggested to Martin that maybe he'd made a mistake, last year, in estimating Butcher's cost of capital. This year, Martin would really make him defend whatever figure he proposed. He could just see himself sitting in the Finance Committee meeting, one week hence, being cross-examined from A to Z and back again—not only by Martin but also by everyone else on the Finance Committee.

Kelley decided that in estimating Butcher's cost of capital for this year, he'd better begin at the very beginning—in order to be sure that he knew what he was doing. He knew that "the beginning" was what he had been taught to think of as the "explicit cost" of each long-term source taken separately. The long-term sources were, apart from depreciation, debt, preferred stock, common stock, and retained earnings.

debt

The explicit cost of long-term debt in percentage terms was, Kelley knew, its yield to maturity calculated on the basis of the amount of money actually received by the company. Thus when Butcher had borrowed $36.8 million in 1966, it had actually received only $36.0 million. The $800,000 difference had been paid to an investment banker as a fee for arranging the loan. But Butcher was obligated, of course, to repay the full $36.8 million. Interest was calculated at 5.5 percent on the outstanding balance. And, therefore, the effective cost to Butcher was almost 6 percent. Table 17.4 shows the calculation—which is nothing more than a rate of return calculation identical in principle to the rate of return calculations we encountered in Chapter 4. The difference is, of course, that in Chapter 4 we were looking at the rate of return to the *lender*. Here we are looking at effective cost to the borrower. The two will be the same only if the borrower receives the full amount he is obliged to repay. But this will rarely, if ever, be the case—because, as mentioned above, raising long-term funds almost always costs money.

preferred stock

Butcher had no preferred stock in its capital structure (see Table 2.1), but Kelley did not wish to exclude the possibility of selling preferred stock now—primarily because he remembered the president's memo of a few weeks ago.

Preferred stock rarely has a maturity date, although it is often redeemable—which means merely that the company can buy it back at some previously specified price, after some previously specified date. Thus

TABLE 17.4

THE BUTCHER COMPANY, EFFECTIVE COST OF $36.8 MILLION, BORROWED IN 1966.

	PAYMENTS ON PRINCIPAL (thousands)	INTEREST ON OUTSTANDING BALANCE AT 5.5% (thousands)	TOTAL ANNUAL PAYMENT (thousands)	PV AT 6% (thousands)
	(1)	(2)	(3)	(4)
1.	$2,300.	$2,024	$4,324	$4,079
2.	2,300.	1,897	4,197	3,735
3.	2,300.	1,771	4,071	3,418
4.	2,300.	1,645	3,945	3,125
5.	2,300.	1,518	3,818	2,853
6.	2,300.	1,392	3,692	2,603
7.	2,300.	1,265	3,565	2,371
8.	2,300.	1,139	3,439	2,158
9.	2,300.	1,012	3,312	1,960
10.	2,300.	886	3,186	1,779
11.	2,300.	759	3,059	1,611
12.	2,300.	633	2,933	1,458
13.	2,300.	506	2,806	1,316
14.	2,300.	380	2,680	1,185
15.	2,300.	253	2,553	1,065
16.	2,300.	127	2,427	955
			TOTAL	$35,671 *

* Amount actually received by Butcher = $36,000,000.

Butcher might sell $8 million of preferred stock to the public or to an insurance company, at 9 percent, redeemable at 109 percent but not earlier than four years from now. This would mean merely that every $100 certificate would receive a $9 dividend every year until that certificate were redeemed. If the certificate were redeemed, the holder would receive $109 for it—plus the $9 dividend due for the year in which redemption occurred.

But the process of selling preferred stock also costs money—and therefore if Butcher did sell an issue of preferred, it would not receive the full amount of the issue. Kelley knew that costs of flotation might be anywhere from one half of 1 percent (if it were sold directly to an insurance company) or 2 or 3 precent if it were sold through an investment banker to the public. Thus if Butcher sold $8 million of preferred to the public with a 9 percent dividend, Butcher would receive only, perhaps, $7.84 million. With a total dividend of $720,000 (= $8 million $\times$ .09), Butcher's effective cost would be 9.18 percent ($=\frac{\$720}{7,840}$) —assuming that the issue remained outstanding forever. And Kelley knew that this was *cost after tax,* not before tax. This was so *because preferred dividends would not be deductible for tax purposes.* This meant that the before tax cost was about twice the after tax cost—which meant, in turn, that a 9 percent preferred was twice as expensive as a 9 percent debt issue.

In order to clarify this latter point in his mind, Kelley drew up Table 17.5. Table 17.5 was based on the assumption that Butcher, next

TABLE 17.5

EFFECT OF 9 PERCENT DEBT AND 9 PERCENT PREFERRED ON EARNINGS FOR COMMON.

	MORE DEBT AT 9% (thousands)	9% PREFERRED STOCK (thousands)
EBIT	$23,497.5	$23,497.5
Interest on present debt	1,897.5	1,897.5
	21,600.0	21,600.0
Interest on new debt	720.0	0
Earnings before taxes	20,880.0	21,600.0
Taxes at 50 percent	10,440.0	10,800.0
Earnings after taxes	10,440.0	10,800.0
Preferred dividend	0	720.0
Earnings for common	$10,440.0	$10.080.0

year, would earn $23,497,500 before interest and taxes, would pay taxes at the rate of 50 percent, and would incur the same dollar cost ($720,000) with new debt as with an issue of preferred (.09 $\times$ $8 million).

Kelley first put down EBIT and then subtracted interest on Butcher's present debt (= $1,897,500). He then subtracted interest on $8 million of new debt at 9 percent (= $720,000). He then calculated and subtracted taxes. This left $10,440,000 to be paid out in common dividends or retained for the benefit of the common stockholders—if Butcher used debt to finance the present projects.

Next, Kelley repeated the calculations, only this time he did not subtract the preferred dividend *before* he calculated taxes—simply because the tax law said he couldn't. So he calculated taxes first and only *then* did he subtract the preferred dividend. The last two lines tell the sad story—a 9 percent preferred issue would really cost the common stockholders $720,000. But a 9 percent debt issue would really cost the common stockholders only $360,000. Thus the after tax cost of a 9 percent debt issue would be only 4.5 percent ($360,000/$8,000,000). But the after tax cost of a 9 percent preferred issue would really be 9 percent (= $720,000/$8,000,000).

common stock

When Kelley, in 1966, two years before, had explained the cost of capital to Butcher's Finance Committee, he had had no trouble at all making them understand what he meant by the cost of debt and the cost of preferred stock. (They had known it already.) But he had lots and lots of trouble making them understand what he meant by the cost of common stock and the cost of retained earnings. He had trouble because nearly every member of the Finance Committee had strongly-held misconceptions about the cost of both. Some thought that the cost of common stock was simply the dividend—which it is *not*. And some thought that retained earnings cost nothing—which they do *not*.

Kelley started by saying that Butcher would certainly not want to sell new common stock and invest the proceeds in new projects unless doing so would improve the position of the present stockholders—or *at least* leave them no worse off.

"Sounds fine," said someone. "We can all agree to that. Now tell us how to do it."

"Butcher's stockholders get two things," said Kelley, "for each share they hold: they get a dividend and they get also an increase in their share of retained earnings. *The sum of those two things is equal to earnings per share.* Suppose Butcher earns $1.90 next year—see Table 7.10—and pays a $1 dividend. Each stockholder will receive $1 in cash for each share he holds. But his investment in the company—his share of retained earnings will have increased by ninety cents. The sum of those two amounts is, of course, exactly equal to EPS of $1.90 a share. EPS is always equal to the dividend we pay plus the change in retained earnings. The dividend can of course be zero—or it can be *higher* than EPS. If it's *higher* than EPS, then retained earnings will decline. Suppose we had a poor year and earned only eighty cents but decided nevertheless to pay a $1 dividend. Retained earnings would go down by twenty cents a share. And the sum of the dividend ($1) and the change in retained earnings would be equal to EPS ($1 — .20 = $.80). In other words, *the reward to Butcher's stockholders, for holding Butcher's stock, is earnings per share.*

"But," said someone, "if we retain earnings, our stockholders will really have received only the dividend."

"Maybe yes, maybe no," said Kelley. "Let's come back to that in a minute."

"Now, as of this moment," said Kelley, "the average expectation of a share of Butcher stock is $1.90—which as we have seen is the mean of our present probability distribution over EPS. That means, of course, that if I now hold a share of Butcher stock, I expect that on the average, year in and year out, I'll be better off by $1.90 a year. In some years, EPS will be more than $1.90 and in others, it will be less, but on the average, I expect EPS to be $1.90. In other words, *if Butcher invested in no new projects,* each Butcher share could expect to earn, on the average, year in and year out, about $1.90."

"You're confusing me," said someone else. "What you're saying will be true only if we pay all our earnings out in dividends. *If we retain earnings, we will invest in new projects.* Otherwise why would we retain earnings? *And if we invest in new projects, our expected EPS next year will be higher than $1.90.*"

"That's right," said Kelley. "But we're going to talk about the effect of growth on the cost of equity later on [Chapter 18]. So right now, in order to make a few basic principles clear, let's just assume *no growth.* In other words, let's just assume that we've been paying all our earnings out in dividends. We've invested in no new projects. All we've done is reinvest depreciation in order to maintain the integrity of our plant and equipment.

"Now, suddenly and unexpectedly," Kelley said, "a new $1 million project appears which promises a DCF rate of return, after taxes, of 12 percent. And we've never heard of debt financing. And if we had heard of it, we wouldn't like it. The question we must answer is thus: Should we sell about 33,333 shares of new common stock at $30 a share —the current price—in order to finance the new project?

"Let me repeat," said Kelley. "We will sell additional stock and invest the proceeds in the new project *if doing so will improve the lot of the present stockholders.* The lot of the present stockholders is an expectation of $1.90 a share. And so, in effect, we are saying that we will sell additional stock and invest the proceeds in the new project *if doing so will raise expected EPS above $1.90.* The quick way to find out whether EPS will go up, if we finance the new project by selling new common stock, is to divide expected EPS *without* the new project (= $1.90) by the price at which we would sell the new shares minus any cost of flotation. Our stock is now selling at $30. Let's suppose that cost of flotation would be $2 a share. We would, thus, receive $28 a share for each share we sold.

"Now let's divide $1.90 by $28, thus," said Kelley, putting on the blackboard:

$$\frac{\$1.90}{\$28.00} = .068$$

"That gives us 6.8 percent. So that," said Kelley, "*is our cost of common stock*—on the assumptions we described above. Now, if we finance a new project which is expected to yield more than 6.8 percent with common stock costing 6.8 percent, *EPS will go up*."

"Very neat," said someone.

"And," said Kelley, "if we finance a new project expected to yield *less* than 6.8 percent with common stock costing 6.8 percent EPS will go *down*."

"All you're saying," said someone, "is that each of our present stockholders can now expect to earn, on the average, year in and year out, about $1.90 a share. If we sell one new share—or ten or 10,000—the proceeds must be invested so as to earn at least $1.90 for each new share we sell. If the proceeds are invested to earn *less* than $1.90 a share, our *present* stockholders *will be worse off*. They will be worse off because their expected EPS will fall below $1.90. They will fall below $1.90 because they will be a weighted average of old earnings of $1.90 a share *and* new earnings of *less* than $1.90 a share. The weighted average *must* therefore be *less* than $1.90."

"Right," said Kelley.

"And therefore if we get $28 net for each new share we sell, that $28 must earn $1.90 in order to maintain the present position of our present stockholders."

"Right," said Kelley.

"That is, those $28 must earn at the rate of 6.8 percent, as you indicated." He pointed to the figures on the board:

$$\frac{\$1.90}{\$28.00} = .068.$$

"Right again," said Kelley.

"In other words, if we sell a new share—or ten or 10,000—we must invest the proceeds to yield 6.8 percent—or present EPS will fall. Thus, 6.8 percent can be regarded as our *cost of money raised by selling common stock*."

"Given the assumptions we've made," said Kelley, "now let's go back to our present problem."

Kelley proceeded to explain that in order to raise $36.8 million, Butcher would have to sell 1,314,285 new shares at $28 a share (1,314,285 shares $\times$ $28 = $36.8 million). This would bring the total number of shares outstanding up to 3,501,785. If the $36.8 million earned at the rate of 6 percent (after taxes), $2,208,000 would be added to earnings after taxes. Total earnings would thus be:

Earnings without any new projects (after taxes)	$4,156,250
Earnings on new projects	2,208,000
TOTAL	$6,364,250

Earnings per share would be $1.82, thus:

$$\frac{\text{Total earnings}}{\text{New number of shares}} = \frac{\$6,364,250}{3,501,785} = \$1.82 \text{ per share}$$

"But," Kelley said, "the present stockholders *without* any new projects are earning $1.90 a share. And they would thus be worse off—not merely because earnings per share had gone down but also because, as a result, the price of the stock would go down. And," he added, "this company is owned by its stockholders."

"All right," said Martin, "but total earnings have gone up. I can't see why that's bad."

"It's bad," said Kelley. "It's bad because I'm a stockholder in this company. I own 280 shares and I'd be unhappy. I want earnings per share to go up—and certainly not down. If you sold stock now at $28 a share, and invested the proceeds in assets yielding only 6 percent, you'd simply be taking some of my present earnings and giving them to the new stockholders."

Kelley said that on each of his 280 shares he could expect to earn, on the average, $1.90 a share given the rate of return Butcher expected to earn on its present assets. But if Butcher sold 1,314,285 shares at $28 a share and invested the proceeds in projects yielding 6 percent, the new shares would be contributing only $1.68 per share to earnings, thus:

$$\frac{\$36.8 \times .06}{\text{Number of new shares}} = \frac{\$2,208,000}{1,314,285} = \$1.68$$

And earnings for all the stockholders *together* would therefore be less than $1.90. New earnings would be, that is, a weighted average of $1.90 and $1.68, thus:

$$\$1.90 \times 2,187.5 = \$4,156.2$$
$$\$1.60 \times 1,314.0 = 2,207.5$$
$$\overline{3,501.5 \qquad 6,363.7}$$

$$\text{Combined EPS} = \frac{\$6,363.7}{3,501.5} = \$1.82$$

"Q.E.D.," said Kelley. "I'd be giving some of my earnings to the new stockholders. That's dilution. I'm worse off than I was before. I'd like to be at least as well off. And, of course, if EPS goes down, the price of our stock will go down, too."

retained earnings

"Now," said Kelley, "let's suppose we have to decide the following question: Should we retain $1 million of earnings in order to finance a new 12 percent project? In other words, instead of planning, this year, to pay all our earnings out in dividends, we would plan to keep $1 million to pay for the new project. *Should we do so?*"

"Of course we should," said someone. "Retained earnings don't cost us anything."

"What do you mean by 'us'?" asked Kelley.

"Us—the company."

"Us is the stockholders," said Kelley, "Suppose," he said, "we do earn $1.90 next year. That's $532 on my 280 shares [280 × $1.90 = $532]. Those $532—each and everyone of them—belong to *me, not* to the company and *not* to the management and *not* to the Board of Directors and *not* to the Finance Committee—but to me. So suppose we paid a $1.00 dividend. I would get $280. But you would have kept $252 of *my* money. And you would have kept it—I might add—without my permission."

"All right," said a banker who had been a member of Butcher's Finance Committee for four years. "It's your money. I'll grant you that. But I don't see why it has to earn 6.8 percent. We can always increase *your* earnings per share by investing retained earnings in any project with a yield higher than zero. If we invested $10 million of retained earnings to yield, say 3 percent after taxes, we'd increase earnings by $300,000 or by about fourteen cents a share. Total expected EPS would then be $2.04 a share—instead of $1.90. What's the matter with that?"

"It makes the company—and I might add, the management—look good to unsophisticated investors—but it's a fraud on the stockholders."

"So?" said the banker, good humoredly.

"Yes," said Kelley. "I'd do better if you paid me my $252 in dividends. Look, suppose you paid me the $252. What could I do with it—if I chose to invest it? I could put it in a savings bank, or I could buy a government bond or I could buy stock in a company like this company or . . ."

"You could buy more stock in Butcher," said Martin.

"Right," said Kelley. "Exactly. Now, suppose I took the $252 and bought Butcher at $30 a share. I'd get exactly 8.4 shares. What would my return be? It would be what those shares could be expected to earn—which would be 8.4 times $1.90 a share or, in total, $15.96 divided by the cost of those shares, $252. $15.96 divided by $252 is exactly 6.3 percent. And Ea/P—that is, expected earnings, without any new projects, divided by the *current* price of the stock is also 6.3 percent [$1.90/30 = .063]. Now, if I can invest my $252 to obtain a return of 6.3 percent, what right does the company have to invest it at less than 6.3 percent?"

"That," said Martin, "is a rhetorical question."

"Rhetorical or not," said the banker, "Kelley's overlooked taxes. If we paid him $252 in dividends, he'd have to pay at least 25 percent, or $63, in taxes. He'd be able to buy only 6.3 shares—not, as he says, 8.4 shares. He would then earn 6.3 times $1.90—not 8.4 times $1.90. His total additional earnings would, thus, be $11.61—not $15.96. Now $11.61 divided by $252 is about 4.6 percent—not 6.3 percent. And so it seems to me that Kelley's wrong. If we, the company, invested Kelley's $252 at a return of 4.6 percent, he, Kelley, would be no worse off."

"Right," said Kelley, "that's why you shouldn't pay it out in dividends."

"You just said we should."

"I was just trying to make clear that the cost of retained earnings is not zero. And I'm glad to see, you've agreed to that. What we *should* do, if we can't invest retained earnings at 6.3 percent, is *buy back Butcher's stock in the market*—that is, we should invest those retained earnings in our own stock. My return on that investment would be 6.3 percent [= $1.90/$30].

"Suppose," Kelley said, "we had $1 million in retained earnings, sitting in the cash account, that we could not invest at 6.3 percent. And suppose therefore that we used it to buy 33,333 shares of Butcher in the open market. This would reduce the number of outstanding shares to 2,154,167 [= 2,187,500-33,333]. But our earnings after tax would, of course, remain the same—$4,156,250. What would happen to earnings per share? They would go up—because the number of shares had been reduced. Earnings per share would be, thus," said Kelley, putting another equation on the board:

$$\frac{\$4,156,250}{2,154,167} = \$1.93$$

"Total additional earnings of about $63,333 [= 33,333 shares $\times$ $1.90] would have thus accrued to the remaining stockholders against an investment of $1 million. This represents a return of almost exactly 6.3 percent. In short, the remaining stockholders have invested $1 million—it's *their* money, remember—and by doing so, they have obtained a return of almost exactly 6.3 percent—which is equal to Ea/P which equals $1.90 divided by $30. Q.E.D.," said Kelley again.

"Sounds pretty theoretical to me," said someone. "First, we'd have brokerage charges on the shares we bought. So, with $1 million we would not be able to buy 33,333 shares."

"That's a detail," said Martin. "It means only that the return is reduced—slightly below 6.3 percent."

"Okay," the someone said, "but if we went into the market and bought 33,333 shares, the price would probably go up."

"Right," said Kelley. "And, if it did, the cost of retained earnings would have been reduced."

"Just a minute," said the banker again. "Now I'm really confused. I think I understood, *in principle,* what you were saying when you talked about the cost of common stock and the cost of retained earnings. *They're opportunity costs.* At least the cost of retained earnings is. I'm not sure about common stock. That means essentially that if the stockholders could invest whatever cash they receive from us at 10 percent, we ought not to invest it for them at 9 percent."

"Right," said Kelley.

"But it seems to me," said the banker, "that the ratio Ea/Pa is the cost of common stock only if no earnings are retained—*because if earnings are retained, and invested profitably, Ea will grow.* To me, that means that the ratio Ea/Pa *would understate our cost of equity.* And if we retain no earnings why should we worry about their cost?"

"That's the growth problem again," said Kelley. "It all depends on how we define *Ea.* We'll come back to that later."

"All right," said the banker. "But don't forget. You've aroused my curiousity."

The foregoing incident took place in 1966 when Butcher's stock was selling at $30 and its expected EPS was $1.90. Butcher's stock is now (early 1968) selling at $51 and expected EPS is now $2.55.

NOTES PAYABLE AND OTHER CURRENT LIABILITIES

Kelley then pointed out that when we talk about long-term capital we mean *all* long-term capital, by whatever means obtained, and regardless of whether it is carried as a current or long-term liability (or equity). In many cases, for example, notes payable, although due on demand or within a year, are regularly renewed and hence provide "permanent" financing. In addition, virtually every firm always has some minimum volume of accounts (including taxes) due and payable. These also provide "permanent" financing and are, therefore, part of the firm's permanent "capital." (If these two types of financing were *not* available, the firm would need more long-term funds, as we saw in Chapters 15 and 16.) Notes payable always have an explicit cost (the interest rate). As we saw in Chapter 11, accounts payable have an explicit cost only if they are not paid on time.

But the amount of financing provided by accounts payable and taxes may be left out of account *provided* that doing so does not significantly change the ratio of total debt to total capital.

COST OF A MIXTURE

Now that we've described the *separate* cost of each type of long-term money, we must ask ourselves how to calculate the cost of *a mixture* of the various types—assuming costs for each type, as above. We don't use just common stock or just retained earnings or just debt. Normally, we use a *mixture* of different types of funds to finance new projects. But before we discuss the method of calculating the cost of a *mixture,* we'd better dispose of the growth problem. In this chapter, we assumed that Butcher was a "no-growth" company—which of course, it is not.

CONCLUSION

In the first part of this chapter we reached the conclusion that *closely-held companies*—most of which are small—do not really have a cost of capital problem. Such companies should not, of course, invest money to yield less than the explicit cost of that money. But whether such companies should invest or not in some proposed new project is a matter for the individual stockholders to decide on the basis of their own attitudes toward risk and return. And if the individual stockholders cannot agree they will have to compromise—as did Clay Company stockholders in Chapter 2.

In the second part of the chapter we turned our attention to *publicly-held companies.* We illustrated the method of calculating the separate cost of each type of long term money—debt, preferred stock and in a simplified, "no-growth" situation, the cost of equity— both common stock and retained earnings.

PROBLEMS

1. You buy a car for $2,250. In order to pay for it, you take $1,250 out of a savings account which pays interest at 5 percent a year and borrow $1,000 from a bank. The bank adds on 8 percent of the loan (= $80) plus a $20 fee—making the total amount of the note $1,100. You are to repay this amount in twelve equal monthly installments.

   You are in a 25 percent tax bracket—which means that your last $2,000 of taxable income is taxed at the rate of 25 percent. The interest you pay the bank is, by the way, tax deductible—which means that you may deduct it from your gross income before you calculate your tax.

   Calculate the after tax cost of each of the two types of capital you have invested in the car.

2. Calculate the weighted average cost after taxes of the two types of capital you have invested in the car.

3. When Kelley calculated Butcher's present cost of debt, he was asleep at the switch. He forgot that Butcher would have to pay legal fees of about $85,000 and a "finder's fee" of about one half of 1 percent of the total amount of the loan. A "finder's fee" is a fee paid to a person who "finds" a loan. In this case, the "finder" would be an investment banker. Both the legal fee and the finder's fee would be current expenses and would be deductible from current income. Butcher's tax rate is 50 percent.

   Assume that Butcher borrows $6 million for ten years, principal to be repaid in equal annual installments of $600,000 each. Interest would be calculated at 8.5 percent on the outstanding balance of the loan, and would also be payable annually. Estimate Butcher's approximate after tax cost of debt, taking account of both the legal fee and the finder's fee.

4. Assume that, instead of selling debt, as in problem 3, Butcher sells

$6 million worth of a 9 percent "callable" preferred—also to a life insurance company. Legal costs would be $80,000 and Butcher, again, would have to pay a one half of 1 percent finder's fee.

"Callable" simply means that after the issue has been outstanding for some specified period—in this case, five years—Butcher would be free to redeem (call) the issue. If it did decide to call the issue, Butcher would simply write a letter to the insurance company saying that, after such and such a date, Butcher would cease paying dividends on the preferred but "would stand ready on that date to redeem the issue, at its offices, at 109 percent of par—or $1,090 for each $1,000 certificate. On the specified day, the insurance company would deliver $6 million worth of preferred stock certificates to Butcher. And Butcher would hand over to the insurance company (actually to its treasurer) a certified check for $6,540,000.

Butcher "calls" the issue exactly five years, to the day, after it was sold. Calculate Butcher's cost of preferred stock for the five year life of the issue. (A cost calculated in this way is called "a cost to first call date.")

5. Why do you suppose a company would wish to be free to "call" a debt issue or an issue of preferred stock?

**APPENDIX
17.A**

LEASING

Your roommate, who just never stops thinking even when he's asleep, wakes you up one morning, just before dawn, and says, "What's that Alfa of yours worth?"

You brush him away and say, "Go away."

He says, "Come on, wake up. Try to be cooperative."

You open one eye and say, "The latest quote in the Chicago market is $2,850. Now go away."

He says, "Okay. I'll give you $2,850 for it—cash—and then lease it back to you for eighteen months for $190 a month."

He reaches into his wallet and extracts two $1,000 bills, eight $100 bills and one $50 bill.

Both your eyes are open now—and they're bulging.

You say, "Where'd you get all that money?"

He says, "If I told you, you'd be an accomplice after the fact."

He pushes a form under your nose and says, "Sign here." He dips his quill pen into the inkwell (your inkwell—he's conducting an economy drive) and hands it to you.

You say, "Whoa! Wait a minute! Who pays for gas and oil?"

He says, "You do."

You say, "Who pays for insurance?"

He says, "You do."

You say, "What happens at the end of eighteen months?"

He says, "You can buy the car back for $285—if you want to."

You look at the money. There are lots of things you could do with $2,850. You could, for example, buy another 570 shares of Roan Selection Trust.

Do you sign or don't you?

What Is Leasing?

What is leasing? In what sense is it a source of financing? What is the difference between buying and leasing? And how does one decide whether to buy or lease?

What is leasing? Everyone, at one time or another, has rented or will rent something—an apartment, a car, a motel room, a tuxedo. Instead of buying the object itself, you buy the right to use it for some specified period of time.

What's the difference? What are the differences between these two ways of acquiring the right to use an asset?

From the point of view of the financial officer, leasing differs from buying in three primary ways—

First, if a company leases an asset—instead of buying it—the asset so leased will *not* be shown on the company's balance sheet. It will not be shown on the company's balance sheet because the company does not own the asset. It owns merely the right to use it.

Second, because the asset is not shown on the company's balance sheet, the corresponding liability is not shown either. The corresponding liability is the lease—that is, the agreement to make a series of specified payments over a specified period of time. The fact that the liability represented by the lease is not shown on the lessee's balance sheet means that the lessee's debt to equity ratio will appear to be less than it actually is.

Finally, when a company leases an asset, the method of financing the asset is "ready-made"—it is intrinsic in the lease itself. When a company *buys* an asset, it must itself provide financing in one way or another—either out of its own funds or by borrowing. But in principle neither method of financing should be more expensive than the other. Why would anyone lease an asset if buying it were cheaper? And why would anyone buy it if leasing it were cheaper?

In short, buying and leasing are essentially the same. Why then should anyone prefer leasing to buying (or, for that matter, buying to leasing)?

Before answering this question let's try to bring out something more clearly, the essential similarity of buying and leasing, and in order to do so, let's go back briefly to Ex-Cello's lathe (see Chapter 7). Suppose, after having thought the matter over and after having discussed it with Ex-Cello's regional sales manager, the Ex-Cello salesman, Roberts, calls Hastings and says, "We've decided to reduce that lathe to $8,400, just for you—provided you buy at least six of them."

"Oh," said Hastings, "very interesting. But the budget's already been approved for the next six months. No money left."

"We'll lease them to you," said Roberts. "I'll send you the details." The next day, Hastings receives from Roberts the information contained in the first two columns of Table 17.6.

In a covering letter Ex-Cello's controller explains that the rental on each lathe would be $1,780 for six years plus $1,360 for the seventh year. The lease agreement would contain a clause giving

TABLE 17.6

SCHEDULE OF LEASING PAYMENTS FROM BUTCHER TO EX-CELLO

YEAR	RENTAL	DISCOUNT FACTORS AT 11%	PRESENT VALUE
(1)	(2)	(3)	(4)
1	$1,780	.901	$1,604
2	1,780	.817	1,454
3	1,780	.731	1,301
4	1,780	.659	1,173
5	1,780	.593	1,056
6	1,780	.535	952
7	1,360 * ⎱ 420 † ⎰	.482	858
			$8,398

* $1,780 less 5 percent of $8,400 (=$420).
† Estimated salvage.

Butcher an option to buy the lathes at the end of the seventh year for $400. Thus if Butcher exercised this option, Ex-Cello would receive $1,780 in the seventh year also. (If Butcher did not buy the lathes at the end of the seventh year, Ex-Cello would sell them in the secondhand market—and would expect to obtain $420 for each one.) Therefore, whether or not Butcher exercised the option, Ex-Cello would expect to receive $1,780 in the seventh year—or shortly after the end of the seventh year—for each lathe.

Ex-Cello's controller pointed out, in his letter, that the rental paid by Butcher to Ex-Cello would be regarded by the Internal Revenue Service as an expense and would therefore be fully tax deductible to Butcher. (Butcher would not, of course, be able to deduct depreciation on the lathe because the lathe would be owned by Ex-Cello.)

Ex-Cello's controller pointed out that the lease liability "would not show" on Butcher's balance sheet—simply because "accepted accounting procedures" allowed liabilities represented by leases *not* to be shown.

Hastings turns the information over to Martin who, in turn, passes it on to Kelley. Kelley calculates the rate of return (to Ex-Cello) on the lease and finds that it is 11 percent—as shown in Table 17.6. Kelley assumed, in making his calculations, that one way or another, Ex-Cello would sell the lathe, at the end of the seventh year for $420.

After having done this calculation, Kelley called a young friend of his—a loan officer—at First National City in order to find out, just for fun, what the bank would charge to lend Butcher money to buy the lathes. The loan officer said that on a seven-year loan of this type, the bank would have to earn 11 percent. He proposed a schedule of payments as shown in Table 17.7. (Look at these payments closely. They are identical to the proposed rental payments shown in Table 17.6!)

TABLE 17.7

SCHEDULE OF PAYMENTS FOR BUYING LATHE

YEAR	PAYMENT
1	$1,780
2	1,780
3	1,780
4	1,780
5	1,780
6	1,780
7	1,780

Then the loan officer said, "Tell me, Kelley. Why would Butcher be interested in an expensive deal like this?"

"We wouldn't," said Kelley. "I'm just amusing myself." He hung up.

This illustration should make clear that leasing is nothing more than debt financing in a flimsy disguise because:

1. In both cases, Butcher is borrowing money at 11 percent to buy the lathes—in one case from the manufacturer (it could, just as well, have been a company specializing in leasing) and, in the other, from a bank.

2. In both cases, all payments made either to Ex-Cello or to the bank would be fully tax deductible—in the first case, as rent, and in the second, as depreciation plus interest. And both sets of deductions would be equal in amount. The rental payments, which would be fully deductible, would be equal to the cost of the lathe less salvage plus compound interest at 11 percent. Under the loan, Butcher would deduct, as depreciation, the full cost of the lathe, less salvage, plus compound interest at 11 percent.

In short, the two arrangements would differ in name only.

Why Lease?

Why then should anyone lease an asset instead of buying it—or, for that matter, buy it instead of leasing it? The reasons are several:

First, lots of assets cannot be bought. They must be leased. Until just recently, for example, IBM would not sell computers; it would only lease them. This was true also of many other producers of electronic equipment.

Second, sometimes a lessor will be able to obtain funds on more favorable terms than the lessee. If in the case described above, Ex-Cello had used a rate less than 10 percent to calculate the annual rental on the lathe, Butcher would have found leasing the lathe cheaper than buying it on the installment plan.

Third, leasing will always finance the full cost of the asset. Borrowing may not—and this fact will weigh heavily with companies which do not have access to unlimited funds. Conceivably, when Kelley called the bank to explore the possibility of an installment purchase, the loan officer might have said: "We'll lend you 80 percent of cost—but not a penny more."

Cautions for Consideration

A word of advice: you should always calculate the implicit rate of return in any lease and you should always compare that rate with the cost of alternative sources of funds—if any.

Go back now to your roommate and his most recent proposal.

First, calculate the rate of return he would earn on the lease if you signed it—both before and after taxes. (Your roommate is in a 40 percent tax bracket.) You know that you could borrow about 60 percent of the value of your car, at 1 percent a month on the outstanding balance. You would, in either case, invest the proceeds in Roan common stock at $5 a share with an expected return of 30 percent.

Would you sign the lease or would you borrow from the bank?

Second, you know that if you do not sell your Alfa to him, your roommate will invest the $2,850 in small loans which will return about 12 percent before taxes. Calculate a series of rental payments, over an 18 month period, such that your roommate would be indifferent between, on the one hand, buying your car and leasing it back to you, and, on the other, investing in small loans returning, on the average, 12 percent before taxes.

18

THE COST
OF
LONG-TERM
CAPITAL
II
growth

Kelley now turned to the growth problem. First he calculated the cost of common stock and the cost of retained earnings based on Butcher's *presently* expected EPS (= $2.55) and the *current* price of Butcher's stock (= $51). If Butcher sold new common stock at the current price, it would realize about $49 after cost of flotation. Thus, its cost of new common stock would be:

$$\frac{E_a}{P_a} = \frac{\$2.55}{49.00} = .052$$

or 5.2 percent. And the cost of retained earnings would be:

$$\frac{E_a}{P} = \frac{\$2.55}{\$51.00} = .05$$

or 5 percent. Both figures seemed very low.

Next, Kelley drew up a table of the price-earnings ratios of all the larger companies in the tool industry. He used, for this purpose, current prices and *expected* earnings for next year as given by the *Value Line Investment Survey* (see Table 18.1). He then converted these price-

TABLE 18.1

PRICE-EARNINGS AND EARNINGS-PRICE RATIOS AS OF DECEMBER, 1968

COMPANY	EXPECTED EARNINGS (1969)	PRICE (DECEMBER 1968)	PRICE/ EXPECTED EARNINGS	EXPECTED EARNINGS */ PRICE
(1)	(2)	(3)	(4)	(5)
Starlett, L. S.	$2.10	$22	10.5	.095
Monarch Machine	4.00	45	11.3	.089
Norton Company	3.00	40	13.3	.075
Nicholson File	2.50	40	16.0	.063
Acme-Cleveland	2.30	30	13.0	.077
Cincinnati Milling	4.50	60	13.3	.075
Stanley Works	3.40	50	14.7	.068
Warner & Swasey	3.00	50	16.7	.060
Carbonundum Company	4.00	50	12.5	.080
Browne & Sharpe	1.40	25	17.9	.056
Black and Decker	2.40	70	29.2	.034
Kearney & Trecker	1.50	14	9.3	.107
Giddings & Lewis	1.35	30	22.2	.045
Butcher Company	2.55	51	20.0	.050

* Figure obtained by dividing the number 1 by the price-earnings ratio.

earnings ratios into earnings-price ratios—by taking the reciprocal of each. Kelley realized, of course, that the *Value Line* estimates were based on expected earnings *for next year*—not on the mean of a probability distribution.

Nevertheless, the figures strongly suggested that Butcher was selling at a very high price relative to its earnings—compared with most other tool manufacturers. (VALUE LINE did not provide data on Butcher. Kelley had added it himself.)

"Why such a high price-earnings ratio?" Kelley asked himself. One thing was obvious—namely, that the investing public was *not* using the same expected earnings figure, $2.55 that Kelley was using. If they were, Butcher's stock would *not* be selling at $51 a share. If the investing public believed, as Kelley did, that on the average, good years and bad, Butcher would earn $2.55, Butcher's stock might be selling at $20 to $25 a share—but certainly not at $51. With expected earnings of $2.55, Butcher offered an earnings yield of 5 percent at a price of $51 a share —half of which was paid out in dividends and half, reinvested. But why should anyone in his right mind buy Butcher to yield 5 percent, when he could buy riskless government bonds to yield more than 7 percent?

"Well," Kelley said to himself," there are two possibilities. Maybe they believe our expected earnings of $4.18 for this year (see Table 2.3) indicate that our earnings will be between $4.00 and $5.00, year in and year out—which would give them an earnings yield of 8 to 10 percent and a dividend yield of 4 to 5 percent.

"But," he said, "that's absurd. Maybe the average individual investor is a fool, but the mutual funds know what they're doing." Twelve funds owned Butcher stock and one had bought 20,000 shares at $49 just two weeks ago. "And the funds know that our earnings are cyclical. They know that this year has been a very good year and that next year will probably be a very good year. But they know perfectly well that with our present assets and efficiency, our earnings could fall to $1.00 a share —if a recession came along. And they know that the probability of a recession is not zero."

And so, Kelley decided, the answer was obvious. The funds and the other sophisticated investors believe that if they bought the stock now they would be buying not merely $2.55 a share *but also a chance to reinvest retained earnings at high rates of return.* This would mean that Butcher's earnings and dividends would grow. Now then, Kelley asked himself, *what does this fact mean for our current cost of capital?*

Kelley knew that the classic examples of this problem were companies like IBM and Xerox, whose earnings and dividends had grown rapidly in the past. Such companies will usually find their stock selling at very high prices *relative to their current EPS*—simply because investors generally will expect growth to continue. In late 1968, for example, IBM was selling at 43 times earnings expected for 1969 and Xerox at 48 times. IBM was selling at $355 a share and its expected EPS for the next twelve months was about $8.20—an earnings yield of slightly more than 2 percent. Xerox was selling at $102 and its expected EPS was about $2.10. Table 18.2 gives earnings per share, and dividends per share, 1954-1968, for IBM and Xerox.

Investors who bought IBM and Xerox in late 1968 expect that over time IBM's and Xerox's EPS will continue to grow—*and without any change in the capital structure mix.* They expect, that is, that both IBM and Xerox will be able to invest their present proportions of debt

TABLE 18.2

IBM AND XEROX, EARNINGS AND DIVIDENDS PER SHARE, 1954-1968

YEAR	IBM		XEROX	
	EPS	DPS	EPS	DPS
(1)	(2)	(3)	(4)	(5)
1954	$ .62	$ .17	$ .02	*
1955	.76	.17	.03	*
1956	.91	.21	.03	$.01
1957	1.05	.24	.03	.01
1958	1.45	.29	.03	.01
1959	1.67	.35	.04	.01
1960	1.94	.52	.04	.02
1961	2.39	.60	.09	.02
1962	2.85	.78	.24	.05
1963	3.39	1.11	.38	.08
1964	4.00	1.54	.63	.14
1965	4.40	1.95	.93	.20
1966	4.71	2.10	1.24	.31
1967	5.81	2.17	1.48	.40
1968	7.71	2.60	1.73	.50
1969	8.21	3.60	2.07	.57
Average Annual Compound Growth Rate	19%	23%	36%	31% *

* Xerox did not pay dividends prior to 1956.

and equity in a "sufficient" number of "high-return" projects. And, as Kelley noted, Butcher now found itself in something of this same position.

"Well," Kelley asked himself again, "what does it all mean for our current cost of capital?"

RETAINED EARNINGS

In order to clarify the problem in his own mind, Kelley began mumbling to himself, as follows, about Company X—one of his favorite nonexistent companies:

"Suppose, for example," he said, "that Company X is earning $5 a share, all of which is paid out in dividends. Company X's stock is selling at $50 a share. Company X has no plans to grow and hence it merely reinvests depreciation in order to maintain the integrity of its plant and equipment. Company X's cost of equity is thus 10 percent [= $5/$50]. This figure is, of course, really meaningless because Company X is happy with its present lot and has no wish to expand—and therefore it has no need to raise new capital.

"But suppose one day," Kelley imagined, "suddenly and unexpectedly, a new project fell from the sky onto the President's desk. It promised to raise EPS next year by 7 percent—to $5.35. Company X would pay for this project by retaining half of *this* year's earnings, or $2.50 a share. Suppose also that Company X, having had its eyes opened by the first project, now anticipates that a similar new project will come along at the beginning of *each* of the four subsequent years. Each of these projects will also raise EPS by 7 percent. And Company X will finance each of *them* by retaining half its earnings." These expectations Kelly summarized in Table 18.3, which shows simply that EPS and DPS, after the first year, are expected to grow at the rate of 7 percent a year—until the sixth year when growth will stop and all earnings will once again be paid out in dividends. We should note that by retaining half of earnings in the first year, Company X has reduced its dividend yield from 10 percent ($5/$50) to 5 percent (= $2.50/$50).

Given these facts and these expectations, what now is Company X's *current* cost of common stock and retained earnings? "In order to answer this question," Kelley said to himself, "let's ask another question: What will investors in Company X now expect to receive over the next five years—and thereafter—given the expectations set forth in Table 18.3 —if everything else remains unchanged? They will expect to receive, as dividends, the amounts listed in Table 18.3. But they will *also* expect to receive at the beginning of the sixth year, *a substantial capital gain.*

Where will this capital gain come from and how much will it be? At the end of the fifth year, Company X's expected earnings will have risen to $7.01—as a result of the five successive new projects undertaken in years 1-5. Company X's stockholders can therefore expect to receive, during the sixth year and thereafter, a dividend of $7.01 a share. But if other things remain the same, Company X will continue to sell on "a 10 percent basis" as it does now. Therefore the price of Company X's stock will be $70.10 (= $7.10/.10).

Two things have happened:

1. Company X's earnings have grown at a compound rate of 7 percent a year to $7.01.
2. And the price of Company X's stock, reflecting the growth in

earnings, has also grown at a compound rate of 7 percent a year [$70.10 = $50 \times (1.07)^5$].

TABLE 18.3

COMPANY X
EXPECTED EARNINGS, RETAINED EARNINGS AND DIVIDENDS

YEAR	EXPECTED * EPS	EXPECTED RETENTIONS PER SHARE	EXPECTED † DPS
(1)	(2)	(3)	(4)
1	$5.00	$2.50	$2.50
2	5.35	2.675	2.675
3	5.72	2.86	2.86
4	6.12	3.06	3.06
5	6.55	3.275	3.275
6	7.01	——	7.01

* Equals current EPS (= $5.00) multiplied by 7 percent growth factors.
† Dividends per share = 50 percent of EPS.

Now then, with these expectations, we can use present value methods to calculate the return a stockholder in Company X will earn on the present price of the stock ($50) —*provided the foregoing expectations are fulfilled.* This is done in Table 18.4. This table tells us that when expected dividends and capital gains are discounted *at 12 percent* they have a present value exactly equal to the present price of the stock.

Now then, what had Kelley done? And what does the foregoing result really mean?

First, Company X—previously stagnant—suddenly sees five new projects lying ahead of it. Each of these projects will raise EPS, DPS and retained earnings by seven percent compounded annually.

Second, looking five years ahead, Company X's stockholders can now expect to receive a capital gain at the end of the fifth year—if they choose, at that time, to sell their stock. If they choose *not* to sell, they would receive a 10 percent dividend (= $7.10/71.10) from that time on.

Third, these two things together mean that Company X's stockholders looking five years ahead, can expect to receive a return—consisting of dividends and capital gain—of 12 percent, given the present price ($50) of the stock.

All this, together, means that if Company X's stockholders do nothing but sit back and relax, they will be presented with opportunities to

TABLE 18.4

COMPANY X, PRESENT VALUE AT 12 PERCENT OF EXPECTED DIVIDENDS PLUS EXPECTED PRICE.

END OF YEAR	EXPECTED DIVIDEND	EXPECTED PRICE	DISCOUNT FACTORS AT 12%	PRESENT VALUE
(1)	(2)	(3)	(4)	(5)
1	$2.50	——	.893	$ 2.23
2	2.675	——	.797	2.13
3	2.86	——	.712	2.04
4	3.06	——	.636	1.95
5	3.275	$70.10	.567	1.86
				39.75 *
				$49.96 †

* Present value of $70.10 to be received five years hence.
† Due to rounding not exactly equal to $50.

invest in five successive projects which will have the effect of raising their return from an expected 10 percent to an expected 12 percent over the next five years.

But if they can now expect to earn 12 percent, *they ought not to dilute this expected return by investing additional equity*—either retained earnings or the proceeds of the sale of a new issue of common stock —*to return less than 12 percent to that equity*. If they sell additional common stock now and invest the proceeds in projects which will return *less* than 12 percent to the equity invested in those projects, the expected return to the common stockholders will be reduced below 12 percent, as we saw in Chapter 17. *It will be a weighted average of 12 percent and something less than 12 percent*. And correspondingly with retained earnings—if they cannot be invested in projects to yield 12 percent, they should be used to buy back the company's stock.

Twelve percent is thus Company X's current cost of equity. It takes account of both Company X's *current EPS and* those opportunities which *are now visible* one, two, three, four and five years ahead.

We should *note carefully* one aspect of the foregoing result: 12 percent is the sum of the current dividend yield plus the growth rate of the dividend! The current dividend yield is:

$$\frac{DPS}{P} = \frac{\$2.50}{50.00} = .05 \text{ or } 5 \text{ percent.}$$

The growth rate of the dividend is 7 percent. And 5 percent plus 7 percent is 12 percent!

In short, we can obtain an estimate of the cost of equity simply by dividing the current dividend (D) by the current price (P) and adding the rate at which the dividend is expected to grow, (g) thus:

$$\text{Cost of equity} = \frac{D}{P} + g$$

This is a very useful little formula—provided g can be estimated with a reasonable degree of confidence—and assuming—as we shall see in Chapters 20 to 22—that if the company has debt in its capital structure, *its debt-equity ratio is not changing.*

How does all this apply to us—to Butcher? Kelley asked himself—after he had stopped muttering. Let's take it slowly he said—and let's keep it simple.

Let us suppose that Butcher has available to it, this year, *one* long-term project, at a cost of $9,052,000 which promises a return, after taxes, of 6 percent. Butcher's apparent cost of common stock as Kelley showed us in the opening lines of this chapter is:

$$\frac{\$2.55}{\$49} = .052$$

or 5.2 percent—which is slightly less than the 6 percent expected return on the project. Butcher decides therefore to finance the purchase of the new assets by using depreciation of $1,720,000 and selling 149,633 shares of stock at $49, net to the company, after fees, etc., of $2 a share.

With this new project Butcher's expected earnings per share will rise from $2.55 to $2.62, thus:

Prior Expected Earnings	=	$5,578,125.
Expected Earnings		
New Project		
(= .06 × $9,052,000)		543,120.
	TOTAL	$6,121,245.

$$\frac{\$6,121,245}{2,187,500 + 149,633} = \$2.62$$

The old stockholders will now appear to be better off than they would have been had the new shares not been sold and the project not undertaken. And, in fact, given the rise in expected EPS, the price of Butcher's stock may rise slightly also—perhaps to $52 to maintain a price-earnings ratio of about 20.

But now suppose that, at the beginning of the next six month period, Butcher's Director of Research stumbles onto a project which will also require $9,052,000—but which would be expected to yield 40 percent! Let us suppose, further, that Butcher decides to finance this project by using $1720 thousand of depreciation and selling 146,640 shares of common stock at $50 net, again after fees, etc., of $2. Expected EPS will now rise from $2.62 to $3.92, thus:

Prior Expected Earnings	=	$6,121,245.
Expected Earnings, New Project		
(= .40 × $9,052,000)	=	3,620,800.
TOTAL		$9,742,045.

$$\frac{\$9,742,045}{2,337,133 + 146,640} = \$3.92$$

And most of the stockholders will, doubtless, jump with joy—especially if the market continues to buy the stock on a 20-times-earnings basis or better—in which case the price of the stock would rise to $78!

But one or two of the *initial* stockholders—that is, those who owned the company before *either* of the above two projects was undertaken—may look a little downcast. They will look a little downcast because they will realize that if the apparently profitable 6 percent project had *not* been undertaken, but only the subsequent 40 percent project, their EPS would now be $3.94 a share instead of $3.92, thus:

Prior Expected Earnings	=	$5,578,125.
Expected Earnings, New Project		
(= .40 × $9,052,000)		3,620,800.
TOTAL		$9,198,925.

$$\frac{\$9,198,925}{2,187,500 + 149,633} = \$3.94$$

In short, they may say, given the fact that a 40 percent project was in the offing, the company's cost of common stock, before it undertook the 6 percent project was decidedly *not* 5.2 percent—it was higher. It was, in fact, expected EPS *with* the 40 percent project, but *without* the 6 percent project—divided by the net price of stock, thus:

$$\frac{\$3.94}{\$49.00} = .080$$

or 8.0 percent.

At the annual meeting, an irate stockholder might jump to his feet and shake his fist at Martin, saying: "Our cost of common stock was 8.0 percent, not 5.2 percent. That 6 percent project never should have been undertaken. You should be fired." Martin would, of course, shrug his shoulders and say: "How the devil did I know a 40 percent project would suddenly appear? And besides the difference is only a few cents a share."

"A few cents might have been a few dollars," the stockholder might say. "You're supposed to maximize the price of the stock."

The above illustration is over-simplified and extreme, but a less extreme illustration would have produced a result different in degree only. In any case, let's be sure, first, that we see why the illustration produced the result it did produce. It produced the result it did produce, simply because the initial stockholders were forced to share, with the stockholders brought in to finance the 6 percent project, the benefits of the 40 percent project. In other words, *given the 40 percent project,* the initial stockholders were rendered worse off. They would clearly have been better off without the stockholders they brought in to finance the 6 percent project. And, obviously, if the 40 percent project had been foreseen when the 6 percent project was being considered, the 6 percent project would have been rejected.

"That's clear enough," said Kelley. "If we *know now*—if we can see *now*—that one, two, three or ten years from now, we will be able to invest in projects which will raise our earnings and dividends, we ought to take those projects into account *now* in estimating our cost of equity. But in the case of Company X, the five projects were *visible now*—and so we knew what *g* would be. What do we do if they are *not* visible—if we merely have a vague feeling that some high-return projects will appear at some time in the reasonably near future? Can we do anything but stand by and wring our hands?"

Kelley was saying, in effect, that the formula Cost of equity = $D/P + g$ was useful—*if* we could estimate *g*. Butcher could calculate D/P easily enough. Expected EPS was $2.55 with a payout ratio of 50 percent, the expected current dividend was about $1.25. *D/P* was therefore about .025. (Kelley knew that Butcher's actual dividend this year (1968) would be nearly $2.40. But this was because Butcher, this year, had been lucky.)

But what was *g*? Now, obviously, said Kelley, the only really satisfactory way to solve this problem is to have perfect foresight! But what does a company do if it *doesn't* have perfect foresight but nevertheless feels sure that some high-return projects will appear in the future? What will those projects look like, what will be the expected rates of return on them, and how much money will they require? All the company knows is that such projects will probably appear—and must somehow be taken into account *now*—or the present stockholders will be less well off than would otherwise have been the case.

Three alternatives are available:

1. We can simply assume that what has happened in the past will happen in the future. Butcher's earnings have grown at the rate of 25 percent for a year and a half. Kelley could assume that they will continue to grow at that rate—forever. Such an assumption would be neither realistic nor sensible.
2. We can assume that earnings will grow, for some specified period of time, say five years, at a rate that seems reasonable in the light of past experience. Kelley might, for example, assume that Butcher's earnings will grow at 10 percent a year for five years, or 15 percent or 25 percent—and would then hold steady thereafter.
3. Kelley might simply try to find out whether any high-return opportunities were likely to become available next year. He would talk to Hastings and the Director of Research and the division heads to find out what they expected. (They would surely expect something.) He would then try to estimate the effect of those projects on EPS. And he would, in turn, estimate the effect of the higher EPS on Butcher's current cost of common stock and retained earnings. This seemed to Kelley more sensible than making highly uncertain assumptions about future growth rates.

But Kelley knew he did not have time, before the meeting of the Finance Committee, to do a lot of talking—to Hastings, the Director of Research and Division—in order to find out whether any high-return projects were just beyond the horizon. He decided therefore to assume that during the next five years, projects would appear which would make Butcher's EPS (the mean of a probability distribution) grow at the rate of 15 percent a year, compounded—as shown in Table 18.5.

TABLE 18.5

THE BUTCHER COMPANY, EXPECTED EPS, FROM 1969

YEAR	EPS ANNUALLY AT 15 PERCENT COMPOUND GROWTH RATE *	DPS
(1)	(2)	(3)
1969	$2.93	1.46
1970	3.37	1.68
1971	3.88	1.94
1972	4.46	2.23
1973 and after	5.13	5.13

* Based on currently expected EPS of $2.55, after taxes.

Butcher's earnings would then level off at $5.13 a share. Kelley assumed also that:

1. In 1969-72, Butcher would pay out 50 percent of EPS in dividends—as shown in Table 18.5.
2. At the end of the fifth year (1973) Butcher's stock would be

TABLE 18.6

COST OF EQUITY CALCULATED ON ASSUMED GROWTH OF EPS OF 15 PERCENT

AT END OF YEAR	EXPECTED DIVIDEND *	EXPECTED PRICE	DISCOUNT FACTORS AT 9%	PRESENT VALUE
(1)	(2)	(3)	(4)	(5)
1969	$1.46	——	.917	$ 1.34
1970	1.68	——	.842	1.41
1971	1.94	——	.772	1.50
1972	2.23	——	.708	1.58
1973	5.13	$64.00 †	.650	{ 3.33 \ 41.60
				——
				$50.76

* From Table 18.5.
† Equals $5.13/.08.

selling to yield 8 percent—based on a dividend of $5.13. Butcher's stock would thus be selling at about $64 a share ($= \$5.13/.08$).

Butcher's stockholders would thus receive a return (consisting of dividends and capital gain) of almost exactly 9 percent, given the present price of the stock ($51)—provided, of course, that the 15 percent growth rate was in fact realized. The present value calculation is given in Table 18.6.

Kelley realized—and you should too—that the process he had gone through, as above, to obtain an estimate of Butcher's cost of equity, was somewhat arbitrary. He might have done the job in a variety of ways. He might, for example, have assumed a declining growth rate—20 percent the first year, 15 percent the second year, and so forth. Or he might have assumed a different level rate. All he could hope was that the rate he had chosen would prove, five years hence, to have led to a reasonable result.

THE COST OF A MIXTURE OF FUNDS

Now that he knew Butcher's cost of equity, adjusted for growth, Kelley was able to calculate the cost of a *mixture* of new funds.

"Suppose," he said, "that we decided to use half debt—costing, say, 4.25 percent after taxes—and half retained earnings—costing 9 percent after taxes—to finance a new project. What would the cost of the mixture be?" It would, Kelley determined, be *a weighted average of the two separate costs, thus*:

TABLE 18.7

COST OF A 50-50 MIXTURE OF FUNDS

TYPE	AMOUNT TO BE USED	PERCENTAGE OF TOTAL AMOUNT	PERCENTAGE COST (AFTER TAX)	WEIGHTED * COST
(1)	(2)	(3)	(4)	(5)
Debt	$ 500,000	50%	4.25%	2.125
Retained earnings	500,000	50%	9.00%	4.500
TOTAL	$1,000,000	100%		6.625

* Percentage of total amount multiplied by percentage cost after tax divided by 100.

Or suppose that we decided to use *30* percent debt and *70* percent retained earnings—instead of 50 percent of each. The cost of the mixture would be 7.575 percent, thus:

TABLE 18.8

COST OF A 70-30 MIXTURE OF FUNDS

TYPE	AMOUNT	PERCENTAGE OF TOTAL AMOUNT	PERCENTAGE OF COST (AFTER TAX)	WEIGHTED COST
(1)	(2)	(3)	(4)	(5)
Debt	$ 300,000	30%	4.25%	1.275
Retained earnings	700,000	70%	9.00%	6.300
TOTAL	$1,000,000	100%		7.575

All we've done, above, is calculate a weighted average cost by multiplying the separate cost of each type, after taxes, by its weight in percent, adding the two products and then dividing by the sum of the weights ($= 100$). The difference between the two results, above, is due *solely to the difference in the weights*. (The process of calculating the weighted average cost of a mixture of different types of capital is no different in principle from calculating the weighted average cost of eight apples costing ten cents each and six pears costing eight cents each.)

Kelley then decided to see what Butcher's weighted average cost of capital was, given Butcher's *actual capital structure*. First, he calculated Butcher's ratio of debt to total capital. He did so by dividing Butcher's debt by Butcher's total capital.

Butcher's total capital was worth $146 million, and its debt, $34.5 million, (see Table 2.1).

Butcher's debt to total capital ratio was, therefore, 23.7 percent, as follows:

$$\frac{\$34.5 \text{ million}}{\$146.1 \text{ million}} = .237$$

or 23.7 percent. Butcher's ratio of equity to total capital was 76.3 percent ($= 100.0 - 23.7$). These figures are given in Table 18.9. Kelley then put in the after-tax cost of each type of money, multiplied it by the percentage of present capital structure it represented, divided by 100 and added. He thus found that Butcher's weighted average cost of capital —based on Butcher's present capital structure—was 7.874 percent.

"So," Kelley said to himself, "that's our cost of capital *if we raise new money in the future, in the ratio of 23.7 parts debt to 76.3 parts equity.*"

What do these weighted average figures mean? They mean simply that if Butcher (or any other company) invested a mixture of funds with a given weighted average cost, say 7.874 percent—as in Table 18.9— in a project with an expected return *exactly equal to that weighted average cost,* everything would "come out even."

To sum it up if Butcher invested $1 million in a new project with an expected rate of return, after taxes, of 7.874 percent, *and* the funds to be invested in that project had been raised in the proportions indicated in Table 18.9, *and* the project did in fact return 7.874 percent

TABLE 18.9

BUTCHER'S WEIGHTED AVERAGE COST OF CAPITAL BASED ON PRESENT CAPITAL STRUCTURE.

TYPE OF LONG-TERM MONEY	PERCENTAGE OF PRESENT CAPITAL STRUCTURE	PERCENTAGE OF AFTER TAX COST	WEIGHTED * COST
(1)	(2)	(3)	(4)
Debt	23.7%	4.25%	1.007
Equity	76.3%	9.00%	6.867
	100.0%		7.874

* Percentage of present capital structure multiplied by after tax cost, divided by 100.

—then the additional EBIT generated by the project would be just sufficient to pay interest on the additional debt at 8.5 percent, and return 9.0 percent to the equity invested in the project. This is illustrated in Table 18.10. This table assumes that a $1 million project would be financed in the proportions indicated in Table 18.9—that is, by selling $237,000 of new debt and by using $763,000 of new equity. Now, a $1 million project which showed a rate of return, after taxes, of 7.874 percent, would show a rate of return *before* taxes (assuming a 50 percent tax rate) of 15.748 percent. This means that, during its first year, a $1 million project would contribute $157,480 to EBIT (see Table 18.10). Of this amount, $20,145 would be paid out in interest (.085 × $237,000 = $20,145). Earnings before taxes would thus be

TABLE 18.10

THE BUTCHER COMPANY, ILLUSTRATION OF MEANING OF WEIGHTED AVERAGE COST OF CAPITAL

1. Increase in EBIT	
.15748 (= 2 × .07874) × $1 million	$157,480
2. Interest on $237,000 at 8.5 percent	20,145
3. Increase in EBT	$137,335
4. Increase in Taxes (at 50 percent)	68,668
5. Increase in EAT	$ 68,667
6. Earnings for new equity	
at 9.0 percent on $763,000	$ 68,670

$137,335 (see Table 18.10). Taxes, at 50 percent, would be $68,668, as would earnings after taxes. But earnings after taxes would be just sufficient to provide a return of 9.0 percent to the $763,000 in new equity. *Nothing is left over*—except a slight amount ($3) due to rounding error.

We should note that the *weighted average cost of capital,* as calculated above, is just the converse of the phenomenon we observed in Chapter 4. In Chapter 4 we defined a DCF rate of return on a proposed project as a "break-even" *rate.* A weighted average cost of capital is a "break-even" *cost.* Thus if we invest in a project with a return less than this "break-even" cost, the stockholders will suffer. This is illustrated in

TABLE 18.11

THE BUTCHER COMPANY, ILLUSTRATION OF RETURN TO COMMON STOCK AND RETAINED EARNINGS WITH 4 PERCENT PROJECT

1. Additional EBIT with 4%	
(after taxes) project costing $1 million	$80,000
2. Interest on $237,000 (at 8.5 percent)	20,145
3. Increase in EBT	$59,855
4. Increase in taxes (at 50 percent)	29,927
5. Increase in EAT	$29,928

Table 18.11, assuming a project yielding 4 percent—after taxes (= 8 percent before taxes). The insurance company would get its 8.5 percent,

but only $29,928 would be left to pay a return on the new equity. This would be a return of less than 4 percent, after taxes, to the new equity raised to help finance the project.

CONCLUSION

In this chapter we have made the following points:

(1) Ea/Pa is not a satisfactory measure of the cost of common stock and Ea/P is not a satisfactory measure of the cost of retained earnings—if earnings are expected to grow.

(2) If earnings are expected to grow, some attempt must be made to estimate the rate at which they will grow—in order to protect the interests of the current stockholders.

(3) Perhaps the most sensible way to do so is by trying to take account of any and all projects which are now "visible"—especially those likely to offer high rates of return. But, if you wish, you can assume some "reasonable" rate of growth—as Kelley did—over some reasonable period of time.

(4) We have also in this chapter illustrated the method of calculating the cost of a *mixture* of funds—sometimes called a weighted average cost of capital. And we have explained what a weighted average cost means.

PROBLEMS

1. In December 1960, IBM was selling at about $100 a share. Using the data given in Table 18.2 and in the text, calculate the percentage return earned by someone who bought the stock on January 1, 1961 and held it until December 31, 1969.

2. In December 1961, Xerox was selling at about $10 a share. Calculate the percentage of return earned by someone who bought the stock then, and sold it on December 31, 1969 at $102.

3. In late 1969 IBM was selling at about $355 a share. Using the data given in Table 18.2—to the extent that it is relevant—estimate the growth rate of EPS which would give you a return of 9 percent—if you bought the stock at $355 and held it for 5 years. Assume that at the end of the fifth year, IBM will be selling at 43 times EPS for the fifth year.

4. Suppose you are Kelley. The day before the Finance Committee is

to meet, Martin hands you a letter from the Plastics Division (located in Old Forge, New York), describing a project, expected to become available next year, which will promise a rate of return before taxes of 62 percent. It will require an investment of $4.25 million. Assume the project will be financed as in Table 18.9, with 24 percent debt at 8.5 percent and 76 percent retained earnings. Butcher's stock is now selling at $56—having gone up $5 in the last few days. Estimate the effect of the project on Butcher's EPS. Recalculate Butcher's current cost of equity and current weighted average cost of capital.

5.   Given the fact that the 62 percent project described in problem 4 is in the offing, would you undertake an 8 percent project this year which would require an investment of $4.25 million? Why or why not?

6.   Suppose the 8 percent project required only $2 million. Would that make any difference?

7.   Just before the Finance Committee meeting, Kelley decides that the 15 percent growth figure he used in Tables 18.5 and 18.6 was too high. He decides to use 12 percent instead. Recalculate the cost of common stock and retained earnings. Then recalculate Butcher's weighted average cost of capital.

RISK, RETURN, AND THE INDIVIDUAL INVESTOR

"Ugh," you say. "What's happened here?"

"What's the matter, dear?" asks your devoted wife. She's sitting across the table from you, munching toast, her hair still up in curlers.

"These corn flakes, they're awful. Ugh." You push the dish away.

"They've added honey to them, honey." she says.

"Don't be funny," you say. "Not at this hour of the morning, and not in these circumstances."

Your wife says, "I think they're very good."

"You would," you say. "They're awful. Ugh."

"The children think they're very good too," she says.

"I don't care what they think," you say. "Have you got something else?"

"An egg, maybe?" she asks.

"I don't like eggs," you say. "And you know it. I want cold cereal —without honey."

"Sorry, dear," she says. "We don't have any."

You heave the dish of corn flakes—with honey—against the kitchen wall and march yourself angrily down to the corner beanery—where they will have corn flakes without honey, you hope.

When you get home that night, you say to your wife, "Lord what a break I had today!"

"What?" she asks, her tone indicating she expects the worst.

"You remember young Kelley? The son of the people who lived next door to us in Metusha?"

"Vaguely," she says.

"Well," you say, "I ran into him at lunch. He's assistant to the financial vice president of Butcher. He gave me a hot tip."

"On what?" she asks.

"On Butcher," you say. "What else? They're expanding again and borrowing more money."

"Yes," she says.

"Yes?" you ask. "How did you know?"

"He didn't tell you anything you couldn't have read in the *Wall Street Journal* this morning," she says, "if you hadn't wasted so much time screaming about those foolish corn flakes."

"I wasn't screaming," you say. "But if I feel like screaming, I will scream. Where's the story?"

She hands you the paper. "Page eighteen."

You say, "Well, that makes it official." You toss the paper on the table. "Anyway, I bought another hundred shares."

"You did!" she exclaims. "With what?"

"I borrowed on the first hundred as security—plus some cash."

"You did?" she says. "That's very interesting. I sold the first hundred right after you left this morning—as soon as I read that story in the journal."

"I know," you say. "The broker called me. I bought them back."

"You did!" she says. "Without calling me!" She walks over to you and says, *"Don't you ever do that again."*

"Those corn flakes with honey made me mad," you say. "You're lucky I came home at all tonight."

"I want you to sell those two hundred shares, first thing in the morning."

"Why?" you ask.

"Butcher is getting too risky," she says, very emphatically. *"They're borrowing too much money."*

You say, "I don't think so."

She says, angrily, "If you don't sell them, I will."

"Oh, no, you won't," you say. "They're now in my name only. You can't sell them."

"You mean you didn't put them in both our names?"

"Exactly," you say. "That'll teach you to serve me corn flakes with honey."

"You ought to be ashamed of yourself," she says.

"I'm not," you say. "But I'll tell you what I'll do. If you'll trot out first thing in the morning and find me some corn flakes *without* honey, I'll put the two hundred shares in both our names."

"I found you some this afternoon," she says, bursting into tears.

THE SATISFIED CUSTOMER

We said in Chapters 1 and 2 that the goal of the firm was to maximize the price of its own common stock. In order to achieve this goal the firm must not only give its customers, the people who buy its products, what they want—corn flakes with more honey or with less, or automobiles with more horsepower or less. It must also give investors, *the people who buy its securities,* what *they* want. If a firm adds more honey to its corn flakes or more horsepower to its automobiles, it will lose some customers —those who thought the prior amount was just right. But it will gain others—those who thought the prior amount was insufficient. If the firm does in fact add more honey to its corn flakes or more horsepower to its automobiles, it is expressing the belief that the gain, in terms of profit, will be larger than the loss.

Correspondingly, if a firm increases—or decreases—the degree of risk it runs, it will annoy some investors and simultaneously please others. And no investor is obliged to buy a firm's common stock any more than any consumer is obliged to buy its corn flakes—with or without honey. Firms can increase the degree of risk they run, as we have seen above, in one or the other (or both) of two ways: by undertaking riskier projects—as did the Clay Company when it bought Mobile Residences, or by borrowing money—especially at long term, as Butcher did when it borrowed $36.8 million to finance its rebuilding program. And if a firm changes the degree of risk it runs, it is *presumably* expressing the belief that the wealth of its stockholders—that is, the value of their shares—will be greater than it would otherwise have been. We will return to this point in Chapters 20 and 21.

This chapter is designed to prepare us for the discussion of leverage in Chapters 20 and 21 and the ensuing discussion of the cost of capital. This chapter describes the various types of investors, what each wants, and how they go about trying to obtain it.

But first we discuss in detail what we mean by return and risk from the point of view of the individual investor.[1]

---

[1] The term "individual investor" is used here to include both individuals as such and financial institutions such as insurance companies, mutual funds, other types of investment funds, and so forth.

RETURN ON A SECURITY

The return on a security is the "average expected payoff," expressed as a percent. In Chapter 3 we calculated the present value of a share of RCA. We might, equally, have calculated an expected rate of return on an investment in a share of the stock at the present price ($43.50). Table 19.1 calculates this expected rate of return for the ten-year period

TABLE 19.1

RATE OF RETURN ON ONE SHARE OF RCA BASED ON CASH FLOWS GIVEN IN TABLE 7.16

YEAR	EXPECTED CASH FLOWS *	DISCOUNT FACTORS AT 9%	PRESENT VALUES (DOLLARS)
(1)	(2)	(3)	(4)
1969	$ 1.07	.917	$ .981
1970	1.14	.842	.960
1971	1.22	.772	.942
1972	1.30	.708	.920
1973	1.39	.650	.904
1974	1.48	.596	.882
1975	1.58	.547	.864
1976	1.68	.502	.843
1977	1.79	.460	.823
1978	1.90 ⎱ 83.00 ⎰	.422	.802 35.026
TOTAL			$43.95

NOTE: Rate of return equal to almost exactly 9 percent.
* From Table 7.16.

1969-1978. The return could just as well have been calculated for a shorter period—one year, two years, five years and so forth.

Or after Butcher in 1966 (repeat *1966*) announced that it had borrowed $36.8 million to undertake a rebuilding program, we could have constructed a probability distribution, similar to that constructed by Kelley (Table 7.11), and then calculated an expected rate of return on investing $30 in a share of Butcher's stock for one year, five years, ten years, or any other period of time. In order to have done so, we would have assumed a payout ratio.

Historically, Butcher has paid out, on the average during the past ten years, about 50 percent of earnings in dividends and we will therefore assume that it will do so during the coming year. Tables 19.2 and 19.3 illustrate the calculation. The EPS in Table 19.2 are taken from Table

T A B L E   1 9 . 2

THE BUTCHER COMPANY EXPECTED CASH FLOW
(STOCK SELLING AT $30)

EPS *	DIVIDEND †	PRICE AT END OF YEAR	CHANGE IN PRICE DURING YEAR	TOTAL CASH ‡ FLOW
(1)	(2)	(3)	(4)	(5)
$4.68	$2.30	$36	+ $6	+ $8.30
3.54	1.75	33	+ $3	+ $4.75
2.40	1.20	30	0	+ $1.20
1.26	.60	27	— $3	— $2.40
0.11	.05	24	— $6	— $5.95
2.06 §	0	20	— $10	— 10.00

* From Table 7.11.
† At approximately 50 percent of EPS.
‡ Dividend plus capital gain or loss shown as change during year.
§ Loss.

7.11. Dividends are given at 50 percent of earnings for each level of earnings. When earnings are negative, dividends are zero. The expected price of the stock at the end of the year is shown for each level of EPS. Thus if earnings are $4.68 during the coming year, we assume that the stock will be selling at $36 at the end of the year—an increase of 20 percent over the price of $30. If earnings are $3.54 during the year, we assume that the stock will be selling at $33—an increase of 10 perecent over the present price. If earnings are $2.40 during the year, or at just about the average expected with debt (see Table 7.11), the price of the stock will remain unchanged, and so forth. If earnings are *below* the average expected, we assume that the price of the stock will decline.

Why will these changes occur in the price of the stock? They will occur because investors will revise their individual probability distributions as soon as new, actual earnings figures become available. If current figures are in the high range, at least some investors will now, rightly or wrongly, attach higher probabilities to the future occurrence of earnings in the high range. And as a result their estimate of average expected earnings and dividends will rise. And if the discount rate has not risen, the price of the stock will rise. The rise would simply mean that some investors now expect the stock to payoff at a higher rate in the future. And correspondingly, if earnings are in the lower range, some investors will now attach higher probabilities to the future occurrence of earnings in the lower range.

The figures shown under Change in Price during Year in Table 19.2 are simply capital gains and losses. They were obtained by subtracting $30, the price of Butcher's stock, from each of the end-of-year prices. Thus if EPS during the year turns out to be $4.68, the price of the stock at the end of the year will be $36. Your capital gain would then be $6. If EPS is just about average, i.e., $2.40, your capital gain would be zero. If EPS is below average, you will have capital *losses* ranging from $3 to $10 a share. We then simply add together the dividend and the capital gain or loss given to obtain a figure for *cash flow* for the year at each level of EPS.

Thus, if EPS turns out to be $4.68 your *total cash flow* will be $8.30— a dividend of $2.30 plus a capital gain of $6.00. If EPS turns out to be $3.54, your total cash flow will be $4.75—a dividend of $1.75 plus a capital gain of $3.00. If EPS turns out to be below average, your total

TABLE 19.3

RATES OF RETURN AND EXPECTED AVERAGE RETURN (STOCK SELLING AT $30)

TOTAL CASH FLOW * (DOLLARS)	PERCENTAGE RETURN BASED ON INITIAL PRICE	PROBABILITY †	PERCENTAGE OF EXPECTED AVERAGE RETURN
(1)	(2)	(3)	(4)
+ $ 8.30	+ 27.66%	.12	+ 3.32%
+ 4.75	+ 15.83%	.23	+ 3.64%
+ 1.20	+ 4.00%	.41	+ 1.64%
− 2.40	− 8.00%	.17	− 1.36%
− 5.95	− 19.83%	.06	− 1.18%
− 10.00	− 33.33%	.01	− 0.33%
TOTAL		1.00	+ 5.73%

* From Table 19.2.
† From Table 7.11.

cash flow will be negative—because in each case the capital loss will be larger than the dividend.

In Table 19.3 we simply transform the dollar cash flow figures given in Table 19.2 into rates of return and, using Kelley's probabilities, compute an average expected rate of return. We start with the *total* cash flow figures given in Table 19.2. These figures are then converted into a percentage by dividing each by $30—the price in 1966 of a share of Butcher stock. Thus if total cash flow is $8.30, the *rate* of return on an investment of $30 now in a share of Butcher stock would be 27.66 percent. If total cash flow is negative, the rate of return will, of course, be negative. Kelley's probabilities are taken from Table 7.11. The average expected return is calculated by multiplying the percentage return by the probability of that return and totaling the column. Looking one year ahead, then, we see that the average expected return is 5.73 percent —on the basis of the probability distribution *you* have used and the assumptions *you* have made about EPS and the changes likely to occur in the price of Butcher's stock.

Other investors would, of course, use their own probability distributions—which might or might not differ materially from yours—and would make their own subjective assumptions about EPS and price changes. But in any event, this is what we mean by *return*—a rate calculated for a specified period of time on an investment made now.

RISK

Now, then, what do we mean by *risk?* We mean, in short, that the actual return on any investment decision may differ from the average expected return. As we look at the percentage returns in Table 19.3, we see that the actual return could range from +27.66 percent to −33.33 percent on the investment of $30 in a share of Butcher stock. And if we buy a share of Butcher stock, we run the risk that the return we will earn will be very low and may reduce our capital by as much as one third.

Risk can be measured in a variety of ways. We used, above, the *range* of the distribution, from +27.66 percent to −33.33 percent as a measure of risk. But the range of a distribution is not really a satisfactory measure of risk because it leaves the probabilities out of account. Suppose that in Table 19.3 the probability of a return of +27.66 had been .01, and the probability of a return of −33.33 had been .12, everything else remaining the same. The two distributions would have the same range, but the second would be riskier simply because it would carry a much larger chance of the lowest return.

average deviation

We need, therefore, a measure of risk which will take account of the probability of each possible outcome. Two such measures are available. They are called the *average* (expected) *deviation* and the *standard* (expected) *deviation*. The average deviation is more straightforward than the standard deviation and therefore easier to understand. It is also easier to calculate. But both measures do essentially the same thing—although in somewhat different ways: each measures the distance from the *mean* (the average expected return) of each possible outcome and then averages all the distances so measured.

Table 19.4 calculates the average deviation from the mean (5.73

TABLE 19.4

ESTIMATED AVERAGE DEVIATION

PERCENTAGE * OF RETURN	DEVIATION FROM AVERAGE †	PROBABILITY	EXPECTED AVERAGE DEVIATION
(1)	(2)	(3)	(4)
+ 27.66%	21.93%	.12	2.632%
+ 15.83%	10.10%	.23	2.323%
+ 4.00%	1.73%	.41	0.709%
− 8.00%	13.73%	.17	2.334%
− 19.83%	25.56%	.06	1.534%
− 33.33%	39.06%	.01	0.391%
TOTAL		1.00	9.923%

* From Table 19.3.
† Average = 5.73 percent. See Table 19.3.

percent) of all the possible percentage returns given in Table 19.3. Table 19.4 simply lists all the possible returns given in Table 19.3 and then subtract them from the *average* expected return of 5.73 percent. Thus, 21.93 percent, the first figure shown under Deviation from Average, is 27.66 percent minus 5.73 percent. The second figure deviation of 10.10 percent is 15.83 percent minus 5.73 percent—and so forth, for the other four deviation figures. Each of the figures thus represents a deviation from the *mean*, the average. In order to obtain an *average* deviation, we weight each individual deviation by the probability that it will occur, and total the products. The sum of the products is 9.923 percent, which is thus the *average amount* by which all the possible returns in column 1 differ (deviate) from the average expected return.

Why do we multiply by the probabilities? We do so because any given deviation will occur with the same frequency as the return from which it is derived. Thus if a return of 27.66 percent will occur 12 percent of the time, then a deviation of 21.93 percent from the average expected return will also occur 12 percent of the time. If a return of 15.83 percent will occur 23 percent of the time, then a deviation of 10.10 percent from the average expected return will also occur 23 percent of the time—and so forth for the other deviations.

standard deviation

The standard deviation is more widely used than the average deviation, although, for reasons which will become clear below, the average deviation is more useful for our purposes. Table 19.5 calculates the standard deviation of all the possible returns given in Table 19.3. Percentage returns and deviations in Table 19.5 are taken directly from Table 19.4.

TABLE 19.5

ESTIMATED STANDARD DEVIATION

PERCENTAGE * OF RETURN	DEVIATION FROM AVERAGE †	DEVIATION SQUARED	PROBABILITY	AVERAGE EXPECTED DEVIATION SQUARED ††
(1)	(2)	(3)	(4)	(5)
+ 27.66%	21.93%	480.92%	.12	57.71%
+ 15.83%	10.10%	102.01%	.23	23.46%
+ 4.00%	1.73%	2.99%	.41	1.23%
— 8.00%	13.73%	188.51%	.17	32.05%
— 19.83%	25.56%	653.31%	.06	39.20%
— 33.33%	39.06%	1525.68%	.01	15.26%
TOTAL			1.00	163.91%

Standard deviation = $\sqrt{168.91}$ = 13.38%.
* From Table 19.3.
† Average = 5.73%. See Table 19.3.
†† Column (3) × Column (4).

Each deviation is squared and *then* multiplied by its associated probability. The products are then totaled. Because the deviations have been *squared,* the *square root* of the sum must be extracted. This is shown at the bottom of Table 19.5—and we find that the standard deviation is 13.00 percent.[2]

The process of squaring the deviations and then extracting the square root of their weighted sums seems "a little artificial"—even to mathematical statisticians.[3] In fact it *is* artificial—but it finds its justification in technical reasons which, happily, need not detain us here.

Before considering what the average and the standard deviation mean, let us look again at what they are. Both are averages of distances from various points (in this case, returns) to a point of reference (in this case, an average expected return). Suppose that we wish to measure the average distance from some point of reference, say the capital, of the ten principal centers of population in the United States and Russia. These two countries have roughly the same population—but Russia is much larger in area. We list the principal cities, as shown in Table 19.6,

TABLE 19.6

DISTANCES OF MAJOR CITIES FROM THEIR CAPITAL

RUSSIAN CITIES	DISTANCE FROM MOSCOW (miles)	U.S. CITIES	DISTANCE FROM WASHINGTON, D.C. (miles)
(1)	(2)	(3)	(4)
Leningrad	400	New York	200
Volgograd	550	Chicago	600
Kharkov	425	Detroit	400
Kuybshev	525	Boston	400
Sverdlovak	850	Los Angeles	2,200
Novosibirsk	1,625	San Francisco	2,350
Krasnoyarsk	2,050	Seattle	2,250
Magnitogorsk	850	New Orleans	950
Ghelyabinsk	900	Minneapolis	900
Tashkent	1,610	Denver	1,400
TOTAL	9,785		11,650
Average	979		1,165

---

[2] For distributions which are more or less symetrical, the average deviation is about 80 percent of the standard deviation.

[3] See Maurice Kendall, *The Advanced Theory of Statistics,* Vol. 1 (New York: Hafner Publishing Company, 1963), p. 39.

measure the distance of each from the capital and compute the average. We find that, on the average, the large centers of population in the United States are nearly 20 percent farther away from the capital than they are in Russia. The results would have been even more striking if we had weighted distance by population—as in fact we should have since several of the most populous cities in the United States are in the West. In Russia, population declines as distance from Moscow increases. We might also have squared the distances from each capital, summed over the squares and taken square roots of the two sums.

What have we done? We have computed the average distance of various outlying points (in this case, the centers of population) from related points of reference (Moscow and Washington, D.C.). When we computed the average and standard deviations for Butcher we did nothing more than this: we measured the distance from various outlying points (the possible returns) to a point of reference (the mean) and averaged.

Now, what do the two deviations mean? Two distributions of expected returns can have averages which are identical but which represent very different degrees of risk. On June 26, 1969, for example, U.S. Treasury notes due in April of 1974, carrying an interest rate of $1\frac{1}{2}$ percent, were selling at $822.00 (per $1,000 note). If bought then and held to maturity, these notes would yield 5.73 percent. This return happens to be exactly the same as the average expected return we calculated in Table 19.3 for Butcher. But the average and standard deviations of the two distributions are very different. The average deviation of the Butcher distribution, as we saw above, is 9.923 percent. The average deviation of the expected return on the Treasury note would be zero—simply because the Treasury note is riskless. If it promises 5.73 percent, the probability is 1.00 that you (or your heirs) would actually receive 5.73 percent. There are no other possible returns and the sum of the deviations (squared or unsquared) would be zero.

Now, the Butcher distribution is obviously riskier than the Treasury note distribution and when we say this, we mean not that the return on Butcher may be *above* the average but rather that it may be *below* the average—and by a large amount if we are unlucky. If a distribution is perfectly symetrical—that is, if the part which lies above the average is a mirror image of the part which lies below the average—we can divide the average (or standard) deviation by two in order to obtain a measure of what we may call the average "downside" deviation, i.e., of the risk of receiving a return below the mean. This is illustrated in Table 19.7 by use of four simple symetrical distributions—all of which have the same mean (5.73 percent) but different average and standard deviations. The average deviation of the first distribution is 2.86; of the

TABLE 19.7

RETURNS AND DEVIATIONS
FOR FOUR SYMMETRICAL DISTRIBUTIONS

PERCENTAGE RETURN	PROBA-BILITY	EXPECTED AVERAGE RETURN	DEVIATION FROM AVERAGE	EXPECTED AVERAGE DEVIATION
(1)	(2)	(3)	(4)	(5)
0 %	.25	0 %	5.73	1.433%
5.73%	.50	2.865 %	—	—
11.46%	.25	2.865 %	5.73	1.433%
	1.00	5.73 %		2.866%
2.86%	.25	.715 %	2.86	.72 %
5.73%	.50	2.865 %	—	—
8.59%	.25	2.148 %	2.86	.72 %
	1.00	5.73 %		1.44 %
4.73%	.25	1.1825%	1.00	.25 %
5.73%	.50	2,8650%	—	—
6.73%	.25	1.6825%	1.00	.25 %
	1.00	5.73 %		.50 %
5.23%	.25	1.3075%	.50	.125%
5.73%	.50	2.8650%	—	—
6.23%	.25	1.5575%	.50	.125%
	1.00	5.73 %		.25 %

second, 1.43; of the third, .50; and of the fourth, .25. And we see under Expected Average Deviation that in each case, the deviations contributed by the returns lying *below* the mean are exactly equal to the deviations contributed by returns lying *above* the mean. Now when we are dealing with symetrical distributions we can obtain a measure of risk, in percentage terms, simply by dividing half of the average (or standard) deviation by the mean—to obtain what we will call here a *risk ratio* [4]—a number which measures the "downside" deviations relative to the mean. This ratio is an index of risk. For the four symetrical distributions given in Table 19.7, the risk-ratios are on page 429.

But the Butcher distribution is *not* symetrical: considerably less than half the deviations lie below the mean. And if we divided the average (or standard) deviation by two, we would overstate the risk of the

---

[4] In the language of statistics, a *coefficient of variation*—divided by two.

MEAN	EXPECTED VALUE OF "DOWNSIDE" DEVIATIONS	RISK RATIO
5.73	1.43	.25
5.73	.72	.125
5.73	.25	.04
5.73	.125	.02

We thus define risk as the ratio of the "downside" deviations to the mean of the distribution. The "downside" deviations can, obviously, range from zero to —100.

distribution. Therefore, in order to obtain a number which is a summary index of risk in the above sense, we simply add up the deviations contributed by those possible returns which lie below the mean. We then divide this sum by the mean. Table 19.4 tells us that of 9.923, the total average deviation, 4.968 (= .709 + 2.334 + 1.534 + .391) is contributed by values which lie below the mean. This figure, 4.968, is 87 percent of 5.73 percent.[5] This figure, 87 percent, is then a measure, albeit again a bit abstract, of the risk of receiving a return on Butcher stock which would be below the average expected return. Or we may say that 87 percent is a measure of the price that an investor in Butcher stock would have to pay *in terms of risk* in order to give himself a chance to earn those returns which are substantially *above* the average expected return. In other words, if an investor in Butcher wants a chance to receive those returns which are above the average, he will have to run the risk of receiving those which are below the average.

THE INDIVIDUAL AND RISK

How does the individual investor deal with this problem? How does he deal, that is, with the *problem of risk?*

The individual deals with risk in one or another of two ways:

1. *Risk–avoiders.* One who invests only in so-called riskless securities (or insured savings accounts) and thus will avoid risk altogether.

---

[5] We cannot obtain a similar "breakdown" of the standard deviation because of the squaring, etc. We can obtain only the percentage of the squared deviations—usually called the "variance"—contributed by those possible returns which lie below the average. They total 87.7 and represent 49 percent of the total variance.

2. *Risk–averters.* One who invests in one or more risky securities, on the basis of his own *subjective* attitude toward risk and re-turn—that is—on the basis of what we will call his own *personal equation between risk and return.*

We discuss each of these types separately.

risk avoiders

The securities of the Federal Government are free of the risk of default because they are, in effect, guaranteed by the power of the Federal gov-ernment to levy taxes. Even if we encountered a depression so severe (a) that no corporation made money and none therefore paid taxes, and (b) taxes collected on personal incomes declined by half, the re-mainder would be sufficient to pay roughly three times the annual in-terest on the Federal debt. The risk that the Federal debt will default seems, therefore, slight if not infinitesimal.[6]

Why do some people invest in this way? In order to understand a bit better investors of this type, let's go back to the individual in Chapter 2 who was confronted with the following choice:

Alternative 1: Invest $10,000 with one possible outcome: a guaran-teed yield of 7 percent.
Alternative 2: Invest $10,000 with two possible outcomes, as follows:

YIELD		PROBABILITY	EXPECTED RETURN
0%		.50	0%
14%		.50	7.00%
	TOTAL	1.00	7.00%

Suppose in considering these two alternatives from Chapter 2 that the individual (you, maybe) had decided he would choose the 7 percent guaranteed return. Now, suppose further that after he made *that* de-cision, he found a third alternative, also risky, on page 439.

What would he have done then? Would he nevertheless have clung to the 7 percent riskless alternative? If he would have, suppose that he had then been offered a risky alternative with an expected return of 15 percent? 20 percent? 100 percent? If there is *no* available expected re-

---

[6] Appendix 19.A at the end of this chapter discusses the two types of risks to which fixed income securities are subject—*market* risk and the risk of *inflation.*

YIELD		PROBABILITY	EXPECTED RETURN
0%		.50	0%
20%		.50	10.00%
	TOTAL	1.00	10.00%

turn which would have induced him to choose *it* rather than the riskless return, he is the kind of person who would invest in nothing but government bonds. He is a *risk-avoider*—which is just another way of saying that he is more conservative than the Chairman of the Finance Committee of the National Association of Widows and Orphans.

What kind of person would he be likely to be—and in what circumstances? First (and perhaps obviously), he would be a person who would be unwilling to take any risk whatever of not having that $700. Perhaps he is a person who works at a relatively low salary and is able to maintain life, barely above subsistence, only with that $700. Or perhaps he's a college student who, without the extra $700, would be unable to finish his education and so forth. You will, doubtless, be able to think of other examples yourself.

risk-averters

Let's go back again to that individual in Chapter 2. And let's suppose that if the expected return on the risky asset is 7 percent, he would choose the riskless alternative. But now let's suppose that he discovers the third alternative above—namely, a risky investment with an expected return of 10 percent. And let's suppose he jumps at it. What has he done? He has, in effect, said that he is willing to accept more risk—but only if the expected return is higher than the certain (guaranteed) return. And one measure of the degree to which he is "risk-averse" is the difference between the expected return on the risky investment (10 percent) and the guaranteed return (7 percent).

Thus investors in this group do not avoid risk—but they are wary of it. And they will never accept additional risk unless it is accompanied by a higher expected return.[7]

---

[7] This is equivalent to saying that such investors will never bet on a fair game— that is, on a game which promises an expected average return of zero. They will not because for them the marginal utility of money is declining. If they bet a dollar and lose it, they will have lost more *utility* than they would have gained if they won—simply because the dollar they now have and might lose, is worth more to them in terms of *utility* than the dollar they would receive if they won.

Each such investor *has his own personal risk-return* on the basis of which he will trade more risk for more expected return. This is just another way of saying that some risk-averters will not accept more risk unless it is accompanied by a large increase in expected return—but others will accept a very large amount of additional risk even if it is accompanied by only a very small increase in expected return.

In order to illustrate this diversity of "risk-return equations," let us suppose that you have an amusement fund of $1,000. And let us suppose, also, that long-term government bonds are available at a yield of 6 percent. As we pointed out above, government bonds are free of the risk of default and therefore their risk ratios are zero. You could invest in such bonds if you wished. At the same time, many other alternatives are available to you—and you have fixed your attention on two. One is a medium grade corporate bond on which you estimate an average expected return for the next year of 6.5 percent, a maximum return of 7.5 percent and a minimum return of 5.5 percent. The probability distribution you have constructed for this bond is as follows:

POSSIBLE RETURNS	PROBABILITY	EXPECTED AVERAGE RETURN
5.50%	.25	1.3750%
6.50%	.50	3.2500%
7.50%	.25	1.8750%
TOTAL	1.00	6.50 %

Average deviation = .50 percent
Risk ratio = .25/6.50 = .038

The other alternative is a common stock on which you estimate an average expected return, for the next year, of 15 percent, a maximum return of 35 percent and a minimum return of minus 5 percent. The probability distribution you have constructed for this stock is as follows:

POSSIBLE RETURNS	PROBABILITY	EXPECTED AVERAGE RETURN
− 5.00%	.25	− 1.25%
+15.00%	.50	+ 7.50%
+35.00%	.25	+ 8.75%
TOTAL	1.00	+15.00%

Average deviation = 10 percent
Risk ratio = 5.0/15.00 = .333

The first alternative offers a modest return of 6 percent, risk free. The second alternative offers a lower return, risk free, of 5.5 percent—provided, of course, you have absolute confidence in your probability distribution!—with a 75 percent chance of a higher return than that offered by the government. The risk-ratio, measuring the risk of receiving a yield below the mean, is low—less than 4 percent of the mean.

The third alternative offers a much higher average expected return than either the government or the corporate bond. But it is also much riskier—its average deviation is 10 percent and its risk ratio is .333 or one third of the mean.

Now, with these three securities, and these three alone, you can obtain a very large number of combinations of risk and return. You could invest all of your amusement fund in one of the three securities. Alternatively you could invest equal amounts in all three securities. If you did so, your expected average return would be the average of the three averages or 9.17 percent, thus:

$$\frac{6.00 + 6.50 + 15.00}{3} = 9.17$$

and your risk ratio would fall somewhere between zero and .333. Or you could invest unequal amounts in the three securities—10 percent of your amusement fund in one, 60 percent in another and 30 percent in the third—or in any other proportions you wished. Or you could invest in any *two* securities in whatever proportions you wished.

And if the risk and return of the riskiest alternative, the common stock were not high enough for your taste, you could borrow money and buy an additional amount of the common stock. By doing so, you would increase both your risk and your average expected return, as follows:

POSSIBLE RETURN	PROBABILITY	EXPECTED AVERAGE RETURN
−10.5%	.25	− 2.625%
+19.5%	.50	+ 9.750%
+49.5%	.25	+12.375%
TOTAL	1.00	+19.50 %

Average deviation = 15 percent
Risk ratio = 7.5 /19.50 = .385

Where do the figures for possible return come from? Bear the following facts in mind: you borrow $500 at 6 percent from a bank or a rich uncle, and buy stock worth a total of $1,500. At the end of the year you must pay the bank (or your uncle) $530—the $500 you borrowed plus $30 in interest. If your return is minus 5 percent on the $1,500, you will have $1,425 at the end of the year ($= .95 \times \$1,500$) of which the bank (or your uncle) will get $530. You will thus be left with $895. Your original investment was $1,000 and your rate of return ($-105/1,000 = -.105$). Your rate of return has declined from minus 5 percent because you have lost $25 of the amount you borrowed—but you must, of course, repay the whole loan. And you have had to pay $30 in interest. These two sums together represent 5.5 percent of your original investment ($\frac{\$25 + \$30}{1,000} = .055$) and 5.5 percent plus 5 percent equals 10.5 percent. You are thus worse off then you would have been had you not borrowed money and bought additional stock.

But now suppose the return on the $1,500 you have invested is 15 percent. At the end of the year you would have $1,725 ($= \$1,500 \times 1.15$). Of this sum you would pay the bank (or your uncle) $530 and you would have $1,195 left. Your return, therefore, on your original investment of $1,000 is thus 19.5 percent ($1,195/1,000 = 1.195$). You have earned much more (15 percent) on the borrowed money than you paid for it (6 percent) and the difference goes into your pocket and increases your return on your original fund. Correspondingly, if the return on the $1,500 turns out to be 35 percent, your return will be 49.5 percent.

CONCLUSION

In short, with just three securities available and assuming you are free to buy "on margin," you can find almost any combination whatever of risk and return—within the limits set by the rate on riskless bonds, the expected average return on the riskiest security available and your borrowing power.

Which combination would *you* choose? And you? And you? And you? The chances are that no two of you would choose the *same* combination. Why? Because, for reasons of circumstance and temperament, some of you are not willing to gamble at all, some of you are willing to gamble a little and some of you are willing to gamble a lot.

Now the fact that each of you will hold different combinations of risk and return means that each of you has a *different subjective risk-return equation*. Some of you will accept a risk ratio of .33 if it is accompanied by an average expected return of 15 percent. But some of you would accept a risk ratio of .33 only if it were accompanied by an average expected return of 20 percent or 25 percent of 30 percent. Your risk-return equations differ.

We can summarize the foregoing discussion in the following way:

(1) As an investor you have a multitude of opportunities available to you. We saw, above, that if just three securities were available, you would be able to construct a very large number of distinct portfolios. In fact, of course, thousands of securities are available.

(2) In constructing a portfolio, you will look at each individual security (or, rather, at a reasonable number of individual securities) in terms of the expected return it offers and in terms of the risk it will add to your portfolio.

(3) You will choose the "best" portfolio available—which is consistent with your own personal risk-return equation. In other words, you will, in effect, construct probability distributions over returns from portfolios made up of the various kinds of financial assets available to you. Each such distribution will have a mean and an average (or standard) deviation. And you will (obviously) choose that portfolio which makes you most comfortable in terms of your own subjective risk-return equation.

Now then, suppose that you have constructed a portfolio in the above way. And suppose also that it includes 100 shares of Butcher which cost you $51 a share. And suppose finally that you pick up the *Wall Street Journal* one morning and find that Butcher has decided to sell more debt.

You know, of course, that the additional debt will make Butcher's stock riskier. This will, of course, affect the risk, overall, of your portfolio. *What will you do? And what will be the effect (if any) of what you do on the price of Butcher's stock?*

In the next two chapters we will explore these questions.

PROBLEMS

1. Using the cash flows given in Table 19.1, calculate an expected rate of return to holding a share of RCA one year, two years, three years, four years and five years. The present price is $43.50 a share. Make appropriate assumptions about the price of the stock one, two, three, four and five years hence.

2. Table 7.16 tells us that if RCA's earnings and dividends grow at the rate of 6.6 percent during the first year, the dividend, for that year,

will be $1.07, approximately. Draw up, as best you can, a proba-
bility distribution of which $1.07 would be the expected value of
the dividend. Calculate an expected return to buying a share of
RCA now, at $43.50, and holding it for one year. The price of the
stock, one year hence, will of course depend on earnings and dividend for the year. Make appropriate assumptions about the price
of the stock at the end of the year.

Calculate also the average and standard deviations of the return,
and a risk ratio.

3. Invest your amusement fund, $1,000, in one or more of the three
securities described in the text, in whatever proportions you wish—
but so as to achieve a result which reflects your preferences for risk
and return. You may borrow up to $500 from a bank at 7 percent.
Calculate the expected average return, the average deviation and
the risk ratio of the "portfolio" you have bought.

Now, assume that you revise your probability distribution for the
common stock as follows:

POSSIBLE RETURNS	PROBABILITY	EXPECTED RETURN
—10.0%	.25	— 2.5 %
+15.0%	.50	+ 7.50%
+40.0%	.25	+10.00%
TOTAL	1.00	+15.00%

Find a new portfolio which gives you the same expected return
and the same risk ratio as the first.

4. In mid-1966 you bought 100 shares of Butcher's stock at $30 a
share and $3,000 of its fifteen-year bonds to yield 5½ percent.
Using the probability distribution given in Table 7.11, calculate
your average expected gain, as of the day you made this investment, for the following year, its average deviation, and your risk
ratio.

Butcher pays interest once a year. You must, of course, make
reasonable assumptions about the price at which both Butcher's
bonds and stock will be selling one year hence.

MARKET RISK
AND
THE RISK OF INFLATION

The federal debt is not, of course, protected against *market risk* and the *risk of inflation*.

Market risk is the risk of capital loss if interest rates rise. Suppose that you buy a ten-year, 6 percent government bond for $100. You will receive $6 a year for ten years and at the end of the tenth year, together with the final interest payment, the principal sum will be returned to you. The rate of return on your investment of $100 is exactly 6 percent. But now suppose that a year after you bought the bond, interest rates rise, and the government finds that in order to sell bonds to the public, it must offer a rate of return of 7 percent. What will happen to the market value of your bond? It will fall, as Table 19.8 shows. Table 19.8 simply calculates the present value of a 6 percent bond, with nine years left to run, *at an opportunity cost (a personal cost of capital) of 7 percent.* Why do we use 7 percent? We do so because 7 percent has now become the opportunity cost to anyone who is considering buying your bond. No one will buy your bond unless he can buy it at a price which will yield 7 percent. Table 19.8 simply tells us what the price would have to be such that your bond would in fact yield seven percent to a new buyer.

As Table 19.8 indicates, the present value of such a bond would be (approximately) $93.50—and you would sustain a capital loss of $6.50 if you were compelled, for whatever reason, to sell the bond one year after you bought it. Of course, if interest rates had gone *down*, instead of up—as they do occasionally—you would have made a capital gain, instead of a capital loss. The loss (or gain) would, of course, be a paper loss (or gain)—unless you actually sold the bond. If you held it to maturity, you would receive back the amount you originally invested. But clearly you would have been better off if you had initially bought a *one-year* bond at something less than 6 percent and, then, one year later bought the 7 percent bond.

TABLE 19.8

PRESENT VALUE OF A 6 PERCENT BOND
AT AN OPPORTUNITY COST OF 7 PERCENT

YEAR	CASH FLOW	DISCOUNT FACTORS AT 7%	PRESENT VALUE
(1)	(2)	(3)	(4)
1	$ 6	.935	$ 5.61
2	6	.873	5.24
3	6	.816	4.90
4	6	.763	4.58
5	6	.713	4.28
6	6	.666	4.00
7	6	.623	3.74
8	6	.582	3.49
9	106	.544	57.66
TOTAL	$154	6.515	$93.50

Alternative calculation:

6.515 $\times$ $6 = $39.09
.544 $\times$ $100 = 54.40
TOTAL $93.49

And, of course, when you buy securities, such as government bonds, the income on which is fixed in dollar terms, you run the risk of *inflation*. If prices rise by 2 percent compounded a year, a 6 percent, ten-year bond would be worth only $85.81 now if you wish to earn 6 percent in *real terms* on your money. Table 19.9 makes this clear by showing cash flow in money terms and in *real terms*—assuming a 2 percent increase in prices a year, compounded annually. The figures show that the price rise would have eaten up 15 percent of your original investment.

TABLE 19.9

PRESENT VALUE OF A 6 PERCENT, TEN-YEAR BOND
(ADJUSTED FOR 2 PERCENT ANNUAL
COST OF LIVING INCREASE)

YEAR	CASH FLOW IN CURRENT DOLLARS	CASH FLOW IN REAL TERMS *	DISCOUNT FACTORS AT 6%	PRESENT VALUE
(1)	(2)	(3)	(4)	(5)
1	$ 6	$ 5.88	.943	$ 5.54
2	6	5.77	.890	5.14
3	6	5.65	.840	4.75
4	6	5.54	.792	4.39
5	6	5.43	.747	4.06
6	6	5.33	.705	3.76
7	6	5.22	.665	3.47
8	6	5.12	.627	3.21
9	6	5.02	.592	2.97
10	6	4.92	.558	2.75
	100	82.03	.558	45.77
				$85.81

* Obtained by dividing cash flow in dollars by appropriate 2 percent growth factor.

20

THE COST OF LONG-TERM CAPITAL III leverage

After he had calculated Butcher's weighted average cost of capital (see Chapter 18), Kelley leaned back in his chair and said:

"So that's our weighted average cost of capital after taxes—assuming we raise new money *in the present proportions:* about 24 percent debt and about 76 percent equity."

He then turned back to Table 15.1 (you should do so too) and did a few quick computations. He said to himself: "If we took all projects with expected rates of return higher than 7.874 percent, we'd need $4,557,000 in outside financing" (see Table 20.1).

Kelley knew that the Finance Committee would be very much against selling common stock now—which probably meant that the whole $4,557,000 would have to be debt. But $4,557,000, as Table 20.1 shows, would be more than 62 percent of the total capital sum to be invested. Kelley divided $4,557,000 by $7,332,000 instead of by $9,052,000 because Butcher's capital structure would be increased only by the sum of retained earnings plus the amount raised externally thus:

$$\$2,775,000 + \$4,557,000 = \$7,332,000.$$

TABLE 20.1

EXTERNAL FUNDS REQUIRED TO ACCEPT ALL HIGH RETURN * PROJECTS

Total long-term projects †		$9,342,000
Minus cost of two projects with rates of return less than 7.874 percent		290,000
	Balance	9,052,000
Depreciation		1,720,000
	Balance	7,332,000
Expected retentions		2,775,000
	Balance	$4,557,000

Percentage of total cost, Less depreciation, to be raised externally $= \dfrac{\$4,557,000}{\$7,332,000} = 61.15\%$

NOTE: Kelley used $7,332,000 (= $9,342,000 — 1.720,000) as the base of this fraction, because only that amount would affect Butcher's capital structure.
* All projects listed in Table 15.1 with rates of return higher than 7.874 percent.
† From Table 15.1.

The difference between $9,052,000 and $7,332,000 was $1,720,000—or Butcher's expected depreciation charges for the first half of the year. This meant, of course, that the purchase of the new assets would be financed partly by expected retained earnings, partly by new debt and partly by reduction in the value of existing assets.

Selling such a large (relatively) amount of new debt would change Butcher's capital structure—as Table 20.2 shows. Debt would be 25.6 percent of the capital structure, instead of 23.7 percent and the percentage of equity would be correspondingly less. These changes were not enormous—but the company would be riskier and would seem so to sophisticated investors.

But at the same time Butcher would be offering its stockholders a higher return—simply because the weighted average expected rate of return on the new projects was 21.8 percent (see Table 20.3)—a rate much higher than Butcher's present average rate of return on its working assets (= total assets minus liquidity). The new projects would raise expected EPS from $2.55 to $3.68—or by about 40 percent. (Kelley was really struck by the latter figure.) And the new projects were, on the average, no riskier than the old projects.

TABLE 20.2

CAPITAL STRUCTURE IF SELL $4,775,000 OF DEBT

	AMOUNT	NEW	OLD *
Debt	$ 39,275,000 †	25.6%	23.7%
Common Stock	21,875,000	14.2%	
Retained			76.3%
Earnings	92,416,000 ‡	60.2%	
TOTAL	$153,566,000	100.0%	100.0%

$34,500. (From Table 2.1)
+ 4,775. (additional debt)
‾‾‾‾‾‾‾
$39,275.

$89,641. (From Table 2.1)
+ 2,775. (additional retained earnings)
‾‾‾‾‾‾‾
$92,416.

* From Table 17.6.

TABLE 20.3

WEIGHTED AVERAGE RETURN ON PROPOSED PROJECTS *

AMOUNT	RATE OF RETURN (AFTER TAX)	DOLLAR RETURN
(1)	(2)	(3)
$ 680,000	42%	$ 286,000
750,000	28%	210,000
3,025,000	24%	726,000
2,464,000	22%	542,000
830,000	21%	174,000
190,000	19%	36,000
925,000	18%	167,000
1,225,000	16%	196,000
730,000	12%	88,000
300,000	10%	30,000
233,000	8%	19,000
$11,352,000		$2,474,000

$$\frac{\$2,474,000}{\$11,352,000} = 21.8\%$$

* Those projects listed in Table 15.1 with rates of return higher than 7.874 percent.

Kelley thought Butcher might have one other alternative—if the President and the Finance Committee continued to feel that Butcher should not sell common stock now. "We might," he thought, "sell just that amount of debt which, together with the earnings we expect to retain, would leave the present debt-equity ratio unchanged." He did a quick computation and found that about $820,000 worth of new debt, combined with $2,775,000 in retained earnings, would leave Butcher's debt-equity ratio unchanged. In that case, Butcher would be able to invest depreciation charges of $1,720,000 plus retained earnings of $2,775,000 plus new debt of $820,000 or, in total, $5,315,000. But this, he noted, as he looked back at Table 15.1, would mean that Butcher would be able to accept only the first four of the sixteen proposed new projects and would have to put the others off until the second half of the year. Expected earnings would go up by eighty cents a share (to $3.35) instead of by $1.13 (to $3.68).

As he was gazing absent-mindedly out the window Kelley suddenly realized that *with the same financial mix* the price of Butcher's stock would go up—if general market conditions did not change. The price would go up because Butcher's earnings per share would go up *with no increase in risk*.

Kelley saw, therefore, that the question he really had to answer was: *Will our stock go up more—or less—if we run more financial risk*—that is, if we increase the percentage of debt in our capital structure?

In this chapter and the next we discuss "leverage." We will be trying to answer the following question: if Butcher (or any other company) increases the percentage of debt in its capital structure, what will happen to the price of its common stock? Will it go up or down—or will it remain unchanged? We will be trying to "get at" the effect of leverage *as such*—by which we mean the effect of leverage *pure and unalloyed*. In order to achieve this objective, we will have to make some assumptions which may startle you.

WHAT IS LEVERAGE?

What do we mean by leverage? We mean, to put the matter in its simplest terms, the use of debt financing, which generally has a low explicit cost, to finance the purchase of assets which will yield a return *which is high relative to that cost*.

Suppose that we are considering starting a new business. The total amount of funds required for investment in liquidity, receivables, inventory and fixed assets is $1 million and we estimate that the rate of return on these assets will be 20 percent before taxes. A large number of financing alternatives is available to us of which we will consider three:

1. The entire $1 million could be financed by equity, that is, by the sale of common stock;
2. $500,000 could be financed by the sale of common stock and $500,000 by the sale of debt at 8 percent;
3. $250,000 could be financed by the sale of common stock and $750,000 by the sale of debt at 10 percent.

The effect of each of these three alternatives on the rate of return on net worth before and after taxes is given in Table 20.4. We can

TABLE 20.4

EFFECT OF LEVERAGE ON RATE OF RETURN, AFTER TAXES ON NET WORTH

		Financing Alternatives		
		NO DEBT	**50% DEBT**	**75% DEBT**
(1)	EBIT (000)	$200.0	$200.0	$200.0
(2)	Interest on debt	——	40.0 *	75.0 †
(3)	EBT (000)	200.0	160.0	125.0
(4)	Taxes (@ 50%)	100.0	80.0	62.5
(5)	EAT (000)	100.0	80.0	62.5
(6)	Net worth ‡ (000)	1,000.0	500.0	250.0
(7)	EBT as percentage of net worth	20%	32%	50%
(8)	EAT as percentage of net worth	10%	16%	25%
(9)	Total assets (000)	1,000.0	1,000.0	1,000.0
(10)	EBIT as percentage of total assets	20%	20%	20%
(11)	Number of shares	20,000	10,000	5,000
(12)	Book value per share	$50	$50	$50
(13)	Expected EPS (after taxes)	$ 5	$ 8	$12.50

* At 8% of $500,000.
† At 10% of $750,000.
‡ Equals total assets minus portion financed by debt.

see readily that as the percentage of debt increases, the rate of return on net worth also increases sharply (lines 7 and 8).

Let's look carefully at this table. We note:

1. No matter which financing alternative we choose, the size of the firm will be unaffected. Total assets will be $1 million whichever financing alternative we choose (line 9).
2. No matter which financing alternative we choose, expected EBIT will be $200,000 and the percentage return, *before* taxes, will

be 20 percent of the value of total assets (lines 1 and 10).

3. But under the second and third alternatives, *the return on net worth* will be higher, both before and after taxes, than the return under the first alternative (lines 7 and 8).

We first encountered this interesting phenomenon in Chapter 2 when we watched Dale Martin, Butcher's financial vice president, weighing the disadvantages of additional risk against the advantages of additional expected return. What's the explanation?

The explanation has two parts—which are brought out by the following little formula:

$$R_{nw} = [r + (r - i) D/E] (1 - t)$$

where:

R_{nw} = return on net worth.
r = rate earned on total assets
i = interest rate paid on debt
D/E = ratio of debt to equity
t = the tax rate

The formula is simply telling us that the return we earn on our own money (that is, on *net worth*) depends on three rates and one ratio as follows:

1. The rate at which the assets we own will earn (r);
2. The rate of interest we are required to pay for the funds we have borrowed (i);
3. The rate (or rates) at which we are required to pay taxes (t); and
4. The ratio of debt to equity in our capital structure (D/E).

In short, given the rate at which our assets are expected to earn and given the rate (or rates) at which we are required to pay taxes —our return on *our own* money will be bigger the more money we borrow, and the less we pay for it. In Table 20.4, column (2), we see, for example, that with debt of $500,000 and net worth of $500,000 ($= D/E$ of 1.00), we would have:

$$R_{nw} = [.20 + (.20 - .08) \frac{500}{500}] .50$$

$R_{nw} = .16$ or 16 percent, as in line 8. With a debt-equity ratio of 3.00 ($= 750/250$)—as in Table 20.4, column (3), we would have:

$$R_{nw} = [.20 + (.20 - .10) 3] .50$$

$R_{nw} = .25$, again as in line 8 of Table 20.4.

And so we see that, by using "leverage"—by putting debt into our capital structure—we can raise dramatically the expected return on our own money. *But does this mean that, by using leverage, we can also raise dramatically the market price of our stock*—or what is the same thing (as we shall see) *the total market value of our company?*

Let's think of each of the three financing alternatives in Table 20.4, as representing *three different companies*—instead of three different ways of financing the *same* company.

Suppose, now you were offered all the stock in Company 2 (Table 20.4). Would you pay more than $500,000 for it—and, if so, how much more? Or suppose you were offered all the stock in Company 3, would you pay more than $250,000 for it—and, if so, how much more? If you would pay more than $500,000 for the stock of Company 2, or more than $250,000 for the stock of Company 3, then you are saying that *you would pay a premium for* the stock of a levered company—presumably to obtain the higher return on net worth the leverage has caused.

Let's put the foregoing questions in a somewhat different way, as follows:

First, suppose that Company 1, which has twice as much equity as Company 2, also has *twice as many shares outstanding* as Company 2. And suppose also that Company 2, which has twice as much equity as Company 3, also has twice as many shares outstanding as Company 3. Company 1 thus has 20,000 shares outstanding, Company 2, 10,000 and Company 3, 5,000 (line 11, Table 20.4). The *book* value (that is, the net worth) of each share in each company is, thus, $50—because Company 1 has twice as many shares and twice as much net worth as Company 2, and four times as much net worth and four times as many shares as Company 3. Therefore, the net worth *per share* for each company must be the same (line 12, Table 20.4).

Second, if the three companies were publicly held and their stock traded on the New York Stock Exchange, *do you think the shares in Company 3 would sell for more than the shares in Company 2? And do you think that the shares in Company 2 would sell for more than the shares in Company 1?*

Now then, in order to throw some light on these questions, let's return for a moment to you and your roommate.

DEBT-EQUITY RATIO

At the end of Chapter 2, you had just inherited $700—which your roommate had urged you to invest in Roan Selection Trust. Roan was then selling at $5 a share and your roommate thought it might go to

$10 a share in the next three months. You thought it might, with equal probability, go to $3:

PRICE OF STOCK	PROBABILITY	PAYOFF	EXPECTED PAYOFF
$10	.50	+100%	+50%
$ 3	.50	− 40%	−20%
	1.00		+30%

An expected return of 30 percent, for three months, looked very attractive and so you bought 140 shares (= $700/$5). Owning all that stock made you feel like a big financial manipulator and you decided therefore to form a corporation to hold the stock. You'd make yourself the president. You filled out the necessary forms—which you had obtained from your lawyer—paid a $10 franchise tax, and presto (!) you were President of Investors Associates Incorporated (of Delaware) with a balance sheet that looked like this:

ASSETS		LIABILITIES AND EQUITY	
Cash	$ 0.	Common stock	
140 shares, Roan		600 shares	
Selection Trust		authorized par	
(at cost)	700.	value $5, 142	
Organization expense	10.	shares outstanding	$710.
Total assets	$710.	Total liabilities and	
		equity	$710.

"All right," you said to yourself. "What do I do now?" You thought about that for a while and finally you said, "Eureka! I've got it!" You would try to persuade your roommate to buy 142 shares in the company at $5 a share. Each of you would then own half the stock. The company would take your roommate's money—$710—and buy another 142 shares of Roan at $5 a share. When your roommate came in, late that night, tired and without much resistance, you put the matter to him. You concluded your sales pitch by saying: "I'll make you a vice president."

"You'll make me a vice president!"

"Yes," you said.

"Okay," he said. "I can't wait to tell my mother. Take the money out of my wallet." He threw himself on his bed and fell asleep instantly.

You took seventy-one ten dollar bills out of his wallet and made out a stock certificate in his name for 142 shares—which you pinned to his pillow. You then rushed down to the bank and made a night deposit. Then you got your broker out of bed and told him to buy 142 more shares of Roan in the morning—as soon as the market opened. Investors Associates balance sheet now looked like this:

ASSETS		LIABILITIES AND EQUITY	
Cash	$ 0	Common stock, 600	
282 shares,		shares authorized,	
Roan Selection		par value $5, 284	
Trust (at cost)	1,410	shares outstanding	$1,420
Organization expense	10	Total liabilities	
Total assets	$1,420	and equity	$1,420

Expected earnings before taxes (EBIT), based on the probability distribution set forth above were $423 (= $1,410 × .30) or $1.49 a share (= $423/284), before taxes—$1.49 was almost exactly 30 percent of $5—the cost of each share.

One piece of financial manipulation almost always leads to another. The next day, at lunch, while you were making a list of the things you would do with your first million dollars, you suddenly realized that you could borrow some money from the bank and buy more stock. This would, of course, raise earnings per share. You rushed out of the restaurant—without finishing your lunch—and over to the bank. You put up the company's 282 shares of Roan as security and signed a note, in the company's name, for $500 for three months at 8 percent. You phoned your broker and bought another 100 shares of Roan. Investors' balance sheet now looked like this:

ASSETS		LIABILITIES AND EQUITY	
Cash	$ 0	Note payable (bank)	$500
382 shares, Roan		284 shares common	
Selection Trust		stock	1,420
(at cost)	1,910		
Organization expense	10	Total liabilities	
Total assets	$1,920	and equity	$1,920

You now had leverage. It felt great and, of course, you now really understood what it was. Investors Associates expected EBIT was still 30 percent, before taxes, of total assets. But expected EPS, before taxes, had "skyrocketed" to $1.88 a share or to nearly 38 percent of the cost of each share.

Why had EPS "skyrocketed"? It had skyrocketed because you had borrowed money ($500) at 8 percent and invested it in 100 shares of Roan with an expected return of 30 percent. Your expected income statement looked like this:

Expected income at 30% of market value
of 382 shares of Roan (= .30 × $1,910) = $573

Interest (for one year) on bank loan—
at 8% of $500   =   40

Net income = $533

Expected net income as percent of
Investors net worth (= $533/1,420 × 100) = 37.5%

Earnings per share of Investors
(= $533/284)   = $1.88

In short, borrowing from the bank had raised Investors' expected return on net worth from 30 percent to about 38 percent and expected EPS, from $1.50 to $1.88.

When you got back to your room that night you explained to your roommate what you had done—that is, about Investors' leverage.

"Great," he said, "absolutely great. You know what we should do now?"

"What?" you asked.

"Sell some of our stock," he said. "By clever manipulation, we've raised our expected earnings from $1.49 to $1.88 a share. Our stock is obviously worth more than $5 a share. Maybe it's worth as much as $6.30—which would be $1.88 discounted at our expected rate of return ($1.88/.30 = $6.30). You sell 60 shares of yours and I'll sell 60 shares of mine."

"Brilliant," you say. "But to whom?"

"That rich kid you roomed with last year. What was his name—the long hair who was majoring in art history?"

"Yes," you said. "He's living in Granville this year. I'll rush right over."

"I'll go with you," said your roommate. "Remember, the deal is 120 shares at $6.30 a share."

After the "rich kid" had listened to the offer, he said (in a rather contemptuous tone), "First, I agree with your probability distribution. The expected return is 30 percent on Roan, before taxes. No doubt about that. But why should I pay you $756 [= 120 × $6.30] for something I can 'manufacture' myself for $596? After we clear away all the financial hocus-pocus, what you're really offering me is a 42.25 percent [= 120/284] interest in Investors Associates. But what does Investors Associates own? It owns 382 shares of Roan.

"So what I'm really buying is 42.25 percent of 382 shares of Roan. That's about 161 shares of Roan, worth about $805 at the present price on the New York Stock Exchange. You understand what I'm saying? On the surface, I'm buying 120 shares of Investors Associates at $6.30 a share—total cost, $756. But what I'm *really* buying is 161 shares of Roan—worth $5 a share or in total $805.

"Moreover," continued the rich kid, "you've borrowed $500—which is 26 percent of your total capital. In other words, Investors Associates holds its stock in Roan on 26 percent margin. If I borrowed 26 percent of $805, my financial risk would be the same. But I'd have to put up only $596 to be able to buy 161 shares of Roan, thus" he scribbled on a tablecloth:

161 shares Roan at $5	=	$805
Borrow 26 percent	=	—209
Balance		$596

"In other words," he said, "you're offering me 161 shares of Roan, on 26 percent margin, for $756. I can 'do it myself,' running exactly the same financial risk, for $596."

"So tell me, oh financial genius," he said, "why I should pay you $756 for something I can 'make' myself for $596?"

As you wandered sadly back to your room, your roommate said, "Was it you who said he was majoring in art history?"

What had gone wrong? You knew—or you thought you knew—that lots and lots of financial manipulators in Wall Street (and Boston), and lots and lots of big butter and egg men from the Midwest had made fortunes by doing nothing more than you had tried to do. They bought a few assets—usually real assets, borrowed some money on them, bought some more assets. These "manipulations" pushed the rate of return on net worth above the rate of return on the assets themselves for, as we have seen above,

$$R_{nw} = r + (r - i) D/E$$

They were then able to sell shares in those assets for more than the assets themselves were "worth"—that is, for more than the going price of such assets. How were they able to do it?

You thought of one possible explanation, as follows:

An individual investor who wants to invest, say, $10,000 in a levered company like Butcher, does not really have the alternative of buying a replica, in miniature, of Butcher's real assets—including its management. When you offered 120 shares of Investors Associates to your friend, the art history major, he saw at once that he was really buying shares in Roan Selection Trust. And he knew that he himself could buy shares in Roan—without any help from you. And, of course, he was not willing to pay you more for shares in Roan than he would have had to pay for them elsewhere.

But when someone offers to sell you 200 shares of stock in Butcher at $51 a share, you may see at once that you are really buying a proportionate share of Butcher's real assets and management—and, of course, a proportionate share of the earnings stream those assets will generate. But you see that you do not really have the alternative of buying real assets which would be a $10,000 replica in miniature of Butcher. Moreover, even if you could, you wouldn't want to.

And so you say to yourself—perhaps *that's* the explanation. Perhaps that's how the financial manipulators do it. They buy real assets, borrow against them, buy some more real assets. And then they sell shares in those assets, at a premium, to small individual investors—like me—who cannot reproduce a replica in miniature of those assets.

But the more you thought about *this* explanation, the less sensible it seemed. There were lots and lots of companies like Butcher—not necessarily in the same industry, but with about the same expected probability distribution over EBIT—that is, with about the same basic expected return on assets and about the same degree of risk. With lots of similar companies available, why would you be required to pay a premium for any one?

In order to illustrate this point, let's suppose that in order to obtain more of the benefits of leverage, Butcher decides to borrow another $51 million at 8 percent, and use that sum to buy back 1 million shares of its own common stock, now selling at $51. This will, of course, raise Butcher's expected EPS both before and after taxes. It will also raise Butcher's debt-equity ratio. (In order to bring out the effect of leverage, *as such*—that is, the leverage effect uncontaminated by other effects—we discuss Butcher's maneuver on the assumption that Butcher pays no corporate taxes.)

Table 20.5 shows Butcher's capital structure before and after the transaction described above. We should note that the *total has not been changed*. By selling debt and repurchasing its own stock, Butcher has

TABLE 20.5

CHANGING CAPITAL STRUCTURE
(BASED ON SALE OF $51 MILLION
SHARES OF COMMON STOCK AT $51)

	BEFORE *		AFTER *	
	(thousands)	Rate	(thousands)	Rate
Debt (old)	$34,500.	22.85%	$ 34,500.	22.85%
Debt (new)	——	——	51,000.	33.77%
Common stock	21,875.†	14.49%	11,875.‡	7.86%
Retained earnings	94,641.	62.66%	53,641.	35.52%
TOTAL	$151,016.	100.00%	$151,016.	100.00%

* See Table 2.1.
† 2,187,500 shares, par value $10.
‡ 1,187,500 shares, par value $10.

simply substituted debt for equity in its capital structure. Total capital is unchanged. Total assets are unchanged and EBIT is unchanged.

EPS, however, before taxes *is* changed—as Tables 20.6 and 20.7 show. *EPS is changed because the number of shares is reduced and because Butcher's rate of return on its basic assets is higher than the rate at which it can borrow.* Table 20.6 shows the calculation of EBT (= EBIT

TABLE 20.6

EXPECTED EARNINGS BEFORE TAXES
(BASED ON SALE OF $51 MILLION DEBT AND REPURCHASE
OF ONE MILLION COMMON AT $51)

EBIT (millions)	INTEREST * (millions)	EBT (millions)
(1)	(2)	(3)
$22.50	$6.08	$16.42
17.50	6.08	11.42
12.50	6.08	6.42
7.50	6.08	1.42
2.50	6.08	—3.58
—2.50	6.08	—8.58

* $2 million on existing debt and $4.08 million on new debt (= $51 million × .08).

TABLE 20.7

EXPECTED EPS (BASED ON SALE OF $51 MILLION DEBT AND REPURCHASE OF ONE MILLION COMMON AT $51)

EBT * (millions)	EPS † (BEFORE TAXES) (millions)	PROBABILITY ‡	EXPECTED VALUE OF EPS (BEFORE TAXES) (millions)
(1)	(2)	(3)	(4)
$16.42	$13.83	.12	$1.66
11.42	9.62	.23	2.21
6.42	5.41	.41	2.22
1.42	1.20	.17	0.20
−3.58	−3.01	.06	−0.18
−8.58	−7.23	.01	−0.07
	TOTALS	1.00	$6.04

* From Table 20.6.
† Based on 1,187, 500 shares.
‡ From Table 7.11.

minus interest). Table 20.7 shows EPS, before taxes, for each level of EBIT. The substitution of debt for equity has raised Butcher's expected EPS, before taxes, from $5.14 to $6.04.

Suppose, now, that as soon as word begins to circulate about Butcher's clever maneuver, your broker calls your friend, the art history major, and suggests that he put in an order to buy 100 shares of Butcher at $52.

Your friend says, "Why $52?"

The broker says, "It will go higher."

Friend: "Why?"

Broker: "Expected EPS has gone up—to about $6 a share before taxes."

Friend: "Because of the leverage effect?"

Broker: "Yes."

Friend: "Where are Alston and United?"

(Alston and United are two of the many companies which are similar to Butcher. Both have the same probability distribution over EBIT as Butcher. Both have about $35 million in debt and 2,187,500 outstanding common shares.)

Broker: "Holding solid as a rock at $51."

Your friend laughs.

The broker says: "What's funny?"

Your friend says: "I don't mind Butcher's additional leverage. In fact, I like it. But why should I pay a premium to get it? Alston, a similar company, is selling at $51. True, Alston has less leverage than Butcher but I'll just make some more of my own. I'll just borrow some money at 8 percent and buy Alston on margin.

"Let's see," he says, "Alston's debt-equity ratio is $34.5/111.6 or about .31 to 1.00. Butcher's debt to equity ratio is $34.5 + $51.0/60.6 or about 1.41 to 1.00 (Table 20.5) I want to put up $5,100 of my own money and then borrow enough more so that after I've bought Alston my *combined debt-equity ratio—including Alston's present debt of $15.77 a share* [= $34.5 million/2,187,500 shares] will be 1.41 to 1.00— like Butcher's.

"This is tricky. First, I buy 100 shares of Alston with my $5,100. Then I borrow $4,295 @ 8 percent from my friendly neighborhood banker and buy another 84.2 shares. My total net expected return is $603.19, as follows" and he scribbles on his wall:

184.2 shares of Alston, expected EPS of $5.14 (before taxes)	$946.79
Less interest at 8 percent on $4,295	--343.60
Net return	$603.19

"And, except for rounding, this is exactly what my expected return would be if I bought 100 shares of Butcher with an expected EPS of $6.04!"

Broker: "Eureka! Why did you borrow exactly $4,295?"

Friend: "So that even though I was buying Alston, my debt-equity ratio would be the same as Butcher's thus" he reads from his wall:

My equity		$ 5,100
Alston debt, $15.77		
a share, 184.2 shares	=	2,905
My personal borrowing	=	4,295
TOTAL		$12,300

"Now then what is my combined debt–equity ratio? It is exactly 1.41 to 1.00 since

$$\frac{\text{Debt} = \$2,905 + 4,295}{\text{Equity} = \$5,100} = 1.41.$$

"Is that clear?" said your friend.

"Maybe," said the broker, "maybe."

"All I've done," said your friend, "is used Alston plus a little home-made leverage to produce a replica of Butcher's expected earnings."

"Wait a minute" said the broker "not so fast. If you buy 100 shares of Butcher and Butcher goes bankrupt, all you've lost is your $5,100. But if you buy Alston on margin, and Alston goes bankrupt, you've lost $9,395—your original $5,100 plus your personal borrowings of $4,295."

"A mere detail" said your friend, "due to the limited liability attached to common stock. But in my world I don't worry about *that*—because in my world bankruptcies never occur. But you do understand what I'm saying, don't you?"

"Of course," said the broker. "By selling $51 million more debt Butcher has put $1.41 worth of debt on top of every $1 of your equity ($34.5 + 51.0/60.6 = 1.41) ."

"Right," says your friend.

"But you can put $1.41 worth of debt on top of every $1 of your equity by buying 184.2 shares of Alston on margin—for, as we saw above, you would have $7,200 of debt working for you-your share of Alston's debt (= $2,905) plus your personal borrowing. And $7,200/$5,100 = 1.41."

Your friend concluded his illustration by saying: "Tell me, oh wise Wall Street Mogul, why should I pay $52 a share for Butcher's leverage when I can do it myself for $51? After all a dollar is a dollar."

"Whoa, wait a minute," said the broker. "Why have you used before tax figures for EPS?"

"To get at the effect of leverage uncontaminated by the tax effect," said your friend, and hung up.

Your friend knew, obviously, that Alston and United offered the same basic probability distribution over EBIT as Butcher—that is, *the same expected stream of earnings before interest and taxes.* And for this reason he had long regarded Butcher, Alston and United as being nearly perfect substitutes for each other—regardless of the fact that the three companies used different types of assets to manufacture different types of products which they sold in different markets to different types of people. Your friend couldn't care less about assets and products. He cared only—and passionately—about EBIT and about probability distributions over EBIT. If two companies had the same probability distribution over EBIT, they were as far as he was concerned, identical twins—two peas in a pod.

And so when his broker offered him 100 shares of Butcher at $52 a share, he just laughed. He laughed because he knew he could buy Alston at $51 a share. And he knew that by borrowing the right amount of money at the right rate of interest, he could himself "manufacture" whatever degree of leverage he wanted. He couldn't make a replica of Butcher's *assets,* as he could have with Investors Associates and Roan Selection Trust. But he *could* make a replica of the levered stream of pretax earnings now owned by Butcher's stockholders.

And so we see that in the foregoing circumstances, market forces would operate to keep Butcher's stock from rising above $51 a share. But if Butcher did, by some chance, rise to $52 a share, all of Butcher's present stockholder's would be able to improve their respective positions by selling Butcher and buying Alston on margin—*"manufacturing" themselves* whatever degree of leverage *they* wanted.

But what's to keep Butcher from falling *below* $51 a share? Suppose all Butcher's stockholders decide they dislike the additional risk and decide to sell. Why won't Butcher plummet to zero? Suppose you were an Alston stockholder, and Alston were selling, as above, at $51. Suppose, further, that Butcher suddenly dropped to $50 a share. How could you, as an Alston stockholder, take advantage of the drop in the price of Butcher—so as to *improve your position with no increase in risk?*

The easiest way to understand this problem is to suppose that you and your wife, together, are as rich as Rockefeller and, together, own all of Alston's common stock and its bonds. You own the common stock and she, the bonds, yielding 5.8 percent. At breakfast, the morning after Butcher's stock has dropped to $50 a share, you adjust your monocle and say, "I see an easy way to make a bit more than $1 million in a bit less than ten minutes."

She says, "Not now dear, I'm doing the crossword puzzle."

You say, "I'm going to sell all my Alston stock at $51—and I want you to sell your bonds—now."

She says, "Just a minute, dear. What's an eight letter word meaning 'mechanical power resulting from use of a bar and fulcrum'?"

"Leverage," you reply. You pick up your direct line to your broker and tell him to sell your 2,187,500 shares of Alston at $51. In a flash you have increased your cash account by $111,562,500 (= 2,187,500 × $51). We disregard your broker's commission—because he enjoys working for you for nothing. Your wife then calls her broker and sells her bonds, realizing $34.5 million. The two of you together now have cash of $146,062,500 as follows:

Sale of 2,187,500 shares Alston at $51	$111,562,500
Sale of $34.5 million Alston bonds	34,500,000
	$146,062,500

You then call your broker back and tell him to buy in all of Butcher's 1,187,500 shares of outstanding stock at $50, its current price. The total cost is $59,375,000 (= 1,187,500 × $50). Thus, after this purchase, you have $86,687,500 left as follows:

Proceeds sale Alston	
stock and bonds	$146,062,500
Purchase 1,187,500	
shares Butcher	59,375,000
BALANCE	$ 86,687,500

You call your broker for the third time and tell him to buy in all Butcher's bonds for $85.5 million—their face value—and to put $34.5 million of those bonds (those yielding 5.8 percent) in your wife's name. *You have $1,187,500 left over.*

Let's summarize:

1. Instead of Alston you now own an identical company—Butcher.
2. Your wife has her $34.5 million in 5.8 percent bonds earning $2 million exactly as before.
3. You own 1,187,500 shares of Butcher stock, with an expected return before taxes of $6.04 a share (see Table 20.7), and $51 million in Butcher's 8 percent bonds. Your total expected return is thus $11,252,500, as follows:

1,187,500 shares at $6.04	=	$ 7,172,500
$51 million, 8 percent bonds	=	4,080,000
TOTAL		$11,252,500

Your total expected return while you were an Alston stockholder was $11,243,750—which is equal to 2,187,500 shares at $5.14 a share. (But the slight difference in your favor is simply due to rounding. Butcher's expected EPS, before taxes, is really somewhere between $6.03 and $6.04.)

In short, your wife has the same return, you have the same return —but you're richer by $1,187,500! And the risk to you must be *exactly* what it was when you owned Alston. Why? Because the two basic income streams—Alston and Butcher—are identical *and* when you owned Alston, your wife, the bondholder, got her $2 million "off the top" and you got the rest. Now that you own Butcher, your wife will get her $2 million "off the top" (hers is the senior bond issue) and you will, again, get the rest.

And, of course, it makes no difference that Alston has thousands of stockholders—not just one. All of them will see an opportunity to make a dollar or two—if Butcher falls to $50, by selling Alston at $51 and buying an appropriate combination of Butcher's stocks and bonds. In sum, Butcher won't sell at $50 for long—market forces will soon drive it back up to $51.

If, now, you read back over the last few pages, you will see that in the restricted circumstances we have described above, *no company can increase its own market value by increasing (or decreasing) its debt-equity ratio.* If, by some chance, the price of Butcher's stock rises slightly above $51, Butcher's stockholder's will be able to improve their respective positions—without jeopardizing their own personal risk preferences—by selling Butcher and buying Alston or United. But if Butcher's stock falls below $51, Alston's and United's stockholders will be able to improve their positions—by selling their holdings and buying appropriate amounts of Butcher's stocks and bonds. This means that Butcher's stock will not be able, for very long, to sell above or below $51 a share. Market forces will see to it that Butcher's stock continues to sell at $51 a share—regardless of Butcher's degree of leverage.

(You yourself should now be able to show what would happen if Butcher had *sold* more *stock* at $51 a share and *redeemed* all or part of its outstanding *debt.*)

Another way of putting the conclusion, to which we have been led by the foregoing discussion, is as follows:

In a no-tax world *a company cannot change its market value*—that is, the combined value of its stock and its bonds—*by changing its capital structure.*

Before Butcher sold the additional $51 million of debt, its total market value was $146,062,500 as follows:

2,187,500 shares common stock at $51 a share	=	$111,562,500
Value of debt	=	34,500,000
TOTAL	=	$146,062,500

After Butcher had sold additional debt its market value was $146,062,500 as follows:

1,187,500 shares common stock at $51 a share	=	$ 60,562,500
Old debt	=	34,500,000
New debt	=	51,000,000
		$146,062,500

All Butcher had done, then, was substitute $51 million of debt for $51 million of common stock. What does this mean? It means that Butcher's stockholders were not one penny better off than they were before. Those who sold their stock back to Butcher had $51 for each share they sold—instead of a stock certificate worth $51. Those who did not sell had exactly what they had had before—a stock certificate worth $51. *Only if the total value of the company had increased would the stockholders have been better off.*

But, you may say, the stockholders *were* better off—leverage had increased their EPS. If you found yourself coming to this conclusion, you overlooked something—you overlooked the fact that *leverage, as it increases return, simultaneously increases risk.* And we have said, in short, that these two effects *are precisely off-setting*—which is why the effect of leverage, *as such,* on the price of the stock, is zero.

But in order to get at the effect of leverage, *as such,* we have made a large number of unrealistic assumptions—among them the assumption that Butcher paid no income taxes. In the next chapter we discuss these assumptions in detail and remove them.

CONCLUSION

The conclusion we reached in this chapter can be summarized in one simple sentence: Leverage *as such* (pure and unalloyed) cannot improve the lot of the stockholders.

PROBLEMS

1. *You are given the following figures for the Keller Company:*
    (a) *Expected percentage return on total assets, before taxes = .20.*
    (b) *Average interest on debt in relation to D/E ratio:*

D/E RATIO	AVERAGE INTEREST RATE
.10	.080
.20	.080
.30	.080
.40	.085
.50	.085
.60	.090
.70	.090
.80	.095
.90	.095
1.00	.100

    (c) *Tax rate = .48*

Calculate rates of return on net worth after taxes, for each of the ten pairs of figures given above.

2. You are given the following additional figures for the Keller Company which at present has no debt:

   (a) Expected EBIT: $905,000.

   (b) Net worth: $2,410,000.

   (c) Number of shares outstanding, 75,000.

Keller suddenly decides to sell $1,205,000 worth of debt (at 8 percent) on the public market and buy back 37,500 shares of its common stock, presently selling at $32.125.

As soon as Keller announces the decision described above, the price of its stock goes up—to $35.

Your roommate offers to sell you 100 shares at $34.50—making much of the fact that Keller's EPS (before taxes) has almost doubled.

What do you say—and why—assuming a world of no corporate taxes?

Suppose now, instead, that your roommate had offered you 100 shares at $29—making much of the fact that Keller was getting "too risky." You don't like Keller's new capital structure any better than he does. What do you do—and why? Again, assume no taxes.

21

THE COST OF LONG-TERM CAPITAL IV
more on leverage

Obviously, now, the discussion in Chapter 20 of what would happen if Butcher did thus and so sounds very theoretical. It sounds very theoretical because, in large part, it is very theoretical. *But it contains nevertheless an important nucleus of truth.* But before we isolate "the nucleus of truth," let's list the principal assumptions on which the foregoing discussion rests. They are:

1. The corporate income tax does not exist. In fact, of course, the corporate income tax *does* exist. And, as we shall see below, this fact makes a difference (a big difference) because *interest on debt is tax deductible.*

2. Individuals can borrow any amount of money they wish—to buy common stocks—at rates equal to the rates at which corporations can borrow. Neither of these assumptions is valid. The amount of money individuals can borrow to buy stocks is regulated by the Federal Reserve Board—and in the recent past has often been less than 50 percent of market value—which means that if you had wished to buy ten shares of AT&T at $50 a share

"on margin," you would have had to "put up" (as they say) *at least* $250 of your own money.

And, in general, individuals will pay more for borrowed money than corporations pay.

3. No firm, no matter how high its debt-equity ratio, will ever default on its debt—that is, fail to pay interest in full when due. Nor will such a firm ever go bankrupt. This means that leverage is assumed to have two—*and only two*—effects. Leverage increases expected EPS and it increases the variability of EPS. And that is all. In other words, if you buy stock in a highly levered firm, you run only the risk that actual EPS may be lower than it would otherwise have been. You run *no* risk that the company's assets will be sold at auction in order to pay off its creditors. This assumption is obviously unrealistic.

Each of these three assumptions is critical. If an individual investor cannot borrow as much as he would like to borrow to buy common stocks, he will not himself be able to manufacture whatever degree of leverage he wants. In such case, he would probably be willing to pay a premium for the stock of a company with either the "right" amount of leverage or with enough leverage so that he himself would be able to "manufacture" the amount he wanted.

And clearly also, if an individual investor cannot borrow at rates as low as those at which corporations can borrow, he will not be able to reproduce the returns corporations can earn. The returns the corporations can earn will be higher. And for this reason also he would probably be willing to pay a premium for the stock of an appropriately levered company.

And if highly levered firms do (and they do) run the risk of bankruptcy, investors will not feel absolutely comfortable about "switching" from the over-valued shares of an unlevered company to the under-valued shares of a highly levered company. Some—or perhaps most—investors would worry that the highly levered company might default and go bankrupt. And this means that the undervalued shares of highly levered companies may go right on being undervalued—that is, the "switching" mechanism we described in Chapter 20 won't work—to the degree necessary to make the price of the stock of the levered company equal to the price of the stock of the unlevered company.

What now is the "nucleus of truth" referred to above?

If a company can in fact raise the price of its stock (and thus lower its cost of capital) by changing its capital structure, it can do so only because interest is tax-deductible or because individuals are not corporations or because highly levered firms run the risk of bankruptcy.

We discuss, first, the effects of the "tax-deductibility" of interest.

TAX DEDUCTIBILITY OF INTEREST

State and federal tax laws, as you know, define *taxable* income as income *after* deduction of interest on debt—short- or long-term. What, now, is the significance of this fact in the present context?

Let's go back to the hypothetical company we introduced at the beginning of Chapter 20 (see Table 20.4). Actually, in Table 20.4 we mixed together two separate effects: The effect of *leverage* on return on net worth and the effect of the *tax-deductibility* of interest. In Table 21.1

TABLE 21.1

EFFECT OF LEVERAGE AND TAX DEDUCTIBILITY OF INTEREST ON RETURN ON NET WORTH

Company 1		Company 2		Company 3	
		50% DEBT-INTEREST		50% DEBT-INTEREST	
NO LEVERAGE		NOT TAX DEDUCTIBLE		TAX DEDUCTIBLE	
(thousands)		(thousands)		(thousands)	
EBIT	$200.0	EBIT	$200.0	EBIT	$200.0
Interest	———	Interest	——— *	Interest	40.0
EBIT	200.0	EBT	200.0	EBT	160.0
Taxes	100.0	Taxes	100.0	Taxes	80.0
EAT	$100.0	EATBI	100.0 †	EAT	80.0
		Interest	40.0		
		EAT	60.0		
Net worth	$1,000.0	Net worth	$500.0	Net worth	$500.0
Return on		Return on		Return on	
net worth	10%	net worth	12%	net worth	16%
No. of shares	20,000		10,000		10,000
EPS	$5.00		$6.00		$8.00

* Interest assumed not tax deductible.
† Earnings after taxes and *before* interest.

we analyze these effects separately. In the "no leverage" situation, EBIT is $200,000, taxes (at 50 percent) are $100,000, net income after taxes is $100,000, net worth is $1 million. And return, after taxes, on net worth is 10 percent. Column 2 shows the effect of leverage alone. EBIT again is $200,000, taxes are $100,000, interest is $40,000 and net income after taxes and interest is $60,000. But, note carefully, *interest is deducted after taxes are calculated—not before*. Net worth is $500,000 and return, after taxes, on net worth is 12 percent—or 2 percentage points more than the return on net worth with no leverage. These two percentage points are thus the effect of leverage alone. They represent the *pure leverage effect*. The pure leverage effect is simply the return after taxes on total assets (*before* deduction of interest) minus the interest rate multiplied by the debt-equity ratio, thus:

Return on total assets, after taxes, before deduction of interest	10.0%
Interest rate	− 8.0%
Difference	2.0%
Debt-equity ratio $= \dfrac{\$500,000}{\$500,000} =$	× 1.0
Pure leverage effect	2.0%

The pure leverage effect is, to repeat, simply the difference between the expected return on assets and the interest rate—multiplied by a number which measures the amount of money borrowed relative to net worth. (You may still be puzzled by the fact that in this case, lenders are putting as much money into the company—$500,000—as are the owners, but are willing to accept less return—4 percentage points less. But you *should*, by this time, know why they are willing to do so.)

the tax effect

The final column of Table 21.1 describes the *combined* leverage *and* tax effects. EBIT is $200,000, interest is $40,000 (deducted *before* computation of taxes), taxes are $80,000, net income after taxes is $80,000, net worth is $500,000 and the return, after taxes on net worth, is thus 16 percent. To repeat: *In this case, interest has been deducted before taxes have been calculated.* And this has produced a "tax effect" which has added 4 percentage points to the return on net worth. The tax effect is simply the interest rate multiplied by the tax rate multiplied by the debt-equity ratio, thus:

Interest rate	8.00%
Tax rate	× .50
	4.00%
Debt-equity ratio	1.00
Tax effect	4.00

And the *combined* effect is the sum of the *two* effects—the pure leverage effect plus the tax effect—2.0 plus 4.0 = 6.0. Or, we might say, the tax effect is equal to the combined effect minus the pure leverage effect. The tax effect arises purely and simply from the fact that the tax authorities are returning to us, that is, *to the common stockholders,* the interest we pay on debt multiplied by the tax rate which in this case is 50 percent.

So what? When, in Chapter 20, we discussed you and Investors Associates, and you and Butcher we disregarded taxes. (We might just as well have assumed that interest on debt was *not* tax deductible.) And we saw that when we disregarded taxes (and some other odds and ends), we concluded that we would be unable to raise the price of our common stock by substituting debt for equity in our capital structure.

Therefore the question now is: Does the tax deductibility of interest make any difference? Does the tax deductibility of interest, by some chance, enable us to raise the price of our stock by substituting debt for equity?

The answer is: *it does.*

In order to understand why this is so, let's look again at Table 21.1 and consider Company 1 and Company 3, two separate but similar companies. Both are listed on the American Stock Exchange. Company 1 is an unlevered company which is sailing smoothly along earning $5 a share. Its 20,000 shares are selling at $50. And so it is earning 10 percent, after taxes, on its equity of $1 million. Its cost of capital is 20 percent (= $10./$50), before taxes, and 10 percent after taxes (= $5/$50). The company expects to earn $5 a share forever. It pays all its earning out in dividends.

Company 3, in which you own 100 shares of stock, was until the day before yesterday identical to Company 1 in every respect—same earnings after taxes, same number of shares, same earnings per share, same business risk. But the day before yesterday, Company 3 borrowed $500,000 at 8 percent and bought back 10,000 shares of its common stock. Its capital structure is therefore 50 percent debt and 50 percent equity. It has in other words, a debt-equity ratio of 1 (= $500,000/$500,000).

As soon as you become aware of this financial coup, you rush over to see your friend, the art history major. You tell him the story about Company 3's new debt-equity ratio. You then pull your stock certificate out of your pocket (100 shares of Company 3) and push it under his haughty nose. You say, "I'll sell you this for $5,100."

He takes the certificate, looks at it, sniffs it, hands it back to you and says, "Just a minute."

He picks up the phone, turns his back to you, dials a number, cups his hand over the mouthpiece so you can't hear what he's saying, and talks for a few seconds. He hangs up, turns back to you and says: "Okay. Endorse the certificate over to me." He hands you an elaborate ball point pen. You sign. He gives you fifty-one crumpled $100 bills which he has mesmerized out of thin air.

You are flabbergasted. You say, "I thought you were one of those do-it-yourself people."

He says, "I am. But you can't do-it-yourself *if interest on debt is tax deductible.*

"Oh," you say. "How so?"

He explains, in a very patronizing way. "First, suppose I own 100 shares of Company 3. And suppose that Company 3's stock now goes to $51 a share. I sell and with the proceeds ($5,100) I buy 204 shares of Company 1 at $50 a share on 50 percent margin—that is, I use my own $5,100 and I borrow $5,100, I pay 8 percent for the $5,100 I borrow —which is the same rate Company 3 is paying. What have I got? I've got only 12 percent on my own money as follows," and he scribbles as usual on the wall:

204 shares at EPS of $5	=	$1,020
Interest at 8% of $5,100	=	− 408
My return in dollars	=	$ 612
My return in percent:	$\dfrac{\$612}{\$5,100} =$	.12

"or exactly 12 percent," he says.

"Now if you look back at Table 21.1," he says, "you'll see that what I've gotten is the *leverage* effect. But doing it myself, I can't get 16 percent, *with the same degree of financial risk Company 3 is running, because I can't reproduce the tax effect.*

"If I want 16 percent on my $5,100 I have to borrow $15,300 and buy 408 shares of Company 1 at $50 a share, thus," he shows on the wall:

My own money	=	$ 5,100
Borrowed at		
8 percent	=	15,300
TOTAL	=	$20,400

"With this $20,400 I buy 408 shares of Company 1 at $50 a share. My return is then 16 percent, thus:"

408 shares at EPS of $5	=	$2,040
Interest at 8% of $15,300	=	−1,224
My return in dollars	=	$ 816
My return in percent:	$\dfrac{\$816}{\$5,100} =$	.16

"or exactly 16 percent. But $15,300 would represent 75 percent of my own personal capital structure [$15,300/$20,400 = .75] and my personal debt-equity ratio would be 3 to 1 [= $15,300/$5,100] instead of 1 to 1.

"Second," he says, "in other words, if I want a 16 percent return, I can get it with a debt-equity ratio of 1 to 1—if I buy the stock of Company 3. But if I try to do it myself, I can get a 16 percent return only with much greater risk.

"Peculiar, isn't it?" he said.

"Very," you said.

"Well," he said, "if you'll just go back and study Table 21.1 hard and reread the last few pages of text you'll understand what's really happening. It's all because of the corporate income tax and because corporations can deduct interest from EBIT to get taxable income."

"Nonsense," you say. "If I do it myself, I can deduct interest to get my *personal* taxable income. If I buy Company 3, I have no interest to deduct. Interest is being deducted once in both cases."

"Don't try to confuse me," he says. "Your personal tax situation is irrelevant. No matter what tax bracket you're in, your return will be higher for the same degree of risk, *if you don't do it yourself*. If you're in a 50 percent bracket, your return will be 6 percent after taxes, if you do it yourself with Company 1. But 8 percent if you just buy Company 3."

"Very peculiar," you say.

"Not at all," he says. "Just think about it. Just use your old noodle. What it means, of course, is that the two stocks won't sell at the same price. The stock of the levered company will command a premium."

And so you say, "I shouldn't have sold you that stock at $51 a share."

"No, you shouldn't," he said.

You say, "Maybe I should buy it back."

He says, "It's now selling at $56."

You say, "$56! How do you know that?"

He says, "I called my broker before I bought it from you."

You say, "Do you mean to say you let me sell it to you at $51 when you knew it was selling on the exchange at $56?"

"Of course," he says. "But it'll go higher."

You say, "How much higher?"

He says, "Let's figure it out."

• PRICING A STOCK

First, suppose you own 100 shares of stock in Company 1 worth $50 a share, or $5,000 in total. You are earning a return of $5 a share, or 10 percent, at the current market price ($5/$50 = .10).

Now, Company 3 sells $500,000 of debt and, as above, buys back 10,000 shares of its stock at $50. Obviously, before the price of Company 3's stock starts to rise, you can increase your return by selling your 100 shares in Company 1 and investing the proceeds in the stock *and* the bonds of Company 3.

In what proportions should you invest so as to have the same degree of risk? You decide to try 50-50, which corresponds to Company 3's debt-equity ratio. You buy 50 shares of Company 3's stock at $50 a share and $2,500 worth of its 8 percent bonds. Your return is 12 percent thus:

$$
\begin{array}{lll}
\text{50 shares at EPS of \$8 a share} & = & \$400 \\
\text{\$2,500 worth of bonds at 8\%} & = & \underline{200} \\
& \text{TOTAL} & \$600 \\
\end{array}
$$

$$\frac{\$600}{\$5,000} = .12$$

or exactly 12 percent.

You then say to yourself: "All right, now how much would I be willing to pay for the stock of Company 3—so as to have the same *return* I had in Company 1?" You decide you would pay $66.67 a share for Company 3—for at that price your return from investing 50-50 in the stock and the bonds of Company 3 would be exactly 10 percent as follows:

$$
\begin{array}{lll}
\text{37.5 shares ($= \$2500/\$66.67$)} & & \\
\quad \text{at EPS of \$8 a share} & = & \$300 \\
\text{\$2,500 worth of bonds at} & & \\
\quad \text{8 percent} & = & \underline{200} \\
& \text{TOTAL} & \$500 \\
\end{array}
$$

$$\frac{\$500}{\$5,000} = .10$$

or exactly 10 percent. So, you say, when the price of Company 3's stock reaches $66.67 everything will be in "equilibrium" at which point no one will have any incentive to switch one way or the other.

The art history major, who has been looking over your shoulder while you've been doing these calculations, now says in a loud irritated voice, "No! No! *That's wrong.*"

You say, "Wrong? Why is it wrong? Company 3 now has a 50-50 debt-equity ratio. I undo its leverage by investing my funds 50-50 in its stock and its bonds. Just plain common sense."

"No," says the art history major, "but in order to keep the explanation simple, let's just suppose you own *all* the stock in Company 1—not just a miserable 100 shares. You've paid $50 a share for it—or total of $1,000,000 [= $50 × 20,000 shares]. But you bought it on 25 percent margin—borrowing $250,000 from your broker at 8 percent. The stock is still selling at $50. Expected EPS is $5 a share and your expected income from Company 1, before deduction of the $20,000 in interest you must pay your broker, is $100,000 [= $5 × 20,000 shares].

"Your expected return from Company 1 is 10.7 percent, thus," as he scribbles again:

Income from 20,000 shares
   at $5 a share   = $100,000
Less interest at 8% on $250,000 = −20,000

Your net return in dollars   = $ 80,000
Your return in percent on
   your own money: $\dfrac{\$80,000}{\$750,000}$ = .107

"or 10.7 percent."

But, of course, expected EPS of $5 a share is just the mean of a probability distribution. The distribution itself is shown in Table 21.2, together with your income both before and after deduction of the interest you're paying on the $250,000 you borrowed.

Now, your problem, in three parts, is as follows:

1. Company 3 has sold $500,000 in debt at 8 percent (to Fidelity, let's say) and has bought back half (= 10,000 shares) of its common stock.

2. At the same time, you sell your 20,000 shares in Company 1 at $50 a share, which is the present market price. Your broker sends you a check for $750,000, which is equal to $1,000,000 (= $50 × 20,000 shares) minus the $250,000 you borrowed from him. So now you have $750,000 to invest in the stock of Company 3.

3. The question you must answer is: *How many shares* should I buy in Company 3 so that my income will be exactly what it was before—*with the same probability distribution?*

You know that Company 1 and Company 3 are similar companies and therefore they will have the same expected EBIT and the same probability distribution over EBIT—as shown in Table 21.2. Now, let's see what Company 3's income after taxes (EAT) will be—after interest has been deducted and taxes paid. This is shown in the final column of Table 21.3. The probabilities and EBIT in Table 21.3 are taken from Table 21.2. We then deduct interest to obtain EBT and we deduct taxes to obtain EAT.

You say, "EAT in Table 21.3 is *exactly the same as Income after Personal Interest in Table 21.2*. But exactly."

"Right!" says the art history major. "But exactly. And what does that mean?"

TABLE 21.2

PROBABILITY DISTRIBUTION OVER YOUR INCOME FROM COMPANY 1

PROBABILITY	EBIT	EAT *	PERSONAL † INTEREST	INCOME AFTER PERSONAL INTEREST
			(thousands)	
(1)	(2)	(3)	(4)	(5)
.01	$ 50	$ 25	$20	$ 5
.02	60	30	20	10
.04	100	50	20	30
.06	120	60	20	40
.07	140	70	20	50
.08	160	80	20	60
.10	180	90	20	70
.24	200	100	20	80
.10	220	110	20	90
.08	240	120	20	100
.07	260	130	20	110
.06	280	140	20	120
.04	300	150	20	130
.02	320	160	20	140
.01	340	170	20	150
1.00				

* = EBIT —.50 EBIT = EBIT (1 —.50).
† = $250,000 × .08.

You think a minute and then say, "If I use my $750,000 to buy *all* the stock in Company 3—I'll have the same expected dollar return with the same probability distribution—as I had when I owned Company 1 on 25 percent margin! I don't need to buy any of Company 3's bonds at all!"

"Right again!" says the art history major. "And so . . . ?"

"And so," you say, "I should be willing to pay up to $750,000 for all the stock in Company 3—or $75 for each of its 10,000 shares. In which case my expected *percentage* return would be exactly what it was before," you say as you scribble on his wall:

$$\frac{\$80,000}{\$750,000} = .107$$

"or 10.7 percent—*with the same probability* distribution!"

TABLE 21.3

PROBABILITY DISTRIBUTION OVER COMPANY 3'S EBIT, EBT AND EAT

PROBABILITY	EBIT	INTEREST	EBT	TAXES	EAT
			(thousands)		
(1)	(2)	(3)	(4)	(5)	(6)
.01	$ 50	$40	$ 10	$ 5	$ 5
.02	60	40	20	10	10
.04	100	40	60	30	30
.06	120	40	80	40	40
.07	140	40	100	50	50
.08	160	40	120	60	60
.10	180	40	140	70	70
.24	200	40	160	80	80
.10	220	40	180	90	90
.08	240	40	200	100	100
.07	260	40	220	110	110
.06	280	40	240	120	120
.04	300	40	260	130	130
.02	320	40	280	140	140
.01	340	40	300	150	150

"Right! Right! Right!" says your friend. "Now, then, do you notice anything peculiar about the result?"

"Yes, indeed!" you say. "When I held all the stock in Company 1, I owned all its assets, in effect, on 25 percent margin. And my debt-equity ratio was 1 to 3 [= $250,000/$750,000]. Now I own all the assets in Company 3—but in effect on 50 percent margin. And my debt-equity ratio is 1 to 1 [= $500,000/$500,000]. But my own income, before my personal income taxes, is *the same in both cases—with the same probability distribution!* Remarkable!"

"Not remarkable at all," he says. "Just look back at Table 21.1. Because interest is tax deductible, the stockholders of Company 3 are receiving $20,000 more than they would otherwise receive—$80,000 after taxes instead of $60,000. *And that $20,000 is certain. And because it's certain it offsets part of the financial risk Company 3 is running.* Is that clear?"

"Why do you say it's certain?" you ask. "It's not certain if Company 3 loses money and pays no taxes. If it pays no taxes it won't get the $20,000 back."

"It's certain if Company 3 can carry the loss forward and offset it against next year's income—or backward and offset it against last year's income."

"Now," says the art history major, "let's go back to your miserable 100 shares in Company 1—which you had owned outright and which had cost you $50 a share—or $5,000 in total. You've sold them at $50 a share, and your problem now is how to invest that $5,000 in the stock *and* bonds of Company 3.

"But before we go to work on the problem, let's get a few things clearly in mind. *First,* that $5 a share return you got, when you owned Company 1, was, of course, the mean of a probability distribution—as in Columns (1), (2), (3), and (4) of Table 21.4. Look at these columns carefully," he admonishes you. "Column (1) is the probability distribution itself. (It's the same as Column (1) of Table 21.2.) Column (2) is

TABLE 21.4

PROBABILITY DISTRIBUTIONS OVER EARNINGS FOR COMPANIES 1 AND 3.

	Company 1			Company 3	
PROBABILITY	EPS (BEFORE TAXES) *	EPS (AFTER TAXES) *	YOUR SHARE (100 SHARES)	EPS (BEFORE TAXES) †	EPS (AFTER TAXES) †
(1)	(2)	(3)	(4)	(5)	(6)
.01	$ 2.50	$1.25	$125	$ 1.00	$ .50
.02	3.00	1.50	150	2.00	1.00
.04	5.00	2.50	250	6.00	3.00
.06	6.00	3.00	300	8.00	4.00
.07	7.00	3.50	350	10.00	5.00
.08	8.00	4.00	400	12.00	6.00
.10	9.00	4.50	450	14.00	7.00
.24	10.00	5.00	500	16.00	8.00
.10	11.00	5.50	550	18.00	9.00
.08	12.00	6.00	600	20.00	10.00
.07	13.00	6.50	650	22.00	11.00
.06	14.00	7.00	700	24.00	12.00
.04	15.00	7.50	750	26.00	13.00
.02	16.00	8.00	800	28.00	14.00
.01	17.00	8.50	850	30.00	15.00
1.00					

* Based on 20,000 shares.
† Based on 10,000 shares—after Company 3 sells $500,000 of debt and buys back 10,000 shares at $50 a share.

Company 1's EPS before taxes. Column (3) is Company 1's EPS after taxes and Column (4) was your total share after taxes, of the earnings of Company 1—before you sold your 100 shares. The figures in Columns (2) and (3) of Table 21.4 are just the figures in Table 21.2 divided by 20,000. And the figures in Column (4) are the figures in Column (3) multiplied by 100. Is that clear?"

You look at Table 21.4 carefully and you say, "Yes, that's clear. Company 1 was expected to earn $2.50 a share before taxes and $1.25 after taxes with probability .01. If Company 1 did earn $1.25 a share, after taxes, my total share would have been $125 [= $1.25 × 100 shares]. If Company 1 earned $1.50, after taxes (with probability .02), my share would have been $150 [= $1.50 × 100 shares], and so forth."

"You've got it!" he said. "Now, the second thing you've got to get clearly in mind is this: You want to buy the stock *and* the bonds of Company 3 in such proportions that you will have *the same total income you would have had in Company 1 with the same probability distribution.*"

"You mean," you say "that I'm to buy the stock and the bonds of Company 3 in such proportions that I'll have an income of $125 with probability .01, $150 with probability .02, and so forth. Then Probability and my Share are the critical columns as far as I'm concerned."

He slapped you on the back. "By Jove," he said, "you've got it."

"Now," he continued, "let's study in Table 21.4 EPS, before and after taxes, for Company 3. These figures are simply the figures for EBT and EAT in Table 21.3, divided by 10,000. Company 3, you will remember, now has only 10,000 shares outstanding—because it has borrowed $500,000 and bought back half its shares. Are you with me?" he asks.

"More or less," you say.

(If you, the reader, are not, go back and read the last page or so carefully. And be sure you understand columns 4 and 6 of Table 21.4.)

"Now," says your friend, "let's look at column (4) and column (6) of Table 21.4 *very carefully*. You want to buy Company 3's stock *and* the interest on its bonds (8 percent on whatever you invest) *in such* proportions that your total income from both stocks *and* bonds will be equal to your share of return from Company 1—that is, $125 with probability .01, $150 with probability .02, $250 with probability .04—and so forth. Is that clear?"

"That's exactly what I said just a minute ago."

"Don't be unpleasant," he says.

"Sorry," you say, "but now, tell me, oh, wise one, how do I do it?"

The art history major then explained to you that the simplest way to do it was by trial and error.

trial and error

It was obvious, he said, that your income from holding Company 3's bonds would have to be less than $125. If your income from holding Company 3's bonds *exceeded* $125, your total share would (column (4) of Table 21.4) be more than $125 when EBIT was at its lowest possible level—that is, at $50,000. And if your income from holding Company 3's bonds were *exactly* $125, then you could hold none of Company 3's stock —for if you received $125 in interest and you owned also as much as one share of stock, your total share, again, would exceed $125 when EBIT was at its lowest level. And so your income from interest must be less than $125.

q.e.d.

You decide to try $100 of interest income. At 8 percent, $100 of interest income equals $1,250 worth of bonds ($\frac{\$100}{.08} = \$1,250$ and $\$1,250 \times .08 = \$100$). So far so good.

Now how many shares of stock should you buy? Obviously, the art history major told you, you want a number of shares which, when multiplied by the EPS figures in column (6) of Table 21.4 and added to your interest income (= $100), will give you the figures in column (4) of Table 21.4. Thus, when EBIT is $50,000 and EPS is 50 cents a share you would need fifty shares:

Interest income	=	$100
50 shares at EPS of $.50	=	25
TOTAL		$125

But if EBIT were $200,000 and EPS is $8, fifty shares would also be the right number, thus:

Interest income	=	$100
50 shares at EPS of $8	=	400
TOTAL		$500

And when EBIT is at its maximum (= $340,000), fifty shares would again be the right number thus:

Interest income	=	$100
50 shares at EPS of $15	=	750
TOTAL		$850

And so forth. And so, he says, you should buy $1,250 worth of Company 3's 8 percent bonds and fifty shares of its stock. You will then have the same total income, with the same probability distribution, as you had when you owned outright 100 shares of stock in Company 1.

"You should note again," he says, "that even though only 25 percent of your income comes from Company 3's bonds, and Company 3's debt to equity ratio is 1 to 1 [$500,000/$500,000], you are now running no more risk than you did when you owned outright 100 shares in an unlevered company. You now have the same expected income you had before—with the same probability distribution. You did *not* have to split your $5,000 equally between the stock and the bonds of Company 3.

"The tax effect again," you say.

"Right," he says.

"But now," you say, "two questions. *First,* I've invested only $3,750 as follows," and you scribble:

$1,250 in bonds	=	$1,250
50 shares of stock at $50	=	2,500
TOTAL		$3,750

"I have $1,250 left. I'm no longer fully invested. And *second,* we want to decide how high the price of Company 3's stock will go."

"The two questions are related," says your friend. "The question you are now asking is: How much should I have been willing to pay for my fifty shares of Company 3 so that my expected *percentage* return from investing in Company 3 would be the same as my expected percentage return from Company 1—with, of course, the same probability distribution."

"That's easy," you say. "My expected percentage return from Company 1 was 10 percent, thus:"

Expected return in dollars	$500
My investment	$5,000

"If I had paid $3,750 for my fifty shares of stock in Company 3, I would have been fully invested, and my percentage return would have equally been 10 percent—because my expected *dollar* return would have been $500, just as it had been before—and I would have had $5,000 invested in total."

"Right," says your friend. "And so . . . ?"

"And so I should have been willing to pay up to $75 a share for my fifty shares of Company 3 [$75 × 50 = $3,750]."

"And if that's what *you* think," he says, "that's what lots of others will think too!"

"Which means, of course," you say, "that Company 3's stock will go to $75 a share!"

"Assuming, of course," said the art history major, "that everything else remains the same."

"Of course," you said. You call your broker immediately and buy back your 100 shares in Company 3 at $57 a share. And the next day, of course, the Commissioner of Labor Statistics announces that the unemployment rate has risen to 5 percent of the labor force. The stock market drops sharply—and Company 3 falls seven points to $50 a share.

THE VALUE OF A LEVERED COMPANY

What, now, do we see? We see that the stock of Company 3 should rise in value to $750,000 (= $75 × 10,000 shares) —other things remaining the same (!). Company 3's bonds are worth $500,000 and the total value of the company is therefore $1,250,000 (= $750,000 + $500,000). The value of Company 3, the levered Company, is thus equal to the value of Company 1, the unlevered company, plus the tax rate (.50) multiplied by Company 3's debt, thus:

Value of unlevered company (V_u)	=	$1,000,000
Tax rate multiplied by Company 3's debt		
(= .50 × $500,000) = td_L	=	250,000
V_L		$1,250,000

This relationship can be expected to hold for one simple reason: If it does not hold, stockholders in unlevered companies (as you, above) will be able to improve their return—with no increase in risk—by selling their shares and buying an appropriate combination of the stock *and* the bonds of the levered company. The relationship will not, of course, hold exactly. But, other things the same, we would expect the total market value of a levered company to be noticeably greater than the total market value of a similar unlevered company—just because of the tax effect alone.

OTHER ASSUMPTIONS

And so that's the effect of the tax deductibility of interest—provided, of course, we can assume investors behave in a rational way. What, now, does it mean for Butcher?

Butcher's stock is now selling at $51 a share and the total value of the company is $146,062,500, thus:

2,187,500 shares of	
common stock at $51	$111,562,500
Face value of outstanding debt	34,500,000
Total value of company	$146,062,500

Now, what would the total value of Butcher be if it had *no debt?* It would be the present market value of the company minus the amount of our outstanding debt multiplied by the tax rate, thus:

Present market value (V_L)	=	$146,062,500
Debt $\times$ .50 (td)		
(= $34,500,000 $\times$ .50)	=	−17,250,000
Present market value, if		
we had no debt (V_u)	=	$128,812,500

To get this figure, we've simply used a variation on the formula we used above, thus:

$$V_L = V_u + td$$

or

$$V_L - td = V_u.$$

"Something wrong," someone said. "If I divide $128,812,500 by 2,187,500 shares, I get nearly $59 a share. That would seem to mean that we could increase the value of our stock by reducing our debt to zero. How about that, Kelley?"

"Well, no," said Kelley, who had suddenly decided to be very polite. "If we reduced our debt to zero, we could do so only by selling additional shares of common stock. Presumably, we'd sell those shares at $51. And in order to redeem $34.5 million of debt we'd have to sell about 680,000 additional shares [= $34.5 million/$51]. Now, if we add 680,000 shares to our present 2,187,500 shares and then divide the total into $128.8 million, we find that if we had no debt, our stock would be selling at about $45 a share, thus:"

$$\frac{\$128.8}{2187.5 + 680.0} = \$44.92$$

"In short, because we have taken advantage, to some extent of the tax deductibility of interest, our stock is selling for about $6 more a share than would otherwise be the case.

"What does all this mean? It means—it must mean—that the more debt we have the higher will be the price of our common stock. If $V_L = V_u + td$ and $V_u = \$128.8$ million (as we showed above), then the more debt we have, the higher V_L will be. And the higher V_L is, the higher will be the price of our stock."

"It still sounds very theoretical to me," said someone sputtering.

"Very theoretical." The sputterer was a retired banker, named Worthington, who divided his time equally between clipping coupons and dozing in a big armchair at the Union League Club. "You're up in the clouds. How can you possibly know what would *really* happen if there *really* were a Company 1 and it *really* substituted debt for half its equity? And how can you possibly know that our stock would be selling at $44 if we had no debt? Humbug!"

Kelley disregarded Worthington. He said, "In addition to the no-tax assumption, we've made three other assumptions:

"First, that investors can borrow as much money as they like to buy common stocks.

"Second, that they can borrow at the same rates at which corporations can borrow.

"Third, that no matter how big its debt-equity ratio, no company will ever default on its debt—or go bankrupt.

"We know that all three assumptions are wrong. What, now, does that mean for us? The fact that the first two assumptions are wrong means that investors who want *more* leverage than they are allowed to make themselves, would probably pay a premium for our stock if it were more highly levered. Lots of people buy stocks on margin. Why do they do so? They do so because they cannot find stocks that are risky enough for them. Why else would they buy stocks on margin—paying premium interest rates, in order to do so—and sacrificing tax benefits they would otherwise be able to obtain?"

"Because they're irrational," said Worthington. "They'd rather pay 9 percent to buy their favorite unlevered stock on 30 percent margin than buy stock in a company which is just as good, has 30 percent debt in its capital structure and borrows its money at 7.5 percent. And that's that."

"We don't need to assume," said Martin, "that every single individual investor is perfectly rational—that he spends every moment of his time looking in every nook and cranny of the *Wall Street Journal* for every opportunity to maximize his wealth. We need only assume that the great bulk of investors do not try to be *irrational*—and that many try hard to find opportunities to increase their wealth. In this latter category, for example, we would certainly put mutual funds, closed-end funds, other financial institutions such as insurance companies and bank trust departments, and also large highly sophisticated individual investors. Mutual funds, bank trust departments and insurance companies hold huge amounts of common stocks. And such financial institutions are run by highly sophisticated investors whose livelihood depends on their doing well with the funds they manage."

Worthington interjected, "Mutual funds, bank trust departments and insurance companies are *not* allowed to borrow to buy securities."

"True," said Kelley," which makes the point even stronger. Many of them are not able therefore to obtain as much leverage as they would like. If we had more leverage, financial institutions would find it easier to satisfy their own risk-return equations.

"And so," Kelley went on, "the more leverage we have, the more attractive our stock will be to: One, individuals who can't now get the combination of risk and return they really want—because of restrictions on margin buying and because they can't borrow at rates as low as the rates at which we can borrow. In addition, if we do the borrowing for them, they get the benefit of the tax effect—which, as we've seen, they can't get by themselves.

"Two, to financial institutions—such as mutual funds—which are prohibited by law from borrowing to buy common stocks. And if we increase our leverage, those of our stockholders who think we have taken too much *financial* risk, can always sell some of their stock and use the proceeds to buy our bonds. They can, that is, 'undo' our leverage, and run whatever degree of *financial* risk they want."

"Provided," said Worthington, "we run no risk of default or bankruptcy."

"Yes," said Kelley. "We'll come back to that later."

where are we now?

The President of Butcher looked perplexed, so Kelley said, "We've said, in effect, that if we increase our debt-equity ratio, the price of our stock will go up for two reasons. First, our stockholders will get the benefit of the tax effect and second, we will make our stock more attractive to people and to financial institutions who cannot now themselves make as much leverage as they want—and who, when they do make their own leverage, pay higher interest rates than we do.

"But we've said also—and this is very important—that, *regardless of what we do,* any one of our stockholders can get whatever degree of leverage he wants *by buying appropriate amounts of our stock and our bonds.*

"And that means—except for the possibility of bankruptcy—*all* of our stockholders will be better off the more leverage we have."

the possibility of bankruptcy

"Except for the possibility of bankruptcy," said Worthington, derisively.

"Yes," said Kelley. "Obviously, beyond a certain point, more leverage does carry with it the risk of bankruptcy. And therefore beyond that certain point, more leverage might well depress the price of our stock.

"In addition," he said, "we must take account of our special position as managers. Our reputations are at stake. If we borrow too much and we run into a succession of poor years, we may go bankrupt. A company such as this—of this size, using the latest techniques to manufacture a large number of diversified basic products—would probably survive. Our factories would survive, our labor force would survive and our markets would survive. But our stockholders would probably lose at least part of their investment and we would probably be replaced by a whole new set of managers and directors. I don't think I'd like that."

"Well, young man," said Worthington, "I'm glad you're finally showing a little sense."

"And so," said Kelley, "we should probably try to decide on a 'reasonable' debt-equity ratio—which we would try to maintain over the long run."

a "reasonable" debt-equity ratio

"What's reasonable?" asked Worthington.

"We can decide that," said Kelley, "in one or the other of two ways. We can either fix the ratio ourselves or we can allow it to be fixed by our lenders."

"It will be fixed by our lenders—no matter what we do," said Worthington. "We can't borrow more money without Fidelity's permission. And they'll do one or the other—or both—of two things. They'll either raise the interest rate to the point at which we would no longer find it worthwhile to borrow. Or they'll refuse to lend us more than a fixed amount—say, one third of our capital structure."

"Right," said Kelley, "they'll fix the upper limit. But we could, if we wished, borrow less—at lower rates."

Kelley then explained that just before the meeting, he had received from Morton of Fidelity a schedule of the additional amounts Fidelity would now be willing to lend Butcher, as follows:

1. $11 million, subordinated to the present debt at 7.5 percent on the outstanding balance. Total long-term debt would then be $45.5 million (= $34.5 million plus $11.0 million). This loan would be repaid in fifteen annual installments of $733,000 each. With this loan Butcher would be able to finance all the projects listed in Table 15.1 with debt—and have something left over.
2. $25.5 million, also subordinated to the present debt, at 8.0 percent. Total long-term debt would then be $60 million (= $34.5 million plus $25.5 million). This loan would be repaid in fifteen annual installments of $1.7 million each. With the addi-

tional $14.5 million Butcher would be free, if it wished, to invest in (about) 280,000 shares of its own common stock.

Kelley explained that for ten years Fidelity would *not* allow Butcher to repay either loan with money borrowed elsewhere—which meant that if interest rates went down Butcher would have been better off to borrow as much as possible short-term from the bank.

"Let's worry about that after we get the main question settled," said Martin. "What's a reasonable debt-equity ratio? Or to put it bluntly, how much risk are we, as managers, willing to take?"

During the ensuing discussion the following points were made:

1. With debt of $60 million ($= 34.5$ million $+ 25.5$ million) annual interest the first year would be about $4 million before taxes. Amortization of $4 million after taxes would be equal to $8 million before taxes, assuming a 50 percent tax rate—because amortization is *not* tax deductible. Interest plus amortization would thus be equal to $12 million in total, in before tax dollars.

2. With debt of $45.5 million interest and amortization before taxes would be $2.7 million (interest) and about $6 million (amortization) —a total of $8.7 million.

3. At present, interest and amortization on a before-tax basis were together about $6.5 million.

4. Depreciation, including depreciation on the new projects, would run about $5 million a year.

5. And expected EBIT would go up by about $5 million—if all the new projects were accepted. It would, of course, go up less than that amount in poor years and more in boom years.

Kelley then passed around a probability distribution over earnings before depreciation, interest and taxes (EBDIT). This distribution which was similar to, but not identical to, Table 7.7 is given in Table 21.5. This table *includes depreciation;* Table 7.7 did not. Kelley passed out copies of Table 7.7—which the Finance Committee had not seen— and explained how it had been drawn up. (You should refresh your memory on this.) He then explained that the EBDIT figures in Table 21.5 had been obtained by adding $10 million to each of the EBIT figures given in Table 7.7. Thus the first EBIT interval in Table 7.7, $15.1–20.0 million, became in Table 21.5, $25.1–30.0. Of the $10 million so added, $5 million was an estimate of depreciation and $5 million was an estimate of the average before-tax profits expected to be generated by the new projects.

The Finance Committee then asked several hundred questions of which the following were the most important:

TABLE 21.5

PROBABILITY DISTRIBUTION OVER EBDIT *

ECONOMIC CONDITIONS	EBDIT (millions)	MIDPOINT OF EBDIT (millions)	PROBABILITY	EXPECTED VALUE † (millions)
Boom				
With MTR	$25.1-30.0	27.5	.03	0.825
Without MTR	30.1-35.0	32.5	.12	3.900
Very Good				
With MTR	20.1-25.0	22.5	.05	1.125
Without MTR	25.1-30.0	27.5	.20	5.500
Good				
With MTR	15.1-20.0	17.5	.09	1.575
Without MTR	20.1-25.0	22.5	.36	8.100
Recession				
With MTR	10.0-15.0	12.5	.02	0.250
Without MTR	15.1-20.0	17.5	.08	1.400
Depression				
With MTR	5.0-10.0	7.5	.01	0.075
Without MTR	10.0-15.0	12.5	.04	0.500
		TOTALS	1.00	$23.250

* See Table 7.7 for definitions.
† Based on midpoints of EBDIT.

Question: Where do those probabilities come from?

Answer: From past history. I dug them out of our own records and out of material published by the National Bureau of Economic Research.

Question: What do you think they mean?

Answer: Given past history—that is, given the number of recessions in general business and in machine tools which we've had since World War II . . .

Worthington: You're just projecting the past into the future.

Answer: That's right. I don't know what else to do. But if you think the probabilities are wrong, I hope you'll say so.

Question: Why do we need them at all? Why can't we use the good old-fashioned rule based on interest coverage? Average EBDIT should cover interest charges two to three times. Your Table 21.5 indicates that average EBDIT would be about $23 million. To me that means that we could borrow an additional $11 million—but not an additional $25 million.

Answer: You can use a times interest earned ratio if you want to. But

Table 21.5 gives you more information than a mere average. The question can then be put in the following way: would we—that is, the management—feel comfortable with a 1 percent probability that we'd be unable to pay interest and amortization out of EBDIT? 2 percent? 5 percent? 10 percent? And so forth. Table 21.5 indicates that if we allow our long-term debt to rise to $60 million, we would run about a 7 percent chance of being unable to pay interest and amortization of $12.8 million (before taxes) out of EBDIT. And we would run about a 3 percent risk with $45.5 million of debt. Neither risk seems very big to me.

Martin: Especially when we take account of two facts: First, if business fell off—for whatever reason—both receivables and inventory would run off into cash. Both fluctuate with sales and that 'cash run off' would be available to pay interest and amortization. In addition, our cash and securities tend to average more than $10 million. We hold so much liquidity just so we'll be able to meet contingencies.

Second, we must decide what assumption to make about the future. Do we think that we will have another prolonged severe depression such as the one we had in the thirties? I don't. I think Kelley's probabilities will probably prove to be conservative. Anyway, it seems to me we must base our financial policy on the assumption that, if we continue to be efficient, we will have an occasional bad year and an occasional poor year. But we will not be pushed to the wall and into bankruptcy by a long, severe depression.

After discussing the pros and cons for another hour, the Finance Committee voted to recommend to the board, a debt level of $60. million.

"We have three questions left for next week's meeting," said Martin:

"One: Do we borrow $25.5 at long-term at current rates—or do we try to borrow part of it short-term?

Two: Kelley thinks we should stop paying cash dividends. Should we or should we not?

Three: We have changed our debt-equity ratio. What, now, is our cost of capital?

CONCLUSION

This chapter has reached the following conclusions:

(1) Because interest on debt is tax deductible, the total market value of a levered company will noticeably exceed the total market value of an unlevered company—provided leverage is not pushed too far.

(2) In addition—again provided we do not push leverage too far—the

more leverage we have the more our stock will appeal to investors who are prevented by law (or administrative regulation) from making their own leverage—or making as much leverage as they would like.

(3) But if we do push leverage too far—to the point at which bankruptcy seems to investors to be a real possibility—the additional leverage may depress the price of our stock instead of raising it.

(4) We should therefore try to achieve a debt-equity ratio which will take the fullest possible advantage of the tax (and other) benefits of leverage but which will not raise, appreciably above zero, the possibility of bankruptcy.

PROBLEMS

1. Let's substitute the following abbreviations for some of the words and terms we've used in the preceding chapters:

    EBIT, in dollars $= x$
    EAT in dollars $= (x - R)(1 - t)$
    Tax rate in percent $= t$
    Total interest in dollars $= R$

    Now, refer to Table 21.1.

    Using these symbols, we can define EAT as follows for the case in which interest was not tax deductible:

    $$EAT = x(1 - t) - R$$

    And we can define EAT as follows for the case in which interest was tax deductible:

    $$EAT = (x - R)(1 - t)$$

    Now, subtract column 2 from column 3.

    What do you see? And what does what you see tell you about the effect of the tax-deductibility of interest on the return to the common stockholders and the bondholders?

2. Now, go back to column 1 of Table 21.1, and set it up as an equation—using the abbreviations given above. Now assume that you had bought all the stock in Company 1 (20,000 shares at $50 each) on 50 percent margin, paying 8 percent for the $500,000 you borrowed. Deduct the interest. Compare the final result with the equation set up above, for Company 2 (column 2).

    Now do you see why you can't "do it yourself" if corporate interest is tax deductible?

3. You own 100 shares of Butcher, now selling at $51 a share. Butcher now sells another $25.5 million of debt (at 8 percent), bringing its

total debt up to $60 million ($34.5 million + $25.5 million). This makes you feel that Butcher is now too risky. But you don't want to sell all your Butcher stock. What do you do? Use the probability distribution over EBIT given in Table 7.11.

4. If everything else remains the same, what will be the approximate price of Butcher's stock after the new debt has been sold?

5. Redo Table 21.1 using
     (a) a 40 percent tax rate
     (b) a 60 percent tax rate.

6. What danger do you see in setting a target debt ratio which most investors would consider to be too low?

22

THE COST OF LONG-TERM CAPITAL

V
recapitulation and conclusion

Before we take up the three questions which were put on the agenda for the next meeting of Butcher's Finance Committee, let's glance back quickly at the rocky terrain we've traversed in Chapters 17 through 21.

We began the discussion by asking: *What is the cost of capital and why do we care about it?* In its simplest terms, we said, the cost of capital is the cost of the money we will raise *now—but have not yet raised—*to finance *new* projects.

The phrase "have not yet raised" is very important—because *we will not know how much new money we will in fact raise until we have estimated the cost of new money.* After we have estimated the cost of new money, we will compare that cost with expected rates of return on proposed new projects (as in Table 15.1). This comparison—between the cost of new money and the expected returns on proposed new projects—will tell us which projects to accept. (We will, of course, accept only those projects which have *an expected rate of return higher than the cost of capital.*) We will, then, add up the cost of all the projects we have decided to accept—and we will, then, know how much new money we will have to raise.

This, then, is why we care about the cost of capital—it enables us to choose from among all *proposed* new projects *those which have an expected return higher than the cost of the funds invested in them.*

In order to estimate the cost of capital, we proceeded in six stages, as follows:

1. We estimated the *separate* cost of each type of money—debt, common stock, retained earnings (Chapter 17).
2. We then adjusted the cost of equity for expected growth. *This adjustment was arbitrary.* It was arbitrary because we were trying to do something which really cannot be done—but which, nevertheless, must be done. We were trying to keep ourselves from investing equity—either retained earnings or the proceeds of the sale of new common stock—in such way that the *present* expected return of our stockholders would be reduced (Chapter 18).
3. We obtained a *weighted average cost of capital* by multiplying the separate cost of each type of money by its weight in our *present* capital structure (Chapter 18).
4. We then began to explore the effect of leverage on the value of the firm and on the cost of capital. We saw, first, that additional leverage raises the common stockholder's *expected return* —provided that the expected percentage return on assets is higher than the rate of interest. But we saw also that additional leverage increases the *variability* of the common stockholder's return and thus, his risk (Chapter 20).
5. We then asked whether leverage, *as such,* could be expected to raise the price of a company's common stock. By "leverage as such," we meant pure unadulterated leverage. But in order to be able to explore the effect of *pure unadulterated leverage,* we had to remove the adulterants—by making a number of unrealistic assumptions—no corporate income taxes, no risk of bankruptcy or default regardless of the degree of leverage, no margin restrictions—and so forth. And *on these assumptions,* we found that no company could increase its own market value by using leverage (Chapter 20).
6. Finally in Chapter 21, we removed these assumptions—in order to be able to examine the effect of leverage in the real world.

We came to the following conclusions:

CONCLUSION 1

Because interest on debt is tax deductible, leverage would increase the value of the firm without limit—were it not for the bankruptcy effect. This, of course, is *not* the effect of leverage *as such*. It is the effect of the tax-deductibility of interest. But without leverage, the firm would have no interest to deduct! We summarized this effect by showing that, *other things remaining the same:*

$$V_L = V_u + tD$$

where

$V_L =$ the total market value of a *levered* firm
$V_u =$ the total market value of an unlevered firm,
$tD =$ the tax rate (t) multiplied by the dollar amount of debt (D) in the levered company's capital structure.

This little equation means something very simple. It means that if Company 1 sells $500,000 worth of debt and buys back half its common stock (see Table 21.1), the value of Company 1 will rise from $1 million to $1.25 million, thus:

$$\$1,250,000 = \$1,000,000 + .50(\$500,000)$$

provided the $500,000 of debt does not create the possibility that Company 1 will go bankrupt. If the total value of Company 1 *does* go up to $1.25 million, the value of Company 1's remaining stock—which had previously been worth $500,000—will go up to $750,000. In other words, the total increase in the total value of the company will accrue to the common stockholders—who will now have $500,000 in cash and stock worth $750,000—instead of the $1 million in stock they had before.

We must, of course, be careful about taking this relationship too literally. But it *does* mean that leverage, properly used, can benefit the common stockholders.

CONCLUSION 2

We found *in addition* that for one other reason, levered firms may command a premium over unlevered firms.

A firm which is highly levered, relative to other firms, will be "all things to all people." It will enable investors who want a lot of leverage to obtain it—without suffering the diseconomies of "doing it themselves." But it will not hurt those stockholders who want little leverage or none. The latter will always be able, at slight cost, to "manufacture" themselves whatever degree of leverage they want—by holding "appropriate" combinations of the levered company's stock *and* its bonds.

CONCLUSION 3

But we concluded also that if leverage is pushed *too* far, the price of the firm's stock may be adversely affected—because too much leverage carries with it the risk of default and bankruptcy. Thus we said that leverage is "a good thing"—provided it is not carried too far.

CONCLUSION 4

We concluded finally that we should have a "target" long-term debt-equity ratio. This ratio might vary over time—depending on circumstances and on our own risk preferences.

THE WEIGHTED AVERAGE COST OF CAPITAL

"Now," said Kelley, "we must decide what the real cost of the additional debt is—the additional debt we propose to sell now. Is it the interest rate on the debt—8 percent—or is it something else?"

"All right," said Worthington, "but before we do that would you please show us how we will calculate our weighted average cost of capital *after* we have reached our 'target' debt-equity ratio. Just assume that after we've reached the 'target,' our stock is selling at $56 a share."

"Simplicity itself," said Kelley. "We would proceed as follows: First, we calculate the cost of equity, using the technique we used in Chapter 18. We would assume a payout ratio and a growth rate over some relatively short period of time—say five years. Both the rate and the period would depend on our own evaluation of our opportunities—the way our markets looked, what our research divisions were doing and so forth. And we would assume a price for our stock at the end of that period of time. We would then use present value methods to estimate the rate of return our stockholders could expect to receive—given the price of our stock, as of the moment we were making the calculation (see Table 18.4). This would give us a cost of equity. Let's suppose it were 10 percent, after taxes.

"We cannot, of course, foresee where interest rates will be a year from now, but let's suppose that as this year (1968), we'd have to pay 8 percent (before taxes, of course), for modest amounts of additional debt.

"Having determined the cost of each type of money, we need only fix the proportions in which each is to be raised. When we decided at the last meeting to raise $25.5 million more in debt, we were in effect fixing our long-term target debt-equity ratio. Debt would be $60 million in total—our present debt of $34.5 million plus the new debt of $25.5 million. After annual retentions of about $6 million, our equity would be about $117 million (see Table 2.1). Total capital would thus be about $177 million. The ratio of debt to total capital would be

$$\frac{\$60 \text{ million}}{\$177 \text{ million}} = .339$$

or 33.9 percent and the ratio of equity to total capital would be

$$\frac{\$117 \text{ million}}{\$177 \text{ million}} = .661$$

or 66.1 percent.

These then would be the proportions in which we would raise any *new* money. Using these percentages, our weighted average cost of new long-term capital would be almost exactly 8 percent, as Table 22.1 indicates.

Kelley put the figures given in Table 22.1 on the board. He had simply multiplied the *percent* of each type of long-term money by the *cost*, after taxes, of each type to obtain the figures in the final column, which show Butcher's (hypothetical) *weighted average cost of capital* based on the new long-term debt-equity ratio.

Eight percent, to repeat, said Kelley, would be our weighted average after tax cost of capital on the following assumptions:

1. The cost of new equity would be 10 percent after taxes.
2. The cost of new long-term debt would be 4 percent after taxes and
3. We would raise new long-term capital in the proportions 33.9 percent debt and 66.1 percent equity.

Equity, of course defined to include both any expected retained earnings and any new common stock.

"Is that clear?" Asked Kelley. "The question we've asked (and answered) is very much like the question: How much *per pound on the average,* would a bag of vegetables cost containing two pounds of peas at 40 cents a pound and one pound of broccoli at $1 a pound.

"60 cents," said Worthington.

"Absolutely right," said Kelley.

"Let me repeat," said Kelley. "This is not our present cost of capital. All I've done is illustrate the way we would calculate our cost of capital *after* we've reached our target ratio. Our present cost of capital is the cost of the debt we will raise *now*. Let's talk . . ."

"Just a minute," said Worthington, who was now really having a hard time staying awake. "I have several hundred questions:

"First, our retentions have been running a little less than $3 million

every six months or a little less than $6 million annually. Future reten-
tions would be included in your equity figure in Table 22.1. Right?"

TABLE 22.1

WEIGHTED AVERAGE COST OF CAPITAL (BASED ON NEW LONG-TERM TARGET DEBT-EQUITY RATIO)

TYPE OF LONG-TERM MONEY	PERCENTAGE OF TOTAL RAISED	COST (AFTER TAXES)	WEIGHTED COST *
(1)	(2)	(3)	(4)
Long-Term Debt	33.9%	4.00%	1.36%
Equity	66.1%	10.00%	6.61%
	100 %		7.97%

* Percentage of total $\times$ after tax cost divided by 100.

"Oh, yes," said Kelley.

"Suppose retentions were not sufficient to make up 67 percent of the
cost of the projects we wanted to finance," asked Worthington. *"What
then?"*

"We'd have to sell common stock," said Kelley, "unless we were willing
to change our debt-equity ratio again—or cut the dividend—that is,
increase retentions."

"Cut the dividend! Never!" said the President, who had just arrived
at the meeting after a hard afternoon at his favorite turkish bath. "What
about preferred stock?"

"May we come back to that, sir?" said Kelley.

"All right, Kelley" said the President. "But *don't forget.*"

"Second," said Worthington," it might be inconvenient and un-
economical to raise money in those proportions, year in and year out."

"That's right," said Kelley. "Suppose we wanted to raise $10 million
and retentions were expected to be $6 million, or just 60 percent of the
total instead of 67 percent. We might sell $4 million of debt (instead
of $3.3 million of debt) plus $700,000 of common stock. Selling such
a small amount of stock would probably be unnecessarily expensive.
We'd balance things off the next time we raised external funds—six
months or a year later.

"Or suppose our stock was selling at a price that was much too low simply because the stock market was down. We'd sell debt instead of *both* debt *and* common. And, again, we'd balance things off the next time we raised external funds."

"If you did that," asked Worthington, "how would you estimate your weighted average cost of capital? You wouldn't be able to."

"Well," said Kelley, "we'd use either the current price of the stock or we'd have to guess about the future price."

"Even though you weren't selling any common stock?"

"Yes," said Kelley.

"But, then," said Worthington, "your weighted average cost would not really represent the cost of the funds to be invested in new projects. Isn't that right?"

"That's right," said Kelley.

"In effect," Worthington went on (he was enjoying himself now), "you'd be investing equity funds you hadn't raised. If you haven't raised them, you can't know their cost. If you don't know their cost, you can't calculate a weighted average cost. And if you can't calculate a weighted average cost, you don't know which projects to accept. And if you don't know which projects to accept, you don't know how much money to raise. Isn't that so, young man?"

"Yes," said Kelley. "Strictly speaking."

"It's a vicious circle," said Worthington, as he fell back in his chair.

Martin said, "I don't think there's any ideal solution to that problem. But we'd be able to estimate our weighted average cost within a relatively small margin of error."

"*Do we use the same cost of capital for all projects?* Some projects are riskier than others. I think we should use a lower cost of capital for less risky projects. And vice versa. But all you've given us is one single cost of capital."

"May we come back to that, too?" asked Kelley.

"All right," said Worthington. "But *don't forget.*"

COST OF NEW DEBT

Now, as to the cost of the additional $25.5 million of debt we have decided to sell. The nominal before-tax cost is 8 percent and the nominal after-tax cost is about half that or about 4 percent. The question is —is that the real cost?

"What's the problem," said Worthington testily. "8 percent is 8 percent, and 4 percent is 4 percent."

Kelley said, "Let's go back to Company 1 for a minute." (See Table 21.1.)

"I've had enough of Company 1," said Worthington. "Let's stick to Butcher."

"We'll come right back to Butcher," said Kelley. "But first, what was Company 1's cost of capital, after taxes, before it sold $500,000 worth of debt and bought back half its common stock? It was, as we saw, 10 percent, thus:"

$$\frac{Ea}{Pa} = \frac{\$5}{\$50} = .10$$

or exactly 10 percent. Company 1, you will remember, paid out all its earnings in dividends. This is, of course, equivalent to calculating a weighted average cost of capital for Company 1, based on the market value of its stock, thus:"

TYPE	COST	AMOUNT	WEIGHT	WEIGHTED COST
Common stock	.10	$1,000,000	1.00	.10
Debt	—	——	—	—
Total	—	$1,000,000	1.00	.10

We can also state Company 1's cost of capital in terms of its *total* after-tax earnings ($= \$100,000$) and its *total* market value—which with no debt in its capital structure, is simply the market value of its common stock ($= \$1,000,000$). We get the same figure, of course, because all we've done is multiply both Ea and Pa by the number of shares outstanding, thus:

$$\frac{\$5.00 \times 20,000}{\$50.00 \times 20,000} = .10$$

or exactly 10 percent.

"What are you getting at?" growled Worthington.

"You'll see in a minute," said Kelley.

"I hope so," said Worthington.

In other words, we can reach the same result in either of two ways —either by dividing Ea by Pa or by dividing total after tax earnings by the total market value of the company. We are, for the moment, disregarding the *cost* of selling additional common stock. The figure means, of course, that if Company 1 raised new money by selling additional common stock, its cost of capital, after taxes, would be 10 percent.

Now, then, what happened to Company 1's cost of capital after it sold $500,000 worth of debt at 8 percent and bought back half its common stock?

We know that the total market value of Company 1, after the debt had been sold, and everything had settled down, was $1,250,000 thus:

Debt	$500,000
10,000 shares of common stock at $75 a share	750,000
	$1,250,000

We can now calculate a weighted average cost of capital for Company 1 as follows:

cost of debt

We know that the net dollar cost of Company 1's debt is $20,000. It is $20,000 and *not* $40,000 because the tax effect has added $20,000 to the earnings of the common stockholders—which, without the tax effect would be $60,000 instead of $80,000 (see Table 21.1). In other words, the gross cost of the debt is $40,000—but of this sum, $20,000 is being returned to the common stockholders via the tax effect. *Ergo,* the net cost is $20,000. The percentage cost of debt, after taxes, is therefore 4 percent, thus:

$$\frac{\$20,000}{\$500,000} = .04$$

or exactly 4 percent.

Cost of Equity. Company 1 is now earning $80,000 after taxes—or $8 a share on the 10,000 shares now outstanding. It's cost of equity is therefore 10.67 percent, thus:

$$\frac{\$80,000}{\$750,000} = .1067 \text{ or } \frac{\$8}{\$75} = .1067$$

or 10.67 percent.

We can therefore calculate a weighted average cost of capital, thus:

TYPE	COST	AMOUNT AT MARKET VALUE	WEIGHT	WEIGHTED COST
Common stock	.1067	$ 750,000	.60	.0640
Debt	.04	500,000	.40	.0160
Total	——	$1,250,000	1.00	.0800

or 8 percent.

What's happened? Two things: *First,* the weighted average cost of capital has declined—from 10 to 8 percent—but, *second,* the cost of equity has gone not *down* but *up*—from 10 percent to 10.67 percent. *This increase in the cost of equity is due directly to the fact that Company 1 now has debt in its capital structure.*

(If you, the reader, are puzzled by this statement, you'd better go back and reread Chapter 21. Ask yourself especially whether you would now be happy with a 10 percent yield on Company 1's stock—if you had been happy with a 10 percent yield before it sold debt.)

And so the increase in Company 1's cost of equity is part of the cost of Company 1's debt. In other words, the cost of Company 1's debt *is more than 4 percent, after taxes.*

How much more? We can find the answer to this question by solving a very simple equation:

Let $x =$ real cost of debt then:

$$.08 = .40x + .60(.10) = .05$$

or 5 percent. We have simply answered the question: with Company 1's after-tax cost of capital reduced to 8 percent, what is the cost of debt *if the cost of equity is held constant at 10 percent.* And the answer, we see, is 5 percent.

"That's a very curious result," said Worthington.

"It is," said Kelley.

"It's not a coincidence?" asked Worthington.

"No," said Kelley. "Company 1's real after-tax cost of debt is equal to its original, *unlevered* cost of capital multiplied by the number 1 minus the tax rate [$.10 \times .50 = .05$]. And Company 1's levered, after-tax, cost of capital, 8 percent, is just a weighted average of its *real* after tax cost of debt and its *unlevered* after tax cost of equity:

$$.08 = .40(.05) + .60(.10)$$

Now, what does all this mean for us, for Butcher? It means that if we had no debt, our after-tax cost of equity would be somewhat less than 9 percent. (See Table 18.7.) And it means also that after we add the additional $25.5 million of debt our cost of equity will be somewhat *higher* than it is now. But this rise in the cost of equity will be attributable to the additional debt and will be part of the cost of that additional debt.

What, then, is the after tax cost of the new debt? I don't believe we can be very precise about it (Kelley said). "But we do know that it can't be more than 4.5 percent. Why? Because if our present cost of equity—with debt in our capital structure—is about 9 percent, well, then our cost of equity *if we had no debt would be a bit less than that.*

"Just plain logic," said Worthington.

"I just don't think we can go far wrong if we assume that the real after-tax cost of the new debt is between 4 and 4.5 percent."

"That means," said Martin, "that we accept all the projects listed in Table 15.1—except the last two."

"Right," said Kelley.

"I so move," said Worthington, who was starting to fall asleep again and wanted to get through the agenda.

The motion was seconded and carried—without a single dissenting vote.

BORROW LONG TERM NOW?

Martin then asked the committee what it thought should be done with the extra funds which would become available after they had sold the additional debt to Fidelity.

Worthington said, "We should decide first whether to borrow long-term now—or whether to borrow short-term or medium-term—in the hope that interest rates will come down. If we borrowed short-term, we wouldn't borrow $15 million extra."

"I don't suppose so," said Martin.

Worthington continued, "Corporate interest rates are at an all-time high. And I do not see how they can go any higher. We're going to have a mild recession. And if we do, corporate rates will come down."

He pulled a piece of paper out of his pocket and said: "Let me read you Sidney Homer's latest comment:

> "The momentum of the current rally was carried into this week as both municipals and corporates posted their largest gains since late March. This is the fourth consecutive week in which most sectors of the bond market have rallied. Government bond prices turned down late in the week, and, as a result, most Governments declined fractionally on the week.
>
> "Short term rates were mixed. The three month Treasury bill rate rose 23 basis points early in the week and then settled down to close the week unchanged. Rates on both Federal agencies and bankers acceptances declined while most other money market rates were unchanged.
>
> "Corporate bond prices continued to rally smartly. Seasoned discount utilities rose over 2 points, one of their largest weekly price advances in the past 2 years. Deep discount utilities are now 3 points above their late June lows. High grade new issue

utilities came to market yielding as much as 40 basis points below the level of last week's offerings. On average, new issue reception was good. New issue yields now stand about 70 basis points below their all time high."

"I should think we'd be able to borrow $10 to 12 million on a three year term basis. We'd simply be betting that, sometime in the next three years we'd be able to borrow, at long-term, at rates below the present level. That seems like a good bet to me."

"You said about the same thing last year," said someone in the back of the room. "And interest rates have been going up ever since. The fact that corporate rates are at an all-time high doesn't mean they can't go higher. And if they go higher, we'll wish that we'd taken Fidelity's $25 million at 8 percent."

"We don't have to decide this today," said Martin. "Let's think about it. I'll talk to Raimondi and see what terms he'd give us on a three or four year $12 million term loan. But amortization would be a problem—he'd probably want us to amortize it at the rate of $3-4 million a year."

"There's one other minor problem," said the President. "If we borrow from Fidelity, we know the cost of the money we will invest in new projects. If we borrow short- or medium-term, we don't. Suppose we invest now in a 5 percent project with short- or medium-term funds costing 4 percent, after taxes. And suppose interest rates keep going up. And as a result, we *have* to borrow at long-term, three years from now at 5.5 percent, after taxes. If we borrow short- or medium-term now, we're gambling—as I see it."

"Well let's think about it," said Martin.

The committee agreed to allow Martin and the President to make the decision—after Martin had heard from Raimondi and had discussed the outlook for interest rates with some money market experts.

"Just a minute," said Kelley, "I have an idea. We should draw up a probability distribution before we decide anything."

"Over what?" asked Martin.

"Well," said Kelley, "if we borrow long-term now instead of short- or medium-term, we are saying in effect that we don't want to take the risk that *at no time in the next year or two or three* will long term rates be below their present level."

Someone said, "Say that again, please."

Kelley said, "We can borrow at long-term now—that is, for fifteen years—at 8.0 percent. If we were *certain* that at some time during the next year or two or three, long-term rates would drop to 7.9 percent, we'd borrow short- or medium-term, wait for long-term rates to come down, and *then* borrow long-term.

"But now suppose that we think that there are ninety-nine chances out of a hundred that sometime in the next three years, long-term rates will drop below 8 percent. What do we do then? Or ninety out of a hundred, or seventy-five or fifty? What then?

"I'm suggesting," said Kelley, "that we should draw up probability distributions for one year, two years and three years. They would answer the question: What are the chances that long-term corporate rates will drop below 8 percent in the next year, the next two years, and the next three years. Three distributions."

"Where would the probabilities come from," asked Worthington? "Out of your hat or Martin's?"

"Neither," said Kelley, "we'd have to do some money and capital markets analysis. Talk to some people."

"Good idea," said Martin, "Do it."

"Who?" said Kelley.

"You," said Martin. "Write a memo telling us what you think will happen to corporate bond rates during the next year, the next two years and the next three years—and *why*. Don't forget the *why*. Send a copy to each of us—with your estimate of the probabilities. Then perhaps we can have a short meeting just before we make the final decision."

"All right," said Kelley gloomily. He had planned to take ten days of vacation—in Switzerland—beginning tomorrow and had already paid for his (and his wife's) plane tickets and hotel reservations.

DIVIDEND POLICY

In order to speed up discussion of dividend policy, Kelley had put the questions (as he saw them) and the alternative courses of action into a memorandum. The memorandum had been sent under Martin's signature to the members of the Finance Committee a week before the present meeting. The memorandum read as follows:

To: Members of Finance Committee

From: Dale Martin

Subject: *Dividend Policy*

We hope to be able to discuss the following questions at the next meeting of the Finance Committee:

Question 1: How should we decide how much earnings to retain?

The alternatives are as follows:

(1) Retain, as we do now, a fixed percentage of earnings. Actually, our present policy is a base dividend of ninety cents a share plus "extras" during the third and fourth quarters suffi-

cient to bring the total up to about 50 percent of whatever our earnings happen to be for the whole year. In effect, then, as a matter of policy we retain about 50 percent of earnings. But we decide *first* how much to pay out. This means, of course, that we subtract dividends from earnings and retain what's left. Retained earnings are thus obtained *as a residual*.

(2) But obviously we could treat *dividends* as the residual. In such case, we would retain earnings to the extent that we could invest them profitably—and pay out the remainder. We might, in any year, retain all our earnings or none. We would have no fixed "payout" policy.

Question 2: But whichever of the above two policies we follow, we must decide whether we should pay cash dividends.
The alternative is to use any excess funds to repurchase our own stock.

After the memorandum was brought up for discussion, the following questions arose:
President: Are you suggesting, as a serious alternative, that if our investment opportunities are good enough, we ought to disburse *nothing* to our stockholders?
Martin: Yes.
President: If we pay no dividends, why should anyone buy our stock? You've been saying, ever since I can remember, that the present price of our stock is simply the discounted value of expected future dividends. You finally convinced me you were right. Now you say we ought to pay no dividend. I repeat: if we pay no dividends, why should anyone buy our stock?
Martin: He'd get a capital gain—on which his personal income tax would be less.
President: How would he get a capital gain?
Martin: If we invest a million dollars of earnings, together with the amount of debt indicated by our target debt-equity ratio in a project with an expected rate of return higher than our cost of capital, the market value of our stock will go up by *more than* a million dollars.
Someone: Other things equal.
Martin: Other things equal. Provided, that is, the market doesn't collapse on our heads—for one reason or another. And our stockholders, if they chose to do so, would then be able to sell some of their stock and get a capital gain. The capital gain would be larger than the dividend our stockholders had forgone. And it would be taxable at capital gains rates—which, of course, are lower than rates on ordinary income.
Worthington: Do you mean to say that if we paid the million dollars out in dividends, we wouldn't undertake the project? Why can't we have *both* the dividend *and* the capital gain?

Martin: We could, of course, pay the million dollars out in dividends and then sell a million dollars worth of new stock which—with the appropriate amount of debt—would enable us to invest in the project. And so the answer to your question is: Yes, we could have both. And *that* means we must ask ourselves what the *real* difference is between the two alternatives. What *is* the real difference? In order to make the difference clearer, let's suppose that if we decide to retain the million dollars, we will pay a *stock* dividend of a million dollars, calculated at the present market price of the stock [= $51 a share]. What would this mean concretely? It would mean that if we retained earnings of $1 million, we would distribute about 196,000 new shares of stock *to our present stockholders* in proportion to their present holdings [196,000 = $1 million/$51]. They could sell those shares if they wished. If they did, they would receive cash—which would be taxable not at ordinary rates but rather *at capital gains rates*—assuming they had owned our stock for at least six months. Those of our stockholders who needed cash would sell. But only those who did sell would pay any tax at all. Conceivably, of course, *all* of them might sell. If all of them did sell, they would be in the same position they would have been in had we paid out the million dollars in dividends—with one important difference.

Worthington: They'd pay less taxes and actually have more dollars to spend.

Martin: Right!

Worthington: That assumes that the price of the stock won't go down —because of the issuance of 196,000 shares of new stock. We would have increased the *supply* of our stock by 196,000 shares. When I went to school, if the supply of a commodity went up, the price would go down, other things equal.

Martin: Other things would *not* be equal. The million dollars of retained earnings would be invested in a project which would return more than our cost of capital—which means that the equity in the project would return more than the cost of equity. Our expected return on equity would rise—with no increase in risk. Nothing else would be changed. The price of our stock *should* go up—not down. If it went down, it would certainly not be because 196,000 additional shares were outstanding. That would really make no sense.

Worthington: All right.

Martin: Now let's look at the other alternative. We pay a cash dividend totaling a million dollars. This would be taxable to *all* our stockholders at ordinary, rather than capital gains rates. Remember under the other alternative, I would pay a capital gains tax—but only if I sold my stock dividend.

Now, having paid out the million dollars in cash dividends, we must sell new common stock in order to be able to finance the new project. But selling new stock will cost us perhaps one dollar a share —even if we offer it first to our own stockholders. That means we would receive only fifty dollars a share—if it were offered to the public at fifty-one dollars a share. The investment bankers would keep the extra dollar. And *that* means that we'd have to sell 200,000 shares of stock in order to raise $1 million. The total number of Butcher shares outstanding would be larger—by 4,000 shares [= 200,000 — 196,000] and our expected EPS and return to equity would be less. And as a result the price of our stock would go up less.

In short, our stockholders are worse off in every way if we pay cash dividends instead of stock dividends. They pay more taxes and their expected return is less than it otherwise would be. And they have less 'flexibility.' Suppose that someone who receives a cash dividend doesn't need the cash but wants instead to increase his investment in Butcher. He pays taxes at ordinary rates first and reinvests the balance. But obviously, because of taxes, he is able to buy fewer shares than he would have received as a stock dividend.

Suppose, on the other hand, that someone who receives a stock dividend needs cash. He sells and pays taxes at capital gains rates. And he will have more cash than he would have had if he had received a cash dividend!

That's all I have to say on that subject. The conclusion seems to me to be obvious.

President: Martin, you've been brainwashed—and I think I know by whom. Your reasoning is just plan specious.

Martin: Specious?

President: Yes! Specious! If we cut our cash dividend in half, the price of our stock would drop substantially.

Martin: Makes no sense.

Worthington: Yes it does! If we cut our cash dividend, most of our stockholders would think we had gotten pessimistic about the future. What we do about dividends conveys information to the public. If we raise the dividend, the public thinks we take a rosy view of the future. If we cut the dividend, they think we're gloomy.

President: Let me say this: When I got this memo of yours, I asked my assistant to see whether he could find any expert opinion on this subject. He found several articles. (The president held them up and waved them around.) All of them—I repeat—all of them conclude that those companies that pay higher dividends sell at higher prices. What do you make of that, Kelley?

Kelley: I know the articles. I think they're wrong. Or perhaps the public is just irrational—they'd rather have less money than more money.

Martin: Which means that we ought to try to educate our stockholders.

President: I don't have any objection to trying to educate our stock-holders. But that will take time. Meanwhile, I move that we maintain our present dividend policy.

Worthington: Second.

The president's motion carried by eleven to two with Martin not voting. Kelley would, of course, have voted no if he had had a vote. But he was not, formally, a member of the committee.

Martin: Now that we've voted my suggestion down, I think the com-mittee ought to face up to the implications of what its done.

President: What is that remark supposed to mean?

Worthington: He means that we've said, in effect, that we should raise the dividend.

Martin: Right!

President: Because I said these studies showed that those companies that paid higher dividends sold at higher prices?

Martin: Of course. What you said means that if we raise the dividend, the price of our stock will go up.

President: I said that what we do about the dividend conveys informa-tion to the public. If we raise the dividend, they think we expect our earnings to go up. And so they bid up the price of our stock.

Martin: We do expect our earnings to go up. So we should raise the dividend.

President: That's taken care of automatically by our fixed payout policy. The dividend increases automatically as our earnings go up.

Martin: But why not raise our payout? Let's be logical. The higher the dividend, the higher the price of our stock.

President: Must be one best payout policy.

Martin: I don't know what it is—and I don't think anyone else does either.

President: Not even Kelley.

Kelley: Not even me.

President: Perhaps we'd better think about how to educate our stock-holders.

Martin: Perhaps we'd better.

Worthington: Now what about the second question in this memo of yours?

President: reaching for his reading glasses: What question?

Martin: If we decide to pay out, say, two dollars a share, should we pay it out in cash dividends to each stockholder, or should we instead use it to repurchase our stock? If we decided to pay out two dollars a share, that would be a total of $4,375,000. At the present price of our stock, we would be able to buy back about 86,000 shares.

Worthington: The idea being, again, that those of our stockholders who really wanted cash, would sell some part of their holdings. But they would be taxable only at capital gains rates. The rest of our stockholders would get a paper capital gain because the total 'pie' would be cut up into a smaller number of pieces. We'd have 86,000 fewer shares outstanding and each therefore would be worth more.

Martin: Right.

President: I thought we had just voted to maintain our present dividend policy.

Martin: I took that to mean that we would continue to pay out 50 percent of earnings. We can pay it out either as a cash dividend—or by repurchasing stock.

President: You're quibbling. The whole point of what I said earlier was that each of our stockholders expects to receive a check from us four times a year. I understand the logic of what you're saying. But our stockholders won't—until you've reeducated them.

CONCLUSION

We began this chapter with a review of the conclusions we had come to in Chapters 17 through 21. In addition, we came to the following further conclusions:

(1) The real cost of debt is higher than its nominal cost—because the inclusion of debt in a company's capital structure raises that company's *cost of equity*. We saw, for example, that the inclusion of debt in Company 1's capital structure raised Company 1's cost of equity from 10 percent to 10.67 percent.

Despite this, of course, the inclusion of debt in its capital structure, reduced Company 1's *cost of capital* from 10 percent to 8 percent. Company 1's cost of capital came down because the rise in its cost of equity was more than offset by the low cost of debt. Previously, all of Company 1's capital had cost 10 percent. After it had sold debt, 40 percent of its capital structure cost only 5 percent.

(2) Theoretically, no company should ever pay a cash dividend—simply because dividends are taxable at ordinary rates and capital gains are taxable at capital gains rates. Tax rates on capital gains are lower than tax rates on ordinary income. But unless an effort has been made to educate them, stockholders may misinterpret a cut in the dividend. They may conclude that the management of the company is pessimistic about the future. And they may rush to sell their

stock. And if they rush to sell their stock the price of that stock may fall.

1. Look up AT&T in the latest issue of the Value Line and in Moody's. Estimate, after taxes, AT&T's
    (a) cost of equity
    (b) cost of debt
    (c) weighted average cost of capital—assuming maintenance of AT&T's present ratio of debt to equity.
2. How much debt do you think AT&T should have? Why?
3. Suppose AT&T had no debt—but, of course, the same total assets. Estimate the market value of the company.
4. Suppose AT&T sold another $200 million of long-term debt at 8 percent and used the proceeds to buy back its common stock at $45 a share. Where would the price of a share of AT&T tend to settle after the purchase had been completed?
5. Use the answer you obtained to problem 4 to recalculate, after taxes, AT&T's cost of equity and its weighted average cost of capital, with the additional $200 million of debt.

V

CONCLUSION

COMPLICATIONS

In a word—we are finally in position to grasp the real meaning of Chapters 1 and 2.

What did we say in Chapters 1 and 2? (Perhaps you'd better go back and reread them!) In *Chapter 1,* after describing the proposed new projects which lay on Martin's desk, we said that Finance bears the primary responsibility for worrying about:

1. Whether new proposals should be undertaken.
2. How they should be financed.

We said also that a firm cannot cope in a rational way with these two problems unless it has a goal. And—provided it is run by economic men—the goal of the firm should be, we said, to maximize the market value of its own common stock.

In Chapter 2 we explained why we chose this goal rather than maximization of profits. Mere maximization of profits, we said, does *not* take account of *risk*. And perhaps we now know what we *really* mean by *risk*.

In Chapter 2 we also explained how a finance officer goes about maximizing—or doing his best (!) to maximize the market value of his company's common stock. He calculates expected rates of return on proposed new projects. And he estimates his company's cost of capital. And now, perhaps, we understand what's really involved in calculating rates of return on the various kinds of assets the firm holds. And perhaps also we understand what's really involved in estimating a company's cost of capital.

But, as we went along, a question or two may have arisen in your mind—and, of these, some may still remain unresolved. For example:

QUESTION 1

As Worthington pointed out (in Chapter 22) all the projects Butcher is now considering are *not* equally risky. This being so, is Butcher justified in using a *single* cost of capital as a cutoff? Shouldn't Butcher use a lower cost of capital for *less* risky projects and a higher cost of capital for the *more* risky projects?

QUESTION 2

Kelley has made Finance appear to be (by far!) the most important part of the firm—it (Finance) is in charge (Kelley seems to have been saying) of maximizing the value of the firm's common stock. How could any job in the firm be any more important than *that*?

We discuss these two questions below.

A SINGLE COST OF CAPITAL?

Let's begin by asking a question to which we all know the answer: Why is the rate of interest on government bonds less than Butcher's cost of equity? The answer is, of course, that we are sure (or, rather, as sure as we can be of anything) that government bonds will not default. We are sure that if we buy a government bond for $1,000 which promises (a) to pay us $42.50 in interest each year and (b) to repay our principal at the end of the tenth year—both parts of that promise will be kept in full.

But what does Butcher really promise? In fact, Butcher promises nothing—except an uncertain return which, conceivably, could be less than zero. Therefore we would expect the *expected* return on Butcher stock—the mean of a probability distribution—to be higher than the certain return on governments—simply because the expected return on

Butcher stock is *not* certain. If an investor is risk averse (go back and look at Chapter 19), he will not accept *additional risk* unless it is accompanied by *additional* expected return—which means that you (or I) will invest in Butcher stock only if it offers an expected return higher than the return on governments.

But suppose now, that Butcher suddenly came across a number of new less risky projects—which would reduce the riskiness of Butcher's *total* investment—while simultaneously and correspondingly reducing Butcher's expected return. And suppose also that Butcher wanted to undertake these projects but did *not* wish to reduce either the total risk of or the total return to its common stock. What could Butcher do? *It could finance the projects with relatively more debt and relatively less equity than would otherwise be the case.* Thus if it found a project which promised an absolutely certain return of 5 percent after taxes, it would finance that project entirely with debt costing, say, 4.5 percent after taxes. The risk of the firm as a whole would not have been increased—because the certain 5 percent return on the new project would more than cover the interest payable on the additional debt. In addition, of course, the return to the common stockholders would have been increased by the difference between the after-tax return on the project (5 percent) and the after-tax cost of debt (4.5 percent).

This means two things:

First, if the riskiness of a new project differs from the overall present riskiness of the firm, the riskiness of the firm can be maintained by financing the new project with relatively *more* debt if the new project is *less* risky than the firm itself—or relatively *less* debt if the new project is *more* risky than the firm itself. We were exposed in Chapter 21 to the kind of process the firm would go through to maintain the same degree of risk. It is analogous to the process by which the individual investor maintains the same degree of risk in his portfolio—regardless of what the firm does to its capital structure.

Second, if proposed new projects are more or less risky than the firm itself, the cost of financing them will *not* be the same as the firm's average cost of capital. Worthington's intuition was right. If Butcher invests in a riskless project, the cost of the money invested in that project is the rate at which Butcher can borrow, adjusted for taxes. And this, of course, will be less than Butcher's average cost of capital. If at the other extreme, it invests in a new project which is much riskier than its existing investments, the cost of the money invested in that project will be *higher* than its average cost of capital. Why? Because if it wishes to maintain the same degree of *total* risk, Butcher will have to finance such a project with relatively more equity and relatively less debt.

This probably sounds very complicated and formidable. But we should bear in mind that from a practical point of view this problem will be important only if a firm begins to undertake new projects which differ substantially in riskiness from those it is now undertaking —as, for example, Clay Company in Chapter 2—and wishes, at the same time, to maintain the same degree of total risk.

WHO MAXIMIZES WHAT?

Finance tries to maximize the price of the firm's common stock *given the opportunities currently available*. But whether a firm does well or not will depend, for the most part, *on whether or not high return opportunities are in fact available*. And whether high return opportunities are in fact available will depend on finance hardly at all. It will depend primarily on the other parts of the company—especially on research and product development.

To repeat: Finance's job is to maximize *given the opportunities which are, in fact, actually available*.

COMPOUND
GROWTH FACTORS

The attached growth factors can be used in a variety of ways:

SUGGESTION 1

They can be used to estimate the rate of growth of a sum of money between two points in time. When in Chapter 4 we wanted to estimate the rate of return on a single payment, ten-year bond, we simply divided the amount we expected to receive in 1978 by the cost of the bond, thus:

$$\frac{\$160}{100} = 1.60$$

We then looked *across ten years* until we came to the number closest to 1.60. This number was 1.6289 under 5.0 percent. This told us that the annual compound rate of return on the bond was slightly less than 5 percent.

Correspondingly, suppose you are asked to invest $256 in some asset on the promise that you will receive $643 exactly seven years from now. At what rate will your original investment accumulate?

First, divide 643 by 256, thus:

$$\frac{643}{256} = 2.5117$$

Second, look up 2.5117 across seven years. The number closest to 2.5117 in the seven year row is 2.5023—which means that your funds would accumulate at a rate of about 14.0 percent a year.

SUGGESTION 2

The first column is labeled "Year" but it might just as well have been labeled "Month," or "Day" or (as in Tables 3.6 and 4.9) just "Period." Suppose your roommate wants to borrow five dollars and promises to give you, in return, $6.25 in two months. At what compound rate would your five dollars accumulate—provided your roommate keeps his promise?

First, divide $6.25 by $5.00:

$$\frac{6.25}{5.00} = 1.25$$

Second, look up 1.25 across two years. The closest number is 1.2544 under 12 percent. This is, of course, 12 percent a *month* or 144 percent a year.

"Not bad," you think, and hand him the five dollars.

Two months later you say to him, "Where's my money?"

He says, "What money?"

You remind him of the loan and he says, "Oh, that. Listen loan shark, will you settle for $5.25?"

"Cash?" you ask.

"Yes," he says.

Okay you say and grab the money.

At what rate, now, has your five dollars *actually* accumulated over the two month period? First divide 5.25 by 5:

$$\frac{5.25}{5.00} = 1.05$$

Then look up 1.05 across two years. The closest number is 1.0609 under 3.0 percent. Your money has thus accumulated at the rate of, say, 2.5 percent a *month* or 30 percent a year—not bad either.

SUGGESTION 3

Or suppose that you want to use a discount rate not given in Table 3.6, for example, 9 percent. You simply take the reciprocal of the appropriate growth rate for the necessary number of years. This is, in fact, how the 9 percent factors used in Table 18.6 were obtained. You should check this yourself. The reciprocal of 1.09 is:

$$\frac{1}{1.09} = .917$$

The reciprocal of 1.1881 is $\dfrac{1}{1.1881} = .842$, and so forth for each successive year.

The essential idea of growth rates is simple. If you invest one dollar at 9 percent a year, you will have $1.09 at the end of the first year. Assuming you do *not* withdraw interest, you will have at the end of the second year, $1.09 \times 1.09 = 1.09^2 = 1.1881$. At the end of the third year you will have $1.09 \times 1.09 \times 1.09 = 1.09^3 = 1.2950$, and so forth.

Growth rate calculations can be applied to any type of number—population, national income, weight, height, and so forth. If you were eighteen inches tall the day you were born and are six feet tall now, at what compound rate a year have you grown?

YEAR	1.0 %	2.0 %	3.0 %	4.0 %	5.0 %
1	1.0100	1.0200	1.0300	1.0400	1.0500
2	1.0201	1.0404	1.0609	1.0816	1.1025
3	1.0303	1.0612	1.0927	1.1249	1.1576
4	1.0406	1.0824	1.1255	1.1699	1.2155
5	1.0510	1.1041	1.1593	1.2167	1.2763
6	1.0615	1.1262	1.1941	1.2653	1.3401
7	1.0721	1.1487	1.2299	1.3159	1.4071
8	1.0829	1.1717	1.2668	1.3686	1.4775
9	1.0937	1.1951	1.3048	1.4233	1.5513
10	1.1046	1.2190	1.3439	1.4802	1.6289
11	1.1157	1.2434	1.3842	1.5395	1.7103
12	1.1268	1.2682	1.4258	1.6010	1.7959
13	1.1381	1.2936	1.4685	1.6651	1.8856
14	1.1495	1.3195	1.5126	1.7317	1.9799
15	1.1610	1.3459	1.5580	1.8009	2.0789
16	1.1726	1.3728	1.6047	1.8730	2.1829
17	1.1843	1.4002	1.6528	1.9479	2.2920
18	1.1961	1.4282	1.7024	2.0258	2.4066
19	1.2081	1.4568	1.7535	2.1068	2.5270
20	1.2202	1.4859	1.8061	2.1911	2.6533
21	1.2324	1.5157	1.8603	2.2788	2.7860
22	1.2447	1.5460	1.9161	2.3699	2.9253
23	1.2572	1.5769	1.9736	2.4647	3.0715
24	1.2697	1.6084	2.0328	2.5633	3.2251
25	1.2824	1.6406	2.0938	2.6658	3.3864
26	1.2953	1.6734	2.1566	2.7725	3.5557
27	1.3082	1.7069	2.2213	2.8834	3.7335
28	1.3213	1.7410	2.2879	2.9987	3.9201
29	1.3345	1.7758	2.3566	3.1187	4.1161
30	1.3478	1.8114	2.4273	3.2434	4.3219
31	1.3613	1.8476	2.5001	3.3731	4.5380
32	1.3749	1.8845	2.5751	3.5081	4.7649
33	1.3887	1.9222	2.6523	3.6484	5.0032
34	1.4026	1.9607	2.7319	3.7943	5.2533
35	1.4166	1.9999	2.8139	3.9461	5.5160
36	1.4308	2.0399	2.8983	4.1039	5.7918
37	1.4451	2.0807	2.9852	4.2681	6.0814
38	1.4595	2.1223	3.0748	4.4388	6.3855
39	1.4741	2.1647	3.1670	4.6164	6.7048
40	1.4889	2.2080	3.2620	4.8010	7.0400
41	1.5038	2.2522	3.3599	4.9931	7.3920
42	1.5188	2.2972	3.4607	5.1928	7.7616
43	1.5340	2.3432	3.5645	5.4005	8.1497
44	1.5493	2.3901	3.6715	5.6165	8.5572
45	1.5648	2.4379	3.7816	5.8412	8.9850
46	1.5805	2.4866	3.8950	6.0748	9.4343
47	1.5963	2.5363	4.0119	6.3178	9.9060
48	1.6122	2.5871	4.1323	6.5705	10.401
49	1.6283	2.6388	4.2562	6.8334	10.921
50	1.6446	2.6916	4.3839	7.1067	11.467

YEAR	6.0 %	7.0 %	8.0 %	9.0 %	10.0 %
1	1.0600	1.0700	1.0800	1.0900	1.1000
2	1.1236	1.1449	1.1664	1.1881	1.2100
3	1.1910	1.2250	1.2597	1.2950	1.3310
4	1.2625	1.3108	1.3605	1.4116	1.4641
5	1.3382	1.4026	1.4693	1.5386	1.6105
6	1.4185	1.5007	1.5869	1.6771	1.7716
7	1.5036	1.6058	1.7138	1.8280	1.9487
8	1.5938	1.7182	1.8509	1.9926	2.1436
9	1.6895	1.8385	1.9990	2.1719	2.3579
10	1.7908	1.9672	2.1589	2.3674	2.5937
11	1.8983	2.1049	2.3316	2.5804	2.8531
12	2.0122	2.2522	2.5182	2.8127	3.1384
13	2.1329	2.4098	2.7196	3.0658	3.4523
14	2.2609	2.5785	2.9372	3.3417	3.7975
15	2.3966	2.7590	3.1722	3.6425	4.1772
16	2.5404	2.9522	3.4259	3.9703	4.5950
17	2.6928	3.1588	3.7000	4.3276	5.0545
18	2.8543	3.3799	3.9960	4.7171	5.5599
19	3.0256	3.6165	4.3157	5.1417	6.1159
20	3.2071	3.8697	4.6610	5.6044	6.7275
21	3.3996	4.1406	5.0338	6.1088	7.4003
22	3.6035	4.4304	5.4365	6.6586	8.1403
23	3.8197	4.7405	5.8715	7.2579	8.9543
24	4.0489	5.0724	6.3412	7.9111	9.8497
25	4.2919	5.4274	6.8485	8.6231	10.835
26	4.5494	5.8074	7.3964	9.3992	11.918
27	4.8223	6.2139	7.9881	10.245	13.110
28	5.1117	6.6488	8.6271	11.167	14.421
29	5.4184	7.1143	9.3173	12.172	15.863
30	5.7435	7.6123	10.063	13.268	17.449
31	6.0881	8.1451	10.868	14.462	19.194
32	6.4534	8.7153	11.737	15.763	21.114
33	6.8406	9.3253	12.676	17.182	23.225
34	7.2510	9.9781	13.690	18.728	25.548
35	7.6861	10.677	14.785	20.414	28.102
36	8.1473	11.424	15.968	22.251	30.913
37	8.6361	12.224	17.246	24.254	34.004
38	9.1543	13.079	18.625	26.437	37.404
39	9.7035	13.995	20.115	28.816	41.145
40	10.286	14.974	21.725	31.409	45.259
41	10.903	16.023	23.462	34.236	49.785
42	11.557	17.144	25.339	37.318	54.764
43	12.250	18.344	27.367	40.676	60.240
44	12.985	19.628	29.556	44.337	66.264
45	13.765	21.002	31.920	48.327	72.891
46	14.590	22.473	34.474	52.677	80.180
47	15.466	24.046	37.232	57.418	88.198
48	16.394	25.729	40.211	62.585	97.017
49	17.378	27.530	43.427	68.213	106.72
50	18.420	29.457	46.902	74.358	117.39

YEAR	11.0 %	12.0 %	13.0 %	14.0 %	15.0 %
1	1.1100	1.1200	1.1300	1.1400	1.1500
2	1.2321	1.2544	1.2769	1.2996	1.3225
3	1.3676	1.4049	1.4429	1.4815	1.5209
4	1.5181	1.5735	1.6305	1.6890	1.7490
5	1.6851	1.7623	1.8424	1.9254	2.0114
6	1.8704	1.9738	2.0820	2.1950	2.3131
7	2.0762	2.2107	2.3526	2.5023	2.6600
8	2.3045	2.4760	2.6584	2.8526	3.0590
9	2.5580	2.7731	3.0040	3.2519	3.5179
10	2.8394	3.1058	3.3946	3.7072	4.0456
11	3.1518	3.4786	3.8359	4.2262	4.6524
12	3.4985	3.8960	4.3345	4.8179	5.3503
13	3.8833	4.3635	4.8980	5.4924	6.1528
14	4.3104	4.8871	5.5348	6.2613	7.0757
15	4.7846	5.4736	6.2543	7.1379	8.1371
16	5.3109	6.1304	7.0673	8.1372	9.3576
17	5.8951	6.8660	7.9861	9.2765	10.761
18	6.5436	7.6900	9.0243	10.575	12.375
19	7.2633	8.6128	10.197	12.056	14.232
20	8.0623	9.6463	11.523	13.743	16.367
21	8.9492	10.804	13.021	15.668	18.822
22	9.9336	12.100	14.714	17.861	21.645
23	11.026	13.552	16.627	20.362	24.891
24	12.239	15.179	18.788	23.212	28.625
25	13.585	17.000	21.231	26.462	32.919
26	15.080	19.040	23.991	30.167	37.857
27	16.739	21.325	27.109	34.390	43.535
28	18.580	23.884	30.633	39.204	50.066
29	20.624	26.750	34.616	44.693	57.575
30	22.892	29.960	39.116	50.950	66.212
31	25.410	33.555	44.201	58.083	76.144
32	28.206	37.582	49.947	66.215	87.565
33	31.308	42.092	56.440	75.485	100.70
34	34.752	47.143	63.777	86.053	115.80
35	38.575	52.800	72.069	98.100	133.18
36	42.818	59.136	81.437	111.83	153.15
37	47.528	66.232	92.024	127.49	176.12
38	52.756	74.180	103.99	145.34	202.54
39	58.559	83.081	117.51	165.69	232.92
40	65.001	93.051	132.78	188.88	267.86
41	72.151	104.22	150.04	215.33	308.04
42	80.088	116.72	169.55	245.47	354.25
43	88.897	130.73	191.59	279.84	407.39
44	98.676	146.42	216.50	319.02	468.50
45	109.53	163.99	244.64	363.68	538.77
46	121.58	183.67	276.44	414.59	619.58
47	134.95	205.71	312.38	472.64	712.52
48	149.80	230.39	352.99	538.81	819.40
49	166.27	258.04	398.88	614.24	942.31
50	184.56	289.00	450.74	700.23	1083.7

YEAR	16.0 %	17.0 %	18.0 %	19.0 %	20.0 %
1	1.1600	1.1700	1.1800	1.1900	1.2000
2	1.3456	1.3689	1.3924	1.4161	1.4400
3	1.5609	1.6016	1.6430	1.6852	1.7280
4	1.8106	1.8739	1.9388	2.0053	2.0736
5	2.1003	2.1924	2.2878	2.3864	2.4883
6	2.4364	2.5652	2.6996	2.8398	2.9860
7	2.8262	3.0012	3.1855	3.3793	3.5832
8	3.2784	3.5115	3.7589	4.0214	4.2998
9	3.8030	4.1084	4.4355	4.7854	5.1598
10	4.4114	4.8068	5.2338	5.6947	6.1917
11	5.1173	5.6240	6.1759	6.7767	7.4301
12	5.9360	6.5801	7.2876	8.0642	8.9161
13	6.8858	7.6987	8.5994	9.5964	10.699
14	7.9875	9.0075	10.147	11.420	12.839
15	9.2655	10.539	11.974	13.590	15.407
16	10.748	12.330	14.129	16.172	18.488
17	12.468	14.426	16.672	19.244	22.186
18	14.463	16.879	19.673	22.901	26.623
19	16.777	19.748	23.214	27.252	31.948
20	19.461	23.106	27.393	32.429	38.338
21	22.574	27.034	32.324	38.591	46.005
22	26.186	31.629	38.142	45.923	55.206
23	30.376	37.006	45.008	54.649	66.247
24	35.236	43.297	53.109	65.032	79.497
25	40.874	50.658	62.669	77.388	95.396
26	47.414	59,270	73.949	92.092	114.48
27	55.000	69.346	87.260	109.59	137.37
28	63.800	81.134	102.97	130.41	164.84
29	74.009	94.927	121.50	155.19	197.81
30	85.850	111.06	143.37	184.68	237.38
31	99.586	129.95	169.18	219.76	284.85
32	115.52	152.04	199.63	261.52	341.82
33	134.00	177.88	235.56	311.21	410.19
34	155.44	208.12	277.96	370.34	492.22
35	180.31	243.50	328.00	440.70	590.67
36	209.16	284.90	387.04	524.43	708.80
37	242.63	333.33	456.70	624.08	850.56
38	281.45	390.00	538.91	742.65	1020.7
39	326.48	456.30	635.91	883.75	1224.8
40	378.72	533.87	750.38	1051.7	1469.8
41	439.32	624.63	885.45	1251.5	1763.7
42	509.61	730.81	1044.8	1489.3	2116.5
43	591.14	855.05	1232.9	1772.2	2539.8
44	685.73	1000.4	1454.8	2109.0	3047.7
45	795.44	1170.5	1716.7	2509.7	3657.3
46	922.72	1369.5	2025.7	2986.5	4388.7
47	1070.3	1602.3	2390.3	3553.9	5266.5
48	1241.6	1874.7	2820.6	4229.2	6319.7
49	1440.3	2193.3	3328.3	5032.7	7583.7
50	1670.7	2566.2	3927.4	5988.9	9100.4

YEAR	21 %	22 %	23 %	24 %	25 %
1	1.2100	1.2200	1.2300	1.2400	1.2500
2	1.4641	1.4884	1.5129	1.5376	1.5625
3	1.7716	1.8158	1.8609	1.9066	1.9531
4	2.1436	2.2153	2.2889	2.3642	2.4414
5	2.5937	2.7027	2.8153	2.9316	3.0518
6	3.1384	3.2973	3.4628	3.6352	3.8147
7	3.7975	4.0227	4.2593	4.5077	4.7684
8	4.5950	4.9077	5.2389	5.5895	5.9605
9	5.5599	5.9874	6.4439	6.9310	7.4506
10	6.7275	7.3046	7.9259	8.5944	9.3132
11	8.1403	8.9117	9.7489	10.657	11.642
12	9.8497	10.872	11.991	13.215	14.552
13	11.918	13.264	14.749	16.386	18.190
14	14.421	16.182	18.141	20.319	22.737
15	17.449	19.742	22.314	25.196	28.422
16	21.114	24.086	27.446	31.243	35.527
17	25.548	29.384	33.759	38.741	44.409
18	30.913	35.849	41.523	48.039	55.511
19	37.404	43.736	51.074	59.568	69.389
20	45.259	53.358	62.821	73.864	86.736
21	54.764	65.096	77.269	91.592	108.42
22	66.264	79.418	95.041	113.57	135.53
23	80.180	96.889	116.90	140.83	169.41
24	97.017	118.21	143.79	174.63	211.76
25	117.39	144.21	176.86	216.54	264.70
26	142.04	175.94	217.54	268.51	330.87
27	171.87	214.64	267.57	332.95	413.59
28	207.97	261.86	329.11	412.86	516.99
29	251.64	319.47	404.81	511.95	646.23
30	304.48	389.76	497.91	634.82	807.79
31	368.42	475.50	612.43	787.18	1009.7
32	445.79	580.12	753.29	976.10	1262.2
33	539.41	707.74	926.55	1210.4	1577.7
34	652.68	863.44	1139.7	1500.9	1972.2
35	789.75	1053.4	1401.8	1861.1	2465.2
36	955.59	1285.2	1724.2	2307.7	3081.5
37	1156.3	1567.9	2120.7	2861.6	3851.9
38	1399.1	1912.8	2608.5	3548.3	4814.8
39	1692.9	2333.6	3208.5	4399.9	6018.5
40	2048.4	2847.0	3946.4	5455.9	7523.2
41	2478.6	3473.4	4854.1	6765.3	9404.0
42	2999.1	4237.5	5970.6	8389.0	11755.
43	3628.9	5169.8	7343.8	10402.	14694.
44	4390.9	6307.1	9032.9	12899.	18367.
45	5313.0	7694.7	11110.	15995.	22959.
46	6428.8	9387.5	13666.	19833.	28699.
47	7778.8	11453.	16809.	24593.	35873.
48	9412.3	13972.	20675.	30496.	44842.
49	11389.	17046.	25430.	37815.	56052.
50	13781.	20797.	31279.	46890.	70065.

YEAR	26 %	27 %	28 %	29 %	30 %
1	1.2600	1.2700	1.2800	1.2900	1.3000
2	1.5876	1.6129	1.6384	1.6641	1.6900
3	2.0004	2.0484	2.0972	2.1467	2.1970
4	2.5205	2.6014	2.6844	2.7692	2.8561
5	3.1758	3.3038	3.4360	3.5723	3.7129
6	4.0015	4.1959	4.3980	4.6083	4.8268
7	5.0419	5.3288	5.6295	5.9447	6.2749
8	6.3528	6.7675	7.2058	7.6686	8.1573
9	8.0045	8.5948	9.2234	9.8925	10.604
10	10.086	10.915	11.806	12.761	13.786
11	12.708	13.862	15.112	16.462	17.922
12	16.012	17.605	19.343	21.236	23.298
13	20.175	22.359	24.759	27.395	30.288
14	25.421	28.396	31.691	35.339	39.374
15	32.030	36.062	40.565	45.587	51.186
16	40.358	45.799	51.923	58.808	66.542
17	50.851	58.165	66.461	75.862	86.504
18	64.072	73.870	85.071	97.862	112.46
19	80.731	93.815	108.89	126.24	146.19
20	101.72	119.14	139.38	162.85	190.05
21	128.17	151.31	178.41	210.08	247.06
22	161.49	192.17	228.36	271.00	321.18
23	203.48	244.05	292.30	349.59	417.54
24	256.39	309.95	374.14	450.98	542.80
25	323.05	393.63	478.90	581.76	705.64
26	407.04	499.92	613.00	750.47	917.33
27	512.87	634.89	784.64	968.10	1192.5
28	646.21	806.31	1004.3	1248.9	1550.3
29	814.23	1024.0	1285.6	1611.0	2015.4
30	1025.9	1300.5	1645.5	2078.2	2620.0
31	1292.7	1651.6	2106.2	2680.9	3406.0
32	1628.8	2097.6	2696.0	3458.4	4427.8
33	2052.2	2663.9	3450.9	4461.3	5756.1
34	2585.8	3383.2	4417.1	5755.1	7483.0
35	3258.1	4296.7	5653.9	7424.0	9727.9
36	4105.3	5456.7	7237.0	9577.0	12646.
37	5172.6	6930.1	9263.4	12354.	16440.
38	6517.5	8801.2	11857.	15937.	21372.
39	8212.0	11178.	15177.	20559.	27784.
40	10347.	14195.	19427.	26521.	36119.
41	13037.	18028.	24866.	34212.	46955.
42	16427.	22896.	31829.	44133.	61041.
43	20698.	29078.	40741.	56932.	79353.
44	26080.	36929.	52148.	73442.	
45	32861.	46899.	66750.	94741.	
46	41404.	59562.	85439.		
47	52169.	75644.			
48	65733.	96068.			
49	82824.				
50					

YEAR	31 %	32 %	33 %	34 %	35 %
1	1.3100	1.3200	1.3300	1.3400	1.3500
2	1.7161	1.7424	1.7689	1.7956	1.8225
3	2.2481	2.3000	2.3526	2.4061	2.4604
4	2.9450	3.0360	3.1290	3.2242	3.3215
5	3.8579	4.0075	4.1616	4.3204	4.4840
6	5.0539	5.2899	5.5349	5.7893	6.0534
7	6.6206	6.9826	7.3614	7.7577	8.1722
8	8.6730	9.2170	9.7907	10.395	11.032
9	11.362	12.166	13.022	13.930	14.894
10	14.884	16.060	17.319	18.666	20.107
11	19.498	21.199	23.034	25.012	27.144
12	25.542	27.983	30.635	33.516	36.644
13	33.460	36.937	40.745	44.912	49.470
14	43.833	48.757	54.190	60.182	66.784
15	57.421	64.359	72.073	80.644	90.158
16	75.221	84.954	95.858	108.06	121.71
17	98.540	112.14	127.49	144.80	164.31
18	129.09	148.02	169.56	194.04	221.82
19	169.10	195.39	225.52	260.01	299.46
20	221.53	257.92	299.94	348.41	404.27
21	290.20	340.45	398.92	466.88	545.77
22	380.16	449.39	530.56	625.61	736.79
23	498.01	593.20	705.65	838.32	994.66
24	652.40	783.02	938.51	1123.4	1342.8
25	854.64	1033.6	1248.2	1505.3	1812.8
26	1119.6	1364.3	1660.1	2017.1	2447.2
27	1466.6	1800.9	2208.0	2702.9	3303.8
28	1921.3	2377.2	2936.6	3621.9	4460.1
29	2516.9	3137.9	3905.7	4853.3	6021.1
30	3297.2	4142.1	5194.6	6503.5	8128.6
31	4319.3	5467.5	6908.8	8714.6	10974.
32	5658.2	7217.2	9188.7	11678.	14814.
33	7412.3	9526.6	12221.	15648.	19999.
34	9710.1	12575.	16254.	20968.	26999.
35	12720.	16599.	21618.	28098.	36449.
36	16664.	21911.	28751.	37651.	49206.
37	21829.	28922.	38239.	50452.	66428.
38	28596.	38178.	50858.	67606.	89677.
39	37461.	50395.	67642.	90591.	
40	49074.	66521.	89963.		
41	64287.	87807.			
42	84216.				
43					
44					
45					
46					
47					
48					
49					
50					

YEAR	36 %	37 %	38 %	39 %	40 %
1	1.3600	1.3700	1.3800	1.3900	1.4000
2	1.8496	1.8769	1.9044	1.9321	1.9600
3	2.5155	2.5714	2.6281	2.6856	2.7440
4	3.4210	3.5228	3.6267	3.7330	3.8416
5	4.6526	4.8262	5.0049	5.1889	5.3782
6	6.3275	6.6119	6.9068	7.2125	7.5295
7	8.6054	9.0582	9.5313	10.025	10.541
8	11.703	12.410	13.153	13.935	14.758
9	15.917	17.001	18.151	19.370	20.661
10	21.647	23.292	25.049	26.925	28.925
11	29.439	31.910	34.568	37.425	40.496
12	40.037	43.717	47.703	52.021	56.694
13	54.451	59.892	65.831	72.309	79.371
14	74.053	82.052	90.846	100.51	111.12
15	100.71	112.41	125.37	139.71	155.57
16	136.97	154.00	173.01	194.19	217.80
17	186.28	210.98	238.75	269.93	304.91
18	253.34	289.05	329.48	375.20	426.88
19	344.54	396.00	454.68	521.53	597.63
20	468.57	542.51	627.45	724.93	836.68
21	637.26	743.24	865.89	1007.7	1171.4
22	866.67	1018.2	1194.9	1400.6	1639.9
23	1178.7	1395.0	1649.0	1946.9	2295.9
24	1603.0	1911.1	2275.6	2706.2	3214.2
25	2180.1	2618.3	3140.3	3761.6	4499.9
26	2964.9	3587.0	4333.7	5228.6	6299.8
27	4032.3	4914.2	5980.5	7267.7	8819.8
28	5483.9	6732.5	8253.0	10102.	12348.
29	7458.1	9223.5	11389.	14042.	17287.
30	10143.	12636.	15717.	19518.	24201.
31	13795.	17312.	21690.	27131.	33882.
32	18761.	23717.	29932.	37711.	47435.
33	25514.	32492.	41306.	52419.	66409.
34	34699.	44514.	57002.	72862.	92972.
35	47191.	60985.	78663.		
36	64180.	83549.			
37	87285.				
38					
39					
40					
41					
42					
43					
44					
45					
46					
47					
48					
49					
50					

YEAR	41 %	42 %	43 %	44 %	45 %
1	1.4100	1.4200	1.4300	1.4400	1.4500
2	1.9881	2.0164	2.0449	2.0736	2.1025
3	2.8032	2.8633	2.9242	2.9860	3.0486
4	3.9525	4.0659	4.1816	4.2998	4.4205
5	5.5731	5.7735	5.9797	6.1917	6.4097
6	7.8580	8.1984	8.5510	8.9161	9.2941
7	11.080	11.642	12.228	12.839	13.476
8	15.623	16.531	17.486	18.488	19.541
9	22.028	23.474	25.005	26.623	28.334
10	31.059	33.334	35.757	38.338	41.085
11	43.794	47.334	51.132	55.206	59.573
12	61.749	67.214	73.119	79.497	86.381
13	87.066	95.444	104.56	114.48	125.25
14	122.76	135.53	149.52	164.84	181.62
15	173.10	192.45	213.82	237.38	263.34
16	244.07	273.28	305.76	341.82	381.85
17	344.13	388.06	437.23	492.22	553.68
18	485.23	551.05	625.24	708.80	802.83
19	684.17	782.49	894.10	1020.7	1164.1
20	964.68	1111.1	1278.6	1469.8	1688.0
21	1360.2	1577.8	1828.3	2116.5	2447.5
22	1917.9	2240.5	2614.5	3047.7	3548.9
23	2704.2	3181.5	3738.8	4388.7	5145.9
24	3812.9	4517.7	5346.4	6319.7	7461.6
25	5376.2	6415.2	7645.4	9100.4	10819.
26	7580.5	9109.6	10933.	13105.	15688.
27	10688.	12936.	15634.	18871.	22748.
28	15071.	18368.	22357.	27174.	32984.
29	21250.	26083.	31970.	39130.	47827.
30	29962.	37038.	45717.	56348.	69349.
31	42247.	52594.	65376.	81140.	
32	59568.	74684.	93487.		
33	83991.				
34					
35					
36					
37					
38					
39					
40					
41					
42					
43					
44					
45					
46					
47					
48					
49					
50					

YEAR	46 %	47 %	48 %	49 %	50 %
1	1.4600	1.4700	1.4800	1.4900	1.5000
2	2.1316	2.1609	2.1904	2.2201	2.2500
3	3.1121	3.1765	3.2418	3.3079	3.3750
4	4.5437	4.6695	4.7979	4.9288	5.0625
5	6.6338	6.8641	7.1008	7.3440	7.5938
6	9.6854	10.090	10.509	10.943	11.391
7	14.141	14.833	15.554	16.304	17.086
8	20.645	21.804	23.019	24.294	25.629
9	30.142	32.052	34.069	36.197	38.443
10	44.008	47.117	50.422	53.934	57.665
11	64.251	69.261	74.624	80.362	86.498
12	93.807	101.81	110.44	119.74	129.75
13	136.96	149.67	163.46	178.41	194.62
14	199.96	220.01	241.92	265.83	291.93
15	291.94	323.41	358.04	396.09	437.89
16	426.23	475.42	529.89	590.17	656.84
17	622.30	698.87	784.24	879.36	985.26
18	908.56	1027.3	1160.7	1310.2	1477.9
19	1326.5	1510.2	1717.8	1952.3	2216.8
20	1936.7	2220.0	2542.3	2908.9	3325.3
21	2827.5	3263.4	3762.7	4334.2	4987.9
22	4128.2	4797.1	5568.8	6458.0	7481.8
23	6027.2	7051.8	8241.8	9622.4	11223.
24	8799.7	10366.	12198.	14337.	16834.
25	12848.	15238.	18053.	21363.	25251.
26	18757.	22400.	26718.	31830.	37877.
27	27386.	32928.	39543.	47427.	56815.
28	39983.	48404.	58523.	70667.	85223.
29	58376.	71155.	86614.		
30	85229.				
31					
32					
33					
34					
35					
36					
37					
38					
39					
40					
41					
42					
43					
44					
45					
46					
47					
48					
49					
50					

YEAR	60 %	70 %	80 %	90 %	100 %
1	1.6000	1.7000	1.8000	1.9000	2.0000
2	2.5600	2.8900	3.2400	3.6100	4.0000
3	4.0960	4.9130	5.8320	6.8590	8.0000
4	6.5536	8.3521	10.497	13.032	16.000
5	10.485	14.198	18.895	24.760	32.000
6	16.777	24.137	34.012	47.045	64.000
7	26.843	41.033	61.222	89.387	128.00
8	42.949	69.757	110.19	169.83	256.00
9	68.719	118.58	198.35	322.68	512.00
10	109.95	201.59	357.04	613.10	1024.0
11	175.92	342.71	642.68	1164.9	2048.0
12	281.47	582.62	1156.8	2213.3	4096.0
13	450.35	990.45	2082.2	4205.2	8192.0
14	720.57	1683.7	3748.1	7990.0	16384.
15	1152.9	2862.4	6746.6	15181.	32768.
16	1844.6	4866.1	12143.	28844.	65536.
17	2951.4	8272.4	21859.	54803.	
18	4722.3	14063.	39346.		
19	7555.7	23907.	70823.		
20	12089.	40642.			
21	19342.	69091.			
22	30948.				
23	49517.				
24	79228.				
25					
26					
27					
28					
29					
30					
31					
32					
33					
34					
35					
36					
37					
38					
39					
40					
41					
42					
43					
44					
45					
46					
47					
48					
49					
50					

SOURCE MATERIAL
AND
SUGGESTIONS
FOR
FURTHER READING

CHAPTERS 1 AND 2

The discussion in these two chapters is based very heavily on the following major works:

Dean, Joel, *Capital Budgeting*. New York: Columbia University Press, 1951, Chapters I–III.

Durand, David, "The Cost of Debt and Equity Funds for Business," *Conference on Research in Business Finance*. New York: National Bureau of Economic Research, 1952, pp. 215–47.

Lutz, Vera, and Lutz, Friedrich, *The Theory of Investment of the Firm*. Princeton, N. J.: Princeton University Press, 1951.

Solomon, Ezra, *The Theory of Financial Management*. New York: Columbia University Press, 1963, Chapters I and II.

The following are worthwhile supplementary readings:

Anthony, Robert, "The Trouble with Profit Maximization," *Harvard Business Review*, vol. 38, (November–December 1960), pp. 126–34.

Porterfield, James, *Investment Decisions and Capital Costs*. Englewood Cliffs, N. J.: Prentice–Hall, Inc., 1965, Chapters II, V, and VI.

Robichek, Alexander, and Myers, Stewart, *Optimal Financing Decisions*. Englewood Cliffs, N. J.: Prentice–Hall, Inc., 1965, Chapter 1.

CHAPTERS 3, 4, AND 5

The ideas in these chapters derive primarily from *The Theory of the Investment Firm* (1951) by Lutz and Lutz, previously cited, Chapter 1; and from Joel Dean's *Capital Budgeting* (1951), previously cited, Chapter II.

James Porterfield's, *Investment Decisions and Capital Costs* (1965), previously cited, provides a useful supplementary discussion not only of rates of return and present value but also of net terminal value and multiple rates of return. See also Ezra Solomon's, *Theory of Financial Management* (1963), previously cited, Chapter X, and his compilation, *The Management of Corporate Capital*, Chicago: Free Press, 1959, Part II, "Measuring Investment Worth," especially the articles by Dean, Hill, Lorie and Savage, and Solomon himself.

CHAPTERS 9 AND 10

See especially:

Lutz, Vera, and Lutz, Friedrich. *The Theory of Investment of the Firm*, Chapters XVII and XX.

Tobin, James, "Liquidity Preference as Behavior Towards Risk," *The Review of Economic Studies*, 26, no. 1 (February 1958), pp. 65–86.

For a different perspective on the liquidity problem see:

Archer, Stephen H., "A Model for the Determination of Firm Cash Balances," *The Journal of Financial and Quantitative Analysis*, vol. 1 (March 1966), pp. 1–11.

Baumol, William J., "The Transactions Demand for Cash: An Inventory Theoritic Approach," *The Quarterly Journal of Economics*, 66, (November 1952), pp. 545–56.

Beranek, William, *Analysis for Financial Decisions*, Homewood, Ill.: Richard D. Irwin, 1963, pp. 345–87.

Miller, Merton H., and Orr, Daniel, "The Demand for Money by Firms: Extensions of Analytic Results," *The Journal of Finance*, vol. 23 (December 1968), pp. 735–59.

Sprenkle, Case M., "The Uselessness of Transactions Demand Models," *The Journal of Finance*, vol. 24 (December 1969), pp. 835–47.

Whalen, Edward L., "An Extension of the Baumol–Tobin Approach to the Transactions Demand for Cash," *The Journal of Finance*, vol. 23 (March 1968), pp. 113–34.

——————. "A Rationalization of the Precautionary Demand for Cash" *The Quarterly Journal of Economics*, vol. 80 (May 1966), pp. 314–24.

For a very interesting discussion and treatment of the problems involved in constructing probability distributions over net cash flows, see William F. Hardin's unpublished doctoral dissertation, *Cash Management in a Small*

Manufacturing Firm: The Assessment and Application of Probability, University of North Carolina, Chapel Hill, North Carolina, 1966.

For a provocative discussion of techniques of forecasting interest rates, see:

Freund, William C., and Zinbarg, Edward D., "Application of Flow of Funds to Interest–Rate Forecasting," *The Journal of Finance,* 18, no. 2 (May 1963), pp. 231–48.

CHAPTER 11

Altman, Edward I., "Financial Ratios, Discriminant Analysis and the Prediction of Corporate Bankruptcy," *The Journal of Finance,* 23, no. 4 (September 1968), pp. 589–609.

Beranek, William, *Analysis for Financial Decisions.* Homewood, Ill.: Richard D. Irwin, 1963, Chapter 10.

Greer, Carl C., "The Optimal Credit Acceptance Policy," *Journal of Financial and Quantitative Analysis,* vol. 2 (December 1967), pp. 399–415.

Mehta, Dileep, "The Formulation of Credit Policy Models," *Management Science,* 15, no. 2 (October 1968), pp. 30–50.

Orgler, Yair E., "Selection of Bank Loans for Evaluation: An Analytical Approach," *The Journal of Finance,* vol. 24 (March 1969), pp. 75–80.

Reinhardt, H., and Schulta, W., *Problems in Credits and Collections.* New York: Dun and Bradstreet, Inc., 1967.

Smith, Paul, "Measuring Risk on Consumer Installment Credit," *Management Science,* vol. 11 (November 1964), pp. 327–40.

CHAPTER 12

For a point of view different from the one presented here see:

Snyder, Arthur, "Principles of Inventory Management," *Financial Executive,* vol. 32 (April 1964), pp. 13–21.

CHAPTER 13

Cord, Joel, "A Method for Allocating Funds to Investment Projects When Returns are Subject to Uncertainty," *Management Science,* 10, no. 2 (January 1964), pp. 335–41.

Dean, Joel, *Capital Budgeting.* New York: Columbia University Press, 1951, Chapters V–IX.

Dyckman, T. R., "Allocating Funds to Investment Projects When Returns are Subject to Uncertainty: A Comment," *Management Science,* 11, no. 2 (November 1964), pp. 348–50.

Hertz, David B., "Risk Analysis in Capital Investment," *Harvard Business Review,* 42, no. 1 (January–February 1964), pp. 95–106.

Hillier, Frederick S., "The Derivation of Probabilistic Information for the Evaluation of Risky Investments," *Management Science,* 9, no. 3 (April 1963), pp. 443–57.

Libik, George, "The Economic Assessment of Research and Development," *Management Science,* 16, no. 1 (September 1969), pp. 33–66.

McLean, John G., "How to Evaluate New Capital Investments," *New Decision Making Tools for Managers.* Cambridge, Mass.: Harvard University Press, 1963.

For different perspectives, see:

Bennion, Edward G., "Capital Budgeting and Game Theory," *Harvard Business Review,* 34, no. 6 (November–December 1956), pp. 115–23.

Charnes, A., Cooper, W. W., and Miller, M. H., "Application of Linear Programming to Financial Budgeting and the Costing of Funds," *The Journal of Business,* 32, no. 1 (January 1959), pp. 20–46.

CHAPTER 14

Alberts, William, and Segall, Joel, The Corporate Merger. Chicago: The University of Chicago Press, 1966.

Gort, Michael, "An Economic Disturbance Theory of Mergers," *Quarterly Journal of Economics,* vol. 83 (November 1969), pp. 624–42.

Mueller, Dennis C., "A Theory of Conglomerate Mergers," *Quarterly Journal of Economics,* vol. 83 (November 1969), pp. 643–59.

Smith, K., and Schreiner, J., "A Portfolio Analysis of Conglomerate Diversification," *Journal of Finance,* vol. 24 (June 1969), pp. 413–27.

CHAPTERS 17, 18, 20, 21, AND 22

These chapters are based very heavily on previously cited Joel Dean's, *Capital Budgeting* (1951), Chapter III; Ezra Solomon's *The Theory of Financial Management* (1963), Chapters III–IX; G. Donaldson's, *Corporate Debt Capacity,* Harvard Business School, Division of Research, 1961, and on the following articles:

Baumol, William, and Malkiel, Burton, "The Firm's Optimal Debt–Equity Combination and the Cost of Capital," *The Quarterly Journal of Economics,* vol. 81 (November 1967), pp. 547–78.

Elton, Edwin J., and Martin J. Gruber, "The Cost of Retained Earnings— Implications of Share Repurchase," *Industrial Management Review,* 9, no. 3 (Spring 1968), pp. 87–104.

——————. "The Effect of Share Repurchase on the Value of the Firm," *The Journal of Finance,* 23, no. 1 (March 1968) pp. 135–49.

Modigliani, Franco, and Merton H. Miller. "The Cost of Capital, Corporation Finance, and the Theory of Investment," *The American Economic Review,* 48, no. 3 (June 1958), pp. 261–97.

——————. "Corporate Income Taxes and the Cost of Capital: A Correction," *The American Economic Review,* 53, no. 3 (June 1963), pp. 433–43.

Schwartz, Eli, "Theory of the Capital Structure of the Firm," *The Journal of Finance,* 14, no. 1 (March 1959), pp. 18–39.

Solomon, Ezra, "Leverage and the Cost of Capital," *The Journal of Finance,* 18, no. 2 (May 1963), pp. 273–79.

See also:

Bodenhorn, Diran, "On the Problem of Capital Budgeting," *The Journal of Finance,* 14, no. 4 (December 1959), pp. 473–92.

Arditti, Fred D., "Risk and The Required Return on Equity," *The Journal of Finance,* vol. 22 (March 1967), pp. 19–36.

Boness, A. James, "A Pedagogic Note on the Cost of Capital," *The Journal of Finance,* 19, no. 1 (March 1964), pp. 99–106.

Malkiel, Burton, "Equity Yields, Growth and the Structure of Share Prices," *American Economic Review,* vol. 48 (December 1963), pp. 1004–31.

On dividend policy see the following:

Brigham, Eugene F., and Myron J. Gordon, "Leverage, Dividend Policy, and the Cost of Capital," *The Journal of Finance,* vol. 23 (March 1968), pp. 85–103.

Friend, Irwin, and Puckett, Marshall, "Dividends and Stock Prices," *American Economic Review,* vol. 54 (September 1964), pp. 656–82.

Gordon, M. J., "Optimal Investment and Financing Policy," *The Journal of Finance,* 18, no. 2 (May 1963), pp. 264–72.

Lintner, John, "Optimal Dividends and Corporate Growth Under Uncertainty," *The Quarterly Journal of Economics,* 78, no. 1 (February 1964), pp. 49–95.

Miller, Merton H., and Franco Modigliani, "Dividend Policy, Growth and the Valuation of Shares," *The Journal of Business of the University of Chicago,* 34, no. 4 (October 1961), pp. 411–33.

Walter, James E., "Dividend Policy: Its Influence on the Value of the Enterprise," *The Journal of Finance,* 18, no. 2 (May 1963), pp. 280–91.

Wippern, Ronald F., "Financial Structure and the Value of the Firm," *The Journal of Finance,* vol. 21 (December 1966), pp. 615–633.

CHAPTER 19

Bernoulli, Daniel, "Exposition of a New Theory on the Measurement of Risk," *Econometrica,* 22, no. 1 (January 1954), pp. 23–36.

Markowitz, Harry, "Portfolio Selection," *The Journal of Finance,* 7, no. 1 (March 1952), pp. 77–91.

Sharpe, William F., "Capital Asset Prices: A Theory of Market Equilibrium

Under Conditions of Risk," *The Journal of Finance,* 19, no. 3 (September 1964), pp. 425–42.

CHAPTER 23

This chapter derives from Solomon, *The Theory of Financial Management* (1963), previously cited, Chapter VI; and Donald L. Tuttle and Robert H. Litzenberger's, "Leverage Diversification and Capital Market Effects on a Risk-Adjusted Capital Budgeting Framework," *The Journal of Finance,* 23, no. 3, June 1968, pp. 427–43.

GLOSSARY

ACCELERATED DEPRECIATION. Methods of depreciation in which the cost of an asset is written off faster than under the straight line method.

ACCOUNTS RECEIVABLE. Amounts due from trade customers on open account. Chapter 11.

ACID-TEST RATIO. Current assets minus inventory, divided by current liabilities. Chapter 1.

ACQUISITION. All forms of external growth such as buying all the outstanding stock of a company, or a majority of it, from that company's stockholders, or buying the assets of the company, or some of them, from the company itself. Chapter 14.

ANNUITY. A series of payments of definite amount to be received periodically for a specified number of periods.

ASSETS. Everything owned by a business, the value of which can be stated in money terms.

AVERAGE COLLECTION PERIOD. Accounts receivable divided by sales per day.

AVERAGE DEVIATION. The arithmetic average of the deviations about the mean of a distribution.

BALANCE SHEET. A statement of what the firm owns—its assets, and what it owes—its liabilities, at the close of business on the date indicated. Chapter 1.

BANKER'S ACCEPTANCES. See Appendix to Chapter 10.

BANKRUPTCY. A legal procedure for the formal liquidation of a corporation declared insolvent by a court of law. Chapter 21.

BOND. A certificate of indebtedness issued by a government or corporation, promising payment of principal plus interest at a future date or dates, more than one year away. Chapter 16.

BANKS FOR COOPERATIVES. See Appendix to Chapter 10.

BOOK VALUE PER SHARE. The total net worth of a corporation divided by the number of shares outstanding.

BREAKEVEN RATE OF RETURN. The rate at which an investor could borrow money (or raise it in other ways), to pay for an investment, and be neither better nor worse off after the investment had terminated. Chapter 4.

CALL PREMIUM. The amount in excess of par which a corporation must pay to exercise the privilege of redeeming its outstanding debt or preferred stock prior to maturity.

CALL PRICE. The price that a corporation must pay to redeem its securities—usually the par value of the securities plus a call premium.

CAPITAL BUDGET. List of new projects, either proposed or approved.

CAPITAL GAIN. Profit from the sale of capital assets.

CAPITAL LOSS. Loss on the sale of capital assets.

CAPITALIZATION RATE. The rate used to find the present value of a stream of future cash flows. Also called discount rate. Chapter 3.

CAPITAL STRUCTURE. Composition of the firm's long-term capital. Chapters 20, 21.

CARRY-BACK; CARRY-FORWARD. The process of carrying losses backward or forward to reduce federal income taxes.

CASH. Cash on hand and demand deposits. Chapter 9.

CASH BUDGET. A statement showing the firm's expected future cash receipts and expected future cash disbursements by periods (months, weeks, days). Chapter 9.

CASH CYCLE. The firm's normal period from disbursements to receipts. The length of the cash cycle will depend on the firm's production period and the credit terms it grants its customers. Chapter 9.

CASH FLOW. Earnings after taxes plus non cash expense.

CERTIFICATES OF DEPOSIT. See Appendix to Chapter 10.

CERTIFICATE OF INDEBTEDNESS. See Appendix to Chapter 10.

CHATTEL MORTGAGE. A mortgage on durable goods—such as cars, machines and so forth.

CIRCULAR FLOW OF WORKING CAPITAL. The flow of working capital in a firm from cash to raw materials to work-in-process to finished goods to accounts receivable and, finally, back to cash. Chapter 9.

COMMERCIAL PAPER. See Appendix to Chapter 10.

COMMON STOCK. Certificates evidencing the ownership of a corporation. Chapter 16.

COMPENSATING BALANCE. Balances maintained with commercial banks to compensate them for services rendered.

COMPOUND EVENTS. A succession (or the simultaneous occurrence) of two or more events—such as two heads on two tosses of a single coin or on one toss of a pair of coins. Chapter 6.

COMPOUND INTEREST. Interest earned in this period on interest earned in prior periods. Chapters 3 and 4.

CONVERTIBLE SECURITIES. Securities, usually bonds or preferred stock, which may be exchanged for the common stock of the issuing corporation at the option of the holder.

COST OF CAPITAL. The minimum rate the firm should require on new investments. Chapters 17-22.

COST OF COMMON STOCK. The cost, expressed as a rate, to a firm of new funds raised through the issuance of common stock. Chapter 18.

COST OF DEBT. The cost, expressed as a rate, to a firm of new funds raised through the issuance of debt. The nominal cost of debt sold at par is the interest rate on the debt. Chapter 17.

COST OF PREFERRED STOCK. The cost, expressed as a rate, to a firm of new funds raised through the issuance of preferred stock. The nominal cost of preferred stock sold at par is the dividend rate. Chapter 17.

COST OF RETAINED EARNINGS. The rate the firm could earn by repurchasing its own common stock at the current market price, plus transactions costs. Chapter 17.

COST OF FLOTATION. The cost of selling an issue of securities—legal fees, fees to investment bankers, and so forth.

CREDIT REPORT. A report on the credit worthiness of a present or potential customer. Chapter 11.

CURRENT ASSET. An asset which is expected to convert itself into cash within a year.

CURRENT LIABILITY. An obligation due within a year.

CURRENT RATIO. Current assets divided by current liabilities. This ratio is often used to assess a firm's ability to meet its current obligations.

DCF. Discounted cash flow.

DCF RATE OF RETURN. The rate which, plus one, makes the present value of a set of cash flows equal to the cost of obtaining those cash flows. Chapter 4.

DEBENTURES. Bonds secured only by the general credit of the borrowing corporation.

DEBT-EQUITY RATIO. The ratio of a firm's long-term debt to its equity.

DEPRECIATION EXPENSE. Amounts carried to the income account for the purpose of recovering the cost of long-lived assets.

DIVIDEND YIELD. The ratio of a stock's current dividend to its current market price.

DOWNSIDE DEVIATION. The risk of receiving a return less than the expected return. Chapter 19.

DPS. Dividends per share, usually stated on an annual basis.

EAT. Earnings after taxes.

EBT. Earnings before taxes.

EBIT. Earnings before interest and taxes.

EBIDT. Earnings before interest, taxes and depreciation.

EQUITY. The net worth of a firm, comprising capital stock, capital surplus, and retained earnings.

EPS. Earning per share of common stock.

EXPORT IMPORT BANK. See Appendix to Chapter 10.

FACTORS. Financial concerns which supply funds by purchasing accounts receivable, and in other ways.

EXPECTED PAYOFF. The mean of a probability distribution in which the events are possible payoffs.

FACTORING. Selling accounts receivable to a factor.

FEDERAL HOME LOAN BANKS. See Appendix to Chapter 10.

FEDERAL INTERMEDIATE AUDIT BANKS. See Appendix to Chapter 10.

FEDERAL LAND BANKS. See Appendix to Chapter 10.

FEDERAL NATIONAL MORTGAGE ASSOCIATION. See Appendix to Chapter 10.

FINANCIAL MANAGEMENT. The art of maximizing the market value of a company's common stock—given the opportunities available to the firm. Chapter 2.

FINANCIAL LEVERAGE. The use of debt to finance the purchase of assets. Chapters 20 and 21.

FINANCIAL RISK. Risk due to the presence of debt in the capital structure.

FINANCIAL STRUCTURE. The way in which the assets of a firm are financed—the entire right hand side of the balance sheet. Chapters 17-22.

FREQUENCY DISTRIBUTION. A tabulation of the number of events, in a specified group (age of students, weight of babies, etc.), by numerical intervals. Chapter 6.

FUTURE VALUE. The future value of a dollar is the value of that dollar compounded at a specified rate per period for a specified number of periods. Chapter 3.

GOAL OF THE FIRM. The goal of the firm is the maximization of the market value of its own common stock—the maximization, that is, of the value of the equity owned by its stockholders. Chapter 2.

INCOME STATEMENT. A statement describing a firm's operating results for a given accounting period.

INCREMENTAL COST. The difference in total cost expected to result from choosing one alternative instead of another.

INCREMENTAL PROFIT. The difference in net cash flow, usually after taxes, expected to result from choosing one alternative instead of another.

INFLATION RISK. The risk of a loss of purchasing power of bond, interest and principal should prices rise. Chapter 19.

INSTALLMENT LOANS. Loans which are repaid in periodic payments or installments, usually monthly.

INTERNAL RATE OF RETURN. See DCF rate of return.

INVENTORY. Those items which are held for sale in the ordinary course of business (finished goods) or are in the process of production for such sale (work in process) or are to be used in the production of goods or services (raw materials and supplies). Chapter 12.

INVENTORY LOAN. A loan secured by the firm's inventory.

INVENTORY TURNOVER. Cost of goods sold divided by average or ending inventory.

LEASING. Buying the right to use an object for some specified period of time. Chapter 17.

LIABILITIES. Amounts owed to the firm's creditors.

LINE OF CREDIT. A statement by a lender that it will be prepared, for a specified period of time, to lend the firm up to a stated amount, on specified terms and conditions.

LIQUIDITY. Cash on hand plus demand deposits plus savings deposits plus marketable (usually short-term government) securities. Chapters 9 and 10.

LISTED SECURITIES. Securities traded on an organized security exchange, such as the New York Stock Exchange.

LONG-TERM ASSETS. Assets which are expected to convert themselves into cash over a period of time longer than a year. Chapter 14.

LONG-TERM DEBT. All of the firm's liabilities not classified as current, i.e., not due within one year.

MARKET RISK. The risk of capital loss on bonds if interest rates rise. Chapter 19.

MARGIN BUYING. Purchase of securities in part by use of borrowed funds.

MARGIN REQUIREMENTS. The percent of total purchase price a buyer of securities is allowed to borrow from a bank or a broker. Margin requirements are set by the Federal Reserve Board.

MARKETABLE SECURITIES. Ordinarily all securities which have a ready market. Chapter 10.

MAXIMIZING. Choosing from among the total of currently available opportunities those which will contribute most to the achievement of the firm's goal. Chapter 2.

MERGER. The formation of one company by combining two or more previously existing companies. See acquisition. Chapter 14.

MORTGAGE. Pledging of property to a lender as security for a debt.

NPV. Net present value.

NET PRESENT VALUE. The present value of an asset, calculated at the required rate of return, minus the cost of the asset. Chapter 3.

NET WORTH. A firm's capital and surplus—capital stock, capital surplus, and retained earnings.

OPPORTUNITY COST. The rate of return available to a firm or individual on the best alternative investment.

PAR VALUE. An assigned value representing part or all of the original price paid—in cash, property, or services—for a share of corporate stock.

PAY BACK PERIOD. The period of time, measured in years, an investment will take to return its cost. Chapter 5.

PAYOUT RATIO. The percentage of earnings paid out in dividends.

PRE-EMPTIVE RIGHT. The right of common stockholders to be given first refusal of new issues of common stock or new issues of securities convertible into common stock. The primary purpose is to protect the equity of present stockholders from dilution.

PREFERRED STOCK. Stock which has preference over common stock with respect to payment of dividends. Chapter 17.

PRESENT VALUE. The value now of money to be received at some time in the future—obtained by discounting expected future receipts at some appropriate rate. Chapter 3.

P/E. Price-earnings ratio.

PRICE-EARNINGS RATIO. The current price of a share of stock divided either by current earnings per share or expected earnings per share.

PRIME RATE. The rate of interest which commercial banks charge their strongest customers for loans.

PROBABILITY. A weight assigned to a particular future event which indicates the chances of the occurrence of that event. Chapter 6.

PROBABILITY DISTRIBUTION. The system of individual weights assigned to the events in some group of events—one or another of which will occur in the future. Chapter 6.

PROFIT AND LOSS STATEMENT. See income statement.

PRO FORMA STATEMENT. A projected statement—usually a projected income account or balance sheet. Chapters 9 and 15.

PURE LEVERAGE EFFECT. The difference between a firm's expected rate of return on assets and the interest rate at which it borrows—multiplied by a number which measures the amount of money borrowed relative to net worth. Chapter 20.

PRIVATE PLACEMENT. Securities sold directly by the firm to a financial institution(s), such as a life insurance company. Sometimes called direct placements.

PV. Present value.

RATE OF RETURN ON AVERAGE INVESTMENT. The net income on the investment after taxes, divided by half of the total amount invested. Capter 5.

RATE OF RETURN ON ORIGINAL INVESTMENT. The net income on the investment after taxes, divided by the total amount invested. Chapter 5.

RATIO ANALYSIS. The process of deriving numerical relationships from financial statements.

RECEIVABLES TURNOVER. The ratio of credit sales to average receivables outstanding.

REFUNDING. Redeeming one bond issue with the proceeds of another.

REPURCHASE AGREEMENTS. See Appendix to Chapter 10.

REQUIRED RATE OF RETURN. A firm's cost of capital or an individual's opportunity cost. The minimum return firms or individuals will accept on new investments.

RETAINED EARNINGS. The balance of net profits and losses of a corporation from its inception after subtracting distributions to shareholders and transfers to capital stock or capital surplus accounts.

RETURN ON NET WORTH. Earnings after taxes divided by net worth. Chapter 20.

RISK. The degree to which the actual return on any investment may differ from the expected return. Chapter 19.

RISK AVERTERS. Investors who will not undertake a risky investment unless the expected return (the mean of a probability distribution) is sufficiently higher than the return on a riskless investment. Chapter 19.

RISK AVOIDERS. Investors who try to avoid risk altogether. Chapter 19.

RISK PREMIUM. The excess return an investor requires as risk increases—calculated by subtracting the rate of return on a riskless asset from the expected rate of return on a risky asset of the same maturity. Chapter 19.

RISK RATIO. A number which measures the downside deviations relative to the mean, found by dividing the sum of the deviations lying below the mean by the mean. Chapter 19.

RISK-RETURN EQUATION. A subjective equation which an investor uses to balance risk and return on an investment. Chapter 19.

SALVAGE VALUE. The residual value of a capital asset at the end of its life.

SECURED DEBT. Debt which is secured by pledge of specific assets—such as real estate or inventory. Chapter 16.

SECURITIES MARKETS. Places where stocks and bonds of all types are bought and sold.

SHORT COST. The cost of running out of anything—for example, cash liquidity, inventory. Chapter 10.

SHORT TERM DEBT. See—current liabilities.

SOURCES AND USES STATEMENT. A financial statement which shows how funds were obtained and how they were used during a specified period.

SPIN-OFF. Distribution by a company of claims to part of its assets—either to its own stockholders or to the public-at-large.

STANDARD DEVIATION. A measure of variability equal to the square root of the weighted sum of the squares of the deviations from the mean. Chapter 19.

STOCK DIVIDEND. A dividend paid in stock instead of in cash. Chapter 22.

STOCK SPLIT. Issuance of new *whole* shares for each share outstanding, as a 2 for 1 split or a 3 for 1 split.

SUBORDINATED DEBT. Debt of lower rank in liquidation than senior (non-subordinated) debt.

TAX ANTICIPATION SECURITIES. See Appendix to Chapter 10.

TAX EFFECT (OF LEVERAGE). The interest rate multiplied by the tax rate multiplied by the debt-equity ratio. Chapter 21.

TENDER OFFER. A proposal made directly by one firm to the stockholder of another firm to buy their stock at a specified price.

TERM LOAN. Loans made by banks and insurance companies for intermediate terms—usually from 3 to 5 years.

TRADE CREDIT. Short term debt arising through credit sales by one firm to another.

TREASURY BILLS. See Appendix to Chapter 10.

TREASURY BONDS. See Appendix to Chapter 10.

TREASURY NOTES. See Appendix to Chapter 10.

UNSECURED DEBT. Debt which is backed by the general credit of the corporation and without pledge of specific assets.

WARRANT. A long term option to buy a specified number of shares of common stock in a particular company at a specified price.

WEIGHTED AVERAGE COST OF CAPITAL. The cost of new long term capital when more than one type is raised. Chapter 18.

WORKING CAPITAL. Current assets minus current liabilities.

PERIODS HENCE	1%	2%	4%	6%	8%	10%	12%	14%	15%	16%	18%	20%	22%	24%	25%	26%	28%	30%	35%	40%	45%	50%
1	0.990	0.980	0.962	0.943	0.926	0.909	0.893	0.877	0.870	0.862	0.847	0.833	0.820	0.806	0.800	0.794	0.781	0.769	0.741	0.714	0.690	0.667
2	0.980	0.961	0.925	0.890	0.857	0.826	0.797	0.769	0.756	0.743	0.718	0.694	0.672	0.650	0.640	0.630	0.610	0.592	0.549	0.510	0.476	0.444
3	0.971	0.942	0.889	0.840	0.794	0.751	0.712	0.675	0.658	0.641	0.609	0.579	0.551	0.524	0.512	0.500	0.477	0.455	0.406	0.364	0.328	0.296
4	0.961	0.924	0.855	0.792	0.735	0.683	0.636	0.592	0.572	0.552	0.516	0.482	0.451	0.423	0.410	0.397	0.373	0.350	0.301	0.260	0.226	0.198
5	0.951	0.906	0.822	0.747	0.681	0.621	0.567	0.519	0.497	0.476	0.437	0.402	0.370	0.341	0.328	0.315	0.291	0.269	0.223	0.186	0.156	0.132
6	0.942	0.888	0.790	0.705	0.630	0.564	0.507	0.456	0.432	0.410	0.370	0.335	0.303	0.275	0.262	0.250	0.227	0.207	0.165	0.133	0.108	0.088
7	0.933	0.871	0.760	0.665	0.583	0.513	0.452	0.400	0.376	0.354	0.314	0.279	0.249	0.222	0.210	0.198	0.178	0.159	0.122	0.095	0.074	0.059
8	0.923	0.853	0.731	0.627	0.540	0.467	0.404	0.351	0.327	0.305	0.266	0.233	0.204	0.179	0.168	0.157	0.139	0.123	0.091	0.068	0.051	0.039
9	0.914	0.837	0.703	0.592	0.500	0.424	0.361	0.308	0.284	0.263	0.225	0.194	0.167	0.144	0.134	0.125	0.108	0.094	0.067	0.048	0.035	0.026
10	0.905	0.820	0.676	0.558	0.463	0.386	0.322	0.270	0.247	0.227	0.191	0.162	0.137	0.116	0.107	0.099	0.085	0.073	0.050	0.035	0.024	0.017
11	0.896	0.804	0.650	0.527	0.429	0.350	0.287	0.237	0.215	0.195	0.162	0.135	0.112	0.094	0.086	0.079	0.066	0.056	0.037	0.025	0.017	0.012
12	0.887	0.788	0.625	0.497	0.397	0.319	0.257	0.208	0.187	0.168	0.137	0.112	0.092	0.076	0.069	0.062	0.052	0.043	0.027	0.018	0.012	0.008
13	0.879	0.773	0.601	0.469	0.368	0.290	0.229	0.182	0.163	0.145	0.116	0.093	0.075	0.061	0.055	0.050	0.040	0.033	0.020	0.013	0.008	0.005
14	0.870	0.758	0.577	0.442	0.340	0.263	0.205	0.160	0.141	0.125	0.099	0.078	0.062	0.049	0.044	0.039	0.032	0.025	0.015	0.009	0.006	0.003
15	0.861	0.743	0.555	0.417	0.315	0.239	0.183	0.140	0.123	0.108	0.084	0.065	0.051	0.040	0.035	0.031	0.025	0.020	0.011	0.006	0.004	0.002
16	0.853	0.728	0.534	0.394	0.292	0.218	0.163	0.123	0.107	0.093	0.071	0.054	0.042	0.032	0.028	0.025	0.019	0.015	0.008	0.005	0.003	0.002
17	0.844	0.714	0.513	0.371	0.270	0.198	0.146	0.108	0.093	0.080	0.060	0.045	0.034	0.026	0.023	0.020	0.015	0.012	0.006	0.003	0.002	0.001
18	0.836	0.700	0.494	0.350	0.250	0.180	0.130	0.095	0.081	0.069	0.051	0.038	0.028	0.021	0.018	0.016	0.012	0.009	0.005	0.002	0.001	0.001
19	0.828	0.686	0.475	0.331	0.232	0.164	0.116	0.083	0.070	0.060	0.043	0.031	0.023	0.017	0.014	0.012	0.009	0.007	0.003	0.002	0.001	
20	0.820	0.673	0.456	0.312	0.215	0.149	0.104	0.073	0.061	0.051	0.037	0.026	0.019	0.014	0.012	0.010	0.007	0.005	0.002	0.001	0.001	
21	0.811	0.660	0.439	0.294	0.199	0.135	0.093	0.064	0.053	0.044	0.031	0.022	0.015	0.011	0.009	0.008	0.006	0.004	0.002	0.001		
22	0.803	0.647	0.422	0.278	0.184	0.123	0.083	0.056	0.046	0.038	0.026	0.018	0.013	0.009	0.007	0.006	0.004	0.003	0.001	0.001		
23	0.795	0.634	0.406	0.262	0.170	0.112	0.074	0.049	0.040	0.033	0.022	0.015	0.010	0.007	0.006	0.005	0.003	0.002	0.001			
24	0.788	0.622	0.390	0.247	0.158	0.102	0.066	0.043	0.035	0.028	0.019	0.013	0.008	0.006	0.005	0.004	0.003	0.002	0.001			
25	0.780	0.610	0.375	0.233	0.146	0.092	0.059	0.038	0.030	0.024	0.016	0.010	0.007	0.005	0.004	0.003	0.002	0.001	0.001			
26	0.772	0.598	0.361	0.220	0.135	0.084	0.053	0.033	0.026	0.021	0.014	0.009	0.006	0.004	0.003	0.002	0.002	0.001				
27	0.764	0.586	0.347	0.207	0.125	0.076	0.047	0.029	0.023	0.018	0.011	0.007	0.005	0.003	0.002	0.002	0.001	0.001				
28	0.757	0.574	0.333	0.196	0.116	0.069	0.042	0.026	0.020	0.016	0.010	0.006	0.004	0.002	0.002	0.002	0.001	0.001				
29	0.749	0.563	0.321	0.185	0.107	0.063	0.037	0.022	0.017	0.014	0.008	0.005	0.003	0.002	0.002	0.001	0.001	0.001				
30	0.742	0.552	0.308	0.174	0.099	0.057	0.033	0.020	0.015	0.012	0.007	0.004	0.003	0.002	0.002	0.001	0.001	0.001				
40	0.672	0.453	0.208	0.097	0.046	0.022	0.011	0.005	0.004	0.003	0.001	0.001										
50	0.608	0.372	0.141	0.054	0.021	0.009	0.003	0.001	0.001	0.001												

PERIODS	1%	2%	4%	6%	8%	10%	12%	14%	15%	16%	18%	20%	22%	24%	25%	26%	28%	30%	35%	40%	46%	50%
1	0.990	0.980	0.962	0.943	0.926	0.909	0.893	0.877	0.870	0.862	0.847	0.833	0.820	0.806	0.800	0.794	0.781	0.769	0.741	0.714	0.690	0.667
2	1.970	1.942	1.886	1.833	1.783	1.736	1.690	1.647	1.626	1.605	1.566	1.528	1.492	1.457	1.440	1.424	1.392	1.361	1.289	1.224	1.165	1.111
3	2.941	2.884	2.775	2.673	2.577	2.487	2.402	2.322	2.283	2.246	2.174	2.106	2.042	1.981	1.952	1.923	1.868	1.816	1.696	1.589	1.493	1.407
4	3.902	3.808	3.630	3.465	3.312	3.170	3.037	2.914	2.855	2.798	2.690	2.589	2.494	2.404	2.362	2.320	2.241	2.166	1.997	1.849	1.720	1.605
5	4.853	4.713	4.452	4.212	3.993	3.791	3.605	3.433	3.352	3.274	3.127	2.991	2.864	2.745	2.689	2.635	2.532	2.436	2.220	2.035	1.876	1.737
6	5.795	5.601	5.242	4.917	4.623	4.355	4.111	3.889	3.784	3.685	3.498	3.326	3.167	3.020	2.951	2.885	2.759	2.643	2.385	2.168	1.983	1.824
7	6.728	6.472	6.002	5.582	5.206	4.868	4.564	4.288	4.160	4.039	3.812	3.605	3.416	3.242	3.161	3.083	2.937	2.802	2.508	2.263	2.057	1.883
8	7.652	7.325	6.733	6.210	5.747	5.335	4.968	4.639	4.487	4.344	4.078	3.837	3.619	3.421	3.329	3.241	3.076	2.925	2.598	2.331	2.108	1.922
9	8.566	8.162	7.435	6.802	6.247	5.759	5.328	4.946	4.772	4.607	4.303	4.031	3.786	3.566	3.463	3.366	3.184	3.019	2.665	2.379	2.144	1.948
10	9.471	8.983	8.111	7.360	6.710	6.145	5.650	5.216	5.019	4.833	4.494	4.192	3.923	3.682	3.571	3.465	3.269	3.092	2.715	2.414	2.168	1.965
11	10.368	9.787	8.760	7.887	7.139	6.495	5.988	5.453	5.234	5.029	4.656	4.327	4.035	3.776	3.656	3.544	3.335	3.147	2.752	2.438	2.185	1.977
12	11.255	10.575	9.385	8.384	7.536	6.814	6.194	5.660	5.421	5.197	4.793	4.439	4.127	3.851	3.725	3.606	3.387	3.190	2.779	2.456	2.196	1.985
13	12.134	11.343	9.986	8.853	7.904	7.103	6.424	5.842	5.583	5.342	4.910	4.533	4.203	3.912	3.780	3.656	3.427	3.223	2.799	2.468	2.204	1.990
14	13.004	12.106	10.563	9.295	8.244	7.367	6.628	6.002	5.724	5.468	5.008	4.611	4.265	3.962	3.824	3.695	3.459	3.249	2.814	2.477	2.210	1.993
15	13.865	12.849	11.118	9.712	8.559	7.606	6.811	6.142	5.847	5.575	5.092	4.675	4.315	4.001	3.859	3.726	3.483	3.268	2.825	2.484	2.214	1.995
16	14.718	13.578	11.652	10.106	8.851	7.824	6.974	6.265	5.954	5.669	5.162	4.730	4.357	4.033	3.887	3.751	3.503	3.283	2.834	2.489	2.216	1.997
17	15.562	14.292	12.166	10.477	9.122	8.022	7.120	6.373	6.047	5.749	5.222	4.775	4.391	4.059	3.910	3.771	3.518	3.295	2.840	2.492	2.218	1.998
18	16.398	14.992	12.659	10.828	9.372	8.201	7.250	6.467	6.128	5.818	5.273	4.812	4.419	4.080	3.928	3.786	3.529	3.304	2.844	2.494	2.219	1.999
19	17.226	15.678	13.134	11.158	9.604	8.365	7.366	6.550	6.198	5.877	5.316	4.844	4.442	4.097	3.942	3.799	3.539	3.311	2.848	2.496	2.220	1.999
20	18.046	16.351	13.590	11.470	9.818	8.514	7.469	6.623	6.259	5.929	5.353	4.870	4.460	4.110	3.954	3.808	3.546	3.316	2.850	2.497	2.221	1.999
21	18.857	17.011	14.029	11.764	10.017	8.649	7.562	6.687	6.312	5.973	5.384	4.891	4.476	4.121	3.963	3.816	3.551	3.320	2.852	2.498	2.221	2.000
22	19.660	17.658	14.451	12.042	10.201	8.772	7.645	6.743	6.359	6.011	5.410	4.909	4.488	4.130	3.970	3.822	3.556	3.323	2.853	2.498	2.222	2.000
23	20.456	18.292	14.857	12.303	10.371	8.883	7.718	6.792	6.399	6.044	5.432	4.925	4.499	4.137	3.976	3.827	3.559	3.325	2.854	2.499	2.222	2.000
24	21.243	18.914	15.247	12.550	10.529	8.985	7.784	6.835	6.434	6.073	5.451	4.937	4.507	4.143	3.981	3.831	3.562	3.327	2.855	2.499	2.222	2.000
25	22.023	19.523	15.622	12.783	10.675	9.077	7.843	6.873	6.464	6.097	5.467	4.948	4.514	4.147	3.985	3.834	3.564	3.329	2.856	2.499	2.222	2.000
26	22.795	20.121	15.983	13.003	10.810	9.161	7.896	6.906	6.491	6.118	5.480	4.956	4.520	4.151	3.988	3.837	3.566	3.330	2.856	2.500	2.222	2.000
27	23.560	20.707	16.330	13.211	10.935	9.237	7.943	6.935	6.514	6.136	5.492	4.964	4.524	4.154	3.990	3.839	3.567	3.331	2.856	2.500	2.222	2.000
28	24.316	21.281	16.663	13.406	11.051	9.307	7.984	6.961	6.534	6.152	5.502	4.970	4.528	4.157	3.992	3.840	3.568	3.331	2.857	2.500	2.222	2.000
29	25.066	21.844	16.984	13.591	11.158	9.370	8.022	6.983	6.551	6.166	5.510	4.975	4.531	4.159	3.994	3.841	3.569	3.332	2.857	2.500	2.222	2.000
30	25.808	22.396	17.292	13.765	11.258	9.427	8.055	7.003	6.566	6.177	5.517	4.979	4.534	4.160	3.995	3.842	3.569	3.332	2.857	2.500	2.222	2.000
40	32.835	27.355	19.793	15.046	11.925	9.779	8.244	7.105	6.642	6.234	5.548	4.997	4.544	4.166	3.999	3.846	3.571	3.333	2.857	2.500	2.222	2.000
50	39.196	31.424	21.482	15.762	12.234	9.915	8.304	7.133	6.661	6.246	5.554	4.999	4.545	4.167	4.000	3.846	3.571	3.333	2.857	2.500	2.222	2.000

INDEX

INDEX